D0204231

Comic Art of Europe

Comic Art of Europe

An International, Comprehensive Bibliography

Compiled by **John A. Lent**

Foreword by David Kunzle

Bibliographies and Indexes in Popular Culture,
Number 5

Greenwood Press
Westport, Connecticut • London

Library of Congress Cataloging-in-Publication Data

Lent, John A.
  Comic art of Europe : an international, comprehensive bibliography
/ compiled by John A. Lent ; foreword by David Kunzle.
      p.   cm.—(Bibliographies and indexes in popular culture,
ISSN 1066–0658 ; no. 5)
  Includes indexes.
  ISBN 0–313–28212–9 (alk. paper)
    1. Caricatures and cartoons—Europe—Bibliography. 2. Wit and
humor, Pictorial—Bibliography. I. Title. II. Series.
Z5956.C3L46   1994
[NC1465]
016.7415′94—dc20   94–14432

British Library Cataloguing in Publication Data is available.

Library of Congress Catalog Card Number: 94–14432
ISBN: 0–313–28212–9
ISSN: 1066–0658

First published in 1994

Greenwood Press, 88 Post Road West, Westport, CT 06881
An imprint of Greenwood Publishing Group, Inc.

Printed in the United States of America

The paper used in this book complies with the
Permanent Paper Standard issued by the National
Information Standards Organization (Z39.48–1984).

10 9 8 7 6 5 4 3 2

Contents

A Backward Looking Foreword
by David Kunzle

As one who never read comics as a child (in England during the 1940s I drifted into adventure story magazines with nary a comic strip in sight), I could not have expected my academic life to be overwhelmed by them—or their early history (before 1896). The cartoon and satiric art was however there for me from the beginning, from the moment I discovered, aged about seven years, a huge volume of Hogarth plates I could barely lift, kept in an ornate and magical cupboard ten feet tall in my grandfather's house. All human life was there, as they say, sex, vice, death—and laughter. I still regard the modern comic strips as the myriad miniature offspring of that monumental seed.

In 1960 Rodolphe Töpffer was revealed to me in an epiphany by Ernst Gombrich's *Art and Illusion*, at the very moment when I was looking for a Ph.D. topic. Emerging from a haze of enchantment in the British Museum library, then the only repository of Töpffer in England, I found myself seduced into Gombrich's invitation, in *Art and Illusion*, to track the fate of the picture story (read: comic strip) from Hogarth to Töppfer. Töppfer is the Krazy Kat of the romantic era in the 19th century and still, amazingly, not translated into English (anglophone publishers of the world, wake up!).

Treasures of a comic strip-like kind emerged galore even before Hogarth, in broadsheets hidden in print rooms and libraries all over Europe: voilà, by 1967 a Ph.D. thesis rewritten and accepted for publication, and in a twinkling, five plus years later, printed by the University of California Press under the title *Early Comic Strip* (c. 1450-1825). In this immodestly-sized tome the asseverations of comic strip "historians" that the ancestry of the comic strip was to be found everywhere (from Trajan's Column to the Bayeux Tapestry) and nowhere (the comic strip being born, of virgines intactae, in the U.S. newspaper 1896) were ground into fine academic dust. Only one viewer hated my book, unable to bear the sight of the teeming broadsheets, and denied the ancestral claim I was making for them, on the grounds that comic and strippy as they may be, they were but dumb and senseless things without the benefit of the speech balloon, as if *this* were the defining constituent of the comic strip.

As a result of my labors on comic strip history (two large volumes on the history before 1896), great honors were showered upon me, like an invitation to advise a multi-million dollar TV series on the comic strip, the script of which started out with authoritative assertion that the comic strip was born in 1896 and in the U.S. This kind of American chauvinism drove me to my kind of European chauvinism, and convinced me that older is better. Allowing for some singular glories in the 20th century comic strip, I can't help regarding the impossible proliferation of our century (six million images!?) as a massified degeneration. I used genuinely to believe, in my English innocence and credulity that Americans could make machines do anything, that Rex Morgan was conceived and drawn by a machine, and not a very clever one. To this day I shun the comic strip page of newspapers, for the perfect awfulness of so many strips, whose crime is not awfulness as such—we live in a democracy—but the fact that they are preferred (by editors, by the public) to others less awful, and maybe even good or novel, which never get syndicated.

To complain that Töpffer and Busch remain unequalled, and that Cham, Doré, Leonce Petit, Marie Duval, Willette and Caran d'Ache might still serve as models today is self-serving, and probably academic snobbery: for they are the heroes (and one heroine) I sing in my Volume II (1826-1895). Has Herriman done a depression-era Töpffer, Walt Kelly or Carl Barks a cold-war Busch? Could be. But one factor above all, militates against quality and creativity: the crushing tyranny of treadmill periodicity. The Trudeau-style sabbatical, now the exception, needs to become a norm. Let's have fewer and better strips—and lessen the sisyphean labors of John Lent.

David Kunzle, a professor of the history of art at the University of California, is a multi-lingual (competent in about a half-dozen languages) scholar of comic art. Among his pathfinding books are two volumes that trace the European comic strip from 1450 through the nineteenth century (*The Early Comic Strip* and *The History of the Comic Strip: Nineteenth Century*), as well as *Fashion and Fetishness*, *Posters of Protest*, and studies of Latin American revolutionary art.

Preface

European academicians and journalists realized the importance of comic art study earlier than their counterparts in other areas of the world. While myopic academic departments and often snobbish professors in the United States resisted the serious scrutiny of comic art throughout the 1950s and 1960s, already in Europe a coterie of writers (some from academic circles) were in the midst of developing this new field of study. The names of many of these prolific writers dotted the popular, trade, and academic press, in the process, making them the pioneers in comic art literature. Among them are Sergio Augusto, Claudio Bertieri, Giani Bono, Gianni Brunoro, Michel Caen, Piero Carpi, Alfredo Castelli, Pierre Couperie, Franco De Giacomo, Oreste Del Buono, Carlos Della Corte, Umberto Eco, Henri Filippini, Franco Fossati, Edouard François, Luis Gasca, Sture Hegerfors, Maurice Horn, Wolfgang Kempkes, D. Labesse, Francis Lacassin, Claude Le Gallo, Claude Moliterni, David Pascal, F. Rivière, Jacques Sadoul, Numa Sadoul, Rinaldo Traini, Sergio Trinchero, and Piero Zanotto.

During the same period, comics-related periodicals grew up, chief among them were *Comics*, *Comics Club*, *Giff-Wiff*, *Les Cahiers de la Bande Dessinée*, *Linus*, *Phénix*, *Rantanplan*, and *Sgt. Kirk*. Many articles on comics appeared in the popular press, and serious study on this topic was broached at congresses in Lucca, while exhibitions were held in Austria, Finland, and Germany. Additionally, Wolfgang Kempkes brought out his *International Bibliography of Comics Literature*, certainly one of the first such works in the world.

When the second major bibliography, Renate Neumann's *Bibliographie zur Comic-Sekundärliteratur* appeared almost a generation later in 1987, the most frequently-listed writers, in addition to some of those above, were Sylvain Bouyer, Jean-Marc Caré, Javier Coma, Luc Dellisse, Jean-Claude Faur, Pierre Fresnault-Deruelle, Wolfgang Fuchs, Thierry Groensteen, Bruno Lecigne, Gerd Lettkemann, Jean Léturgie, Antoine

Roux, Klaus Strzyz, Markus Tschernegg, and Jutta Wermke. Obviously, the continual attracting of writers indicated that comic art was growing as a field of study.

Many more periodicals devoted to comic art sprouted, including *Apropos, Bédésup, Caricature et Caricaturistes, Comic Forum: Das Magazin für Comicliteratur, Comixene: Das Comicfachmagazin, El Wendigo, Icom Info, Il Fumetto, Neuróptica,* and *Storyboard.*

Preserving and studying comic art was earnestly undertaken in most parts of Europe by the time Neumann's bibliography appeared, with the inauguration of private and university comic art collections in Belgium, England, France, Germany, Sweden, Switzerland, and Yugoslavia. Cartoon courses and even whole academic programs also appeared in England and elsewhere, along with more congresses, exhibitions, and associations.

This bibliography, one of four dealing with various parts of the world, and all published by Greenwood, is an attempt to capture the history and contemporary status of European comic art as it was reflected in the literature.

Organization, Objectives, Emphases

Comic art in this volume represents animation, caricature, comic books, comic strips, gag, illustrative, magazine, and political cartoons. At times, it was difficult determining genre because of the terminology. The word "caricature" in some countries of Europe takes on more meanings than in the United States, including that of cartooning in a general sense.

The bibliography covers 29 countries for which sources were available. Because of the collapse of the Soviet Union and the dramatic changes in East Europe, geopolitical areas and names have changed, which presented a problem when I was organizing the bibliography. In some cases, I did not change anything. Czechoslovakia, for example, remained the same because all of the sources related to that country before its split into Czech Republic and Slovakia. In other instances, the splintered countries were given separate categories, e.g., Croatia, Estonia, and Macedonia. The old German Democratic Republic was subsumed under Germany, although it retained a subcategory.

Chapter one includes continental, regional, and comparative perspectives, starting with a references section containing entries on overviews, histories, encyclopedias, and a periodical directory. The latter provides names, addresses, typical contents, and inaugural dates of at least 81 comic art-related journals, magazines, and fanzines. A general studies section consists of items that either are too general or too vague to fit elsewhere or that are cross category in nature. A regional aspects part subdivides into Federation of European Cartoonists Organizations (FECO), festivals, French-language (mainly French-Belgian), and Scandinavia. The rest of the first chapter covers region-, not country-specific aspects of animation, caricature, comic books, comic strips, and political cartoons.

In chapter two, Albania, Austria, Belgium, Bulgaria, Croatia, Czechoslovakia,

Denmark, Estonia, and Finland are treated with a category scheme that usually includes general studies and genres that apply. The Belgium chapter stands out with a more expanded categorization. Besides having parts dealing with animation, comic books (further divided into comic books and cinema and television, festivals, and genres), and comic strips, the chapter also has sections on general studies, broken into children's press and festivals; cartoonists, listing 33 individually; and characters and titles, singling out 11. If a cartoonist or character/title is the subject of at least two citations, it is given a separate listing in this and subsequent chapters. Because it is very difficult to delineate between some Belgian and French cartoonists and their works, the user of this bibliography is encouraged to cross reference the Belgium and France chapters.

The chapter on France, consisting of about 2,800 citations, begins with a references section, made up of bibliographies, collections, museums, dictionaries, directories, and encyclopedias, followed by a general studies part, broken into children's press, festivals, and periodicals (particularly *Charivari* and *Le Canard Enchaine*). The various types of cartooning (caricature, comics, graphic arts, and political cartoons) are dealt with individually under historical aspects. The cartoonists and caricaturists subcategory includes hundreds of names with 119 singled out; many names appear under characters and titles as well, where 36 are listed individually.

The rest of the chapter provides citations on animation, caricature, cartoons, comic books, and comic strips. Because of the abundance of materials on comic books, subcategories were expanded to include *anthologies*, usually multi-author collections of cartoons and some reviews; *art, aesthetics, and architecture*; *cinema, theater*, the use of comics in and their relationship to these media; *education, culture*, including literacy, reading, and schooling; *genres*, broken down into animal, crime, erotic and pornographic, heroes, parody, science fiction, and western; *industry*, pertaining to production, distribution, sales, marketing, advertising, and the state of the industry; *language, semiotics*; *legal aspects*, including censorship, creator's rights, legal suits, libel, copyright, plagiarism, contracts, guidelines, regulations, and ethics; *psychology*, including psychoanalysis and psychiatry; *religion*, including myths; *sociopolitical*, and *technical aspects*. Some of these subcategories, identically defined, appear in subsequent chapters.

Germany is the subject of the fourth chapter, which has references and general studies parts, the latter subdivided into children's media, periodicals (singling out *Fliegenden Blätter*, *Kladderadatsch*, and *Simplicissimus*), and women (images and cartoonists). The German Democratic Republic is treated separately, followed by historical aspects of animation, caricature, comics, graphic arts, and political cartoons. Under the cartoonists and caricaturists part, 39 individuals were given special treatment, while 19 characters and titles were listed separately. The remainder of the Germany chapter includes animation, caricature, cartoons, comic books, comic strips, and political cartoons. Comic books as a category is expanded into *art*; *children*, especially cartoons for children; *cinema, television, theater*; *education, culture*; *effects debate*, especially in the 1950s concerning possible negative effects of violence/horror comics, and the Komischen Streifen; *genres*, singling out adventure, alternative and underground, education, erotic and pornographic, heroes and superheroes, horror, and science fiction; *industry*, with subcategories on the companies of Carlsen-Verlag, Ehapa-Verlag, and

Kauka-Comics, and on advertising; *literature*; *psychology*; *religion*; *semiotics and language*; *socio-political*, and *technical aspects*.

Chapter five is devoted to Great Britain with the usual sections on references and general studies, the latter subdivided by anthologies, children, professionalism (cartoonists' organizations, congresses, schools, and festivals), technical aspects, television, film, radio, and women. The historical aspects section consists of parts on animation, caricature and cartoons, comic books, comic strips, and political cartoons. Scores of cartoonists and caricaturists are cited, with 41 given special listings; in the characters and titles part, 17 are treated individually. Periodicals, with *Punch* and *Viz* singled out, is next, followed by animation, caricature, comic books, comic strips, and political cartoons. Comic books has subheadings of anthologies, anti-comics campaign of 1949-1955, censorship, effects debate, genres, industry, and underground.

The sixth chapter includes Greece, Hungary, and Ireland; chapter seven, Italy, and chapter eight, Luxembourg, Macedonia, the Netherlands, Norway, Poland, Portugal, Romania, Russia (Soviet Union), Spain, Sweden, Switzerland, Turkey, and Yugoslavia.

The chapter on Italy has major sections on references and resources, general studies (broken into children and youth, festivals, and women), historical aspects (caricature, comics), legal aspects, cartoonists and caricaturists (10 individualized), characters and titles (25 singled out), animation, caricature, comic books, comic strips, and political cartoons. Comic books is further divided into anthologies, cinema, television, and theater, collecting and fandom, commercial aspects, culture and society, education, fascism, genres (adventure, crime, erotic and pornographic, fantasy, horror, humor, new wave and underground, science fiction, superhero, war, and western), psychology, structure (including format, language, theme), and technical aspects.

Throughout the entire book, it was often difficult categorizing cartoonists by genre, and especially by country. For example, Grosz spent important periods of his career in both his native Germany and his adopted United States, and Uderzo, Pratt, and Cadelo have done much of their work in France, although they are Italian-born. Arbitrarily, I decided to keep these individuals in their countries of origin. The category problem was compounded when dealing with some French and Belgian cartoonists and their characters. For example, "Lucky Luke," among a number of strips, can be called French as well as Belgian. As indicated earlier, the user of this bibliography must use the French and Belgian comics sections interchangeably.

A serious effort was put forth to compile a comprehensive and usable bibliography. No item was too small or insignificant to be listed; if it dealt with comic art, it could become a citation. The compiler works on the premise that both systematically-researched and ephemeral materials are useful during the course of developing a field of study.

Having said that, I must point out some limitations on comprehensiveness. The accelerated interest in comic art (unfortunately, too often as a commercial investment, rather than reading experience) in recent years has seen a proliferation of literature, usually in quickly-slapped-together anthologies and collections. Not all of these books are included. The necessity to drop some was based on expediency, rather than evaluative, decisions. They were not readily available physically or accessible in library and other research depositories. In some other cases where materials were obtainable, a selective process had to be used because of the volume. For example, not all the collections of Disney character stories are here, nor are all the references to famous cartoonists who also excelled in painting or other arts. The German artist/caricaturist George Grosz comes to mind here. I saw hundreds of citations about him, but for the most part, chose those that dealt with him as a caricaturist.

The bibliography is representative in covering various publications, writing formats and styles, time periods, and languages. Most of the citations are current, ranging from the 1960s to present, although some date back to the eighteenth and nineteenth centuries.

Many problems surfaced in the course of doing this work. Dealing with such a voluminous amount of information presented (sometimes inaccurately) in different bibliographic styles can lead to much duplication. Although I have attempted to eliminate, or at least, to minimize duplication, some is bound to exist, for which I apologize.

As indicated already, categorization gave me a few headaches. In a number of periodicals, cartoonist profiles are intermingled with accounts of their characters or the titled works for which they are known. Thus, the user of this bibliography will find in the sections on characters and titles much biographical information about the creators of those works, and conversely, much on characters and titles in cartoonists' profiles and interviews.

At times it has been difficult to determine dates of periodicals. Some magazines, especially fanzines, are not dated. Others change series or alternate, without any seeming logic, between using dates and volume numbers or months and seasons of the year.

The citations are arranged alphabetically by author, or by article title when an author is not listed, and are numbered consecutively.

Search Process

The search for literature was mostly manual, since that is the way the compiler works, and because much of the literature, being journalistic, anecdotal, or brief, is not in computerized databases. Many bibliographies, indices, and bibliographic periodicals, too numerous to list here, were used. It is worth noting, however, that all volumes of *Reader's Guide to Periodical Literature*, 1890 to 1992, were searched.

On a regular basis and rather systematically, the compiler has attempted to keep abreast of the literature on mass communications and popular culture for at least 30 years. For the most part, works on comic art are expected to be found in those fields, as well as in art. Hundreds of journal titles in these three fields and others, published on all continents, are scanned regularly by the compiler.

No effort will be made to list all of these periodicals, only those that would be expected to yield some articles. Among these, all numbers of the following were searched: *Animag, Apropos, Art? Alternatives, Artsy, Breaking In, Canadian Cartoonist, The Cartoonist (Nigeria), Cartoonist PROfiles, Cine Cubano, Citizens Publishing, Comic Art Studies, Comicist, Comics Collector, Comics Interview, Comics Journal, Comics News Service from Poland, Comics Scene, Communication Abstracts, Communication Booknotes, Communication Monographs, Communication Quarterly, Critical Studies in Mass Communication, European Journal of Communication, Fat Comic, FCA S.O.B., FECO News, Fort Mudge Most, The Funnie's Paper, Gannett Center Journal, Gauntlet, Gazette, Hollywood Eclectern, Humerus, Humor, Index on Censorship, Journal of Communication, Journal of Popular Culture, Journal of Popular Film, Journalism History, Journalism Monographs, Journalism Quarterly, Kayhan Caricature, L'Ecran, Mass Comm Review, Media Development, Media History Digest, Minnesota Cartoonist, Nemo, Nordic Comics Revue, Public Culture, Puck Papers, The Quill, Seriejournalen, Studies in Latin American Popular Culture, Talking Turkey, Target, Trix, Watcher,* and *WittyWorld.*

Additionally, the compiler looked at the following periodicals with varying degrees of exhaustiveness, depending upon availability and relevance: *AAEC Notebook, Akrep, Albany Cartoon Journal, Amazing Heroes, Amazing World of DC Comics, Animation, Animato, Anime-zine, Archie, Association of Comics Enthusiasts Newsletter, Comic Cuts, (A Suivre), Baby Sue, B & W, Barks Collector, Bédésup, Big O, La Borsa del Fumetto, Bulls' Eye, Caniffites, CAPS, Caricature, Cartoon Art Museum Newsletter, Cartoon Quarterly, Cartoons, Cartoon Times, Chapters, Collector's Club Newsletter, Collectors Dream, Comic Art, Comic Book Marketplace, Comic Book Newsletter, Comic Book Price Guide, Comic Cellar, Comicguia, Comic Informer, Comic Reader, Comic Relief, Comics Business, Comics Buyer's Guide, Comics Feature, Comic Shop News, Comics International, Comics Release, Comics Retailer, Comics Review, Comics Score Board, Comic Strip News, Comics Values Monthly, The Comics World, Comix, Corto Maltese, Daredevil Chronicles, Dreamline, The Duckburg Times, East Coast Animation, El Wendigo, FA, Fandom Annual, Fanfare, The Fans of Central Jersey, The Fan's Zine, FCA and Me, Too! Newsletter, Fenix, Foom, Four-Color Magazine, Fred Greenberg's Omnibus, Funny Times, Funnyworld, The Gag Recap, Get Animated!, Graphixus, Granma Weekly Review, Heroic Fantasy, Humour and Caricature, ICOM/INFO, Il Fumetto, Infinity, Inkspot, Inside Comics, Inspirational Comics, In Toon, IPI Report, Itchy Planet, Japanimation, The Jester, Kever, Keverinfo, Kitchen Sink Pipeline, The Licensing Book, Linus, LOC, Locus, Mangajin, Manhattan Comic News, Menomonee Falls Gazette, Menomonee Falls Guardian, Mieux Vaut en Rire, Monokel, National Cartoonists Society Newsletter, Near Mint, The New Comic News, Newsletter of Northern California Cartoon and Humour Association, Newtype, Okefenokee Star, Orion, Outworld's Bi-Monthly, Overstreet's Price Update, Panels, Penstuff, Pogo Is Back, Qua Brot, RBCC, Retail Express, Robin Snyder's History of the Comics, SAF Reporter, Serieskaberen, Sick, Small Press Comics Explosion, Society of Strip Illustration Newsletter, Speakeasy, Squa Tront, Story Board, TEGN, Transformation, Tratto, Triangle Comic Review, TV Guide, Twinkles, UCLA, Uncle Jam Quarterly, Vot der Dumboozle?, Wizzard, Witzend, World Cartoon Gallery (Skopje) Catalogue, The World of Comic Art, Worldwide Classics Newsletter,* and *Yellow Press.*

"Fugitive" materials, such as dissertations not indexed through the University of Michigan system, theses, catalogues, conference papers, and pamphlets also make up part of the bibliographies.

Besides using scores of libraries in the United States and beyond, as well as the interlibrary loan services, the compiler found other ways to gather sources on comic art. Some key writers in the field were asked to submit bibliographies of their works, and advertisements were placed in *WittyWorld International Cartoon Magazine* soliciting citations. The compiler became familiar with much literature as he prepared his regular bibliographic column for *WittyWorld* during the past seven years. Additional sources became available during my interviews with hundreds of cartoonists and comic art specialists around the world.

Acknowledgments

Bibliographic work, tedious and time-consuming as it is, can have its moments of pleasure and fulfillment. In the course of finishing this bibliography, there were a number of such times—while scavenging through stacks of books and periodicals at comics festivals and stores, while finding a cache of fanzines or a list of references in library and commercial catalogues, or while interviewing cartoonists and comics authorities worldwide.

The latter deserve my first words of gratitude. The hundreds of cartoonists I have interviewed in Asia, Canada, Caribbean, Europe, South America, and the United States are the most interesting, flexible, and generous professionals I have known. They have shared with me their experiences, cartoons, and scrapbooks and clippings, the latter useful for bibliographic purposes. They have showered me with hospitality, motored me around crowded cities, provided me translations, and, in some cases, given me the benefits of their own comic art research.

They should all be mentioned, but space does not permit. Especially helpful, and to whom I am very thankful, are: Norman Isaac and Deng Coy Miel in the Philippines; Ramli Badrudin and Gerardus Sudarta in Indonesia; Suresh Sawant, Abu Abraham, Sudhir Tailang, Anant Pai, and Pran in India; K.M.K. Madagama and W.R. Wijesoma in Sri Lanka; Harunoor Rasheed Harun, Nazrul Islam, and the staffs of *Cartoon* and *Immad* magazines in Bangladesh; the entire cartoonists club of Myanmar, and particularly U Ngwe Kyi and Maung Maung Aung; Chai Rachawat in Thailand; Lat and Zunar in Malaysia; Zhan Tong and his talented cartooning family in China; Zunzi, Chan Ya, Larry Feign, and Jimmy Pang in Hong Kong; Johnny Lau and Heng Kim Song in Singapore; Yukio Sugiura, Sampei Sato, and Yoshiro Kato in Japan; Tom Hoong and Shan Li in Taiwan; Polito, Ares, Boligán, and Lillo in Cuba; Bohuslav Pernecký, Viliam Živický, Koloman Leššo in Slovakia; Ane Vasilevski and other personnel at the Osten Gallery and *Osten* magazine in Macedonia; Chris Browne, Jerry Robinson, and Mort

Walker in the United States; Robert LaPalme in Canada, and Flavio Mario De Alcantava Calazans in Brazil.

Other individuals were also very kind during my travels in search of cartooning information: Milan Šoltés, Rev. Samuel Meshack, Dr. Josephine Joseph, Dr. B.P. Sanjay, Lim Cheng Tju, Fong Pick-Huei, Sankaran Ramanathan, Mohd. Hamdan Adnan, Marcel and Viviane Sadarnac, Hane Latt, U. Thiha (a) Thiha Saw, Kyaw Lin, Klára Kubičková, Keiko Tonegawa, Yutaka Kaneko, Toshiko Nakano, and Katsuhisa and Midori Ichitsuka.

Former and current students, whose graduate work I proudly supervised during the past 20 years, lent much appreciated support: Professor Oranuj Lertchanyarak (and husband, Kanongdej) and Dr. Charles Elliott, in Thailand and Hong Kong, respectively; Dr. Hongying Liu-Lengyel (and husband, Dr. Alfonz Lengyel) in China; Dr. John V. Vilanilam in India; Dr. Myung Jun Kim, Dr. Hoon Soon Kim, and Sang Kil Lee in Korea, and Dr. Hsiao Hsiang-wen and Chu-feng Tang in Taiwan. Others, such as Rei Okamoto and Aruna Rao, provided sources and insights concerning Japanese and Indian cartoons, respectively, and Dr. Fei Zhengxing, Kohava Simhi, Jim Dever, Dr. Maria Santana, Chyun-Fung Shi, and Betsi Grabe helped in recording and translating sources.

Cartoonists and comic art specialists who kindly sent information, especially lists of their own works, were John J. Appel, Jean-Claude Faur, Axel Frohn, Denis Gifford, Harold Hinds, Maurice Horn, Nat Karmichael, Les Lilley, Richard Langlois, Leonard Rifas, and Jerry Robinson. Horn donated a part of his library to me. Also providing sources were Gary Groth, Pete Coogan, Randall Scott, German Caceres, Robert Roberts, Joseph G. Szabo, and Tim Ernst. Mort Walker, Jerry Robinson, David Kunzle, and Maurice Horn gave these bibliographies much respectability by writing forewords that are informative and interesting.

Roseanne Lent typed the 1986 bibliography on comic art which I self published, and Michael Taney readied this one for publication.

The reader of any scholarly work has a right to know who paid the research bill, for here lies the potential for influence peddling. As with my previous works, this bibliography was completed without grants and with very minimal (and that given begrudgingly) help from my workplace. Instead, it was financed by my summer earnings, meager savings, and income tax refunds, as well as a loan from what I good naturedly, but gratefully, call the Bovalino's Ristorante "Foundation," my brother Russ's restaurant in Westlake, Ohio.

To all the people mentioned above, and hundreds of others, I express my sincerest appreciation.

John A. Lent

1

Continental, Regional, Comparative Perspectives

REFERENCES

Overviews, Histories

1. Baron-Carvais, Annie. *La Bande Dessinée*. Paris: Presses Universitaires de France, 1985.

2. Baumgärtner, Alfred Clemens. *Die Welt der Comics*. Probleme Einer Primitiven Literaturform. 5. erw. Auflage. Bochum: Kamp, 1972.

3. Baur, Uwe. "Für Eine Gattungstheorie des Comics." In Zdenko Škreb and Uwe Baur, eds. *Erzählgattungen der Trivialliteratur*. Innsbruck: Institut für Germanistik, Universität, 1984.

4. Beauregard, Jacques and Léandre Trucotte. *La Bande Dessinée*. Montreal: Ed. Beauchemin, 1973.

5. Bergeron, Francis and Alain Sanders. "La B.D. C'Est Beaucoup Plus Que de la Bande Dessinée." *L'Astrolabe* (Paris). 1:80 (1985), pp. 2-4.

6. Bouyer, Sylvain. "Il n'y a Pas de Spécificité au Numéro Que Vous Avez Demandé." *Les Cahiers de la Bande Dessinée*. 72, 1986, pp. 46-47.

7. Coupal, Michel. "Terminologie de la Bande Dessinée." *Meta* (Montreal). 23:4 (1978), pp. 311-314.

8.   Couperie, Pierre, Proto De Stefanis, Edouard François, Gérald Gassiot-Talabot, Maurice Horn, Claude Moliterni. *Bande Dessinée et Figuration Narrative*. Histoire, Esthétique, Production et Sociologie de la Bande Dessinée Mondiale, Procédés Narratifs et Structure de l'Image dans la Peinture Contemporaine. Musée des Arts Décoratifs, Palais du Louvre, Pavillon de Marsan (exposition). Paris: S.E.R.G., 1967.

9.   Cronel, Hervé. "L'Image et la Référence." *La Nouvelle Revue Française* (Paris). 226, 1971, pp. 179-192.

10.   Denni, Michel and Françoise Thonet. "La Rage de Collectionner." *Les Cahiers de la Bande Dessinée*. 69, 1986, pp. 49-54.

11.   Filippini, Henri and Michel Bourgeois. *Le Bande Dessinée en 10 Leçon, de Zig et Puce á Tintin et Astérix*. Paris: Hachette, 1976.

12.   François, Edouard. *L'Age d'Or de la Bande Dessinée*. Ivry (Val-de-Marne): S.E.R.G., 1974.

13.   Frémion, Yves. "Le Tournant des Années '80." *Magazine Littéraire* (Paris). 180, 1982, pp. 71-73.

14.   Fuchs, Wolfgang J. *Comics im Medienmarkt, in der Analyse, im Unterricht*. Opladen: Leske und Budrich, 1977.

15.   Fuchs, Wolfgang J. and Reinhold Reitberger. *Comics-Handbuch*. Reinbek bei Hamburg: Rowohlt Taschenbuch Verlag, 1978.

16.   Fuchs, Wolfgang J. and Reinhold C. Reitberger. *Das große Buch der Comics*. Anatomie Eines Massenmediums. Mit Schallplatte. Heinz Moos Verlag, 1971; Reinbek bei Hamburg: Rowohlt Taschenbuch Verlag, 1973; Dreieich: MeCO Verlag GmbH, 1982.

17.   Gonzales, Christian. "Promenade en 'BD.'" *Le Spectacle du Monde. Réalités* (Paris). 256, 1983, pp. 87-91.

18.   Gubern, Román. *Comics*. Kunst und Konsum der Bildergeschichten. Aus dem Französischen übertragen von Hainer Kober. Reinbek bei Hamburg: Rowohlt Taschenbuch Verlag, GmbH, 1973. (Originally, *Literatura de la Imagen*); Barcelona: Salvat Editores, 1973; Lausanne: Editions Grammont, S.A., 1978.

19.   Herdeg, Walter and David Pascal, eds. *The Art of the Comic Strip/ Die Kunst des Comic Strip/ L'Art de la Bande Dessinée*. Zürich: Walter Herdeg The Graphis Press, 1972.

20.   Hoffmann, Detlef and Sabine Rauch, eds. *Comics: Materialien zur Analyse Eines Massenmediums*. Frankfurt, Berlin, Munich: Diesterweg, 1975.

21.   Holtz, Christina. *Comics, Ihre Entwicklung und Bedeutung*. Munich, New York, London, Paris: K.G. Saur, 1980.

22.   "La Bande Dessinée Aujourd'hui." *Magazine Littéraire* (Paris). 95, 1974, pp. 8-37.

23.   Lacassin, Francis. *Pour un Neuvième Art. La Bande Dessinée*. Paris, Geneva: Slatkine, 1971, 1982.

24.   Li Pera Pignato, Rosathea. *Attraverso il Fumetto. I. Alla Ricerca dei Meccanismi. II. Alla Ricerca dei Personaggi*. Messina, Firenze: Casa Editrice G. D'Anna, 1977.

25.   Marny, Jacques. *Le Monde Étonnant des Bandes Dessinées*. Preface by René Goscinny. Paris: Eds. du Centurion, 1968.

26.   Metken, Günter. *Comics*. Frankfurt, Hamburg: Fischer Taschenbuch-Verlag, 1971.

27.   Micheli, S., ed. *Parole e Nuvole*. Atti del Corso Sulla Letteratura per Immagini per Insegnanti della Scuola dell'Obbligo Organizzato dal Centro Studi sul Cinema e Sulle Communicazioni di Mussa. Universita degli Studi di Siena, Provincia di Siena tenuto a Siena nel Novembre-Dicembre 1982. Rome: Bulzoni, 1985.

28.   Pernin, Georges. *Un Monde Etrange, la Bande Dessinée*. Paris: Ed. Cledor, 1974.

29.   Pierre, Michel. *La Bande Dessinée*. Paris: Librairie Larousse, 1976.

30.   Pleuß, Alfred. *Bildergeschichten un Comics. Grundlegende Informationen und Literaturhinweise für Eltern, Erzieher, Bibliothekare*. Bad Honnef: Bock und Herchen, 1983.

31.   Rey, Alain. *Les Spectres de la Bande. Essai sur la B.D.* Paris: Minuit, 1978.

32.   Riha, Karl. *Zok Roarr Wumm. Zur Geschichte der Comics Literatur*. Steinbach: Anabas Verlag Kämpf, 1970.

33.   Schnurrer, Achim and Riccardo Rinaldi. *Die Kunst der Comics*. Reinbek bei Hamburg: Carlsen Verlag, 1984.

34.   Setterblad, Svante. "Vom Künstler zum Leser. Die Internationale Produktion und Distribution von Comics." *Communications* (Sankt Augustin). 10:1/3 (1984), pp. 129-137.

35.   Strazzulla, Gaetano. *Fumetti di Ieri e di Oggi*. Bologna: Cappelli Editore, 1977.

36.   Suchan, Eric. "Geschichte der Comics. 1. Teil." *Comic Forum. Das Österreichische Fachmagazin für Comicliteratur.* 3:11 (1981), pp. 29-31.

37.   Suchan, Eric. "Geschichte der Comics. 2. Teil." *Comic Forum. Das Österreichische Fachmagazin für Comicliteratur.* 3:12 (1981), pp. 43-45.

38.   Suchan, Eric. "Geschichte der Comics. 3. Teil." *Comics Forum. Das Österreichische Fachmagazin für Comicliteratur.* 4:14 (1982), pp. 18-20.

39.   Tremblay, Roger. "La Bande Dessinée: Une Typologie." *The Canadian Modern Language Review.* 36:3 (1980), pp. 504-513.

40.   Verweyen, Annemarie. *Comics. Eine Ausstellung im Rheinischen Freilichtmuseum, Landemuseum für Volkskunde Kommern.* Cologne: Rheinland-Verlag GmbH, 1986.

41.   Zimmermann, Hans Dieter, ed. *Comic Strips. Geschichte Struktur, Wirkung und Verbreitung der Bildergeschichten.* (Catalog). Berlin: Ausstellung in der Akademie der Künste vom December 13, 1969 to January 25, 1970.

42.   Zimmermann, Hans Dieter, ed. *Vom Geist der Superhelden. Comic Strips. Zur Theorie der Bildergeschichte.* Munich: Deutscher Taschenbuch Verlag, 1973, 1975.

43.   Zureddu, Gérard. "*La BD 'Un Art Moyen.*'" In *A la Rencontre de... Jacques Tardi*, edited by Gari, pp. 9-15. Marseilles: Bédésup, 1982.

Encyclopedias

44.   Alessandrini, Marjorie *et al. Encyclopédie des Bandes Dessinées.* Paris: Albin Michel, 1979, 1986.

45.   Anónimas y Colectivas *Historia de los Comics.* 4 Vols. Barcelona: Editor José Toutain, 1983.

46.   Couperie, Pierre, Henri Filippini, and Claude Moliterni. *Encyclopédie de la Bande Dessinée.* Ivry: S.E.R.G., Vol. 1, 1974; Vols. 2-3, 1975.

47.   Crawford, Hubert H. *Crawford's Encyclopedia of Comic Books.* Middle Village, New York: Jonathan David Publishers, 1978.

48.   Fossati, Franco. *I Fumetti in 100 Personaggi.* Milan: Longanesi & Co., 1977.

49.   Fossati, Franco. *Guida al Fumetto Satirico & Politico.* Milan: Gammalibri, 1979.

50. Frémion, Yves. "Petit Dictionnaire des Auteurs de B.D." *Magazine Littéraire* (Paris). 95, 1974, pp. 27-36.

51. Fuchs, Wolfgang J. *Compact-Minilexikon. Comic Helden von Asterix bis Zorro.* Munich: Compact-Verlag, 1984.

52. Kousemaker, Kees and Evelien, Rob Richard, Jan Smet, and Albert Tol, eds. *Wordt Vervolgd-Stripleksikon der Lage Landen.* Utrecht, Antwerp: Het Spectrum B.V., 1979.

53. Moliterni, Claude *et al. Histoire Mondiale de la Bande Dessinée.* Paris: P. Horay, 1980.

54. Sadoul, Jacques. *Panorama de la Bande Dessinée.* Paris: J'ai Lu, 1976.

55. Strazzula, Gaetano. *I Fumetti. 2. ed. Totalmente Rifatta.* 2 Vols. Firenze: Sansoni, 1980.

Periodical Directory

56. *Anuscha Mascha.* Fanzine. Wolfgang Höhne, Rudolfstr. 26, 7500 Karlsruhe 1, Germany.

57. *Apropos.* Published twice yearly as "Almanac of the Humour and Satire of Nations." Includes cartoons, illustrations, cartoonists' profiles, histories of humor magazines, interviews. Approximately 130-175 pp. Published by House of Humour and Satire, 5300 Gabrovo, P.O Box 104, Bulgaria. Editions in Bulgarian, Russian, English, and French. Since 1983.

58. *Association of Comics Enthusiasts Newsletter. Comic Cuts.* Founded 1977 as organ of A.C.E. by Denis Gifford. Mainly newspaper clippings about comics. Address: 80 Silverdale, Sydenham, London, England SE26-4SJ. A.C.E. is England's first club for collectors of British comics.

59. *(A Suivre).* French monthly consisting mainly of cartoon strips, but also occasional articles and news notes. No. 177 in October 1992. Jean-Paul Mougin, 66, rue Bonaparte, 75006 Paris, France.

60. *Bédésup.* Major, regularly published periodical dealing mainly with French comic art; includes reviews, news, articles, interviews. Jean-Claude Faur, BP 14, 13234 Marseilles Cedex 4, France.

61. *Le Nouveau Bédésup.* Quarterly. Jean Arrouye or Jean-Claude Faur, BP 14, 13234 Marseilles, Cedex 4, France.

62.   *Bild and Bubbla*. Focus on comics in Europe, especially Sweden. No. 2 in 1989. Address: *Serieframjandet*, Kungsholm Strand 135 B, 112 48 Stockholm.

63.   *Black and White*. Fanzine of articles, strips, letters. Daniel Slingsby, 25 Cottingham Rd., Hull HU5 2PP, England. Mid-1980s.

64.   *Caricature et Caricaturistes*. Twenty-three numbers by 1992 with profiles of France's top cartoonists. Bimester. Interviews, showcases. Edited by Solo, Groupe Té Arte, 65 rue Blomet, 75015 Paris, France.

65.   *The Cartoon Art Trust Newsletter*. Newsletter of Cartoon Art Trust and National Museum of Cartoon Art, "Carriage Row," 163-203 Eversholt St., London NW1, England.

66.   *The Cartoonist*. Started as fortnightly in early 1993; oversized newspaper full of British (some U.S.) cartoons on newsworthy events. 14 Utopia Village, Chalcot Road, London NW18LH.

67.   *Comic Art*. Articles on foreign and Italian cartoons, characters, and artists; news, reviews, letters, and many full color strips. Via Flavio Domiziano, 9-00145 Rome, Italy.

68.   *Comic Forum*. Austrian periodical dealing mostly with Germanic comics, but others as well. Zöllergasse 15, A-1070 Vienna, Austria.

69.   *Comicgraph*. Published by Wolfgang Brenner, Luisenstr. 8, D-6070 Langen, Germany.

70.   *Comicguia*. Cuaderno de la historieta. Published quarterly by Francisco Tadeo Juan, Editor Manuel Aquilar 17, 46001 Valencia, Spain. Deals with Spanish and other comic books. No. 23 in Summer 1992.

71.   *Comic Media News*. Newszine for comics fans of Britain. 42 pp. News, reviews, interviews. Richard Burton, 22 Woodhaw, Egham, Surrey TW209AP England.

72.   *Comic Reddition*. Published by Volker Hamann, Edition Alfons, Schöneberger, Str. 12, D-2080 Pinneberg, Germany.

73.   *Comics Express*. German periodical. Olpener Str. 767, D-5000 Cologne 91, Germany.

74.   *Comics International*. Monthly independent trade paper for US and British industry. News, listings, features. 77 Oxford St., London W1R1RB, England.

75.   *Comics News Service from Poland*. Started as mimeographed newsletter in 1991. English language account of Polish comics: news, reviews, prizes, exhibitions, interviews. Witold Traczyk, ul. Nowina 15/1, 60-589 Poznań, Poland. Quarterly.

76. *Comikazin.* Fanzine. Henning Way, Hagenstraße 23, 3000 Hannover 1, Germany.

77. *Comix.* Il Giornale dei Fumetti. Tabloid of 32 pages devoted to U.S., European strips, essays. Via Corassori 24, 41100 Modena, Italy.

78. *Comixene.* Fanzine of articles, letters, and its own strip, "Auntie Mayme." Howard Stangroom, 10, Geneva Drive, Redcar, Cleveland TS10 1JP, England. Mid-1980s.

79. *Corto Maltese.* Showcasing numerous cartoons, strips, and comics. Articles on the field of comics, artists, and characters. Casa Editrice R.C.S. Rozzoli Periodici S.p.A., Via A. Rizzoli 2, 20132 Milan, Italy.

80. *Die Sprechblase.* Eight times yearly comics magazine. 105 number in 1990. 64 pages. Norbert Hethke, P.O.B., D-6917 Schönau, Germany.

81. *El Wendigo.* Published since 1974 by Faustino Rodríguez Arbesú, Apartado de Correos 461, Gijón, Spain. Mostly about U.S. comic book artists and characters, but also deals with Spanish cartoonists.

82. *Fantasy Advertiser (FA).* Bimonthly since about early 1980s. Current news, reviews, and articles on role playing games, TV, cinema, sci-fi, comics in Great Britain and U.S. Address in early years: Martin Lock, 3, Marlow Ct., Brittania Square, Worcester WR1 3DP, England. Succeeded by Martin Skidmore, 25, Cornleaze, Withywood, Bristol, England.

83. *Fantazia. The Definitive Superhero Magazine.* Published beginning about 1990, at 69 Hurst St., Birmingham B5 4TE, England. U.S. and British comic books, as well as strips, video, film. Interviews, articles, news, reviews.

84. *Fat Comic.* Danish periodical. Started in 1980. After 32 numbers, merged with *Serieskaberen* to form *Seriejournalen.* Tegnestuen Gimle, Husumgade 2, 2200 Copenhagen N, Denmark.

85. *FECO News.* Published as newsletter of Federation of European Cartoonists Organizations by Ronald Libin. Includes FECO news, selected cartoon works from various countries, short articles. In 1992 FECO included Belgium, Great Britain, Holland, Russia, Czechoslovakia, Bulgaria, USA, Yugoslavia, Japan, Colombia, Cyprus, Australia, Ireland, and Germany. Gelijkheidstraat 10- 8400 Oostende, Belgium.

86. *Fusion.* "The far-out fanzine for fantasy fans." Hugh Campbell, 46 Kirkland Rd., Kilbirnie, Ayrshire, KA25 6HU, England. No. 2, 1984.

87. *Giff-Wiff.* Three-times-yearly periodical on comic art of U.S. and Europe published from 1964 to 1967 in Paris. Jean-Jacques Pauver, editor.

88. *Graphixus.* Published ten times yearly by Media and Graphic Creations, 81 Herries St., London W10 4LE. Adult comix showcase and review of visual entertainment. News, interviews, articles. Beginning in 1978.

89. *Haga.* Bimonthly review of comic books since 1972. Address: Rue de Périole, 31500 Toulouse, France.

90. *Icom Info.* Magazine for those interested in comics, cartoons, trick film, and illustration. Official organ of Interessenverband Comic e.V. Monthly in German. Includes news items, letters, calendar of festivals, interviews, articles, reviews, advertisements. Includes other countries besides Germany. *Icom Info*, c/o Gerd Zimmer, Holzäckerstrasse 32, 8551 Wimmelbach, Germay.

91. *Il Fumetto.* Revista dei Comics a Cura Dell'Anaf. Published monthly beginning in 1972, with ties to Associazione Nazionale Amici del Fumetto in Bologna. News notes, articles, interviews, portfolios of American and some Italian cartoonists.

92. *Infinity.* Fanzine for underground comics enthusiasts. Articles, letters, strips. Russell Willis, 6, Shutler Rd., Broadstairs, Kent, England. Mid 1980s.

93. *Jester.* Organ of Cartoonists Club of Great Britain. Monthly with news, profiles, reprinted clippings. Clive Collins, editor, 251 Highlands Blvd., Leigh-on-Sea, England SS9 3TN.

94. *Kever.* Cartoon magazine published by Kartoenistenvereniging, Mortsel, The Netherlands.

95. *Keverinfo.* Monthly cartoon newsletter of 42 pages, published by Kever Kartoenistenvereniging, Belgium. News, advertisements, interviews, festival announcements. Bob Vincke, Eikhof 20, 3540 Heusden-Zolder, Haasrode, Belgium.

96. *Kuk.* Published as four-page Czech cartoon magazine, beginning in 1990. Parizska 9, 11630 Prague 1, Czechoslovakia.

97. *La Borsa del Fumetto.* Published beginning in 1979 at Viale Tunisia No. 30, 20124 Milan, Italy. Provides prices, illustrations, portfolios and short articles about US, Italian, other European comic books.

98. *La Lettre de Bédésup.* Published three times yearly as eight-page newsletter about comic books, primarily French. B.P. 14, 13234 Marseilles Cedex 4, France. In French.

99. *L'Année de la Bande Dessinée.* Annual dealing with comics. Paris, 1981-1983; Grenoble, 1984-.

100. *Le Collectionneur de Bandes Dessinée.* Monthly dealing with comics out of Paris.

101. *Les Cahiers de la Bande Dessinée (Schtroumpf)*. Since 1969; published by Editions Jacques Glénat, 6, rue Lieutenant-Charror, 38000 Grenoble, France. Monthly. Deals with comic books.

102. *Lippe*. Fanzine. Andreas Anger. Schreibersgasse 7, 8710 Kitzingen, Germany.

103. *Mieux Vaut en Rire*. Published by André Baur, 24 rue du Chardon, 57100 Thionville, France. Interviews, reprinted articles mostly about French cartoonists; many cartoons and caricatures.

104. *Monokel*. Short-lived (ca. 1990) satirical magazine at Humonarchie, 1041 Vienna, Pf. 508. Color, black and white cartoons, news, advertisements.

105. *Neuróptica. Estudios Sobre el Cómic*. Spanish periodical devoted to various aspects of comics. Zaragoza. Since 1983.

106. *Nilus*. Started in 1987 or 1988 by Agostino and Franco Origone and published by Edition Glénat, Genoa, Italy. Cartoons.

107. *Nordic Comics Revue International*. Published quarterly by the Nordic magazines, *Seriejournalen, Bild and Bubbla, Bobbla, TEGN,* and *Sarjainfo*. Letters, news items from individual Scandinavian countries, interviews, reviews. Since 1992. Frank Madsen, editor, Tegnestuen Gimle, Husumgade 2, 1. th., DK 2200, Copenhagen, Denmark.

108. *Norsk Tegneserieforum*. Magazine on comics. Westbye Egebergsgt. 8C, N0172 Oslo 1, Norway.

109. *Outside*. Fanzine. Toni Momper, Linnichstr. 29, 5110 Asldorf, Germany.

110. *Phénix*. Published from 1966 by Éditions Serg, Paris. Articles on U.S., European comic books and strips.

111. *Plop*. Fanzine. Bernhard Bollen, Ludwig-Beck-Str. 12, 4000 Düsseldorf, Germany.

112. *Ran-Tan-Plan*. Since 1966, in Brussels, Belgium.

113. *Rraah! Neues aus der Comicszene*. Four times yearly German comic news magazine of 52 pp. New books, trends, profiles. Comicplus, Verlag Sackman und Hörndl, Eppendorfer Weg 67, D-2000 Hamburg 20, Germany.

114. *The SAF Reporter*. Published by Ervin Rustemagic in English and French editions for Strip Art Features, PO Box 38, 71210 Ilidza, Sarajevo, Yugoslavia. Reports on activities of artists who are part of SAF; mainly about strip cartooning. Since late 1980s.

115. *Sarjainfo*. Magazine on comics. Pl. 927, SF00101 Helsinki, Finland.

116. *Schatten.* Fanzine. Auroragraphics, Küsnachter Str. 15, CH-8126 Zwmikon, Germany.

117. *Seriejournalen.* Published four times a year as Danish magazine on comics. First number September 1990. Frank Madsen, Tegnestuen Gimle, Ahlefeldtsgade 27, DK 1359 Copenhagen K, Denmark.

118. *Serieland-Magasinet.* Comics-oriented magazine. Attn: Sölve Dahlgren, Safirgatan 6, S26700 Bjuv, Sweden.

119. *Shadows.* Fanzine of articles, strips, letters. Pete Howard, 18. Anderson Crescent, Great Barr, Birmingham B43 7SU, England. Mid 1980s.

120. *Signum.* Fanzine. Lars Vollbrecht, Columbusstr. 2, 2850 Bremerhaven, Germany.

121. *Society of Strip Illustration Newsletter.* Monthly periodical of England's Society of Strip Illustration, 7 Dilke St., London SW34JE. News, exhibitions, cartoons, reprints from newspapers and magazines.

122. *Speakeasy. The Origin of the Comics World.* Monthly of John Brown Publishing, The Boathouse, Crabtree Lane, Fulham, London SW68NJ, England. Mainly U.S. and British comic books; news, articles, and reviews. Since about 1980.

123. *Storyboard.* Published irregularly, beginning in September 1981, with information on Nordic animation. Interviews, reports about festivals, and articles about Nordic, other European, U.S. animation. Mattias Gordon, Slathults Norrgard, S-57800 Aneby, Sweden. In Swedish.

124. *Strapazin—Comic Art Magazine.* Edited by David Basler and Herbert Meiler. Comic art periodical since 1985 with international news, reviews, profiles, new publications. Meiler, Oberländerstr 31, D-8000 Munich 70, Germany.

125. *Talking Turkey.* Published by Galaxy Publications Ltd., PO Box 312, Witham, Essex CM8 3SZ. Mix of European, American, and British cartooning. Launched October 1991.

126. *TEGN.* Norwegian periodical dealing with Scandinavian and other comics. Number 3, October 1989. Address: Postboks 162, N1473 Skårer, Norway.

127. *Tratto, Revista di Humus Grafico ed Altro.* Six times a year. Mostly gag cartoons, some political and one strip. Address: Strada Perugia-S. Marco 4/A, 06100 Perugia, Italy.

128. *Trööt!* Fanzine. Friesgasse 9, A-1150 Vienna, Austria.

129. *Utopische Welt.* Fanzine. Katrin Friedrich, Gerstäckerstr. 18, 3000 Hannover, Germany.

130. *Watcher*. Started in October 1988 as international magazine of fantasy, horror, and science fiction, devoted to comics and films of Germany, Finland, France, Italy, Canada, and U.S. Mostly illustrations. Chris Dohr, Weidegasse 1, D-5500 Trier, Germany.

131. Wilhelm-Busch-Gesellschaft. *Wilhelm-Busch-Jahrbuch 1988*. Hannover. Wilhelm-Busch-Museum, 1989. 148 pp. Yearbooks of Wilhelm-Busch-Society have been published since 1932.

132. *Worlds Collide*. Articles on most aspects of comics; letters; illustrations. Howard Stangroom, 10, Geneva Drive, Redcar, Cleveland TS10 IJP, England. Mid 1980s.

133. *Yellow Press*. Started 1991 by NBJ Publications, P.O. Box 3315, Dublin 12, Ireland. Full of cartoons.

134. *Zebra*. Fanzine. Georg K. Berres, Giselherstr. 19, 5000 Cologne, Germany.

135. *Zelot*. Fanzine published by Ragnar Fyri, Solliveien 37, 1370 Asker, Norway, in early 1980s.

GENERAL STUDIES

136. "As Ações da Cartoon." *Corto Circuito*. April 1992, pp. 42-44.

137. Auquier, Jean. "La République des Bulles." *Coccinelle*. June 1990, p. 7.

138. "The Biggest Cartoon: Save the North Sea!" *FECO News*. No. 5, 1987, p. 12.

139. Blanco, Francisco. "Antifascist Cartoons." *CEMEDIM*. September-October 1985, pp. 6-7.

140. Burke, Peter. *Popular Culture in Early Modern Europe*. New York: New York University Press, 1978.

141. "Cartoons by Frank Hoffmann." *FECO News*. No. 13, 1992, p. 7.

142. *C'Est le Bouquet!* Paris: Albin Michel, 1976. 114 pp.

143. Clements, R.J. "European Literary Scene: Penetration into Precincts of Art and Literature." *Saturday Review*. September 3, 1966, p. 23.

144. Cole, William and Mike Thaler. *The Classic Cartoons*. Cleveland, Ohio: World Publishing, 1966. 336 pp. ("America," "England," "The Continent").

145.   Coyne, Jean A. "Vint Lawrence." *Communication Arts*. March/April 1988, pp. 42-49.

146.   De Laet, Danny. "Hans Kresse, ou l'Homme Qui Se Perdit au Nord." *Phénix*. No. 12, 1969.

147.   Desutter, Manu. "25 Jaar Humor." *FECO News*. No. 2, 1986, p. 5.

148.   *Euro-Kartoenale 1989. "Luchtvaart. Kruishoutem-Belgie."* 1989.

149.   "Euro News." *Comic Forum. Das Österreichische Fachmagazin für Comicliteratur* (Vienna). 1:1 (1979) to 5:19 (1983). Series.

150.   "European Audiovisual Communication Centre." *FECO News*. No. 6, 1988, p. 6.

151.   "European War Cartoons—Chiefly German." *Review of Reviews*. October 1915, pp. 418-424.

152.   Fernández, Norman. "Cuando lo Viejo se Viste Nuevo." *El Wendigo*. Año 15, No. 46, 1989, pp. 6-7.

153.   Fronval, George. "La Dynastie des Offenstadt." *Phénix*. No. 3, 1967, pp. 40-43; No. 5, 4. Trimestre 1967, pp. 21-26; No. 7, 3. Trimestre 1968, pp. 13-16.

154.   Gifford, Denis. "Now It's Eurohumor." *Graphics World* (London). November 1978.

155.   Gonzalez, Cristine. "Life Inside Daffy Duck Is Hot, and Sometimes Your Ribs Get Broken." *Wall Street Journal Europe*. August 6-7, 1993, pp. 1, 8.

156.   Hammerl, Thomas. "New Cartoons by Erich Paulmichl." *Novum Gebrauchsgraphik*. October 1986, pp. 38-43.

157.   Hartau, Johannes. "Don Quijote in der Kunst. Wandlungen Einer Symbolfigur in Deutschland, England und Frankreich." Doctoral dissertation, University of Hamburg, 1983.

158.   Hartung, Peter. "Strid om Jacobs Efterladte Vaerk." *Serieskaberen*. June 1990, pp. 19-20.

159.   "Humor in Art and Cartooning." In *Humor Scholarship: A Research Bibliography*, edited by Don Nilsen, pp. 243-249. Westport, Connecticut: Greenwood Press, 1993.

160.   "Jack Markow." *Cartoonist PROfiles*. March 1980, pp. 72-78.

161. Jarrase, Dominique. "A la Barbe d'Haussmann." *Revue de l'Art*. 84 (1989), pp. 81-82.

162. *Jeux D'Hiver Jeux D'Humour*. Paris: HA! Les Humoristes Associes, 1991.

163. Knigge, Andreas C. "Der Einfluß der Amerikanischen Abenteuer-Serien auf die Europäischen Comics." In *Comic-Jahrbuch 1986*, edited by Martin Compart and Andreas C. Knigge, pp. 37-43. Berlin: Ullstein GmbH, 1985.

164. Kobylinski, Szymon. *Eskapaden*. Berlin: Eulenspiegel-Verlag, 1962.

165. Kolditz, Niels. "Fanszene." *ICOM*. January 1993, pp. 60-61.

166. Lengyel, Alfonz. *Selected Prints from the Goebel Collection*. St. Davids, Pennsylvania: Eastern College Printing Press, 1988. (Rowlandson, pp. 48-49; Daumier, pp. 54-55; Gavarni, pp. 64-65).

167. "Liars, Damn Liars—and Cartoonists." *Access Magazine*. Winter 1985, pp. 18-23.

168. Lipinski, Eryk. *Rätsel um Otek*. Berlin: Eulenspiegel-Verlag, 1969.

169. Lofficier, Randy and Jean-Marc. "Comics in Europe." *Uncle Jam Quarterly*. Fall 1989, pp. 5-6.

170. Neal, Jim. "Europeans Prefer Florida's Disney World to Euro-Disney." *Comics Buyer's Guide*. September 3, 1993, p. 28.

171. "One-Man Crusade; European Cartooning." *Newsweek*. September 14, 1959, pp. 114-115.

172. Petersen, Teddy, Claus Seidel and Arne Sørensen. *Drawing the Line*. Copenhagen: AIDA, 1992. (Denmark, Estonia, Latvia, Lithuania).

173. Piotrowsky, Mieczystaw. *Pas Zweite Gesicht*. Berlin: Eulenspiegel-Verlag, 1982.

174. Reber, László. *Hokuspokus*. Berlin: Eulenspiegel-Verlag, 1962.

175. Reguera, Constantino. "Mas Alla de los Pirineos." *El Wendigo*. Winter 1988-1989, p. 36. (France, Italy).

176. Risley, John. "Between Two Rounds." *Apropos*. No. 1, 1983, pp. 157-158.

177. "Salute to Pavel Constantin, Sergei Tjunin and Ane Vasilevski." *WittyWorld*. Summer/Autumn 1991, p. 83.

178. Sanders, Jan. *La Barre à Babord*. Grenoble: Glénat, 1983. 71 pp.

179.   Shaw, R. "Europa Pokes Fun." *Review of Reviews*. April 1930, pp. 42-45.

180.   Shikes, Ralph E. *Slightly Out of Order. Best Cartoons from the Continent by the Members of the Association Internationale des Humoristes*. New York: Viking Press, 1958.

181.   *Silence, On Coule....* Lausanne: Kesseling, 1986. 96 pp.

182.   Søndergaard, Carsten. "Tam Messe." *Serieskaberen*. June 1990, p. 21.

183.   Tscherepanow, Juri. *Der Dressierte Pegasus*. Berlin: Eulenspiegel-Verlag, 1978.

184.   Tschernegg, Markus. "Euro-News." *Comic Forum. Das Magazin für Comicliteratur*. 7:28 (1985), pp. 52-55.

185.   Tschernegg, Markus. "Euro-News." *Comic Forum. Das Magazin für Comicliteratur*. 7:30 (1985), pp. 14-17.

186.   Tschernegg, Markus and Dinu Logoz. "Euro-News." *Comic Forum. Das Magazin für Comicliteratur*. 7:29 (1985), pp. 17-20.

187.   Vasvári, Anna. *Wo Sind Meine Wimpern?* Berlin: Eulenspiegel-Verlag, 1975.

188.   Williams, Michael. "Euro Disney Awash in Red Ink." *Variety*. July 19, 1993, p. 38.

REGIONAL ASPECTS

Federation of European Cartoonists Organizations (FECO)

189.   "A Brief History of FECO." *FECO News*. Special Edition, 1989, pp. 4-5.

190.   "FECO Meeting Skopje." *FECO News*. No. 12, 1991, p. 11.

191.   Hartmann, Paul. "A Report on the FECO Meeting in December 1986." *FECO News*. No. 3, 1987, p. 15.

192.   Libin, Ronald. "The FECO Constitution." *FECO News*. No. 7, 1989, pp. 14-15.

193.   Lilley, Les. "First FECO Meeting in Jugoslavia." *FECO News*. No. 5, 1987, pp. 14-15.

194.   Lilley, Les. "The President's Report from Skopje." *FECO News*. No. 12, 1991, p. 5.

195.   Lilley, Les. "A Report from the President General." *FECO News*. No. 13, 1992, p. 15.

196.   "Minutes of the FECO Meeting." *FECO News*. No. 1, 1986, p. 4.

197.   Moolenaar, Ab. "Feco Meeting 05-10-91 Beringer-Belgium." *FECO News*. No. 13, 1992, p. 23.

198.   Nieuwendijk, Peter. "History of the Federation of European Cartoonists Organisations." *FECO News*. No. 1, 1986, pp. 4-5.

Festivals

199.   Bleicher-Viehoff, Thomas A.T., Dinu Logoz, and Martin Frenzel. "'BD' 86. Festivals." *Comic Forum. Das Magazin für Comicliteratur* (Vienna). 8:33 (1986), pp. 45-56.

200.   "Durbuy 1990." *Seriejournalen*. December 1990, pp. 23-24.

201.   Knigge, Andreas C., Ole Steen Hansen, and Cuno Affolter. "Die Festivals." In *Comic-Jahrbuch 1986*, edited by Martin Compart and Andreas C. Knigge, pp. 293-302. Berlin: Ullstein GmbH, 1985. (Comic festivals of Angoulême, Frankfurt, Barcelona, Sierre, and Munich).

French-Language

202.   Barets, Stan and Thierry Groensteen, eds. *L'Année de la Bande Dessinée 84-85*. Grenoble: Eds. Jacques Glénat, 1984. (Belgium, France).

203.   Barets, Stan and Thierry Groensteen, eds. *L'Année de la Bande Dessinée 85-86*. Grenoble: Eds. Jacques Glénat, 1985 (Belgium, France).

204.   Béra, Michel, Michel Denni and Philippe Mellot. *Trésors de la Bande Dessinée: B.D.M.* Paris: L'Amateur, 1979-.

205.   Bleicher-Viehoff, Thomas A.T. "Euro News." *Comic Forum. Das Magazin für Comicliteratur*. 32, 1986, pp. 9-10. (Belgium, France).

206.   Caré, Jean-Marc. "Bande Dessinée. Les Années 1980 (1.)." *Le Français dans le Monde* (Paris). 170, 1982, pp. 20-22. (Belgium, France).

207.   Caré, Jean-Marc. "Bande Dessinée: Les Années 80 (2.)." *Le Français dans le Monde*. 172, 1982, pp. 11-14.

208.   Caré, Jean-Marc. "BD: le Droit à la Différence." *Le Français dans le Monde*. 200, 1986, pp. 12-17. (Belgium, France).

209.   Chante, Alain. "De Révolution en Contre-Révolution." *Le Français dans le Monde*. 200, 1986, pp. 18-20. (Belgium, France).

210.   Ciment, Gilles and Anne Lescaut. "Présence de la Bande Dessinée dans les Bibliothèques Publiques: C'Est le Fonds Qui Manque le Plus." *Les Cahiers de la Bande Dessinée*. 70, 1986, 37-42. (Belgium, France).

211.   Combet, Claude. "Succès 1985 et Projets 1986." *Livres Hebdo* (Paris). 8:4 (1986), pp. 73-76, 86, 90-95. (Belgium, France).

212.   de Hassonville, Alain. "La Fascination de Eglises dans la Bande Dessinée." *Coccinelle*. January-April 1990, pp. 19-21. (Belgium, France).

213.   Delpierre, J.C. "Comment Caser la Bulle. Quelques Bulles, Quelques Cases, Quelques Héros Qui Ont Fait et Font de la Bande Dessinée." *Bibliographie de la France* (Paris). CLXVII, 2e partie, 1978, Chronique: pp. 2,274-2,306.

214.   Derouet, Paul. "Frankreich/Belgien." In *Comic-Jahrbuch 1986*, edited by Martin Compart and Andreas C. Knigge, pp. 230-252. Berlin: Ullstein GmbH, 1985.

215.   Filippini, Henri. "BD Jeunesse: Pas Morte." *Le Français dans le Monde*. 200, 1986, pp. 58-59. (Belgium, France).

216.   Filippini, Henri, Jacques Glénat, Thierry Martens, and Numa Sadoul. *Histoire de la Bande Dessinée en France et en Belgique: Des Origines à Nos Jours*. Grenoble: Eds. Jacques Glénat, 1979, 1984.

217.   Groensteen, Thierry. "Dernières Nouvelles de l'Édition." *Les Cahiers de la Bande Dessinée*. No. 69 (1986), p. 60. (Belgium, France).

218.   Groensteen, Thierry. "Où Va la Bande Dessinée? *Les Cahiers de la Bande Dessinée*. No. 68, 1986, pp. 41-48.

219.   Jaffray, Patricia. "La BD Franco-Belge à la Conquête du Monde." *Livres Hebdo*. 6:3 (1984), pp. 83-88.

220.   Joor, Thierry. "Vu de New York." *Les Cahiers de la Bande Dessinée*. No. 56, 1984, pp. 40-41. (French-language comics in U.S.).

221.   Mills, T.F. "Franco-Belgian Comics: A Success Story." *Comics Journal*. February 1986, pp. 75-85.

222.   Moliterni, Claude, ed. *Histoire de la Bande Dessinée d'Expression Française*. Ivry (Val-de-Marne): S.E.R.G., 1972.

223. Scholz, Claus D. "Von Raumschiffen und Rieseninsekten. Science Fiction-Comics in Frankreich und Belgien." *Comixene. Das Comicfachmagazin* (Hannover). 7:30 (1980), pp. 15-20. (Belgium, France).

224. Taillandier, François. "Les Grandes Manoeuvres Ont Commencé." *Livres Hebdo*. 8:4 (1986), pp. 66-71. (Belgium, France).

225. "Writer: Thierry Smolderen." *Comics Interview*. No. 75, 1989, pp. 15-42.

Scandinavia

226. "Exklusiv Bob Godfrey Intervju." *Story Board*. No. 7, 1988, pp. 12-13.

227. "Fanzines." *Seriejournalen*. March 1992, p. 18.

228. "Fri oss Fra Masseproduksjonen." *TEGN*. No. 3 (13), 1989, pp. 16-21.

229. Gordon, Mattias. "Flip Johnson: Bildstormare." *Story Board*. No. 7, 1988, pp. 4-7.

230. Jørgensen, Anders. "Skandinavien." In *Comic-Jahrbuch 1986*, edited by Martin Compart and Andreas C. Knigge, pp. 255-262. Berlin: Ullstein GmbH, 1985. (Denmark, Sweden).

231. Larsen, Guttorm. "Animation: Skolproblemets Losning?" *Story Board*. No. 7, 1988, p. 14.

232. Larsen, Guttorm. "Annecy: En Levande Malming." *Story Board*. No. 7, 1988, pp. 8-9.

233. Larsen, Guttorm. "Annecy: Ett Markligt Val." *Story Board*. No. 7, 1988, p. 10.

234. Larsen, Guttorm. "Annecy: Inte Bara Prisvinnare." *Story Board*. No. 7, 1988, p. 11.

235. Larsen, Guttorm. "Asifa Norden Endrer Ansikt?" *Story Board*. No. 7, 1988, p. 17.

236. Larsen, Guttorm. "Kreativt Mote." *Story Board*. No. 7, 1988, p. 15.

237. Madsen, Frank. "Tegneserieal Bums Koster 10 Kr. for Meget." *Serieskaberen*. December 1989, pp. 36-39.

238. Milton, Freddy. "Kommentar til Albumpris-undersøgelsen." *Serieskaberen*. December 1989, pp. 39-40.

239.   "Min Animagiska Penna." *Story Board*. No. 7, 1988, p. 3.

240.   "Nordic Comics Revue." *Seriejournalen*. March 1992, p. 11.

241.   "Nordic Light." *Story Board*. No. 7, 1988, pp. 18-19.

242.   "Nordic News." *Story Board*. 1, 1989, pp. 6-7.

243.   Plaschke, Niels. "Liller Mollers Sex-Film Blev Stor Succes...." *Story Board*. No. 7, 1988, p. 31.

244.   Plaschke, Niels. "Mens Vi Leder Efter Troldeskoven." *Story Board*. No. 7, 1988, pp. 28-29.

245.   Roland, Niels. "Fra Flip til Flop." *Seriejournalen*. March 1992, pp. 16-17.

246.   "Skoll!" *ICOM*. January 1993, p. 12.

247.   Strom, Gunnar. "Animation in the Nordic Countries." *Animation*. Winter 1989, pp. 80-82.

248.   "Strom in ASIFA." *Story Board*. No. 1, 1989, p. 15.

249.   Vainio, Paiso [sic]. "Lettre de Scandinavie: Finlande et Suède." *Les Cahiers de la Bande Dessinée*. 62, 1985, pp. 40-42.

250.   Vainio, Pasi. "Lettre de Scandinavie (2): Norvège, Islande et Danemark." *Les Cahiers de la Bande Dessinée*. 64, 1985, pp. 47-49.

251.   Von Jacobson, O. *Adamson*. Berlin: D. Eysler and Co., n.d.

ANIMATION

252.   "Bluth Negotiating with New Euro Investors." *Variety*. May 27, 1991, p. 69.

253.   Edera, Bruno. *Evocation Synoptique des Origines et des Pionniers du Film d'Animation en Europe, 1888-1928*. Annecy: Tournée Internationale d'Animation, 1971.

254.   Edera, Bruno. "Les Pionniers Européens de l'Animation." *Ecran*. 11 (1973), pp. 12-19.

255.   Erneux, Jean-Louis. "EC's Cartoon Project: The $6-Million Mandate." *Variety*. May 27, 1991, p. 58.

256.   "European Animation Funding, 1988-91." *Variety*. May 27, 1991, p. 75.

257. Fitzgerald, Theresa. "Eastern Conflict: Art Vs. Commerce." *Variety*. September 21, 1992, p. 67.

258. "Forum Agenda: Mixing Speed with Finance." *Variety*. September 21, 1992, pp. 61, 66.

259. Groves, Don. "Mouse Not Meek in Distrib Jungle." *Variety*. November 2, 1992, pp. 34, 40.

260. Groves, Don. "'Princess Ann and the Goblin' Enters an Eastern European Alliance." *Variety*. November 5, 1990, p. 60.

261. Halas, John. "Humour and Satire in Animated Film." *Apropos*. No. 1, 1983, pp. 138-139.

262. Hardy, Phil. "Europeans Animated by Cartoon Boom." *Variety*. November 5, 1990, p. 55.

263. Pitman, Jack. "Kitty Comes on Strong in Europe." *Variety*. May 27, 1991, p. 75.

264. Popescu-Gopo, Jon. "Films, Films, Films." *Apropos*. No. 3, 1986, pp. 152-154.

265. "Tom and Jerry Gain Additional Exposure in U.K., Germany." *The Licensing Book*. October 1990, p. 12.

266. Truck, Walter. "Die Axt im Walde." *Comic Info*. No. 1, 1993, pp. 52-53.

267. Williams, Michael. "Ani Market Adds Kidvid, Live Action to Its Line up." *Variety*. June 7, 1993, p. 28.

268. Williams, Michael. "Annecy Animation Fest Kicks Off." *Variety*. June 7, 1993, p. 28.

269. Williams, Michael. "Don't Delay! Buy into the Studio." *Variety*. May 27, 1991, p. 73.

270. Williams, Michael. "Euros Go Global at Toon Meet." *Variety*. October 7, 1991, pp. 63, 66.

271. Williams, Michael. "Euro Tooners Come of Age." *Variety*. September 21, 1992, p. 61.

272. Williams, Michael. "Toonsters Insist Plan Just Doesn't Compute." *Variety*. October 7, 1991, p. 66.

CARICATURE

273.   Barros, Bernardo G. *La Caricatura Contemporánea. Italia. España. Portugal. Inglatera. Otras Naciones. América.* 2 Vols. Madrid: Editorial América, n.d. (ca. 1920, 1925).

274.   Cundall, Joseph. *Hans Holbein. The Great Artists.* London: Sampson Low Marston and Co. Ltd., n.d.

275.   "Europeans in the Public Eye, a Caricaturists' Symposium." *Living Age.* December 5, 1925, pp. 492-494.

276.   Fuchs, Eduard. *Die Karikatur der Europäischen Völker von Altertum bis zur Neuzeit.* 2 Vols. Berlin: A. Hoffmann, 1902. 4th Ed. Munich: Albert Langen, 1921.

277.   Gauthiez, Pierre. *Holbein.* Coll. "Les Grands Artistes." Paris: Henri Laurens, Éd., 1907.

278.   Gianeri, Enrico. *Storia della Caricatura Europea.* Firenze: Vallecchi, 1967.

279.   Gopnik, Adam. "High and Low: Caricature, Primitivism, and the Cubist Portrait." *Art Journal.* Winter 1983, pp. 371-372.

280.   Grand-Carteret, John. *Contre Rome. La Bataille Anti-Clericale en Europe.* Paris: Louis Michaud, n.d.

281.   Grand-Carteret, John. *Le Jeune Premier de l'Europe devant l'Objectif Caricaturale* (Alfonso XIII). Paris: Louis Michaud, Éditeur, n.d.

282.   Grand-Carteret, John. *Les Moeurs et la Caricature en Allemagne, en Autriche, en Suisse.* Paris: Louis Westhausser Éditeur, 1885.

283.   "Gute Kritische Grafik Hat Kein Verfalldatum." *Rhein-Main-Presse.* November 11, 1991, p. 22.

284.   Hartau, Johannes. "Don Quixote in Broadsheets of the Seventeenth and Early Eighteenth Centuries." *Journal of the Warburg and Courtauld Institute.* 48 (1985), pp. 234-238.

285.   "Hewison, William: 1925-: Reproductions: Caricatures of Barry Humphries, Elizabeth Quinn, Judi Dench, Anton Lesser and Elizabeth Taylor." *Art and Artists.* February 1985, p. 43.

286.   Hofmann, Werner. *Die Karikatur von Leonardo bis Picasso.* Vienna: 1956.

287.   "Jack Markow." *Cartoonist PROfiles.* September 1981, pp. 14-17.

288. Kahn, Gustave. *Europas Fürsten im Sittenspiegel der Karikatur*. Berlin: Hermann Schmidts Verlag, 1907/1908. 472 pp.

289. Koch, Ursula E. "From the Revolution (1848) to the Franco-Prussian War (1870/71): The Image of the Neighbour in Satirical Comparison from the Examples of the Paris Daily Newspaper *Le Charivari* and the Berlin Weekly *Kladderadatsch*. "Paper presented at International Association for Mass Communication Research, Bled, Yugoslavia, August 26-31, 1990.

290. Levy, Paul. "Euro-Caricatures: Of Frogs and Scabrous Scotsmen." *AAEC Notebook*. Spring 1993, pp. 17-18.

291. Malcolm, J.P. *An Historical Sketch of the Art of Caricature*. London: 1813.

292. "Old-Time Caricatures—No. 15." *Twinkles*. May 8, 1897, p. 13.

293. Perrine-Wittkamp, Francine. "Caricature: An Art As Old As Time." *Media History Digest*. Fall 1985, pp. 14-16.

294. Piltz, Georg. *Geschichte der Europäischen Karikatur*. Berlin: VEB Deutscher Verlag der Wissenschaften, 1976. 328 pp.

295. Roger-Marx, Claude. *La Caricature Étrangère. Espagne et Italie*. No. 5. Paris: Laboratoires Le Brun and Mictasol, n.d.

296. Roger-Marx, Claude. *La Caricature Étrangère. Flandres et Pays du Nord*, No. 2. Paris: Laboratoires Le Brun and Mictasol, n.d.

297. Sherry, James. "Four Modes of Caricature: Reflections Upon a Genre." *Bulletin of Research in the Humanities*. 87 (1986), pp. 29-62.

298. Sternberg, Jacques, "La Caricature Est l'Un des Beaux Arts?" *Arts et Spectacles* (Paris). September 26 to November 6, 1956. (Series of 5 articles on England, France, and U.S.).

COMIC BOOKS

299. Affolter, Cuno and Bruno Haldner. *Comics: Fünf Westschweizer Zeichner: Ab'Aigre, Ceppi, Cosey, Derib, Poussin: (Ausstellung)*. Graphische Sammlung der Eidgenössichen Technischen Hochschule Zürich, 18 Dezember 1982 bis 27 Februar 1983. Catalogue. Zürich: Graphische Sammlung der Eidgenössischen Technischen Hochschule, 1982.

300. Allwood, Martin S. *The Impact of the Comics on a European Country*. Marston Hills, Mullsjo: The Institute of Social Research, 1956.

301.   Chemin, Jean-Paul. *Dossier B.D.: Le Langage de la Bande Dessninée, la B.D. Engagée de par le Monde*. Brussels: Centre Audio-Visuel, CEDOC/CCID, 1979.

302.   "Comicorama: Deutschland, Österreich, Schweiz." *ICOM*. October 1992, pp. 6-11.

303.   "Comicorama: Frankreich, Belgien, Europa." *ICOM*. October 1992, p. 12.

304.   Decker, Dwight R. "Memoirs of a Foreign Comics Fan." *Comics Journal*. October 1984, pp. 103-106, 108-109.

305.   Dooley, Michael. "Comic Iconoclasm: A Catalog Review." *Comics Journal*. June 1988, pp. 53-55.

306.   "East, West Meet in Breakthrough." *Comics Journal*. April 1990, p. 18.

307.   Fromental, J.L. and F. Landon. "Science-Fiction et Bande Dessinée." *Magazine Littéraire* (Paris). 88, 1974, pp. 25-27. (Buzzelli, Druillet, Lob, Bielsa, Mandryka, Mézières).

308.   Ghosh, Arup. "Comics Are Wow!" *Saturday Statesman* (Delhi). February 2, 1991, pp. 1, 8.

309.   Glénat, Jacques, *et al. Histoire de la BD en France et en Belgique*. 2nd. Ed. Grenoble: Glénat, 1984.

310.   Gravett, Paul. "Euro-Comics: A Dazzling Respectability." *Print*. November-December 1988, pp. 74-87.

311.   Groth, Gary. "Kurtzman." *Comics Journal*. October 1992, pp. 62-69. (On European comics).

312.   Horn, Maurice. "Fantasy and the Fantastic in European Comics." *Epic Illustrated*. No. 2, 1980.

313.   Hunter, Mark. "Holy Respectability Batman! In Europe Comics Are More Than Just Kids' Stuff." *TWA Ambassador*. January 1986, pp. 41-46.

314.   Ihme, Burkhard. "Montage im Film und im Comic." *Comic Info*. 1/1993, pp. 33-36.

315.   "Inn i 1990: 80-Tallets Beste Tegneserier." *TEGN*. No. 1, 1990, pp. 10-15. (Belgium, France, Scandinavia, U.S.).

316.   Kronborg, Steffen. "Tegneserier for Hjernen, for Hjertetog for Underlivet." *Seriejournalen*. March 1991, pp. 30-32.

317.   Lofficier, J.M. and Fred Patten. "The Great European Comic Heroes." *Nemo*. December 1984, pp. 40-44.

318.   Peeters, Benoît. *Case, Planche, Récit. Comment Lire Une Bande Dessinée*. Brussels: Casterman, n.d. 144 pp.

319.   Roland, Niels. "Manarrefisse." *Seriejournalen*. March 1991, pp. 27-29.

320.   Tennant, Neil. "Mighty Marvel Mags in Europe." *Foom*. June 1977, pp. 6-7.

321.   Thompson, Don. "Dargaud Brings European Comics to the New World." *Comics Buyer's Guide*. July 8, 1983, pp. 38, 47-48, 52.

322.   Tschernegg, Markus and Paul Derouet. "...Und Es Gibt sie Doch! Der Versuch Einer Bestandsaufnahme in Sachen Deutschsprachiger Comic-Zeichner." *Comic Forum*. 6:23 (1984), pp. 62-75. (Bender, Brons, Deix, Grimm, Hau, Hondo, Kalenbach, Reiche, Roos, Scheuer, Schroeder, Schultheiß, Thorin Grave).

323.   "Um die Comics in USA, England und der Schweiz." *Jugendliteratur*. 1, 1955, p. 43.

324.   "Undergrounds: New Formats and European Invaders." *Comics Journal*. March 1981, pp. 21-22.

COMIC STRIPS

325.   Hill, Draper. "Establishing an Honorable Cartoon Pedigree. It Ain't Easy To Convince America That It Didn't Invent the Comic Strip." *Association of American Editorial Cartoonists Notebook*. Winter 1991, pp. 20-24.

326.   Kunzle, David. *The Early Comic Strip. Narrative Strips and Picture Stories in the European Broadsheet from c. 1450 to 1825*. Berkeley, California: University of California Press, 1973. 471 pp.

327.   Kunzle, David. *The History of the Comic Strip. The Nineteenth Century*. Berkeley, California: University of California Press, 1990. 411 pp.

328.   Moliterni, Claude and Pierre Couperie. "Die Comic-Forschung in Europa." Colloquium on "Theorie der Comic Strips," Akademie der Künste, Berlin, January 18, 1970.

329.   "Profil Jagoan Komik." *Jakarta*. May 27-June 2, 1988, pp. 14-15. ("Asterix," "Lucky Luke," "Smurfs," "Tintin").

330.   Stack, Frank. "Comic Strip Family Tree." *Comics Journal*. May 1992, pp. 45-47.

POLITICAL CARTOONS

331. *Exposition Dessins d'Humour 72.* Avignon: Galerie Gérard Guerre, 1972.

332. Joseph, Joe. "Humourless Eurocrats Get Last Laugh." *Notebook.* Summer 1992, p. 8.

333. Wolf, Reva. *Goya and the Satirical Print in England and on the Continent, 1730 to 1850.* Boston, Massachusetts: David R. Godine in association with Boston College Museum of Art, 1991. 109 pp.

2

Country Perspectives—Albania to Finland

ALBANIA

General Studies

334. "Kidz International Sneak Preview: Albania." *WittyWorld*. Summer/Autumn 1991, pp. 72-75.

335. Marinova, Marina. "Humour and Satire in Albania Today." *Apropos*. No. 3, 1986, p. 83.

AUSTRIA

General Studies

336. Bamberger, Richard. *Dein Kind und Seine Bücher*. Vienna: Verlag Jugend und Volk, Taschenbuch No. 5, 1957.

337. Bamberger, Richard. *Jugendlektüre*. Vienna: Verlag für Jugend und Volk, 1955.

338. Ecker, Hans. "Zur Frage der Desillusionierung." *Österreichische Pädagogische Warte* (Vienna). 52, 1964, pp. 71-74.

339. *Klassiker der Karikatur: No. 7. Ferdinand von Reznicek*. Berlin: Eulenspiegel-Verlag, 1972.

Comic Books and Strips

340. Alber, Wolfgang. "Columbus." *Comic Forum. Das Österreichische Fachmagazin für Comicliteratur* (Vienna). 2:6 (1980), pp. 37-40. (Norbert Kienbeck, Ferdinand Rieder).

341. Alber, Wolfgang. "Portrait Verlag Pollischansky." *Comic Forum. Das Österreichische Fachmagazin für Comicliteratur.* 2:7/8 (1980), pp. 110-112.

342. Alber, Wolfgang. "Tobias Seicherl. Der Wiener Donald Duck der 30er Jahre." *Comic Forum. Das Österreichische Fachmagazin für Comicliteratur.* 4:13 (1982), pp. 75-76.

343. Frenzel, Martin. "Von Detektiven und Agenten. Eine Bestandsaufnahme zur Geschichte der Detektiv- und Agentencomics. 1. Teil." *Comic Forum. Das Österreichische Fachmagazin für Comicliteratur.* 4:3 (1982), pp. 15-18.

344. Franzel, Martin. "Von Detektiven und Agenten. Eine Bestandsaufnahme zur Geschichte der Detektiv- und Agentencomics. 2. Teil." *Comic Forum. Das Österreichische Fachmagazin für Comicliteratur.* 4:14 (1982), pp. 28-34.

345. Führing, Dr. "Comic-Strips im Vormarsch." *Österreichischer Jugend-Informationsdienst.* 7 (1953), p. 9.

346. Görlich, Ernst J. "Von den Comic-Strips und dem Visuellen Zeitalter." *Neue Wege* (Vienna). October 1954.

347. Görlich, Ernst J. "Zur Frage der Comic Books." *Österreichische Monatschefte* (Vienna). 11:5 (1955), p. 21-22.

348. Görlich, Ernst J. "Zur Frage der Comic-Strips." *Österreichische Lehrer-Zeitung* (Vienna). 8:12 (1954), pp. 182-183.

349. Hon, Walter. "Die Bildersprache der Comics." *Österreichischer Jugendinformationsdienst* (Vienna). 9, 1955, p. 17.

350. Jambor, W. "Comics, Ein Problem für Unsere Jugend? *Österreichischer Jugend-Informationsdienst* (Vienna). 9, 1956, p. 2.

351. Kempkes, Wolfgang. "Comics und Film—Ein Vergleich." *Katalog der Comics-Ausstellung* (Vienna). 2, 1970, pp. 32-35.

352. Kolditz, Niels. "Bilder Machen Geschichte 'Comicwelten in Wien.'" *ICOM.* January 1993, p. 58.

353. Langsteiner, Hans. "Film und Comics." *Comic Forum. Das Österreichische Fachmagazin für Comicliteratur.* 3:9 (1981), pp. 36-39.

354. Leinweber, Horst. "Der Comic-Strip als Publizistisches Phänomen. Seine Entwicklung und Bedeutung. Unter Besonderer Berücksichtigung der Amerikanischen Tagespresse." Dissertation, Vienna, 1958.

355. "'Literatur' der Primitiven. Die Symbolsprache der Comic-Books." *Die Furche* (Vienna). 11:40 (1955), p. 4.

356. Moser, Leopold and Wolfgang J. Fuchs. "Film und Comics." *Comic Forum. Das Magazin für Comicliteratur.* 5:21 (1983), pp. 69-71.

357. Pirkl, Wolfgang and Wolfgang Richter. *Comics im Unterricht. Ein Unterrichtsbeispiel für die Fächer Deutsch und Bildnerische Erziehung. Sekundarstufe 1.* Vienna: Österreichischer Bundesverlag, 1980.

358. Spitta, Theodor. "Die Bildersprache der Comics." Unveröffentlicher Vortrag, gehalten 1955 auf der Kuratoriumstagung, Vienna.

359. Trost, Erwin. "Ein Gesetz Gegen Micky Maus?" *Wiener Kurier.* November 20, 1956.

360. Tschernegg, Markus. "Chris Scheuer—Ein Kurzporträt." *Comic Forum. Das Österreichische Fachmagazin für Comicliteratur.* 5:18 (1983), pp. 67-70.

361. Tschernegg, Markus. "Comicon. Eine Idee. Ein Service-Studio. Ein Verlag. 1. Teil." *Comic Forum. Das Österreichische Fachmagazin für Comicliteratur.* 4:15 (1982), pp. 59-61.

362. Tschernegg, Markus. "Comicon. Eine Idee. Ein Service-Studio. Ein Verlag. 2. Teil." *Comic Forum. Das Österreichische Fachmagazin für Comicliteratur.* 4:16 (1982), pp. 22-25.

BELGIUM

General Studies

363. Bille, Julie. "Tegneserieskolen i Bruxelles." *Seriejournalen.* June 1992, p. 48.

364. Blaes, S. "La 'Comic Art Gallery of Antwerp.'" *Phénix.* No. 12, 1969.

365. "Dødsfald." *Seriejournalen.* December 1990, p. 11.

366. Farnsworth, Clyde H. "Satirical Weekly in Brussels Pricks Bubbles of Hypocrisy." *New York Times.* February 26, 1967.

367. "Gallery—Belgium." *WittyWorld.* Winter/Spring 1989, pp. 54-59.

368. Gassiot-Talabot, Gérald. *La Figuration Narrative dans l'Art Contemporain.* Brussels: Quadrun, Palais des Beaux-Arts, 1967.

369. Grand-Carteret, John. *Popold II, Roi des Belges et de Belles, devant l'Objectif Caricaturale.* Paris: Luis Michaud Éd., 1908.

370. Leborgne, André. "Le Jardin des Curiosités: Le Rayon de la Mort." *Rantanplan* (Brussels). No. 12, 1968, pp. 13-14.

371. Leguebe, Wilbur. *La Société des Bulles.* Brussels: Eds. Ouvrière, 1977.

372. Maeterlinck, L. *Le Genre Satirique dans la Peinture Flamande.* Brussels: 1907.

373. Mallet, Pat. *Les Petits Hommes Verts.* Grenoble: Glénat, 1982. 48 pp.

374. *Musée pour la Culture Flamande. Het Beeldverhaal in Vlaanderen en Elders.* Catalogue. Anvers: 1969.

375. "O-Sekoer." *FECO News.* No. 4, 1987, p. 4.

Children's Press

376. Decaigny, T. *De Kinderpers.* Brussels: Nationale Dienst voor de Jeugd, 1955.

377. Decaigny, T. "La Presse Enfantine." *Service National de la Jeunesse* (Brussels). 1958.

378. Decaigny, T. *La Presse Illustrée pour Enfants et Adolescents.* Brussels: Ministère de l'Éducation et de la Culture, 1965.

379. Geerts, Claude and Edith Watrin. "25 Ans d'Évolution de la Presse Enfantine." *Études et Recherches. Technique de Diffusion Collective.* 9-10 (1963), pp. 25-175.

Festivals

380. "Humour of the People's Society." *Apropos.* No. 7, 1991, pp. 76-78.

381. *Knokke-heist België 1983. Het 20e Humorfestival. Davidsfonds Kartoenboek 17.* Ghent: Erasmus, 1983.

382. *Knokke-heist België 1984. De 23ste Wereldkartoenale. Davidsfonds Kartoenboek 18.* Ghent: Erasmus, 1984.

383. *Knokke-heist 20ste Wereld-Kartoenale 1981. Catalogus.* Ghent: Erasmus, 1981.

Cartoonists

384.   Baur, André. "Bubec." *Mieux Vaut en Rire*. No. 13, 1989, pp. 42-45.

385.   "Berck Kan Niet Alles Alleen Doen." *Hipper*. Nos. 27-28, 1975.

386.   Bouyer, Sylvain. "Le Dossier: Crespin. Crespin Contre l'Héritage d'Hergé ou Tentatives pour Fixer le Temps." *Bédésup. Le Magazine de l'Image et de la B.D.* (Marseilles). 28, 1984, pp. 3-6, 8. (Michel Crespin).

387.   de Saeger, Kris. "Eddy Ryssack." *Comixene. Das Comicfachmagazin* (Hanover). 8:41 (1981), pp. 60-61.

388.   "Dominique Jacquemin, Belgium." *FECO News*. No. 7, 1989, p. 20.

389.   "Een Teken Aan de Wand." *De Post*. January 2, 1972. (Karel Verschuere).

390.   Faur, Jean-Claude. "Interview. Albert Weinberg." *Le Nouveau Bédésup. Magazine de l'Image et de la B.D.* 35, 1985, pp. 2-7.

391.   Faur, Jean-Claude. "Entretien avec... Léo Fabri." *Bédésup*. 8, 1979, pp. 5-6.

392.   Flora, Paul. *Von A (utos) bis Z (entauren)*. Berlin: Eulenspiegel-Verlag, 1977.

393.   Groensteen, Thierry. "Conversation avec Philippe Vandooren." *Les Cahiers de la Bande Dessinée*. 60, 1984, pp. 44-47.

394.   Groensteen, Thierry, Daniel Hugues and Thierry Joor. "Conversation avec Didier Pasamonik." *Les Cahiers de la Bande Dessinée*. 56, 1984, pp. 76-82.

395.   "Kartoenist Emiel de Bolle." *Kever*. June 1993, p. 3-4.

396.   "Kartoens, Moet Ik Er Een Tekening Bij Maken?" *Kever*. June 1993, pp. 7-11. (Bob Vincke).

397.   Kraft, David A. "Alain Baran." *Comics Interview*. No. 59, 1988, pp. 32-37, 39, 41, 43-45.

398.   Léturgie, Jean. "Entretien avec Willy Lambil." *Schtroumpfanzine* (Grenoble). 35, 1979, pp. 3-9. (a.k.a. Willy Lambillotte).

399.   Martens, Thierry. "En Taillant un Crayon avec... Hubuc." *Rantanplan*. No. 5, 1967, pp. 8-10.

400.   Martens, Thierry. "En Taillant un Crayon avec... Mazel." *Rantanplan*. No. 6, 1967, pp. 12-14.

401.   Sterckx, Pierre. "Les Catastrophiques Carrosseries d'Ever Meulen." *Les Cahiers de la Bande Dessinée*. 68, 1986, pp. 78-79. (a.k.a. Eddy Vermeulen).

402.   Tschernegg, Markus. "William Vance und Seine Serien." *Comic Forum*. 4:13 (1982), pp. 47-56. (a.k.a. William Van Cutsem).

403.   Verschooten, Gilbert. "From Felix the Cat to Taxandria: The Wonderful Life of Animation Filmer Raoul Servais." *FECO News*. No. 13, 1992, pp. 11-13.

Biddeloo, Karel

404.   Milan. "Stripgidsprijs 1979 voor Karel Biddeloo." *Jet*. No. 17, November 1979.

405.   Milan. "Striptekenaar Karel Biddeloo." *Kommunikatief*. March 1980.

Cauvin, Raoul

406.   Cance, Louis. "Bibliographie de Cauvin." *Les Cahiers de la Bande Dessinée*. 61, 1985, pp. 30-34.

407.   Groensteen, Thierry. "Entretien avec Raoul Cauvin." *Les Cahiers de la Bande Dessinée*. 61, 1985, pp. 6-12.

408.   Hugues, Daniel. "Les Idées Noires de Cauvin." *Les Cahiers de la Bande Dessinée*. 61, 1985, pp. 15-17.

Charlier, Jean-Michel

409.   Cormier, Sylvain. "L'Oeuvre de Jean-Michel Charlier: Notes de (Re)lectures." *La Nouvelle Barre du Jour* (Outremont, Québec). 110/111, 1982, pp. 53-57.

410.   Filippini, Henri. "L'Humour Chez Jean-Michel Charlier." *Schtroumpf. Les Cahiers de la Bande Dessinée*. 37, 1978, p. 37.

411.   Filippini, Henri and Jean Léturgie. "Entretien avec Jean-Michel Charlier." *Schtroumpf. Les Cahiers de la Bande Dessinée*. 37, 1978, pp. 7-21.

412.   Léturgie, Jean. "Bibliographie de Jean-Michel Charlier." *Schtroumpf. Les Cahiers de la Bande Dessinée*. 37, 1978, pp. 41-46.

413.   Roux, Antoine. "Ce Vieux Rascall." *Schtroumpf Les Cahiers de la Bande Dessinée*. 37, 1978, pp. 35-36.

Comès, Didier (Dieter Hermann)

414.   Chante, Alain. "Montage et Couleurs dans L'Ombre du Corbeau." *Schtroumpf. Les Cahiers de la Bande Dessinée*. 55, 1983, pp. 25-28.

415. Dellisse, Luc. "Les Pannes du Récit." *Schtroumpf. Les Cahiers de la Bande Dessinée*. 55, 1983, pp. 46-47.

416. de Pierpont, Jacques. "Le Choc des Cultures." *Schtroumpf. Les Cahiers de la Bande Dessinée*. 55, 1983, pp. 33-35.

417. Ecken, Claude. "Dans l'Ombre et le Silence, un Itinéraire." *Schtroumpf. Les Cahiers de la Bande Dessinée*. 55, 1983, pp. 20-24

418. Groensteen, Thierry. "Bibliographie de Didier Comès." *Schtroumpf. Les Cahiers de la Bande Dessinée*. 55, 1983, p. 48.

419. Groensteen, Thierry. "Entretien avec Didier Comès." *Schtroumpf. Les Cahiers de la Bande Dessinée*. 55, 1983, pp. 8-18.

420. Groensteen, Thierry. "Marginales sur Comès." *Schtroumpf. Les Cahiers de la Bande Dessinée*. 55, 1983, pp. 40-44.

421. Pinchart, Patrick. "Comèseries Contre Bondieuseries." *Schtroumpf. Les Cahiers de la Bande Dessinée*. 55, 1983, pp 37-39.

Craenhals, François

422. Cance, Luis, V. Passen, V. and Louis Teller, "Bibliographie Craenhals." *Cahiers Universitaires*. No. 11, 1971.

423. De Laet, Danny. "Craenhals, Digne Maitre de l'Humour Dessinée." *Cahiers Universitaires*. No. 11, 1971.

424. de Saeger, Kris. *Dossier Craenhals*. Brussels: Casterman, n.d. 132 pp.

425. Glénat, Jacques and François Rivière. "Schtroumpf Rencontre F. Craenhals." *Cahiers Universitaires*. No. 11, 1971.

426. Rivière, François. "La Part du Rêve Chez F. Craenhals." *Cahiers Universitaires*. No. 11, 1971.

Dany (Daniel Henrotin)

427. Ecken, Claude. "Les Métamorphoses d'Olivier Rameau." *Schtroumpf. Les Cahiers de la Bande Dessinée*. 49, 1981, pp. 27-31.

428. Filippini, Henri. "Bibliographie de Dany." *Schtroumpf. Les Cahiers de la Bande Dessinée*. 49, 1981, pp. 45-49.

429. Filippini, Henri and Jean Léturgie. "Entretien avec Dany." *Schtroumpf. Les Cahiers de la Bande Dessinée*. 49, 1981, pp. 7-23.

430. Lecigne, Bruno. "Hallucinaville, un Monde de Carnaval." *Schtroumpf. Les Cahiers de la Bande Dessinée.* 49, 1981, pp. 35-37.

431. Lehner, René. "Dany." *Comixene. Das Comicfachmagazin.* 8:40 (1981), pp. 56-57.

DeGroot, Robert

432. DeGroot, Bob and Philippe Turk. *Leonard Is a Genius.* New York: Dargaud International, 1983. 48 pp.

433. Martens, Thierry. "En Taillant un Crayon avec...Robert de Groot." *Rantanplan.* No. 7, 1967, pp. 12-13.

de Moor, Bob

434. Bourdil, Pierre-Yves and Bernard Tordeur. *Bob de Moor. 40 Ans de Bande Dessinée. 35 Ans aux Côtés d'Hergé.* Brussels: Eds. du Lombard, 1986.

435. Burgdorf, Paul. "Bob de Moor." *Comixene. Das Comicfachmagazin.* 8:39 (1981), pp. 46-48, 50-51.

436. "De 'Artec-studio's' Werken en Winnen." *Overal.* April 25, 1948.

437. Legardinier, Claudine. "Bob de Moor Prend le Large." *(A Suivre).* October 1992, pp. 104-105.

De Winter, Eddi

438. "Barst, Eddi de Winter." *Apropos.* 7, 1991, pp. 8-9.

439. "The Judging. Eddi de Winter—Belgium." *FECO News.* No. 13, 1992, p. 18.

Franquin, André

440. Alber, Wolfgang, ed. *CF-Spezial: Franquin.* Vienna: Edition Comic Forum, 1986.

441. Baudoux, Vincent and Xavier Zeegers. "L'île Rose." *Schtroumpf. Les Cahiers de la Bande Dessinée.* 47/48, 1980, pp. 61-65.

442. Bleicher-Viehoff, Thomas A.T. "Franquin bei Kauka Oder: Schwarze Gedanken zum 'Lieben Rolf.'" *ICOM-INFO.* February 1990, pp. 34-39.

443. "Franquin et Gillain Répondent aux Questions de Philippe Vandooren." In *Comment on Devient Créateur de Bande Dessinée.* Verviers: Ed. Gérard et Co., 1969.

444. Fuchs, Wolfgang J. "André Franquin Oder: Die Welt von Rotarin und Fantasio." *Comixene. Das Comicfachmagazin.* 6:24 (1979), pp. 4-9.

445. Glénat, Jacques. "Schtroumpf Rencontre Franquin." *Cahiers Universitaires.* No. 10, 1970.

446. Goupil, Jacky, Philippe Isaac, André Franquin, and Vittorio Léonardo. *Livre d'Or: Franquin.* Hounoux: SEDLI; Jacky Goupil, 1982.

447. Léturgie, Jean. "André Franquin. Bibliographie." *Schtroumpf. Les Cahiers de la Bande Dessinée.* 47/48, 1980, pp. 70-80.

448. Léturgie, Jean. "Entretien avec André Franquin." *Schtroumpf. Les Cahiers de la Bande Dessinée.* 47/48, 1980, pp. 7-21.

449. Léturgie, Jean. "Greg: a Propos de Franquin." *Schtroumpf. Les Cahiers de la Bande Dessinée.* 47/48, 1980, pp. 45-47.

450. Loszycer, Charles. "La Vraie Nature de Franquin." *Schtroumpf. Les Cahiers de la Bande Dessinée.* 47/48, 1980, p. 67.

451. Quella, Didier. "A la Rencontre de... Franquin." *Bédésup.* 27, 1983, pp. 7-13.

452. Quella, Didier. "A la Rencontre de... Franquin." *Bédésup.* 28, 1984, pp. 34-47.

453. Quella, Didier. "A la Rencontre de... Franquin. Le Jeu de Mots dans la Série des Gaston Lagaffe de Franquin." *Bédésup.* 26, 1983, pp. 7-11, 13, 15.

454. Rivière, François and J. Topor. "André Franquin Animalier." *Cahiers Universitaires.* No. 10, 1970.

455. Sadoul, Numa. "André Franquin, le Monde de Spirou." *Phénix.* No. 20, 1971.

456. Sadoul, Numa. *Et Franquin Créa Lagaffe: Entretiens avec Numa Sadoul.* Brussels: Distri BD, 1986.

457. Topor, J. "Bibliographie de Franquin." *Cahiers Universitaries.* No. 10, 1970.

Franz (Franz Drappier)

458. Cance, Louis. "Bibliographie de Franz." *Les Cahiers de la Bande Dessinée.* 64, 1985, pp. 36-38.

459. Ecken, Claude. "Entretien avec Franz." *Schtroumpfanzine.* 30, 1979, pp. 3-9.

460. Groensteen, Thierry. "Entretien avec Franz." *Schtroumpf. Les Cahiers de la Bande Dessinée.* 64, 1985, pp. 8-15.

Greg, Michel (Michel Régnier)

461. Di Manno, Yves. "Le Lagage Chez Greg." *Cahiers Universitaires*. No. 17, 1972.

462. Glénat, Jacques and Numa Sadoul. "Entretien avec Greg." *Cahiers Universitaires*. No. 17, 1972.

463. Masson, G. and Louis Teller. "Bibliographie de Greg." *Cahiers Universitaires*. No. 17, 1972.

464. Sadoul, Numa. "Greg et Son Studio." *Cahiers Universitaires*. No. 17, 1972.

465. Sadoul, Numa. "Michel Greg Scénariste." *Cahiers Universitaires*. No. 17, 1972.

466. Tschernegg, Markus. "Portrait: Michel Greg." *Comic Forum. Das Magazin für Comicliteratur*. (Vienna). 7:27 (1985), pp. 46-47.

Hergé (Georges Rémi)

467. *(A Suivre)*. Hors Série. "Spécial Hergé." Paris, Tournai: Casterman, 1983. German ed. Hamburg: comicplus +, Verlag Sackmann und Hörndl, 1986.

468. *Bédésup*. Edition Spéciale. "Hergé N'Est Plus!" Marseilles: *Bédésup*, 1983.

469. Bergeron, Francis. "Pour Comprendre Notre Monde, Lisez Tintin." *L'Astrolabe* (Paris). 1:80 (1985), pp. 10-12.

470. Bourdil, Pierre-Yves. *Hergé. Tintin au Tibet*. Brussels: Labor, 1985.

471. Cance, Luis, Jacques Glénat, and Dominique Labesse. "Bibliographie d'Herge." *Cahiers Universitaires*. No. 14, 1971.

472. Chante, Alain. "La Violence d'Hergé." *Le Nouveau Bédésup*. 32/33, 1985, pp. 8-10.

473. Chion, Michel. "Herge: l'Image et la Lettre." *Cahiers du Cinema*. January 1987, p. xiv.

474. De La Croix, Arnaud. "L'Éternel Retour de Tintin." *Les Cahiers de la Bande Dessinée*. 56, 1984, pp. 42-45.

475. De La Croix, Arnaud and Christophe Brichant. "Les Toiles Mystérieuses." *Les Cahiers de la Bande Dessinée*. 68, 1986, pp. 83-87.

476. "Documents sur Hergé, Préface: A. Saint Ogan." *Cahiers Universitaires*. No. 14, 1971.

477. Faur, Jean-Claude. "A la Rencontre de Tintin." In *À la Rencontre de la Bande Dessinée*, edited by Jean-Claude Faur, pp. 207-220. Marseilles: Bédésup, J.C. Faur, 1983.

478. Fondation Joan Miró. *Hommage à Hergé*. Paris, Tournai: Casterman, 1986. 64 pp.

479. Gauthier, Philippe. 1983. "Adieu à Hergé (alias Georges Rémi)." *Commentaire* (Paris). 6, 1983, pp. 857-864.

480. Giroux, Renée-Héloïse and François Hébert. Êtes-Vous Tintinologue? Fascicule 1.:Sainte-Foy, Québec: Eds. du Royaume de la Bande Dessinée, 1983; Fascicule 2: Paris: Casterman, 1983.

481. Goddin, Philippe. *Comment Naît Une Bande Dessinée? Par-Dessus l'Épaule d'Hergé*. Brussels: Casterman, n.d. 48 pp.

482. Goddin, Philippe. *Hergé et les Bigotudos—Le Roman d'Une Aventure*. Brussels: Casterman, n.d. 288 pp.

483. Goddin, Philippe and Pierre-Yves Bourdil. *Hergé et Tintin. Reporters du Petit Vingtième au Journal Tintin. Le Mythe Hergéen*. Paris, Brussels: Eds. du Lombard, 1986.

484. Greg, Mike. "Hergé: Genius and Friend." *Nemo*. October 1983, pp. 26-32.

485. Groensteen, Thierry. "Les Ménines Selon Hergé." *Les Cahiers de la Bande Dessinée*. 64, 1985, pp. 54-55.

486. Groensteen, Thierry. "Notes sur le Comique Hergéen." *Les Cahiers de la Bande Dessinée*. 59, 1984, pp. 79-81.

487. Groensteen, Thierry, Thierry Joor and Patrick Weber. "Tintin et l'Alph-Art." *Les Cahiers de la Bande Dessinée*. 72, 1986, pp. 51-53.

488. Hergé. *Archives Hergé*. 4 Vols. Brussels: Casterman, n.d. Vol. 1, 420 pp.; Vol. 2, 260 pp.; Vol. 3, 420 pp.; Vol. 4, 420 pp.

489. Hergé. *The Crab with the Golden Claws. The Adventures of Tintin*. Boston, Massachusetts: Little, Brown, 1974. 62 pp.

490. Jacquemin, Roger. "Hergé." *Lectures* (Liège). 12, 1983, pp. 10-17.

491. Knigge, Andreas C. "50 Jahre Tim und Struppi. Die Schule Hergé." *Comixene. Das Comicfachmagazin*. 6:23 (1979), pp. 7-11.

492. Labesse, Dominique. "L'Ampleur d'Un Succès." *Schtroumpf. Les Cahiers de la Bande Dessinée*. 14/15, 1978, pp. 33-36.

493. Labesse, Dominique. "Le Comique Chez Hergé." *Cahiers Universitaires*. No. 14, 1971.

494. Labesse, Dominique. "Le Comique Chez Hergé." *Schtroumpf. Les Cahiers de la Bande Dessinée*. 14/15, 1978, pp. 53-55.

495. Labesse, Dominique. "Les Studios Hergé." *Cahiers Universitaires*. No. 14, 1971.

496. Labesse, Dominique. "Les Studios Hergé." *Schtroumpf. Les Cahiers de la Bande Dessinée*. 14/15, 1978, p. 37.

497. Labesse, Dominique. "Repères Biographiques." *Schtroumpf. Les Cahiers de la Bande Dessinée*. 14/15, 1978, pp. 23-25.

498. Lecigne, Bruno. "Hergé et l'École de Bruxelles: Classicisme et Simulation." *Education 2000* (Paris). 21, 1982, pp. 17-20.

499. Lecigne, Bruno. *Les Héritiers d'Hergé*. Brussels: Magic Strip, 1983.

500. Lecigne, Bruno. "Yves Deloule ou le Miroir Brisé." *Les Cahiers de la Bande Dessinée*. 70, 1986, pp. 82-83.

501. *Le Musée Imaginaire de Tintin*. Paris, Tournai: Casterman, 1980.

502. Madsen, Frank. "Jagten på Hergé's Kilder." *Seriejournalen*. December 1990, pp. 26-31.

503. Peeters, Benoît. *Hergé. Avec 1 Cassette*. Brussels: Eds. Décembre, 1981.

504. Peeters, Benoît. *Hergé, les Débuts d'Un Illustrateur*. Brussels: Casterman, n.d. 216 pp.

505. Peeters, Benoît. *Le Monde d'Hergé*. Paris, Tournai: Casterman, 1983. 216 pp. German ed. *Hergé. Ein Leben für die Comics*. Hamburg: Carlsen Verlag, 1983.

506. Peeters, Benoît. *Tintin and the World of Hergé: An Illustrated History*. Boston, Massachusetts: Little, Brown and Co., 1988. 161 pp.

507. Pierre, Michel. "Tintin Parle aux Jeunes de 7 à 77 Ans." *Phosphore* (Paris). 38, 1984, pp. 50-53.

508. Ponzi, Jacques. "Interview Hergé." *Rantanplan*. No. 2, 1966, pp. 2-3.

509. Quella-Guyot, Didier. "Un Inventaire Épuisant ou la Leçon d'Hergé." *Le Nouveau Bédésup*. 32/33, 1985, pp. 20-26.

510. Rémi, Georges (Hergé). *The Black Island*. Boston, Massachusetts: Atlantic, Little-Brown, 1975.

511. Rémi, Georges (Hergé). *The Blue Lotus*. Boston, Massachusetts: Atlantic, 1984.

512. Rémi, Georges (Hergé). *The Broken Ear*. Boston, Massachusetts: Atlantic, 1978.

513. Rémi, Georges (Hergé). *The Calculus Affair*. Boston, Massachusetts: Atlantic, 1976.

514. Rémi, Georges (Hergé). *The Castafiore Emerald*. Boston, Massachusetts: Atlantic, 1975.

515. Rémi, Georges (Hergé). *Destination Moon*. Boston, Massachusetts: Atlantic, 1976.

516. Rémi, Georges (Hergé). *Explorers on the Moon*. Boston, Massachusetts: Atlantic, 1976.

517. Rémi, Georges (Hergé). *King Ottokar's Scepter*. Boston, Massachusetts: Atlantic, 1974.

518. Rémi, Georges (Hergé). *The Land of Black Gold*. Boston, Massachusetts: Atlantic, 1975.

519. Rémi, Georges (Hergé). *Prisoners of the Sun*. Boston, Massachusetts: Atlantic, 1975.

520. Rémi, Georges (Hergé). *Red Rackham's Treasure*. Boston, Massachusetts: Atlantic, 1974.

521. Rémi, Georges (Hergé). *The Secret of the Unicorn*. Boston, Massachusetts: Atlantic, 1974.

522. Rémi, Georges (Hergé). *The Seven Crystal Balls*. Boston, Massachusetts: Atlantic, 1975.

523. Rémi, Georges (Hergé). *Tintin in America*. Boston, Massachusetts: Atlantic, 1979.

524. Rémi, Georges (Hergé). *Tintin and the Picaros*. Boston, Massachusetts: Atlantic, 1978.

525. Rivière, François. "Dossier 'École d'Hergé.'" *Cahiers Universitaires*. No. 9, 1970.

526. Rivière, François. "Eléments pour Une Présentation d'Hergé." *Cahiers Universitaires*. No. 14, 1971.

527. Rivière, François. *L'Ecole d'Hergé: Logicien du Rêve*. Grenoble: Eds. Jacques Glénat, 1976.

528. Sadoul, Numa. "Bibliographie." *Schtroumpf. Les Cahiers de la Bande Dessinée.* 14/15, 1978, pp. 71-82.

529. Sadoul, Numa. "Déclarations Supplémentaires: A Propos des 'Picaros.'" *Schtroumpf. Les Cahiers de la Bande Dessinée.* 14/15, 1978, pp. 20-22.

530. Sadoul, Numa. "Entretien avec Hergé." *Schtroumpf. Les Cahiers de la Bande Dessinée.* 14/15, 1978, pp. 7-17.

531. Sadoul, Numa. *Entretiens avec Hergé.* Brussels: Casterman, 1983. 256 pp.

532. Sadoul, Numa. "Schtroumpf Rencontre Hergé." *Cahiers Universitaires.* No. 14, 1971.

533. Sadoul, Numa. *Tintin et Moi—Entretiens avec Hergé. Nouvelle Édition Remise à Jour, Augmentée d'un Entretien à Propos des Picaros.* Paris: Tournai: Casterman, 1975, 1983.

534. Sayers, John. "Tintin Creator Dead at 75." *Comics Scene.* July 1983, p. 14.

535. Serres, Michel. "Les Bijoux Distraits ou la Cantatrice Sauve." *Critique* (Paris). 26:277 (1970), pp. 485-497.

536. Serres, Michel. "Tintin ou le Picaresque Aujourd'hui. Hergé: Les Aventures de Tintin: Tintin et les Picaros." *Critique* (Paris). 33:358 (1977), pp. 197-207.

537. Spence, Martin. "Quiff, Plus Fours and a Dog Called Snowy (Key Images from Herge's Adventures of Tintin)." *Art and Artists.* November 1986, pp. 16-22.

538. Sterckx, Pierre. "Tintin el l'Alph'Art." *Les Cahiers de la Bande Dessinée.* 59, 1984, pp. 72-77.

539. Sterckx, Pierre and Benoît Peeters. *Hergé, Dessinateur.* Brussels: Casterman, n.d. 48 pp.

540. Sterckx, Pierre and Thierry Smolderen. *Hergé, Portrait Biographique.* Brussels: Casterman, n.d. 480 pp.

541. Thompson, Kim. "Herge Dead at 75." *Comics Journal.* March 1983, pp. 13-15.

542. Tibi, Jean. *Voyage au Pays de Tintin.* Saint-Etienne: CIEREC, Université de St. Etienne, 1983.

543. "Tintin and Herge." *Cartoonist PROfiles.* September 1977, pp. 63-65.

544. "'Tintin' Creator Herge Dies of Leukemia at 75." *Comics Buyer's Guide.* April 1, 1983, p. 1.

545. "The Tintin Story." *Cartoonist PROfiles*. No. 15, 1972, pp. 4-11.

546. "The Tintin Story." *Cartoonist PROfiles*. March 1980, p. 29.

547. Tuten, F. "Books for Georges Rémi/Hergé." *Artforum*. May 1984, p. 71.

548. "Un Hommage: Hergé." *Le Vif* (Brussels). Special Number, Verschiedene Aufsätze, 1983.

549. Van Belle, Anita. "Rencontre Hergé—Marx au San Salvador." *Les Cahiers de la Bande Dessinée*. 60, 1984, pp. 83-84.

550. Vandromme, Pol. *Le Monde de Tintin*. Paris: Gallimard, 1959.

551. Van Hamme, Jean. "Le Dossier Hergé." *Tintin*. January 14, 1971.

552. Vazquez De Parga, Salvador. "Hergé, Tintin Linea Clara y la Escuela de Bruselas." *Neuróptica. Estudios Sobre el Cómic* (Zaragoza). 2, 1984, pp. 12-20.

Hermann (Hermann Huppen)

553. Groensteen, Thierry. *Hermann*. Paris: Ed. Alain Littaye, 1983.

554. Hermann. *The Survivors: Talons of Blood*. Stamford, Connecticut: Fantagraphics Books, 1982. 48 pp.

555. "Las Torres de Hermann Huppen." *El Wendigo*. No. 59, 1993, pp. 34-35.

556. Lecigne, Bruno. "Bibliographie d'Hermann." *Schtroumpf. Les Cahiers de la Bande Dessinée*. 44, 1980, pp. 45-48.

557. Tschernegg, Markus. "Hermann. Comicographie." *Comic Forum. Das Magazin für Comicliteratur*. 5:19 (1983), pp. 64-65.

558. Tschernegg, Markus. "Hermann—der Künstler... Oder: Auf der Suche Nach Neuen Wegen." *Comic Forum. Das Magazin für Comicliteratur*. 5:19 (1983), pp. 15-18.

559. Warfa, Dominique. "Retour à la Terre, ou Jeremiah et la Science-Fiction Prétexte." *Schtroumpf. Les Cahiers de la Bande Dessinée*. 44, 1980, pp. 38-43.

560. Warfa, Dominique and Serge Delsemme. "Moi, J'Aime l'Odeur du Crottin... Interview d'Hermann." *Schtroumpf. Les Cahiers de la Bande Dessinée*. 44, 1980, pp. 7-16.

Hermans, Eugeen

561.   De Decker, Karel. "Eindelijk: Hier Is PINK." In "Beknopt Verslag." *De Standaard Za.* 25, August 26, 1973.

562.   De Laet, Danny. "Eugeen Hermans: Legende die Nog Niet Vergeten Werd." *De Standaard.* Special number. November 17, 1978.

563.   "De Pionier van het Vlaamse Beeldverhaal Eugeen Hermans." *Kartoen.* September 1978.

564.   Neckers, Jan and Karel Driesen. "Eug. Hermans alias Pink, Striptekenaar van Het le (sic) Uur." *Stripwereld.* No. 3, 1974.

Hubinon, Victor (Victor Hughes)

565.   Filippini, Henri, Jean Léturgie, and André Leborgne. "Bibliographie." *Schtroumpf. Les Cahiers de la Bande Dessinée.* 35, 1978, pp. 43-45.

566.   Forestier, Isabelle and Jean Léturgie. "Entretien avec Victor Hubinon." *Schtroumpf. Les Cahiers de la Bande Dessinée.* 35, 1978, pp. 7-16.

567.   *Hubinon.* Marcinelle: Eds. Jean Dupuis, 1984.

Jacobs, Edgar-Pierre

568.   Bielikoff, Stéphane and François Rivière. "Who's Who in Jacobs." *Schtroumpf. Les Cahiers de la Bande Dessinée.* 30, 1976, pp. 66-70.

569.   Dubois, Daniel. "Bibliographie." *Schtroumpf. Les Cahiers de la Bande Dessinée.* 30, 1976, pp. 71-73.

570.   "Edgar Pierre Jacobs Dies at 83." *Comics Journal.* July 1987, p. 129.

571.   Jacobs, Edgar-Pierre. *Edgar-Pierre Jacobs. Trente Ans de Bandes Dessinées.* Paris: A. Littaye, 1973.

572.   Jacobs, Edgar-Pierre. *Un Opéra de Papier.* Paris: Gallimard, 1981.

573.   Le Gallo, Claude. *Le Monde de Edgar P. Jacobs. Avec un Dossier Complet sur la Marque Jaune par D. Van Kerckhove.* Paris, Brussels: Eds. du Lombard, 1984.

574.   Rivière, François. "Entretien avec Jacobs un Puritain de la B.D." *Schtroumpf. Les Cahiers de la Bande Dessinée.* 30, 1976, pp. 4-16.

575.   Routeau, Luc. "Jacobs: Narration, Science-Fiction." *Communications* (Paris). 24 (1976), pp. 41-61.

576. Steyn, Ivo. "Edgar-Pierre Jacobs." *Comics Journal*. March 1989, pp. 27-28.

577. Tramson, Jacques. "Le Merveilleux aux Écoutes du Réel: L'Historicité Scientifique dans la Saga Jacobsienne." In *Histoire et Bande Dessinée: Actes du 2e Colloque International Éducation et Bande Dessinée*, pp. 138-156. La Roque d'Anthéron: Objektif Promo Durance, 1979.

578. Van Herp, Jacques. "Les Long-Shots de Jacobs." Préface to *Le Rayon U*. Brussels: C.A.B.D., 1967.

Jijé (Joseph Gillain)

579. Filippini, Henri. "Joseph Gillain, Interview." *Phénix*. No. 16, 1970.

580. Filippini, Henri. "L'École Jijé." *Schtroumpf. Les Cahiers de la Bande Dessinée*. 39, 1979, p. 29.

581. Filippini, Henri. "Entretien avec Gillain." *Schtroumpf. Les Cahiers de la Bande Dessinée*. 39, 1979, pp. 7-22.

582. Filippini, Henri and Jean Léturgie. "Bibliographie de Gillain." *Schtroumpf. Les Cahiers de la Bande Dessinée*. 39, 1979, pp. 41-48.

583. Mouminoux. "Gillain par Mouminoux." *Schtroumpf. Les Cahiers de la Bande Dessinée*. 39, 1979, p. 30.

584. Roux, Antoine. "Le Western et Gillain ou Jerry Scott et Randolph Spring Chez les Hommes Qui Rient." *Schtroumpf. Les Cahiers de la Bande Dessinée*. 39, 1979, pp. 33-39.

Leloup, Roger

585. Leloup, Roger. *Vulcan's Forge*. New York: Comcat, 1989.

586. "Radioscopie d'Un Personnage en Quête de Réalité." *Schtroumpfanzine*. 25, pp. 12-15.

Morris (Maurice de Bevere)

587. Gielle, J. "L'Quest pour Rire de Morris." *Schtroumpf. Les Cahiers de la Bande Dessinée*. 43, 1980, pp. 21-23.

588. Lecigne, Bruno. "Morris: des Méchants à Géométrie Variable." *Schtroumpf. Les Cahiers de la Bande Dessinée*. 43, 1980, pp. 35-38.

589. Léturgie, Jean and Henri Filippini. "Bibliographie Morris." *Schtroumpf. Les Cahiers de la Bande Dessinée*. 43, 1980, pp. 44-48.

590. Lérurgie, Jean and Henri Filippini. "Entretien avec Morris." *Schtroumpf. Les Cahiers de la Bande Dessinée.* 43, 1980, pp. 7-19.

591. Morris. *Morris Vous Apprend à Dessiner Lucky Luke.* Paris, Barcelona, Lausanne, New York, Stuttgart: Dargaud Editeur, 1971, 1984.

592. "Morris im Interview. Über die Schwierigkeiten Einen Zeichentrickfilm zu Machen." *Comic Forum. Das Magazin für Comicliteratur.* 5:21, pp. 32-33.

593. Roux, Antoine. "Morris ou un Plongeur Sachant Plonger." *Schtroumpf. Les Cahiers de la Bande Dessinée.* 43, 1980, pp. 29-32.

594. Tibéri, Jean-Paul. *Livre d'Or: Morris.* Hounoux: SEDLI, Jacky Goupil, 1984.

595. Van Herp, Jacques and André Leborgne. "Interview mit Morris. Übersetzt von K. Siepe." *Comic Forum. Das Österreichische Fachmagazin für Comicliteratur.* 1:3 (1979), pp. 31-33.

Paape, Eddy

596. Cance, Louis, Jacques Glénat, and Louis Teller. "Bibliographie de Paape." *Cahiers Universitaires.* No. 17, 1972.

597. Glénat, Jacques. "Le Style d'Eddy Paape." *Cahiers Universitaires.* No. 17, 1972.

598. Glénat, Jacques and Cl. Hebert. "Entretient avec Paape." *Cahiers Universitaires.* No. 17, 1972.

Peyo (Pierre Culliford)

599. "Der Vater der Schlümpfe Ist Tot." *ICOM.* January 1993, p. 14.

600. Peyo. *The Astrosmurf. A Smurf Adventure.* New York: Random House, 1979. 40 pp.

601. Culliford, Pierre (Peyo). *The Astrosmurf.* New York: Random, 1982.

602. Culliford, Pierre. *The Smurfs and the Howlibird.* New York: Random, 1983.

603. Filet, G. and Jacques Glénat. "Bibliographie de Peyo." *Cahiers Universitaires.* No. 12, 1971.

604. Filippini, Henri. "Peyo et Ses Assistants." *Schtroumpf. Les Cahiers de la Bande Dessinée.* 54, 1983, p. 41.

605. Fuchs, Wolfgang J. "Was Schlumpft Denn Da? Peyo und Seine Schlümpfe." *Comixene. Das Comicfachmagazin.* 6:23 (1979), pp. 55-56.

606. Glénat, Jacques. "Schtroumpf Rencontre P. Culliford (Peyo)." *Cahiers Universitaires*. No. 12, 1971.

607. Glénat, Jacques, Thierry Groensteen, and Franz Van Cauwenbergh. "Bibliographie de Peyo." *Schtroumpf. Les Cahiers de la Bande Dessinée*. 54, 1983, pp. 43-48.

608. Groensteen, Thierry. "Entretien avec Peyo." *Schtroumpf. Les Cahiers de la Bande Dessinée*. 54, pp. 9-20.

609. "Peyo, Creator of Smurfs, Dies at 64." *Comics Journal*. February 1993, pp. 16-17.

610. Rivière, François. "Peyo l'Enchanteur." *Cahiers Universitaires*. No. 12, 1971.

611. Wasterlain, Marc. "Je Me Souviens de Peyo et de Quelques Autres." *Schtroumpf. Les Cahiers de la Bande Dessinée*. 54, 1983, p. 23.

Pil

612. Durnez, Gaston. "Comics for Ever." In *Spoedbericht, Davidsfonds*. Leuven: 1963.

613. De Decker, Karel. "Inleiding tot Pils Pilitieke Prentjes." In *De Pilgrimstocht der Mensheid*. VP 215, Heideland, Hasselt, 1967.

614. "Humo Sprak Met Phil." *Humo*. No. 1951, 1978.

615. "Joë Pil Meulepas." *Vlaanderen*. No. 137, 1973.

616. "Met pijl en Pen. Karikaturen van Pil." *De Toerist*. No. 1, 1952.

Schuiten, François

617. "Fiche Bibliographique." *Les Cahiers de la Bande Dessinée*. 69, 1986, p. 48.

618. Groensteen, Thierry. "Schuiten. Plus Dure Sera la Chute." *Les Cahiers de la Bande Dessinée*. 56, 1984, pp. 87-90.

619. Groensteen, Thierry, Daniel Hugues and Thierry Smolderen. "Conversations avec François Schuiten." *Les Cahiers de la Bande Dessinée*. 69, 1986, pp. 8-20.

620. Hugues, Daniel. "L'Effroyable Secret de Monsieur S." *Les Cahiers de la Bande Dessinée*. 56, 1984, pp. 91-93.

Sirius (Max Mayeu)

621. Filippini, Henri. "Entrevue avec Sirius." *Schtroumpfanzine*. 16, 1978, pp. 15-17.

622. Nassaux, Jean-Paul. "Relire Timour... Quelles Images de l'Histoire du Monde."
      Bédésup. 14/15, 1980, pp. 3-12.

623. Rommelaere, Catherine. "1. Asie Antérieure." In *Archéologie, Histoire de l'Art
      et Bande Dessinée*, pp. 25-26. Louvain-la-Neuve: U.C.b. Institut Supérieur
      d'Archéologie et d'Histoire de l'Art, 1980.

624. Terence. "Franquin, Macherot et Sirius en Liberté." *Phénix*. No. 12, 1969.

Tibet (Gilbert Gascard)

625. Hue, François. "Bibliographie de Tibet." *Schtroumpf. Les Cahiers de la Bande
      Dessinée*. 40, 1979, pp. 40-48.

626. Léturgie, Jean. "Entretien avec Tibet." *Schtroumpf. Les Cahiers de la Bande
      Dessinée*. 40, 1979, pp. 7-20; 21: "Post-Face de Tardi."

627. Tschernegg, Markus. "Interview mit Tibet und Duchateau." *Comic Forum. Das
      Österreichische Fachmagazin für Comicliteratur*. 4:16 (1982), pp. 67-69. (Andre-
      Paul Duchateau).

Tillieux, Maurice

628. "Bibliographie de Maurice Tillieux." *Rantanplan*. No. 8-9, 1968, pp. 22-30.

629. Cance, Louis, Henri Filippini and Brigitte Hermann. "Bibliographie de Maurice
      Tillieux." *Schtroumpf. Les Cahiers de la Bande Dessinée*. 34, 1977, pp. 40-46.

630. Doigneaux, Patrick. "A la Rencontre de... Maurice Tillieux: Crouton. Portrait
      Physique et Moral." *Le Nouveau Bédésup*. 29/30, 1984, pp. 69-77.

631. Doigneaux, Patrick. "A la Rencontre de... Maurice Tillieux: La Rédemption de
      Libellule, ou Tillieux Fait Jeu Égal avec les Plus Grands en Matière de
      Psychologie." *Le Nouveau Bédésup*. 29/30, 1984, pp. 78-80.

632. Doigneaux, Patrick. "A la Rencontre de... Maurice Tillieux: Le Comique de
      Libellule." *Le Nouveau Bédésup*. 29/30, 1984, pp. 81-90.

633. Doigneaux, Patrick. "L'Accident: Une Réalité Obsédante Chez Maurice Tillieux."
      Bédésup. 24/25, 1983, pp. 73-79.

634. Doigneaux, Patrick. "Socio-Géographie des Lieux Chez Maurice Tillieux."
      Bédésup. 22/23, 1982, pp. 91-94.

635. Doigneaux, Patrick. "Socio-Géographie des Lieux Chez Maurice Tillieux."
      Bédésup. 27, 1983, pp. 36-40.

636. Doigneaux, Patrick. "Tillieux: La Nuit." *Bédésup*. Nos. 48-49, 1989, pp. 23-33.

637. Faur, Jean-Claude. "Comment J'Ai Fait Connaissance avec Maurice Tillieux." *L'Hebdo de la B.D.* No. 58, 1991, pp. 2-3.

638. Faur, Jean-Claude. "Maurice Tillieux et 'L'Esprit de Finesse.'" *Bédésup.* 2nd Trim. 1988, p. 15.

639. Faur, Jean-Claude. *Tillieux. Écrivain, Dessinateur et Scénariste.* Marseilles: Bibliothèque de Marseille, 1983. 56 pp.

640. François, Edouard. "Le Comique Chez Tillieux." *Schtroumpf. Les Cahiers de la Bande Dessinée.* 34, 1977, pp. 37-39.

641. Hermann, Brigitte. 1977. "Entrevue avec Maurice Tillieux." *Schtroumpf. Les Cahiers de la Bande Dessinée.* 34, 1977, pp. 7-22.

642. Leborgne, André. "Tillieux et le Roman Noir." *Rantanplan.* No. 8-9, 1968, pp. 13-14.

643. Martens, Thierry and Alain Van Passen. "Maurice Tillieux, Une Époque, Une Oeuvre." *Rantanplan.* No. 8-9, 1968, pp. 16-21.

644. Quella, Didier. "Le Jeu de Mots Chez Tillieux." *Bédésup.* 22/23, 1982, pp. 73-79, and continued.

645. Rehm, Dirk. "Maurice Tillieux. Die Abenteuer von Jeff Jordan." *Comic Forum. Das Magazin für Comicliteratur.* 7:27 (1985), pp. 36-38.

646. *Tillieux.* Marcinelle: Jean Dupuis, 1984.

647. Van Herp, Jacques. "Tillieux et Harry Dickson." *Rantanplan.* No. 8-9, 1968, pp. 3-4.

648. Vankeer, Pierre. "A la Rencontre de Maurice Tillieux." *Rantanplan.* No. 8-9, 1968, pp. 3-4.

649. Van Passen, Alain. "L'Univers de Maurice Tillieux." *Rantanplan.* No. 8-9, 1968, pp. 5-12.

Vandersteen, Willy (Willebrord)

650. Burgdorf, Paul. "Willy Vandersteen." *Comixene. Das Comicfachmagazin.* 7:28 (1980), pp. 11-16.

651. de Laet, Danny. *Willy Vandersteen, de Man die Zijn Volk Leerde Lachen.* Antwerp: Vlaamse Toeristenbond Antwerpen, 1982.

652. De Lente, J. "Willy Vandersteen ou la BD Industrialisée." *Phénix.* No. 14, 1970.

653. Durnez, Erik. *Ik Vier Het Elke Dag... Willy Vandersteen 65*. Antwerp: Standaard uitg., 1978.

654. Groensteen, Thierry. "Derrière le Maître, Un Studio." *Schtroumpf. Les Cahiers de la Bande Dessinée*. 51, 1981, pp. 37-39.

655. Groensteen, Thierry. "Entretien avec Willy Vandersteen." *Schtroumpf. Les Cahiers de la Bande Dessinée*. 51, 1981, pp. 9-18.

656. Lucas, Jean. "Une Recette à la Flamande." *Schtroumpf. Les Cahiers de la Bande Dessinée*. 51, 1981, pp. 25-26.

657. Smits, Jean-Marie. "L'Oeuvre Réaliste, de Tijl à Bessy." *Schtroumpf. Les Cahiers de la Bande Dessinée*. 51, 1981, 32-35.

658. Teller, Louis, Alain Van Passen, and Thierry Groensteen. "Bibliographie." *Schtroumpf. Les Cahiers de la Bande Dessinée*. 51, 1981, pp. 41-48.

659. Vandersteen, Willy. *Willy and Wanda*. San Francisco, California: Hiddigeigei Books, 1976-. (Series of graphic albums translated from Flemish).

660. Wèlkom in de *Wereld Suske en Wiske*. Tentoonstelling Casino-Kursaal Oostende. Antwerp, Belgium: Standard Uitgeverij, 1990. 24 pp.

Van Hamme, Jean

661. *Schtroumpf. Les Cahiers de la Bande Dessinée*. 70, 1986, pp. 14-19.

662. Menéndez, Germán. "Un Guionista Excepcional: Jean Van Hamme." *El Wendigo*. No. 50, 1990, pp. 4-7.

663. Van Hamme, Jean. "Chocolates, Beer and Comics." Exhibition Catalogue for "Comic Strip Art from Belgium." Brussels: 1988.

Van Raemdonck, G.

664. De Decker, Karel. *G. Van Raemdonck*. Antwerp: Vlaamse Toeristische Bibliotheek, 1973.

665. Kooijman, Jan and Hans Stoovelaar. *In de Ban van Bulletje en Bonestaak*. uitg. N. Noordermeer, 1977.

Walthéry, François

666. Jour, Jean. *François Walthéry*. Drogenbos, Belgium: Librosciences, 1981; Paris: Dupuis, 1982.

667.   Rehm, Dirk and Werner Hoof. "François Walthéry." *Comic Forum. Das Magazin für Comicliteratur.* 7:30 (1985), pp. 46-50.

Wasterlain, Marc

668.   Arrouye, Jean. "*Wasterlain*: Il Est Minuit Docteur Poche ou le Merveilleux Loufoque." *Les Cahiers de la Bande Dessinée.* 57, 1984, pp. 78-81.

669.   Fano, Daniel. "Wasterlain avant Docteur Poche." *Les Cahiers de la Bande Dessinée.* 67, 1986, pp. 16-18.

670.   Groensteen, Thierry. "Fiche Bibliographique." *Les Cahiers de la Bande Dessinée.* 67, 1986, p. 38.

671.   Groensteen, Thierry and Thierry Smolderen. "Entretien avec Marc Wasterlain." *Les Cahiers de la Bande Dessinée.* 67, 1986, pp. 8-15.

Will (Willy Maltaite)

672.   Filippini, Henri. "Will ou le Modernisme dans l'École Belge." *Schtroumpf. Les Cahiers de la Bande Dessinée.* 45, 1980, pp. 23-25.

673.   Filippini, Henri and Jean Léturgie. "Bibliographie de Will." *Schtroumpf. Les Cahiers de la Bande Dessinée.* 45, 1980, pp. 44-49.

674.   Filippini, Henri and Jean Léturgie. "Entretien avec Will." *Schtroumpf. Les Cahiers de la Bande Dessinée.* 45, 1980, pp. 7-21.

675.   Lecigne, Bruno. "La Renaissance de Will." *Schtroumpf. Les Cahiers de la Bande Dessinée.* 45, 1980, pp. 31-35.

Characters and Titles

676.   Ecken, Claude. "De la Lecture pour Buddy." *Schtroumpf. Les Cahiers de la Bande Dessinée.* 50, 1981, p. 23-29.

677.   Groensteen, Thierry. "Pirlouit, ou le Bon Petit Diable." *Schtroumpf. Les Cahiers de la Bande Dessinée.* 54, 1983, pp. 29-30.

678.   Groensteen, Thierry and Franz Van Cauwenbergh. "Benoît Brisefer, Supergamin." *Schtroumpf. Les Cahiers de la Bande Dessinée.* 54, 1983, pp. 37-39.

679.   Janssen, Otto. "Durango." *Comic Forum. Das Magazin für Comicliteratur.* 7:29 (1985), pp. 46-54.

680.   Lecigne, Bruno. "Go West: l'Épopée des Braves Gens." *Schtroumpf. Les Cahiers de la Bande Dessinée.* 50, 1981, pp. 36-37.

681.   Lehner, René. "Jugurtha." *Comixene. Das Comicfachmagazin.* 8:36 (1981), pp. 17-20.

682.   Léturgie, Jean. "Chick Bill, l'Invincible." *Schtroumpf. Les Cahiers de la Bande Dessinée.* 40, 1979, pp. 23-27.

683.   Martens, Thierry. "Le Jardin des Curiosités, Jonny Viking." *Rantanplan.* No. 12, 1968, pp. 9-10.

684.   Pasamonik, Didier. "Son Altesse Riri. La BD Dont le Prince Est un Enfant." *Schtroumpf. Les Cahiers de la Bande Dessinée.* 51, 1981, pp. 27-29.

685.   Pasamonik, Didier. "'Un Petit Ketje des Marolles' ou les Sources Bruxelloises de Bob Fish." *Les Cahiers de la Bande Dessinée.* 60, 1984, pp. 95-97.

686.   Steyn, Ivo. "Lava #1 Published." *Comics Journal.* July 1987, p. 131.

"Astérix Chez les Belges."

687.   Kramer, Johannes. "'Astérix Chez les Belges' und die Landeskunde Belgiens." *Die Neueren Sprachen* (Frankfurt). 80:1 (1981), pp. 35-42.

688.   Voisin, Marcel. "Notes pour l'Analyse de l'Album 'Astérix Chez les Belges' par Goscinny et Uderzo, Ed. Dargaud, Paris, 1979." *Französisch Heute.* March 1987, pp. 112-119.

"Blake et Mortimer"

689.   Jacobs, Edgar-Pierre. *Un Opéra de Papier. Les Mémoires de Blake et Mortimer.* Paris: Gallimard, 1981.

690.   Le Gallo, Claude. "Blake, Mortimer et la Science-Fiction." *Phénix.* No. 4, 3 Trim. 1967, pp. 23-26.

691.   Populaire, Alain. "Le Secret de l'Espadon ou la Troisième Guerre Mondiale." *Schtroumpf. Les Cahiers de la Bande Dessinée.* 30, 1976, pp. 18-20.

692.   Souchet, Philippe. "Les Rapports Est-Quest et les Tensions Raciales dans les Aventures de Blake et Mortimer." In *La Message Politique et Social de la Bande Dessinée*, edited by Charles-Olivier Carbonell, pp. 9-78. Toulouse: Publications de l'Institut d'Etudes Politiques de Toulouse 8, 1975.

"Bob et Bobette"

693. Berger, Thomas. "Bobette, Stakkels Tøs!" *Seriejournalen.* September 1992, p. 15.

694. Groensteen, Thierry. "Bob et Bobette ou la Famille Qui n'Existe Pas." *Schtroumpf. Les Cahiers de la Bande Dessinée.* 51, 1981, pp. 20-24.

695. Hjorth-Jørgensen, Anders. "Et Album til 19, 75 Kr." *Seriejournalen.* September 1992, p. 14.

"Buck Danny"

696. Pierre, Michel. "Buck Danny." *Schtroumpf. Les Cahiers de la Bande Dessinée.* 37, 1978, pp. 31-33.

697. Rodier, Alain. "1947-1977: le Climat d'une Époque." *Schtroumpf. Les Cahiers de la Bande Dessinée.* 35, 1978, pp. 18-35.

"Comanche"

698. Lecigne, Bruno. "Comanche: de l'Image du Conflit au Conflit de l'Image." *Schtroumpf. Les Cahiers de la Bande Dessinée.* 44, 1980, pp. 33-36.

699. Tschernegg, Markus. "Comanche. Eine Frau im Wilden Westen." *Comic Forum. Das Magazin für Comicliteratur.* 5:19 (1983), pp. 34-35, 47.

"Gaston Lagaffe"

700. Jeancharles, Louis. "Gaston Lagaffe: 'Plutôt Rouge Que Mort.'" *Le Nouveau Bédésup.* 29/30, 1984, pp. 45-46.

701. Picco, J.L. "Gaston Lagaffe Héros Tous Emplois." *Cahiers Universitaires.* No. 10, 1970.

702. Pillet-Atzori, Thierry. "Gaston Lagaffe: Un Gaffeur de Choc." *Schtroumpf. Les Cahiers de la Bande Dessinée.* 47/48, 1980, pp. 54-58.

"Gil Jourdan"

703. Dellisse, Luc. "Gil Jourdan. Plaisir du Texte." *Les Cahiers de la Bande Dessinée.* 72, 1986, pp. 91-93.

704. Doigneaux, Patrick. "Tillieux: La Mer and Gil Jourdan." *Bédésup.* 2nd Trim., 1988, pp. 13-14.

705. Hermann, Brigitte. "Les Aventures de Gil Jourdan." *Schtroumpf. Les Cahiers de la Bande Dessinée.* 34, 1977, pp. 29-36.

706.   "Tillieux: La Mer and Gil Jourdan." *Bédésup*. 3rd-4th Trim., 1989, pp. 3-7.

"Les Schtroumpfs. "

707.   Ecken, Claude. "Schtroumpf, le Langage Fantôme." *Schtroumpf. Les Cahiers de la Bande Dessinée*. 54, 1983, p. 35.

708.   Goergen, Helene. "Schlümpfe im Unterricht Mit Erwachsenen?" *Zielsprache Französisch* (Munich). 4, 1979, pp. 163-167.

709.   Granja, Vasco. "A Criacao de Banda Desenhada 'Les Schtroumpfs' dá Origem a Uma Série de Filmesanimadas." *República* (Portugal). April 5, 1967, p. 4.

710.   Lannes, J.M. "Chroniques Schtroumpfiennes." *Cahiers Universitaires*. No. 12, 1971.

711.   Lecigne, Bruno. "Le Grand Schtroumpf, Figure, Mythique du Père." *Schtroumpf. Les Cahiers de la Bande Dessinée*. 54, 1983, pp. 31-33.

712.   "Schtroumpfage Subversif." *Spirou*. January 20, 1966.

713.   Simon, André. "La Politique au Pays Schtroumpf." *Bédésup*. 13, 1980, pp. 7-15.

714.   Simon, André. "Schtroumpfs et Publicité." *Bédésup*. 26, 1983, p. 17.

"Lucky Luke"

715.   Baudoux, Vincent, Michel Baudson, Yvan Delporte, *et al. La Bande à 4 ou la Victoire de Waterloo avec les Auteurs de Jerry Spring, Lucky Luke, Tif and Tondu, Gaston*: Jijé, Morris, Will, Franquin. Album Édité à l'Occasion de l'Exposition Organisée par le Ministère de la Communauté Française de Belgique en Coll. avec la Société des Expositions du Palais des Beaux-Arts de Bruxelles. Marcinelle: J. Dupuis S.A., 1981.

716.   Caré, Jean-Marc. "Lucky Luke, Un Pauvre Gardien de Vaches Solitaire..." *Le Français dans le Monde*. 159, 1981, pp. 17-18.

717.   Lacassin, Francis. "Lucky Luke." *Giff-Wiff*. No. 5, 1965, p. 22.

718.   Le Gallo, Claude. "Lucky Luke, a Poor Lonesome Cow-boy." *Phénix*. No. 3, 1967, pp. 31-32.

719.   Leguebe, Eric. "Lucky Luke Story." *Phénix*. No. 19, 1971.

720.   "Lucky Luke—Comicographie." *Comic Forum. Das Magazin für Comicliteratur*. 5:21 (1983), pp. 43-47.

721. "Lucky Luke. Die Autoren." *Comic Forum. Das Magazin für Comicliteratur.* 5:21 (1983), pp. 17-20.

"Silence"

722. Everaert, Nicole and Bernard Hervé. "'Silence' de Comès. La Différence et la Norme." *Bédésup.* 16, 1981, pp. 25-29.

723. Lecigne, Bruno and Jean-Pierre Tamine. "Silence, Traité de Mécanique Générale." *Schtroumpf. Les Cahiers de la Bande Dessinée.* 55, 1983, pp. 30-32.

"Spirou"

724. Benatar, Simy, Mazaltob Emergui, and Dominique Liatchein. "L'Image de la Femme dans Spirou." In *Le Message Politique et Social de la Bande Dessinée,* edited by Charles-Olivier Carbonell, pp. 149-181. Toulouse: Publication de l'Institut d'Etudes Politiques de Toulouse 8, 1975.

725. Bleicher, Thomas A.T. "Houba! Houba! Ein Nachruf auf das Marsupilami." *Comixene. Das Comicfachmagazin.* 8:41 (1981), pp. 14-15.

726. Brun, Philippe. *Histoire du Journal Spirou et des Publications des Éditions Dupuis.* Grenoble: Glénat, 1975, 1981.

727. Brunoro, Gianni. "Eloge d'un Animal Fantastique Appelé Marsupilami." *Schtroumpf. Les Cahiers de la Bande Dessinée.* 47/48, 1980, pp. 42-44.

728. Burdeyron, François-Xavier. *L'Âge d'Or du Journal Spirou.* Marseilles: Bédésup, 1988.

729. Ecken, Claude. "Un An de Spirou." *Les Cahiers de la Bande Dessinée.* 60, 1984, pp. 48-49.

730. Fermín Pérez, Ramón. "Introducción a Spirou (y a Franquin)." *El Wendigo.* March-May 1986, pp. 18-20.

731. Glénat, Jacques. "Spirou et Fantasio." *Cahiers Universitaires.* No. 10, 1970.

732. "Komik Riwayatmu Dulu (2)." *Jakarta.* May 27-June 2, 1988, pp. 20-21.

733. Leborgne, André. "Spirou." *Phénix* SP.

734. Léturgie, Jean. "Spirou: Grandeur et Décadence d'un Journal.' *Schtroumpfanzine.* 33, 1979, pp. 14-20.

735. Mietzsch, Andreas. *Huba. Huba. Das Marsupilami-Buch.* Hamburg: comicplus +, Verlag Eckart Sackmann, 1985.

736.   Moliterni, Claude. "8 Dessinateurs de Spirou à Paris." *Phénix*. No. 15, 1970.

737.   Sadoul, Numa. "Le Monde de Spirou et Fantasio." *Schtroumpf. Les Cahiers de la Bande Dessinée*. 47/48, 1980, pp. 25-41.

738.   "*Spirou* Turns 50." *Comics Journal*. October 1988, p. 31.

739.   Vankeer, Pierre. "Spirou." *Rantanplan*. No. 12, 1968, p. 5.

"Tintin"

740.   Altarriba, Antonio. "La Intrincada Intriga de las Joyas Intrinsecas o la Casta-Flor des-Nojada." *Neuróptica. Estudios Sobre el Cómic* (Zaragoza). 2, 1984, pp. 32-50.

741.   Apostolidés, Jean-Marie. "Anatomie d'un Succès: Les Aventures de Tintin." *Liberté* (Montreal). 26:4 (1984), pp. 11-24.

742.   Apostolidés, Jean-Marie. *Les Métamorphoses de Tintin*. Paris: Seghers, 1984.

743.   Apostolidés, Jean-Marie. "L'Unique et les Doubles: Tintin dans *L'Oreille Cassée*." *Stanford French Review*. Spring 1984, pp. 87-103.

744.   Apostolidès, Jean-Marie. "Tintin and the Family Romance." *Children's Literature*. 13 (1985), pp. 94-108.

745.   Bergeron, Francis. "50 Ans avant Soljénitsyne. Tintin au Pays des Soviets." *Est and Quest* (Paris). 4, 1984, p. 26-28.

746.   Bertieri, Claudio. "Il Sucessi di Tintin, dal Cinema alle Edicole." *Il Lavoro* (Genoa). November 11, 1965.

747.   Bertieri, Claudio. "Tin-Tin: Cinema o Fumetto." *Il Lavoro*. November 23, 1965.

748.   Brault, Colette. "Tintin, l'Enchanteur." *Tele-Magazin* (Paris). No. 571, 1966.

749.   C.H. "Aprés Indiana Jones, Spielberg Choisit Tintin." *Livres Hebdo* (Paris). 6:40 (1984), p. 97.

750.   de Cours Saint-Gervasy, Pierre-Louis. "Tintin au Pays des Fascistes?" In *Le Message Politique et Social de la Bande Dessinée*, edited by Charles-Olivier Carbonell, pp. 119-147. Toulouse: Institut d'Etudes Politiques de Toulouse, 1975.

751.   De La Croix, Arnaud. "L'Art Nécrophile du Portrait." *Les Cahiers de la Bande Dessinée*. 72, 1986, pp. 70-71.

752.   De La Croix, Arnaud. "Une Dynamique de la Violence." *Les Cahiers de la Bande Dessinée*. 59, 1984, pp. 82-84.

753. Di Manno, Yves. "Le Fantastique dans Tintin." *Cahiers Universitaires*. No. 14, 1971.

754. Di Manno, Yves. "Le Fantastique dans Tintin." *Schtroumpf. Les Cahiers de la Bande Dessinée*. 14/15, 1978, pp. 57-59.

755. Filippini, Henri. "Tintin." *Phénix* SP.

756. Fjorklid, Finn. "Litteraturen om Tintin." *TEGN*. 1, 1990, p. 46-48.

757. Goddin, Philippe. *L'Aventure du Journal Tintin: 40 Ans de Bandes Dessinées*. Paris, Brussels: Eds. du Lombard, 1986.

758. Hausser, Michel. "Mots de Jeu dans 'Les Aventures de Tintin.'" *Eidôlon* (Talence). 26, 1985, pp. 191-250.

759. "Here's a Good Comic: Tintin Books." *Newsweek*. February 22, 1960, p. 104.

760. Jenkins, Iain. "'Nazi' Tintin Gives Belgium a Nasty Turn." *The Jester*. August 1992, p. 8.

761. Labesse, Dominique. "A Propos du Racisme." *Schtroumpf. Les Cahiers de la Bande Dessinée*. 14/15, 1978, pp. 45-48.

762. Labesse, Dominique. "Les Régimes Politiques." *Schtroumpf. Les Cahiers de la Bande Dessinée*. 14/15, 1978, pp. 49-50.

763. Labesse, Dominique. "Les Voyages et l'Aventure." *Schtroumpf. Les Cahiers de la Bande Dessinée*. 14/15, 1978, pp. 43-44.

764. Laurenceau, Georges. "La Syldavie et la Bordurie." *Schtroumpf. Les Cahiers de la Bande Dessinée*. 14/15, 1978, pp. 51-52.

765. Le Gallo, Claude. "Brave Capitaine Haddock." *Phénix*. No. 23, 1972.

766. Le Gallo, Claude. "Tintin Héros de XXe Siècle." *Phénix*. No. 4, 3 Trim., 1967, pp. 3-17.

767. *Le Point* (Paris). September 25, 1972 to February 5, 1973. (16 specials on French media. No. 15: "Les Tintins de la Vᵉ.").

768. Lerman, Alain. *Histoire du Journal Tintin*. Grenoble: Eds. Jacques Glénat, 1979.

769. "Les Aventures de Tintin." *La Nation Européenne*. October 1967, p. 45.

770. Luciano, Dale. "Tintin's America." *Comics Journal*. September 1981, pp. 33-35.

771.   MacIntyre, Mac. "Tintin Grows Up and Discovers Sex." London *Times* dispatch in *Statesman* (New Delhi). July 6, 1993, p. 1.

772.   Martens, Thierry. "Tintin au Tournant." *Rantanplan.* No. 12, 1968, pp. 7-8.

773.   Masson, Pierre. "Morphologie d'un Conte en Bandes Dessinées. 'Les Bijoux de la Castafiore,' de Hergé." *L'Ecole des Lettres* (Paris). 1, 1983, pp. 37-44.

774.   Mills, T.F. "America Discovers Tintin." *Comics Journal.* November 1983, pp. 60-69.

775.   M.L. and G.M. "Tintin au Pays de l'Ornière." *Libération.* Supplement Special Angoulême 1992, p. xi.

776.   Moliterni, Claude. "Tintin Présente l'Univers de la BD." *Phénix.* No. 19, 1971.

777.   Morin, E. "Tintin Héros d'une Génération." *La Nef* (Paris). No. 13, 1958.

778.   Moutet, Anne-Elisabeth. "Tintin Cleans Up His Act." *The Jester.* August 1992, p. 12.

779.   Mozgovine, Cyrille. *Dictionnaire Tintin "D' Abdallah à Zorrino."* Brussels: Casterman, 1993. 264 pp.

780.   Muñoz Zielinski, Manuel. "La Función de los Personajes Secundarios: El Capitan Haddock." *Neuróptica. Estudios Sobre el Cómic* (Zaragoza). 2, 1984, pp. 22-29.

781.   Peeters, Benoît. *Les Bijoux Ravis. Une Lecture Moderne de Tintin.* Brussels: Magic Strip, 1984.

782.   Roland, Niels. "Tintins Museum." *Seriejournalen.* December 1990, pp. 36-38.

783.   Sadoul, Numa. "Galeries de Portraits." *Schtroumpf. Les Cahiers de la Bande Dessinée.* 14/15, 1978, pp. 38-42.

784.   Sadoul, Numa. *Tintin et Moi. Entretien avec Hergé.* Paris, Tournai: Casterman, 1975.

785.   Sadoul, Numa and Francis Groux. "Tintin et les Phénomènes Paranormaux." *Schtroumpf. Les Cahiers de la Bande Dessinée.* 14/15, 1978, pp. 60-63.

786.   Saunier, Henri. "Tchiize Special Tintin." *Bédésup.* Nos. 48-49, 1989, pp. 54-55.

787.   Sterckx, Pierre. "Tintin au Congo ou le Guerrier Attrapé par la Queue..." *Schtroumpf. Les Cahiers de la Bande Dessinée.* 14/15, 1978, p. 56.

788.   "Tintin Cans Book." *Comics Journal.* October 1991, p. 29.

789. "Tintin Lives." *Comics Journal*. March 1988, p. 16.

790. "*Tintin* Magazine: The End or the Beginning?" *Comics Journal*. July 1988, p. 22.

791. Tisseron, Serge. *Tintin Chez la Psychanalyste. Essai sur la Création Graphique et la Mise en Scène de Ses Enjeux dans l'Oeuvre d'Hergé*. Paris: Eds. Aubier Montaigne, 1985.

792. Valeix, Christian. "Tintin, Son Papa et Son Grand-père." *Le Nouveau Bédésup*. 32/33, 1985, pp. 11-18.

793. Vandromme, Pol. *Le Monde de Tintin*. Paris: Gallimard, Coll. "L'Air du Temps," 1959.

794. Vanherpe, Henri. "La Bande Dessinée et la Politique. Un Exemple. Le Contenu Politique des Albums de Tintin." Paper presented for graduate diploma, Lille, 1968.

795. Vanherpe, Henri. "Les Idées Politiques de 'Tintin.'" *Revue Politique et Parlementaire* (Paris). 72:811 (1970), pp. 39-55.

796. Van Lierde, Henry and Gustave du Fontbare. *Le Colloque de Moulinsart*. Brussels: Rossel; Paris: Futuropolis, 1983.

797. Williams, Michael. "'Tintin' Rewrites the Rules for French Primetime." *Variety*. May 25, 1992, p. 34.

798. Williams, Michael. "'Tintin' Rides into Sunset, Leaving France 3 Glowing." *Variety*. November 23, 1992, p. 24.

Animation

799. Levie, Pierre. "Belgique: Terre de Dessins Animés." *Corto Circuito*. April 1992, p. 34.

800. Moins, Philippe. "Animation in Belgium." *Animation*. Winter 1989, p. 83.

Comic Books

801. Bertran, Serge F. "Illustrés Oubliés: Wonderland." *Rantanplan*. No. 12, 1968, pp. 10-12.

802. Blanchard, Gérard. *La Bande Dessinée. Histoire des Histoires en Images de la Préhistoire à Nos Jours*. Verviers: Gerard Ed., 1969.

803.   Boisdequin, Michel. "Coup de Coeur pour le Flibustier de Dieu!" *Coccinelle.* January-April 1990, pp. 10-11.

804.   Bosmans, Serge and Marc Michetz. *Kogaratsu, the Lotus of Blood.* London: Acme Press, 1987. 48 pp.

805.   Boudre, Alain. "Broussaille. Un Héros au Coeur pur." *Coccinelle.* June 1990, p. 27.

806.   Clausse, Roger. "A Propos de la Bande Dessinée." Preface to *La Bande Dessinée Belge*, pp. 7-9. Brussels: 1968.

807.   Doutreligne, Michel. "La Bande Dessinée." In *Littérature Française de Belgique. Publié Sous la Direction de Robert Frickx et Jean Muno*, pp. 98-118. Sherbrooke, Québec: Eds. Naaman, 1979.

808.   "Editorial: Comics." *Rantanplan.* No. 2, 1966, p. 1.

809.   "Editorial: Le Temps de la Patience...." *Rantanplan.* No. 3, 1966, p. 1.

810.   "Editorial: Un An Déjà...." *Rantanplan.* No. 4, 1966/1967, p. 1.

811.   Eskenazi, Frank. "L'Art Peellaert." *Libération.* Supplement Special Angoulême 1992, p. vii.

812.   Feron, Michel. "Bandes Dessinées pour les Jeunes." *Vo n' Polez Nin Comprind.* No. 4-5, 1967.

813.   Feron, Michel. "Comic-Books. Courtres Considérations Critiques." *Le Sac à Charbon.* No. 1, 1965.

814.   Feron, Michel. "La Première Assemblée Pléniere du CABD." *Vo n'Polez Nin Comprind.* No. 2, 1957.

815.   Frémion, Yves. "L'École Belge." *Magazine Littéraire* (Paris). 95, 1974, pp. 34-35.

816.   Greg, Michel. *La Bande Dessinée, Phénomène Social?* Brussels: Bibliotheque Royale de Belgique, 1968.

817.   Greg, Michel. "La Bande Dessinée, Phénomène Social?" Preface to *La Bande Dessinée Belge*, pp. 14-17. Brussels: 1968.

818.   Groensteen, Thierry. "La BD Belge au Féminin Pluriel." *Les Cahiers de la Bande Dessinée.* 58, 1984, pp. 43-45.

819.   Guichard-Meili, Jean. "Les Loisirs d'Illico." *Rantanplan.* No. 6, 1967, pp. 4-6.

820. Herman, Paul. "Bande Dessinée: L'École Belge en Veilleuse." *Magazine Littéraire* (Paris). 118, 1976, pp. 62-63.

821. Hermann, Brigitte. *Index de la Bande Dessinée Belge*. Grenoble: J. Glénet, 1976 (?).

822. *Introduction à la Bande Dessinée Belge*. (Exposition, Bibliothèque Albert ler, Brussels, June 29 to August 25, 1968). Brussels: Bibliothèque Royale de Belgique, 1968.

823. "La BD Agit Comme Trait d'Union Entre le Québec et la Belgique." *Coccinelle*. June 1990, p. 21.

824. Lacassin, Francis. "Les Bandes Dessinées, Produit d'une Civilisation." Conference d'un congres international d'éditeurs de Comics du marché commun, Brussels. April 1966.

825. *La Jeune Bande Dessinée Liégoise*. (Exposition). Liège: Affaires Culturelles, 1984.

826. Leborgne, André. "Belgique." In *Histoire Mondiale de la Bande Dessinée*, edited by Pierre Horay, pp. 154-170. Paris: Pierre Horay Editeur, 1989.

827. Leborgne, André. "Safari en Italie." *Rantanplan*. No. 7, 1967, pp. 4-8.

828. Lefevre, Gaston. "Bandes pour Vieux." *Rantanplan*. No. 5, 1967, pp. 12-13.

829. "Les Bandes Dessinées à l'Université." *Rantanplan*. No. 2, 1966, p. 8.

830. "Le Centre de la Bande Dessinée Belge, Enfin!" *Les Cahiers de la Bande Dessinée*. 68, 1986, p. 59.

831. Leguebe, Wilbur. *La Société des Bulles*. Brussels: La Vie Ouvrière, 1977.

832. Martens, Thierry. "Bande Dessinée et Figuration Narrative." *Rantanplan*. No. 7, 1967, p. 9.

833. Martens, Thierry. "Cheneval, de Bimbo aux Heroic-Albums." *Rantanplan*. No. 12, 1968, pp. 7-8.

834. Martens, Thierry. *Réalisme et Schematisme dans les Bandes Dessinées Belges Contemporaines*. Brussels: 1967. 278 pp.

835. Martens, Thierry. "Réalisme et Schematisme dans les Bandes Dessinées Hebdomadaires Belges Contemporaines (1945-1965)." Thesis, l'Université Catholique de Louvain, Institut des Sciences Politiques et Sociales, 1966.

836. Martens, Thierry. "Tribune d'Éssai...." *Vo n'Polez Nin Comprind*. No. 4-5, 1967.

837. Matthys, Francis. "Bulles et Planches en Nouvelle-France: Le Missionnaire Pierre-Joseph Chaumonot Reçoit Une Coccinelle." *Coccinelle*. January-April 1990, p. 15.

838. Morris and Pierre Vankeer. "9e Art: Musée de la Bande Dessinée." *Spirou*. 1967.

839. Picco, J.L. "Luc Orient ou la Nouvelle SF Belge." *Cahiers Universitaires*. No. 17, 1972.

840. Sinda, Thierry. "La B.D. et l' Afrique." *Coccinelle*. January-April 1990, p. 30.

841. Ugeux, William. "Introduction à la Bande Dessinée Belge." *Phénix*. No. 7, 3 Trim., 1968, pp. 63-68.

842. Ugeux, William. "Le Neuvième Art. Introduction to *La Bande Dessinée Belge*." *Rantanplan* (Brussels). 1967, pp. 10-13.

843. Vandooren, Philippe. *Comment on Dévient Créateur de Bandes Dessinées*. Verviers: Bibliothéque Marabout MS 120, Gérard Editions, 1969.

844. Van Hamme, Jean. "Introduction à la Bande Dessinée Belge. Inleiding Tot Het Belgish Strip Verhaal." Catalogue. Brussels: Bibliothèque Royal de Belgique, 1968.

845. Van Herp, Jacques. "Urnaghur." *Rantanplan*. No. 12, 1968, p. 9.

846. Vankeer, Pierre. "Chronique de l'Âge d'Or." *Rantanplan*. No. 2, 1966, p. 4; No. 3, 1966, p. 4; No.4, 1966/1967, pp. 2-3; No. 5, 1967, p. 11; No. 6, 1967, pp. 15-17; No. 7, 1967, pp. 14-16; No. 12, 1968, p. 4.

847. Vankeer, Pierre. "Editorial." *Rantanplan*. No. 7, 1967, p. 3.

848. Vankeer, Pierre. "Editorial." *Rantanplan*. Supplement of No. 8-9, 1968, p. 1.

849. Vankeer, Pierre. "Le Rayon U ou le Maillon Retrouve." Preface to *Le Rayon U*. Brussels: C.A.B.D., 1967.

850. Vankeer, Pierre. "Quelques Mots Sur l'Évolution des Bandes Dessinées en Belgique de 1946 à 1966." *I Fumetti* (Rome). No. 9, 1967, pp. 135-137.

851. Van Passen, Alain. "Fuisons le Point...." *Rantanplan*. No. 3, 1966, pp. 7-8.

Cinema, Television

852.   "Bande Dessinée et Cinéma." *Amis du Film et de la Télévision* (Brussels). 1966, pp. 7-13.

853.   Chevron, Alain. "Bande Dessinée et Cinéma." *Amis du Film et de la Télévision.* Nos. 144-145, 1968.

854.   De Seraulx, Micheline. "TV: l'Enfant Jaune ou la Bande Dessinée." *Vo n'Polez Nin Comprind.* No. 2, 1967.

855.   Godin, Noel. "Anatomie d'Une Bande Dessinée." *Amis du Film et de la Télévision.* No. 137, 1967, pp. 10-11.

856.   Godin, Noel. "Bandes Dessinées et Cinéma." *Amis du Film et de Télévision.* No. 127, 1966.

857.   Oreche, J. "Les Bandes Dessinées Qui Inspirent le Cinéma." *Cine-Revue* (Brussels). October 20, 1966.

858.   Peeters, Benoît. "Autour du Scénario. Cinéma, Bande Dessinée, Roman-Photo, Vidéo-Clip, Publicité, Littérature." *Revue de l'Université de Bruxelles.* 1986, pp. 1-2.

859.   Van Passen, Alain. "Petit Écho sur le Cinéma et la Bande Dessinée." *Rantanplan.* No. 4, 1966/1967, p. 16.

Comic-Verlag Dupuis

860.   de Laet, Danny. *L'Affaire Dupuis. Dallas sur Marcinelle.* Brussels: News, Comics and Média sprl., 1985.

861.   "Dupuis: Accord Enfin Conclu." *Livres Hebdo.* 7:37 (1985), p. 52.

862.   Zecchini, Alain. "Libraire BD Recherche Nouveaux Héros." *Livres Hebdo.* 8:27 (1986), pp. 53-55.

Festivals

863.   "BD Durbuy 90, Les Prix: des References." *Coccinelle.* June 1990, p. 11.

864.   Moliterni, Claude. "La 1ère Convention de la BD Belge." *Phénix.* No. 13, 1969.

865.   Moliterni, Claude. "2ème Convention de la BD Belge." *Phénix.* No. 17, 1970.

866.   Passamonick, Didier. *L'Expo 58 et le Style Atome.* Brussels: Magic Strip, 1983.

867.   "Propos à Bâtons Rompus." *Les Cahiers de la Bande Dessinée*. 70, 1986, pp. 59-61.

Genres

868.   "Le Western dans la Bande Dessinée." Brussels: Maison des Jeunes d'Auderghem, 1974.

869.   Van Herp, Jacques. "Les Bandes Dessinées de Science-Fiction." *Rantanplan*. No. 4, 1966/1967, pp. 6-9.

870.   Van Herp, Jacques. "Les Bandes Dessinées de Science-Fiction. Robida: Saturnin Farandoul." *Rantanplan*. No. 5, 1967, pp. 3-5.

871.   Van Herp, Jacques. "Science-Fiction et Bande Dessinée." *Rantanplan*. No. 6, 1967, pp. 18-19; No. 7, 1967, pp. 18-20.

Comic Strips

872.   "Bruno Brazil: from James Bond to the A-Team and Back Again." *Nemo*. December 1985, pp. 51-53.

873.   De Bree, Kees, Rob Van Eijck, and Martin Wassington. *Strips*. Haarlem: Oberon, 1979.

874.   De Laet, Danny. *De Vlaamse Strip Auteurs*. Antwerp: De Dageraad, 1982. 317 pp.

875.   De Laet, Danny. *Het Beeldverhaal in Vlaanderen*. Breda: Brabantia Nostra, 1977.

876.   De Laet, Danny and Varende. *De Zevende Kunst Voorbij: Geschiedenis van Het Beeldverhaal in Belgie*. Brussels: Ministerie van Buitenlandse Zake, Buitenlandse Handel en Ontwikkelings-Samenwerking, 1979. 302 pp. (History of newspaper comic strips in Belgium).

877.   De Laet, Danny and Yves Varende. *Mehr als Siebente Kunst. Geschichte der Belgischen "Comic Strips" (Bildgeschichten)*. Brussels: Ministerium für Auswärtige Angelegenheiten, für Außenhandel und Entwicklungszusammenarbeit, 1979.

878.   De Saeger, Kris *De Nieuwe Heldenmakers*. Leuven: KUL, 1978.

879.   De Saeger, Kris *Het Belgisch Stripverhaal*. Leuven: KUL, 1979.

880.   Dessicy, Guy. "Belgium: A Kingdom Where the Comic Strip Is King." Exhibition of "Comic Strip Art from Belgium," Brussels, 1988.

881. Groensteen, Thierry. "Belgium, the Comic Strip Paradise." Exhibition Catalogue for "Comic Strip Art from Belgium," Brussels, Belgium, 1988.

882. *Inleiding Tot Het Belgisch Stripverhaal*. Brussels: KB, 1968.

883. Kousemaker, Evelien and Kees *Wordt Vervolgd, Stripleksikon der Lage Landen*. Utrecht: Het Spectrum, 1979.

884. Lachartre, Alain. *Objectif Pub*. Brussels: Eds. Robert Laffont-Magic Strip, 1986.

885. Manderveld, Manu. *Strip-script, op Zoek Naar een Mogelijke Plaats in de OB-afdeling Volwassen*. Antwerp: STLB, 1976.

886. Martens, Thierry. "Survey of the Belgian Comic Strip." Exhibition Catalogue for "Comic Strip Art from Belgium," Brussels, Belgium, 1988.

887. *Ontwikkelingssamenwerking. 1979*. 302 pp. (History of Belgian newspaper comics).

BULGARIA

General Studies

888. "Bulgaran." *Apropos*. No. 3, 1986, pp. 157-159.

889. "Bulgarian Cartoon-Magazines." *FECO News*. No. 12, 1991, p. 23.

890. "Eastern European and Russian Humor." In *Humor Scholarship: A Research Bibliography*, edited by Don L.F. Nilsen, pp. 197-199. Westport, Connecticut: Greenwood, 1993.

891. Gerasimov, Bogomil. "Humour: The Gift of Gabrovo." *UNESCO Courier*. 29 (1976), pp. 9-11.

892. Ivanova, Nina. "Laughter As a Curse: (The Comic Press in the National Revival Period)." *Apropos*. No. 6, pp. 116-117.

893. Ivanova, Nina. "Satirists and Politicos: (The Bulgarian Comic Press from the Liberation in 1878 to the Union with Eastern Rumelia in 1885)." *Apropos*. No. 7, 1991, pp. 116-117.

894. Kraev, Georg. "The Capital of Humor." *Discover Bulgaria*. January-February-March 1991, pp. 28-29.

895. Nilsen, Don L.F. "Inside Bulgaria's House of Humour." *Humor Events*. June 1988, pp. 3-4.

896. Popov, Yordan. "To Gobrovo with a Smile." *Discover Bulgaria*. January-February-March 1991, pp. 26-27.

897. Purvova, Fani. "A Story with a Happy Ending." *Discover Bulgaria*. January-February-March 1991, p. 34.

898. Shterev, Nikolai. "From Don Quixote to Sly Peter." *Discover Bulgaria*. January-February-March 1991, p. 35.

Cartoonists

899. "Alla and Chavdar Georgiev." *Apropos*. No. 7, 1991, pp. 32-34.

900. "Angela Minkova." *Apropos*. No. 5, 1988, p. 67.

901. "Anri Kulev, Satirist." *Index on Censorship*. October 1992, pp. 32-33.

902. "Bulgarian Cartoonists." *Apropos*. No. 2, 1986, pp. 78-79.

903. "Despó-sition." *Apropos*. No. 7, 1991, pp. 80-83, 89-90, 95-98, 102-104. (Stefan Despodov).

904. "Iliya Beshkov about Alexander Bozhinov." *Apropos*. No. 3, 1986, pp. 147-149.

905. *Klassiker der Karikatur: No. 20. Jules Pascin*. Berlin: Eulenspiegel-Verlag, 1981. (a.k.a. Julius Pincas).

906. Sivriev, Stanislav. "Iliya Beshkov on Laughter, Derision, the Comic and All That." *Apropos*. No. 1, 1983, pp. 123-126.

907. Tsokev, Peter. "The Quickest Way To Bring People Together: Interview with Hristo Penchev." *Discover Bulgaria*. January-February-March 1991, pp. 30-33.

CROATIA

General Studies

908. "Croatian Cartoonists Association, Croatian Anti War Cartoons." *FECO News*. No. 13, 1992, p. 2.

909. "English Exhibition in Zagreb." *FECO News*. No. 5, 1987, p. 8.

910. *91. Primirje Karikature. Hrvatsko Društvo Karikaturista. Galerija Galženica, Nov. 28-Dec. 12, 1991*. Zagreb, 1991.

Animation

911.   Givens, Bill. "Zagreb Animation." *Animation*. Winter 1989, pp. 74-75.

912.   Holloway, R. *Z is for Zagreb*. New York: Barnes, 1972; London: Tantivy Press, 1972.

CZECHOSLOVAKIA

General Studies

913.   *Archikatúra 1992 Bratislava*. Bratislava: Spolok Architektov Slovenska, Pro Slovakia, and Galeria Mesta Bratislavy, 1992. 60 pp. Catalogue of architecture cartoons, June 4-July 12, 1992.

914.   Clair, René and Jaroslav Tichý. *Comics*. Prague: 1967. 60 pp.

915.   "CSSR-Schund, Kitsch, Comics." *Bulletin: Jugend + Literatur*. No. 6, 1972, p. 15.

916.   Kumermann, Daniel. "And the Winner of This Year's 'Emil' Is...." *WittyWorld*. Summer 1988, pp. 44-45.

917.   Kumermann, Daniel. "Many Problems Abound To Account for the Sad State of Czech Graphic Humor." *WittyWorld*. Summer/Autumn 1989, pp. 40-41.

918.   "A Long Trip by Car... Bratislava to Belgium." *FECO News*. No. 13, 1992, p. 17.

919.   "New Cartoon Magazine in Czechoslovakia—Kuk." *FECO News*. No. 10, 1990, p. 16.

920.   Riha, Karl. "Die Blase im Kopf." *Knizni Kultura* (Prague). No. 2, 1965.

921.   Sliva, Jiri. "A Tradition Continues: Czechoslovakian Cartoons." *WittyWorld*. Summer 1988, pp. 44-45.

Cartoonists and Their Works

922.   *Čim Drží Svět Pohromadě*. Prague: Mladá Fronta, 1990. 240 pp.

923.   Haas, Leo. *Links Überholt*. Berlin: Eulenspiegel-Verlag, 1961.

924. *Jesters in Earnest.* Cartoons by Czechoslovak Artists Z.K., A. Hoffmeister, A. Pelc, Stephen, W. Trier. Preface by David Low. London: John Murray, 1944.

925. "Laco Torma, Czechoslovakia." *FECO News.* No. 7, 1989, p. 24.

926. *72 Drawings by Jiří Jirásek.* Newcastle upon Tyne: Stand, 1968. 20 pp.

927. Szobel, Geza. *Civilisation.* Foreword by Jan Stransky. Middlesex: Penguin Books Harmondsworth, 1942.

928. Vanek, Marián. *Tribúny.* Bratislava: Slovenský Spisovatel, 1990.

929. Vico. *Eko Vico. Obrázky Z Páte Výstavy Časopisu Krkonoše.* Pardubice, 1989.

930. "Viliam Živický, Czechoslovakia." *FECO News.* No. 7, 1989, p. 25.

Born, Adolf

931. Born, Adolf. *Bilderbuch der Reisekunst.* Berlin: Eulenspiegel-Verlag, 1982.

932. Born, Adolf. *Bilderbuch der Verführungskunst.* Berlin: Eulenspiegel-Verlag, 1975.

933. Born, Adolf. *The International Pavilion of Humor of Montreal Presents Adolf Born. 1974 Cartoonist of the Year.* Montreal: 1974. Unpaginated.

934. Born, Adolf. *Nachmittage Eines Clowns.* Berlin: Eulenspiegel-Verlag, 1967.

935. "I Remain Loyal to Humour." *Apropos.* No. 1, 1983, pp. 95-101.

936. Posova, Katerzhina. "Revealing the Truth (about Adolf Born)." *Apropos.* No. 1, 1983, pp. 90-94.

Kotrha, Lubomir

937. "Lubomir Kotrha, Cartoonist from Czechoslovakia." *FECO News.* No. 6, 1988, p. 5.

938. "Lubomir Kotrha, Czechoslovakia." *FECO News.* No. 7, 1989, p. 23.

Sliva, Jiri

939. Christoph, Tobias. "Cartoons by Jiri Sliva." *Novum Gebrauchsgraphik.* December 1988, pp. 56-60.

940. "Jiri Sliva." *Apropos.* No. 6, pp. 40-44.

941. Sliva, Jiri. *Allerlei Zirkus.* Berlin: Eulenspeigel-Verlag, 1979.

Animation

942. Asad Binakhahi. [Animation in Czechoslovakia]. *Kayhan Caricature*. June 1993.

943. Assadolah Binakhahi. [Animation in Czechoslovakia]. *Kayhan Caricature*. July 1993.

944. Assadolah Binakhahi. "Czech Animator Karel Zaman." *Kayhan Caricature*. April 1993.

945. Cohen, Karl. "More Alive Than Humans: The Surreal World of Jan Svankmajer." *Animation*. Winter 1989, pp. 36-37.

946. Malek, Michael. "Painful Changes on Tap for Czech Anim Biz." *Variety*. November 5, 1990, p. 60.

DENMARK

General Studies

947. Bjorklid, Finn. "Fraksjoner. Lett Fravaerende i Goteborg." *TEGN*. No. 3 (13), 1989, p. 10.

948. "Bonniers Satser på Blade." *Seriejournalen*. September 1990, p. 7.

949. "Dansk Tegneserie—Museum Åbner i Ubby." *Seriejournalen*. June 1992, pp. 9-10.

950. *Fat Comic*. Index. Danske Tegneserieudgivelser i 80-erne
   Af Frank Madsen med hjælp af Rune Kidde

ARBSK	Arbejderbevægelsens Skolekontaktudvalg
B&B	Balder & Brage
BF	Bogfabrikken (viderefører Borgens serier fra 1986)
BORG	Borgens Forlag
BRØN	Brøndums Forlag
CC	Carlsen Comics (slået s.m. Interpresse til SEMIC 1986)
DNG	Dansk Natur Gas
DONNA	Forlaget Donna (Jussi Olsen/C.M.Drastrup (nu SEMIC))
EBF	Ekstra Bladets Forlag
Eget	Udgivet på ophavsmandens eget forlag
FAGB	Fagbladet
HF	Huset Forlag
INF	Informations Forlag
IP	Interpresse (slået sammen med Carlsen til SEMIC 1986)
KBF	Københavns Bogforlag

LABL	Landsforeningen af Bøsser and Lesbiske
LEGO	LEGO Publishing
MAL	Mallings Forlag
RP	Runepress (Interpresse)
SF	Serieforlaget (Gutenberghus)
SOC	Socialdemokratiet
STAVN	Forlaget Stavnsager
TEL	Tellerups Forlag
ULFSV	U-landsforeningen Svalerne
UNDVN	Undervisningsministeriet
VIBM	Viborg Museum
WF	Winthers Forlag (Ejet af Gutenberghus)

1980

Lasse S. Nielsen	Blot	B&B
C & V Hansen	Rasmus Klump bygger radiostation	CC
Arne Ungermann	Hanne Hansen	CC
Werner Wejp Olsen	Felix 8: Den nye engergikilde	CC
Antologi	Hård kost 3	HF
J & C. Deleuran	Pirelli & Firestone 2: Occidentens Lys	INF
Rune Kidde	Rune T. Kidde	IP
Rune Kidde	Man siger så meget	IP
Madsen/Vadmand/ Kure	Valhalla 2: Thors brudefærd	IP
Jørgen Mogensen	Poeten & Lillemor minialbum	IP
Jesper T Petersen	Mandag	MAL

1981

Rune Kidde	Fuglene	B&B
C & V Hansen	R Klump møder Tik Tak og andre venner	CC
Thomas Kjellerup	Uffe Hin Spage	Eget
Rina Dahlerup	Kanindræberen Kaj	IP
Orla Klausen	Jens Langkniv 1	IP
Jørgen Mogensen	Poeten & Lillemor minialbum	IP
O Pihl/J Tofteskov	Som blommen i et æg	IP
Karsten Hansen	48 sider af Karsten Hansen	WF

1982

Rasmus Bregnhøi	Hvor deprimerende	B&B
Kirsten Schmidt	Sødsuppemagasinet	B&B
Antologi	Menneskefiskeren	B&B
Henning Gantriis	Livet går videre i Lidenlund	CC
C & V Hansen	Rasmus Klump i vanskeligheder	CC
P Ehlers/T Prehn	Kosmo	HF
Orla Klausen	Jens Langkniv 2: Landsknægte	IP
Madsen/Vadmand/ Kure	Valhalla 3: Odins væddemål	IP
Freddy Milton	Villiams Verden	IP

Jørgen Mogensen	Poeten & Lillemor Minialbum	IP
Hans Qvist	Skrækkelige Olfert Minialbum	IP
C & J Deleuran	Pirelli & Firestone: Occidentens Lys 2	INF
Kim Fupz Aakeson	Gå løs på livet	KBF
Jesper T Petersen	Tirsdag	MAL
Rune Kidde	Gal og normal	RP
Sussi Bech	Hvor går du hen?	UNDVM

1983

Antologi	Fuga i E-mol	B&B
J P Agger/O Munk	Felix 9: Jagten på u-båden	CC
J P Agger/O Munk	Felix 10: Felix og våbensmuglerne	CC
C & V Hansen	Rasmus Klump klarer en rævestreg	CC
C & V Hansen	Rasmus Klump henter juletræ	CC
Karl Oskar Jæger	Historien om Ben Hadj	CC
Thomas Kjellerup	Bjarke og Hjalte	Eget
Stefan Fjeldmark	Snedronningen	IP
Orla Klausen	Jens Langkniv 3: Heksene	IP
Klausen/Sanderhage	H. Kure's Skjoldungesagaen 1	IP
Peter Madsen	Hen ad vejen	IP
Jørgen Mogensen	Poeten & Lillemor Minialbum	IP
Hans Qvist	Skrækkelige Olfert Minialbum	IP
Pia Thavlov	En uheldig dag	IP
Werner Wejp-Olsen	Momsemor Minialbum	IP
Peter Kielland	Kun i aften	RP
J. Deleuran	Søren Dum si'r de andre	SOC.
J. Deleuran	Et valg for livet - Søren Dum	SOC.

1984

Rune Kidde	Må jeg høfligst anmode Dem om at...	BORG
Freddy Milton	Drømmen om Vagn	BORG
Freddy Milton	Villiams anden verden	BORG
Trine Vester	Alice Cool	BORG
Per Sanderhage	Felix 11: De overjordiske	CC
C & V Hansen	Rasmus Klump har fart på	CC
Michael Jensen	Lykkeridderne 1: I fjendens sold	CC
Jørgen Mogensen	Poeten & Lillemor i sommerhuset	CC
P Ehlers/T Prehn	Kosmo 2	HF
Claus Deleuran	Mikkeline på Skattejagt	INF
Carsten Graabæk	Statsministeren 1: Her går det godt	IP
Carsten Graabæk	Statsministeren 2: Hjælp regeringen...	IP
Dan Skat Kaplan	Helt ude i sovsen	IP
Jørgen Mogensen	Poeten & Lillemor minialbum	IP
Torben Osted	Fodring forbudt minialbum	IP
O Pihl/K Korsgaard	Reporterne 1: Det hvide guld	IP
Hans Qvist	Skrækkelige Olfert minialbum	IP
Werner Wejp-Olsen	Fridolin minialbum	IP
Werner Wejp-Olsen	Momsemor 1	IP

Kim Fupz	Langt ud af halsen	KBF
Mads Rye	Kurt Kapok	KBF
Jesper T Petersen	Onsdag	MAL
Peter Kielland	En dæmonhistorie	RP
Mårdon Smet	Spildte Guds ord på Balle-Lars	RP
J. Deleuran	Søren Dum på krigsstien	SOC.
Claus Deleuran	Vi, verden og de andre	ULFSV
Karsten Hansen	Firserfars	WF

1985

Per Vadmand	Ole & Linda	B&B
Freddy Milton	Sanne og Pamfilius	BORG
Freddy Milton	Hvem dræbte Koch-Robin?	BORG
J P Agger/O Munk	Felix 12: Kong Fido	CC
C & V Hansen	Rasmus Klump i spøgelseshuset	CC
Michael Jensen	Lykkeridderne 2: I Wallensteins Lejr	CC
Karl Oskar Jæger	Farlig Last	CC
A. Stahlschmidt	Gastyvene	DNG
Ivar Gjørup	Egoland 1	INF
Sussi Bech	Zainab 1	IP
Carsten Graabæk	Statsministeren 3	IP
Orla Klausen	Rakkertøsen 1: Herle	IP
S Lindskrog/P Stein	Manden der kunne undværes	IP
Pia Thaulov	Pariseranekdoter	IP
Werner Wejp Olsen	Momsemor 2	IP

1986

P Vadmand/O Munk	Felix 13: Gummihønen	CC
Sussi Bech	Nofret 1: Flugten fra Babylon	CC
Hesseldahl/Hauge	Et spørgsmål om Wagner	CC
Michael Jensen	Lykkeridderne 3: Møde ved Breitenfeld	CC
Nikoline Werdelin	Café 1	CC
Nikoline Werdelin	Café 2	CC
Hesseldahl/H Rehr	Julius 1: Tågernes Dal	DONNA
Holger Philipsen	Carlt nemli´	DONNA
Ivar Gjørup	Egoland 2: Røven af 4. dimension	INF
Antologi	Kulørte Sider 1	IP
Antologi	Kulørte Sider 2	IP
Antologi	Kulørte Sider 3	IP
Poul Benedikt	Phoenix i flammer	IP
Kræsten Krum Byskov	Hævngerrige Høvdinge	IP
Carsten Graabæk	Statsministeren 4	IP
T & P Hansen	Unoder	IP
T & P Hansen	Adolf Johansen, Viceværd	IP
Peter Heydenreich	Johnny Starfighter 1	IP
Orla Klausen	Rakkertøsen 2: Stimænd	IP
S Lindskrog/P Stein	Dr. Vogels sanatorium	IP

Freddy Milton	Gnuff 1: Ballade i Nørregade	IP
Freddy Milton	Gnuff 2: Den store Teknokrak	IP
Jørgen Mogensen	Poeten & Lillemor	IP
O Pihl/K Korsgaard	Reporterne 2: Nordstjernen	IP
Niels Roland	Atelieret	IP
Morten Schmidt	Rejsen til Alabama	IP
Morten Schmidt	Smukke Fie	IP
Pia Thaulov	Øst for Hebriderne	IP
Werner Wejp Olsen	Momsemor 3	IP
Frank Madsen	Jim Spaceborn: Den ukendte galakse	LEGO
L.O. Nejstgaard	Thybald og Lyzette i ØDelia	SOC.
Michael Jensen	Mordet i Finnerup Lade	VIBM

1987

Michael Kvium	Performance	BF
Antologi	København	BF
P Jadmand/ Munk	Felix 14: Atomterroristerne	CC
Sussi Bech	Nofret 2: Amons gemalinde	CC
Lasse Holm	Jakob og Diana 1: Terroristerne	CC
Henrik Rehr	Drømmen om langskibene	CC
Rune Kidde	Den lilla Møghætte og Pulven	EBF
Anders H-Jørgensen	Diverse tegnerier 1977-87	Eget
Ivar Gjørup	Egoland 3: Hunnen er menn. bedst. ven	INF
Antologi	Kulørte Sider 4	IP
Antologi	Kulørte Sider 5	IP
Antologi	Kulørte Sider 6	IP
Antologi	Kulørte Sider 7	IP
Kim Annweiler	Quark fra Valhalla 1	IP
Kræsten Krum Byskov	Dværgenes Dal	IP
Carsten Graabæk	Statsministeren 5	IP
P Heydenreich	Johnny Starfighter 2	IP
Peter Kielland	Herbert i junglen	IP
Orla Klausen	Rakkertøsen 3: Sjællænderen	IP
Orla Klausen	Da Hans blev bange	IP
Freddy Milton	Søren Spætte: Rejsen til Ramashanka	IP
Freddy Milton	Gnuff 3: Graffiti-mesteren	IP
Jørgen Mogensen	Poeten & Lillemor	IP
Ole Pihl	Slangens bud	IP
Roland/K Mortensen	New Roses Rock	IP
Kim Fupz	Kys!	KBF
Freddy Milton	Drøje dage i job-junglen	STAVN
Karsten Hansen	Stille og roligt	WF

1988

Benny Dahl Hansen	Til laveste bud	ARBSK
Erik Hjorth Nielsen	Hvid og Sort som mælk og blod	BF
Henriette Westh	Hamlet, 5. akt, 2. scene	BF

Peter Kielland	Ulvevinter	BF
Freddy Milton	Rig eller ærlig?	BF
Antologi	Danske Fristelser	BF
Bo Torstensen	Sammen vi stå	BF
Ejler Krag	Casanova 1	BRØN
P Vadmand/O Munk	Felix 15: Rumolympiaden	CC
Sussi Bech	Nofret 3: Kætterkongens Hof	CC
A Carlsen/L Refn	Boris 1: Hvor er Glasnost?	CC
Nikoline Werdelin	Café 3	CC
Gert Henrik Poulsen	Jungleland	CC
Lasse Holm	Jakob og Diana 2: Græsk Intermezzo	CC
Schiøtt/Sanderhage/		
Gil Johansen	Kjøwenhawnstrup	CC
S Rislund/M Schack	Nådada	CC
Nikoline Werdelin	Café 4	CC
Claus Deleuran	Ill. Danmarkshistorie for folket 1	EBF
Rune Kidde	Litterærlige klassikere	EBF
Paul Arne Kring	Manden paa stranden	EBF
Niels Roland	Succés	EBF
N H Frey/K Kynde	ETC.	Eget
Ivar Gjørup	Egoland 4: Hjertets renhed er at...	INF
Antologi	Kulørte Sider 8	IP
Antologi	Kulørte Sider 9	IP
Carsten Graabæk	Statsministeren 6	IP
Knøchel/F Jeppesen	TVRK 1	IP
Madsen/Vadmand/		
Kure	Valhalla 4: Historien om Quark	IP
Freddy Milton	Gnuff 4: Gribedyrets hemmelighed	IP
Jørgen Mogensen	Poeten & Lillemor	IP
Henning Nielsen	Zoto og Zym	IP
Torben Osted	Quark fra Valhalla 2	IP
Niels Roland	Firbenenes By	IP
Jesper T Petersen	Når enden er go´1-6	LABL
Bikki I. Pingel	Gøngehøvdingen	SF
Werner Wejp Olsen	Krimi-quiz	SF
Nikoline Werdelin	Rose 1	SF

1989		
Eiler Krag	Casanova 2	BRØN
Eiler Krag	Lyndetektiven	BRØN
Freddy Milton	Jagten på den vise sten	BF
Freddy Milton	Hvem dræbte Koch-Robin, 2. udgave	BF
Morten Schmidt	Dæmonen	BF
Morten Schmidt	Når en lille djævel frister	BF
Henrik Rehr	Kvikleif 1	BF
Nikoline Werdelin	Café 5	CC
Sussi Bech	Nofret 4: Den sidste Minos	CC
Carsten Graabæk	Statsministeren 7	CC

Jørgen Mogensen	Poeten & Lillemor 4	CC
Claus Deleuran	Ill. Danmarkshistorie for folket 2	EBF
Niels Roland	Gunnar taf kampen op	FAGB
Kim Fupz	Op og stå!	IP
Hesseldahl/Heydenr.	Panik	IP
Orla Klausen	Gøngehøvdingen 1: 50.000 Rigsdaler	IP
Madsen/Vadmand/		
Kure	Valhalla 5: Rejsen til Udgårdsloke	IP
Freddy Milton	Søren Spætte: Opstand i Storskoven	IP
Torben Osted	Quark 3	IP
Thomas Hauge	Faldet ved Resaca o.a. fortællinger	SF
Freddy Milton	Svenderik og Gylledrikken	SOC.
Hesseldahl/Rehr	Julius 1: Tågernes dal	TEL
Hesseldahl/Rehr	Julius 2: Sørøver Skummelskræks skat	TEL

951. Grasten, Bent. *Dansk Humor i Streg, Fra til Idag.* Copenhagen: Hans Reitzel, 1962.

952. "Hvorfor Jeg Ikke Abonnerer på Seriejournalen." *Seriejournalen.* September 1990, p. 5.

953. Kidde, Rune T. "Rune Kiddes Åbningstale." *Seriejournalen.* March 1992, pp. 44-45.

954. "Kilroys Lukning Rammer Branchen Hårdt." *Seriejournalen.* September 1990, p. 8.

955. Kruuse, Jens. *Danske Streger; Dansk Humoristisk Tegnekunst Gennem 100 Aar.* Copenhagen: P. Haase and Sons Forlag, 1946.

956. Larsen, Tom Erik. "Et Halvt år I Løvens Hule." *Seriejournalen.* September 1992, pp. 4-5.

957. Madsen, Frank. "Det Kulørte Bibliotek." *Seriejournalen.* March 1992, pp. 42-43.

958. "Mikkel Mus Ved Computeren." *Serieskaberen.* September 1989, p. 11.

959. Rögind, Carl. *50 Tegninger: Tekst fra "Punch" or "Puk."* Hilleröd: Knud Poulsens, n.d.

960. "Udstillingsvindue." *Seriejournalen.* September 1990, pp. 24-25.

961. *Verdensdramaet I Karikaturer.* Copenhagen: Commodore, 1945. 422 pp.

Festivals

962. Berger, Thomas. "Tegneseriefestival Tager Form." *Seriejournalen.* December 1991, pp. 10-11.

963.   Christensen, Ole C. "Seriejournalen i Erlangen." *Seriejournalen*. September 1992, pp. 42-47.

964.   "Erlangen Saetter Focus þa Danmark." *Seriejournalen*. June 1992, p. 11.

965.   Mathiasen, Paw and Teddy Kristiansen. "Danskere i San Diego." *Seriejournalen*. September 1992, pp. 48-49.

Cartoonists and Their Works

966.   AIDA. *Hunting Life: Danish Cartoonists*. Copenhagen: Association Internationale de Défense des Artistes, 1992.

967.   "Bille, Erik." *Seriejournalen*. June 1992, p. 3.

968.   Bojesen, Bo. *Parade*. Copenhagen: Hans Reitzel, 1958.

969.   "Cosper." *Seriejournalen*. June 1992, p. 4. (Siegfried "Cosper" Cornelius).

970.   Dam, Mogens. *Årets, der gik; Ver og Tegninger af Mogens Dam (and) Otto F.* Årgang: Berlingske Forlag, 1963.

971.   "Engholm, Kaj." *Seriejournalen*. September 1992, p. 7.

972.   Frikvarter Med Den Glydenblonde. *Tegninger af Jensenius*. Copenhagen: Rasmus Navers, 1947.

973.   Hjorth-Jørgensen, Anders. "Interview med GIL." *Seriejournalen*. March 1991, pp. 35-39.

974.   "Jussi Olsen ny Chef for Interpresse." *Seriejournalen*. December 1990, p. 6.

975.   Kronborg, Steffen. "Endansk Sture Hegerfors." *Seriejournalen*. December 1990, p. 5.

976.   Mathiasen, Paw. "Rune Kidde." *Nordic Comics Revue*. Winter 1992-1993, pp. 6-7.

977.   "Mogens Dalgaard Død, 62 År." *Seriejournalen*. September 1989, pp. 4-5.

978.   Roland, Niels. "Bonderøve og Bataljemaleri." *Seriejournalen*. December 1991, pp. 32-35. (Michael Jensen).

979.   Roland, Niels. "Byen Hvor Alt Kanske." *Seriejournalen*. June 1992, pp. 39-41. (Per Vadmand).

980. Schlüter, Paul. "Schlüters Ping Pristale." *Seriejournalen*. March 1991, p. 4.

981. Smet, Mårdøn and Paw Mathiasen. "Bums Finder Madrester i Konservesdåse." *Seriejournalen*. September 1992, pp. 29-35. (Jonas Wagner).

982. Smet, Mårdøn and Paw Mathiasen. "Interview med Bent Nielsen." *Seriejournalen*. September 1992, pp. 38-39.

983. Vadmand, Per. "Litterer Tegning. Svar til Jesper Jensen." *Politiken*. 15. August 1989.

984. Waller, Klaus. "Interview mit Per Carlsen." *Comixene. Das Comicfachmagazin*. 7:33 (1980), pp. 7-8.

Bech, Sussi

985. "Bech, Sussi." *Seriejournalen*. June 1992, p. 2.

986. Smet, Mårdøn. "Ikke et Ord Om Tintin." *Seriejournalen*. December 1991, pp. 26-31.

Bidstrup, Herluf

987. Bidstrup, Herluf. *Augelacht und Angelacht*. Berlin: Eulenspiegel-Verlag, 1955.

988. Bidstrup, Herluf. *Das Dicke Bidstrup-Buch*. Berlin: Eulenspiegel-Verlag, 1973.

989. Bidstrup, Herluf. *Einfälle und Reinfälle*. Berlin: Eulenspiegel-Verlag, 1957.

990. Bidstrup, Herluf. *Gewitzles und Verschmitzles*. Berlin: Eulenspiegel-Verlag, 1955.

991. "Bidstrup, Herluf." *Seriejournalen*. June 1992, p. 2.

Byskov, Kraesten Krum

992. "Byskov, Kraesten Krum." *Seriejournalen*. June 1992, p. 3.

993. Roland, Niels. "Flaeskesvaer og Kunsten at Vaere Ansvarsløst Skør!" *Seriejournalen*. September 1992, pp. 36-37.

Deleuran, Claus

994. "Deleuran, Claus." *Seriejournalen*. September 1992, pp. 5-7.

995. Roland, Niels. "Interview med Claus Deleuran." *Serieskaberen*. March 1990, pp. 24-30.

Gantriis, Henning

996. "Gantriis, Henning." *Seriejournalen*. September 1992, p. 4.

997. "Henning Gantriis Død, 71 År." *Serieskaberen*. March 1990, p. 5.

Giese, Suzanne

998. Giese, Suzanne. "Løn Efter Indsats Om Biblioteksafgiften, fmd. for S-gruppen i DF." *Politiken*. June 1989, p. 26.

999. Kronborg, Steffen. "Kilopris pa Bøger. Svar til Suzanne Giese." *Politiken*. June 1989, p. 29.

1000. Lindstrøm, Curt. "Bytter Gerne med Thorup. Svar til Suzanne Giese." *Politiken*. July 1989, p. 4.

1001. Madsen, Frank. "Kan Giese Lese. Svar til Suzanne Giese." *Politiken*. July 1989, p. 14.

Jepsen, Hans Lyngby

1002. "Bogfabrikanter OG Ridefogeder. Hans Lyngby Jepsen om biblioteksafgiften." *Information*. June 1989, p. 9.

1003. Koefoed, Ingerlise. "Voksenbogens Don Quixote. Svar til Hans Lyngby Jepsen." *Politiken*. 7. August 1989.

1004. Tellerup, Kristian. "Tågesnak, Svar til Hans Lyngby Jepsen." *Politiken*. 1. August 1989.

1005. Urwald, Ann Mari. "Børn og Bøger. Svar til Hans Lyngby Jepsen." *Politiken*. 31. July 1989.

Koefoed, Ingerlise

1006. "Giv Bogen Nyt Liv Kronik af Ingerlise Koefoed (SF)." *Weekendavisen*. 7. July 1989.

1007. Jepsen, Hans Lyngby. "Forfatterafgiften Og Ef Svar til Ingerlise Koefoed." *Politiken*. 11. August 1989.

1008. Jepsen, Hans Lyngby. "Til Børnebogens Beskytterinde. Svar til Ingerlise Koefoed." *Politiken*. 21. July 1989.

Kring Sorensen, Paul Arne

1009. Jorgensen, Karsten Juhl and Benni Bodker Nielsen. "Carnivorous Beets and Beautiful Women—A Talk with the Multitalented Danish Comic Artist Paul Arne Kring." *Nordic Comics Revue International.* Autumn 1992, pp. 16-17.

1010. "Omkring en Dansk Tegner. Interview med Paul Arne Kring Sørensen." *Seriejournalen.* June 1992, pp. 29-37.

Madsen, Frank

1011. Madsen, Frank. *Kurt Dunder i Afrika.* Copenhagen: Carlsen Comics, 1991. 46 pp.

1012. Milton, Ingo. "En Rigtig Helt." *Seriejournalen.* December 1991, pp. 36-40.

Madsen, Peter

1013. "Pris til Peter Madsen." *Serieskaberen.* March 1990, p. 4.

1014. Roland, Niels. "Interview med Peter Madsen." *Seriejournalen.* September 1990, pp. 34-39.

1015. Trine, Sick. "Tykke Divus Madsen er Årets Tegnemand Tegneseriekonventet 1989." *Politiken.* 17. June 1989.

Milton, Freddy

1016. Jensen, Jesper. "Tegneserien er Ligeberettiget. Svar til Freddy Milton." *Politiken.* 31. July 1989.

1017. Milton, Freddy. "Status ved Gammel Dok." *Serieskaberen.* September 1989, p. 14.

1018. Milton, Freddy. "Tegneserierne 1 Kulturpolitikken." *Politiken.* 23. July 1989.

1019. Møller, Kurt. "Disney-Zeichner in Europa. (2) Interview mit Freddy Miltion. Übersetzt von Klaus Strzyz." *Comixene. Das Comicfachmagazin.* 7:33 (1980), pp. 54-57.

1020. Møller, Kurt. "Disney-Zeichner in Europa. (3) Interview mit Fred Milton. Übersetzt und Bearbeitet von Klaus Strzyz." *Comixene. Das Comicfachmagazin.* 8:34 (1981), pp. 46-49.

Storm Petersen, Robert

1021. Burgdorf, Paul. "Storm P. Clown Oder Sozialkritiker?" *Comixene. Das Comicfachmagazin.* 8:36 (1981), pp. 45-48.

1022. Petersen, Robert Storm. *Storm P.* Copenhagen: Carit Andersen's Forlag, 1942.

Animation

1023. Decker, Dwight R. "Woody Woodpecker's Finest Hour." *Comics Journal.* September 1981, pp. 306-309.

1024. Hansen, Peter R. "Danes Lead Scandi Pack." *Variety.* September 21, 1992, pp. 70-71.

1025. Patten, Frederick. "Subway to Paradise." *Animation.* Winter 1989, p. 82.

1026. Plaschke, Niels. "Dodsfald." *Story Board.* 1, 1989, p. 7.

Comic Books

1027. "B and U-Gruppens Forslag til Biblioteksafgift." *Serieskaberen.* December 1989, p. 6.

1028. Baudry, Jean. "Danemark: Une Autre Image du Français." *Le Français dans le Monde.* 200, 1986, pp. 74-76.

1029. "Biblioteksafgift Efter Sidetal." *Seriejournalen.* December 1990, p. 6.

1030. "Bogillustratorernes Årsmøde." *Serieskaberen.* December 1989, p. 6.

1031. Burgdorf, Paul. "Comics in Dänemark." *Comixene. Das Comicfachmagazin.* 6:27 (1979), pp. 4-8.

1032. "Comic Book Confidential Vist i Danske Biografer." *Serieskaberen.* March 1990, p. 7.

1033. "Coming Attractions from Danish Writers and Artists." *Nordic Comics Revue International.* Autumn 1992, p. 15.

1034. "The Danes Buy Judge Dredd." *Comics Journal.* February 1992, p. 16.

1035. "Danish Breakthrough in USA." *Nordic Comics Revue* . Winter 1992-1993, p. 15.

1036. "Danish Comics in Brussels." *Nordic Comics Revue.* Winter 1992-1993, p. 15.

1037. "Danske Serier på Vej." *Serieskaberen.* December 1989, pp. 14-18; March 1990, pp. 20-23; June 1990, pp. 22-23.

1038. "Dansk Tarzan—Blad ud i USA." *Seriejournalen.* December 1991, p. 9.

1039. Deleuran, Claus. "Bertel Haarders Ping Pris Tale." *Seriejournalen.* March 1992, pp. 8-9.

1040. "Fat Comic." *Serieskaberen.* December 1989, p. 4.

1041. "Fat Comic Fylder 10 År." *Serieskaberen.* March 1990, p. 5.

1042. "Flere Sider, Faerre Serier." *Seriejournalen.* March 1991, p. 6.

1043. "Gimle og Pinligt Selskab Flytter Sammen." *Seriejournalen.* September 1990, p. 7.

1044. Graabaek, Carsten. "Danske Tegneserier i Finland." *Serieskaberen.* September 1989, p. 17.

1045. Hammer, Peter. "Comics: Something That's Not So Rotten in Denmark." *Comics Journal.* May 1981, pp. 256-257.

1046. "Hård Hud Savnes Hos Forlaeggernel." *Seriejournalen.* March 1991, p. 5.

1047. Hartung, Peter. "En Anmelders Bekendelser." *Serieskaberen.* March 1990, pp. 59-60.

1048. Hartung, Peter and Paw Mathiasen. "Dansk Efterårs-boom." *Seriejournalen.* December 1990, pp. 13-15.

1049. Hesseldahl, Morten. "En Ny Begyndelse." *Seriejournalen.* September 1992, p. 19.

1050. Hjorth-Jørgensen, Anders. "Dansk Tegneserie Leksikon." *Seriejournalen.* June 1992, insert, pp. 1-4.

1051. Hjorth-Jørgensen, Anders. "Flere Børne-serier, Tak!" *Seriejournalen.* June 1992, p. 14.

1052. Hjorth-Jørgensen, Anders. "Lårbasser og Patvaerk." *Seriejournalen.* March 1991, pp. 12-13.

1053. Hjorth-Jørgensen, Anders. "Tegneserie-Markedet Netop Nu." *Seriejournalen.* December 1990, pp. 12-13.

1054. Hjorth-Jørgensen, Anders. "Tyndt." *Seriejournalen.* December 1991, p. 18.

1055. "Hvem er Bibliotekslektørerne?" *Serieskaberen.* December 1989, pp. 33-35; March 1990, pp. 46-50.

1056. Jensen, Jesper. "Biblioteksafgift og Tegneserier." *Serieskaberen*. September 1989, p. 24.

1057. Jensen, Jesper. "Ren Hokus-Pokus Om Politikens leder 26.6." *Politiken*. 28. June 1989.

1058. Jensen, Nils Aage. "Danske Forfattere Forener Eder." *Politiken*. 6. July 1989.

1059. Kerte, Jens. "Lavere Takst Til Striber Fra Danske Tegneserieskaberes Pressemeddelelse." *Politiken*. 1. July 1989.

1060. Kidde, Rune T. "Indfald & Udfald." *Seriejournalen*. March 1992, pp. 14-15; June 1992, p. 49-50.

1061. Kidde, Rune T. "Tegneserie-Radio Lukket Indtil Videre." *Seriejournalen*. March 1991, p. 7.

1062. Knudsen, Ole, Kristoffer Mogensen, and Jakob Stegelmann. *Gyldendals Tegneserieleksikon. Argh til Zap*. Copenhagen: Gyldendal, 1991.

1063. Koefoed, Ingerlise. "Det er Ingen Vaegtafgift Biblioteksafgiften Skal Ikke Gøre Forskel þa Tykke og Tynde Bøger." *Politiken*. 14. July 1989.

1064. "Korte Nyheder." *Serieskaberen*. June 1990, pp. 5-7.

1065. Kronborg, Steffen. "Året I Striber Den Danske Tegneseriescene 1988." *BUM*. No. 6, 1989.

1066. Kronborg, Steffen. "Billedbøger For Voksne." *Bogens Verden*. No. 2, 1989.

1067. Kronborg, Steffen. "De Gratis Tegneserieglaeder." *Serieskaberen*. December 1989, pp. 30-33.

1068. Kronborg, Steffen. "Hvor Blev de Af?" *Seriejournalen*. December 1991, pp. 41-46.

1069. Kronborg, Steffen. "Succes Eller Fiasko." *Serieskaberen*. March 1990, pp. 56-58.

1070. "Kulørte Siders Iaeserundersøgelse." *Seriejournalen*. December 1990, p. 8.

1071. Larsen, Steffen. "Rundt Om Ruderne. Om Serieskaberen nr. 7." *Det Fri Aktuelt*. 20. June 1989.

1072. Lind. "Tegneserien Sultes Ihjel Fra Danske Tegneserieskaberes Pressemeddelelse." *Fyens Stiftst*. 9. July 1989.

1073. Lindhardt, Karsten. "Og Alle Klappede Tegneseriekonventet 1989." *B.T.* 17. June 1989.

1074. "Loven om Biblioteksafgift Vedtages Juni 1990." *Serieskaberen.* December 1989, p. 6.

1075. Madsen, Frank. "Det Danske Tegneserieskonvents Pris 1989." *Serieskaberen.* September 1989, p. 15.

1076. Madsen, Frank. "En Bog Er Ikke En Bog Biblioteksafgiften til Tegneserier." *Weekendavisen.* 16. June 1989.

1077. Madsen, Frank. "Gimle—Tegneserievaerksted, 1980-1990." *Serieskaberen.* March 1990, pp. 38-45.

1078. Madsen, Frank. "Komiklex 3 Udkommet." *Serieskaberen.* March 1990, pp. 5-6.

1079. Madsen, Frank. "Op Med Tegnebogen Om Biblioteksafgiften." *Politiken.* 19. June 1989.

1080. Madsen, Frank. "Regnefejl til 170 Mio. Kr. I Dansk Forfatterforenings Forslag til Biblioteksafgift." *Serieskaberen.* June 1990, pp. 24-25.

1081. Madsen, Frank. "Tag Hensyn Til Tegneserierne Om Biblioteksafgiften." *Berlingske Tidende.* 11. July 1989.

1082. Madsen, Frank. "Tegneseriekonvent på Søpavillonen." *Seriejournalen.* December 1990, pp. 19-22.

1083. Madsen, Frank. "Tegneseriealbums Burde Producerers, Så de Kunne Saelges 10 Kroner Billigere." *Serieskaberen.* March 1990, pp. 55-56.

1084. Madsen, Frank. "Vikings in Germany." *Nordic Comics Revue International.* Autumn, 1992, p. 15.

1085. Madsen, Preben Juul. "For Dumt At Være Dansker Om Biblioteksafgiften." *Politiken.* 7. August 1989.

1086. "Masser af Danske Albums i Efteråret." *Seriejournalen.* December 1991, p. 20.

1087. "Masser af Danske Albums på Vej." *Seriejournalen.* June 1992, pp. 8-9.

1088. Mathiasen, Paw. "Mathiasens Danmarks-Krønnike 1: Sådan Gik 80-erne." *Serieskaberen.* March 1990, pp. 31-37.

1089. Milton, Freddy. "Dødskys II." *Seriejournalen.* March 1992, p. 7.

1090. Milton, Ingo. "'Håndtekstning.' på Computer." *Seriejournalen.* September 1992, pp. 50-51.

1091. Mogensen, Jørgen. "Cosper 80 År." *Seriejournalen.* March 1991, p. 7.

1092. "Niels Roland ny Kilroy-Tegner." *Serieskaberen*. December 1989, p. 5.

1093. "Ny Udgave af Komiklex til November." *Serieskaberen*. September 1989, pp. 5-6.

1094. Roland, Niels. "Den Omvendte Verden." *Seriejournalen*. March 1992, p. 46.

1095. Roland, Niels. "Judaskys til Danske Tegneserier." *Seriejournalen*. March 1992, p. 6. Reprinted from: *Berlingske Tidende*. January 28, 1992.

1096. Roland, Niels. "Med Banalitetens Speeder i Bund." *Seriejournalen*. December 1990, pp. 34-35.

1097. Roland, Niels. "Sandheden er Altid det Første Offer." *Serieskaberen*. June 1990, pp. 26-32.

1098. Roland, Niels. "Udgivelsesaftalerformalitet Eller Sikkerhed?" *Serieskaberen*. December 1989, pp. 22-23.

1099. Rossa-Fischer, Doris. "Das Problem der Comics in Dänemark." *Jugendliteratur*. 2:8 (1956), p. 393.

1100. Rostbøll, Grethe F. "Grethe Rostbøll om Tegneserier." *Seriejournalen*. September 1992, pp. 6-7.

1101. "Seriefonden." *Seriejournalen*. June 1992, p. 22.

1102. "Serieskaberen Fusionerer Med Fat Comic." *Serieskaberen*. March 1990, p. 3.

1103. Sick, Trine. "Tegneserieforfattere i Klemme Revisionen af Biblioteksloven et Problem, en Reportage fra Tegneseriekonventet 1989." *Politiken*. 2. July 1989.

1104. "Sidste Nummer af Fat Comic." *Serieskaberen*. June 1990, pp. 4-5.

1105. "'Slim'—Dansk Skraekblad fra Tellerup." *Seriejournalen*. December 1990, p. 6.

1106. Smet, Mårdøn. "Fra Almagt til Afmagt." *Seriejournalen*. March 1992, pp. 30-35.

1107. Søndergaard, Carsten. "Bibliotekerne Udlåner 14 Mio. Tegneserier om Året." *Seriejournalen*. September 1992, p. 9.

1108. Søndergaard, Carsten. "Bort med Berger." *Seriejournalen*. June 1992, p. 5.

1109. Søndergaard, Carsten. "Efterårets Medieskabte Tegneserie 'Krise.'" *Seriejournalen*. December 1990, pp. 4-5.

1110. Søndergaard, Carsten. "Interpresse Fyrer Super-Ove Efter 27 År." *Seriejournalen*. September 1992, p. 10.

1111. Søndergaard, Carsten. "Talk Dirty—en Erotisk Leg." *Seriejournalen*. June 1992, p. 6.

1112. Søndergaard, Carsten. "Tegne-seriealbum Koster 20 Kroner for Lidt!" *Serieskaberen*. March 1990, pp. 54-55.

1113. Søndergaard, Carsten. "'Tegneserier Skaber Racister.'" *Seriejournalen*. September 1992, pp. 20-21.

1114. Stegelmann, Jakob. "Niels Roland Hyler Som en Stukket Gris." *Seriejournalen*. June 1992, p. 4.

1115. Stegelmann, Jakob. "Tegneserieforfatterne Gør Oprør. Om Biblioteksafgiften." *Berlingske Tidende*. 17. June 1989.

1116. "Støt Litteraturen Leder om Biblioteksafgiften." *Politiken*. 26. June 1989.

1117. Stubkjær, Niels. "Forfatterpenge. Ef og Biblioteksafgiften." *Politiken*. 31. July 1989.

1118. "Tegneserie-Forfatterne Gået fra Dansk Forfatterforening." *Serieskaberen*. June 1990, p. 4.

1119. "Tegneserier Med i Lovforslag." *Seriejournalen*. March 1991, p. 7.

1120. Vadmand, Per. "Carlt 50 År." *Seriejournalen*. December 1990, p. 7.

1121. Vadmand, Per. "Tegninger Og Tågeslør Om Biblioteksafgiften." *Politiken*. 5. July 1989.

Comic Strips

1122. Bojesen, Bo. *Årets Tegninger fra Politiken 1961*. Copenhagen: Politikens Forlag, 1961.

1123. Kidde, Rune. "The Prime Minister's Comments on 'The Prime Minister.'" *WittyWorld*. Winter/Spring 1992, pp. 30-31.

1124. Mathiasen, Paw. "Nye Tider for Avisstrips." *Seriejournalen*. March 1992, pp. 40-41.

1125. Simonsen, Claus. "Kollecting Kelly in Kopenhagen." *Fort Mudge Most*. March 1989, pp. 10-13.

1126. Smet, Mårdøn. "The Magic of Egypt." *Nordic Comics Revue*. April 1992, pp. 3-5.

1127. "WOW: Danish Cartoonist." *Cartoonist PROfiles*. June 1977, pp. 82-84.

ESTONIA

Animation

1128. Assenin, Sergei. *Estonian Animated Films and Their Creators*. Tallinn: Perioodika, 1986. 320 pp.

1129. Deneroff, Harvey. "Estonian Animation." *Animation*. Winter 1989, pp. 46-47.

FINLAND

General Studies

1130. "Comics-Ausstellung im Amos Anderson Museum." *Comics* (Helsinki). August 15-October 3, 1971.

1131. Emerson, Hunt. "IV Suomalainen Sarjakuvafestivaali." *Society of Strip Illustration Newsletter*. May 1989, pp. 12-19.

1132. Jokinen, Osmo. "Nootteja Sarjakuvista." *Piirretty jä Sarjoja* (Katalog der Comic-Ausstellung). August 25-October 3, 1971.

1133. "Karicatures." *Time*. March 16, 1959.

1134. Kaukoranta, Heikki. "Sanasia Sarjakuvan Kehitysvaiheista." *Piirretty jä Sarjoja* (Katalog der Comic-Ausstellung). August 25-October 3, 1971.

1135. Kaukoranta, Heikki. "Suoma Laisista Sarjakuvista." *Piirretty jä Sarjoja* (Katalog der Comic-Ausstellung). August 25-October 3, 1971.

1136. Kaukoranta, Heikki. "Yhdeksännen Taiteen Noususta." *Bibliophilos*. No. 4, 1970, pp. 94-104; No. 1, 1971, pp. 15-22.

1137. Packalén, Bengt. "Lapsisarjakuvia Ja Sarjakuvalapsia." *Piirretty jä Sarjoja* (Katalog der Comic-Ausstellung). August 25-October 3, 1971.

1138. *Piirrettyjä Sarjoja: Ausstellungskatalog der Comic-Ausstellung in Helsinki*. August 15-October 3, 1971. Helsinki.

1139. Vainio, Pasi. "Ever Meulen au Sauna. Situation de la BD Étrangère en Finlande." *Les Cahiers de la Bande Dessinée*. 72, 1986, p. 45.

1140. Zimmermann, Hans D. "Esipuhe." *Piirretty jä Sarjoja* (Katalog der Comic-Ausstellung), August 25-October 3, 1971, p. 1. Helsinki.

Comic Books

1141. Hänninen, Harto. "Blood and Perversions: Nalle Virolainen Produces Horror." *Nordic Comics Revue.* Winter 1992-1993, pp. 3-5.

1142. Hänninen, Harto. "Girls Just Wanna Have Fun—Women Renew Finnish Comics." *Nordic Comics Revue International.* Autumn 1992, pp. 11-13.

1143. Kaukoranta, Heikki. *Comic Books in Finland 1904-1966.* Helsinki: Publications of the University Library of Helsinki, 1968.

1144. Kaukoranta, Heikki. "Finlande." In *Histoire Mondiale de la Bande Dessinée,* edited by Pierre Horay, pp. 202-205. Paris: Pierre Horay Éditeur, 1989.

1145. "Mumi Rekord." *Seriejournalen.* September 1992, p. 10.

1146. "Newsflash." *Nordic Comics Revue International.* Autumn, 1992, p. 13.

Comic Strips

1147. Apunen, Matti and Hildi Hawkins. "Cartoon Town: Tarmo Koivisto's Mämilä." *Books from Finland.* 21:2 (1987), pp. 103-105.

1148. Paul, Bill. "Donald Duck Faces a Morals Charge in Western Europe." *The Barks Collector.* July 1981, pp. 13-16. From *Wall Street Journal.* February 10, 1978.

3

Country Perspectives—France

REFERENCES

Bibliographies

1149. "Bande Dessinée et Peinture: Une Bibliographie." *Les Cahiers de la Bande Dessinée*. 72, 1986, p. 80.

1150. Caré, Jean-Marc. "Petit Quid de la BD." *Le Français dans le Monde*. April 1986, pp. 84-85.

1151. Groensteen, Thierry. "Fiche Bibliographique." *Les Cahiers de la Bande Dessinée*. 68, 1986, p. 40.

Collections, Museums

1152. Bertieri, Claudio. "Dagli Anni Trenta Alle Sale del Louvre." *Il Lavoro*. June 30, 1967.

1153. Caen, Michel. "Notre Musée Permanent de la Bande Dessinée." *Plexus* (Paris). 1967.

1154. Caré, Jean-Marc. "Faire Savoir et Faire Aimer: Le Point de Vue du Libraire Spécialisé à Paris." *Le Français dans le Monde*. April 1986, pp. 51-53.

1155. Cendre, Anne. "La Bande Dessinée Entre au Louvre." *La Tribune de Genève*. April 24, 1967, p. 5.

1156. Faur, Jean-Claude. "Bibliothèques et Bande Dessinées." *Journée d' Etude des Bibliothécaires Flamands* (Turnhout, Belgium). 24. November 1979.

1157. Faur, Jean-Claude. "Comment Créer un Fonds B.D. en Bibliothèque." *Livres de France*. No. 16, 1981, pp. 59-63.

1158. Faur, Jean-Claude. "Les Bandes Dessinées dans les Bibliothèques." *Bulletin d'Analyse des Livres pour Enfants*. No. 27, 1972, pp. 3-4.

1159. Lefort, Didier. "Bibliotheques: Conservation et/ou Entomologie?" *Bédésup*. Nos. 48/49, 1989, p. 16.

1160. Moliterni, Claude. "Dessin d'Humour à la Bibliothèque Nationale." *Phénix*. No. 17, 1970.

Dictionaries, Directories, Encyclopedias

1161. Alberelli, Christian. "Who's Who." *Le Français dans le Monde*. 200, 1986, pp. 79-83.

1162. Alessandrini, Marjorie, ed. *Encyclopédie des Bandes Dessinées*. Paris: Michel, 1979.

1163. Bénézit, Emmanuel. *Dictionnaire Critique et Documentaire des Peintres, Sculpteurs, Dessinateurs et Graveurs*. 8 Vols. Paris: 1976.

1164. Bronson, Philippe. *Guide de la Bande Dessinée*. Paris: Temps Futurs, 1984.

1165. Bronson, Philippe. *Guide de la Bande Dessinée. 300 Auteurs, 4000 Titres, 6000 Références*. Grenoble: Editions Jacques Glénat, 1986.

1166. Collectif (Marjorie Alessandrini, Marc Duveau, Jean-Claude Glaiser and Marion Vidal). *Encyclopédie des Bandes Dessinées*. Paris: Albin Michel, 1979.

1167. Dityvon, Claude. *Cinquante-Neuf Auteurs de Bande Dessinée*. Paris: Futuropolis, 1981.

1168. Filippini, Henri. *Dictionnaire de la Bande Dessinée*. Paris: Editions Bordas, 1989.

1169. Filippini, Henri and Fr. Solo. "Encyclopédie de la Bande Dessinée." *Noir et Blanc* (Paris). June 1971.

1170. Horn, Pierre L., ed. *Handbook of French Popular Culture*. Westport, Connecticut: Greenwood Press, 1991.

GENERAL STUDIES

1171. "Bicentenaire de la Revolution. 5 Humoristes Celebrent le Bicentenaire...." *Mieux Vaut en Rire*. No. 12, 1989, pp. 44-46.

1172. Boussel, Patrice. "Qu'est-ce Que l'Humour?" *Rabelais* (France). May 1955.

1173. Brion, Marcel. "Félix le Chat ou la Poésie Créatrice." *Le Rouge et le Noir*, July 1928.

1174. Brisson, Adolphe. *Nos Humoristes*. Paris: 1960.

1175. "Cartoon Cancels TV Producer." *Comics Journal*. January 1988, p. 18.

1176. Chapelain, Maurice. "Pourquoi les Écrivains Dessinent-ils?" *Le Figaro Illustré* (Paris). June 24, 1950.

1177. "Connaissez-Vous les Dessins de George Sand Dont on Fête le 150ᵉ Anniversaire?" *Le Figaro Illustré*. May-June 1954.

1178. Dancette, Victor and Edmond-François Calvo. *The Beast Is Dead*. Abi Melzer Productions, 1984. 92 pp.

1179. "Det Franske Bladmarked Smuldrer." *Serieskaberen*. March 1990, p. 12.

1180. "Frankrig." *Serieskaberen*. June 1990, pp. 11-12.

1181. Freymann, Jean Richard. "Le Witz: Introduction au Witz." *Mieux Vaut en Rire*. No. 13, 1989, pp. 59-62.

1182. Grimmer, Georges. *Cinq Essais Nadariens*. Paris: Libr. Jammes, 1956.

1183. Hamman, Joe. "Le 47ᵉ Salon des Humoristes. 50 ans d'Histoire." *Rabelais*. May 1955.

1184. Hansi. "Imagier de Colmar en France, Incarnait l'Alsace au Coeur Fidèle." *Carréfour* (Paris). June 20, 1951.

1185. La Borderie, René. *Les Images dans la Société et l'Éducation*. Paris: Casterman, coll. "E3," 1972.

1186. "La RFA en Pointe." *Mieux Vaut en Rire*. No. 13, 1989, pp. 2-8.

1187. Larrain, Jean. *Les Estampes.* Paris: Presses Universitaires de France, 1943.

1188. Le Blanc, Charles. *Manuel de l'Amateur d'Estampes.* 4 Vols. Paris: Emile Bouillon, 1854-1888.

1189. Leguebe, Eric. *Voyage en Cartoonland.* Paris: 1977.

1190. "Les Bandes des Vieux." *Candide.* No. 272, 1966, p. 20.

1191. "L'Humour Est Aussi Une Forme d'Information!" *Mieux Vaut en Rire.* No. 5 (n.d.), pp. 66-72.

1192. "Meli-Melo." *Mieux Vaut en Rire.* No. 5 (n.d.), pp. 78-80.

1193. Mespoulet, M(arguerite). *Creators of Wonderland.* New York: Arrow Editions, 1934.

1194. "Mickey Chernobyl." *Asiaweek.* May 1, 1992, p. 22. (Theme park).

1195. Moliterni, Claude. "Cartoon et Comic Strip Art." *Phénix.* No. 23, 1972.

1196. Morin, Louis. *Le Dessin Humoristique.* Paris: 1913.

1197. Nye, R.B. "Miroir de la Vie: The French Photoroman and Its Audience." *Journal of Popular Culture.* Spring 1977, pp. 744-751.

1198. Pagnol, Marcel. *Notes sur le Rire.* Paris: Les Éditions Nagel, 1947.

1199. Pascal, David. "Our Man in Paris." *Newsletter.* November 1964.

1200. Pérez, Ramón Fermín. "Una Calle Demaisiado Larga." *El Wendigo.* Año 15, No. 46, 1989, pp. 10-12.

1201. "Quand Eros Fait des Bulles." *Le Nation Européenne.* No. 19, 1967, pp. 16-20.

1202. Ragón, Michel. *Le Dessin d'Humor.* Paris: Arthème Fayard, 1960.

1203. *San Julian (Période 1970-1984).* Grenoble: Glénat, 1985.

1204. Sternberg, Jacques. *Un Siècle d'Humour François.* Paris: 1961.

1205. Suarés, André. "Yorick, Essai sur le Clown." *Verve* (Paris). November 15, 1938.

1206. "Thionville." *Mieux Vaut en Rire.* No. 13, 1989, pp. 63-68.

1207. Trez,. *A.B.C. pour Rire.* Paris: Robert Laffont, 1956.

1208. Trez. *De Language des Feuilles.* Paris: Pierre Horay, 1958.

1209. Valton, Edmond. *Les Monstres dans l'Art: Êtres Humains et Animaux, Bas-Reliefs, Rinceaux, Fleurons, etc.* Paris: Ernest Flammarion, Éditeur, n.d.

1210. Veber, Jean. *L'Oeuvre Lithographiée.* Text by Louis Lacroix and Pierre Veber. Paris: Libr. Floury, 1931.

1211. Victoroff, David. *Le Rire et le Risible.* Paris: Presses Universitaires de France, 1955.

1212. Walker, Brian. "American Cartoonist Shocks France!!!" *Cartoonist PROfiles.* June 1979, pp. 46-47.

1213. Yaki, Paul. *Le Montmartre de Nos Vingt Ans.* Paris: Éditions Talardier, 1933.

Children's Press

1214. Ballande, Bernard. "Journaux d'Enfants." *Educateurs.* No. 7-8, 1947.

1215. Bauchard, Philippe. "*The Child Audience. A Report on Press, Film and Radio for Children.* Paris: UNESCO, 1952. 198 pp.

1216. Bauchard, Philippe. "Les Mythes de la Presse pour Enfants." *Observateur.* August 27, 1953.

1217. Brauner, A. "Poissons sans Paroles." In *Les Journaux pour Enfants.* Paris: Presses Universitaires de France, 1954.

1218. Cappe, Jeanne. "Les Illustrés pour la Jeunesse." *Littérature de la Jeunesse* (Paris). 1951, p. 9.

1219. Cappe, Jeanne. "Littérature Enfantine et Sens International." *Educateurs.* No. 40, 1952.

1220. Chombart de Lauwe, Marie-José. "L'Enfant et Ses Besoins Culturels dans la Cité Contemporaine." *Images de la Culture.* Paris: Payot No. 163, 1970.

1221. Dela Potterie, Eudes. "La Presse Enfantine Face aux Techniques Audiovisuelles." *Temps Libre.* No. 3, 1964.

1222. Dela Potterie, Eudes. "Le Marché de la Presse Enfantine en 1956." *Educateurs.* No. 61, 1956, pp. 3-18.

1223. Dela Potterie, Eudes. "Nouvelles Observations sur la Presse Enfantine." *Educateurs.* No. 73, 1958, pp. 28-37.

1224. Dela Potterie, Eudes. "Presse Enfantine et Famille." *Educateurs*. No. 48, 1953, pp. 533-541.

1225. Dubois, Raoul. "La Mauvaise Presse pour Enfants, Est-Elle un Mal Nécessaire?" *Education Nationale*. No. 5 and 12, 1953.

1226. Dubois, Raoul. "La Presse Enfantine Française." *Franc et Franches Camarades*. Paris: 1957.

1227. Dubois, Raoul. "La Presse pour Enfants de 1934-1953." In *Les Journaux pour Enfants*. Paris: Presses Universitaires de France, 1954.

1228. Dubois, Raoul. "Les Journaux pour Enfants." *La Pensée*. No. 37, 1951.

1229. Dubois, Raoul. "Une Bibliographie sur les Études Concernant les Publications Destinées à la Jeunesse." *Vers l'Education Nouvelle*. No. 107, 109, 1956-1957.

1230. Durand, Marion and Bertrand Gérard. *L'Image dans le Livre pour Enfants*. Paris: L'École des Loisirs, 1975.

1231. Empaytaz, Frédéric F., ed. *Les Copains de Votre Enfance*. Paris: Denoël, 1963.

1232. Escarpit, Denise. *Les Exigences de l'Image dans le Livre de la Première Enfance*. Paris: Magnard, 1973.

1233. Faur, Jean-Claude. "La Presse Illustrée pour la Jeunesse: 1890-1950." Documents Annexes au Colloque Education et Bande Dessinée, La Roque d'Anthéron, 1977, pp. 9-17.

1234. Fouilhé, Pierre. *Journaux d'Enfants, Journaux pour Rire?* Paris: Centre d'Activité Pédagogique, 1955, pp. 30-31.

1235. Fouilhé, Pierre. "La Presse Enfantine." *L'Ecole des Parents*. March 1965.

1236. Fouilhé, Pierre. "La Presse Enfantine et Son Public." In *Evantail de l'Histoire Vivante, Hommage à Lucien Febvre*. Paris: 1953. 385 pp.

1237. Fouilhé, Pierre. "L'Enfant Devant Son Journal." *L'Ecole des Parents*. No. 9, 1953, pp. 39-42.

1238. Fouilhé, Pierre. "Les Héros et Ses Ombres." *Les Journaux pour Enfants*. Numéro spéciale de "Enfance," 1954.

1239. Fronval, George. "Sur les Journaux de Jeunes d'Autrefois." *Phénix SP*. 1971.

1240. Gerin, Elisabeth. *Tout sur la Presse Infantine. Collection Pédagogique "Connaître et Juger," No. 1*. Paris: Centre de Recherches de la Bonne Presse, 1958. 190 pp.

1241. Henriot, Jean Jacques. *L'Enfant, l'Image et les Media*. Dammarie les Lys, France: SDT, 1982. 264 pp.

1242. "Journaux des Jeunes à Traves l'Europe." *Record*. Supplément, No. 70, 1967. 16 pp.

1243. Lacroix, S. "La Presse pour Enfants en France." *Bulletin des Bibliothéques de France*. 1:2 (1956).

1244. Mareuil, André. *Littérature et Jeunesse d'Aujourd hui*. Paris: Flammarion, Coll., "Nouvelle Bibliothèque Scientifique," 1971.

1245. Ménard, P. "Journaux d'Enfants, Journaux Encore Dangereux." *Hygiene Mentale*. 2 (1957), p. 198.

1246. Peignot, Joseph. *Les Copains de Votre Enfance*. Paris: Denoël, 1963. 191 pp.

1247. Raillon, Louis. "Où en Est la Question des Journaux d'Enfants." *Educateurs*. No. 14, 1948.

1248. Rouvroy, Maurice A. "Images et Enfants." *Littérature de Jeunesse*. 1951, p. 11.

1249. Soriano, Marc. *Guide de Littérature pour la Jeunesse*. Paris: Flammarion, 1969, 1978.

1250. Vurpillot, Eliane. *La Monde Visuel du Jeune Enfant*. P.U.F., Coll. "Bibliothèque Scientifique Internationale," Section "Pyschologie." Paris: 1971.

Festivals

1251. "Angoulême Lives." *Comics Journal*. May 1989, pp. 23-24.

1252. "Angoulême 19 au Rayon Succés." *Charente Libre*. January 27, 1992, pp. 1, 8-9, 16.

1253. *Bande et Ciné*. Official program of Angoulême 15, Salon International de la Bande Dessinée, Angoulême, 1988. 64 pp. Dossier on "Cinema et B.D."

1254. "Bulles de Salon." *Libération*. Supplement Special Angoulême 1992. 16 pp.

1255. Dutrey, Jacques. "Angoulême at 18: Coming of Age." *Comics Journal*. July 1991, pp. 29-30.

1256. Dutrey, Jacques. "Angoulême '92: A Dizzying Display of Comic Art." *Comics Journal*. May 1992, pp. 35-36.

1257. Dutrey, Jacques. "Europe's Largest Con Draws Media." *Comics Journal.* July 1987, p. 130.

1258. Dutrey, Jacques. "Lauzier Wins Grand Prize at Angoulême." *Comics Journal.* May 1993, pp. 35-36.

1259. Dutrey, Jacques. "Le Salon d' Angoulême Celebrates 20th Anniversary." *Comics Journal.* May 1993, pp. 33-34.

1260. Emerson, Hunt. "Ah... Angoulême!! How Well I Recall." *Comics Journal.* February 1993, pp. 104-110.

1261. Faur, Jean-Claude. "Bédésup Fête Ses Dix Ans." *Impressions du Sud* (Aix). No. 14, 1986, pp. 42-43.

1262. Faur, Jean-Claude. "Regionalisme et Bande Dessinée Table Ronde du Festival International du Livre de Nice." *Provence Ligurie* (Nice). No. 16, 1980, pp. 8-9.

1263. "Final au Week-end: Cohue-Bohu." *Charente Libre.* January 27, 1992, p. 9.

1264. Hartung, Peter. "Stor Interesse om Grenoble-Festival." *Serieskaberen.* June 1990, pp. 16-18.

1265. Heimann, Rolf. "A Cangarou in the Bidet." *Inkspot* (Australia). Spring/Summer 1992, pp. 20-21.

1266. Jaffray, Patricia and François Taillandier. "Angoulême. Le XIIIe Salon de la BD. Sous le Signe le l'Affluence." *Livres Hebdo.* 8:6 (1986), pp. 92, 97.

1267. J.-F. L. "Angoulême 'Bulle.'" *Figaroscope.* January 22, 1992, pp. 4-5.

1268. Kolditz, Niels. "Stagnation auf Hohern Niveau." *Comic Info.* 1/1993, pp. 46-49.

1269. Lent, John A. "St. Just Le Martel: The Festive Cartoon Salon." *WittyWorld.* Winter 1993, pp. 26-27.

1270. "Les Dix Commandments." *Libération.* Supplement Special Angoulême 1992, p. xii.

1271. Mathiasen, Paw. "Angoulême 1990." *Serieskaberen.* March 1990, pp. 18-19.

1272. Moliterni, Claude. "La 2ᵉᵐᵉ Convention de la BD." *Phénix.* No. 13, 1969.

1273. Moliterni, Claude. "3ᵉᵐᵉ Convention de la BD." *Phénix.* No. 17, 1970.

1274. Moliterni, Claude. "4ᵉᵐᵉ Convention de la BD." *Phénix.* No. 23, 1972.

1275. Petersen, Poul. "Angoulême." *Seriejournalen.* March 1992, pp. 22-29.

1276. *Program.* 11th Salon International du Dessin de Presse et d'Humour, St. Just le Martel, France, du 3 au 11 Octobre 1992. St. Just le Martel, 1992. 152 pp.

1277. Quella-Guyot, Didier. "Angoulême Passionnement." *Bédésup.* Nos. 48/49, 1989, pp. 44-51.

1278. Rebiére, Michel. "Angoulême Épate des Américains." *Charente Libre.* January 25, 1992, p. 11.

1279. "Salon International du Dessin de Presse et d'Humour—Saint Just Le Martel." *FECO News.* No. 8, 1989, pp. 16-17.

1280. "Salon: la Ruée des Mickeys." *Charente Libre.* January 24, 1992, pp. 1, 10-11, 22, 24.

1281. "Salon: Lucien Académicien." *Charente Libre.* January 24, 1992, pp. 1, 10-11, 23, 26.

1282. Szabo, Joseph G. "Angoulême, A Meeting Place for Newton, Mice, Turtles, Ducks, Mr. Natural, Some Bad Girls, and Columbus." *WittyWorld.* Winter/Spring 1992, p. 40.

Periodicals

1283. Bachollet, Raymond. "Le Catalogue des Journaux Satiriques: Le Mot." *Le Collectionneur Français.* 195 (1982), pp. 10-11; 196 (1982), pp. 7-8; 197 (1983), pp. 5-7.

1284. Brisson, Jules and Félix Ribeyre. *Grands Journaux de France.* Paris: Jouast Père, 1862.

1285. Couperie, Pierre. "Des Suppléments du Dimanche aux Journaux Illustrés." *Giff-Wiff.* No. 8, 1963.

1286. Filippini, Henri. *Histoire du Journal et des Éditions Vaillant.* Grenoble: Eds. Jacques Glénat, 1978.

1287. Filippini, Henri. "Les Années Cinquante aux Éditions de Fleurus." *Schtroumpfanzine.* 26, 1979, pp. 14-23.

1288. Groensteen, Thierry. "Histoire de la Revue PHENIX." *Les Cahiers de la Bande Dessinée.* 62, 1985, pp. 48-52.

1289. Groensteen, Thierry. "La Vie des Revues." *Les Cahiers de la Bande Dessinée.* 67, 1986, pp. 62-63. (*Pilote, Charlie, Fluide Glacial, L'Echo des Savanes, Métal Hurlant, Circus, (A Suivre), Vécu,* etc.).

1290. Groensteen, Thierry. "Le Cas Bédésup." *Les Cahiers de la Bande Dessinée.* 71, 1986, p. 89.

1291. Jannet, Philippe. "Les Revues de Bandes Dessinées." *Presse Actualité* (Paris). 172, 1983, pp. 18-24. (*Fluide Glacial, Métal Hurlant, Pilote, (A Suivre), L'Echo des Savances, Charlie Mensuel, Circus,* etc.).

1292. Sanders, Alain. "Le P.C. par la Bande." *L'Astrolabe* (Paris). 1:80 (1985), p. 32. (*Vaillant, Pif-Gadget, Rahan*).

1293. Tschernegg, Markus. "Die Großen Europäischen Comic-Magazine. Eine Neue Comic-Forum-Serie." *Comic Forum. Das Magazin für Comicliteratur.* 7:27 (1985), p. 25. (*Vécu*).

1294. Tschernegg, Markus. "Die Großen Europäischen Comic-Magazine." *Comic Forum. Das Magazin für Comicliteratur.* 7:28 (1985), p. 57. (*Charlie Mensuel*).

1295. Warfa, Dominique. *79 Clins d'Oeil (A Suivre) sur la BD.* Liège: Ed. Groupe PHI, 1984.

Charivari

1296. *Album Charivarique.* Magazin des Dessins, Croquis, Charges et Caricatures par les Artistes du *Charivari,* du *Figaro* et de *La Caricature.* Paris: n.d.

1297. Czyba, Lucette. "Féminisme et Caricature. La Question du Divorce dans *Le Charivari.*" In *Proceedings* of Colloquium, "La Satire Imagée et la Caricature entre la République et la Censure de 1830 à 1900," Frankfurt, 1988.

1298. Koch, Ursula E. and Pierre-Paul Sagave. *Le Charivari: Die Geschichte Einer Pariser Tageszeitung im Kampf um die Republik, 1832 bis 1882.* Cologne: C.W. Leske, 1984.

Le Canard Enchaine

1299. Egen, Jean. *Le Canard Enchaine.* Paris: Seghers, 1978. 187 pp.

1300. "France's 'Chained Duck': Humor Journal." In *Modern Mass Media,* edited by John C. Merrill, John Lee, and Edward J. Friedlander, p. 160. New York: Harper and Row, 1990.

1301. Tomlins, James. "They All Quake When the Chained Duck Quacks." *Editor and Publisher.* December 8, 1973, p. 48.

Women

1302. Amiel, Vincent. "Indices ou Féminin." *Les Cahiers de la Bande Dessinée.* 71, 1986, pp. 25-27.

1303. "Astérix et les Femmes?" *Le Vasistas* (Göttingen). 57/58, 1981, p. 17.

1304. "B.D.: de l'Air Neuf. Les Héroïnes Prennent Leur Revanche." *Le Vasistas* (Göttingen). 57/58, 1981, pp. 19-22.

1305. Benatar, Simy. "La Vision de la Femme, à Travers la Bande Dessinee." *Revue Politique et Parlementaire* (Paris). 865, 1976, pp. 63-77.

1306. Billard, Pierre. "Des Filles pour les Bandes." *L'Express* (Paris). October 17-23, 1966.

1307. Carlier, Abel. "La Femme dans la BD: à Propos des "Passagers du Vent" de François Bourgeon." *Dossier Comu* (Louvain-La-Neuve). 10, 1982, pp. 4-21.

1308. Chambon, Jacques. J.P. Fontana, and G. Temey. "Statut de la Femme dans les Bandes Dessinées d'Avantgarde." *Mercury* (Paris). No. 7, 1965, pp. 51-57.

1309. De La Croix, Arnaud. "Femmes Nues avec Ceintures." *Les Cahiers de la Bande Dessinée.* 64, 1985, pp. 24-25.

1310. de Pierpont, Jacques. "Esclavage et Condition Féminine." *Les Cahiers de la Bande Dessinée.* 65, 1985, pp. 23-25.

1311. de Pierpont, Jacques. "Isabelle Fantouri: Mieux Vaut en Rire." *Les Cahiers de la Bande Dessinée.* 56, 1984, pp. 27-29.

1312. de Pierpont, Jacques. "Les Dames de F'Murr." *Les Cahiers de la Bande Dessinée.* 60, 1984, pp. 30-31.

1313. Doreille, Robert. "Une Femme...dans Chaque Port." *Bédésup.* 17, 1981, pp. 23-27.

1314. Eubben, Marie-Claire, and Claire Vanderhaeghen. "Feminine and Masculine Stereotypes in French-Language Comic Strips for Children and Adolescents. Les Stereotypes Feminin et Masculin dans la Bande Dessinée pour Enfants et Adolescents d'Expression Française." *Revue de l'Institut de Sociologie* (Solvay). 3:4 (1982), pp. 433-457.

1315. Falardeau, Mira. "Les Bédéssinatrices." *La Nouvelle Barre du Jour* (Outremont, Québec). 110/111, 1982, pp. 81-87.

1316. Fatou, Hélène. "Cartoon Heroine, Who Are You?" *EBU Review* November 1983, pp. 9-12.

1317. Fernández, Norman. "La Trampa Que No Es Mujer." *El Wendigo*. Autumn/Winter 1989-1990, pp. 13-15.

1318. Frémion, Yves. "Dix Nanas pas Comme les Autres." *Le Français dans le Monde*. 200, 1986, pp. 25-26.

1319. Goimard, Jacques. "La Déesse-Fille." *Fiction*. No. 137, 1965, pp. 152-156.

1320. Groensteen, Thierry. "Filles des Pierres." *Les Cahiers de la Bande Dessinée*. 69, 1986, pp. 34-35.

1321. Groensteen, Thierry. "La Femme Est l'Avenir du Héros." *Les Cahiers de la Bande Dessinée*. 58, 1984, pp. 29-31.

1322. Hugues, Daniel. "Singulier pour Elles." *Les Cahiers de la Bande Dessinée*. 62, 1985, pp. 22-23.

1323. "Idées Reçues sue les Femmes." *Le Vasistas* (Göttingen). 57/58, pp. 3-13.

1324. "Isabelle Rabarot Donne de l'Auteur à la Couleur." *Charente Libre*. January 25, 1992, p. 11.

1325. Kahn, Gustave. *La Femme dans la Caricature Française*. Paris: A. Méricaut, n.d.

1326. "La 'Drague' en Textes et en Images." *Le Vasistas*. 57/58, pp. 24-27.

1327. Leguebe, Eric. "Les Avators de l'Éternel Féminin." *Arts*. April 27, 1966.

1328. "L'Image de la Femme dans la Bande Dessinée." *Le Vasistas*. 57/58, pp. 14-16.

1329. Roux, Antoine. "'Occupe-toi d'Amélie!'...et Will Créa Kiki!" *Schtroumpf. Les Cahiers de la Bande Dessinée*. 45, 1980, pp. 37-42.

1330. Sadoul, Jacques. *L'Enfer des Bulles*. Paris: Jean-Jacques Pauvert, 1968.

1331. Sadoul, Jacques. *Les Filles de Papier*. Paris: Ed. Elvifrance, J.-J. Pauvert, 1971.

1332. Sullerot, Eveline. "La Presse Féminine." Paris: A. Colin, 1963.

HISTORICAL ASPECTS

1333. Brisson, Adolphe. "Les Humoristes." *Les Annales* (Paris). No. 1381.

1334. Brisson, Adolphe. *Nos Humoristes*. Paris: Soc. d'Édition Artistique, 1900.

1335. Chanfrault, Bernard. "The Stereotypes of 'Deep France' in the *Almanach Vermot*." *Humor*. 5:1/2 (1992), pp. 7-31.

1336. Halimi, André. *Ce Qui a Fait Rire les Français sous l'Occupation*. Paris: Lattès, 1979.

1337. Parménie, A(ntoine) and C. Bonnier de la Chapelle. *Histoire d'Un Éditeur et de Ses Auteurs: P.-J. Hetzel (Stahl)*. Paris: Albin Michel, 1953.

1338. Roudevitch, Michel. "L'Animation Française: le Taureau par les Cornes ou le Diable par la Queue." *Corto Circuito*. April 1992, pp. 5-9.

Caricature

1339. Adhémar, Jean, ed. *Dessin d'Humour du XVe Siècle à Nos Jours*. Paris: Bibliothéque Nationale, 1971.

1340. Alexandre, Arséne. "French Caricature of To-day." *Scribner's Monthly*. April 1894, pp. 477-488.

1341. Alexandre, Arséne. *L'Art du Rire et de la Caricature*. Paris: Quatin Librairies-Imprimeries Réunies, 1892.

1342. Alexandre, Arséne. *L'Espirit Satirique en France*. Paris: Berger Levrault, 1917.

1343. Alvarus (Álvaro Cotrim). "A Caricatura e a Revolução Francesa." *Vamos Ler!* (Rio de Janeiro). July 15, 1943.

1344. "American and French Caricature." *Literary Digest*. April 26, 1913, pp. 948-949.

1345. Appelbaum, Stanley, ed. *French Satirical Drawings from "L'Assiette au Beurre."* New York: Dover, 1978.

1346. Baudelaire, Charles. *De l'Essence du Rire et Géneralement du Comique dans les Arts Plastiques. Quelques Caricaturistes Français. Quelques Caricaturistes Étrangers*. Paris: Éditions René Kiefer, 1925.

1347. Baudelaire, Charles. *Oeuvres en Collaboration: Le Salon Caricaturale*. Intro. by Jules Mouquet. Paris: *Mercure de France*, 1932.

1348. Bayard, Emile. *La Caricature et les Caricaturistes*. Paris: Libraire Delagrave, 1913. 398 pp.

1349. Béchu, Jean Pierre. *La Belle Époque et Son Envers*. Paris: André Sauret, 1980.

1350. Beraldi, H. *Un Caricaturiste Prophète. La Guerre Telle Qu'elle Est Prevue par A. Robida Il y a Trent-Trois Ans*. Paris: Dorbon-Ainé, 1916.

1351. Berleux (Jean), pseud. of Quentin-Bauchart (Maurice). *La Caricature Politique en France Pendant la Guerre, le Siège de Paris et la Commune (1870-1871)*. Paris: Labitte, Ém. Paul and Cie, 1890. 319 pp.

1352. Blum, André. "La Caricature Politique en France Pendant la Guerre de 1870-1871." *Revue Etudes Napoléoniennes*. November-December 1919, pp. 301-311.

1353. Blum, André. "La Caricature Politique en France sous le Second Empire." *Revue Etudes Napoléoniennes*. March-April 1919, pp. 169-183.

1354. Blum, André. "La Caricature Politique Sous a Monarchie de Juillet." *Gazette des Beaux-Arts*. March 1920, pp. 257-277.

1355. Blum, André. *La Caricature Révolutionnaire, 1789-1795*. (Thesis, Doctor of Letters). Paris, Jouve and Cie, 1916.

1356. Blum, André. *L' Estampe Satirique en France Pendant les Guerres de Religion*. Paris: M. Girard and E. Bière. 1913.

1357. Blum, André. "L'Estampe Satirique et la Caricature en France au XVIIIᵉ Siècle." *Gazette des Beaux-Arts*. May 1910, pp. 379-392; July 1910, pp. 69-87; August 1910, pp. 108-120; September 1910, pp. 243-254; October 1910, pp. 275-292; November 1910, pp. 403-420; December 1910, pp. 447-467.

1358. Boime, Albert. *Art in an Age of Revolution*. Chicago, Illinois: University of Chicago Press, 1987.

1359. Bornemann, Bernd. *La Caricature: Art et Manifeste, du 16ᵉ à Nos Jours*. Geneva: Skira, 1974.

1360. Broadley, A.M. *Napoleon in Caricature. 1795-1821*. Intro. by J. Holland Rose. 2 Vols. New York, London: John Lane Co., 1911.

1361. Burlingame, Cynthia and James Cuno. *French Caricature and the French Revolution 1789-1799*. Chicago, Illinois: University of Chicago Press, 1989. 280 pp.

1362. Cabanés, Dr. *La Médecine en Caricatures*. Paris: P. Longet, editor, 1925-1928.

1363. Cabanés, Dr. *Le Costume du Médicin en France. Des Origines au XVIIᵉ Siècle*. Paris: P. Longet, editor, n.d.

1364. *Cahiers de l'Art Mineur* (Paris). From 1975 onwards, many issues on Caran d'Ache, Callot, Cham, Grandville, Doré, Robida, Steinlen, Daumier, Jossot, Johannot, etc.

1365. Cain, George. "Caricatures d'Antan." *Variétés* (Paris). February 1911.

1366. *Caricature de la "Conférence de la Paix."* 233 Images de Tous les Pays, by Beer, Bobb Boscovitz, Job, etc. Paris: Librairie Nilsson, 1908.

1367. *Caricature, Presse Satirique: 1830-1918.* Paris: Bibliothèque Forney, 1979.

1368. Carteret, Léopold. *Le Trésor du Bibliophile Romantique et Moderne 1801-1875.* Vol. 3: "Livres Illustrés du XIXᵉ Siècle." Paris: L. Carteret, 1927.

1369. Chadefaux, Marie-Claude. "Le Salon Caricatural de 1846 et les Autres Salons Caricaturaux." *Gazette des Beaux-Arts.* March 7, 1968, pp. 161-176.

1370. "The Challenge to Rule: Confrontations with Louis XVI." *Art Journal.* Summer 1989, pp. 150-154.

1371. Champfleury (Jules-François-Félix Husson). *Histoire de la Caricature Antique.* Paris: E. Dentu Éditeur, n.d.

1372. Champfleury. *Histoire de la Caricature au Moyen Âge et Sous la Renaissance.* Paris: E. Dentu Éditeur, n.d.

1373. Champfleury. *Histoire de la Caricature Moderne.* 4 Vols. Paris: E. Dentu, 1863-1865.

1374. Champfleury. *Histoire de la Caricature Sous la Réforme et la Ligue, de Louis XIII à Louis XVI.* Paris: E. Dentu Éditeur, 1880.

1375. Champfleury. *Histoire de la Caricature Sous la République, l'Empire, et la Restauration.* Paris: E. Dentu, 1874.

1376. Champfleury. *Musée Secrète de la Caricature.* Paris: E. Dentu Éditeur, 1888.

1377. Chatelus, Jean. "Thèmes Picturaux dans les Appartements de Marchands et Artisans Parisiens au XVIIIᵉ Siècle." *Dix-Huitième Siècle.* 6 (1974), pp. 309-324.

1378. "Comment." *The Nation* (Napoleon and Bessie Bigotry). May 14, 1947, pp. 531-532.

1379. Cuno, James. *French Caricature and the French Revolution, 1789-1795.* Los Angeles, California: Grunwald Center for the Graphic Arts, Wight Art Gallery, University of California, Los Angeles, 1988.

1380. Dacier, Émile, Albert Vuaflart, and Jacques Herold. *Jean de Jullienne et les Graveurs de Watteau au XVIIIᵉ Siècle Paris.* 4 Vols. Paris: N.p., 1921-1929.

1381. Dayot, Armand. *Les Maîtres de la Caricature Française au XIX Siècle.* Paris: Maison Quantin, n.d.

1382. Dayot, Armand. "Napoléon et la Caricature." *Je Sais Tout* (Paris). October 1910.

1383. de Baeque, Antoine. *La Caricature Révolutionnaire*. Paris: Presses du CNRS, 1988.

1384. Deberdit, Raoul. *La Caricature et l'Humour au XIX Siécle*. Paris: Libr. Larousse, n.d. (1898-1899).

1385. Deberdit, Raoul. "La Caricature et l'Humour au XIXᵉ Siècle." *Revue Encyclopédique*. 1898, Vol. 1, pp. 1-40.

1386. de la Vaissière, Pascal, ed. *L'Art de l'Estampe et la Révolution Française*. Paris: Musée Carnavalet, 1977.

1387. Dickey, Stephanie. "The Passions and Raphael's Cartoons in Eighteenth-Century British Art." *Marsyas*. 22 (1983-1985), pp. 33-46.

1388. Diehl, Gaston. *Le Dessin en France au XIXᵉ Siècle. Romantiques et Realistes*. Paris: Éditions Hyperion, n.d.

1389. Dixmier, Élizabeth. *L'Assiette au Beurre*. Paris: Maspero, 1974.

1390. Duche, Jean. *1760-1960. Deux Siècles d'Histoire de France, par la Caricature*. Paris: Éditions du Port Royal, 1961.

1391. Duhem, Pierre. *Un Écho de la Révolution: Au Pays des Gorilles*. Paris: Beauchesne, 1989.

1392. du Seigneur, Maurice. "L'Exposition de la Caricature et de la Peinture de Moeurs au XIXᵉ Siècle." *Artiste*. 1988, pp. 433-439.

1393. Eudel, Paul. *Catalogue des Faux-Fortes, liths., Caricatures, Vignettes Romantiques, Dessins et Aquarelles Formant la "Collection Champfleury."* Paris: Léon Sapin, Libr., 1891.

1394. Farwell, Beatrice. *The Charged Image: French Lithographic Caricature, 1816-1848*. Santa Barbara, California: Santa Barbara Museum of Art, 1989. 188 pp.

1395. Farwell, Beatrice. *French Popular Lithographic Imagery, 1815-1870*. 12 Vols. Chicago, Illinois: University of Chicago Press, 1981.

1396. Fels, Florent. "La Caricature Française de 1789 à nos Jours. La Caricature Sous la Révolution et le Premier Empire." *Crapouillot*. Special number. April 1959.

1397. Fleury, Jules. *Histoire de la Caricature Antique par Champfleury*. Paris: E. Dentu, 1865. 248 pp.

1398. Fournel, Victor. "La Caricature au XIX° Siècle." *Les Artistes Français Contemporains (Peintres et Sculpteurs)*. Tours: Alfred Mame et Fils, 1884.

1399. *French Caricature and the French Revolution, 1789-1799*. Chicago, Illinois: University of Chicago Press, 1988. 279 pp.

1400. "French Caricaturists and Caricature." *Current Literature*. January 1904, pp. 76-77.

1401. "French View of American Caricature." *Review of Reviews*. July 1913, pp. 97-98.

1402. *Galerie Comique du XIX° Siècle*. (Album of 400 works of Daumier, Boilly, Draner, Beaumont, Gavarni, Stop, Grévin, Forain, Caran d'Ache, etc.). Paris: G. Hazard, n.d.

1403. Gallotti, Jean. "A Propos de l'Éxposition Victor Hugo." *L'Art Vivant* (Paris). September 15, 1930.

1404. Gaultier, Paul. *Le Rire et la Caricature*. Paris: 1911.

1405. Georgel, Pierre. "Dessins de Victor Hugo dans les Collections Publiques Françaises." *Revue du Louvre et des Musées de France*. 21:4-5 (1971), p. 251.

1406. Goldstein, Robert J. "Approval First, Caricature Second: French Caricaturists, 1852-81." *The Print Collector's Newsletter*. May/June 1988, pp. 48-50.

1407. Goldstein, Robert J. *Censorship of Political Caricature in Nineteenth-Century France*. Kent, Ohio: Kent State University Press, 1989. 293 pp.

1408. Goldstein, Robert J. "The Debate over Censorship of Caricature in Nineteenth-Century France." *Art Journal*. Spring 1989, pp. 9-15.

1409. Grand-Carteret, John. *Caricatures et Images de Guerre. La Kultur et Ses Hauts Faits*. Paris: Librairie Chapelot, 1916.

1410. Grand-Carteret, John. *Die Erotik in der Französischen Karikatur*. Leipzig: C.W. Stern, Verlag, 1909.

1411. Grand-Carteret, John. *Images Galantes et l'Esprit de l'Étranger*. Paris: La Librairie Mondiale, n.d.

1412. Grand-Carteret, John. *La Crète Devant l'Image*. Paris: Libr. Henry May, Éditeur d'Art, 1897.

1413. Grand-Carteret, John. *La Femme en Culotte*. Paris: Ernest Flammarion Ed., 1899.

1414. Grand-Carteret, John. *L'Affaire Dreyfus et l'Image*. Paris: Ernest Flammarion, n.d.

1415. Grand-Carteret, John. *Les Caricatures sur l'Alliance France-Russie*. Paris: Librairies-Imprimeries Réunies, n.d.

1416. Grand-Carteret, John. *Les Moeurs et la Caricature en France*. Paris: G. Decaux Éd., 1888.

1417. Grand-Carteret, John. *"L'Oncle de l'Europe" Devant l'Objectif Caricatural*. Paris: Louis Michaud, ca. 1905. 285 pp.

1418. Grand-Carteret, John. *"Lui" Devant l'Objectif Caricatural*. Paris: Libraire Nilsson, n.d. 295 pp.

1419. Grand-Carteret, John. *Nicolas, Ange de la Paix, Empereur du Knout Devant l'Objectif Caricaturale*. Paris: Louis Michaud Éditeur, n.d.

1420. Grand-Carteret, John. *Une Turquie Nouvelle pour les Turcs*. Paris: Édition Photographique, n.d.

1421. Grand-Carteret, John. *Verdun, Images de Guerre*. Paris: Librairie Chapelot, 1916.

1422. Grand-Carteret, John. *Zola en Images*. Paris: Libr. Félix Juven, 1908.

1423. Grand-Carteret, John and Léo Delteil. *La Conquête de l'Air Vue par l'Image. 1495-1909*. Paris: Librairie des Annales, 1910.

1424. Guillemin, Henri. "Victor Hugo Avaitil de l'Humour?" *Le Figaro Illustré* (Paris). October 28, 1950.

1425. Hadol. *Le Grand Vautour de Sédan. La Ménagerie Impériale Composée de Ruminants et d'Autres Qui ont Devoré la France Pendant 20 Années*. Paris: Bureau de *L'Eclipse*, 1870.

1426. Hartau, Johannes. "Don Quixote in Broadsheets of the Seventeenth and Early Eighteenth Centuries." *Journal of the Warburg and Courtauld Institutes*. 48 (1985), pp. 234-238.

1427. Helfand, William H. "The Poisoning of the Sick at Jaffa." In *Die Vortrage der Hauptversammlung in Paris*, edited by Wolfgang-Hagen Hein and Karlheinz Bartels, pp. 79-97. Stuttgart: Wissenschaftliche Verlagsgesellschaft MBH, 1975.

1428. Helfand, William H. and Pierre Julien. "Medicine and Pharmacy in French Political Prints—The Franco-Prussian War and the Commune." In *Acta Congressus Internationalis Historiae Pharmaciae Bremae MCMLXXV*, edited by Wolfgang-Hagen Hein, pp. 237-269. Stuttgart: Wissenschaftliche Verlagsgesellschaft MBH, 1978.

1429. Henderson, Ernest Flagg. *Symbol and Satire in the French Revolution*. New York: G.P. Putnam's Sons, 1919. 456 pp.

1430. Herding, Klaus and Rolf Reichardt. *Die Bild Publizistik der Franzosischen Revolution*. Frankfurt: Suhrkamp, 1989. 178 pp.

1431. Heredia, Luis F. "Los Apaches y la Caricatura Francesca." *La Esfera* (Madrid). December 11, 1915.

1432. Hunt, Lynn. "Engraving the Republic: Prints and Propaganda in the French Revolution." *History Today*. October 1980, pp. 11-17.

1433. Huyghe, René. *Le Dessin Français au XIXᵉ Siècle*. Lausanne: Éditions Mermod, 1948.

1434. Jaime, E. *Musée de la Caricature ou Recueil des Caricatures les plus Rémarquables Publiées en France depuis le XIVᵉ Siècle Jusqu'à nos Jours.* 2 Vols. Paris: Chez Delloye, Libr. Éditeur, 1838.

1435. Jones, Philippe. "La Liberté de la Caricature en France au XIXᵉ Siècle." *Synthèse.* February 1960, pp. 1-11.

1436. Jones, Philippe. *La Presse Satirique Illustrée entre 1860 et 1890*. Tours: Institut Français de Presse, 1956.

1437. Kahn, Gustave. *Das Weib in der Karikatur Frankreichs*. Stuttgart: H. Schmidt, 1907. 472 pp.

1438. Künnemann, Horst. "L'Imagérie Populaire. Epinal, die Französische Stadt der Bilderbogen." *Zeitschr. für Jugendliteratur.* 1:2 (1967), pp. 415-418.

1439. Lambert, Susan. *The Franco-Prussian War and the Commune in Caricature 1870-71*. London: Victoria and Albert-Museum, 1971. 119 pp.

1440. Langlois, Claude. *La Caricature Contre-Révolutionnaire*. Paris: Presses du CNRS, 1988.

1441. Lankheit, Klaus. "Die Leiden der Freiheit. Über Einige 'Karikaturen' aus der Julimonarchie." In *"La Caricature." Bildsatire in Frankreich 1830-1835*, pp. 15-25. Munich: Westfälisches Landesmuseum für Kunst und Kulturgeschichte, 1980.

1442. *Les Présidents et la Caricature, 1841-1900.* Vol. V. Paris: Libraires de la Curiosité et des Beaux Arts, 1928.

1443. Lethève, Jacques. *La Caricature et la Presse Sous la IIIe République.* Paris: Armand Colin, 1961.

1444. McCauley, Anne. "Caricature and Photography in Second Empire Paris." *Art Journal.* Winter 1983, pp. 355-360.

1445. Malvano, Laura. "Le Sujet Politique en Peinture: Evénements et Histoire Pendant les Années de la Révolution." *Histoire et Critique des Arts.* Spring 1980, pp. 31-65.

1446. "Napoleão e os Caricaturistas." *Carioca* (Rio de Janeiro). December 28, 1935.

1447. "Notes sur les Caricatures Napoleoniennes." In *L'Histoire, la Vie, les Moeurs et la Curiosité par l'Image, le Pamphlet et le Document (1450-1900).* Vol. IV. Paris: Libraires de la Curiosité et des Beaux Arts, 1928.

1448. Parent, Françoise. "Les Cabinets de Lecture dans Paris: Practiques Culturelles et l'Espace Social Sous la Restauration." *Annales E.S.C.* 34, 1979, pp. 1016-1038.

1449. Parent, Françoise. "Lire à Paris au Temps de Balzac." *Editions de L'Ecole des Hautes Études en Sciences Sociales.* Paris: 1981.

1450. Perrout, R. *Les Images d'Epinal.* Paris: 1910.

1451. *Politique et Polémique: La Caricature Françoise de la Revolution, 1789-1799.* Paris: Bibliothéque Nationale, and Los Angeles, California: University of California at Los Angeles, 1988.

1452. Price, Aimée Brown. "Official Artists and Not-So-Official Art: Covert Caricaturists in Nineteenth-Century France." *Art Journal.* Winter 1983, pp. 365-370.

1453. Revel, Jean-François. "L'Invention de la Caricature." *L'Oeil.* January 1964, pp. 12-21.

1454. *Rire et Galanterie. Recueil Hebdomadaire d'Images Galantes.* Nos. 1-100. Paris: Chez Offenstadt Éd., 1903-1904.

1455. Riverain, Jean. "La Caricature Française du XVIe au XVIIIe Siècle." *Larousse Mensuel* (Paris). July 1950.

1456. Riverain, Jean. "La Caricature Française au XIXe Siècle." *Larousse Mensuel* (Paris). October 1950.

1457. Riverain, Jean. "La Caricature Françoise de 1900 à 1950." *Larousse Mensuel* (Paris). February 1951.

1458. Roberts'-Jones, Philippe. *La Caricature du Second Empire à la Belle Epoque, 1850-1900.* Paris: 1963.

1459. Romi: *Histoire des Faits Divers.* Paris: Éditions du Pont Royal, 1962.

1460. Schmidt, Karl Eugen. *Deutschland und die Deutschen in der Franzoischen Karikatur seit 1848.* Stuttgart: Emil Muller Verlag, 1907.

1461. Seguin, Jean-Pierre. *Canards du Siècle Passé.* Paris: Pierre Horay, 1969.

1462. Seguin, Jean-Pierre. *Nouvelles à Sensation: Canards du XIXᵉ Siècle.* Paris: Colin, 1959.

1463. Sorel, Philippe. "Les Dantan au Musee Carnavalet: Portraits-Charges Sculptes de l'Epoque Romantique." *Gazette des Beaux-Arts.* January 1986, pp. 1-38; February 1986, pp. 87-102.

1464. Teper, E. *Die Revolutionare Karikatur der Pariser Kommune.* Moscow: 1961.

1465. Thackeray, William M. "Caricature and Lithography in Paris." In *The Paris Sketch Book.* 1840.

1466. Thackeray, William. "Parisian Caricatures: Lithography." *London and Westminster Review.* April 1839, pp. 282-305.

1467. Traviés et Numa. *Caricatures Antilériques.* Paris: Chez Aubert, éditeur de la *Caricature*, Lithographies de Bernard, 1833.

1468. Warnod, André. "A Vida Boêmia de Montmartre." *Dom Casmurro* (Rio de Janeiro). May 15-September 6, 1943.

1469. Warnod, André. *Ceux de la Butte.* Paris: René Juillard Sequana, 1947.

1470. Warnod, André. *Fils de Montmartre. Souvenirs.* Paris: Libr. Arthème Fayard, 1955.

1471. Warnod, André. *Les Berceaux de la Jeune Peinture. Montmartre, Montparnasse.* Paris: Albin Michel Éd., n.d.

1472. Warnod, André. *Les Peintres de Montmartre. Gavarni, Toulouse-Lautrec, Utrillo.* Paris: La Renaissance du Livre, n.d.

1473. Wechsler, Judith. *A Human Comedy: Physiognomy and Caricature in 19th Century Paris.* Chicago, Illinois: University of Chicago Press; London: Thames and Hudson, 1982. 208 pp.

1474. Wilker, Jenny. "French Caricature and the French Revolution." *The Print Collector's Newsletter*. May/June 1989, pp. 69-72.

Comics

1475. *Archéologie, Histoire de l'Art et Bande Dessinée*. Neuve: U.C.b. Institut Supérieur d'Archéologie et d'Histoire de l'Art, 1980. (Exposition, March 20-April 14, 1980).

1476. Arrouye, Jean. 1979. "Bandes à Part." In *Histoire et Bande Dessinée: Actes du 2e Colloque International Éducation et Bande Dessinée*, pp. 105-126. Lo Roque d' Anthéron: Objectif Promo-Durance, 1979.

1477. Aziza, Claude. "L'Antiquité dans la Bande Dessinée: Un Racisme Insolite." *Bédésup*. 24/25, 1983, pp. 27-29.

1478. Barrera-Vidal, Albert. "Les Relations Franco-Allemandes dans la BD d'Expression Française où l'Histoire Revue et Non Corrigée. In *Histoire et Bande Dessinée: Actes du 2e Colloque International Éducation et Bande Dessinée*, pp. 86-97. Lo Roque d' Anthéron: Objectif Promo-Durance, 1979.

1479. Barrera-Vidal, Alberto. 1984. "L'Histoire par la Bande... Dessinée." Faculté de Philosophie et Lettres, l'Université de Liège, Section d'Histoire B 20, 1984.

1480. Baur, André, Patrick Dillies, Noël Nel, and Pierre Pegeot. "Mise en Bandes et Mise en Pièces de l'Histoire. L'Histoire de France en Bandes Dessinées. No. 2." *Pratiques* (Metz). 18/19, 1978, pp. 30-48.

1481. Becker, Hartmut. "Comics und Geschichte. Teil 2. Historische Serien bei Carlsen." *Comixene. Das Comicfachmagazin*. 6:23 (1979), pp. 12-24.

1482. Blanchard, Gérard. *Histoire de la Bande Dessinée*. Verviers, Belgium: Marabout, 1969.

1483. Blanchard, Gérard. *La Bande Dessineé Histoire des Histoires en Images de la Préhistoire à Nos Jours*. Paris: Marabout Université, No. 179, 1979.

1484. Caré, Jean-Marc. "Histoire et Bande Dessinée: Le Moyen Age." *Le Français dans le Monde*. 162, 1981, pp. 18-19.

1485. Carrez, Claude. *Naissance d'une Bande Dessinée: La Crète Minoenne.*" *Education 2000*. 21, 1982, pp. 73-78.

1486. Colini, Serge. "Histoire des Bandes Dessinées." *Minou* (Paris). August 5, 1965.

1487. Couperie, Pierre, Edouard François, Henri Filippini, Claude Moliterni, Michel Denni, and Philippe Mellot. "France." In *Histoire Mondiale de la Bande Dessinée*, edited by Pierre Horay, pp. 20-101. Paris: Pierre Horay, 1989.

1488. Dovetto, Joseph and Raymond Roge. "La Croisade Contre les Albigeois dans la Bande Dessinée." In *Histoire et Bande Dessinée: Actes du 2e Colloque International Éducation et Bande Dessinée*, pp. 35-43. Lo Roque d' Anthéron: Objectif Promo-Durance, 1979.

1489. Eloy, Michel. "L'Antiquité dans la Bande Dessinée." *Français 2000* (Brussels). 105, 1982, pp. 39-47.

1490. Faur, Jean-Claude, ed. *À la Rencontre de la Bande Dessinée*. Marseilles: Bédésup, 1983.

1491. Faur, Jean-Claude. "Bande Dessinée ou Histoire?: Caligula dans l'Imagerie Populaire." In *Histoire et Bande Dessinée: Actes du 2e Colloque International Éducation et Bande Dessinée*, pp. 17-25. Lo Roque d'Anthéron: Objectif Promo-Durance, 1979.

1492. Faur, Jean-Claude. "De Gaulle en BD: Sur Deux Albums Récents." In *À la Rencontre de la Bande Dessinée*, edited by Jean-Claude Faur, pp. 59-60. Marseilles: Bédésup, J.-C. Faur, 1983.

1493. Faur, Jean-Claude. *Diabédé*. Série 1: *Histoire de la Bande Dessinée: Des Cavernes à Épinal*; Série 2: *Histoire de la Bande Dessinée: D'Épinal à Winsor MacCay*. La Roque d'Anthéron: Objectif Promo Durance, 1978.

1494. Faur, Jean-Claude. "Enseigner l'Histoire par la Bande Dessinée? Qui! Mais Il n'y a Pas de 'Recette'!" In *À la Rencontre de la Bande Dessinée*, edited by Jean-Claude Faur, pp. 121-123. Marseilles: Bédésup, J.-C. Faur, 1983.

1495. Faur, Jean-Claude. *Histoire et Bande Dessinée*. Marseilles: Bédésup, 1979.

1496. Faur, Jean-Claude. "La B.D. a Dix Ans." *Livres Hebdo*. No. 49. 1981, pp. 92-95.

1497. Faur, Jean-Claude. "L'Image de l'Empereur Caligula dans la BD." In *À la Rencontre de la Bande Dessinée*, edited by Jean-Claude Faur, pp. 23-26. Marseilles: Bédésup, J.-C. Faur, 1983.

1498. Faur, Jean-Claude. "Pour une Histoire de la Bande Dessinée dans la Région." *Les Carnets de la Region Provence-Alpes-Cote d'Azur* (Marseilles). No. 14, 1985, pp. 4-9.

1499. Faur, Jean-Claude. *Un Grand Illustré pour la Jeunesse Sous l'Occupation—le Téméraire*. Marseilles: Bédésup, 1981. 31 pp.

1500. Filippini, Henri. "80ᵉᵐᵉ Anniversaire de la BD." *Phénix*. No. 18, 1971.

1501. Filippini, Henri. *Histoire de Journal et des Éditions Vaillant*. Grenoble: Glénat, 1978.

1502. Filippini, Henri. *Les Années Cinquante*. Grenoble: Eds. Jacques Glénat, 1977.

1503. Francart, Roland. *Tresors de la B.D. [Bande Dessinée] Religieuse de 1941 a 1985*. Brussels: CRIABD [Centre Religieux d'Information et d'Analyse de la Bande Dessinée], 1985. 56 pp.

1504. François, Édouard. "Histoire de la Bande Dessinée." *Française* (Paris). 1972, p. 31.

1505. François, Édouard. *L'Âge d'Or de la Bande Dessinée*. Paris: Serg, 1971.

1506. Fresnault-Deruelle, Pierre. "L'Effet d'Histoire." In *Histoire et Bande Dessinée: Actes du 2e Colloque International Éducation et Bande Dessinée*, pp. 98-104. La Roque d'Anthéron: Objectif Promo-Durance, 1979.

1507. Garçon, François. "Clio en Bulles." *Education 2000*. 21, 1982, pp. 79-85.

1508. Groensteen, Thierry. *La Bande Dessinée Depuis 1975*. Paris: MA Editions, 1985.

1509. "Histoire de la Bande Dessinée d'Expression Française." *Bédésup*. Special Number (Ed. Serg, Paris), 1972.

1510. *Histoire et Bande Dessinée: Actes du 2e Colloque International Éducation et Bande Dessinée*. La Roque d'Anthéron: Objectif Promo-Durance, 1979.

1511. *Histoire et Bande Dessinée: Projet d'Étude sur la B.D. d'Expression Française*. Besançon: Direction Régionale des Affaires Culturelles, 1983.

1512. Horn, Maurice. "Histoire de la Bande Dessinée." *Informations et Documents* (Paris). No. 243, 1967, pp. 20-27.

1513. Horn, Maurice. "70 Années de Bandes Dessinées." *Phénix*. October 1966.

1514. Lebrette, François. "L'Histoire en Bandes Dessinées." *Le Spectacle du Monde* (Paris). 1979, pp. 81-85.

1515. Lecigne, Bruno. *Avanies et Mascarade*. Paris: Futuropolis, 1981.

1516. Moliterni, Claude, ed. *Histoire de la Bande Dessinée d'Expression Françise*. Paris: Editions Serg, 1972.

1517. Moliterni, Claude. *Histoire Mondiale de la Bande Dessinée*. Paris: Pierre Horay, 1989.

1518. Mouchel, Gérard-Guy. "Le Monde Antique dans la B.D." *L'Ecole des Lettres* (Paris). 8, 1984, pp. 53-56.

1519. *Le Moyen Âge par la Bande Dessinée*: Exposition, 1 au 15 Juin (Salle des Chevaliers), Cité de Carcassonne, 15 Juin au 31 Juillet 1978, Bibliothèque Municipale. Carcassonne: Groupe d'Animation Culturelle de Carcassonne, 1978.

1520. Pierre, Michel. "Les Histoires de l'Oncle Paul: Mythologie ou Mystification?" In *Histoire et Bande Dessinée: Actes du 2e Colloque International Éducation et Bande Dessinée*, pp. 51-58. Lo Roque d'Anthéron: Objectif Promo-Durance, 1979.

1521. Prost, Jean and André Pelletier. "Histoire et Bande Dessinée: A Propos de 'Il Était une Fois Lugdunum' (T. 1: De l'Histoire de Lyon en Bandes Dessinée)." *Histoire et Bande Dessinée: Actes du 2e Colloque International Éducation et Bande Dessinée*. pp. 26-34. Lo Roque d'Antéron: Objectif Promo-Durance, 1979.

1522. Renard, Jean-Bruno. "L'Histoire Mythique de la Technique dans la Bande Dessinée." In *Histoire et Bande Dessinée: Actes du 2e Colloque International Éducation et Bande Dessinée*, pp. 157-167. Lo Roque d'Anthéron: Objectif Promo-Durance, 1979.

1523. Saint-Michel, Serge. 1979. "Les Amazones de l'Empire d'Abomey." In *Histoire et Bande Dessinée: Actes du 2e Colloque International Éducation et Bande Dessinée*, pp. 71-78. Lo Roque d'Anthéron: Objectif Promo-Durance, 1979.

1524. Schneider, Hagen. "Comics und Epochensensibilität." *Neue Unterrichtspraxis* (Hanover). 9:4 (1976), pp. 210-213.

1525. Thonet, Françoise. "Une Chine Débridée." *Les Cahiers de la Bande Dessinée*. 72, 1986, pp. 85-86.

1526. Tisseron, Serge. *Contribution à l'Utilisation de la B.D. Comme Instrument Pédagogique: Une Tentative Graphique sur l'Histoire de la Psychiatre.* Lyon: Université Claude Bernard à Lyon, 1975.

1527. Vankeer, Pierre. "L'As: Histoire d'un Illustré Entre la Tradition et le Modernisme." *Giff-Wiff.* No. 22, 1966.

Graphic Arts

1528. Adhémar, Jean. *Graphic Art of the Eighteenth Century.* Trans. by M.I. Martin. New York: McGraw-Hill, 1964.

1529. Adhémar, Jean. *Imagerie Populaire Française.* Milan: Electra, 1968.

1530. Agulhon, Maurice. *Marianne into Battle: Republican Imagery and Symbolism in France, 1785-1880*. Trans. by Janet Lloyd. Cambridge, Massachusetts: Cambridge University Press, 1981.

1531. Arasse, Daniel. *La Guillotine dans la Révolution*. Exhibition Catalogue. Vizille: Musée de la Révolution Française, 1987.

1532. Arnauldet, Thomas. "Estampes Satiriques, Bouffonnées ou Singulières. Relative à l'Art et aux Artistes Français Pendant les XVIIe Siècles." *Gazette des Beaux-Arts*. September 1859, pp. 342-361.

1533. Art Council of Great Britain. *French Popular Imagery: Five Centuries of Prints*. Exhibition Catalogue. London: Hayward Gallery, 1974.

1534. Brieger, Lothar. *Das Goldene Zeitalter der Franzoischen Illustration*. Berlin-Vienna: Benjamin Harz Verlag, n.d.

1535. Carlson, Victor I. and John W. Ittman. *Regency to Empire: French Printmaking, 1715-1814*. Exhibition Catalogue. Baltimore, Maryland and Minneapolis, Minnesota: The Baltimore Museum of Art and the Minneapolis Institute of the Arts, 1984.

1536. Casselle, Pierre. "Sur le Commerce de l'Estampe à Paris dans la Seconde Moitié du XVIIIe Siècle." Ph.D. dissertation, Ecole Nationale des Chartes, 1976.

1537. Crow, Thomas E. "The Oath of the Horatii in 1785: Painting and Pre-Revolutionary Radicalism in France." *Art History*. December 1978, pp. 424-471.

1538. Dacier, Émile. *La Gravure Française*. Paris: Libr. Larousse, 1944.

1539. de Goncourt, Edmond and Jules de Goncourt. *L'Art du XVIIIme Siécle*. 2nd Ed. 3 Vols. Paris: G. Charpentier, 1881-1882.

1540. de la Sizeranne, Robert. *Le Miroir de la Vie*. Paris: Libr. Hachette, 1912.

1541. The Detroit Institute of Arts and the Metropolitan Museum of Art, New York. *French Painting 1774-1830: The Age of Revolution*. Exhibition Catalogue. Detroit, Michigan: Detroit Institute of Arts, 1975.

1542. Duverger, Erik. *Réflixions sur le Commerce d'Art au XVIIIe Siècle*. Acts of the Twenty-First International Congress for Art History, Vol. 3. Princeton, New Jersey: Princeton University Press, 1964.

1543. Faure, Élie. *Histoire de l'Art*. Paris: Libr. Plon, Éditions d'Histoire et d'Art, 1941.

1544. Gabey, Georgette. "La Naissance du Désir de Lire." *Le Monde*. June 12, 1971.

1545. Henderson, Ernest F. *Symbol and Satire in the French Revolution*. New York and London: G.P. Putnam's Sons, 1912.

1546. Hourticq, Louis. "Les Parisiens aux Salons de Peinture." In *La Vie Parisienne au XVIIIe Siècle*. Conférences du Musée Carnavalet. Paris: Payot, 1928.

1547. Isherwood, Robert M. *Farce and Fantasy: Popular Entertainment in Eighteenth-Century Paris*. Oxford: Oxford University Press, 1986.

1548. Johnson, W. McAllister. "Affiche, Annonces et Avis Divers: The 'Estampe-Publicité' in Eighteenth-Century France." *Gazette des Beaux-Arts*. 6th ser., 102 (1983), pp. 121-128.

1549. Lacassin, Francis. "Histoire de la Littérature Populaire." *Magazine Littéraire*. No. 9, 1967, pp. 10-15.

1550. Leith, James A. *The Idea of Art As Propaganda in France, 1750-1799: A Study in the History of Ideas*. Toronto: University of Toronto Press, 1965.

1551. Lorentz, O.J. *Fiasque, Melé d'Allegories. Illustré. Illustrations d'Illustres Illustralisés, Illustrée par un Illustrissime Illustrateur Illustrement Illustré*. 2 Vols. Paris: August 1840.

1552. Lorentz, O.J. *Polichnel. Ex-Roi des Marionettes Devenu Philosophe* (Louis Philippe). Paris: Willermy, Éd. Libraire, 1848.

1553. Mitchell, Hannah. "Art and the French Revolution: An Exhibition at the Musée Carnavalet." *History Workshop*. Spring 1978, pp. 123-145.

1554. Morin, Louis. *Le Dessin Humoristique*. Paris: Henri Laurens Éditeur, n.d.

1555. Morin, Louis. "Nos Humoristes et la Guerre." *Je Sais Tout* (Paris). February 15, 1916.

1556. Musée Carnavalet, Paris. *L'Art de l'Estampe et la Révolution Française*. Exhibition Catalogue. Paris: Musée Carnavalet, 1977.

1557. *Musée Comique. Toutes Sortes de Choses en Images*. Doré, Bertall, Nadar, etc. Faisant suite à la *Revue Comique*. Paris: Aubert and Cie, 1850.

1558. *Musée Dantan*. Galerie des Charges et Croquis des Celebrités de l'Epoque. Avec Texte Explicatif et Biographique. Paris: Chez H. Delloye, Libraire Éditeur, 1839.

1559. *Musée pour Rire, Le*. Dessins par Tous le Caricaturistes de Paris, Daumier, Gavarni, etc. Text by Maurice Alhoy, Louis Huart, and Charles Philipon. 2 Vols. Paris: Chez Aubert, 1839.

1560. *Pendant la Guerre. L'Esprit Satirique en France.* Preface by Arsène Alexandre. Paris: Berger Levrault, 1916.

1561. Pigal (Edme-Jean). *Recueil de Scènes de Societé.* Lithographies de Langlemé, coloriées. Paris: Chez Martinet, vers, 1830.

1562. Plée, Léon. "La Comédie Picturale." (Caran d'Ache, Cappiello etc.). *Les Annales* (Paris). No. 1381.

1563. Plée, Léon. "Le Salon des Humoristes." *Les Annales* (Paris). Nos. 1300 to 1351.

1564. Plée, Léon. "Le Salon des Humoristes." *Les Annales* (Paris). No. 1381.

1565. Renouvier, Jules. *Histoire de l'Art Pendant la Révolution.* 2 Vols. Paris: Vve Jules Renouard, 1863.

1566. Richard, Marius. "Leurs Dessins Leur Ressemblent. Les Peynet." *Points de Vues* (Paris). February 12, 1955.

1567. Roberts-Jones, Philippe. *La Presse Satirique Illustrée Entre 1860 et 1890.* Paris: Institut Français de la Presse, 1956.

1568. Saulnier, Adam. "Histoire d'un Homme sans Nom Qui Rendra Célèbre un Jeune Danois." *Varietés* (Paris). August 7/13, 1952.

1569. Scheifley, W.H. "French Pictorial Humor." *Catholic World.* May 1926, pp. 175-178.

1570. Schneider, Helmut. "Französische Bilderbogen des 19. Jahrhunderts im Museum." (Hamburg). May 12, 1972, p. 18.

1571. Voll, Karl. *Frankreichs Klassischer Zeichner im XIX Jahrhundert.* Berlin-Vienna: Benjamin Harz, Verlag, 1913.

Political Cartoons

1572. Auclert, Jean-Pierre. *La Grande Guerre des Crayons:... 1914-1918.* Paris: Laffont, 1981.

1573. Helfand, William H. "Medicine and Pharmacy in French Political Prints." *Trans. and Studies Coll. Phys.* (Philadelphia). 4th Series, July 1974, pp. 14-33.

1574. Helfand, W.H. and Pierre Julien. "Medicine and Pharmacy in French Political Prints." In *Acta Congressus Internationalis XXIV Historiae Artis Medicinae*, pp. 1145-1160. Budapest: Museum, Bibliotheca et Archivum; 1976.

1575. "La Révolution Française 1789-1989." *Mieux Vaut en Rire*. No. 12, 1989, pp. 1-42.

1576. Loquai, Franz. "De Gaulle Tonton Valery et Cie..." *Mieux Vaut en Rire*. No. 13, 1989, pp. 16-17.

1577. Rifkin, Adrian. "Well Formed Phrases: Some Limits of Meaning in Political Print at the End of the Second Empire." *Oxford Art Journal*. 8:1 (1985), pp. 20+.

CARTOONISTS and CARICATURISTS

1578. "A la Decouverte de... Pierre Brochard." *Coccinelle*. January-April 1990, pp. 8-9.

1579. "A la Rencontre de WEYLAND." *Bédésup*. Nos. 40-41, 1987, pp. 3-8.

1580. "Anthea Shackleton." *Comics Interview*. No. 69, 1989, pp. 46-58.

1581. Aymé, Marcel. "Il y a Dix Ans Mourait Chas Laborde." *Les Nouvelles Littéraires* (Paris). February 15, 1951.

1582. Bachollet, Raymond. "Paul Iribe 'Témoin' de Son Temps." *Le Collectionneur Français*. 184 (1981), pp. 7-8.

1583. Bajard, Annie. *B.D. Flash!* St. Etienne: Le Hénaff, 1982. (Biard, Chaland, Claveloux, Clerc, Cornillon, Montellier, Terpant, Tranchand, Vallès).

1584. Bilger, Philippe. "Comptes et Mécomptes de Jacques Calvet." *La Lettre*. July-August 1992, p. 28.

1585. Boime, Albert. *Thomas Couture and the Eclectic Vision*. New Haven, Connecticut: Yale University Press, 1980.

1586. Bonnot. *Bonnot. 60 Dessins d'Observation Faits a la Maison*. Preface by Jacques Sternberg. Grenoble: Glénat-Guttin, 1972.

1587. Bouyer, Sylvain. "Tripp et Barcelo. L'Itinéraire en Peau de Banane." *Les Cahiers de la Bande Dessinée*. 65, 1985, pp. 90-91. (Marc Barcelo).

1588. Burdeyron, François-Xavier. "Lug et les Super-Héros: Une Interview de Marcel Navarro." *Le Nouveau Bédésup*. 34, 1985, pp. 31-37.

1589. "Burki." *Mieux Vaut en Rire*. No. 14, 1989, pp. 2-16.

1590. Capet, B. and Th. Defert. "François Roy Vidal." *Phénix*. No. 18, 1971.

1591. Carco, Francis. *Les Humoristes*. Paris: Librairie Paul Ollendorf, 1921.

1592. Charrier, Christian and Michel Jans. "Interview mit Jordi Bernet und Enrique Sanchez Abuli." *ICOM*. January 1993, pp. 28-34.

1593. Chery, Christian. "Avec Paul Colin et Gen Paul." *Les Lettres Françaises* (Paris). No. 1138, 1966.

1594. Claretie, Jules. *Peintres et Sculpteurs Contemporains*. 2 Vols. Paris: Lib. des Bibliophiles, 1882-1884.

1595. Couffon, Claude. "Entretien avec Evelyne Sullerot." *Les Lettres Françaises*. June 30, 1966, pp. 17-18.

1596. de Banville, Théodore. "Les Grands Chroniqueurs: Gavarni, Daumier, Cham." *Gil Blas*. December 19, 1879.

1597. Defert, Th. "Ricord Mulatier." *Phénix*. No. 19, 1971.

1598. Delorme, Hughes. *L'Humour Contemporain*. I—Albert Guillaume; II—Jean Veber; III—Abel Faivre; IV—Dubout; V—Poulbot; VI—Grassier. Paris: Édit. Les Laboratoires Le Brun and Mitasol, n.d.

1599. Delperdange, Patrick. "Rivière et Co, Enquêtes en Tous Genres." *Les Cahiers de la Bande Dessinée*. 68, 1986, pp. 36-39.

1600. Di Manno, Yves. "Martin Milan ou la Poétique Réaliste." *Cahiers Universitaires*. No. 19, 1972.

1601. "D. Jon Zimmerman." *Comics Interview*. May 1983, pp. 57-59.

1602. Dubout, Albert. *Total Verrückt*. Berlin: Eulenspiegel-Verlag, 1956.

1603. Ellmar, Paul. "Der Eiffelturm Verläßt Seinen Platz... Ein Französischer Walt Disney." *Die Zeit*. July 16, 1953.

1604. "Entretien avec Sylvan Byck." *Mongo*. No. 0, 1967.

1605. Enu, Henri J. "Un Monde à Décrypter. Quatre Créateurs de Bandes Dessinées Vous Parlent." *La Quizaine Littéraire* (Paris). 169, 1973, pp. 17-19. (Claire Bretécher, Danie Dubos, Jean-Claude Forest, Paul Gillon).

1606. Farinole. *C'Était pour Rire*. Vingt Ans d'Humour et de Vie Parisienne avec les Dessinateurs Humoristes (Carrizey, Dubout, Jean Effel, Bellus etc.). Paris: Jacques Vautrain, 1953.

1607. Faur, Jean-Claude. "Grenoble 1: Le Pari Gagne de Pierre Pascal." *Bédésup*. 1st-2nd Trim., 1989, p. 12.

1608. Faur, Jean-Claude. "Rencontre avec... Francis Bergèse." *Le Nouveau Bédésup.* 29/30, 1984, pp. 4-9.

1609. Faur, Jean-Claude. *Rétrospective Robert Velter: de Spirou à Nimbus.* Toulouse: Bibliothéque Municipale, 1975. Unpaginated.

1610. Faur, Jean-Claude. *Un Grande Illustré d'Après-Guerre: Garth.* Marseilles: Bédésup, 1981. 14 pp.

1611. Fels, Florent. "Robert Macaire." *L'Art Vivant* (Paris). August 1926.

1612. Ferment, Claude. "Le Caricaturiste Traviès: La Vie et l'Oeuvre d'un 'Prince de Guignon.' (1804-1859)." *Gazette des Beaux-Arts.* February 1982, pp. 63-77.

1613. Filippini, Henri. *Carnet de Dédicaces: Arnal, Bretécher, Charlier, Chéret.* Ivry (Val-de-Marne): S.E.R.G., 1974.

1614. Filippini, Henri. "Entretien avec Annie Goetzinger." *Schtroumpfanzine.* 19, 1978, pp. 3-9.

1615. Filippini, Henri. "Entretien avec Claude Moliterni." *Schtroumpfanzine.* 24, 1978, pp. 14-21.

1616. Filippini, Henri. "Entretien avec Jean-Paul Mougin." *Schtroumpfanzine.* 27, 1979, pp. 14-19.

1617. Filippini, Henri. "Entretien avec Michel de France." *Schtroumpfanzine.* 31, 1979, pp. 3-5.

1618. Filippini, Henri. "Entretien avec Patrice Sanahujas." *Schtroumpfanzine.* 33, 1979, pp. 3-12.

1619. Filippini, Henri. "Entretien avec Philippe Luguy." *Schtroumpfanzine.* 36, 1979, pp. 14-20. (a.k.a. Philippe Liéron).

1620. Filippini, Henri. "Les Dessinateurs Larousse." *Schtroumpfanzine.* 31, 1979, pp. 5-10. (Battaglia, Bielsa, Buzzelli, Coelho, Crepax, Gattia, Manara, Marcello, Marzal-Canos, Poïvet, Toppi).

1621. Filippini, Henri. "Marcel Mat." *Schtroumpfanzine.* 30, 1979, pp. 17-20.

1622. Fourié, Jean. "Mouminoux. Une Carrière en Dents de Scie." *Les Cahiers de la Bande Dessinée.* 63, 1985, pp. 87-90. (Guy Mouminoux, a.k.a. Dimitri).

1623. François, Edouard. "G. Omry." *Phénix.* No. 12, 1969.

1624. François, Edouard. "Raymond Macherot." *Phénix.* No. 5, 4 Trimestre 1967, pp. 1-15.

1625. Frantz, Henri and Octave Uzanne. *Daumier and Gavarni.* New York, 1904.

1626. Fronval, George. "Hommage à Marcel Alain." *Phénix.* No. 12, 1969.

1627. Gauthier, Guy and Philippe Pilard. "René Goscinny e Albert Uderzo." *Républica* (Lisbon). May 24, 1967.

1628. Gautier, Théophile. "Gavarni, Gustave Doré." *L'Artiste.* 1857, pp. 243-245.

1629. Gib. "Chez les Humoristes." *Je Sais Tout* (Paris). 7e année, I sem. IV.

1630. "Gibo." *Mieux Vaut en Rire.* No. 14, 1989, pp. 72-75.

1631. Girerd, J.P. *The International Pavilion of Humor of Montreal Presents Jean Pierre Girerd. 1986 Cartoonist of the Year.* Montreal: 1986. Unpaginated.

1632. Groensteen, Thierry. "Calligaro et le Texte Pictural." *Les Cahiers de la Bande Dessinée.* 71, 1986, pp. 58-61.

1633. Groensteen, Thierry. "Conversation avec Dominique Leroy." *Les Cahiers de la Bande Dessinée.* 58, 1984, pp. 72-73.

1634. Groensteen, Thierry. "Hislaire, Yann, Le Gall, Cossu et les Autres..." *Les Cahiers de la Bande Dessinée.* 70, 1986, pp. 75-81.

1635. Groensteen, Thierry. "L'Édition Selon ARTEFACT. Conversation avec Jean-Pierre Mercier." *Les Cahiers de la Bande Dessinée.* 64, 1985, pp. 44-46.

1636. Groensteen, Thierry. "Le Glénat Nouveau Est Arrivé. Entretien avec Marcel-Didier Vrac." *Les Cahiers de la Bande Dessinée.* 67, 1986, pp. 56-58.

1637. Groensteen, Thierry. "Makyo, Alchimiste du Rire et de la Peur." *Les Cahiers de la Bande Dessinée.* 58, 1984, pp. 82-87. (Pierre Fournier).

1638. Groensteen, Thierry and Bruno Lecigne. "Marginal et Fier de l'Étre. (Conversation avec Etienne Robial)." *Les Cahiers de la Bande Dessinée.* 62, 1985, pp. 35-39.

1639. Guérin, Raoul. *L'Humour Contemporain, II—Raoul Guérin.* Paris: Laboratoires Le Brun et Mitasol, n.d.

1640. Guilmer, André. *À la Manière de...,* Gus Bofa, L. Boucher, Carlègle, Dubout, Joseph Hémard, Chas Laborde, etc. Preface by Raymond Escolier. Grenoble: Éditions de l'Imprimerie Génerale Marcel Bessons, n.d.

1641. *Gus. Arrêts sur Images. 15 Ans d'Actualités TV.* Preface by Pierre Tchernia. Geneva: Editions Rousseau, 1991. 160 pp.

1642. Henry, Maurice. *Voyages du Rêveur*. Paris: Albin Michel, 1979. 160 pp.

1643. Henry, Maurice. *Vive la Fuite!* Paris: Pierre Horay, 1958.

1644. Hervé. *Hervé Présente Martine et Cie*. Preface by Carmen Tessier. Paris: Presses Mondiales, 1953.

1645. Hesse, Raymond. *Louis Morin*. Paris: Henri Babon Éd., 1930.

1646. Holme, Charles, ed. *Daumier and Gavarni*. New York: Offices of 'The Studio,' 1904. Unpaginated.

1647. Hommerie, Bernard. "Bretagne et B.D. Reynald Secher." *La Lettre de Bédésup*. No. 58, 1992, p. 5.

1648. Hommerie, Bernard. "René Le Honzec." *La Lettre de Bédésup*. No. 58, 1992, p. 5.

1649. *Hotel des Voyageurs*. Paris Crapule Productions, 1986. (Gilles Bachelet).

1650. Huart, Louis. *Physiologie du Flaneur*. Vignettes de Adolphe, Daumier et Maurisset. Paris: Aubert et Cie, n.d.

1651. "Ils Nous Ont Quitté (Zac-Lap)." *Mieux Vaut en Rire*. No. 5 (n.d.), pp. 12-13.

1652. "Interview: Jean-Claude Faur." *Le Nouveau Bédésup*. Nos. 40-41, 1987, pp. 55-62.

1653. "Jean-Marc Lofficier." *Comics Interview*. No. 45, 1987, pp. 17-21.

1654. "Jean Morette Collaborateur au Républicain Lorrain." *Mieux Vaut en Rire*. No. 5 (n.d.), pp. 14-24.

1655. Jeanniot, Georges. *Georges Jeanniot*. Coll. "Les Maîtres Humoristes." Paris: Libr. Félix Juven, 1908.

1656. Lacassin, Francis. "Alain Resnais et les Bandes Dessinées." *L'Avant Scène du Cinéma* (Paris). No. 61-62, 1966, pp. 51-57.

1657. Lacoubre, Roland. "H.G. Clouzot et la Language Dessinée." *Giff-Wiff*. No. 10, 1965, p. 25.

1658. "La Couleur dans Dinghys Dinghys: Sensibilité du Grain et des Ombres Claires. Interview Réalisée par Correspondance par 'Les Cahiers.'" *Les Cahiers de la Bande Dessinée*. 65, 1985, p. 91. (Anne Fougerouse).

1659. "La Palme à Roland." *Lui*. No. 53, 1968.

1660. "L. Berrings." Souvenir program of exhibition, 11th Salon International du Dessin de Presse et d'Humour, St. Just le Martel, France. St. Just: 1992.

1661. "Lebon." *Mieux Vaut en Rire*. No. 14, 1989, pp. 33-51.

1662. Lecigne, Bruno. "Edmond Baudoin. Un Rubis au Bout du Pinceau." *Les Cahiers de la Bande Dessinée*. 70, 1986, pp. 90-93.

1663. *Le Diable à Paris. Paris et les Parisiens à la Plume et au Crayon*. 4 Vols. Paris: J. Hetzel Libr. Éditeur, 1866-1869. (Gavarni, Grandville, Bertall, Cham, etc.).

1664. *Lefranc*. Brussels: Casterman, n.d. 48 pp.

1665. Léturgie, Jean. "Entretien avec Guy Vidal." *Schtroumpfanzine*. 19, 1978, pp. 10-16.

1666. Léturgie, Jean. "Entretien avec Jean-Claude Denis." *Schtroumpfanzine*. 36, 1979, pp. 3-8.

1667. Léturgie, Jean. "Entretien avec Jean Tabary." *Schtroumpfanzine*. 32, 1979, pp. 15-21.

1668. Léturgie, Jean. "Entretien avec Max Cabanes." *Schtroumpfanzine*. 28, 1979, pp. 3-11.

1669. Léturgie, Jean. "Entretien avec Michel Blanc-Dumont." *Schtroumpfanzine*. 22, 1978, pp. 3-10.

1670. Léturgie, Jean. "Entretien avec Pétillon." *Schtroumpfanzine*. 24, 1978, pp. 3-13.

1671. Léturgie, Jean. "Entretien avec Pierre Wininger." *Schtroumpfanzine*. 18, 1978, pp. 3-12.

1672. Lima, Herman. "Bonecos de Paris." *Rio Magazine* (Rio de Janeiro). April 1949. (Grambert).

1673. Lindekens, René. "Analyse Structurale de la Stripsody de Cathy Berberian." *Communications* (Paris). 24 (1976), pp. 140-176.

1674. Marijac. *Souvenirs de Marijac et l'Histoire de Coq Hardi*. Grenoble: Eds. Jacques Glénat, 1978. (Jacques Dumas).

1675. Marmonnier, Christian. "Des Echos d'Albin Michel. Conversation avec Thierry Souccar." *Les Cahiers de la Bande Dessinée*. 57, 1984, pp. 76-77.

1676. "Mattauer." *Mieux Vaut en Rire*. No. 13, 1989, pp. 51-52.

1677. Mellquist, Jerome. *Les Caricatures de Jacques Villon*. Paris: P. Cailler, 1960. 38 pp., 85 plates.

1678. Métivet, Lucien. *Lucien Métivet. Les Maîtres Humoristes*. Preface by Pierre Valdagne. Paris: Libr. Félix Juven, 1907.

1679. Mick. *Les Grands Humoristes Français*. No. 3, *Variations de Mick*. Preface by Yvan Andouard. Paris: Éditions Presses Mondiales, 1953.

1680. "Millon." *Mieux Vaut en Rire*. No. 14, 1989, pp. 27-32.

1681. *Mirande*. Coll. "Les Maîtres Humoristes." Paris: Libr. Félix Juven, 1907.

1682. Moliterni, Claude. *Entretiens avec Gir, Jean-Michel Charlier, Robert Gigi, Hugo Pratt, Fred, Gotlib, Philippe Druillet*. Ivry: S.E.R.G., 1973.

1683. "Monet the Caricaturist." *Kayhan Caricature*. September 1992.

1684. *Montmartre et Ses Artistes*. Paris: *L'Art et le Beau*, No. 4, Librairie Artistique et Littéraire, n.d.

1685. "Narcisse." *Mieux Vaut en Rire*. No. 5 (n.d.), pp. 43-45.

1686. Pica, Vittorio. *Attraverso Gli Albe e le Cartelle*. Vol. IV of *Tres Maestri della Caricatura in Francia: Daumier, Gavarni, Forain*. Bergamo: 1904.

1687. Pinson, Daniel. "Esprit Sportif et Paranoia dans l'Oeuvre de F. Masse." *Bédésup*. 14/15, 1980, pp. 35-40.

1688. "Piskorski." *Mieux Vaut en Rire*. No. 13, 1989, pp. 53-58.

1689. Poinsignon, Jean-Claude. "Félix Auvray (1800-1833), Caricaturiste Occasionnel." *Gazette des Beaux-Arts*. March 1989, pp. 121-134.

1690. Pontes, Elõi. "Victor Hugo, Desenhista e Caricaturista." *O Globo*. August 4, 1952.

1691. Raynal, Maurice. *De Goya a Gauguin*. Coll. "Les Grands Siècles de la Peinture." Geneva, Paris, New York: Skira, 1951.

1692. Ribaud-Moisan, André. *Dix Ans d'Histoire en Cent Dessins*. Paris: Albin Michel, 1968.

1693. Ries, Gregor. "Pierre Serons 'Kleine Welten.'" *ICOM*. October 1992, pp. 48-51.

1694. "Rolandael." *Mieux Vaut en Rire*. No. 14, 1989, pp. 77-80.

1695. Rudwick, M.J.S. "Caricature As a Source for the History of Science: De la Beche's Anti-Lyellian Sketches of 1831." *Isis.* December 1975, pp. 534-560.

1696. Sadoul, Numa. *Portraits à Plume et au Pinceau.* Grenoble: Eds. Jacques Glénat, 1976. (Interviews with Bretécher, Dubos, Forest, Godard, Goscinny, Macherot, Mandryka, Morris, Pichard, Roba, Tabary, Uderzo).

1697. Samson, Jacques. "Quelle Critique pour la Bande Dessinée?" *Les Cahiers de la Bande Dessinée.* 63, 1985, pp. 52-55.

1698. Sanders, Alain and Sophie Leroy de Harbonville. "À la Rencontre de Georges Fronval." *Le Nouveau Bédésup.* 31, pp. 4-7.

1699. Schwarz, Heinrich. "Daumier, Gill and Nadar." *Gazette des Beaux-Arts.* 19 (1957), pp. 89-106.

1700. Scotto, U. "Enrico De Seta." *Phénix.* No. 20, 1971.

1701. Scotto, U. "Les Cauchemars de J. Le Gall." *Phénix.* No. 22, 1972.

1702. Somm, H. *Somm.* Coll. "Les Maîtres Humoristes." Paris: Libr. Félix Juven, 1907.

1703. Taillandier, François. "'L'Esprit Humanos' de Salvador Soldevila." *Livres Hebdo.* 8:38 (1986), pp. 60-61.

1704. Tibéri, Jean-Paul. *Dossier Pieds Nickelés.* Hounoux: SEDLI; Jacky Goupil, 1984. (Louis Forton).

1705. "Une Bande Dessinée pour l'Amour de Régine Crespin." *Marie Claire.* No. 181, 1967.

1706. Vallotton, Felix, Ashley St.-James, and André Berelowitch. *Vallotton: Dessinateur de Presse.* Paris: Chêne, 1979. 186 pp.

1707. Van Belle, Anita and Marie Mandy. "Ah, Vous Vous Éditez?" *Les Cahiers de la Bande Dessinée.* 61, 1985, pp. 35-39.

1708. Vandooren, Philippe. *Comment on Devient Créateur de Bande Dessinées.* (Interviews with Franquin and Gillain). Ed. Gerard and Co., Marabout, coll. "Reussir," No. MS120. Verviers: 1969.

1709. "Vuillemin." *Mieux Vaut en Rire.* No. 13, 1989, pp. 46-50.

1710. Wolinski, Georges. *Wolinski dans l'Huma.* Paris: Mazarine, 1980.

Ache, Jean

1711. Faur, Jean-Claude. "Comment Je n'Ai Pas Réédité Tout Jean Ache." *L'Hebdo de la B.D.* Nos. 101-102, 1991, pp. 5-6.

1712. Faur, Jean-Claude. *Jean Ache: Peinture et Bande Dessinée.* Marseilles: Bibliothéque Municipale, 1981. 8 pp.

Alexis (Dominique Vallet)

1713. Filippini, Henri. "Bibliographie d'Alexis." *Schtroumpf. Les Cahiers de la Bande Dessinée.* 38, 1978, pp. 39-47.

1714. Filippini, Henri. "Hommages et Interviews en Forme d'Hommages: Gotlib." *Schtroumpf. Les Cahiers de la Bande Dessinée.* 38, 1978, pp. 15-18.

1715. Filippini, Henri. "Hommages et Interviews en Forme d'Hommages: Lob." *Schtroumpf. Les Cahiers de la Bande Dessinée.* 38, 1978, p. 22.

1716. Filippini, Henri. "Hommages et Interviews en Forme d'Hommages: Olivier Hugla." *Schtroumpf. Les Cahiers de la Bande Dessinée.* 38, 1978, p. 12.

1717. Filippini, Henri. "Hommages et Interviews en Forme d'Hommages: Lauzier." *Schtroumpf. Les Cahiers de la Bande Dessinée.* 39, 1978, p. 20.

1718. Léturgie, Jean. "Hommages et Interviews en Forme d'Hommages: Guy Vidal." *Schtroumpf. Les Cahiers de la Bande Dessinée.* 38, 1978, p. 36.

1719. Sotto, Jean-Michel. "Entretien avec Alexis." *Schtroumpf. Les Cahiers de la Bande Dessinée.* 37, 1978, pp. 7-10.

Auclair, Claude

1720. Cance, Louis. "Bibliographie de Claude Auclair." *Les Cahiers de la Bande Dessinée.* 59, 1984, pp. 41-42.

1721. Chante, Alain. "L'Eau, le Feu, la Terre et le Ciel dans l'Oeuvre d'Auclair." *Les Cahiers de la Bande Dessinée.* 58, 1984, pp. 25-28.

1722. de Pierpont, Jacques. "Auclair avant Simon." *Les Cahiers de la Bande Dessinée.* 58, 1984, pp. 14-16.

1723. Deschamps, Alain. "Bran Ruz, Histoire d'Une Rencontre." *Les Cahiers de la Bande Dessinée.* 58, 1984, pp. 32-34.

1724. Groensteen, Thierry. "Entretien avec Claude Auclair." *Les Cahiers de la Bande Dessinée*. 58, 1984, pp. 7-13.

1725. "Interview mit Claude Auclair. (Aus dem Französischen Übersetzt von Cuno Affolter)." *Comixene. Das Comicfachmagazin*. 8:37 (1981), pp. 6-9.

1726. Jonsson, Jon Sveinbjorn. "Claude Auclair er Død." *TEGN*. 1, 1990, p. 33.

1727. Lehner, René. "Claude Auclair und die Chronik Einer Kommenden Zeit." *Comixene. Das Comicfachmagazin*. 8:37 (1981), pp. 4-6.

Avelot, Henri

1728. Avelot, Henri. *Henri Avelot*. Coll. "Les Maîtres Humoristes." Les Meilleures Dessins. Les Meilleures Légendes. Paris: Libr. Félix Juven, 1908.

1729. Avelot, Henri. *Traité Pratique de la Caricature et du Dessin Humoristique*. Paris: Henri Laurens, 1932.

Avoine

1730. Avoine. *Eclats de Sourire*. Tournai: Casterman, 1988.

1731. Avoine. *Faites-Moi Rire, Je Pars Dans Quatre Minutes*. Paris: B. Diffusion, n.d. 93 pp.

1732. Avoine, *et al. Le Ski*. Grenoble: Glénat, 1982.

1733. Avoine, *et al. Le Vin*. Paris: HA! Humoristes Associes, 1980.

Bac, Ferdinand

1734. Bac, Ferdinand. *Belles de Nuit*. Preface by Pierre Veber. Paris: H. Simonis Empis Éditeur, n.d.

1735. Bac, Ferdinand. *Des Images*. 100 Dessins. Paris: H. Simonis Empis Éditeur, 1901.

1736. Bac, Ferdinand. *Femmes de Théâtre*. 20 Dessins en Couleurs. Prologue by Yvette Guilbert. Paris: H. Simonis Empis Éditeur, n.d.

1737. Bac, Ferdinand. *Fernand* (sic) *Bac*. Coll. "Maîtres Humoristes." Preface by Marcel Prévost. Paris: Librairie Félix Juven, 1907.

1738. Bac, Ferdinand. *La Comédie Féminine*. 100 Dessins. Preface by F. Bac. Paris: H. Simonis Empis Éditeur, 1899.

1739. Bac, Ferdinand. *La Femme Intime*. Preface by Marcel Prévost. Paris: H. Simonis Empis Éditeur, n.d.

1740. Bac, Ferdinand. *Les Alcôves*. Preface by Richard O'Monroy. Paris: H. Simonis Empis Éditeur, n.d.

1741. Bac, Ferdinand. *Les Amants*. 100 Dessins en Couleurs. Preface by Un Amant. Paris: H. Simonis Empis Éditeur, 1898.

1742. Bac, Ferdinand. *Les Fêtes Galantes*. 20 Dessins en Couleurs. Preface by Arsène Houssaye. Paris: H. Simonis Empis Éditeur, n.d.

1743. Bac, Ferdinand. *Les Maîtresses*. Album en Couleurs. Preface by Félicien Champsaur. Paris: H. Simonis Empis Éditeur, 1897.

1744. Bac, Ferdinand. *Modèles d'Artistes*. Paris: H. Simonis Empis Éditeur, n.d.

1745. Bac, Ferdinand. *Nos Amoureuses*. 20 Dessins en Couleurs. Paris: H. Simonis Empis Éditeur, n.d.

1746. Bac, Ferdinand. *Nos Femmes*. 20 Dessins en Couleurs. Preface by Maurice Donnay. Paris: H. Simonis Empis Éditeur, n.d.

1747. Bac, Ferdinand. *Petites Folies*. 100 Dessins. Preface by Bernard Vandérem. Paris: H. Simonis Empis Éditeur, 1903.

1748. Bac, Ferdinand, Albert Guillaume, Guydo, Charles Léandre, *et al. Quelques Tranches de Vie*. Album en Couleurs. Paris: Chez Charpentier et E. Fasquelle Éditeurs, 1896.

1749. Lima, Herman. "Ferdinand Bac e a Dança das Suas Libélulas." *Rio Magazine* (Rio de Janeiro). August 1948.

1750. Puech, Lucien. "Ferdinand Bac Intime." In *L'Album*. Paris: Montgrédien et Cie, 1901.

Baissat, Bernard

1751. Didier, Pascal and André Baur. "Baissat." *Mieux Vaut en Rire*. No. 13, 1989, pp. 69-70.

1752. "Le Canard Enchaîné: Entretien avec Bernard Baissat." *Mieux Vaut en Rire*. No. 13, 1989, pp. 71-72. (Reprinted from *Le Monde Libertaire*. October 8, 1988).

Barbe

1753. Barbe. *Le Condottiere*. Grenoble: Glénat, 1980.

1754. Barbe. *Nous Sommes Trop*. Grenoble: Glénat, 1981.

Baudelaire, Charles

1755. Hofmann, Werner. "Baudelaire et la Caricature." *Preuves*. 207 (1967), pp. 38-43.

1756. McLees, Ainslie A. "*Argot Platique*: Baudelaire and Caricature." Ph.D. dissertation, University of Virginia, 1980.

1757. McLees, Ainslie A. "Baudelaire and Caricature: Argot Plastique." *Symposium*. Fall 1984, pp. 221-233.

1758. McIntosh, Malcolm. "Baudelaire's Caricature Essays." *Modern Language Notes*. 71:7 (1956), pp. 1503-1507.

1759. Pichois, Claude. "La Date de l'Essai de Baudelaire sur le Rire et les Caricaturistes." *Lettres Romanes*. August 1, 1965, pp. 213-216.

Bélom

1760. Bélom. *Ça Occupe*. Grenoble: Glénat, 1983.

1761. Bélom. *Et Que Ça Saute!* Grenoble: Glénat, 1984.

Benoit, Ted (Thierry)

1762. Delavaud, Gilles and Pierre Donnadieu. "Entretien avec Ted Benoit." *Éducation 2000*. 21, 1982, pp. 21-28.

1763. Glénat, Jacques. "Benoit Brisefer." *Cahiers Universitaires*. No. 12, 1971.

Bertall

1764. Bertall. *Album de Caricatures*. Paris: Au Bureau du Journal *La Semaine*, 1848.

1765. Bertall. *Le Grélot au Salon*. Le Salon de 1872 Depeint et Dessiné par Bertall. En Couleurs. Paris: Malu, Éd., 1872.

Bilal, Enki

1766. Andrevon, Jean-Pierre. "Bilal, Un Itinéraire de la Déglingue." *Schtroumpf. Les Cahiers de la Bande Dessinée*. 53, 1982, pp. 33-38.

1767. Bergeron, Francis. "Relecture(s): "Partie de Chasse" de Christin et Bilal." *Le Nouveau Bédésup*. 29/30, 1984, pp. 32-33.

1768. Bernardi, Luigi. "Bilal? E in Fuorigioco." *Comic Art*. No. 46, 1988, p. 31.

1769. Bilal, Enki. *The Call of the Stars*. Syracuse, New York: Flying Buttress, 1978. 46 pp.

1770. Bilal, Enki. *Gods in Chaos*. New York: Catalan Communications, 1987.

1771. Bilal, Enki. *The Woman Trap*. New York: Catalan, 1988.

1772. Bilal, Enki and Jean-Pierre Dionnet. *Exterminator 17*. New York: Catalan Communications, 1986. 62 pp.

1773. "Enki Bilal." *Society of Strip Illustration Newsletter*. April 1989, pp. 6-11.

1774. Filippini, Henri. "Bibliographie." *Schtroumpf. Les Cahiers de la Bande Dessinée*. 53, 1982, pp. 47-50.

1775. Filippini, Henri. "Entretien avec Enki Bilal." *Schtroumpfanzine*. 18, 1978, pp. 13-19.

1776. Giacobbi, Carole. "Bilal et Littérature." *Figaroscope*. January 22, 1992, p. 9.

1777. Gisle, Jon. "Enki Bilal—Realisten i Virkelighetens Grenseland (og Hinsides...)." *TEGN*. 1, 1990, pp. 20-25.

1778. Groensteen, Thierry. "'Comme un Diament Noir.' La Foire aux Immortels." *Schtroumpf. Les Cahiers de la Bande Dessinée*. 53, 1982, pp. 39-43.

1779. Kaps, Joachim. "Endstation Äquator Enki Bilals Werk Seit Beginn der 80er Jahre." *Comic Info*. 1/1993, pp. 16-25.

1780. Lecigne, Bruno. "Enki Bilal ou le Pouvoir Ironisé." *Schtroumpf. Les Cahiers de la Bande Dessinée*. 53, 1982, pp. 15-20.

1781. Lecigne, Bruno and Jean-Pierre Tamine. "Bilal Coloriste." *Schtroumpf. Les Cahiers de la Bande Dessinée*. 53, 1982, pp. 23-31.

1782. Lesueur, Patrick. "Enki Bilal: 'Genau Nach Süden.'" *Comic Info*. 1/1993, p. 26.

1783. Léturgie, Jean and Henri Filippini. "Enki Bilal (Entretien)." *Schtroumpf. Les Cahiers de la Bande Dessinée*. 53, 1982, pp. 7-13.

1784. Pomerleau, Luc. "Pierre Christin and Enki Bilal: Called to Comics." *Comics Journal*. May 1989, pp. 62-77.

1785. Thévenet, Jean-Marc. *Images pour Un Film: les Décors d'Enki Bilal pour 'La Vie Est un Roman' d'Alain Resnais*. Paris: Dargaud, 1983. 80 pp.

Binet, Christian

1786. Binet. *Les Bidochon: Roman d'Amour*. Paris: France Loisirs, 1986. 52 pp.

1787. Frémion, Yves. *"Dossier Binet."* Hounoux: SEDLI; Jacky Goupil, 1984.

Blondeau, Georges (Gé Bé)

1788. Carano, Ranieri. "Gé Bé, l'Incubo Buono." *Linus*. No. 41, 1968, pp. 1-9.

1789. "Gébé." *Mieux Vaut en Rire*. No. 14, 1989, pp. 17-25.

Bofa, Gus

1790. Bofa, Gus. *Slogans*. Paris: Librairie des Champs-Elysées, 1940.

1791. Charensol, Georges. "Gus Bofa." *Le Portique* (Paris). No. 6, 1947.

1792. Edelman, Jean. *Gus Bofa et les Illustrateurs de l'Entre-Deux-Guerres*. Paris: Musée-Galerie de la SEITA, 1983.

Bonnet, Honoré

1793. Bonnet, Honoré. *Honoréquiem.* Paris: A.C.R.I., 1986.

1794. Bonnet, Honoré. *La Voix des Sports "Traits Honoré."* Villeneuve d'Ascq: Author, n.d.

Bosc, Jean-Maurice

1795. Bosc. *Boscaves au Feu.* Paris: Jean-Jacques Pauvert, 1959.

1796. Bosc. *J'Aime Beaucoup Ce Que Vous Faites.* Paris: Denoël, 1985.

1797. Bosc. *Je T'Aime.* Paris: Albin Michel, 1969.

1798. Bosc, Jean-Maurice. *L'Armée.* Paris: Denöel, 1987. 62 pp.

1799. Bosc. *Le Fleur dans Tous Ses États.* Paris: Tchou, 1968.

1800. Bosc. *Les Boscaves.* Paris: Éditions Denoël, 1965.

1801. Bosc. *Mort au Tyran.* Paris: Jean-Jacques Pauvert, 1959.

1802. Bosc. *Petit Biens.* Paris: Fernand Hazan, 1956.

1803. Bosc. *Si de Gaulle Était Petit.* Paris: Jean-Jacques Pauvert, 1968. 120 pp.

1804. Mohamad Ali Baniasadi. [Bosc]. *Kayhan Caricature.* June 1993.

Bouchard, Gilbert

1805. "Rencontre avec Gilbert Bouchard." *Bédésup.* 1st-2nd Trim., 1989, pp. 8-9.

1806. "Rencontre avec Gilbert Bouchard." *Bédésup.* No. 48/49, 1989, pp. 8-11.

Bouchot, Henri

1807. Bouchot, Henri. "Charges d' Horace Vernet d' Après Ses Confrères de l'Institut." *Gazette des Beaux-Arts.* November 1, 1897, pp. 393-408.

1808. Bouchot, Henri. *Les Livres à Vignettes du XIXe Siècle.* Paris: Edouard Rouveyre, Ed., 1891.

Bourgeon, François

1809. Alexandre, Pierre. "La Côte des Esclaves." In *Bourgeon à la Hune*, edited by L'Association Clovis, pp. 32-36. Grenoble: Eds. Jacques Glénat, 1986.

1810. Boudriot, Jean. "La Mer au Quotidien." In *Bourgeon à la Hune*, edited by L'Association Clovis, pp. 22-27. Grenoble: Eds. Glénat, 1986.

1811. Cance, Louis and Thierry Groensteen. "Fiche Bibliographique." *Les Cahiers de la Bande Dessinée*. 65, 1985, p. 38.

1812. Corteggiani, François. *François Bourgeon. Le Passager du Temps*. Grenoble: Eds. Jacques Glénat, 1983.

1813. Forni, Pierre and Yves Frémion. "Bourgeon's Story." In *Bourgeon à la Hune*, edited by L'Association Clovis, pp. 4-13. Grenoble: Eds. Jacques Glénat, 1986.

1814. Groensteen, Thierry. "Entretien avec François Bourgeon." *Les Cahiers de la Bande Dessinée*. 65, 1985, pp. 8-16.

1815. "Interview mit François Bourgeon." *Comixene. Das Comicfachmagazin*. 8:37 (1981), pp. 18-20.

1816. L'Association Clovis. *Bourgeon à la Hune*. Grenoble: Eds. Jacques Glénat, 1986.

1817. Léturgie, Jean. "Entretien avec François Bourgeon." *Schtroumpfanzine*. 29, 1979, pp. 13-19.

1818. Luxardo, Hervé. "Révoltes et Conflits, le Monde en 1780." In *Bourgeon à la Hune*, edited by L'Association Clovis, pp. 28-31. Grenoble: Glénat, 1986.

1819. Saouter Caya, Catherine and Philippe Sohet. L' Esthétique de Bourgeon." *Les Cahiers de la Bande Dessinée*. 65, 1985, pp. 17-21.

Bretécher, Claire

1820. Bretécher, Claire. "Claire Bretécher's Comedie Français: Trials of Raoul." *Ms*. March 1978, pp. 64-66.

1821. Bretécher, Claire. *More Frustration*. London: Methuen, 1983.

1822. Bretécher, Claire. *Still More Frustration*. London: Methuen, 1986.

1823. Destombes, Patrick and Jean-Pierre Tamine. "Le Miroir Immobile de Bretécher." *Bédésup*. 20, 1982, pp. 39-45.

1824. Kaeppelin, Philippe. "A Propos des Mères de Claire Bretécher." *Education 2000*. 21, 1982, pp. 40-44.

1825. *National Lampoon Presents Claire Bretécher*. New York: National Lampoon, 1978. 96 pp.

1826. Settekorn, Wolfgang. "Zur Konstituierung von Sprechaktsequenzen (Bretécher, Claire: 'La Gueule.')." In *Bildung und Ausbildung in der Romania. Bd. 1: Literaturgeschichte und Texttheorie*, edited by Rolf Kloepfer, Arnold Rothe, Henning Kraus, and Thomas Kotschi, eds., pp. 522-548. Munich: Fink, 1979.

1827. "Slicing the Baloney with Style; Work of C. Bretecher." *Time*. May 8, 1978, p. 91.

Bridenne

1828. Bridenne, Michel. *Saison des Amours*. Paris: Glénat, 1984.

1829. "Bridenne." *Mieux Vaut en Rire*. No. 5 (n.d.), pp. 29-39.

Cappiello, Leonetto

1830. Bousquet, Jacques. "Leonetto Cappiello et Son Oeuvre." *Comédia Illustré* (Paris).

1831. Cappiello, Leonetto. *Album. 70 Caricatures*. Paris: H. Floury, Éditeur, 1905.

1832. Cappiello, Leonetto. *Album. 70 Dessins*. Paris: H. Flory, Éditeur, 1905.

1833. Chevalier, Denys. "L. Cappiello." *Arts-Spectacles* (Paris). January 17, 1947.

1834. Lo Duca. *L'Affiche*. Paris: Presses Universitaires de France, 1945.

1835. Nathanson, Thadée. "Cappiello." *Arts-Spectacles* (Paris). January 17, 1947.

1836. Vienot, Jacques. *L. Cappiello, Sa Vie et Son Oeuvre*. Preface by Jean Cocteau. Paris: Éditions de Clermont, 1946.

Caran d'Ache

1837. Beerbohm, Max. "Caran d'Ache, a Forgotten Artist." *Liliput* (London). September 1942.

1838. Brisson, Adolphe. "Caran d'Ache." In *Nos Humoristes*. Paris: Soc. d'Édition Artistique, n.d.

1839. Caran d'Ache. *Album*. Ière, IIᵉ et IIIᵉ Séries. Paris: Plon-Nourit et Cie, n.d.

1840. Caran d'Ache. *Bric à Brac*. Paris: Plon-Nourit et Cie, n.d.

1841. Caran d'Ache. *Carnet de Chèques*. Paris: Plon-Nourit et Cie, 1892.

1842. Caran d'Ache. *C'Est à Prendre ou à Laisser*. Paris: Plon-Nourit et Cie, n.d.

1843. Caran d'Ache. *Gros et Détail*. Paris: Plon-Nourit et Cie, n.d.

1844. Caran d'Ache. *Histoires en Images*. Preface by Jean-François Borv. Paris: 1979.

1845. Caran d'Ache. *Les Courses dans l'Antiquité*. Paris: Plon-Nourit et Cie, 1900.

1846. Caran d'Ache. *Les Lundis de Caran d'Ache* (4 Albums). Paris: Libraire Plon et Librairie du Figaro, n.d.

1847. Caran d'Ache. *Pages de Histoire*. Paris: n.d.

1848. Caran d'Ache. *Pssit!* Em Colaboração com Forain. Paris: 1898.

1849. Caran d'Ache. *Caran d'Ache*. Coll. "Les Maîtres Humoristes," Ière, et IIᵉ Series. Paris: Librairie Félix Juven, n.d.

1850. "Caran d'Ache. Fabricante de Bonecos." *Serões* (Lisbon). No. 29.

1851. "Échos de Paris, Les." *Les Annales* (Paris). March 7, 1909.

1852. Maurice, A.B. "Art of Caran d'Ache." *Bookman*. April 1909, pp. 132-139.

Cardon

1853. "Interview: Cardon." *Kayhan Caricature*. June 1992.

1854. "Interview: Cardon." *Kayhan Caricature*. August 1992.

Carlègle

1855. Carlègle. *C'Est un Oiseau Qui Vient de France*. Paris: Soc. Littèraire de France, 1916.

1856. Carlègle. *La Chasse à l'Élephant ou "les Vertus Menagères."* Paris: Éditions Bourrelier-Chimènes, 1931.

Chaland, Yves

1857. Arrouye, Jean. "La Courte Échelle." *Les Cahiers de la Bande Dessinée.* 60, 1984, pp. 92-94.

1858. Bouyer, Sylvain. "Le Retour de la Comète." *Les Cahiers de la Bande Dessinée.* 71, 1986, pp. 92-93.

1859. Faur, Jean-Claude. "À la Rencontre de... Y. Chaland." *Le Nouveau Bédésup.* 36/37, 1986, pp. 3-13.

1860. Kronborg, Steffen. "Yves Chaland Død, 33 År." *Seriejournalen.* September 1990, p. 15.

1861. Lecigne, Bruno. "Chaland. L'Art Utéro-Narratif." *Les Cahiers de la Bande Dessinée.* 60, 1984, pp. 86-87.

1862. Steacy, Ken. "Yves Chaland: Visionary of Europe's Atomic Age." *Comics Journal.* February 1991, pp. 29-30.

Cham (Charles-Henri Amédée de Nóe)

1863. Cham. *Actualistés 1850-51.* 2 Vols. Paris: Chez Aubert et Cie, 1851.

1864. Cham. *Assemblée National Comique.* Text by Auguste Liseux. Illustrations by Cham. Paris: Michel Levy Frères, Librs. Edts., 1850.

1865. Cham. *Au Bal de l'Opéra.* Paris: Au Bureau de Journal *Le Charivari,* n.d.

1866. Cham. *Au Diable les Domestiques.* Paris: 1857.

1867. Cham. *Baigneurs et Buveurs d'Eau.* Paris: Au Bureau du Journal *Le Charivari,* n.d.

1868. Cham. *Ces Jolis Messieurs,* Paris: Arnauld de Vresse, n.d.

1869. Cham. *Croquis en l'Air.* Paris: Au Bureau du Journal *Le Charivari,* n.d.

1870. Cham. *Cours de Physique.* Paris: Maison Martinet, n.d.

1871. Cham. *Émotions de Chasse.* Paris: Librairie Nouvelle, n.d.

1872. Cham. *La Bourse Illustrée*. Paris: Au Bureau du Journal *Le Charivari*, n.d.

1873. Cham. *Les Folies Parisiennes: Quinze Années Comiques, 1864-1879*. Intro. by Léon Gérome. Paris: Calman, 1883.

1874. Cham. *Le Salon de 1869 Charivarisé*. Paris: Arnauld de Vresse, n.d.

1875. Cham. *Mélanges Comiques*. Paris: Au Bureau du Journal *Le Charivari*, n.d.

1876. Cham. *Nouvelles Croquades*. Paris: Au Bureau du Journal *Le Charivari*, n.d.

1877. Cham. *Nouvelles Leçons de Civilité*. Paris: Arnauld de Vresse, n.d.

1878. Cham. *Promenades à l'Exposition*. Paris: Au Bureau du Journal *Le Charivari*, n.d.

1879. Cham. *Proudhoniana*. Paris: Au Bureau du Journal *Le Charivari*, n.d.

1880. Cham. *Revue du Salon de 1853*. Paris: Au Bureau du Journal *Le Charivari*, n.d.

1881. de Saliès, Alexandre. "Preface to Ignotus du Figaro." *Album Cham*. Paris: n.d.

1882. Halévy, Ludovic. *Douze Années Comiques par Cham 1868-1879*. Paris: C. Lévy, 1880.

1883. Kunzle, David. "Cham., the Popular Caricaturist—Cham and Daumier: Two Careers, Two Reputations, Two Audiences." *Gazette des Beaux-Arts*. December 1980, pp. 213-224.

1884. Kunzle, David. "Les Miserables de Victor Hugo, Lus, Medites, Commentes et Illustres par Cham." *Gazette des Beaux-Arts*. July/August 1985, pp. 22-34.

1885. Picard, Gaston. "Cham Auteur Dramatique." *Revue Mondiale*. September 1929, pp. 301-306.

1886. Ribeyre, Félix. *Cham, Sa Vie et Son Oeuvre*. Paris: E. Plon-Nourit, Éd., 1884.

1887. Vachon, Marius. "Cham." *Gazette des Beaux-Arts*. 20 (1879), pp. 443-446.

1888. Whiteing, Richard. "Cham." *Scribner's Monthly*. March 1880.

Charlier, Jean-Michel

1889. Cormier, Sylvain. "L'Oeuvre de Jean-Michel Charlier: Notes de (re)Lectures." *La Nouvelle Barre du Jour*. February 1982, pp. 53-57.

1890. Filippini, Henri. "Entretien avec Jean-Michel Charlier." *Schtroumpf.* No. 37, 10th year, p. 16.

1891. "Jean-Michel død, 64 År." *Serieskaberen.* December 1989, p. 8.

1892. Léturgie, Jean. "Un Conteur d'Histoires." *Schtroumpf. Les Cahiers de la Bande Dessinée.* 37, 1978, pp. 23-24.

1893. Moliterni, Claude. "J.-M. Charlier." *Phénix.* No. 6, 1st Trim., 1968, p. 48.

Chaval

1894. Bostel, Honoré. "Ses Dessins de Match Que Chaval Préferait." *Paris-Match.* No. 982, 1968.

1895. Chaval. *L'Animalier.* Paris: Albin Michel, 1970.

1896. Chaval. *L'Homme.* Paris: Albin Michel, 1970.

1897. Chaval. *Vive Guttenberg!* Paris: Robert Laffont, 1956.

Chéret, André

1898. Filippini, Henri. "Bibliographie." *Schtroumpf. Les Cahiers de la Bande Dessinée.* 46, 1980, pp. 42-50.

1899. Filippini, Henri. "Rahan C'Est André Chéret." *Schtroumpf. Les Cahiers de la Bande Dessinée.* 46, 1980, p. 17.

1900. Filippini, Henri and Jean Léturgie. "Entretien avec André Chéret." *Schtroumpf. Les Cahiers de la Bande Dessinée.* 46, 1980, pp. 7-16, 20-25.

1901. Roux, Antoine. "Pour une Poignée de Dents de Machaidorus en Plus ou André Chéret, le Roi des Roués." *Schtroumpf. Les Cahiers de la Bande Dessinée.* 46, 1980, pp. 31-40.

Christin, Pierre

1902. Christin, Pierre. *Heroes of the Equinox.* New York: Dargaud, 1984.

1903. Christin, Pierre. *Welcome to Alflofol.* New York: Dargaud, 1984.

1904. Christin, Pierre. *The World Without Stars*. New York: Dargaud, 1984.

1905. Christin, Pierre and Jean-Claude Mézières. *Ambassador of the Shadows*. New York: Dargaud, 1984.

1906. Zanotto, Piero. "Anche Il Franchesi Hanno Il Loro Linus." *Carlino Sera* (Bologna). July 13, 1966; *Nazione Sera* (Firenze). July 12, 1966.

Christophe (Georges Colomb)

1907. Caradec, François. *Christophe*. Paris: Grasset, 1956.

1908. Caradec, François. "Genèse et Métamorphose des Oeuvres de Christophe." In *Les Faceties du Sapeur Camember*. Paris: 1958.

Cocteau, Jean

1909. Faur, Jean-Claude. *Jean Cocteau Poète Graphique*. Marseilles: Bibliothèque Municipale, 1983. 45 pp.

1910. Faur, Jean-Claude. "Jean Cocteau Poète Méditerranéen." *Impressions du Sud* (Aix). No. 4, 1984, pp. 16-17.

1911. *Jean Cocteau. Drawings: 129 Drawings from "Dessins."* Foreword by Edouard Dermit. New York: Dover, 1972. 129 pp.

Cuvelier, Paul

1912. Bourdil, P.Y. "La Beauté du Corps ou l'Art de P. Cuvelier." *Cahiers Universitaires*. No. 8, 1970.

1913. Cance, Luis. "Bibliographie de Cuvelier." *Cahiers Universitaires*. No. 8, 1970.

1914. Glénat, Jacques. "Schtroumpf Rencontre Cuvelier." *Cahiers Universitaires*. No. 8, 1970.

1915. Goddin, Philippe. *Paul Cuvelier. L'Aventure Artistique. Etude Biographique et Critique*. Brussels: Magic Strip, 1981.

1916. Goddin, Philippe. *Corentin et les Chemins du Merveilleux. Paul Cuvelier et la Bande Dessinée. Avec un Témoignage de Hergé*. Brussels, Paris: Eds. du Lombard, 1984.

1917. Ponzi, Jacques. "Cuvelier." *Rantanplan*. No. 12, 1968, p. 3.

Daumier, Honoré

1918. Adhémar, Jean. "Daumier 1808-1879." In *Les Peintres Célèbres*. Genèva, Paris: Éditions d'Art, Lucien Mazenod, 1948.

1919. Adhémar, Jean. *Daumier, le Peintre Graveur*. Exhibition Catalogue. Preface by Julien Cain. Paris: Bibliothèque Nationale, 1958.

1920. Adhémar, Jean. *Daumier. Lithographies, Gravures sur Bois Sculptures*. Exhibition Catalogue. Foreword by P.A. Lemoisne and J. Laran. Paris: Bibliotheque Nationale, 1934.

1921. Adhémar, Jean. *Honoré Daumier*. Paris: Éditions Pierre Tisné, 1954.

1922. Adhémar, Jean. *Honoré Daumier: Drawings and Watercolours*. Preface by Claude Rogér-Marx. New York: Macmillan; Basle: Holbein-Verlag, 1954.

1923. Adhémar, Jean, ed. *Doctors and Medicine in the Works of Daumier*. London: Peter Owen, 1965; Boston: Boston Book and Art Publishers, 1970.

1924. "Aesculape." *Revue Médicale* (Paris). Articles on Daumier in December 1958, January 1959, March 1959.

1925. Alexandre, Arséne. *Daumier*. Coll. "Maîtres de l'Art Moderne." Paris: Les Éditions Rieder, 1928.

1926. Alexandre, Arséne. *Honoré Daumier: L'Homme et et l'Oeuvre*. Paris: H. Laurens, 1888.

1927. Alvarus (Álvaro Cotrim). *Daumier e Pedro I*. Rio de Janeiro: Ministério da Educação e Cultura, Serviço de Documentação, 1961.

1928. Alvarus (Álvaro Cotrim). "Jean Cherpin Restabelece a Verdade Sôbre a Vida de Daumier." *Leitura* (Rio de Janeiro). May 1959.

1929. Armingeat, Jacqueline. *Honoré Daumier, Les Gens du Spectacle*. Foreword by François Périer. Paris: 1973.

1930. Balzer, Wolfgang. *Der Junge Daumier und Seine Kampfgefährten*. Dresden: 1965.

1931. Baty, Gaston. "La Légende de Robert Macaire." In *Hommes et Mondes*. Paris: Éditions Jacques Vautrain, April 1947, tome II, n.° 9.

1932. Baudelaire, Charles. *Les Dessins de Daumier*. Coll. "Ars Graphica," Études et Documents. Paris: Aux Éditions G. Crés et Cie, 1924.

1933. Bell, Clive. "Daumier." In *Landmarks in Nineteenth Century Painting*. London: Chatto and Windus, 1928.

1934. Bertels, Kurt. *Honoré Daumier als Lithograph*. Coll. "Klassiche Illustratoren." Vol. 4 Munich, Leipzig: R. Piper, Verlag, 1908.

1935. Bertram, Anthony. *Daumier 1808-1897*. Coll. "The World's Masters." New York, London: The Studio Publications Inc., 1934.

1936. Beytout, Gavarni and Louis Sergent. *La Pharmacie et la Médecine dans l'Oeuvre de Daumier*. Paris: Les Pharmaciens Bibliophiles, 1932.

1937. Billioud, J. *Daumier*. Exhibition Catalogue, Musée Cantini, Marseilles, June 1947.

1938. Bouchot, Henri. *Les Livres à Vignettes du XIX Siècle*. Paris: Edouard Rouveyre, Éd., 1891. (Daumier, Gavarnia, Grandville).

1939. Bouvy, Eugéne. *Daumier: L'Oeuvre Gravé du Maître. Reproduction de Toutes les Planches; Notices Sur Chaque Ouvrage et Sur Chaque Planche, Introduction Historique et Index Alphabétique*. 2 Vols. Paris: Maurice Le Garrec, 1933.

1940. Bouvy, Eugéne. *Trente-six Bustes de H. Daumier*. Paris: Maurice Le Garrec, 1932.

1941. Brughetti, Romualdo. "Daumier Piadoso y Rebelde." *Leoplan* (Buenos Aires). November 19, 1947.

1942. Carelli, André. "Daumier, um Gênio do Jornalismo Ilustrado." *Vamos Ler!* (Rio de Janeiro). January 28, 1943.

1943. Cary, Elisabeth L. "Daumier's Caricatures." *Putnam's*. August 1907, pp. 580-590.

1944. Cary, Elisabeth L. *Honoré Daumier. A Collection of His Social and Political Caricatures*. New York, London: G.P. Putnam's Son, 1907.

1945. Cassou, Jean. *Daumier*. Coll. "Artistes de Jadis et d'Aujourd'hui." Lausanne: Éditions Jean Marguerat, 1949.

1946. Cassou, Jean. "Daumier, l'Homme des Foules (1848-1948)." *Arts de France* (Paris). No. 21-22, 1948.

1947. *Catalogue de l'Exposition à la Bibliotèque Nationale 1934*. Paris: Éditions des Bibliotèques Nationales de France, 1934.

1948. Chambers, R.K. "Daumier's 'Histoire Ancienne': Art and Politics." *Arts*. September 1980, pp. 156-157.

1949. Champfleury. "Daumier." In *Histoire de la Caricature Moderne*. Paris: E. Dentu, Éd., n.d.

1950. Champfleury. *Daumier. Essais de Catalogue de l'Oeuvre Lithographié*. Paris: Librairie Parisienne, 1878.

1951. Champfleury. *H. Daumier. Catalogue de l'Oeuvre Lithographié et Gravé*. Paris: H. Heyman et J. Perois, Éditeurs, 1878.

1952. Champfleury. "Les Illustrateurs de Livres au XIXᵉ Siècle. Daumier." In *Le Livre*, Revue du Monde Littéraire. Paris: 1883.

1953. Charensol, Georges. "Daumier Peintre et Historien." *Historia* (Paris). May 1954.

1954. Cherpin, Jean. *Daumier et le Théâtre*. Paris: Bibliothèque du T.N.P. L'Arche Éd., 1958.

1955. Cherpin, Jean. "Daumier et le Théâtre." In *Arts et Livres de Provence*. Edisud: 1978.

1956. Cherpin, Jean. "Daumier et le Théâtre." *Aesculape* (Paris). March 1959.

1957. Cherpin, Jean. "L'Acte de Baptème de Daumier." *Aesculape* (Paris). March 1959.

1958. Cherpin, Jean. "Les Amis de Daumier." *Arts-Spectacles* (Paris). July 13, 1951.

1959. Cherpin, Jean. "Les Premiers Amis de Daumier." In *La Revue Française*. Paris: Noël 1951.

1960. Cherpin, Jean, André Negis, and Louis Sergent. "De la Maison de Santé à l'Imagination." *Aesculape* (Paris). March 1959.

1961. Childs, Elizabeth C. "Honoré Daumier and the Exotic Vision: Studies in French Caricature and Culture, 1830-1870." Ph.D. dissertation, Columbia University, 1989.

1962. Childs, Elizabeth C. "The Secret Agents of Satire: Daumier, Censorship, and the Image of the Exotic in Political Caricature, 1850-1860." *Proceedings of the Western Society for French History*. Forthcoming.

1963. Cochet, Gustavo. *Honoré Daumier*. Buenos Aires: Editorial Poseidon, 1945.

1964. Coquiot, Gustave. *H. Daumier. 1808-1979*. Paris: Larousse, 1901.

1965. Coquiot, Gustave. *Des Peintres Maudits*. Paris: André Delpeuch, Éd., 1924.

1966. Courthion, Pierre, ed. *Daumier Raconté par lui-Même et par Ses Amis*. Vésenaz, Geneva: Pierre Cailler, 1945.

1967. Craven, Thomas. "Daumier." In *Men of Art*. New York: Simon and Schuster, 1940.

1968. Daumier, Honoré. *Catalogue de l'Oeuvre Lithographiée de Daumier*. Collection du "Peintre-Graveur Illustré." Par Loys Delteil. 11 Vols. Paris: Chez l'Auteur, 1925-1930.

1969. Daumier, Honoré. *Catalogue des Peintures, Aquarelles et Dessins au Musée de l'Orangerie 1934*. Intro. by Claude Roger-Marx. Paris: Éditions des Musées Nationaux, 1934.

1970. Daumier, Honoré. *Croquis Variés*. Paris: Au Bureau du Journal *Le Charivari*, n.d.

1971. Daumier, Honoré. *Daumier und das Theater*. Intro. by Hans Rothe. Leipzig: Paul List, Verlag, 1925.

1972. Daumier, Honoré. *Daumier und der Krieg*. Intro. by Hans Rothe. Leipzig: Paul List, Verlag, 1926.

1973. Daumier, Honoré. *Daumier und die Ehe*. Intro. by Hans Rothe. Leipzig: Paul List, Verlag, 1927.

1974. Daumier, Honoré. *Daumier und die Justiz*. Intro. by Hans Rothe. Leipzig: Paul List, Verlag, 1928.

1975. Daumier, Honoré. *Daumier und die Politik*. Intro. by Hans Rothe. Leipzig: Paul List, Verlag, 1924.

1976. Daumier, Honoré. *Dessins et Aquarelles de la Coll. Holbein*. Intro. by Jean-Adhémar. Preface by Claude Roger-Marx. Paris: Les Éditions Braun, n.d.

1977. Daumier, Honoré. *Law and Justice*. New York: Pantheon Books, Inc., n.d.

1978. Daumier, Honoré. *Les Cent et un Robert Macaire*. Composés Sur les Idées et les Légendes de Charles Philipon. 2 Vols. Paris: Chez Aubert et Cie, Éditeurs du *Musée pour Rire*, 1839. Reprinted. Paris: Pierre Horay, 1979.

1979. Daumier, Honoré. *Les Gens de Justice*. Preface by Jules Cain. Monte-Carlo: Éditions du Livre, 1954.

1980. Daumier, Honoré. *Maler und Kunstliebhaber*. Zurich: Rascher Verlag, 1945.

1981. Daumier, Honoré. *Married Life*. New York: Pantheon Books Inc., n.d.

1982. Daumier, Honoré. *120 Lithographiques de Honoré Daumier*. Intro. by Jean Laran. Paris: Éditions d'Études et Documents, 1929.

1983. Daumier, Honoré. *Plaisirs de l'Été*. Paris: Bureau du *Journal Amusant* et Bureau du *Charivari*, n.d.

1984. Daumier, Honoré. *Physiologie de Robert Macaire*. Text by James Rousseau. Paris: Jules Laisné, Éd., 1842.

1985. Daumier, Honoré. *Physiologie du Poète*. Text by Sylvius. Paris: Aubert et Cie, 1842.

1986. Daumier, Honoré. *Politische Karikaturen*. Zurich: Rascher Verlag, 1944.

1987. Daumier, Honoré. *Revolution und Krieg*. Zurich: Rascher Verlag, 1945.

1988. Daumier, Honoré. *Theater und Publikum*. Zurich: Rascher Verlag, 1945.

1989. Daumier, Honoré. *Third-Class Railway Carriage*. The Metropolitan Museum of Art, New York. Intro. by S.L. Faison Jr. London: Percy Lund Humphries Publisher, n.d.

1990. Daumier, Honoré. *20 Litografias*. Prologue of Julio Rinaldini. Buenos Aires: Editorial Kraft Limitada, n.d.

1991. Daumier, Honoré. *240 Lithographien, Ausgewählt und Eingeleitet von Wilhelm Wartmann*. Zurich: Manesse, 1946. 240 pp.

1992. "Daumier." Special number of *Arts et Livres de Provence* (Marseilles). No. 8, 1948.

1993. *Daumier*. Coll."Les Maîtres Humoristes." Paris: Libr. Félix Juven, 1907.

1994. *Daumier, Eyewitness of an Epoch*. Intro. and notes by J.R. Kist. London: Victoria and Albert Museum, 1976.

1995. *Daumier Polemiste*. Catalogue des Lithogs. et Sculptures de Daumier au Musée Galliera, 1945. "Front National des Arts." Paris: 1934.

1996. *Daumier. Premier Bulletin Daumier* (Marseilles, Arts et Livres de Provence). No. 18, 1950.

1997. *Daumier Raconté par Lui-Même et par Ses Amis*. Genèva: Pierre Cailler, Éd. 1945. (Th. de Banville, Ch. Baudelaire, Henri Focillon, Jean Laran, Paul Valery).

1998. "Daumier, the Lawyer's Bane." *Literary Digest*. October 15, 1927, pp. 28-29.

1999. Dayot, Armand. "Daumier." *Les Annales* (Paris). August 12, 1900.

2000. Dayot, Armand. "Honoré Daumier." *Revue Rhénane*. April-May 1923.

2001. de Amador, Fernan Felix. "El Genio Vengativo de Daumier." *La Prensa* (Buenos Aires). Reprinted in *Vamos Ler!* (Rio de Janeiro). October 29, 1942.

2002. Delteil, Loys. *Le Peintre-Graveur Ilustré: Daumier*. 11 Vols. Paris: Chez l'Auteur, 1925-1930.

2003. Descaves, Lucien. "Honoré Daumier!" *Vamos Ler!* (Rio de Janeiro). February 18, 1943.

2004. Dété, Eugene. *Physionomies et Physiologies*. Foreword and catalogue by Louis Dimier, Paris: 1930.

2005. Drost, Wolfgang. "Daumier, Critique de la Civilisation Décadente." *Aesculape* (Paris). March 1959.

2006. Duranty. "Daumier." *Gazette des Beaux Arts* (Paris). May-June 1878.

2007. Durbé, Dario. *Daumier Scultore*. Milan: Poldi Pezzoli, 1961.

2008. Erio, Paul. "À la Mémoire de Daumier." *La Vie Illustrée* (Paris). August 3, 1900.

2009. Escholier, Raymond. *Daumier*. Paris: Michaud, 1913.

2010. Escholier, Raymond. *Daumier*. Coll. "Anciens et Modernes." Paris: H. Floury, Éditeur, 1934.

2011. Escholier, Raymond. *Daumier*. Coll. "Les Écrits et la Vie Anecdotique et Pittoresque des Grands Artistes." Paris: Louis Michaud, n.d.

2012. Escholier, Raymond. *Daumier et Son Monde*. Nancy: Berger-Levrault, 1965.

2013. Escholier, Raymond. *Daumier, Peintre et Lithographe*. Coll. "La Vie et l'Art Romantiques." Paris: H. Floury, Éditeur, 1923.

2014. Escholier, Raymond. "Daumier." In *La Peinture Française au XIXe Siècle*. Vol. 2. Paris: Libr. Floury, 1943.

2015. Fels, Florent. *Les Cent Robert Macaire de Daumier*. Coll. "L'Art et la Vie." Paris: Les Arts et les Livres, 1926.

2016. Fischer, Marcel. *Daumier der Maler*. Bern: Alfred Scherz, Verlag, 1950.

2017. Focillon, Henri. "Daumier." In *Maîtres de l'Estampe. Peintres-graveurs*. Paris: H. Laurens, Éd., 1930.

2018. Fontaines, André. *Daumier*. Albums d'Art Druet IV. Paris: Librairie de France, 1927.

2019. Fontaines, André. *La Peinture de Daumier*. Coll. "Ars Graphica." Paris: Aux Éditions G. Crés et Cie., 1923.

2020. Fosca, François. *Daumier*. Coll. "Les Maîtres de l'Art." 6th Ed. Paris: Libr. Plon, 1933.

2021. Fougerat, Emmanuel, *Honoré Daumier. 1808-1879*. Coll. "Album d'Art Retrospectif. Drogues et Peintures." Paris: Pavillée, Éd., n.d.

2022. Fouras, Hugues. "Pour Mieux Honoré Daumier Ses Amis Comptent 'Taper' l'État." *Le Figaro-Littéraire* (Paris). August 14, 1954.

2023. Foyer, Jean. *Daumier au Palais de Justice*. Paris: La Colombe, 1958.

2024. Frantz, Henri. *Daumier and Gavarni*. Notes by Henri Frantz and Octave Uzanne. London: Offices of *The Studio*, 1904.

2025. Fuchs, Eduard. *Der Maler Daumier*. Munich: Albert Langen, Verlag, 1930.

2026. Fuchs, Eduard. *Der Maler Daumier (Nachtrag Supplement)*. Munich: Albert Langen, Verlag, 1930.

2027. Fuchs, Eduard. *H. Daumier. Holzchnitte 1833-1870*. Munich: Albert Langen, Verlag, 1923.

2028. Fuchs, Eduard. *H. Daumier. Lithographien 1828-1851*. Munich: Albert Langen, Verlag, 1923.

2029. Fuchs, Eduard. *H. Daumier. Lithographien 1852-1860*. Munich: Albert Langen, Verlag, 1923.

2030. Gauthier, Maximilen. *Daumier 1808-1879*. "Coll. des Maîtres." Paris: Les Éditions Braun et Cie., 1939.

2031. Geoffroy, Gustave. "Daumier." In *Revue de l'Art Ancien et Moderne*. Paris: 1901.

2032. Geoffroy, Gustave. *Daumier*. Coll. "Les Artistes de Tous les Temps." Paris: Libr. de L'Art Ancien et Moderne, n.d.

2033. Gobin, Maurice. *Daumier Sculpteur (1808-79). Avec un Catalogue Raisonné et Illustré de l'Oeuvre Sculpté*. Paris: Pierre Cailler, Geneva, 1952.

2034. Goldstein, Ben. "Daumier's Spirit in American Art." *Print Review*. 11 (1980), pp. 127-144.

2035. Grappe, Georges. "Honoré Daumier." *L'Art Vivant* (Paris). May 1934.

2036. Grass, Mick. "L'Affiche du Charbonnier ne Serait-Elle pas de Daumier?" *Arts et Spectacles* (Paris). April 1950.

2037. Grass, Mick. *La Lumière sur Daumier. Etudes sur l'Artist et Son Oeuvre*. Marseilles: A. Tacussel, 1931.

2038. Grass, Mick. "Les Logis Parisiens d'Honoré Daumier." *Arts et Spectacles* (Paris). September 2, 1949.

2039. Gretton, T. "Daumier, Artist for All Time?" *History Today*. May 1981, pp. 50-51.

2040. Gutiérrez, Ricardo. "Honorato Daumier, Intérprete de la Vida Social." *La Prensa* (Buenos Aires). September 12, 1937.

2041. Harris, Bruce and Seena Harris, eds. *Honoré Daumier, Selected Works*. New York: Bounty Books, 1969.

2042. Harzard, N.A. and Loys Delteil. *Catalogue Raisonné d'Oeuvre Lithographiée de H. Daumier*. Ourry (Oise): Chez N.A. Hazard, 1904.

2043. Herding, Klaus. "Daumier, Critique des Temps Modernes. Recherches sur l'Histoire Ancienne." *Gazette des Beaux-Arts*. January 1989, pp. 29-44.

2044. Herding, Klaus. "Le Citadin à la Campagne: Daumier Critique du Comportement Bourgeois Face à la Nature." *Nouvelles de l'Estampe*. July-October 1979, pp. 28-40. (Special issue on Daumier).

2045. Hofmann, Werner. "Ambiguity in Daumier (and Elsewhere)." *Art Journal*. Winter 1983, pp. 361-364.

2046. Hofmann, Werner. "Daumier." In *La Caricature de Vinci à Picasso*. Grund-Paris: Editions Aimery Somogy, 1958.

2047. *Honoré Daumier*. Exhibition Catalog. Ingelheim am Rhein, 1971.

2048. James, Henry. *Daumier: Caricaturist*. Emmaus, Pennsylvania: Rodale Press, 1954.

2049. Jones, Philippe. "Les Femmes dans l'Oeuvre Lithographique de Daumier." In *Étapes de l'Art Français*. Intro. by André Castel. Coll. "Connaissance de l'Art. Connaissance de l'Homme," des *Cahiers de Médecine de France*. Paris: Olivier Perrin, Éd., 1951.

2050. *Klassiker der Karikatur: No. 12. Honoré Daumier.* Berlin: Eulenspiegel-Verlag, 1974.

2051. Klossowski, Erich. *Honoré Daumier.* Munich: R. Piper and Co., Verlag, 1908; 2nd Ed, 1923.

2052. Knauf, Erich *Daumier.* Berlin: 1931.

2053. Langemeyer, Gerhard. *Honoré Daumier, 1808-79.* Bildwitz und Zeitkritik. Sammlung Horn. Münster: 1978; Bonn: 1979.

2054. Larguier, Léo. "Le Wagon de Troisième-Classe" and "Les Vieux Amis." In *En Compagnie des Vieux Peintres.* Paris: Albin Michel, 1927.

2055. Larkin, Oliver W. "Daumier, Bourgeois Playgoer." *Theatre Arts.* March 1940, pp. 182-193.

2056. Larkin, Oliver W. *Daumier: Man of His Time.* New York: McGraw-Hill, 1966.

2057. Lassaigne, Jacques. *Daumier.* Paris: Éditions Hyperion, 1938.

2058. Lassaigne, Jacques. *Daumier.* Coll. "Les Grandes Maîtres de la Peinture." Paris: Édition Hyperion, 1946.

2059. Lecomte, Marcel. *H. Daumier.* Catalogue of René Gaston-Dreyfus Collection. 3 Vols.: June 1966, December 1966, and May 1968.

2060. Lejeune, Robert. *Honoré Daumier.* French adaptation of Gustave Roud. Lausanne: Éditions Clairefontaine, 1953.

2061. Lejeune, Robert. *Honoré Daumier. Der Künstler und Kämpfer.* Zurich: 1945.

2062. Lelheire, Jacques. "Daumier, Fuselli et le Cauchemar." *Aesculape* (Paris). March 1959.

2063. Lemann, Bernard. "Daumier and the Republic." *Gazette des Beaux Arts.* February 1945.

2064. Lemann, Bernard. *Honoré Daumier.* Intro. by Bernard Lemann. New York: Reynal and Hitchcock, 1946.

2065. Lewisohn, Sam A. "Daumier." In *Painters and Personality.* New York: Harper and Brothers Publishers, 1937.

2066. *Lithographs and Drawings by Daumier Lent by Lessing J. Rosenwald.* Philadelphia, Pennsylvania: The Free Library, 1930.

2067. *L'Oeuvre d'Honoré Daumier 1808-1879*. Catalogue des Peintures, Sculptures, Dessins, Lithographies et Livres Illustrés au Musée Cantini de Marseille du 14 juin au 6 juillet 1947. Intro. by Jean Cristofol. Marseilles: Musée Cantini, 1947.

2068. Maison, Karl E. *Daumier. Drawings. Reproductions*. New York: Thomas Yoseloff, 1960.

2069. Maison, Karl E. "Daumier Studies." *The Burlington Magazine* (London). March-April 1954.

2070. Maison, Karl E. *Honoré Daumier: Catalogue Raisonné of the Paintings, Watercolours, and Drawings*. 2 Vols. London and Greenwich, Connecticut: New York Graphic Society, 1967-1968.

2071. Maison, Karl E. "Sur les Dessins de Daumier." *Aesculape* (Paris). December 1958.

2072. Marcel, Henri. *Daumier, Biographie Critique*. Paris: 1907.

2073. Marcel, Henri. *Honoré Daumier*. Coll. "Les Grandes Artistes, Leur Vie, Leur Oeuvre." Paris: H. Laurens, Éd., 1929.

2074. Maroger, Jacques. "La Technique de Daumier dans les Tableaux du Musée du Louvre." Thesis, l'Ecole du Louvre, 1936.

2075. Marotte, Léon. *Daumier*. Paris: Helleu et Sergent, 1924.

2076. Martine-Charles and Marotte-Léon. *Honoré Daumier*. Coll. "Dessins des Maîtres Français." Paris: Helleu et Sergent, Éd., 1924.

2077. Martins, Luís. "Daumier e as Preocupações Sociais." *A Evolução Social da Pintura*. Vol. 27. São Paulo: Departamento de Cultura, 1942.

2078. Maxmin, Jody. "A Hellenistic Echo in Daumier's Penelope?" *Art International*. August 1984, pp. 38-47.

2079. Melot, Michel. "Daumier and Art History: Aesthetic Judgement/Political Judgement." *Oxford Art Journal*. 11:1 (1988), pp. 3-24.

2080. Melot, Michel. "Daumier Devant l'Histoire de l'Art." In *Honoré Daumier 1808-79*. Bildwitz und Zeitkritik. Sammlung Horn. Münster: 1978; Bonn: 1979.

2081. Melot, Michel. "Daumier Devant l'Histoire de l'Art: Judgement Esthétique, Judgement Politique." In *Daumier et le Dessin de Presse*. Grenoble: 1980.

2082. Morrissey, Ann. *Daumier on Women: The Lithographs*. Exhibition Catalogue. Los Angeles, California: University Art Galleries, University of Southern California, 1982.

2083. Nieuwendijk, Peter. "Honoré Daumier." *Sick.* 22/23 (1991), pp. 4-14.

2084. Osiakowski, Stanislas. "Daumier et la Lutte pour la Libération Politique et Sociale (la Pologne, l'Irlande)." *Aesculape* (Paris). March 1959.

2085. Otto, Benesch. *Artistic and Intellectual Trends from Rubens to Daumier.* Cambridge: 1943.

2086. Parturier, Françoise and Jacqueline Armingeat. *Daumier: Intellectuelles ("Les Bas-Bleus" et "Femmes Socialistes").* Paris: Editions Vilo-Paris, 1974.

2087. Passeron, Roger. *Daumier.* Oxford: Phaidon, 1981.

2088. Passeron, Roger. *Daumier et la Satire d'Aujourd'Hui.* Paris: Vision Nouvelle, 1974.

2089. Passeron, Roger. "Daumier: Lithographe et Sculpteur." *L'Oeil* (Lausanne). April 1989, pp. 52-59.

2090. Passeron, Roger. *Hommage à Daumier.* Exhibition Catalogue. Château de Blois, 1968.

2091. Penzoldt, Ernst. *Honoré Daumier. Gotter und Helden. Funzig Lithographien.* Munich: R. Piper and Co., Verlag, 1947.

2092. Phillips, Duncan. "Daumier." *Art and Understanding* (New York). November 1929.

2093. Phillips, Duncan. *Honoré Daumier. Appreciations of His Life and Works.* New York: Phillips Publications, No. 2, 1922.

2094. Picard, Raymond. *Honoré Victorin Daumier, 1808-79. Daumier and the University. Teachers and Students..* Trans. by Arnold Rosin. Boston: Boston Book and Art Publishers, 1970.

2095. Piltz, Georg, ed. *Honoré Daumier [Karikaturen].* Munich: 1974.

2096. Plée-Léon and Jules Bertaut. "Le Centenaire de H. Daumier." *Les Annales* (Paris). No. 1287, 1908.

2097. Powell, Kirsten and Elizabeth C. Childs. *Femmes d'Esprit: Women in Daumier's Caricature.* Hanover and London: University Press of New England, 1990. 146 pp.

2098. Prevost, Louis. *Honoré Daumier: A Thematic Guide to the Oeuvre.* Ed. by Elizabeth C. Childs. New York and London: Garland Publishing, 1989.

2099. Raynal, Maurice. *Daumier.* Geneva, Paris: Albert Skira, n.d.

2100. Read, Herbert. "Daumier." In *Art and Society*. London: Faber and Faber, 1945.

2101. "Rediscovered Caricaturist of Genius: Honoré Daumier." *Current Literature*. July 1907, pp. 50-54.

2102. Rentmeister, Cäcilia. "Daumier und das Häsliche Geschlecht." In *Honoré Daumier und die Ungelösten Probleme der Bürgerlichen Gesellschaft*. Exhibition Catalogue. Berlin: Neue Gesellschaft für Bildende Kunst für Schloss Charlottenburg, 1974.

2103. Rey, Robert. *Daumier*. Coll. "Les Contemporains. Oeuvres et Portraits du XXᵉ Siècle." Paris: Libr. Stock, 1923.

2104. Rey, Robert. "Daumier et le Sentiment de la Solitude." *Aesculape* (Paris). December 1958.

2105. Rey, Robert. *Honoré Daumier*. New York: Abrams; London: Thames and Hudson, 1966.

2106. Rey, Robert. *Honoré Daumier, 1808-79*. London: Collins, 1960.

2107. Rim, Carlo. *Au Temps de Daumier ou les Régimes à l'Essai*. Coll. "Arc en Ciel." Grenoble: B. Arthaud, Éd., 1935.

2108. Rim, Carlo. *Honoré Daumier. Son Oeuvre*. Coll. "Célébrités Contemporaines." Paris: Nouvelle Revue Critique, Éd., 1929.

2109. Roberts-Jones, Philippe. *De Daumier à Lautrec*. Paris: 1960.

2110. Roberts-Jones, Philippe. *Honoré Daumier. Moeurs Conjugales*. Monte Carlo: 1967.

2111. Roberts-Jones, Philippe. "Les Femmes dans l'Oeuvre Lithographique de Daumier." *Médecine de France*. 23 (1951), pp. 29-32.

2112. Roberts-Jones, Philippe. "Les Types Physionomiques Chez Daumier." Thesis, University of Brussels, 1952.

2113. Roger-Marx, Claude. *Daumier*. Paris: Libr. Plon, Éditions d'Histoire et d'Art, 1938.

2114. Roger-Marx, Claude. "Daumier et le Peuple." *L'Art Vivant* (Paris). May 1934.

2115. Roger-Marx, Claude. "Daumier Illustrateur." In *Crapouillot*. Paris: Noël, 1929.

2116. Roger-Marx, Claude. *Daumier. Paintings*. London: Methuen, 1962.

2117. Roger-Marx, Claude. "Grandeur de Daumier." In *Maîtres du XIXe Siècle et du XXe*. Coll. "Les Problèmes de l'Art." Genèva: Pierre Cailler, Éd., 1954.

2118. Roger-Marx, Claude. "Les Dernières Lithographies de Daumier." *L'Art Vivant* (Paris). 1930.

2119. Rosenthal, Léon. *Preface à un Tirage de 36 Bois de Daumier*. Paris: Meynial, 1921.

2120. Rosenthal, Léon and J. Laran. *Daumier*. Coll. "L'Art de Notre Temps." Paris: Libr. Central des Beaux-Arts, 1921.

2121. Rossel, André. *H. Daumier Oeuvres Politiques et Sociales. Prend Parti*. Paris: Editions Hier et Demain, 1971. 317 pp.

2122. Rousseau, James. *Physiologie de la Portière*. Dessins de Daumier. Paris: Jules Laisné Éd., 1841.

2123. Rousseau, James. *Physiologie de Robert Macaire. Vignettes de Daumier*. Paris: Jules Laisné, 1842.

2124. Roy, Claude. "Daumier." In *L'Amour de la Peinture. Descriptions Critiques*. Paris: N.R.F. Gallimard, 1956.

2125. Roy, Claude. *Daumier. Dessins*. Geneva: Skira, 1971.

2126. Rumann, Arthur. *Honoré Daumier sein Holzschnittwerk*. Munich: Delphin, Verlag, 1914.

2127. Rumann, Arthur. *Daumier als Illustrator*. Munich: Delphin, Verlag, 1919.

2128. Rumann, Arthur. *Honoré Daumier*. Berlin: Martin Wasservogel, 1926.

2129. Sachs, Maurice. *Honoré Daumier*. Paris: Éditions Pierre Tisné, 1939.

2130. Sadler, Michael. *Daumier, the Man and the Artist*. London: Halton and Truscott Smith, Ltd, 1924.

2131. Saint Guilhem, F. and Klaus Schrenk. *Honoré Daumier: l'Oeuvre Lithographique*. Foreword by Charles Baudelaire. 2 Vols. Paris: 1978.

2132. Salazar, Abel. "Exposição das Obras de Daumier nas Tulherias e na Biblioteca Nacional." In *Paris, em 1934*. Pôrto: Tip. Civilização, 1938.

2133. Samson, Mireille. *Honoré Daumier. Centenaire de Sa Mort*. Valmondois, 1979.

2134. Sauret, André, comp. *H. Daumier: Teachers and Students*. Dijon: Imprimerie Darantiere, 1970. 95 pp.

2135. Scheiwiller, Giovanni. *Honoré Daumier*. Coll. "Arte Moderna Straniera." Milan: Ulrico Hoepli, Editore, 1942.

2136. Schneider, P. "Daumier: Gagged Again." *Encounter*. April 1980, pp. 48-49.

2137. Schweicher, Curt. *Daumier*. Paris: Édition Aimery Somogy, 1953; London: Hienemann, 1954.

2138. Sergent, P.J. "Daumier et la Médecine." *Aesculape* (Paris). December 1958.

2139. Sicre, José Gomes. "Daumier." *Norte* (Buenos Aires). August 1947.

2140. Stahl, Fritz. *Honoré Daumier*. Berlin: Rudolf Mosse, Buchverlag, 1930.

2141. Sterling, Ch. *Daumier*. Exhibition Catalogue (L'Orangerie). Foreword by Calude Roger-Marx. Paris: 1934.

2142. Stoll, André. *Die Rückkehr der Babaren: Europäer und 'Wilde' in der Karikatur Honoré Daumiers*. Exhibition Catalogue. Hamburg: Hans Christians für the Kunsthalle der Stadt Bielefeld, 1985.

2143. Teüchi, Hyïkata. *Honoré Daumier*. Tokyo: *Mainichi Shimbun*, Kamakura, 1974.

2144. Tyler, Francine. "The Impact of Daumier's Graphics on American Artists: c.1863-c.1923." *Print Review*. 11 (1980), pp. 109-126.

2145. Valéry, Paul. *Daumier*. Coll. "Les Trésors de la Peinture Française au XIXᵉ Siècle." Paris: Albert Skira, Éd., 1938.

2146. Venturi, Lionello. "Daumier." In *Modern Painters*. London: Charles Scribner's Sons, 1947.

2147. Venturi, Lionello. *Pour Comprendre la Peinture de Giotto à Chagal*. Paris: Albin Michel, Éd., 1950.

2148. Vincent, Howard P. *Daumier and His World*. Evanston, Illinois: Northwestern University Press, 1968.

2149. Waldmann, Emil. *Honoré Daumier*. Berlin: Hyperion Verlag, 1918-1919.

2150. Waldmann, Emil. *Daumier*. Leipzig: 1923.

2151. Wartmann, W. *Honoré Daumier*. Foreword by B. Lemann. Zurich: 1945; London: 1946.

2152. Wassermann, Jeanne L. *Daumier Sculpture*. Exhibition Catalogue. In Collaboration with Joan M. Lukach and Arthur Beale. Cambridge, Massachusetts: Fogg Art Museum, Harvard University, 1969.

2153. Wolff, Albert. *La Gloire à Paris (Mémoires d'un Parisien)*. Paris: Victor Havard, Éd., 1886.

2154. Wurmser, André. *H. Daumier*. Paris: Éditions Cercle d'Art, 1951.

David, Jacques-Louis

2155. Boime, Albert. "Jacques-Louis David, Scatological Discourses in the French Revolution, and the Art of Caricature." *Arts Magazine*. February 1988, pp. 72-81.

2156. Boime, Albert. "Marmontel's Bélisaire and the Pre-Revolutionary Progressivism of David." *Art History*. 3 (1980), pp. 81-101.

2157. Bordes, Philippe. *Le Serment du Jeu de Paume de Jacques-Louis David: Le Peintre, Son Milieu et Son Temps de 1789 à 1792*. Paris: Editions de la Réunion des Musées Nationaux, 1983.

2158. Brookner, Anita. *Jacques-Louis David*. London: Chatto and Windus, 1980.

2159. Crow, Thomas E. "'Gross David, with the Swoln Cheek': Review of *Jacques-Louis David*, by Anita Brookner." *Art History*. 5 (1982), pp. 109-117.

2160. Delécluze, E.J. *David, Son École et Son Temps: Souvenirs*. 2nd Ed. Paris: Didier et Cie, 1980.

2161. Dowd, David L. *Pageant-Master of the Republic: Jacques-Louis David and the French Revolution*. Lincoln, Nebraska: University of Nebraska Press, 1948. Reprinted: Freeport, New York: Books for Libraries Press, 1969.

2162. Ettlinger, L.D. "Jacques-Louis David and Roman Virtue." *Journal of the Royal Society of Arts*. 115 (1967), pp. 105-123.

2163. Hautecoeur, Louis. *Louis David*. Paris: Editions de la Table Ronde, 1954.

2164. Lortel, J. "David Caricaturiste." *L'Art et les Artistes*. March 1914, pp. 273-275.

2165. Schnapper, Antoine. *Jacques-Louis David, Témoin de Son Temps*. Paris: Bibliothéque des Arts; Fribourg: Office du Livre, 1980.

2166. Wildenstein, G. "David, Auteur de Caricatures Contre les Anglais Commandées par la Convention." In *Omagiu lui George Oprescu cu Prilejul Împlinirii a 8o de Ani*. Edited by T. Vianu and M. Popescu. Bucharest: Editura Academiei Republicii Populare Romine, 1961.

Desclozeaux, Jean-Pierre

2167. Desclozeaux. *Entre Chien et Chat*. Paris: Denoël, 1983.

2168. Desclozeaux. *Mine de Rien*. Paris: Donoël, 1984.

2169. "Jean-Pierre Desclozeaux." *Apropos*. No. 6, pp. 25-28.

Dionnet, Jean-Pierre

2170. Dionnet, Jean-Pierre. "Blackmark." *Phénix*. No. 17, 1970.

2171. Dionnet, Jean-Pierre. "Entre Mongo et Ranagar." *Galaxie*. (Ed. Opta, Paris). No. 102, 1972.

2172. Dionnet, Jean-Pierre and Gal. *Conquering Armies*. New York: Heavy Metal, 1977. 59 pp.

2173. Filippini, Henri. "Entretien avec Jean-Pierre Dionnet." *Schtroumpfanzine*. 21, 1978, pp. 14-21.

2174. Groensteen, Thierry and Bruno Lecigne. "Citizen Dionnet." *Les Cahiers de la Bande Dessinée*. 59, 1984, pp. 45-49.

Doré, Gustave

2175. Alem, Conrado. "Gustavo Doré y Sus Dibujos de Parlamentarios." *Correo Literario* (Buenos Aires). October 1, 1944.

2176. Doré, Gustave. *Das Graphische Werk*. Ed. by Gabriele Forberg. Munich: 1975.

2177. Doré, Gustave. *Histoire Pittoresque, Dramatique et Caricaturale de la Sainte Russie*. Paris: J. Bry Ainé Libr. Éditeur, 1854. Reprinted: 1967.

2178. Doré, Gustave. *L'Oeuvre de Doré*. Exhibition Catalog, Museé de l'Ain, Brou, 1963.

2179. Doré, Gustave. *Two Hundred Sketches Humorous and Grotesque*. Boston: 1867.

2180. Doré, Gustave. *Versailles et Paris en 1871*. Preface by Gabriel Hanotaux. Paris: Plon, Nourit et Cie Imp. Édit., 1907.

2181. Farner, Konrad. *Gustave Doré, der Industrialisierte Romantiker*. Dresden: 1963.

2182. Gosling, Nigel. *Gustave Doré*. New York: 1973.

2183. "Gustave Dore, Comics Pioneer." *Comics Buyer's Guide*. March 27, 1992, pp. 1, 22.

2184. Jerrold, William D. *Life of Gustave Doré*. London: 1891.

2185. Maass, John. "Doré's Politicians." *Target*. Winter 1986, pp. 7-10.

2186. Pagáno, José L. "Pulvis de Chavannes y Gustavo Doré Caricaristas." In *Formas de Vida*. Buenos Aires: El Ateneo, n.d.

2187. Roosevelt, Blanch. *Life and Reminiscences of Gustave Doré*. New York: 1885.

2188. Valmy-Baysse, J. *Gustave Doré. Bibliographie et Catalogue Complet de l'Oeuvre par Louis Dézé*. 2 Vols. Paris: 1930.

2189. Varschavski, L.R. *Gustave Doré*. Moscow: 1966.

Druillet, Philippe

2190. Bataille, C. "Bibliographie de Philippe Druillet." *Schtroumpf. Les Cahiers de la Bande Dessinée*. 42, 1979, pp. 55-62.

2191. Bataille, C. "L'Écriture Graphique Automatique Chez Ph. Druillet." *Schtroumpf. Les Cahiers de la Bande Dessinée*. 42, 1979, p. 53.

2192. Chénetier, Marc and Pierre Fresnault-Deruelle. "Vive la B.D.!" *La Quinzaine Littéraire* (Paris). 163, 1973, pp. 32-33.

2193. Druillet, Philippe. *Lone Sloane-Delirius*. Paris: Dragon's Dream, 1973. 136 pp.

2194. Druillet, Philippe. *Yragael-Urm*. Paris: Dragon's Dream, 1975. 120 pp.

2195. Dutrey, Jacques. "Philippe Druillet." *Comics Journal*. July 1988, pp. 24-26.

2196. Groensteen, Thierry. "BD, Cinéma, Peinture, Animation, Architecture. Druillet: L'Explosion." *Les Cahiers de la Bande Dessinée*. 67, 1986, pp. 77-83.

2197. Léturgie, Jean. "Entretien avec Philippe Druillet." *Schtroumpf. Les Cahiers de la Bande Dessinée*. 42, 1979, pp. 7-41.

2198. Moliterni, Claude. "Philippe Druillet, Interview." *Bédésup*. No. 13, 1969.

Dubout, Jean

2199. Dubout, Jean. *Album*. Preface by Marcel Aymé. Nice: Éditions d'Art et Technique, 1942.

2200. Dubout, Jean. *Album*. Preface by Gabriel Chevalier. Monte-Carlo: Éditions du Livre, n.d.

2201. Dubout, Jean. *Cartoons*. London: Neville Spearman, 1957.

2202. Dubout, Jean. *Dessins*. Monte-Carlo: Éditions du Livre, 1947.

2203. Dubout, Jean. *Du Bout de la Lorgnette de Dubout*. Preface by Philippe Soupault. 11th Ed. Paris: N.R.F. Gallimard, 1937.

2204. Dubout, Jean. *Dubout... en Train*. Monte-Carlo: Éditions du Livre, n.d.

2205. Dubout, Jean. *Dubout's Raillery*. London: Putnam, 1956.

2206. Dubout, Jean. *La Mythologie de Dubout*. Paris: Maurice Gonon, Éd., 1954.

2207. Dubout, Jean. *La Rue Sans Loi*. Carlo: Éditions du Livre, 1944.

2208. Dubout, Jean. *Les Aventures de la Famille Anatole*. Paris: Comptoir Internationale du Livre, n.d.

2209. Dubout, Jean. *Les Chats de Dubout*. Sanit-Amand: Editions Hoëbeke, 1987. 98 pp.

2210. Dubout, Jean. *Les 64 Poses*. Paris: Les Jarres d'Or, n.d.

2211. Dubout, Jean. *Total Verruckt Vorwot Kurt Kusenberg*. Hamburg: Rowholt Verlag, n.d.

2212. Dubout, Jean. *Tour de France*. Monte-Carlo: Éditions du Livre, n.d.

2213. Lima, Herman. "Dubout e a Sua Fauna de Mulheres Rabelaisianas." *Rio Magazine* (Rio de Janeiro). June 1948.

2214. Saucet. "Dubout." *Les Nouvelles Littéraires*. Paris: n.d.

Dupuis, Pierre

2215. De Laet, Danny. "Pierre Dupuis, un Diabolik Qui s'Ignore." *Cahiers Universitaires*. No. 12, 1971.

2216. Filippini, Henri. "Entretien avec Pierre Dupuis." *Schtroumpfanzine*. 29, 1979, pp. 3-11.

2217. Glénat, Jacques. "Schtroumpf Rencontre P. Dupuis." *Cahiers Universitaires*. No. 12, 1971.

2218. Cance, Luis and Marteens. "Bibliographie de Dupuis." *Cahiers Universitaires*. No. 12, 1971.

Duveaux, Michel

2219. Bouyer, Sylvain. "Michel Duveaux. La Tentation des Extrêmes." *Les Cahiers de la Bande Dessinée*. 67, 1986, pp. 86-91.

2220. "Entretien avec Michel Duveaux." *Schtroumpfanzine*. 34, 1979, pp. 15-21.

Effel, Jean

2221. Effel, Jean. *Adam und Eva*. Vols. 1, 2. Berlin: Eulenspiegel-Verlag, 1968.

2222. Effel, Jean. *Album*. Preface by Léon Fargue. Monaco: Édition d'Art et Technique, n.d.

2223. Effel, Jean. *Das Dicke Effel-Buch*. Berlin: Eulenspiegel-Verlag, 1979.

2224. Effel, Jean. *De la Troisième République à la Seconde Restauration*. Paris: Temps Actuels, 1981.

2225. Effel, Jean. *Ent Deckung der Liebe durch Adam und Eva*. Berlin: Eulenspiegel-Verlag, 1983.

2226. Effel, Jean. *Historio-Grafik*. Berlin: Eulenspiegel-Verlag, 1970.

2227. Effel, Jean. *La Création du Monde*. Paris: Gallimard Libr., 1951, 1952.

2228. Effel, Jean. *La Création du Monde. Le Ciel*. Paris: Gallimard Libr., 1954.

2229. Effel, Jean. *La Création du Monde. Les Eaux*. Paris: Gallimard, Libr., 1953.

2230. Effel, Jean. *La Vie Naïve d'Adam et Ève*. Paris: Julliard, Séquana, 1946.

2231. Effel, Jean. *Le Diable et Son Train*. Paris: René Julliard, 1951.

2232. Effel, Jean. *Le Jardin d'Éden*. Paris: Éditions Cercle d'Art, 1956.

2233. Effel, Jean. *Le Roman d'Adam et Ève. La Création de l'Homme*. Paris: Éditions Cercle d'Art, 1953.

2234. Effel, Jean. *Le Roman d'Adam et Ève. L'École Paternelle*. Paris: Éditions Cercle d'Art, 1954.

2235. Effel, Jean. *Toujours Occupés*. Paris: Éditions Cercle d'Art, 1955.

Ernst

2236. Ernst. *Ciel, Mon Paris!* Preface by Christophe Dechavanne. Paris: Éditions de la Sabliere, 1990. 48 pp.

2237. Ernst. *Clin D'Oeil*. Brussels: Éditions du Lombard, annual series, 1980-1988.

2238. Ernst. *Les Meilleurs Gags Clin d'Oeil*. Paris: Editions du Lombard, 1989. 112 pp.

Faivre, Abel

2239. Faivre, Abel. *Abel Faivre. L'Album. IX*. Paris: Librairie Illustrée, 1901.

2240. Faivre, Abel. *Abel Faivre. I et II*ᵉ *Albuns*. Coll. *"Les Maîtres Humoristes."* Paris: Libr. Félix Jouven, 1907, 1909.

2241. Puech, Lucien. "Abel Faivre Intime." In *L'Album*, IX. Paris: Libr. Illustrée, 1901.

Faizant, Jacques

2242. Faur, Jean-Claude. "Advice of Jacques Faizant: 'Evolve Endlessly, Do Not Hurry, and Be Opinionated.'" *WittyWorld*. Summer 1988, pp. 34-35.

2243. Faur, Jean-Claude. "Faizant, Jacques." In *Contemporary Graphic Artists*, Vol. 3, pp. 63-64. Detroit, Michigan: Gale, 1988.

2244. Saunier, Henri, *et al.* "Jacques Faizant: La Vielle Dame du Quai Conti." *Le Nouveau Bédésup*. 1-2 Trim. 1987, pp. 14-21.

Floc'h, Jean-Claude

2245. Groensteen, Thierry. "Entretien avec Floc'h et Rivière." *Les Cahiers de la Bande Dessinée*. 68, 1986, pp. 8-16.

2246. Léturgie, Jean. "Entretien avec Floc'h." *Schtroumpfanzine*. 16, 1978, pp. 3-9.

F'Murr (Richard Peyzaret)

2247. Baudin, Henri. "Le Décor Comique de F'Murr dans Sa Série: 'Le Génie des Alpages.'" *Cahier Comique Communication* (Grenoble). 1, 1983, pp. 95-110.

2248. F'Murr. *Vingts Dieux. C'Est Le Synode*. Paris: Gilles Tautin, 1977.

2249. Groensteen, Thierry. "Entretien avec F'Murr." *Les Cahiers de la Bande Dessinée*. 60, 1984, pp. 7-14.

2250. Groensteen, Thierry. "Un Espace Entre Quatre F'Murr." *Les Cahiers de la Bande Dessinée*. 60, 1984, pp. 18-21.

2251. Léturgie, Jean. "Entretien avec F'Murr." *Schtroumpfanzine*. 17, 1978, pp. 3-12.

2252. Van Cauwenbergh, Franz. "Bibliographie de F'Murr." *Les Cahiers de la Bande Dessinée*. 60, 1984, pp. 32-34.

Folon, Jean-Michel

2253. Faur, Jean-Claude. "Folon, Jean-Michel." *Contemporary Graphic Artists*, Vol. 3, pp. 66-68. Detroit, Michigan: Gale, 1988.

2254. Soavi, Giorgio. "Vita Anche Sentimentale, di J.M. Folon." *Linus*. 5:46 (1969), pp. 1-10.

Forain, Jean Louis

2255. Alvarus (Álvaro Cotrim). "Jean Louis Forain." *Vamos Ler!* (Rio de Janeiro). April 29, 1943.

2256. Alvarus (Álvaro Cotrim). "O Forain Pouco Conhecido." *Vamos Ler!* (Rio de Janeiro). November 12, 1942.

2257. Azorin. "Forain." *La Prensa* (Buenos Aires). March 19, 1933.

2258. Bauer, Bérard. "Forain, Crítico de umo Época." *O Jornal* (Rio de Janeiro). September 14, 1952.

2259. Bauer, Bérard. "Le Souvenir de Forain." *Le Figaro Illustré* (Paris). June 21, 1952.

2260. Bostel, Honoré. "La Belle Époque." *Paris-Match*. June 14, 1958.

2261. Daudet, Alphonse. "Préface." In *Forain-Album*. Paris: H. Simonis Ed., n.d.

2262. de Fornaro, C. "Famous Illustrator of French Manners, J.L. Forain." *Arts and Decoration*. October 1923, pp. 26-27.

2263. Forain, Jean-Louis. *Album*. "Avant-Propos" by Maurice Talmeyr. Paris: Plon-Nourit et Cie, 1896.

2264. Forain, Jean-Louis. *Album*. Preface by Alphonse Daudet. Paris: H. Simonis Empis, Édit., n.d.

2265. Forain, Jean-Louis. *De la Marne au Rhin*. Album de Dessins des Années de Guerre (1914-1919). 2 Vols. Paris: Lafitte Éditeur, 1920.

2266. Forain, Jean-Louis. *Doux Pays*. Paris: Libr. Plon, n.d.

2267. Forain, Jean-Louis. *J.L. Forain. Coll. Les Maîtres Humoristes*. I et IIe Albuns. Paris: Libr. Félix Juven, 1908, 1909.

2268. Forain, Jean-Louis. *La Comédie Parisienne*. Paris: G. Charpentier et E. Fasquelle, Édts., 1892; IIe Série, Paris: Librairie Plon, n.d.

2269. Forain, Jean-Louis. *La Vie*. Paris: Libr. Félix Juven, Éditeur, n.d.

2270. Forain, Jean-Louis. "Le Fifre." *Journal Hebdomadaire de J.L. Forain*. February 23, 1889; June 1, 1889.

2271. Forain, Jean-Louis. *Les Temps Difficiles*. Paris: G. Charpentier et E. Fasquelle, Édts., 1895.

2272. Forain, Jean-Louis. *Rires et Grimaces*. Paris: Librairie d'Art, Ludovic Basquet, Éditeur, n.d.

2273. Geoffroy, Gustave. "Forain." *Arts et les Artistes*. Special number. New series, November 21, 1921.

2274. Guérin, Marcel. *J.L. Forain—Aquafortiste. Catalogue Raisonné de l'Oeuvre Gravée de l'Artiste*. 3 Vols. Paris: H. Floury, 1912.

2275. Gutiérrez, Ricardo. "J.L. Forain: Un Acusador Público." *La Prensa* (Bueno Aires). March 15, 1937.

2276. Henriot, Émile. "Forain: Les Dessins. Les Légendes." *Je Sais Tout* (Paris). April 15, 1914.

2277. *Jean Louis Forain—Peintre, Dessinateur et Graveur. Catalogue de l'Exposition Organisée pour le Centénnaire de Sa Naissance à la Bibliotèque Nationale.* June-September 1952. "Avant Propos" by Jules Cain. Intro. by Paul Léon. Paris: Conservateur au Cabinet des Estampes, 1952.

2278. Kunstler, Charles. *Forain.* Paris: Les Éditions Rieder, 1931.

2279. *Les Maîtres Modernes de l'Eau-Forte. Jean Louis Forain.* Intro. by Malcolm G. Salaman. London: *The Studio*; Paris: Librairie Ernest Flammarion, 1925.

2280. Puech, Lucien. "Forain Intime." In *L'Album*, XVIII. Paris: Montgrédien et Cie, Édts., 1901.

2281. Rocha, Camile. "O Forain Pouco Conhecido." *Vamos Ler!* (Rio de Janeiro). November 12, 1942.

2282. Sem. "Forain Est Mort." *Illustration Française* (Paris). July 18, 1931.

2283. Vaillat, Léandre. *En Écoutant Forain.* Paris: Ernest Flammarion, Éd., 1931.

2284. Vaillat, Léandre. "O Centenário de Forain." *O Jornal* (Rio de Janeiro). August 17, 1952.

2285. Vauxcelles, Louis. "Forain Peintre." *Le Monde Illustré* (Paris). November 20, 1937.

Forest, Jean-Claude

2286. Andrevon, Jean-Pierre. "Forest et les Couvertures de S.F." *Schtroumpf. Les Cahiers de la Bande Dessinée.* 26, 1975, pp. 30-32.

2287. Cance, Louis and Jean-Pierre Andrevon. "Bibliographie de Jean-Claude Forest." *Schtroumpf. Les Cahiers de la Bande Dessinée.* 26, 1975, pp. 37-40.

2288. Di Manno, Yves. "Jean-Claude Forest et Ses Mythes." *Schtroumpf. Les Cahiers de la Bande Dessinée.* 26, 1975, pp. 23-25.

2289. Forest, Jean-Claude and Paul Gillon. *Lost in Time.* New York: NBM, 1986.

2290. "Jean Claude Forest. Un Intervista con l'Autore di Barbarella." *Linus*. No. 31, 1967, pp. 1-4.

2291. Lob, Jacques and Jean-Claude Forest. "Entretien." *Autour du Scénario*. 1986, pp. 103-109.

2292. Sadoul, Numa. "Entretien avec Jean-Claude Forest." *Schtroumpf. Les Cahiers de la Bande Dessinée*. 26, 1975, pp. 8-17.

Franc, Régis

2293. Groensteen, Thierry. "Entretien avec Régis Franc." *Les Cahiers de la Bande Dessinée*. 57, 1984, pp. 6-10.

2294. Groensteen, Thierry, Christian Marmonnier, Frédéric Niffle and Franz Cauwenbergh. "Bibliographie de Régis Franc." *Les Cahiers de la Bande Dessinée*. 57, 1984, pp. 35-36, 97.

2295. Lecigne, Bruno. "Sous le Café, la Plage." *Les Cahiers de la Bande Dessinée*. 57, 1984, pp. 22-23.

François, André

2296. François, André. *The Half-Naked Knight*. New York: Alfred Knopf, 1958.

2297. François, André. *Mit Gesträubten Federn*. Berlin: Eulenspiegel-Verlag, 1956.

2298. François, André. *The Penguin André François*. Ringwood, Victoria, Australia: Penguin, 1964. Unpaginated.

2299. François, André. *The Tattooed Sailor. Cartoons from France*. Intro. by Walt Kelly. New York: Alfred A. Knopf, 1953.

2300. *Manigances*. Les Meilleurs Dessins Humoristiques d'Andrés François, Chaval et Mose. Paris: Revue Neuf, n.d.

2301. Searle, Ronald. *The Biting Eye of André François*. London: Perpetua, 1960.

Fred (Othon Aristides)

2302. Glénat, Jacques. "Bibliographie de Fred dans Pilote." *Cahiers Universitaires*. No. 9, 1970.

2303. Glénat, Jacques. "Schtroumpf Rencontre Fred." *Cahiers Universitaires*. No. 9, 1970.

2304. Moliterni, Claude. "Fred, Interview." *Phénix*. No. 22, 1972.

2305. Sadoul, Numa. "Bibliographie de Fred dans Hara-Kiri." *Cahiers Universitaires*. No. 9, 1970.

2306. Toussaint, Bernard. *Fred*. Paris: Albin Michel, 1975.

Gavarni (Guillame Sulpice Chevallier)

2307. Alhoy, Maurice M. *Physiologie de la Lorette*. Vignettes de Gavarny [sic]. Paris: Aubert et Cie., n.d.

2308. Armelhaut, J. and E. Boucher. *L'Oeuvre de Gavarni. Lithographies Originales et Essais d'Eau-Forte et de Procédés Nouveaux. Catalogue Raisonné*. Paris: 1873.

2309. Bouchot, Henri. "Gavarni." *Bulletin de l'Art Ancien et Moderne*. October 1904, pp. 301-302; January 1905, p. 6.

2310. Brocos, Maximino. "Gavarni, Dibujante Social." *Correo Literario* (Buenos Aires). April 1, 1944.

2311. Burty, Philippe. "Gavarni." *Chronique des Arts et de la Curiosité*. December 2, 1866, pp. 275-276.

2312. Cain, Julien and Jean Vallery-Radot. *Gavarni*. Paris: 1954.

2313. Carrillo, E. Gomez. "El Pintor de la Galanteria." In *El Cuarto Libro de las Crónicas*. Madrid: Mundo Latino, 1921.

2314. Chennevières, Philippe de. "Gavarni: Souvenirs d'un Directeur des Beaux-Arts." *L'Artiste*. June 1885, pp. 406-423.

2315. de Goncourt, Edmond and Jules. *Gavarni: L'Homme et l'Oeuvre*. Paris: Henri Plon, 1873. 432 pp.

2316. Delaborde, Henri. "Gavarni, Sa Vie et Ses Oeuvres." *Revue des Deux Mondes*. 1873, pp. 158-182.

2317. de Mirecourt, Eugene. *Gavarni*. Paris: Librairie des Contemporains, 1870.

2318. de Mirecourt, Eugene. *Gavarni. Histoire Contemporaine. Portraits et Silhouettes au XIXe Siècle*. Paris: 1867.

2319. Duplessis, Georges. *Gavarni*. Paris: 1876.

2320. Escholier, Raymond. "Gavarni et les Femmes." *Le Figaro. Supplément Artistique*. May 31, 1923.

2321. Forgues, Émile. *Gavarni*. Paris: Librairie de l'Art, n.d.

2322. Forgues, Eugène. *Gavarni. Les Artistes Célèbres*. Vol. 7. Paris: 1887.

2323. Forgues, Eugène. "Les Illustrateurs de Livres au XIX° Siècle. Gavarni." *Le Livre*. 3 (1882), pp. 116-130.

2324. Gautier, Théophile. "Gavarni: Les Douze Mois." *L'Illustration*. March 20, 1869.

2325. Gavarni. *Caricatures Diverses*. Paris: Chez Bauger, Impr. d'Aubert et Cie, between 1839-1841.

2326. Gavarni. *D'Après Nature*. Album avec 40 Dessins. Texts of Jules Janin, Paul de Saint Victor, Edmond Texier, and Edmond and Jules de Goncourt. Paris: Movisot, Libr. Éditeur, 1859.

2327. Gavarni. *Fourberies de Femmes en Matière de Sentiment*. Paris: Chez Bauger, Impr. d'Aubert et Cie, between 1839-1841.

2328. Gavarni. *Gavarni*. Coll. "Les Maîtres Humoristes." Paris: Libr. Félix Juven, 1909.

2329. Gavarni. *La Masquerade Humaine*. Intro. by Ludovic Halévy. Paris: Calmann Lévy Éditeur, 1881.

2330. Gavarni. *Leçons et Conseils*. 28 lithographs published by *Le Charivari*. Paris: Impr. d'Aubert et Cie, 1839.

2331. Gavarni. *Le Diable à Paris. Paris et les Parisiens. Moeurs, Costumes, Caractères et Portraits des Habitants de Paris*. 2 Vols. Paris: J. Hetzel Libr. Éd., 1845-1846.

2332. Gavarni. *Les Gens de Paris*. Paris: n.p., n.d.

2333. Gavarni. *Les Lorettes*. Premier Tirage des 79 Lithographies de Gavarni en Couleurs. Paris: Bauger et Pannier, Impr. d'Aubert et Cie, 1841-1848.

2334. Gavarni. *Les Lorettes Vieillies. Oeuvres Nouvelles*. Vol. 2. Paris: ca. 1850.

2335. Gavarni. *Masques et Visages*. Paris: Librairie du *Figaro*, 1868.

2336. Gavarni. *Oeuvres Choisies*. Special edition published by *Le Figaro*, consisting of: *Les Enfants Terribles. Traduction en Langue Vulgaire. Les Lorettes. Les Actrices. Fourberies de Femmes en Matière de Sentiment. Clichy. Paris le Soir. Carnival à Paris. Paris le Matin. Les Étudiants à Paris. La Vie de Jeune Homme. Les Débardeurs. Les Gens de Paris*. Paris: 1857.

2337. Gavarni. *Oeuvres Choisies*. Paris: Horizonts de France, 1944.

2338. Gavarni. *Scenes de la Vie Intime*. Album Romantique. Paris: S.I. Édit, 1837.

2339. *Gavarni*. Paris: Bibliothéque Nationale, 1954. 80 pp.

2340. Halévy, Ludovic. "Gavarni e a Sua Obra." *Vamos Ler!* (Rio de Janeiro). June 10, 1943.

2341. H., C. "Les Fêtes Gavarni." *Revue Universelle*. May 1, 1902, pp. 229-231.

2342. James, David. "Gavarni and His Literary Friends." Ph.D. dissertation, Harvard University, 1942.

2343. *Klassiker der Karikatur: No. 5. Paul Gavarni*. Berlin: Eulenspiegel-Verlag, 1970.

2344. Landre, Jeanne. *Gavarni*. Paris: 1912.

2345. Lemoisne, Paul-André. *Gavarni, Peintre et Lithographe*. Vols. 1, 2. Paris: H. Floury, 1924-1928.

2346. Lemoisne, Paul-André. *La Vie et l'Art Romantiques. Gavarni, Peintre et Lithographie*. 2 Vols. Paris: H. Floury Ed., 1924.

2347. Lima, Herman. "Gavarni, Classificador de Borboletas." *Rio-Magazine* (Rio de Janeiro). April 1948.

2348. Monnier, Albert. "Théâtre de Gavarni." *Journal pour Rire*. June 26, 1852.

2349. Monteiro, Mário. "Gavarni Até em Londres foi Mestre." *Vamos Ler!* (Rio de Janeiro). April 16, 1942.

2350. Pierret, Paul. "Gavarni au Théâtre." *Figaro Illustré*. June 1894, pp. 108-112.

2351. Pierrot, Roger. "Balzac et Gavarni: Documents Inédits." *Etudes Balzaciennes*. December 1958, pp. 153-159.

2352. Quenell, Peter. "Gavarni: The Butterfly-Chaser." *Liliput* (London). October 1944.

2353. Robiquet, Jean. *L'Oeuvre Inédit de Gavarni*. Paris: H. Floury Éd., 1912.

2354. Sainte-Beuve, C.-A. "As Lengendas de Gavarni." *Vamos Ler!* (Rio de Janeiro). June 3, 1943.

2355. Sainte-Beuve, C.-A. "Gavarni." In *Nouveaux Lundis*. Vol. VI. Paris: 1866.

2356. Sinn, René. "Dessinateur Charmant des Grisettes et des Lorettes, Gavarni Conquit la Celebrité en Croquant sur le Vif ses Contemporains." *L'Hérisson* (Paris). January 12, 1956.

2357. Smith, Albert. *Gavarni in London*. London: D. Bogne, 1849.

2358. Stamm, Therese Dolan. *Gavarni and the Critics*. Ann Arbor, Michigan: UMI Research Press, 1979. 216 pp.

2359. Tardieu, Charles. "Gavarni." *L'Art*. 1 (1875), pp. 53-59.

2360. Uzanne, Octave. "Gavarni as Draughtsman and Lithographer-Designer of Fashions—Humorist-Satirist-Book Illustrator." In *Daumier and Gavarni*, edited by Charles Holme. London: Offices of *The Studio*, 1904.

2361. Warnod, André. *Gavarni*. Paris: F. Rieder et Cie, 1926.

Gerbault, Henri

2362. Gerbault, Henri. *Ach'tez-Moi, Joli Blond!* Preface by Charles Mong. Paris: H. Simonis Empis, Éd., 1900.

2363. Gerbault, Henri. *Bonjour, M'sieurs Dames*. Preface by Paul Guillain. Paris: H. Simonis Empis, Éd., 1903.

2364. Gerbault, Henri. *Boum!... Voilá*. Preface by Sully Prudhomme. Paris: H. Simonis Empis, Éd., n.d.

2365. Gerbault, Henri. *Broutilles Parisiennes*. 36 Dessins. Paris: Publication de La Vie Parisienne, n.d.

2366. Gerbault, Henri. *Henri Gerbault. Les Maîtres Humoristes. Les Meilleurs Dessins. Les Meilleurs Légendes*. I^e et IIe Albuns. Paris: Libr. Felix Juven, 1907-1908.

2367. Gerbault, Henri. *Parisiennettes*. Paris: Publication de La Vie Parisienne, 1894.

Gigi, Robert

2368. Léturgie, Jean. "Entretien avec Gigi." *Schtroumpfanzine*. 34, pp. 3-10.

2369. Moliterni, Claude. "Robert Gigi, Interview." *Phénix.* No. 18, 1971.

Gill, André (Louis Gosset de Guines)

2370. Baysse, J. Valny. *Le Roman d'Un Caricaturiste.* Paris: Éditions Marcel Seheur, 1927.

2371. Fontane, Charles. *André Gill. Un Maître de la Caricature (1840-1885).* 2 Vols. Paris: Aux Éditions du Livre, 1927.

2372. Gill, André. *20 Portraits Contemporains.* Paris: M. Magniers et Cie, 1886.

2373. Lods, Armand and Vega. *André Gill. Sa Vie. Bibliographie de Ses Oeuvres.* Paris: Léon Vanier, Libr. Éditeur, 1887.

2374. Valmy-Baysse, J. *Le Roman d'Un Caricaturiste André Gill.* Paris: Seheur, 1927. 323 pp.

Gillon, Paul

2375. Akoun, André. "La Bande Dessinée: Nouveau Langage? Interview de Paul Gillon par André Akoun." *Communication et Langages* (Paris). 34, 1977, pp. 94-105.

2376. Dupuis, Pierre. "Paul Gillon." *Schtroumpf. Les Cahiers de la Bande Dessinée.* 36, 1978, pp. 23-24.

2377. Filippini, Henri. "Bibliographie de Paul Gillon." *Schtroumpf. Les Cahiers de la Bande Dessinée.* 36, 1978, pp. 43-46.

2378. Filippini, Henri. "Un Dessin Qui Sent Bon l'Aventure." *Schtroumpf. Les Cahiers de la Bande Dessinée.* 36, 1978, p. 29.

2379. Filippini, Henri. "Entretien avec Paul Gillon." *Schtroumpf. Les Cahiers de la Bande Dessinée.* 36, 1978, pp. 7-21.

2380. Frémion, Yves. "Gillon du Lac, Opéra." *Schtroumpf. Les Cahiers de la Bande Dessinée.* 36, 1978, p. 26.

2381. Roux, Antoine. "Paul Gillon, Jérémie et la Peau de Chagrin." *Schtroumpfanzine.* 19, 1978, pp. 18-22.

Giraud, Jean (Gir, Moebius)

2382. Cance, Louis and Numa Sadoul. "Bibliographie de Jean Giraud." *Schtroumpf. Les Cahiers de la Bande Dessinée*. 25, 1974, pp. 38-41.

2383. Caré, Jean-Marc. "Les Humanoïdes à Angoulême: Giraud Est-Il Bon?" *Le Français dans le Monde*. 154, 1980, pp. 17-18.

2384. Clarke, Anthony. "Time Masters: The Moebius Epic." *Comics Scene*. September 1982, pp. 25-28.

2385. "Entretien avec Jean Giraud." *Schtroumpf. Les Cahiers de la Bande Dessinée*. 25, pp. 8-16.

2386. Faur, Jean-Claude. "Comment Je n'Ai Pas Découvert Moebius." *L'Hebdo de la B.D.* No. 70, 1991, p. 5.

2387. Fermín Pérez, Ramón. "Cancion de Cuna para Moebius." *El Wendigo*. October 1986, pp. 8-15.

2388. Giraud, Jean (Moebius). *Moebius: The Collected Fantasies of Jean Giraud*. 6 Vols. New York: Marvel Entertainment Group, 1987-1988.

2389. Giraud, Jean and Alexandro Jodorowsky. *The Incal*. 3 Vols. New York: Marvel, 1988.

2390. Kreinz, Glória. "O Mundo Caótico de Moebius." *Boletim de HQ*. March-April 1992, p. 2.

2391. Léturgie, Jean. "Rencontre avec Jean Giraud." *Schtroumpfanzine*. 34, 1979, pp. 12-14.

2392. "Many To Feature Moebius in 1989." *Comics Journal*. April 1989, pp. 21-22.

2393. Moebius. *Arzach*. New York: Heavy Metal Communications, 1977. 64 pp.

2394. Moebius. *Heavy Metal Presents Moebius*. New York: HM Communications, 1981. 96 pp.

2395. Moebius. *Moebius, the Collected Fantasies of Jean Giraud*. Epic Graphic Novel. New York: Marvel Entertainment Group. 1987-.

2396. "Moebius." *Comics Interview*. No. 45, 1987, pp. 6-16.

2397. "Moebius." *Comics Interview*. No. 64, 1988, pp. 24-37.

2398. Moliterni, Claude. "Gir, Interview." *Phénix*. No. 14, 1970.

2399. Pérez, Ramón F. "Jean Giraud: Gir/Moebius." Program of Centro Cultural Compoamor, Oviedo. November 1988, pp. 45-46.

2400. Rivière, François. "Gir Fantastiqueur." *Schtroumpf. Les Cahiers de la Bande Dessinée*. 25, 1974, pp. 29-31.

2401. Roux, Antoine. "Jean Giraud ou Une Leçon de Montage." *Schtroumpf. Les Cahiers de la Bande Dessinée*. 25, 1974, pp. 35-37.

2402. Sadoul, Numa. *Mister Moebius et Docteur Gir: Jean Giraud*. Paris: Albin Michel, 1976.

2403. Smolderen, Thierry. *Les Carnets Volés du Major, ou les Aventures de Moebius*. Paris: Schlirf Book, 1984.

2404. Smolderen, Thierry and Yves Schlirf. "Jean Gir, le Nouveau Moebius." *Les Cahiers de la Bande Dessinée*. 58, 1984, pp. 88-93.

2405. Thompson, Kim. "The Other Side of Moebius." *Comics Journal*. December 1987, pp. 84-105.

2406. Tschernegg, Markus. "Giraud Oder Moebius? 1. Teil." *Comic Forum. Das Österreichische Fachmagazin für Comicliteratur*. 2:4 (1980), pp. 38-42.

2407. Tschernegg, Markus. "Giraud Oder Moebius? 2. Teil. Leutenant Blueberry." *Comic Forum. Das Österreichische Fachmagazin für Comicliteratur*. 2:5 (1980), pp. 47-54.

2408. Warren, Bill. "On the Moebius Strip." *Comics Scene*. #3 (Vol. 3, Series #14), pp. 24-28, 66.

Godard, Christian

2409. Cance, Louis. "Bibliographie de Christian Godard." *Les Cahiers de la Bande Dessinée*. 59, 1984, pp. 41-44, 60.

2410. Cance, Louis and Louis Teller. "Bibliographie de Godard." *Cahiers Universitaires*. No. 19, 1972.

2411. "Christian Godard Starter Eget Forlag." *Serieskaberen*. December 1989, p. 9.

2412. Filippini, Henri. "Christian Godard, Interview." *Phénix*. No. 23, 1972.

2413. Filippini, Henri. "Entretien avec Christian Godard." *Schtroumpfanzine*. 25, 1978, pp. 3-11.

2414. Godard, Christian and Julio Ribera. *The Vagabond in Limbo: An Ultimate Alchemist*. New York: Dargaud International, 1983. 48 pp.

2415. Godard, Christian and Julio Ribera. *The Vagabond of Limbo: What Is Reality, Papa?* Montreal: Dargaud Canada, 1981. 52 pp.

2416. Hugues, Daniel. "Un Petit Clown en Bas de l'Échelle." *Les Cahiers de la Bande Dessinée*. 59, 1984, pp. 38-40.

2417. Igual, A. "La Production de Godard à Vaillant/Pif." *Cahiers Universitaires*. No. 19, 1972.

2418. Jennequin, Jean-Paul. "Christian Godard." *Comics Journal*. July 1989, p. 46.

2419. Sadoul, Numa. "Entretien avec Ch. Godard." *Cahiers Universitaires*. No. 19, 1972.

2420. Sadoul, Numa. "Entretien avec Christian Godard." *Les Cahiers de la Bande Dessinée*. 59, 1984, pp. 7-17.

2421. Sadoul, Numa. "Godard ou la BD d'Auteur." *Cahiers Universitaires*. No. 19, 1972.

2422. Sadoul, Numa. "Notes Anthrométriques pour une Approche de Godard." *Cahiers Universitaires*. No. 19, 1972.

Goossens, Daniel

2423. Groensteen, Thierry. "Goossens. Le Téléspectateur Flaubert." *Les Cahiers de la Bande Dessinée*. 63, 1985, pp. 72-74.

2424. Lecigne, Bruno and Jean-Pierre Tamine. "Goossens et la Fission Nucléaire." *Les Cahiers de la Bande Dessinée*. 63, 1985, pp. 76-77.

2425. Léturgie, Jean. "Entretien avec Goossens." *Schtroumpfanzine*. 25, 1978, pp. 16-20.

Goscinny, René

2426. Cance, Louis, Henri Filippini, Jacques Glénat, Thierry Martens, Numa Sadoul, and Louis Teller. "Bibliographie de René Goscinny." *Schtroumpf. Les Cahiers de la Bande Dessinée*. 22, 1973, pp. 46-50.

2427. Eudes, Dominique. "René Goscinny." *Linus*. No. 13, 1966, p. 1.

2428. Faur, Jean-Claude. "Adieu René Goscinny!" *Richochet* (Bibliothéque Centrale de Prêt, Montauban). No. 7, 1978, pp. 17-20.

2429. Goscinny, René. "Comics in France." *Cartoonist PROfiles*. No. 19, 1973, pp. 18-25.

2430. Goscinny, René and Tabary. *The Caliph's Vacation*. The Adventures of Caliph Haroun Al Sa'afti. New York: Dargaud International, 1982. 46 pp.

2431. Levy, Francine. "Le Petit Poucet de Perrault à Goscinny." *Humoresques*. 2 (1988), pp. 67-76.

2432. Morand, Claude. "Les Trois Messages de Goscinny." *Arts*. October 19, 1966.

2433. Nye, Russel B. "Death of a Gaulois: René Goscinny and Astérix." *Journal of Popular Culture*. Fall 1980, pp. 181-195.

2434. Philippe, Claude-Jean. *René Goscinny*. Paris: Seghers, 1976.

2435. Potin, Jacques. "René Goscinny Parle de Son Héros: Astérix." *Presse Actualité* (Paris). 34, 1967, pp. 40-47.

2436. "Qui Es-Tu Réné Goscinny? Le Père Tranquille du Bouillant Astérix." *Salut les Copains*. December 1969, pp. 84-86.

2437. Sadoul, Numa. "Entretien avec René Goscinny." *Schtroumpf. Les Cahiers de la Bande Dessinée*. 22, 1973, pp. 5-18.

2438. Sadoul, Numa. "Morris Parle de René Goscinny et de 'Lucky Luke.'" *Schtroumpf. Les Cahiers de la Bande Dessinée*. 22, 1973, pp. 20-23.

2439. Sadoul, Numa. "René Goscinny, Un Humoriste Qui S'Amuse." *Schtroumpf. Les Cahiers de la Bande Dessinée*. 22, 1973, pp. 32-33.

2440. Sadoul, Numa. "Tabary Parle de René Goscinny et du 'Grand Vizir Iznogoud.'" *Schtroumpf. Les Cahiers de la Bande Dessinée*. 22, 1973, pp. 30-31.

2441. Sullerot, Eveline. "Chèr Goscinny, Vous Oubliez Vos Gauloises." *Giff-Wiff*. No. 21, 1966.

Gotlib, Marcel (Marcel Gotlieb)

2442. Dreyfus, Antoine. "Super Gotlib!" *Le Quotidien de Paris*. January 22, 1992, p. iv.

2443. Faur, Jean-Claude. "Comment Je n'Ai Jamais Revu Gotlib." *L'Hebdo de la B.D.* No. 54, 1991, pp. 2-3.

2444. Filet, G., Numa Sadoul, and Jacques Glénat. "Bibliographie de Gotlib." *Cahiers Universitaires.* No. 13, 1971.

2445. Glénat, Jacques and Numa Sadoul. "Schtroumpf Rencontre Gotlieb." *Cahiers Universitaires.* No. 13, 1969.

2446. Lehner, René. "Gotlib." *Comic Forum. Das Österreichische Fachmagazin für Comicliteratur.* 4:15 (1982), pp. 50-56.

2447. Lindon, Mathieu. "Marcel Gotlib, de 'Pif le Chien' à Jean Daniel." *Libération.* Supplement Special Angoulême 1992, pp. viii-ix.

2448. Moliterni, Claude. "Gotlib, Interview." *Phénix.* No. 18, 1971.

2449. "'Pour Moi, C'est l'Equivalent du Nobel.'" *Le Quotidien de Paris.* January 22, 1992, p. v.

2450. Poyet, Marie-Ange. "Les Coups de Coeur de... Gotlib." *Figaroscope.* January 22, 1992, p. 6.

2451. Rebiére, Michel. "La Fête au Président Marcel." *Charente Libre.* January 23, 1992, p. 10.

2452. Sadoul, Numa. *Gotlib.* Paris: Albin Michel, coll. "Graffiti," 1974.

2453. Sadoul, Numa. "Gotlib le Grave, ou la Face Cachée de l'Humour." *Cahiers Universitaires.* No. 13, 1971.

2454. Tua, Christian. "Accusé Marcel G. Inventeur Fou." *Charente Libre.* January 23, 1992, p. 22.

Grandville (Jean Ignace Isidore Gérard)

2455. Alvarus (Álvaro Cotrim). "Grandville, um Caricaturista Perseguido pela Morte." *Vamos Ler!* (Rio de Janeiro). May 7, 1942.

2456. Blanc, Charles. *Grandville.* Paris: Emile Audois, 1855.

2457. Cabanès, (Docteur). "Un Grand Caricaturiste Visionnaire: Grandville." In *Autour de la Vie de Bohème,* pp. 177-204. Paris: Albin Michel, 1938.

2458. *Catalogue Illustré des Dessins et Croquis Originaux Exécutés à l'Aquarelle, à la Sépia, à la Plume et au Crayon par J.-J. Grandville Dont la Vente Aura Lieu*

Après Son Décès à Paris, Rue des Jeûneurs, 42 Salle n° 3 [,] les 4 et 5 Mars 1853 à Une Heure. Paris: Typographie de Plon Frères, 1853.

2459. Cuno, James. Review of *"Grandville: Dessins Originaux* by Clive F. Getty."
Review, *Art Bulletin.* September 1988, p. 533.

2460. de Meixmoron de Dombasle, C. "J.-J. Grandville." *Memoires de l'Académie de Stanislas*, 1893. 5ᵉ Serie, Vol. 11, pp. 300-339. Nancy: 1894.

2461. *Fantastic Illustrations of Grandville. 266 Illustrations from "Un Autre Monde" and "Les Animaux."* Intro. by Stanley Appelbaum. New York: Dover Publications, 1974. 165 pp.

2462. Garcin, Laure. *J.J. Grandville, Révolutionnaire et Précurseur de l'Art du Mouvement.* Paris: Eric Losfeld, 1970.

2463. "Grandville: Opposition Caricature and Political Harassment." *Print Collector's News Letter.* January-February 1984, pp. 197-201.

2464. Grandville, J.J. *Die Phantasien des Grandville.* Paris: Melzer, 1976. 96 pp.

2465. Grandville, J.J. *Galérie Mythologique.* Paris: Bulla Éditeur, n.d., ca. 1830.

2466. Grandville, J.J. *Grandville's Animals, the World's Vaudeville.* Intro. by Bryan Holme. London: Thames and Hudson, 1981. 64 pp.

2467. Grandville, J.J. *Scènes de la Vie Privée et Publique des Animaux.* 2 Vols. Paris: J. Hetzel et Paulin Éditeurs, 1842.

2468. *Grandville: Das Gesamte Werk.* 2 Vols. Munich: Rogner u. Bernhard, 1969.

2469. "Grandville: 1803-1847: Reproductions: Caricatures d'Homme à Tete d'Animal." *Connaissance des Arts.* May 1987, p. 67.

2470. Jakovski, Anatole. "Grandville." *Arts de France* (Paris). Nos. 19-20, 1948.

2471. *J.J. Grandville.* Paris: *Cahier de l'Art Mineur*, No. 1, 1976. 64 pp. Reprinted from *Cahier de l'Art Mineur.* 2nd Trim., 1976.

2472. J(anin), J(ules). "Grandville." In *Biographie Universelle (Michaud) Ancienne et Moderne*, pp. 340-346. Paris: C. Desplaces et M. Michaud, 1854. Vol. XVII.

2473. Kaenel. "Le Buffon de l'Humanité: La Zoologie Politique de J.-J. Grandville (1803-1847)." *Revue de l'Art.* January-February 1986, pp. 21-28.

2474. Münz, Ludwig. "Über die Bildsprache von Jean Ignace Isidore Gérard Dit Grandville (1803-1847)." *Alte und Neue Kunst/Wiener Kunstwissenschaftliche Blätter.* 3:3/4 (1954).

2475. Nawiasky, Mechtild. "Grandville, a Forerunner of Walt Disney." *Liliput* (London). August 1943.

2476. Sello, Gottfried. *Grandville, Das Gesamte Werk.* Munich: 1969.

2477. Vinchon, Jean. "Grandville." *Les Nouvelles Littéraires* (Paris). September 14, 1950.

Grévin, A.

2478. Grévin, A. *A. Grévin.* Coll. "Les Maîtres Humoristes." Preface by Jérôme Ducet. Paris: Libr. Félix Juven, 1907.

2479. Grévin, A. *Les Filles d'Ève.* Paris: Tip. Henri Plon, n.d.

2480. Grévin, A. *Les Nouveaux Travestissements Parisiens.* Paris: Aux Bureaux du *Journal Amusant* et du *Petit Journal pour Rire*, n.d.

2481. Grévin, A. *L'Esprit des Femmes.* Preface by Pierre Veron. Paris: Dusacq et Cie, n.d.

Guillaume, Albert

2482. Alvarus. "Albert Guillaume." *Vamos Ler!* (Rio de Janeiro). September 3, 1942.

2483. G.E.C. "Le Donne e i Caricaturista Albert Guillaume." *Follie dell'Umorismo* (Rome). March 15, 1952.

2484. Guillaume, Albert. *Albert Guillaume. Les Maîtres Humoristes.* Preface by Alfred Capus. Paris: Librairie Félix Juven, 1907.

2485. Guillaume, Albert. *Contre le Spleen.* 100 Dessins. Paris: H. Simonis Empis, Éditeur, 1902.

2486. Guillaume, Albert. *Des Bonshommes.* Iᵉ série. Preface by Francis Chevassu. Paris: H. Simonis Empis, Éditeur, n.d. IIᵉ série. Preface by Henri Lavedan. Paris: H. Simonis Empis, Éditeur n.d.

2487. Guillaume, Albert. *Étoiles de Mer.* Preface by Abel Hermant. Paris: H. Simonis Empis, Éditeur, 1896.

2488. Guillaume, Albert. *Faut Voir.* Preface by Auguste Germain. Paris: H. Simonis Empis, Éditeur, n.d.

2489. Guillaume, Albert. *Les Repas à Travers des Âges*. Paris: Charles Delagrave, n.d.

2490. Guillaume, Albert. *Les Unes et les Autres*. 100 Dessins. Paris: Garnier Frères, 1905.

2491. Guillaume, Albert. *Madame Est Servie*. Paris: H. Simonis Empis, Éditeur, 1896.

2492. Guillaume, Albert. *Madame Veut Rire*. 100 Dessins, Paris: H. Simonis Empis, Éditeur, 1902.

2493. Guillaume, Albert. *Memóires d'une Glace*. Preface by Paul Hervieu. Paris: H. Simonis Empis, Éditeur, n.d.

2494. Guillaume, Albert. *Mes Campagnes*. Preface by Georges Courteline. Paris: H. Simonis Empis, Éditeur, n.d.

2495. Guillaume, Albert. *Mes 26 Jours*. Preface by Edouard Detaille. Paris: H. Simonis Empis, Éditeur, n.d.

2496. Guillaume, Albert. *Mon Sursis*. Preface by Richard Ó. Monroy. Paris: H. Simonis Empis, Éditeur, n.d.

2497. Guillaume, Albert. *Pour Vos Beaux Yeux*. Preface by Coquelin Cadet. Paris: H. Simonis Empis, Éditeur, n.d.

2498. Guillaume, Albert. *P'tites Femmes*. Preface by Fernand Vaudérem. Paris: H. Simonis Empis, Éditeur, n.d.

2499. Guillaume, Albert. *R'vue d'Fin d'Année*. Preface by Miguel Zamacois. Paris: H. Simonis Empis, Éditeur, n.d.

2500. Guillaume, Albert. "Souvenirs d'un Humoriste." *Les Oeuvres Libres* (Paris). September 1951.

2501. Guillaume, Albert. *Y a des Dames*. Preface by Willy. Paris: H. Simonis Empis, Éditeur, n.d.

2502. Puech, Lucien. "Albert Guillaume Intime." In *L'Album*. I. Paris: Montgrédien, 1901.

2503. Sergines. "Les Puzzles d'Albert Guillaume." *Les Annales* (Paris). No. 1410.

Guys, Constantin

2504. Baudelaire, Charles. *Le Peintre de la Vie Moderne*. Paris: Éditions René Kierfer, 1923; Geneva: Éditions La Palatine, n.d.

2505. Duflo, Pierre. *Constantin Guys, Fou de Dessin, Grand Reporter, 1802-1892.* Paris: Seydoux, 1988.

2506. Grigson, Geoffrey. "Constantin Guys: War Correspondent, Dandy and So On." *Liliput* (London). May 1944.

2507. Roger-Marx, Claude. *Constantin Guys.* "Coll. des Maîtres." Paris: Les Éditions Braun et Cie, 1949.

Hémard, Joseph

2508. Hémard, Joseph. *Autobiographie... par Lui-Même.* Preface by Georges Grappe. Paris: Henri Babon, Éd., 1928.

2509. Hémard, Joseph. *Chez les Fritz. Notes et Croquis de Captivité.* Preface by J. Germain. Paris: L'Édition Française Illustrée, 1919.

2510. Hémard, Joseph. *30 Tableaux d'Histoire de France Revue et Corrigée.* Paris: Édition du *Sourire*, 1912.

Hermann-Paul

2511. Hermann-Paul. *Deux Cents Dessins. 1897-1899.* (La Campagne pour la Revision. Affaire Dreyfus). Paris: Éditions de la *Revue Blanche*, 1900.

2512. Hermann-Paul. *Hermann-Paul.* Coll. "Les Maîtres Humoristes." Paris: Libr. Félix Juven, 1907.

2513. Hermann-Paul. *Les Amours de Jules.* Paris: Libr. Félix Juven, n.d.

2514. Lago, Silvio. "Ante Unos Dibujos de Hermann-Paul." *La Esfera* (Madrid). October 7, 1916.

Huard, Charles

2515. Huard, Charles. *Charles Huard.* Coll. "Les Maîtres Humoristes." Paris: Libr. Félix Juven, 1908.

2516. Huard, Charles. *Londres, Comme Je l'ai Vu.* Paris: Eugène Rey, Libr. Éditeur, 1908.

2517. Huard, Charles. *Paris, Province, Étranger.* 100 Dessins. Paris: Eugène Rey, Libr. Éditeur, 1906.

Jossot

2518. Jossot. *Femelles.* Paris: Société d'Éditions Littéraires et Artistiques, 1901.

2519. Jossot. *Mince de Trognes!* Preface by Henri Bauer. Paris: Chez G. Hazard, 1896.

Juillard, André

2520. "Bibliographie de Juillard." *Les Cahiers de la Bande Dessinée.* 56, 1984, pp. 35-36.

2521. Groensteen, Thierry. "Entretien avec André Juillard." *Les Cahiers de la Bande Dessinée.* 56, 1984, pp. 6-14.

2522. Groensteen, Thierry. "Profil d'Une Carrière." *Les Cahiers de la Bande Dessinée.* 56, 1984, pp. 15-17.

2523. Hugues, Daniel. "Entre l'Aigle et l'Épervier." *Les Cahiers de la Bande Dessinée.* 56, 1984, pp. 23-25.

2524. Martin, Jacques. "André Juillard, l'Héritier." *Les Cahiers de la Bande Dessinée.* 56, 1984, pp. 4-5.

2525. Saouter Caya, Catherine. "Le Paysage Selon Juillard." *Les Cahiers de la Bande Dessinée.* 72, 1986, pp. 72-73.

Lauzier, Gérard

2526. Caré, Jean-Marc. "Lauzier: Haro Sur les Cadres." *Le Français dans le Monde.* 164, 1981, pp. 15-16.

2527. Forestier, Isabelle and Jean Léturgie. "Entretien avec Gérard Lauzier." *Schtroumpfanzine.* 26, 1979, pp. 3-11.

Léandre, Charles

2528. Léandre, Charles. *Charles Léandre*. Coll. "Les Maîtres Humoristes." 2 Albums. Paris: Libr. Félix Juven, 1908.

2529. Léandre, Charles. *Croquis d'Audience* (L'Affaire Humbert). 102 Croquis Pris au Tribunal. Paris: Libr. Félix Juven, n.d.

2530. Léandre, Charles. *Nocturnes*. Preface by Pierre Veber. Paris: H. Simonis Empis, Éd., n.d.

2531. Léandre, Charles. *Paris et Provence*. Paris: Libr. Félix Juven, 1897.

2532. Léandre, Charles. *Veber et Cadel, Musée des Souverains*. Paris: Libr. Félix Juven, ed., 1888.

2533. Lima, Herman. "Charles Léandre, Rabelais do Lápis." *Rio Magazine* (Rio de Janeiro). August 1951.

2534. Lima, Herman. "O Rabelaisiano Charles Léandre." *Vamos Ler!* (Rio de Janeiro). November 23, 1944.

Leclerc, Michel-Edouard

2535. Drapeau, Ivan. "Michel-Edouard Leclerc: 'Je n'Embaucherais pas Bidochon.'" *Charente Libre*. January 23, 1992, p. 11.

2536. Nivelle, Pascale. "La Ligne Leclerc." *Libération*. Supplement Special Angoulême 1992, p. xiv.

Loisel, Régis

2537. Kaps, Joachim. "Mit Bildern Träume Erzählen Régis Loisel und Seine Comics." *ICOM*. October 1992, pp. 16-27.

2538. Truck, Walter. "Rosige Zeiten?" *ICOM*. October 1992, p. 28.

Manchette, Jean-Patrick

2539. Costa Magna, Michele. "Les Bandes Dessinées de Jean-Patrick Manchette." *(A Suivre)*. November 1979, pp. 35-36.

2540. "Les Bandes Dessinées de Jean-Patrick Manchette." *(A Suivre)*. November 1979, pp. 35-36.

Mandryka, Nikita

2541. "Bibliographie." *Schtroumpf. Les Cahiers de la Bande Dessinée.* 28, 1975, pp. 37-43.

2542. Filippini, Henri. "Il Était Une Fois... Kalkus." *Schtroumpf. Les Cahiers de la Bande Dessinée.* 28, 1975, pp. 28-29.

2543. Sadoul, Numa. "Entretien avec Mandryka." *Schtroumpf. Les Cahiers de la Bande Dessinée.* 28, 1975, pp. 7-22.

Margerin, Frank

2544. Blanc, Anita. "Margerin: La Nouvelle Idole des Jeunes." *Livres Hebdo.* 5:2 (1983), pp. 88-89.

2545. Jennequin, Jean-Paul. "Frank Margerin." *Comics Journal.* August 1988, pp. 21-22.

2546. Léturgie, Jean. "Entretien avec Frank Margerin." *Schtroumpfanzine.* 27, 1979, pp. 3-10.

Martin, Jacques

2547. *Alix, Lefranc et Jacques Martin.* Brussels: R.T.P., 1975.

2548. Bouyer, Sylvain. "Mais Aussi... Alix, Jhen... et Jacques Martin. La Tour de Babel ou le Symbolisme de l'Échec." In Groupe Interdisciplinaire de Recherche Universitaire sur la Bande Dessinée. *A la Rencontre de Jacques Martin*, pp. 141-151. Marseilles: Bédésup, 1985.

2549. Chaboud, Jack. "Jacques Martin de la Méthode Historique." In Groupe Interdisciplinaire de Recherche Universitaire sur la Bande Dessinée. *A la Rencontre de Jacques Martin*, pp. 153-155. Marseilles: Bédésup, 1985.

2550. Groupe Interdisciplinaire de Recherche Universitaire sur la Bande Dessinée (Université Paul-Valéry de Montpellier). *A la Rencontre de Jacques Martin.* Marseilles: Bédésup, 1985.

2551. Impériali, Guy. "Jacques Martin: Le Précurseur et l'Honneur de l'Antiquité Faite Homme." In Groupe Interdisciplinaire de Recherche Universitaire sur la Bande Dessinée. *A la Rencontre de Jacques Martin*, pp. 171-175. Marseilles: Bédésup, 1985.

2552. Lequeux, Jean Claude. "Jacques Martin: 'Pas de Bing! de Crack! ni de Bong!'" *Français 2000*. 105, 1982, pp. 31-37.

2553. Lequeux, Michel. "Dessiner l'Histoire avec Jacques Martin." *Français 2000*. 105, 1982, pp. 19-30.

2554. "1984. Année Martin." *Les Cahiers de la Bande Dessinée*. 56, 1984, pp. 37-38.

2555. Sanders, Alain. "Jhen: Jacques Martin, C'Est Beaucoup Plus Que Jacques Martin." In Groupe Interdisciplinaire de Recherche Universitaire sur la Bande Dessinée. *A la Rencontre de Jacques Martin*, pp. 167-170. Marseilles: Bédésup, 1985.

2556. Sanders, Alain. "Les Aventures de Jacques Martin au Pays des Sectaires." *L'Astrolabe* (Paris). 1:80 (1985), pp. 33-34.

2557. Sanders, Alain. "Retour aux Sources." *L'Astrolabe*. 1:80 (1985), pp. 24-26.

Mattotti, Lorenzo

2558. Sisci, Francesco. "L'Indispensable: Lorenzo Mattotti." *Les Cahiers de la Bande Dessinée*. 68, 1986, pp. 4-5.

2559. Sterckx, Pierre. "Pleins Feux sur Mattotti." *Les Cahiers de la Bande Dessinée*. 71, 1986, pp. 54-57.

Mezieres, Jean-Claude

2560. Glénat, Jacques. "Schtroumpf Rencontre Linus et Mézières." *Cahiers Universitaires*. No. 7, 1970.

2561. Kraft, David A. "Jean-Claude Mézières." *Comics Interview*. No. 77, 1989, pp. 30-39, 41-45.

2562. Mézières, Jean-Claude and Pierre Christin. *Ambassador of the Shadows*. Valerian Spatiotemporal Agent. New York: Dargaud International, 1981. 52 pp.

2563. Mézières, Jean-Claude and Pierre Christin. *Heroes of the Equinox*. Valerian Spatiotemporal Agent. New York: Dargaud International, 1983. 48 pp.

2564. Mézières, Jean-Claude and Pierre Christin. *Welcome to Alflolol*. Valerian Spatiotemporal Agent. New York: Dargaud International, 1983. 48 pp.

2565. Mézières, Jean-Claude and Pierre Christin. *World Without Stars*. Valerian Spatiotemporal Agent. New York: Dargaud International, 1982. 52 pp.

Monnier, Henry

2566. Champfleury. *Henry Monnier. Sa Vie, Son Oeuvre*. Paris: E. Dentu, Éd., 1879.

2567. Marie, Aristide. *Henry Monnier*. Paris: Librairie Floury, 1931.

2568. Melcher, Edith. *The Life and Times of Henry Monnier, 1799-1877*. Cambridge, Massachusetts: Harvard University Press, 1950.

2569. Monnier, Henry. *À Baton Rompu*. Paris: Éditions Pierre Horay, 1953.

2570. Monnier, Henry. *Moeurs Administratifs, Dessinées d'Après Nature*. Paris: n.p., n.d.

Montellier, Chantal

2571. Bossati, Patrick. "Une Image Juste." *Les Cahiers de la Bande Dessinée*. 65, 1985, pp. 80-81.

2572. de Pierpont, Jacques. "Méfaits Divers." *Les Cahiers de la Bande Dessinée*. 65, 1985, pp. 84-85.

2573. Groensteen, Thierry. "Entretien avec Chantal Montellier." *Les Cahiers de la Bande Dessinée*. 65, 1985, pp. 68-74.

2574. Lecigne, Bruno. "Graffiti et Correspondances." *Les Cahiers de la Bande Dessinée*. 65, 1985, p. 75.

2575. Sterckx, Pierre. "Le Blanc Montellier." *Les Cahiers de la Bande Dessinée*. 65, 1985, pp. 86-87.

Mulatier/Ricord/Morchoisne

2576. "Logic of Exaggeration." *Kayhan Caricature*. November 1992.

2577. Mulatier/Ricord/Morchoisne. *Ces Animaux Qui Nous Gouvernent. Tome 2.* Paris: France Loisirs, 1987. 58 pp.

2578. Mulatier/Ricord/Morchoisne. *Ces Animaux Qui Nous Gouvernent.* Paris: Dervish Publications, 1964. 64 pp.

2579. "Mulatier Morchoisne Ricord." *Kayhan Caricature.* January 1993.

Nitka

2580. Nitka. *Oh Oui Docteur.* Paris: Loempia, 1987.

2581. Nitka. *Rien Que Ça.* Paris: Loempia, 1987.

2582. Nitka. *Vie de Chien.* Paris: Éditions Loempia, 1987.

Norma (Norbert Morandière)

2583. Filippini, Henri. "Entretien avec Norma." *Schtroumpfanzine.* 17, 1978, pp. 15-21.

2584. Tschernegg, Markus. "'Flammender Speer' Eine Comicserie von Norbert Morandiere (Norma) und Roger Lecureux." *Comic Forum. Das Österreichische Fachmagazin für Comicliteratur.* 3:10 (1981), pp. 44-46.

Pesch, Jean-Louis (Jean-Louis Poisson)

2585. Faur, Jean-Claude. "Comment Je Suis Devenu Éditeur Porno Grâce à Jean-Louis Pesch." *L'Hebdo de la B.D.* No. 45, 1990, p. 6.

2586. Faur, Jean-Claude. "Entretien avec... Jean-Louis Pesch." *Bédésup* (La Roque d'Anthéron). 9, 1979, p. 6.

Pellos, René

2587. Faur, Jean-Claude. *Retrospective René Pellos: de Futuropolis aux Pieds Nickelés.* Toulouse: Bibliothèque Municipale, 1974. 9 pp.

2588. Faur, Jean-Claude. "Un Grand Chef-d'Oeuvre de la Bande Dessinée Française: 'Atomas' de René Pellos." *Athanor.* No. 1, 1977, pp. 53-54.

2589. Filippini, Henri. "Entretien avec Pellos." *Schtroumpf. Les Cahiers de la Bande Dessinée*. 31, 1976, pp. 6-19.

2590. Ghébali, Victor-Yves and Catherine, Louis Cance, and Henri Filippini. "Bibliographie." *Schtroumpf. Les Cahiers de la Bande Dessinée*. 31, 1976, pp. 33-42.

2591. Lacassin, Francis. "De Forton à Pellos." *Azur* (Paris). 1965.

2592. Maric, Raymond. "Quarante Ans d'Amitié." *Caricature et Caricaturistes*. August 1992, pp. 779-787.

2593. Pascal, Pierre. *Pellos*. Angoulême: Éditions Sodieg, 1977.

2594. Pellos. "Pellos." *Caricature et Caricaturistes*. August 1992, pp. 769-779.

2595. "Pellos." *Caricature et Caricaturistes*. August 1992, pp. 758-764, 788-793.

2596. Tibéri, Jean-Paul. "Pellos." *Caricature et Caricaturistes*. August 1992, pp. 765-768.

2597. Tibéri, Jean-Paul. "Pellos, Roi des Dessinateurs Sportifs." *Schtroumpf. Les Cahiers de la Bande Dessinée*. 31, 1976, pp. 24-25.

2598. Tibéri, Jean-Paul. "Les Signatures de Pellos." *Schtroumpf. Les Cahiers de la Bande Dessinée*. 31, 1976, p. 21.

Peynet, Raymond

2599. Peynet, Raymond. *Aus Lauter Liebe Ein Bilderbuch für Zartliche Leute*. Hamburg: Rowohlt Verlag, 1953.

2600. Peynet, Raymond. *Les Amoureux de Peynet*. Preface by Max Favalelli. Paris: V. de Valence, Éditeur, 1953.

2601. Peynet, Raymond. *Le Tour du Monde. Les Amoureux de Peynet*. Preface by Paul Guth. Paris: V. de Valence, Éditeur, 1954.

2602. Peynet, Raymond. *Verliebte Welt. Ein Bilderbuch für Liebende und Andere Optimisten*. Hamburg: Rowohlt Verlag, 1949.

Philipon, Charles

2603. Bechtel, Edwin de Turck. *Freedom of the Press and L'Association Mensuelle; Philipon Adversus Louis-Philippe*. New York: New York Album, Grolier Club, 1952.

2604. Cuno, James. "The Business and Politics of Caricature: Charles Philipon and La Maison Aubert." *Gazette des Beaux-Arts*. October 1985, pp. 95-112.

2605. Cuno, James. "Charles Philipon and La Maison Aubert: The Business, Politics, and Public of Caricature in Paris, 1820-1840." Ph.D. dissertation, Harvard University, 1985.

2606. Cuno, James. "Charles Philipon, La Maison Aubert, and the Business of Caricature in Paris, 1829-41." *Art Journal*. Winter 1983, pp. 347-354.

2607. Cuno, James. "Philipon, Desloges and the Politics of 'Les Physiologies,' 1841-1842." *Cahiers de l'Étude de la Presse et l'Opinion*. 1983/1984.

2608. *Musée ou Magazin Comique de Philipon*. Paris: Chez Aubert et Cie, ca. 1842.

Plantu

2609. Plantu. *À la Soupe!* Paris: Imprimerie du "Monde," 1987. 144 pp.

2610. "Quelques Pubs (Plantu)." *Mieux Vaut en Rire*. No. 5 (n.d.), pp. 73-75.

Poïvet, Raymond

2611. Cance, Louis and Henri Filippini. "Raymond Poïvet. Bibliographie." *Schtroumpf. Les Cahiers de la Bande Dessinée*. 33, 1977, pp. 36-42.

2612. Filippini, Henri. "Entretien avec Raymond Poïvet." *Schtroumpf. Les Cahiers de la Bande Dessinée*. 33, 1977, pp. 7-22.

2613. Franso, Pierre. "Un Poète Imagier: Raymond Poivet." *Miroir du Fantastique* (Paris). No. 4, 1968, pp. 182-185.

Poulbot (Francisque)

2614. Poulbot (Francisque). *Des Gosses et des Bonshommes*. 100 Dessins. Paris: Author, n.d.

2615. Poulbot (Francisque). *Encore des Gosses et des Bonshommes*. 100 Dessins. Paris: Author, n.d.

2616. Poulbot (Francisque). *Poulbot*. Coll. "Les Maîtres Humoristes." Paris: Librairie Félix Juven, 1908.

Préjelen, René

2617. Préjelen, René. *La Légende de Béguinette*. Preface by Pierre Veber. Paris: H. Simonis Empis Éditeur, 1903.

2618. Préjelen, René. *L'Amour en Dentelles*. Preface by Willy. Paris: H. Simonis Empis Éditeur, 1902.

2619. Préjelen, René. *René Préjelen. Les Maîtres Humoristes*. Paris: Libr. Félix Juven, 1908.

Puvis de Chavannes, Pierre

2620. Adam, Marcele. *Les Caricatures de Pierre Puvis de Chavannes*. Paris: Libr. Charles Delagrave, 1905.

2621. Pagáno, José. "Puvis de Chavannes y Gustave Doré, Caricaturistas." In *Formas de Vida*. Buenos Aires: El Ateneo, 1941.

2622. Price, Aimée B. "Puvis de Chavannes's Caricatures: Manifestoes, Commentary, Expressions." *The Art Bulletin*. March 1991, pp. 119-140.

2623. Schmidt, K.E. "Puvis als Karikaturenzeichner." *Zeitschrift für Bildende Kunst*. New Series. XVII, 1906, pp. 63-65.

2624. Vauxcelles, Louis. "Puvis de Chavannes Caricaturiste." *L'Art et les Artistes*. 1, 1905, pp. 9-13.

Rabier, Benjamin

2625. Alberelli, Christian. *Benjamin Rabier*. Grenoble: Eds. Jacques Glénat, 1981.

2626. "Benjamin Rabier Intime. Raconté par Lui-Même." In *L'Album*. Paris: Montgrédien et Cie, 1901.

2627. Floch, Jean Marie. "La Spatialisation et Son Rôle dans la Mise en Discours du Récit: Analyse d'un Récit en Images de B. Rabier." *The Canadian Journal of Research in Semiotics* (Edmonton). 6/7, 1979, pp. 123-137.

2628. Horay, Pierre. *Benjamin Rabier.* Paris: Pierre Horay Éditeur, n.d. 128 pp.

2629. Rabier, Benjamin. *Benjamin Rabier. Les Maîtres Humoristes.* Paris: Libr. Félix Juven, 1907.

2630. Rabier, Benjamin. *Escutem!* Rio de Janeiro: Livraria Garnier, 1921.

2631. Rabier, Benjamin. *O Fundo do Saco.* Rio de Janeiro: Livraria Garnier, 1921.

2632. Rabier, Benjamin. *Pages Folles.* Preface by Fred Isly. Paris: G. Richard Éditeur, n.d.

Reding, R.

2633. Cance, Louis and Louis Teller. "Bibliographie de Reding." *Cahiers Universitaires.* No. 16, 1972.

2634. Glénat, Jacques and Cl. Hebert. "Schtroumpf Rencontre R. Reding." *Cahiers Universitaires.* No. 16, 1972.

2635. Rivière, François. "R. Reding et la Littérature Populaire." *Cahiers Universitaires.* No. 16, 1972.

2636. Sadoul, Numa. "L'Imagination de Reding." *Cahiers Universitaires.* No. 16, 1972.

Reiser, Jean-Marc

2637. Bayon. "La Chute de la Maison Reiser." *Liberation.* November 7, 1983.

2638. Cavanna. "Méchant, Reiser? Non, Féroce." *Liberation.* November 7, 1983, p. 28.

2639. "Dossier Reiser." *Mieux Vaut en Rire.* No. 5. (n.d.), pp. 46-65.

2640. Frémion, Yves. *Reiser.* Paris: Albin Michel, 1974.

2641. Millet, Giles. "Vers la Ligne Triste." *Liberation.* November 7, 1983, p. 29.

2642. Reiser. *Vive les Femmes!* Paris: Editions Albin Michel, 1983. 79 pp.

2643. "Reiser de A à Z." *Liberation*. November 7, 1983.

Roba, Jean

2644. Filet, G. and Jacques Glénat. "Bibliographie de Roba." *Cahiers Universitaires*. No. 16, 1972.

2645. Martens, Th. "La Carrière de Roba." *Cahiers Universitaires*. No. 16, 1972.

2646. Sadoul, Numa. "Pour Jean Roba." *Cahiers Universitaires*. No. 16, 1972.

2647. Sadoul, Numa. "Schtroumpf Rencontre Roba." *Cahiers Universitaires*. No. 16, 1972.

Robida, Albert

2648. Beraldi, H. *Un Caricaturiste Prophète*. Paris: Dorbon-Ainé, 1916.

2649. Robida, Albert. *La Vie Électrique*. Paris: à la Librairie Illustrée, n.d.

2650. Robida, Michel. "Le Centenaire d'Albert Robida." *Les Nouvelles Littéraires* (Paris). November 11, 1948.

Rouveyre, André

2651. Pica, Vittorio. "André Rouveyre." *L'Amour de l'Art* (Paris). No. 3, 4ᵉ Année, 1923.

2652. Rouveyre, André. *Carcasses Divines. 1906-1907*. Paris: Société du *Mercure de France*, 1909.

2653. Rouveyre, André. *150 Caricatures Théâtrales, par Rouveyre*. Prefaces by Catulle Mendés and Ernest la Jeunesse. Paris: Albin Michel, 1904.

2654. Rouveyre, André. *La Comédie Française de Rouveyre*. Preface by Robert de Montesquieu. Paris: Albin Michel, 1906.

2655. Thomas, Louis. *André Rouveyre*. Paris: Les Bibliophiles Fantaisistes, Dorbon-Ainé, 1912.

Saint Ogan, Alain

2656. Leguebe, Eric. "Alain Saint Ogan, Médaille d'Argent de Paris." *Phénix*. No. 18, 1971.

2657. Leguebe, Eric. "Alain Saint Ogan." *Phénix*. No. 22, 1972.

Sem (Georges Goursat)

2658. Bouret, Jean. "Deauville Fête Sem." *Arts Spectacles* (Paris). July 20, 1951.

2659. Doumergue, Jean G. "Sem et Son Oeuvre." *Illustration Française* (Paris). December 8, 1934.

2660. Sem. *Album Sem. Consacré aux Types de Montecarlo.* n.p., n.d.

2661. Sem. *Le Vrai et le Faux Chic.* Paris: Copyright by *Succés*, March 25, 1914.

Sempé, Jean-Jacques

2662. Forlani, Remo. "Sempé avec Nous!" *Giff-Wiff*. No. 15, 1965, p. 32.

2663. Sempé, Jean-Jacques. *Bonsoir.* Paris: Éditions Denoël, 1974.

2664. Sempé, Jean-Jacques. *Des Hauts et des Bas.* Paris: Dencil: 1971. 111 pp.

2665. Sempé, Jean-Jacques. *Face à Face.* Paris: Éditions Denoël, 1972.

2666. Sempé, Jean-Jacques. *Marcellin Caillou.* Paris: Éditions Denoël, 1969. 93 pp.

2667. Sempé, Jean-Jacques. *Nothing Is Simple.* London: MacDonald, 1963. 143 pp.

2668. Sempé, Jean-Jacques. *Rien N'Est Simple.* Paris: Dencel, 1970. 127 pp.

Sennep (Jean Pennès)

2669. Sennep, J. *Album.* Preface by Léo Larguier. Collection Art et Technique. Monte-Carlo: Éditions du Livre, 1943.

2670. Sennep, J. *Au Bout du Quai.* Paris: Éditions Bossard, 1929.

2671. Sennep, J. *Départ à Zero.* Paris: Bordas, 1947.

2672. Sennep, J. *Pierre, Edouard et Léon*. Album du *Nouveau Cri*. Paris: n.d.

Serre, Claude

2673. "Claude Serre, France." *FECO News*. No. 3, 1987, p. 5.

2674. Serre, Claude. *Humour Noir et Hommes en Blanc*. Paris: Glénat, 1984.

2675. Serre, Claude. *La Bouffe*. Paris: Glénat, 1982.

2676. Serre, Claude. *La Forme Olympique*. Grenoble: Glénat, 1991.

2677. Serre, Claude. *L'Automobile*. Paris: Glénat, 1988.

2678. Serre, Claude. *Le Bricolage*. Paris: Glénat, 1983.

2679. Serre, Claude. *Le Sport*. Grenoble: Glénat, 1977.

2680. Serre, Claude. *Les Vacances*. Grenoble: Glénat, 1984.

2681. Serre, Claude. *Petits Anges*. Paris: Glénat, 1985.

2682. Serre, Claude. *Rechute*. Paris: Glénat, 1988.

2683. Serre, Claude. *Savoir Vivre*. Paris: Glénat, 1981.

2684. Serre, Claude. *Still Life*. London: Methuen, 1985.

2685. Serre, Claude. *Vice Compris*. Grenoble: Glénat, 1987.

2686. Serre, Claude. *Zoo au Logis*. Paris: Glénat, 1986.

Siné (Maurice Sinet)

2687. Siné. *CIA*. Paris: Jean-Jacques Pauvert, 1968.

2688. Siné. *A Frenchman's Irreverent Look at Life and Love. Sine Qua Non*. New York: E.P. Dutton and Co., 1961. 92 pp.

2689. Siné. *Les Chats de Siné*. Paris: France Loisirs, 1982.

2690. Sinet, Maurice. *The French Cats*. New York: Simon, 1958. Unpaginated.

Solé, Jean

2691. Léturgie, Jean. "Entretien avec Jean Solé." *Schtroumpfanzine*. 21, 1978, pp. 3-11.

2692. Solé, Jean. *Solé. Animaleries et Compagnie*. Paris: Editions Vents d'Ouest, 1991.

2693. Solé, Jean, comp. *Joyeux Noël*. Paris: Éditions Vents d'Ouest, 1987.

Solo

2694. Solo. *Solo: Le Cassegueules*. Paris: Té Arte, 1987. 112 pp.

2695. Szabo, Joe. "Striving To Achieve the Most with the Least. A Visit with Solo." *WittyWorld*. Summer/Autumn 1992, pp. 15-16, 18-19.

Steinlen, Alexandre

2696. de Carvalho, Ronald. "Steinlen." In *O Espelho de Ariel*, edited by Álvaro Pinto. Rio de Janeiro: *Anuário do Brasil*, n.d.

2697. Jourdain, Francis. *Alexandre Steinlen*. Paris: Éditions Cercle d'Art, 1954.

2698. Marguery, Henry. "Les Chats dans l'Oeuvre de Steinlen." *L'Amateur d'Estampes*. 7 (1928), pp. 47-53.

2699. Steinlen, Alexandre. Catálogo da Exposição na Bibliothèque Nationale de Paris, de maio-junho de 1953, com estudos de Julien Cain, Gerard Bauer, Claude Roger-Marx et Jean Valery-Radot. Paris: Bibliothèque Nationale. 1953.

2700. Steinlen, Alexandre. *La Guerre*. Text by C. Marc Clair. Special number of *L'Art et les Artistes* (Paris). 1918.

2701. Steinlen, Alexandre. *L'Oeuvre Gravée et Lithographiée de Steinlen*. Preface by Claude Roger-Marx. Paris: Societé de Propagation des Livres d'Art, 1913.

2702. Steinlen, Alexandre. *Steinlen et la Rue*. By Serge Auriol. *Saint-Lazare*. By Jacques Dyssoud. Paris: Eugene Rey, Éd., 1930.

2703. Warnod, André. "Steinlen." *Vamos Ler!* (Rio de Janeiro). November 5, 1942.

Tardi, Jacques

2704. "Bibliographie de Jacques Tardi." *Les Cahiers de la Bande Dessinée*. 63, 1985, p. 40.

2705. Bouyer, Sylvain. "Tueur de Pingouins." *Les Cahiers de la Bande Dessinée*. 63, 1985, pp. 20-22.

2706. Dellisse, Luc and Thierry Groensteen. "Vingt-Six Leçons sur la Patrie." *Les Cahiers de la Bande Dessinée*. 63, 1985, pp. 27-29.

2707. de Pierpont, Jacques. "14-18: Voyages au Bout de la Mort." *Les Cahiers de la Bande Dessinée*. 63, 1985, pp. 16-17.

2708. Derouet, Paul. "750 000 Tonnen Fleisch und Knochen... Die Visionen des Jacques Tardi." In *Comic Jahrbuch 1986*, edited by Martin Compart and Andreas C. Knigge, pp. 65-73. Berlin: Ullstein GmbH, 1985.

2709. Everaert-Desmedt, Nicole. "Tardi et la Production d'Absurde par les Structures Narratives." In *A la Rencontre de... Jacques Tardi*, edited by Gari, pp. 113-123. Marseilles: Bédésup, 1982.

2710. Faur, Jean-Claude. "L'Évolution Graphique de Tardi." In *A la Rencontre de... Jacques Tardi*, edited by Gari, pp. 85-86. Marseilles: Bédésup, 1982.

2711. Frenzel, Martin. "Illusion der Zerstörung. Martin Frenzel über den Pastiche-Künstler Jacques Tardi." *Comic Forum. Das Magazin für Comicliteratur*. 6:23 (1984), pp. 45-57.

2712. Gari. *A la Rencontre de... Jacques Tardi*. Marseilles: Bédésup, 1982.

2713. Groensteen, Thierry. *Tardi: Monographie*. Brussels: Magic Strip, 1980.

2714. Groensteen, Thierry. "Entretien avec Jacques Tardi." *Les Cahiers de la Bande Dessinée*. 63, 1985, pp. 7-15.

2715. Hurtig, Alain. "Tardi, le Dessinateur au Trait Noir." *Livres Hebdo*. 5:2 (1983), pp. 90-91.

2716. Lecigne, Bruno. "Jacques Tardi: Une Esthétique de la Citation." *Education 2000*. 21, 1982, pp. 34-37.

2717. Lecigne, Bruno. "Les Préfaces Dessinées de Tardi." In *A la Rencontre de... Jacques Tardi*, edited by Gari, pp. 105-112. Marseilles: Bédésup, 1982.

2718. Pinson, Daniel. "Griffu de Tardi—Manchette ou l'Histoire au Présent." In *Histoire et Bande Dessinée: Actes du 2e Colloque International Éducation et Bande Dessinée*, pp. 127-137. La Roque d'Anthéron: Objectif Promo-Durance, 1979.

2719. Pujade, Robert. "L'Inénarrable (Essai sur l'"Autorité' de Tardi)." In *A la Rencontre de... Jacques Tardi*, edited by Gari, pp. 125-131. Marseilles: Bédésup, 1982.

2720. Renard, Emmanuel. "L'Esthétique de la Mort Chez Tardi." In *A la Rencontre de... Jacques Tardi*, edited by Gari, pp. 31-38. Marseilles: Bédésup, 1982.

2721. Simon, André. "La Guerra de 1914-18 Vista por Tardi." *Neuróptica. Estudios Sobre el Cómic* (Zaragoza). 2, 1984, pp. 112-119.

2722. Tardi, Jacques. *Tardi en Banlieue*. Brussels: Casterman, n.d. 48 pp.

2723. Vissière, Jean Louis. "Mais la Guerre Que Je Préfère, C'Est Celle de 14-18... (G. Brassens)." In *À la Rencontre de... Jacques Tardi*, edited by Gari, pp. 63-65. Marseilles: Bédésup, 1982.

2724. Zureddu, Gérard. "Tardi—Ici et là." In *À la Rencontre de... Jacques Tardi*, edited by Gari, pp. 87-104. Marseilles: Bédésup, 1982.

Tetsu

2725. Tetsu. *C'Est Pas Rose*. Grenoble: Glénat, 1982.

2726. Tetsu. *La Vie Est Belle*. Paris: Jean-Jacques Pauvert, 1964.

2727. Tetsu. *La Vie Est Belle*. Grenoble: Glénat, 1985.

Tim (Louis Mitelberg)

2728. Tim. *Décennie Dessinée 1970-1980*. Paris: Albin Michel, 1980.

2729. Tim. *Époque Épique*. Paris: Albin Michel, 1981.

2730. Henry, Maurice. *Voyages du Rêveur*. Paris: Albin Michel, 1979.

Topor, Roland

2731. Mohsen, Ibrahim. "Topor." *Kayhan Caricature*. November 1992.

2732. "Roland Tapor." *Apropos*. No. 5, 1988, pp. 49-50.

2733. Searle, Ronald. "Roland Topor." *Graphis* (Zurich). No. 133, 1968.

Toulouse-Lautrec, Henri

2734. Alexandre, Arséne. "Toulouse-Lautrec." *Le Figaro Illustré* (Paris). April 1902.

2735. Alvarus (Álvaro Cotrim). "Chas Laborde. Um Herdeiro de Toulouse-Lautrec." *Vamos Ler!* (Rio de Janeiro). July 30, 1942.

2736. Gatard, Marie. "C'est le Destin Cruel et Magnifique de Toulouse-Lautrec." *Paris-Match*. January 17, 1959.

2737. Kennedy, Jean-Louis. "Toulouse-Lautrec." *Vamos Ler!* (Rio de Janeiro). October 15, 1942.

2738. Lotte, Jean-A. "Du Nouveau sur Lautrec." *Nouvelles Littéraires*. August 11, 1949.

2739. Mac Orlan, Pierre. "Lautrec Le Peintre." Paris: Libr. Floury, 1934.

2740. Toulouse-Lautrec. Henri. *Yvette Guilbert*. Text by Claude Roger-Marx. Paris: Pont des Arts, 1950.

Uderzo, Albert

2741. Affolter, Cuno. "Albert Uderzo—Ein Leben für den Comic." *ICOM-INFO*. February 1990, pp. 50-52.

2742. Alber, Wolfgang. "Exclusivinterview mit Uderzo. Interview Übersetzt von Ruth Karzel." *Comic Forum*. 2:7/8 (1980), pp. 94-96.

2743. Baccard, Erik. "Le Gag Visuel Secondaire Chez Uderzo." *Schtroumpf. Les Cahiers de la Bande Dessinée*. 23, 1974, pp. 37-38.

2744. Brunoro, Gianni. "Polyvalence Graphique d'Uderzo." *Schtroumpf. Les Cahiers de la Bande Dessinée*. 23, 1974, pp. 39-42.

2745. Cance, Louis and Louis Teller. "Bibliographie d'Albert Uderzo." *Schtroumpf. Les Cahiers de la Bande Dessinée*. 23, 1974, pp. 44-46.

2746. Frémion, Yves. "Tout sur Uderzo en 20 Questions." *Schtroumpf. Les Cahiers de la Bande Dessinée*. 23, 1974, p. 19.

2747. Giromini, Ferruccio. "Uderzo per Scherzo." *Comic Art*. No. 46, 1988, p. 51.

2748. Glénat, Jacques, Numa Sadoul, and Erik Baccard. "Entretien avec... Albert Uderzo." *Schtroumpf. Les Cahiers de la Bande Dessinée*. 23, 1974, pp. 8-18.

2749. Kabatek, Adolf, ed. *Uderzo. Der Weite Weg zu Astérix*. Stuttgart: Ehapa Verlag, 1986.

2750. Knigge, Andreas C. "Albert Uderzo." *Comixene. Das Comicfachmagazin*. 6:24 (1979), pp. 17-19.

2751. *Schtroumpf: les Cahiers de la Bande Dessinée*. No. 23, 1976. Entire issue on Uderzo, including a long interview and Bibliography.

2752. Tschernegg, Markus. "Von Uderzo... bis Astérix. Eine Betrachtung über Serien des Zeichners in der Zeit vor Astérix." *Comic Forum. Das Österreichische Fachmagazin für Comicliteratur*. 2:7/8 (1980), pp. 97-99.

2753. "Uderzo: France's Answer to Walt Disney." *Hindustan Times* (New Delhi). October 29, 1989.

Veyron, Martin

2754. Bouyer, Sylvain. "Enfermer Veyron." *Les Cahiers de la Bande Dessinée*. 62, 1985, pp. 17-19.

2755. Filippini, Henri. "Entretien avec Martin Veyron." *Schtroumpfanzine*. 32, 1979, pp. 3-9.

2756. Groensteen, Thierry and Bruno Lecigne. "Entretien avec Martin Veyron." *Les Cahiers de la Bande Dessinée*. 62, 1985, pp. 7-12.

2757. Lecigne, Bruno. "Bernard Lermite Va au Spectacle." *Les Cahiers de la Bande Dessinée*. 62, 1985, pp. 14-16.

2758. Van Cauwenbergh, Franz. "Bibliographie de Martin Veyron." *Les Cahiers de la Bande Dessinée*. 62, 1985, pp. 33-34.

Vovelle, Michel

2759. Baur, André. "Interview de Michel Vovelle." *Mieux Vaut en Rire*. No. 13, 1989, p. 75.

2760. "Vovelle." *Mieux Vaut en Rire*. No. 13, 1989, pp. 73-74.

Willette, Adolphe

2761. Beuve, Paul. *Iconographie de A. Willette (De 1861-1909)*. Paris: Charles Bosse, Librairie, 1909.

2762. Brisson, Adolphe. "Silhouettes & Croquis. Le Pierrot de Montmartre." *Les Annales* (Paris). February 18, 1906.

2763. Calderon, Ventura. "Melancolia de Payasos." *La Prensa* (Buenos Aires). May 10, 1931.

2764. "Caricaturist Willette." *Current Literature*. May 1900, p. 123.

2765. de Fourcaud, L. "Avant le Salon. Le Peintre Willette et le Cabaret du *Chat Noir*." *Les Annales Politiques et Littéraires* (Paris). March 20, 1892.

2766. Detouche, Henri. *Les Peintres de la Femme Intégrale, Félicien Rops et A. Willette*. Paris: A. Blizot, Éditeur, 1906.

2767. Geoffroy, Gustave. "L'Art de Willette." *Les Annales* (Paris). No. 1182.

2768. Lemaitre, Jules. "Les Pierrots de Willette." *Les Annales* (Paris). No. 1439.

2769. Teall, G.C. "Art of Willette." *The Bookman*. June 1911, pp. 394-398.

2770. Tild-Jean. "Notes sur Willette." *L'Art et les Artistes* (Paris). February 1909.

2771. Willette, Adolphe. *Feu Pierrot*. Paris: H. Floury, 1919. (Autobiography).

2772. Willette, Adolphe. *1914. Sans Pardon. A Feu! à Poils! et à Sang!* Paris: Devambrez Éditeur, 1914.

2773. Willette, Adolphe. *Oeuvres Choisies*. 100 Dessins. Paris: H. Simonis Empis Éd., 1901.

2774. Willette, Adolphe. *Pauvre Pierrot*. Paris: Chez Leon Vanier, 1884.

2775. Willette, Adolphe. *V'là les English*. Special number of *Le Rire* (Paris). n.d.

2776. Willette, Adolphe. *Willette. Les Maîtres Humoristes.* Paris: Félix Juven, 1907.

2777. Willette, H. *Willette en Chandail. Dans l'Intimité des Grands Artistes.* Paris: Éditions Sansot-L. H. Alexandre, 1926.

2778. "Willette Intime." In *L'Album*, XV. Paris: Montgrédien et Cie, 1901.

CHARACTERS and TITLES

2779. Andrevon, Jean-Pierre. "Les Naufragés du Temps, une Interpénétration Conflictuelle." *Schtroumpf. Les Cahiers de la Bande Dessinée.* 36, 1978, pp. 31-35.

2780. Andrevon, Jean-Pierre. "'Les Pionniers de l'Espérance.' Repères Thématiques et Esthétiques." *Schtroumpf. Les Cahiers de la Bande Dessinée.* 33, 1977, pp. 26-29.

2781. "Arabelle la Sirène." *Candide.* No. 305, 1967, p. 20.

2782. Baldrey, Danièle and Jacqueline Demarty. "Du Roman à la Bande Dessinée. Brouillard au Pont de Tolbiac." *Le Français dans le Monde.* 200, 1986, pp. 63-69.

2783. Bergeron, Francis. "Esprit Scout pas Mort! La Patrouille des Castors." *L'Astrolabe.* 1:80 (1985), pp. 17-19.

2784. Bergeron, Francis. "Partie de Chasse (sans Andropov)." *L'Astrolabe.* 1:80 (1985), pp. 35-36.

2785. Bleicher-Viehoff, Thomas A.T. "Bobo 'The King of Knast' 20 Jahre Bobo in Deutschland (1966-1986)." *Comic Forum. Das Magazin für Comicliteratur.* 8:33 (1986), pp. 35-36.

2786. Bouchu, G. "Le Secret de Yakari." *Schtroumpf. Les Cahiers de la Bande Dessinée.* 50, 1981, pp. 31-33.

2787. Brunoro, Gianni. "La Reschtroumpfance du Schtroumpf de Fées." *Cahiers Universitaires.* No. 12, 1971.

2788. "Buck Brady Rides in Paris." *Newsweek.* March 24, 1947, p. 66.

2789. Chante, Alain. "Martin Milan, Un Homme, Un Vrai." *Les Cahiers de la Bande Dessinée.* 59, 1984, pp. 26-28.

2790. Chante, Alain. "Rififi: Altruiste, Philosophe ou Misanthrope?" *Les Cahiers de la Bande Dessinée.* 63, 1985, pp. 94-95.

2791. de Cortanze, Gérard. "Vies et Rêves de Thomas Noland." *Les Cahiers de la Bande Dessinée*. 64, 1985, pp. 29-31.

2792. de Goede, J. "Hans Kresse et Eric l'Homme du Nord." *Phénix*. No. 12, 1969.

2793. Dégru, Alain. "Fantasque et Fantastique Iznogoud." *Schtroumpf. Les Cahiers de la Bande Dessinée*. 22, 1973, pp. 41-43.

2794. Dellisse, Luc. "Le Tube et la Tour." *Les Cahiers de la Bande Dessinée*. 69, 1986, pp. 31-33.

2795. Dellisse, Luc. "Mort de Jeannette Pointu." *Les Cahiers de la Bande Dessinée*. 67, 1986, pp. 34-35.

2796. Dellisse, Luc. "Quelle Jungle? Quelle Folie?" *Les Cahiers de la Bande Dessinée*. 59, 1984, pp. 24-25.

2797. Di Manno, Yves. "Marc Dacier Reporter." *Cahiers Universitaires*. No. 17, 1972.

2798. Di Manno, Yves. and A. Igual. "La Ribambelle aux Galopingos." *Cahiers Universitaires*. No. 16, 1972.

2799. Duveau, Christian and Marc. "The Avengers." *Horizons du Fantastique* (Paris). No. 18, 1971.

2800. Ecken, Claude. "Bernard Prince. Entre l'Eau et le Feu." *Schtroumpf. Les Cahiers de la Bande Dessinée*. 44, 1980, pp 28-31.

2801. Ecken, Claude. "Ce Cochon d'Edmond!" *Les Cahiers de la Bande Dessinée*. 62, 1985, pp. 28-30.

2802. Filippini, Henri. "Olivier Rameau ou un Monde sur Mesure." *Schtroumpf. Les Cahiers de la Bande Dessinée*. 49, 1981, p. 25.

2803. François, Edouard. "La Planète Mongo." *Phénix*. No. 3, 1967, pp. 17-20.

2804. "French Edition of *Dark Knight* Is Critical Success." *Comics Journal*. September 1987, p. 27.

2805. Fresnault-Deruelle, Pierre. "Lilliput en BD." *Phénix*. No. 24, 1972.

2806. Groensteen, Thierry. "Carpets' Bazaar, le Rouleau sans Visage." *Les Cahiers de la Bande Dessinée*. 72, 1986, pp. 87-90.

2807. "Kinky—I Love You et la Prima Donna." *L'Express*. No. 843, 1967, p. 60.

2808. Labesse, Dominique. "Popol et Virginie." *Cahiers Universitaires*. No. 14, 1971.

2809. Labesse, Dominique. "Quick et Flupke." *Cahiers Universitaires*. No. 14, 1971.

2810. Labesse, Dominique. "Zo, Zette et Jocko." *Cahiers Universitaires*. No. 14, 1971.

2811. Laurenceau, Georges. "La Syldavie et le Bordurie." *Cahiers Universitaires*. No. 14, 1971.

2812. Lecigne, Bruno. "Ici Même, le Chaînon Manquant." *Les Cahiers de la Bande Dessinée*. 63, 1985, pp. 30-32.

2813. Le Gallo, Claude. "Elaoin Sdretu." *Phénix*. No. 24, 1972.

2814. Le Gallo, Claude. "Gare à Gaston." *Phénix*. No. 24, 1972.

2815. Le Gallo, Claude. "Iorix." No. 21, 1971.

2816. "Les Increvable Supermen de la Maison-Blanche." In *Paris-Press-L'Intransegeant*. Paris: 1967.

2817. Léturgie, Jean. "Il Était une Fois...Dracurella." *Schtroumpf. Les Cahiers de la Bande Dessinée*. 41, 1979, p. 41.

2818. Léturgie, Jean. "La Justice de Domino." *Schtroumpf. Les Cahiers de la Bande Dessinée*. 46, 1980, p. 29.

2819. Léturgie, Jean. "Tif et Tondu ou les Aventures de M. Choc." *Schtroumpf. Les Cahiers de la Bande Dessinée*. 45, 1980, pp. 27-29.

2820. Marnat, Marcel. "Pim Pam Poum." *Les Lettres Françaises*. June 30-July 7, 1966.

2821. Nassaux, Jean-Paul. "BD et Chevalerie. Les Aventures de Thierry, le Chevalier sans Nom." *Bédésup*. 24/25, 1983, pp. 11-13.

2822. Nassaux, Jean-Paul. "Images d'Ivanhoe d'Eugène Delacroix à Dino Battaglia." *Bédésup*. 26, 1983, pp. 19-24.

2823. Pagnol, Marcel. "La Famille Fenouillard." Preface to *La Famille Fenouillard*. Paris: Le Livre de Poche, Librairie Armand Colin, 1965.

2824. Pascal, Pierre. "Futuropolis." *Schtroumpf. Les Cahiers de la Bande Dessinée*. 31, 1976, pp. 30-31.

2825. Pascal, Pierre. "Junior et les Publications de la SPE." *Cahiers Universitaires*. No. 11, 1971.

2826. Rivière, François. "Un Précieux Chez les Hurons: 'Oumpah-Pah.'" *Schtroumpf. Les Cahiers de la Bande Dessinée*. 22, 1973, pp. 34-35.

2827. Sackmann, Eckart. "Bastos et Zakusky—Eine Neue Dimension des Abenteuers." *Comic Forum. Das Magazin für Comicliteratur.* 8:32 (1986), pp. 26-29.

2828. "Seraphina: Reportage ou Fiction?" *Jeune Africaine.* December 15, 1966, p. 55.

2829. Thonet, Françoise. "Qui Êtes-Vous, Francis Albany?" *Les Cahiers de la Bande Dessinée.* 68, 1986, pp. 17-19.

2830. Trout, Bernard. "En Quelques Lignes...Le Fantôme Contre le Baron Pirate." Paris: CELEG, 1965.

2831. Tschernegg, Markus. "Ann et Dan." *Comic Forum. Das Österreichische Fachmagazin für Comicliteratur.* 3:11 (1981), pp. 56-58.

2832. Tschernegg, Markus. "David Walker. Ein Verkappter Western." *Comic Forum. Das Magazin für Comicliteratur.* 5:19 (1983), pp. 48-53.

2833. Tschernegg, Markus. "Nic." *Comic Forum. Das Magazin für Comicliteratur.* 5:19 (1983), pp. 54-55.

2834. Van Belle, Anita. "Mort Cinder, le Mort Impavide." *Les Cahiers de la Bande Dessinée.* 62, 1985, pp. 82-84.

2835. Warfa, Dominique. "Goulag for Ever." *Les Cahiers de la Bande Dessinée.* 63, 1985, pp. 91-93.

"Achille Talon"

2836. "Achille Talon." *Cartoonist PROfiles.* No. 19, 1973, p. 25.

2837. Brunoro, Gianni. "Notre Talon d'Achille." *Cahiers Universitaires.* No. 17, 1972.

2838. Greg, Michael. "Achille Talon." *Cartoonist PROfiles.* No. 15, 1972, p. 11.

2839. Greg, Mike. *Walter Melon: Magnesia's Treasure.* Montreal: Dargaud Canada, 1981. 51 pp.

2840. Rivière, François. "Le Ballon d'Achille." *Cahiers Universitaires* (Paris). No. 17, 1972.

2841. Rivière, François. "Les Malheurs d'Achille Talon." *Cahiers Universitaires* (Paris). No. 17, 1972.

2842. Tramson, Jacques. "Pour Une Rhétorique de la Bande Dessinée: La Redondance Comme Procédé de l'Humour (Le Cas Achille Talon)." *Humoresques.* 1 (1988), pp. 177-187.

"Adèle Blanc Sec"

2843. Caré, Jean-Marc. "Adèle Blanc Sec: Enfin une Héroïne, une Vraie.... *Le Français dans le Monde*. 174, 1983, pp. 13-15.

2844. Gauthier, Guy. "Aventures d'Hier, Héros d'Aujord'hui." *Le Français dans le Monde*. 200, 1986, pp. 21-24.

"Alix"

2845. Alapetite, Bernard. "Alix ou la Résurrection Roman." Group Interdisciplinaire de Recherche Universitaire sur la Bande Dessinée. *A la Rencontre de... Jacques Martin*, pp. 157-160. Marseilles: Bédésup, 1985.

2846. Association Clovis. *Ave Alix*. Marseilles: Bédésup, 1984.

2847. Dessart, Marie. "3. Antiquité Classique: 1. L'Etrurie." *Archéologie, Histoire de l'Art et Bande Dessinée*, pp. 39-41. Louvain-La-Neuve: U.C.b. Institut Supéreur d'Archéologie et d'Histoire de l'Art, 1980.

2848. Groensteen, Thierry and Jacques Martin. *Avec Alix*. Paris: Tournai: Casterman, 1984.

2849. Pizzotti, Patricia. "3. Antiquité Classique: 3. La Sculpture, Bas-Reliefs et Statuaire, Source d''Alix.'" In *Archéologie, Histoire de l'Art et Bande Dessinée*, pp. 50-51. Louvain-La-Neuve: U.C.b. Institut Supéruer d'Archéologie et d'Histoire de l'Art, 1980.

2850. Roux, Antoine. "Alix l'Intrépide: d'une Histoire sans Histoires à l'Ère du Soupçon." In *Histoire et Bande Dessinée: Actes du 2e Colloque International Éducation et Bande Dessinée*, pp. 9-16. La Roque d'Anthéron: Objectif Promo-Durance, 1979.

2851. Simon, André. "Alix au Miroir de Notre Temps." In Groupe Interdisciplinaire de Recherche Universitaire sur la Bande Dessinée. *A la Rencontre de... Jacques Martin*, pp. 161-166. Marseilles: Bédésup, 1985.

2852. Simon, André. "Alix, Miroir de Notre Temps." *Bédésup*. 9, 1979, pp. 11-14.

2853. Simon, André. "Fiction Gallo-Romaine et Politique Contemporaine." *Les Cahiers Rationalistes* (Paris). 357, 1980, pp. 136-162.

2854. Vereggen, Jean-Pierre. "Les Aventures d'Alix ou l'Intrusion de l'Histoire dans la Bande Dessinée." *Français 2000* (Brussels). 91, 1977, pp. 33-35.

"Ardeur"

2855. Dellisse, Luc. "Un Visage Perdu." *Les Cahiers de la Bande Dessinée*. 69, 1986, pp. 94-96.

2856. de Pierpont, Jacques. "Ardeur. La Grande Fournaise." *Les Cahiers de la Bande Dessinée*. 69, 1986, pp. 90-93.

"Astérix"

2857. Albert, Claudia. "Sprachartistik und Sprachvergleich. Zur Wortschatz-und Wörterbucharbeit am Beispiel von 'Astérix.'" *Der Fremdsprachliche Unterricht*. 15:59 (1981), pp. 220-222.

2858. "Astérix en Fleche." *Bulletin du Livre*. November 15, 1966, pp. 13-14.

2859. Augusto, Sergio. "Astérix, o Popeye de Bela Galia." *Jornal do Brasil*. September 15, 1967.

2860. "Astérix Passe aux Actes." *L'Express* (Paris). No. 855, 1967, p. 60.

2861. Barraud, Hervé and S. de Sède. "La Mythologie d'Astérix." *La Nouvelle Critique* (Paris). September 1969, pp. 35-40.

2862. Baudry, Jean. "Astérix et l'Urbanisme." *Le Français dans le Monde*. 203, 1986, pp. 80-81.

2863. Bergmann, Thomas. "Astérix Macht Abitur? Zur Situation der Comics." *Aspekte*. 4:3 (1971), pp. 42-46.

2864. Bursch, Horst. "'Astérix en Hispania.' Eine Lektüreanregung für den Spanischunterricht der Sekundarstufe II." *Neusprachliche Mitteilungen aus Wissenschaft und Praxis* (Berlin). 36:2, 1983, pp. 97-101.

2865. Cassou-Yager, Hélène. "*Astérix*: A Bouillon Cube of French History, Gaullist Politics, and French Attitudes and Prejudices Towards Other Countries." In *Selected Proceedings: 32nd Mountain Interstate Foreign Language Conference*, edited by Gregorio Martin, pp. 85-92. Winston-Salem, North Carolina: Wake Forest University, 1984. 411 pp.

2866. Chabbi, Jameleddine. "Astérix ou le Français Moyen." *Revue Politique et Parlementaire* (Paris). 814, 1970, pp. 66-79.

2867. "Comicographie. Astérix in Deutschland." *Comic Forum. Das Österreichische Fachmagazin für Comicliteratur*. 2:7/8, pp. 104-105.

2868. "Comic-Strip Über de Gaulle." *Der Spiegel*. No. 52, 1965.

2869. Cuervo, Javier. "Astérix el Macho." *El Wendigo*. No. 54 (1991), p. 39.

2870. Cuesta Fernández, Fernando. "Oum-pah-pah el Piel Roja; Ensayo General de Astérix." *El Wendigo*. December 1985, pp. 12-15.

2871. Decker, Dwight R. "Astérix: 'These Frenchmen Are Crazy!'" *Comics Journal*. February 1977, pp. 20-22, 25-31.

2872. Decker, Dwight R. "Astérix: 'These Frenchmen Are Crazy!'" *Comics Journal*. February 1978, pp. 20-29.

2873. Deguerry, Françoise and René Goscinny. "Astérix Batailleur." *Cahiers Universitaires*. No. 29, 1966, pp. 44-46.

2874. "Ecco el Famoso Astérix." *Epoca*. December 11, 1966, pp. 140-141.

2875. Gargand, Jean-Noël. "Le Phénomène Astérix." *L'Express*. September 19-25, 1966, pp. 24-26.

2876. Goscinny, René. "Découpage Inédit d'une Planche de Astérix et les Normands." *Les Lettres Francaises*. No. 1138, 1966.

2877. Goscinny, René and Albert Uderzo. *Astérix and Cleopatra*. Montreal: Dargaud Canada, 1978.

2878. Goscinny, René and Albert Uderzo. *Astérix and the Great Crossing*. New York: Dargaud, 1984.

2879. Goscinny, René and Albert Uderzo. *Astérix in Britain*. Montreal: Dargaud Canada, 1979.

2880. Goscinny, René and Albert Uderzo. *Astérix the Gaul*. Montreal: Dargaud Canada, 1981. 48 pp.

2881. Goscinny, René and Albert Uderzo. *Astérix the Gladiator*. Montreal: Dargaud Canada, 1979.

2882. Grassegger, Hans. *Sprachspiel und Übersetzung. Eine Studie Anhand der Comics-Serie Astérix*. Tübingen: Stauffenburg, 1985. 105 pp.

2883. "Hail the Great, French Comic-Book Hero; Astérix Le Gaulois." *Time*. December 23, 1966, p. 27.

2884. Hangartner, Urs. "Astérix... Ein Gallisches Phänomen. ZACK!..." *Comic Forum. Das Magazin für Comicliteratur*. 8:31, (1986), pp. 19-20.

2885. Hartmann, Regina. "Betrachtungen zur Arabischen Version von Astérix. Ein Übersetzungsvergleich." *Linguistische Berichte* (Opladen, Wiesbaden). 81, 1982, pp. 1-31.

2886. Hilleret, Georges. "Pierre Tchernia: Astérix Était un Monstre." *Tele 7 Jours.* No. 362, 1967.

2887. Hochstein-Peschen, Rita. "Spaß und Wissen mit Astérix und den 'Schtroumpfs.' Über Möglichkeiten des Einsatzes von Comics im Französischunterricht der Erwachsenenbildung." *Zielsprache Französisch* (Munich). 4, 1979, pp. 153-162.

2888. Jacqmain, Monique and Herman Cole. "Astérix à la Conquête de l'Europe." *Babel* (Gerlingen; Reprint Amsterdam). 16:1 (1970), pp. 4-12, 20.

2889. Kauffmann, Judith. "Astérix, un Humour Pictural et Verbal." *Cahier Comique Communication* (Grenoble). 1, 1983, pp. 48-94.

2890. Kerst, Hans. "Methoden des Umgangs mit Comics im Unterricht. Dargestellt am Beispiel des Heftes 'Astérix der Gallier' in Einer R 8." Hausarbeit zur 2. *Lehrerprüfung* (Hamburg). March 1972.

2891. Lapierre, Marcel. "Après Astérix Le Gaulois, Deux Romains en Gaule." *La Semaine Radio-Tele.* No. 9, 1967.

2892. Lentz, Serge. "La Folie Astérix." *Le Nouveau Candide* (Paris). No. 348, 1967, pp. 4-9.

2893. Litrán, Manuel and Virginie Merlin. "Astérix Devient Star." *Paris-Match.* No. 976, 1967.

2894. Lofficier, Jean-Marc. "One Froggy Evening: Astérix the Gaul." *Comics Buyer's Guide.* October 24, 1986, pp. 28, 32.

2895. Marković, Frauke. "Die 'Astérix'—Serie als Lektüre Heutiger Schüler der Sekundarstufe. Hausarbeit für Die 1. *Staatsprüfung für das Lehramt an Volks-und Realschulen* (Hamburg). May 1971.

2896. Martin, Paul-M. "L'Image de César dans *Astérix*, ou, Comment Duex Français sur Trois Aujourd'hui Voient César." In *Présence de César*, edited by Raymond Chevallier, pp. 459-481. Paris: Belles Letts., 1985. 546 pp.

2897. Meidt, Ernst-Heinrich. "Astérix im Französischunterricht—Zwei Unterrichtsbeispiele." *Neursprachliche Mitteilungen aus Wissenschaft und Praxis* (Berlin). 29, 1976, pp. 202-210.

2898. Meidt, Ernst-Heinrich. "Astérix in der Volkshochschule. Zwei Beispiele für Unterricht mit Comics in der Erwachsenenbildung." *Zielsprache Französisch* (Munich). 3, 1979, pp. 116-129.

2899. Menne, Dieter. "Astérix-Hefte im Deutschunterricht der Unterstufe." *Gegenwartskunde* (Frankfurt, Berlin). 21, 1972, pp. 419-427.

2900. Metken, Günter. "Astérix der Gallier." *Frankfurter Allegemeine Zeitung.* December 6, 1968, p. 32.

2901. Miani, Rozinaldo A. "Astérix, o Herói Gaulês." *Boletim de HQ.* November-December 1991, p. 3.

2902. Mikelbank, Peter. "Astérix Fighting Mickey's Might." *Variety.* August 24, 1992, pp. 35, 45.

2903. Neumann, Danièle. "Astérix dans Tous Ses États." *Livres Hebdo.* 5:46 (1983), pp. 89-90.

2904. Neumann, Renate. "Die Französische Sprache und Ihre Regionalen Eigentümlichkeiten in 'Astérix.'" *Zielsprache Französisch* (Munich). 3, 1981, pp. 125-129.

2905. "Ni Moraliste-ni Critique... Je Suis un Rigolo! (Astérix)." *Le Cid* (Paris). No. 15, 1969.

2906. Nolte, Margarete. "Das Aufgezwungene Leitbild. Kritische Analyse der Astérix-Comic-Produkte." *Lebendige Schule* (Bad Heilbrunn). 29:7 (1974), pp. 258-263.

2907. Nye, Russel B. "Astérix Revisited." *Comics Journal.* May 1982, pp. 59-67.

2908. Perec, Georges. "Astérix au Pouvoir." *Arts.* No. 59, 1966.

2909. Picquenot, Alain. "Le Récit du DEVIN." *Pratiques.* 11/12, (1976), pp. 51-77.

2910. Pinet, Christopher. "Astérix, Brassens, and Cabu: The ABCs of Popular Culture." In *Popular Traditions and Learned Culture in France*, edited by Marc Bertrand, pp. 275-286. Saratoga, California: Anma Libri, 1985. 335 pp.

2911. Pinet, Christopher. "Myths and Stereotypes in Astérix le Gaulois." *Canadian Modern Language Review* (Toronto). 34:2 (1978), pp. 149-162.

2912. Pottar, O. "Astérix, le Druide, le Guide et la Potion Magique." *Arts.* February 23, 1966.

2913. "Pour le Nöel des Gaulois, Astérix et Obelix Ont Conquis les Cinémas." *Paris-Match.* December 23, 1967.

2914. Raether, Martin. "'Astérix' im Frankreichkunde—Unterricht?" In *Literatur im Fremdsprachenunterricht. Beiträge zur Theorie des Literaturunterrichts und zur Praxis der Literaturvermittlung im Fremdsprachenunterricht*, edited by Konrad Schröder and Franz-Rudolf Weller, pp. 211-222. Frankfurt: Diesterweg, 1977.

2915. Rioux, Lucien. "D'Astérix aux Westerns, Ceux Qui Font le Vent, les Snobs et les Intellectuels." *Constellation*. October 1967.

2916. Röhl, Magnus. "Le Cycle d'Astérix—Épopée de la 5e République. Quelques Réflexions." *Moderna Sprak*. 69, 1975, pp. 35-43.

2917. Rothe, Wolfgang. "Astérix und das Spiel mit der Sprache." *Die Neueren Sprachen* (Frankfurt). 73:3 (1974), pp. 241-261.

2918. Rous, Guido. "Herr Sartre Liebt die Vampire (Astérix, der Gallier Oder Die Comic-Strips der Franzosen)." *Christ und Welt* (Stuttgart). February 16, 1968, p. 15.

2919. Roux, Antoine. "Les Adaptations Étrangères d'Astérix." *Schtroumpf. Les Cahiers de la Bande Dessinée*. 22, 1973, pp. 38-40.

2920. Sadoul, Numa. "Astérix Gauchiste." *Schtroumpf. Les Cahiers de la Bande Dessinée*. 22, 1973, p. 44.

2921. Sadoul, Numa. "Les Personnages d'Astérix." *Schtroumpf. Les Cahiers de la Bande Dessinée*. 23, 1974, pp. 20-22.

2922. Schwebbach, Hella. "Analyse des Comic Books 'Astérix' Hinsichtlich Seiner Pädagogischen Bedeutung für Kinder und Jugendliche. Hausarbeit für das 1. "*Staatsexamen für das Lehramt an Volks-und Realschulen* (Hamburg). 1967.

2923. Siepe, Hans T. "Descartes, Astérix und Crédit Agricol: Roland Barthes' Semiologie der Konnotation im Unterricht." *Die Neueren Sprachen* (Frankfurt, Berlin, Bonn). 77:5 (1978), pp. 430-444.

2924. Simon, André. "Les Gaulois dans la B.D." *Le Débat* (Paris). 16, 1981, pp. 96-108.

2925. Stoll, André. *Astérix das Trivialepos Frankreichs. Die Bildund Sprachartistik Eines Bestseller-Comics*. Cologne: DuMont Schauberg, 1974.

2926. Stoll, André. *Astérix, l'Épopée Burlesque de la France*. Paris: Éditions Complexes, 1978.

2927. Thiriant, Jean. "Non à Astérix." *La Nation Européenne* (Paris). No. 19, 1967, p. 15.

2928. "Those Frenchwomen Are Crazy." *Comics Journal*. December 1979, pp. 70-71.

2929. Thürmer, Wilfried. "Comicforschung und Didaktik des Comic. Thesen zur Mediensoziologischen Analyse der Formalstruktur Eines 'Astérix'-Heftes." *Diskussion Deutsch* (Frankfurt, Berlin, Munich). 8, 1977, pp. 626-643.

2930. Uderzo, Albert. *De Flamberge à Astérix*. Paris: Philippsen, 1985.

2931. Verdaguer, Pierre. "Le Héros National et Ses Dédoublements dans *San-Antonio et Astérix*." *French Review*. March 1988, pp. 605-614.

2932. Verg, Erik. "Bei Langeweile: Astérix." *Hamburger Abendblatt*. March 18/19, 1967.

2933. "Viel Astérix und Obelix!" *Eltern* (Munich). No. 9, 1970, pp. 244, 247-249.

2934. Vignier, Gérard. "L''Effet Astérix!'" *Le Français dans le Monde*. 170, 1982, pp. 105-108.

2935. "Vive les Celtes! Astérix." *National Geographic*. May 1977. pp. 632-633.

2936. Walter, Heribert. "Astérix le Gaulois im Französischunterricht." *Französisch Heute* (Frankfurt). 3, 1972, pp. 130-144.

2937. Walter, Heribert. "Astérix le Gaulois im Französischunterricht." *Französisch Heute* (Frankfurt). 4, 1972, pp. 206-215.

2938. Zimmermann, Hans D. "Astérix und Jodelle. Zu Zwei Französischen Comics." In *Comic Strips: Geschichte, Struktur, Wirkung und Verbreitung der Bildergeschichten*. Catalog of Exhibit Berliner Akademie der Künste, December 13, 1969-January 25, 1970, pp. 44-49. Berlin: 1969.

"Barbarella"

2939. "Barbarella." *Adan* (Buenos Aires). No. 15, 1967, pp. 94-97.

2940. "Barbarella." *Continental* (London). October 1967.

2941. "Barbarella." *Welt der Literatur* (Hamburg). April 27, 1967.

2942. "Barbarella als Film." *Er*. December 5, 1967, pp. 33-38.

2943. "Barbarella, la Historieta en Carne y Plastico." *Panorama*. No. 66, 1968, pp. 67-69.

2944. "Barbarella-Pille zur Hand." *Der Spiegel*. No. 44, 1968, p. 202.

2945. "Barbarellas Start ins Weltraumabenteuer." *Welt am Sonntag* (Hamburg). July 15, 1967.

2946. Beraldi, Franco. "Le Ragazze di Parigi si Vestano Come Barbarella." *Tempo* (Milan). November 10, 1965, p. 48-51.

2947. Bertieri, Claudio. "Barbarella Disinvolta Cosmonauta." *Il Lavoro Nuovo* (Genoa). May 8, 1965.

2948. Bertieri, Claudio. "Barbarella: Licenza di Uccidere Mostri." *Il Lavoro* (Genoa). September 21, 1966.

2949. Bertieri, Claudio. "B.C. e Barbarella." *Cinema 60* (Rome). No. 57, 1966.

2950. Bertieri, Claudio. "Personaggi, i Normalissimi Addams, Uup un Cavernicolo Temponanta, Barbarella. L'Antichissimo Mondo di B.C. Su Alcuni Riferimenti Culturali nei Considetti Fumetti Neri." *Fantascienza Minore.* Special number, 1967, pp. 27-35.

2951. Bretagne, Christian. "La Barbarella du Tiers Monde." *Candide* (Paris). No. 292, 1966.

2952. "The Bizarre Beauties of Barbarella." *Playboy.* March 1968, pp. 108-118.

2953. De Turris, Gianfranco and S. Fusco. "Barbarella/Jane." *Sgt. Kirk.* No. 7, 1968, pp. 1-5.

2954. "The Erotic Universe of Barbarella." *Penthouse.* 3:5 (1968), pp. 55-60.

2955. Forest, Jean-Claude. *Barbarella.* New York: Grove Press, 1966.

2956. Forest, Jean-Claude. *Barbarella, the Moon Child.* New York: Heavy Metal Books, 1978. 51 pp.

2957. Giuffredi, E. "Mandato d'Arresto per Barbarella." *Novella.* No. 20, 1965.

2958. Hegerfors, Sture. "Rymdhoppen Barbarella." *Expressen* (Stockholm). January 3, 1965.

2959. Heymann, Danièle. "Barbarella Inspire les Paroliers." *L'Express* (Paris). No. 849, 1967, p. 114.

2960. Heymann, Danièle. "Barbarella, un Nombre de Mujer." *Gaceta Illustrada* (Madrid). No. 569, 1967, p. 93.

2961. Heymann, Danièle. "Barbarella Sous les Lauriers Roses." *L'Express* (Paris). No. 842, 1967, pp. 46-48.

2962. "Jane Fonda: Je Serais Barbarella." *Cancans de Paris.* 1967, pp. 15-16.

2963. Kniewel, Liane. "Bardot-Entdecker Zaubert Nun Barbarella." *Hamburger Abendblatt.* August 26/27, 1967, p. 11.

2964. Legrand, Gerard. "Barbarella, Nouvelle Vamp des Comics Est Française." *Arts* (Paris). February 24, 1965.

2965. Moorcock, Michael and Charles Platt. "Barbarella and the Anxious Frenchman." *New Worlds* (London). No. 179, 1968, pp. 13-25.

2966. Pfeffer, Gottfried. "Barbarella. Comics für die Großen—Parodie oder Pornographie?" *Rheinischer Merkur* (Cologne). February 10, 1967.

2967. Rivière, François. "Barbarella Cache Forest." *Schtroumpf. Les Cahiers de la Bande Dessinée*. 26, 1975, pp. 28-29.

2968. Romer, Jean-Claude. "Bararella, Mon Amour." *Giff-Wiff*. No. 11, 1965, p. 4.

2969. Torrisi, Maurizo. "L'Antibarbarella di Madam de Gaulle." *Settimana Incom* (Milan). November 7, 1965, pp. 30-39.

2970. Trinchero, Sergio. "Il Nonno di Barbarella è Buck Rogers." *Smack*. No. 3, 1968, pp. 21-22.

2971. Truquetit, Andréa. "De Barbarella à Forest." *Miroir du Fantastique*. 1:8 (1968), pp. 388-395.

2972. Wagner, Friedrich A. "Comic-Strip als Filmschau; Roger Vadims 'Barbarella.'" *Frankfurter Allgemeine Zeitung*. October 15, 1968, p. 22.

2973. Zanotto, Piero. "A Proposito di Un Film su Barbarella." *Corriere del Ticino*. November 20, 1965.

2974. Zanotto, Piero. "Barbarella Piace alla Teste d'Uovo." *Il Gazzettino*. September 21, 1965.

2975. Zanotto, Piero. "Costerà Quanto La Biblia, Il Film Dedicato a Barbarella." *Il Gazzettino* (Venice). March 9, 1967.

2976. Zanotto, Piero. "E'Nata a Parigi la Cugina di Barbarella." *Nazione Sera* (Florence). January 21, 1967.

"Bicot et les Rantans—plans" ("Winnie Winkle")

2977. Lacassin, Francis. "Bicot, ou les Charmes de l'Imposture." *Informations et Documents* (Paris). No. 221, 1965. Also in *Azur* (Paris). 1965.

2978. Santelli, Claude. "Bicot, où la Révanche du Naturel." *Azur* (Paris). 1965.

"Boule et Bill"

2979. de Man, Martine and Jean Fr. Malherbe. *Un Ghetto Exemplaire. Analyse Socio-Culturelle d'une Bande Dessinée*. Brussels: Liège: Ed. C. T.L., 1977.

2980. Glénat, Jacques. "Boule et Bill." *Cahiers Universitaires*. No. 16, 1972.

"Chevalier Ardent"

2981. Sadoul, Numa. "Chevalier Ardent." *Cahiers Universitaires*. No. 11, 1971.

2982. Trenquel, Roger. "Etude sur les Cavaliers de l'Apocalypse de Craenhals." *Bédésup*. 27, 1983, pp. 31-35.

2983. Tschernegg, Markus. "Roland. Ritter Ungestüm." *Comic Forum. Das Österreichische Fachmagazin für Comicliteratur*. 3:10 (1981), pp. 50-51.

"Fluide Glacial"

2984. de Pierpont, Jacques. "Un An de Fluide Glacial." *Les Cahiers de la Bande Dessinée*. 61, 1985, pp. 43-44.

2985. Eskenazi, Frank. "Les Farces et Attrapes de Fluide Glacial." *Libération*. Supplement Special Angoulême 1992, p. ix.

2986. Groensteen, Thierry. "'L'Effet Fluide? Conversation avec Jacques Diament." *Les Cahiers de la Bande Dessinée*. 61, 1985, pp. 40-42.

2987. Mathiasen, Paw. "Fluide Glacial." *Serieskaberen*. September 1989, p. 23.

"Guy L'Eclair"

2988. Colini, Serge. "Guy l'Eclair." *Plexus*. No. 8, 1967, pp. 169-171.

2989. "Le Retour de Guy l'Eclair." *Lui* (Paris). 1965.

"Hara Kiri"

2990. Carano, Ranieri. "Hara Kiri per Wolinski." *Linus*. No. 35, 1968, pp. 1-7.

2991. Choron, Odile. *La Petite Histoire de Hara-Kiri et Charlie Hebdo*. Paris: Menges, 1983.

"Jean Valhardi"

2992. Glénat, Jacques. "Jean Valhardi, Dernier Justicier." *Cahiers Universitaires*. No. 17, 1972.

2993. Léturgie, Jean. "Valhardi, Héros d'Une Génération." *Schtroumpf. Les Cahiers de la Bande Dessinée*. 39, 1979, pp. 25-26.

"Jodelle"

2994. Bartier, Pierre and Guy Pellaert. *The Adventures of Jodelle*. New York: Grove Press, 1967. 68 pp.

2995. Burguet, Franz-André. "Jodelle Mon Amour." *Arts* (Paris). June 29, 1966.

2996. Chambon, Jacques. "Un Delire Barroque: Les Aventures de Jodelle." *Mercury* (Paris). No. 11, 1966, pp. 85-87.

2997. Längsfeld, Wolfgang. "Die Schöne Jodelle." *Süddeutsche Zeitung Literaturbeilage* (Munich). December 7, 1967, p. 6.

2998. Sternberg, Jacques. *Les Aventures de Jodelle*. (Préface). Paris: Le Terrain Vague, 1966.

"La Grande Menace"

2999. Carbonell, Charles-Olivier. "Approche Politique de 'La Grande Menace.'" In Groupe Interdisciplinaire de Recherche Universitaire sur la Bande Dessinée. *A la Rencontre de Jacques Martin*, pp. 41-51. Marseilles: Bédésup, 1985.

3000. Chante, Alain. "L'Expression du Pouvoir dans 'La Grande Menace': Essai d'Étude Quantitative." In Groupe Interdisciplinaire de Recherche Universitaire sur la Bande Dessinée. *A la Rencontre de Jacques Martin*, pp. 53-71. Marseilles: Bédésup, 1985.

3001. Chante, Alain. "Organisation de la Planche et du Récit dans 'La Grande Menace.'" In Groupe Interdisciplinaire de Recherche Universitaire sur la Bande Dessinée. *A la Rencontre de Jacques Martin*, pp. 73-89. Marseilles: Bédésup, 1985.

3002. Farisse, Jacques. "'La Grande Menace' de Jacques Martin. Réflexion sur l'Aspect Morphologique des Personnages." In Groupe Interdisciplinaire de Recherche Universitaire sur la Bande Dessinée. *A la Rencontre de Jacques Martin*, pp. 91-102. Marseilles: Bédésup, 1985.

"Les Chevaliers du Ciel"

3003. Charlier, Jean-Michel. "Les Revoici!... Treize Nouveaux Épisodes des Chevaliers du Ciel." *Pilote*. No. 440, 1968, pp. 36-39.

3004. Lanot, Jean-François. "La Politique Étrangère de la France et le Racisme dans Les Chevaliers du Ciel." In *Le Message Politique et Social de la Bande Dessinée*, edited by Charles-Olivier Carbonell, pp. 79-97. Toulouse: Institut d'Etudes Politiques de Toulouse, 1975.

"Les Frustrés"

3005. Barrera-Vidal, Albert. "Clés Pour une Lecture des Frustrés." *Le Français dans le Monde*. 200, 1986, pp. 36-39.

3006. Bretécher, Claire. *Frustration*. New York: Grove Press, 1987.

3007. Lamy, Marie-Noëlle. "Le Langage des Frustrés: Recherche d'une Méthode d'Analyse." *Grazer Linguistische Studien*. 15, 1981, pp. 143-165.

"Les Passagers du Vent"

3008. Chaboud, Jack. "Marine à Voile et Bateaux de Papier." In *Bourgeon à la Hune*, edited by L'Association Clovis, p. 14-17. Grenoble: Eds. Jacques Glénat, 1986.

3009. Dellisse, Luc. "La Course au Savoir." *Les Cahiers de la Bande Dessinée*. 65, 1985, pp. 26-28.

3010. Groensteen, Thierry. "La Raison du Plus Mort." *Les Cahiers de la Bande Dessinée*. 65, 1985, pp. 29-31.

3011. Van Belle, Anita. "Un Art du Secret." *Les Cahiers de la Bande Dessinée*. 65, 1985, pp. 32-34.

3012. Vermeil, Frantz. "Mon Ancêtre, Négrier Nantais." In *Bourgeon à la Hune*, edited by L'Association Clovis, pp. 42-46. Grenoble: Eds. Jacques Glénat, 1986.

3013. Villiers, Patrick. "La Traite des Noirs Vers les Antilles Françaises Sous le Règne de Louis XVI." In *Bourgeon à la Hune*, edited by L'Association Clovis, pp. 36-41. Grenoble: Eds. Jacques Glénat, 1986.

"Le Vagabond des Limbes"

3014. Ecken, Claude. "Le Rêve, Cette Autre Réalité." *Les Cahiers de la Bande Dessinée*. 59, 1984, pp. 35-37.

3015. Turlan, Gilbert. "Axle Munshine, le Vagabond des Limbes." *Schtroumpf. Les Cahiers de la Bande Dessinée*. 41, 1979, pp. 37-39.

"Lone Sloane"

3016. Everaert, Nicole. "Lone Sloane. Pourquoi ce Malaise?" *Bédésup*. 14/15, 1980, pp. 48-53.

3017. Goimard, Jacques. "Lone Sloane." *Fiction* (Paris). No. 162, 1967, pp. 129-131.

3018. Juin, Hubert. "Lone Sloane." *Les Lettres Françaises*. No. 1160, 1967, p. 10.

"Lt. Blueberry"

3019. Charlier, J.M. and Moebius. *The Man with the Silver Star. A Lieutenant Blueberry Adventure*. New York: Dargaud International, 1983. 47 pp.

3020. Cuervo, Javier. "Moebius: 'Inconscientemente Empece a Dibujar Teniente Blueberry por Gustar a las Mujeres.'" *El Wendigo*. Winter 1988-1989, pp. 34-35.

3021. Funhoff, Jörg. "Analyse Eines Comics mit Realistischen Anstrich. Durchgeführt an der Serie 'Fort Navajo' ('Lieutenant Blueberry')." *Medien + Erziehung* (Leverkusen). 20:1 (1976), pp. 35-45.

3022. Illien, Philippe. "Blueberry." *Schtroumpf. Les Cahiers de la Bande Dessinée*. 37, 1978, pp. 26-30.

3023. Jacquin, Louis-Hugues and Christophe Sarrotte. "Petit Dictionnaire des Personnages des Aventures de 'Blueberry.'" *Schtroumpf. Les Cahiers de la Bande Dessinée*. 25, 1974, pp. 22, 24.

3024. Lozano, Dominique. "Blueberry et le Western Crépusculaire." *Schtroumpf. Les Cahiers de la Bande Dessinée*. 25, 1974, pp. 17-19.

3025. Pérez, Ramón F. "Blueberry." *El Wendigo*. May 1983, pp. 32-37.

"Lucky Luke"

3026. "A Comic Book Hero Goes off the Weed." *World Health*. March 1984, p. 30.

3027. Filippini, Henri. "Les 'Seconds Rôles' dans Lucky Luke." *Schtroumpf. Les Cahiers de la Bande Dessinée*. 43, 1980, pp. 24-25.

3028. Goscinny, René. "Les Dalton." *Schtroumpf. Les Cahiers de la Bande Dessinée*. 43, 1980, p. 42.

3029. Goscinny, René and Morris. *Lucky Luke: The Tenderfoot*. Montreal: Dargaud Canada, 1981. 47 pp.

3030. Jonsson, Jon Sveinbjorn. "Lucky Luke Går i Kloster?" *TEGN*. 1, 1990, pp. 16-18.

3031. Lacassin, Francis. "Lucky Luke." *Giff-Wiff*. No. 5, 1965, p. 22.

3032. Lacassin, Francis. "Lucky Luke à l'Université." *Giff-Wiff*. No. 16, 1965, p. 3.

3033. "Lucky Luke: Die Jagd Nach dem Phantom." *ICOM*. October 1992, p. 64.

3034. "'Lucky Luke'—Multimedial Zerkocht." *Bulletin: Jugend + Literatur*. No. 4, 1972, Beiträge 5, p. 26.

3035. Morris. "Les Dalton Versus Lucky Luke." *Schtroumpf. Les Cahiers de la Bande Dessinée*. 43, 1980, pp. 39-40.

3036. Prange-Cramer, Christa and Erich Schinkel. "Unterrichtsentwurf. Fach: Deutsch; Thema: Merkmale der Comic-Sprache; Kurz-Comic 'Lucky Luke'; Klasse: 6 Einer Hauptschule." *Schwarz auf Weiß* (Dortmund). 10:2 (1986), pp. 29-32.

3037. Stocker, M. and H.-P. Stähli. "Lucky Luke. Legendäre Verbrecher." *Comic Forum. Das Magazin für Comicliteratur*. 5:21 (1983), pp. 23-28.

3038. Tschernegg, Markus. "Lucky Luke der und Wilde Westen." *Comic Forum. Das Magazin für Comicliteratur*. 5:21 (1983), pp. 21-23.

3039. "Wilder Western bei der Post." *ICOM*. January 1993, p. 6.

"Marie Math"

3040. Lob, Jacques. "Marie Math." *Giff-Wiff*. No. 22, 1966.

3041. Zanotto, Piero. "Forest Ha Creato Marie-Math Inspirandosi a BB." *Stampa Sera* (Turin). January 22, 1967.

"Metal Hurlant"

3042. "French Magazines Cut Back; *Metal Hurlant* Folds." *Comics Journal*. September 1987, pp. 23-24.

3043. Frenzel, Martin. "Über Form und Substanz." *Comic Forum. Das Magazin für Comicliteratur*. 8:31 (1986), p. 6.

3044. "The Rise and Fall: *Metal Hurlant*." *Comics Journal*. September 1987, p. 24.

"Norbert et Kari"

3045. De La Croix, Arnaud. "Norbert et Kari, Philosophes du Langage." *Les Cahiers de la Bande Dessinée*. 59, 1984, pp. 21-23.

3046. Glénat, Jacques. "Norbert et Kari." *Cahiers Universitaires*. No. 19, 1972.

3047. Van Belle, Anita. "Godard Est un Zozo." *Les Cahiers de la Bande Dessinée*. 59, 1984, pp. 29-31.

"Philémon"

3048. Brunoro, Gianni. "Invitation à Une Lecture Psycologique de Philémon." *Cahiers Universitaires*. No. 9, 1970.

3049. Ducoffre, Marie-Jeanne. "Philémon, Naufragé de l'Écriture." *Français 2000*. 105, 1982, pp. 83-87.

"Pif le Chien"

3050. Amengual, Barthélemy. *Le Petit Monde de Pif le Chien: Essai sur un 'Comic' Français*. Alger: Ed. de Travail et Culture d'Algérie, 1955.

3051. Moliterni, Claude. "Pif." *Phénix*. SP.

3052. Moreau, René, Jean Ollivier and Georges Wolinski. *Claude Arnal. Une Vie de Pif*. Paris: Ed. Messidor, 1983.

Pilote

3053. Dionnet, J.P. "Pilote." *Phénix*. SP.

3054. Dutrey, Jacques. "*Pilote*: A Retrospective and Eulogy." *Comics Journal*. April 1990, pp. 21-23.

3055. Filippini, Henri. *Histoire du Journal Pilote et des Publications des Editions Dargaud*. Grenoble: Eds. Jacques Glénat, 1977.

3056. Filippini, Henri. "Pilote a Vingt Ans." *Schtroumpfanzine*. 35, 1979, pp. 14-16.

3057. Vidal, Guy, Marie-Ange Guillaume and François Gorin. *Pilote, Raconté par Ceux Qui l'Ont Fait*. Neuilly-sur-Seine: Dargaud, 1980.

"Ric Hochet"

3058. Dellisse, Luc. "Relecture: Ric Hochet." *Les Cahiers de la Bande Dessinée*. 67, 1986, pp. 92-95.

3059. Filippini, Henri. "Ric Hochet ou le Réalisme Made in Belgique." *Schtroumpf. Les Cahiers de la Bande Dessinée*. 40, 1979, pp. 34-36.

3060. Tschernegg, Markus. "Rick Master." *Comic Forum. Das Österreichische Fachmagazin für Comicliteratur*. 4:16 (1982), pp. 61-66.

"Saga de Xam"

3061. Chambon, Jacques. "Saga de Xam." *Fiction*. No. 175, 1968, pp. 138-140.

3062. "Saga de Xam, Queen Mystère Magazine." *Ellery* (Paris). No. 242, 1962, p. 113.

"Satanik"

3063. Fermigier, André. "Satanik, Barbarella et Cie." *Le Nouvel Observateur* (Paris). April 19, 1967, pp. 31-33.

3064. Cournot, Michel. "Satanik, où la Métamorphose des Amants." *Le Nouvel Observateur* (Paris). April 19, 1967, pp. 34-35.

"Thorgal"

3065. Ciment, Gilles. "Le Mythe Fondateur: Une Stratégie de l'Effacement." *Les Cahiers de la Bande Dessinée.* 70, 1986, pp. 25-27.

3066. Ecken, Claude. "Thorgal à la Croisée des Genres." *Les Cahiers de la Bande Dessinée.* 70, 1986, pp. 20-23.

3067. Van Hamme, Jean and Gregor Rosinski. *Thorgal, Child of the Stars.* Virginia Beach, Virginia: Donning, 1986.

3068. Van Hamme, Jean and Gregor Rosinski. *Thorgal: The Archers.* Virginia Beach, Virginia: Donning, 1987.

3069. Van Hamme, Jean and Gregor Rosinski. *Thorgal: The Sorceress Betrayed.* Virginia Beach, Virginia: Donning, 1988.

"Tonton Marcel"

3070. de Pierpont, Jacques. "Tonton Marcel, Génial et Too Much." *Les Cahiers de la Bande Dessinée.* 57, 1984, pp. 30-32.

3071. Van Belle, Anita. "Tonton Marcel Se Déguise." *Les Cahiers de la Bande Dessinée.* 57, 1984, pp. 33-34.

"Ulysse"

3072. Brunon, Claude-Françoise. "Un Mythe Déplacé: Ulysse, d'Homère, Lob et Pichard." *Haga Sup. Revue de la Bande Dessinée* (La Roque d'Anthéron). 3, 1977, pp. 3-6.

3073. Lob, Jacques and Georges Pichard. *Ulysses.* New York: Heavy Metal, 1978. 60 pp.

3074. Pinson, Daniel. "Le Lexique Sonore dans Ulysse de Lob et Pichard." *Education 2000*. 21, 1982, pp. 66-72.

"Valérian"

3075. Brunoro, Gianni. "Valérian aux Yeux de Perle." *Cahiers Universitaires*. No. 7, 1970.

3076. Glénat, Jacques. "Valérian." *Cahiers Universitaires*. No. 7, 1970.

3077. Knutsson, Magnus, Henning Kure, Pierre Christin, Jean-C. Mézières, and Horst Schröder. "Valérian. Eine Artikelcollage." *Comixene. Das Comicfachmagazin*. 6:23 (1979), pp. 17-21.

3078. Lofficier, Jean-Marc and Randy. "Valérian: Not Just Another French Hero." *Comics Scene*. March 1983, pp. 25-28.

3079. Pérez, Ramón. "Valérian." *El Wendigo*. January 1984, pp. 30-38.

3080. Rosier, Jean-Maurice. "Une B.D. Engagée: Les Héros de l'Equinoxe." *Français 2000*. 105, 1982, pp. 75-82.

"Zig et Puce"

3081. Glénat, Jacques. "Le Retour de Zig, Puce et Quelques Autres." *Cahiers Universitaires*. No. 17, 1972.

3082. Saint-Ogan, Alain. *Je Me Souviens de Zig et Puce et de Quelques Autres*. Paris: La Table Ronde, 1961.

3083. Vankeer, Pierre. "Le Supplement aux Voyages de Zig et Puce." *Rantanplan*. No. 6, 1967, pp. 10-11, 17; No. 7, 1967, p. 10-11, 17.

ANIMATION

3084. Amengual, Barthélemy. "Le Cinéma d'Animation, Expression Privilégiée du Surréalisme à l'Écran." *Etudes Cinématographiques*. 40-42, 1965.

3085. Auriol, Jean-Georges. "Les Dessins Animés Avant le Cinéma: Emile Reynaud." *La Revue du Cinéma*. December 1929.

3086. Auriol, Jean-Georges. "Les Premiers Dessin Animés Cinématographiques: Emile Cohl." *La Revue du Cinéma*. January 1930, pp. 12-19.

3087. Baze, Robert. "Le Théâtre d'Ombres en France: Ancêtre du Dessin Animé et du Cinéma." In *Théâtres d'Ombres: Tradition et Modernité*, edited by Stathis Damianakos and Christine Hemmet, pp. 251-254. Paris: L'Harmattan, 1986. 317 pp.

3088. Beiman, Nancy. "Animation Training Paris Style." *Cartoonist PROfiles*. June 1990, pp. 18-23.

3089. Beiman, Nancy. "Annecy 1989." *Cartoonist PROfiles*. December 1989, pp. 35-37.

3090. Benayoun, Robert. *Le Dessin Animé Après Walt Disney*. Lausanne: J.J. Pauvert, 1961.

3091. Bessy, Maurice. "Dessins Animés: Koko, Mickey, Félix and Co." *Ciné Magazine*. February 1930, pp. 28-30.

3092. Blanchard, Gérard. *La Bande Dessinée: Histoire des Histoires en Images*. Verviers: Marabout University, 1969.

3093. Bofa, Gus. "Du Dessin Animé." *Les Cahiers du Mois*. 16-17 (1925), pp. 50-56.

3094. Bonitzer, Pascal. "De la Bande Dessinée au Dessin Animé." *Education 2000*. 21, 1982, pp. 38-39.

3095. Borde, Raymond. "Notes sur l'Histoire du Dessin Animé." *Positif*. July-August 1963, pp. 15-23.

3096. Cohl, Emile. "Dessin Animés." *Larousse Mensuel*. August 1925, pp. 816-864.

3097. Cohl, Emile. "Les Dessins Animés et à Trucs, Causerie Faite au Ciné-Club le 12 Juin, 1920." *Le Journal du Ciné-Club*. n.d.

3098. Cohl, Emile. "Sur les Dessin Animés." *Ciné-Tribune*. July 15, 1920.

3099. Collin, P. "L'Evolution Dramatique du Dessin Animé." Unpublished manuscript, IDHEC, Paris, 1952.

3100. Couperie, Pierre. "Bande Dessiné et Figuration Narrative." Exhibit Catalog, Musé des Arts Décoratifs, Paris, 1967.

3101. Crafton, Donald. *Emile Cohl, Caricature, and Film*. Princeton, New Jersey: Princeton University Press, 1990. 400 pp.

3102. Dauven, L.R. "En Visite Chez M. Emile Cohl Qui Inventa les Dessins Animés." *Pour Vous*. August 1933.

3103. de Tronquières, J.B. (pseud. of Emile Cohl). "Dessins Animés." *Larousse Mensuel*, August 1925.

3104. Duca, Lo. *Le Dessin Animé*. Paris: Prima, 1948.

3105. "Francia: Se Firmó una Resolución Que Otorga Apoyo Económico al Cine de Animación." *Corto Circuito*. April 1992, p. 51.

3106. "French Cartoon Biz Losing Color As Largest Animator Shuts Down." *Variety*. January 13, 1988, pp. 40, 48.

3107. Gaumont, Léon. "Système de Production de Bandes Cinématographiques Reproduisant des Événements, Actualités ou Autres, par la Représentation de Déplacements Simulés d'Objets, Corps, Masses Quelconques, Troupees [*sic*] en Actions, Navires, etc." French patent no. 296.016, 1900.

3108. Gill, Andy. "Beyond the Storyboard." *The Independent* (England). March 29, 1989.

3109. Goscinny, René and Morris. *Histoire d'un Dessin Animé: Lucky Luke. Le Scénario, la Réalisation, les Sources du Film*. Neuilly sur Seine: Dargaud, 1971.

3110. Hofferman, Jon. "Light Years." *Animation*. December 1987, pp. 21-22.

3111. Hurtubise, Jacques. "*Les Images Dessinées*." *La Revue du Cinéma—Image et Son*. June-July 1974.

3112. "La Technique du Dessin Animé Trent Ans Aprés Son Invention." *La Nature*. October 1, 1938, pp. 201-210.

3113. Le Maire, Eugéne. "L'Industrie du Dessin Animé." *Bulletin de la Société pour l'Encouragement pour l'Industrie Nationale*. March-April 1937, pp. 151-175.

3114. Lo Duca, Giuseppe. "Du Dessin Animé à la Plastique Animée." *La Nature*. May 1939, pp. 314-319.

3115. Lo Duca, Giuseppe. *Le Dessin Amimé; Histoire, Esthétique, Technique*. Paris: Prisma, 1948.

3116. Lo Duca, Giuseppe. "L'Industrie du Dessin Animé." *Génie Civil*. October 31, 1936.

3117. Lo Duca, Giuseppe and Maurice Bessy. *Méliès Mage*. Paris: Prisma, 1948.

3118. Maillet, Raymond. "Emile Cohl." *L'Anthologie du Cinéma X*. No. 98, 1978, pp. 221-244.

3119. Maillet, Raymond. "Les Pionniers Français de l'Animation." *Ecran* 73:11 (1973), pp. 20-28.

3120. Mitry, Jean. *Histoire du Cinéma*. 5 Vols. Paris: Editions Universitaires, 1967-1980.

3121. Orange, François. "Computer Generated Cartoons." In *The Use of Computers in Broadcasting Organizations*, pp. VII. 1/1. Singapore: French Singapore Institute/AIBD, 1989.

3122. Perrault, Charles. *Contes*. Paris: Garnier Frères, 1967.

3123. Poncet, Marie-Thérèse. "Dessin Animé, Art Mondial." In *Le Cercle du Livre*. Paris: 1956. 413 pp.

3124. Poncet, Marie-Thérèse. *L'Esthétique du Dessin Animé*. Paris: Nizet, 1952.

3125. Poncet, Marie-Thérèse. *Etude Comparative des Illustrations du Moyen Âge et des Dessins Animés*. Paris: Nizet, 1952.

3126. Prieto-Goubert, Martha. "Cinéma d'Animation et Télévision en France." *Corto Circuito*. April 1992, p. 47.

3127. Sadoul, Georges. *Histoire Générale du Cinéma*. 5 Vols. Paris: Denoël, 1973.

3128. Sadoul, Georges. "Le Cinéma et les Bandes Dessinées." *Les Lettres Françaises*. July 6, 1966.

3129. Sadoul, Georges. "Sur le Huitième Art." *Cahiers du Cinéma*. June 1962, pp. 8-13.

3130. Valleiry, François. "Doit-on le Dire; Réponse à M. Méliès." *Phono-Ciné-Gazette*. June 15, 1908.

3131. Williams, Michael. "As Output Falls, French Say: 'We're OK.'" *Variety*. May 27, 1991, pp. 56, 58.

3132. Williams, Michael. "French Indies Are Alive and Well and on the Tube." *Variety*. November 5, 1990, pp. 58, 64.

3133. Williams, Michael. "He-Men Yield to Humor as Kidvid Defends Niche." *Variety*. July 27, 1992, pp. 39, 41.

3134. Williams, Michael. "Loss of La 5 Smacks French with a Wollop." *Variety*. September 21, 1992, pp. 63, 72.

3135. Williams, Michael. "Market Keeps Many from Fest at Animation Meet." *Variety*. June 10, 1991, p. 39.

CARICATURE

3136. Ansa, Luis. "The Caricature Triumvirate." *Target*. Spring 1987, pp. 9-12.

3137. Baudelaire, Charles. *Curiosités Esthétiques: L'Art Romantique*. Paris: Garnier Frères, 1962.

3138. Baudelaire, Charles. "Qeulques Caricaturistes Français." In *Oeuvres Complètes*. 2 Vols. Paris: Gallimard, 1976.

3139. Baudelaire, Charles. "Some French Caricaturists." In *Baudelaire: Selected Writings on Art and Artists*. Trans. by P.E. Charvet. London: 1972.

3140. Bayard, Emile. *La Caricature et les Caricaturistes*. Paris: Librairie Charles Delagrave, 1900.

3141. Benoist, Luc. "Portraits et Caricatures." In *La Sculpture Romantique*. Paris: La Renaissance du Livre, n.d.

3142. Campagne, Jean-Marc. "La Caricature et les Médecins." *Carpouillot* (Paris). April 1958.

3143. "Caricature et la Photographie, La." *Photo Cinéma* (Paris). March 1951.

3144. *Caricatures Françaises et Etrangères d'Autrefois et d'Aujourd'hui*. Special number of *Arts et Métiers Graphiques* (Paris). September 15, 1932.

3145. Chabanne, Thierry. "L'Autocaricature de l'Ariste." *Humoresques*. 1 (1988), pp. 174-176.

3146. Feuerhahn, Nelly. "Caricature, Humour et Représentation des Droits de l'Homme." *Humoresques*. 1 (1988), pp. 194-205.

3147. "Fôrça da Caricatura e a Fragilidade das Estátuas, A. Postais de Paris." *O Globo* (Rio de Janeiro). February 28, 1950.

3148. G.E.C. (Enrico Gianeri). *L'Intesa Cordiale. L'Inghilterra, nella Caricatura Francese*. Milan: Garzante, Editore, 1940.

3149. Gaultier, Paul. *Le Rire et la Caricature*. Paris: Libr. Hachette, 1911.

3150. Giraudoux, Jean. "Sur la Caricature." *Caricatures. Arts et Métiers Graphiques* (Paris). September 15, 1932.

3151. Haraucourt, Edmond D'. "L'Amour de la Caricature." "L'Humour et les Humoristes." In *L'Amour et l'Esprit Gaulois à Travers l'Histoire, du XV° au XX° Siècles*. Paris: Libr. Martin Dupuis, 1929.

3152. Kunzle, David. "L'Illustration, Journal Universel." *Nouvelles de l'Estampe*. January-February 1979, pp. 8-19.

3153. Melot, Michel. *L'Oeil Qui Rit—le Pouvoir Comique des Images*. Paris: 1975.

3154. Morin, Violette. "Le Dessin Humoristique." *Communications*. 15 (1970).

3155. Newcomb, Timothy. "Caricature Across the Water." *Target*. Summer 1982, pp. 9-12.

3156. Oberthür, Mariel. "Autour du 'Chat Noir.'" *Connaissance des Arts*. August 1981, pp. 68-73.

3157. Prinet, Jean and Antoinette Dilasser. *Nadar*. Paris: 1966.

3158. Ragón, Michel. *Les Maîtres du Dessin Satirique*. Paris: Pierre Horay, 1972.

3159. Ragón, Michel. *Witz und Karikatur in Frankreich*. Hamburg: Nannen-Verlag, 1961.

3160. Refort, Lucien. *La Caricature Littéraire*. Paris: Libr. Armand Colin, 1932.

3161. Reshef, Ouriel. "Le Hulan et la Paysanne: Lecture d'une Image Editee Chez Pinot et Sagaire." *Gazette des Beaux-Arts*. February 1987, pp. 75-80.

3162. Roger-Marx, Claude. "La Caricature en France." *Arts et Métiers Graphiques*. September 15, 1932, pp. 57-114.

3163. Saulnier, Claude. *Le Sens du Comique. Essai sur le Caractère Esthétique du Rire*. Paris: Libr. Philosophique, J. Vrin, 1940.

3164. "Teaching Caricature." *Kayhan Caricature*. May 1992, pp. 47-48.

3165. Topuz, Hifzi. *Caricature et Société*. France: Maison Mame, 1974.

3166. Weber, A. *Tableau de la Caricature Médicale Depuis les Origines Jusqu'à Nos Jours*. Preface by Laignel Lavastine. Paris: Dépot Général: *Le François*, 1936.

Anthologies

3167. *Album, L'*. Monthly publication with text by Lucien Puech. Paris: Montgrédien et Cie, Éditeurs, 1902. (Each number dedicated to an artist: I—Albert Guillaume;

II—Ferdinand Bac; III—Ch. Huard; IV—H. Gerbault; V—Caran d'Ache; VI—Ch. Léandre; VII—Job; VIII—Benjamin Rabier; IX—Abel Faivre; X—A. Robida; XI—Steinlen; XII—Hermann-Paul; XIII—Grün; XIV—Paul Baluriau; XV—A. Willette; XVI—Lucien Métivet; XVII—J.L. Forain; XVIII—"La Pléiade des Jeunes").

3168. Aldebert, Bernard. *Jeux de l'Auto*. Paris: De Valence, Éd., 1955.

3169. *Caricatures de Tout le Monde*. Series of 32 printings. Paris: Maison Aubert et Cie, n.d.

3170. D'Alessio, Gregory. *The Gregory d'Alessio Pocket Book*. New York: 1945.

3171. *Eux et Nous. 100 Caricatures Politiques Françaises et Etrangères*. Paris: "Les Cahiers de la République des Lettres," Les Beaux Arts, 1926.

CARTOONS

Anthologies

3172. Badert, A.G. *Drôle d'Ère*. Lyon: Roger Bonnefon, 1945.

3173. Batellier, J.F. *Is Anybody Out There?* Intro. by Denis Postle. London: Free Association Books, 1984.

3174. Bébin. *Les Parodies des Grands Chefs d'Oeuvre*. Louvre et Luxemborg. Text, Preface by J. de Montfrileux, Paris: Imprimerie Kapp, n.d.

3175. Bellus, Jean. *Clementine Cherie. The Rage of Paris*. New York: Grayson Publishing Company, 1955.

3176. Bennett, Edna, compiler. *The Best Cartoons from France*. New York: Simon and Schuster, 1953.

3177. Bergson, Henri. *Le Rire*. Paris: Presses Universitaires de France, 1947.

3178. Carrizey, Robert. *Album*. Preface by Pierre Mac Orlan. "Collection Art et Technique." Monte Carlo: 1943.

3179. Cavell, Philippe. *Transes Mécaniques*. Paris: Éditions Dominique Leroy Snel, 1979. 63 pp.

3180. Coq. *Mam'zelle Souris*. Paris: Éditions Les Presses Mondiales, n.d.

3181. de Banville, Théodore. *Mes Souvenirs*. Paris: Eugène Fasquelle, Éditeur, n.d.

3182. de Beaumont, Édouard. *Parisiens et Parisiennes*. Croquis. Paris: Au Bureau du Journal *Le Charivari*, n.d., ca. 1840.

3183. de Brunhoff, Laurent. *À Tue-Tête*. Paris: Julliard, 1957.

3184. Degano, Marino. *Pleins Feux sur les Dragons*. Grenoble: Glénat, 1986.

3185. De Losques. *Oh! Nos Grandes Actrices Parisennes et leur Opinion sur Le Quina-Laroche*. Paris: Devambez, n.d.

3186. "Dessin Pub (Cabu, Font, and Val)." *Mieux Vaut en Rire*. No. 5. (n.d.), pp. 25-28.

3187. *Dessins Inavouables*. Paris: Jean-Jacques Pauvert, 1965. 109 pp.

3188. Dimier, Louis. *Physionomies et Physiologies*. Paris: Émile Nourry, Éd., 1930.

3189. Don. *Rien Que des Souvenirs...* Paris: N.R.F. Gallimard, 1955.

3190. *Frivoiltés*. Cartoons by Bosc, Lauzier, Maurice, Henry, Mose, Trez. Paris: Hazan Fernand, 1955. 70 pp.

3191. Granger, Michel. *Granger: L'État des Lieux*. Paris: Glénat, 1985. 79 pp.

3192. Henriot. *Henriot*. Coll. "Les Maîtres Humoristes." Paris: Libr. Félix Juven, 1909.

3193. Job. *Mes 21 Jours*. Paris: Ancienne Maison Quantin, Librs. Imprimeries Réunies, n.d.

3194. *Keskidi. Special Humour*. Brussels: Raymond Burini, 1991. 49 pp.

3195. Labeyrie, L. *A Rebrousse-Poil*. Grenoble: Glénat, 1984.

3196. *La Table*. Paris: HA! Humoristes Associes, 1985.

3197. Lenormant, François. *Histoire Ancienne de l'Orient Jusqu'aux Guerres Médiques*. Paris: A. Lévy, 1881.

3198. Lenormant, François. *Histoires des Peuples Orientaux*. Paris: A. Lévy, n.d.

3199. *Le Petit Zizi Illustré. Dessins de: Jicka, Pichon, Yak Rivais*. Preface by Pierre Perret. Paris: Le Cherche Midi Éditeur, 1985. 144 pp.

3200. *Les 7 Péchés Capitaux*. Paris: HA! Humoristes Associés, 1983.

3201. *Liberte Cherie*. Cartoons by Bosc, Lauzier, Maurice, Henry, Mose, Trez. Paris: Fernand Hazan, n.d. 68 pp.

3202. Lui. *Les Meilleurs Dessins de Lui*. Paris: Denoël, 1966. 110 pp.

3203. Macé, Gabriel. "Lap n'Est Plus Là." *Canard Enchaîné*. January 17, 1987.

3204. Manfredini. *Dessins et Légendes. 1914-1917*. Preface by Louis Vauxcelles. Paris: A. Michel Éditeur, ca. 1918.

3205. Mars. *Mesdames les Cyclistes*. Paris: Plon, Nourit et Cie Éditeurs, n.d.

3206. Mars. *Paris Brilliant*. Paris: Libr. Plon, n.d.

3207. *Mieux Vaut Rire!*... Recueil de Dessins Humoristiques Choisis par J.E. Ponterman et Presentés par Tristan Bernard. Paris: Éditions Arts et Métiers Graphiques, n.d.

3208. Mitelberg, Louis. *Das Vierte Reich*. Berlin: Eulenspiegel-Verlag, 1955.

3209. Mitelberg, Louis. *Album*. Présentation de Pierre Constade. Paris: Éditions Cercle d'Art, 1953.

3210. Mohiss. *Tout Passe. Dieu Merci*. Preface by Marie José Gaucher. Paris: Syros Alternatives, 1987. 43 pp.

3211. Mose. *À la Mer*. Paris: Le Cherche Midi Éditeur, 1992.

3212. Mose. *Mécanique Ondulatoire de la Haute Couture*. Paris: Pierre Horay, 1958.

3213. Mose. *Noirs Desseins*. Paris: Fernand Hazan, n.d.

3214. Pichard, Georges. *Marie-Gabrielle de Saint-Eutrope*. Preface by Numa Sadoul. Grenoble: Glénat, 1977.

3215. Piem. *Un Coeur Gros Comme Ça*. Paris: Le Cherche Midi Éditeur, 1986. 62 pp.

3216. Rip and Aghion. *Dans le Tass*. Preface by Pierre Wolf. Paris: n.p., n.d.

3217. *Rires en Chaînes. Television et Humour*. Preface by Pierre Tchernia. Paris: Le Cherche Midi Éditeur, 1987. 128 pp.

3218. Roger, Milés L. *Vingt Peintres du XIXe Siècle*. Paris: Impr. Georges Petit, 1911.

3219. *Royal Menageries, The*. A Collection of the Best Caricatures Which Have Appeared in Paris since the Late Revolution. London: Charles Tilt, 1831.

3220. Samivel. *L'Opera de Pics. Précédé de La Réponse des Hanteurs*. Grenoble, Paris: B. Arthaud, 1944.

3221. Sarjon, A. *Les Plaisirs de Baden*. Paris: Au Bureau du *Charivari*, n.d.

3222. Silvius. *Physiologie du Poéte*. Paris: Jules Laisné, 1842. (Daumier).

3223. Swinglehurst, Edmund. *French Lovers Are Lovely*. London: Arco Publications Ltd., 1957.

3224. Thomas, J. *Aidons la Nature!* Grenoble: Glénat, 1985.

3225. Trez. *Jeux à Trez*. Grenoble: Glénat, 1982.

3226. Wattier, Ed. *La Jeunesse d'une Actrice ou 12 Scènes de Jour et de Nuit*. Paris: Sazerac et Duval Eddos, 1826.

3227. Zislin. *Sourires d'Alsace*. Preface by Paul Deroulède. Paris: Les Marches de l'Est, 1913.

COMIC BOOKS

3228. Aeschimann, Eric. "Bulles-Canto." *Libération*. Supplement Special Angoulême 1992, p. xiii.

3229. Alain, P. "Le Calembour Dessiné." *Cahiers Universitaires*. No. 13, 1971.

3230. "A La Rencontre de Durango." *Bédésup*. 4th Trim. 1987, pp. 4-8.

3231. Adhemar, Jean. "Cinq Siècles de Bandes Dessinées." *Les Lettres Françaises*. No. 1138, 1966.

3232. Alberelli, Christian. "Who's Who." *Le Français dans le Monde*. April 1986, pp. 79-83.

3233. "All Change in French Comics Magazines." *Comics Journal*. November 1989, pp. 25-27.

3234. *Apprendre l'Anglais par la Bande Dessinée*. Paris: Marabout, Coll. "Voyages et Langues," 1972.

3235. Augusto, Sergio. "As Bandas Francesas." *Jornal do Brasil*. March 3, 1967.

3236. Baron-Carvais, Annie. *La Bande Dessinée*. Paris: Ed. Presses Universitaires de France, Collection "Que Sais-Je?" #2212, 1985.

3237. Baudou, Jacques. *La Bande Dessinees*. Reims: Maison de la Culture de Reims, 1971.

3238. "BD: en Route, Gais Lurons!" *Charente Libre*. January 23, 1992, pp. 1, 10, 11, 20, 22.

3239. Benayoun, Robert. "Le Ballon dans les Bandes Dessinées." *La Brèche* (Paris). 1965.

3240. Benayoun, Robert. *Le Ballon dans la B.D.* Paris: Balland, 1978.

3241. Benayoun, Robert. *Le Ballon dans la Bande Dessinée: Vroum, Tchac, Zowie.* Paris: A. Ballard, 1968. 110 pp.

3242. Béra, Michel, Michel Denni, and Philippe Mellot. *Trésors de la Bande Dessinée.* Paris: Éditions de l'Amateur, 1988.

3243. Beylie, Claude. "Démons et Merveilles." *Giff-Wiff*. No. 17, 1966, p. 29.

3244. Boivin, Jacques. "Sexophonie dans le Planetarium." *Miroir du Fantastique*. 1:8 (1968), pp. 401-402.

3245. Boltanski, Luc. "La Constitution du Champ de la Bande Dessinée." *Actes de la Recherche en Science Sociales*. January 1975, pp. 37-59.

3246. Bonnemaison, Guy Charles. "Les Ballons dans les Bandes Dessinées." *Giff-Wiff*. No. 8, 1965, p. 39.

3247. Boudard, Alphonse. "Pour un Boulevard des Pieds Nickelés." *Azur* (Paris). 1965.

3248. Boujut, Michel. "Le Jazz avec Nous!" *Giff-Wiff*. No. 22, 1966.

3249. Bouquet, Jean-Louis. "Beauté en Graine." *Giff-Wiff*. No. 7, 1965.

3250. Bourgeois, Michel and Henri Filippini. *La Bande Dessinée en 10 Leçons.* Paris: Hachette, 1975.

3251. Bremond, Claude. "Pour une Gestuaire des Bandes Dessinées." *Langages* (Paris). No. 19, 1968.

3252. Brunoro, Gianni. "Le Crépuscule des Immortels." *Cahiers Universitaires*. No. 8, 1970.

3253. Brunoro, Gianni. "Un Classique d'Une Autre Dimension." *Cahiers Universitaires*. No. 13, 1971.

3254. Cabanes, Max *et al*. "Quatre Regards, I: BD: Le Droit à la Différence, II: Nulle, la Critique? III: Le Jour où Il n'y Aura plus de Fanzines; IV: Politiques Éditoriales: Vendre ou Mourir." *Le Français dans le Monde*. April 1986, pp. 12-17, 44-45, 48, 54-55.

3255. Caen, Michel, Jacques Lob, and Jacques Sternberg. *Les Chefs d'Oeuvre de la Bande Dessinée.* Paris: Editions Planete, 1967.

3256. Caen, Michel. "La Blonde Explosive." *Giff-Wiff*. No. 14, 1965, p. 14.

3257. Cantenys, A. "Le Monde Clos des Illustrés." *Les Lettres Françaises*. April 23, 1956.

3258. Carano, Ranieri. "A Propos de Lucques." *Linus*. No. 29, 1967, pp. 1-3.

3259. Carbonell, Charles-Olivier, ed. *Le Message Politique et Social de la Bande Dessinée*. Toulouse: IEPT/Privat, 1975.

3260. Caré, Jean-Marc and Jacques Pécheur. "C'Est la Crise... Alors, ou Cohabite?" *Le Français dans le Monde*. April 1986, pp. 56-57.

3261. "Carte Blanche a la B.D." *Figaroscope*. January 22, 1992.

3262. "Cent-Vingt Millions des Lecteurs." *Arts et Loisirs* (Paris). No. 34, 1966, p. 13.

3263. Chante, Alain. "De Révolution en Contre-Révolution." *Le Français dans le Monde*. April 1986, pp. 18-20.

3264. Chapeau, Bernard. "La Franglais dans les Bandes Dessinées." *Giff-Wiff*. No. 12, 1965, p. 1.

3265. Chateau, René, Claude Guillot, and Jean Guichard-Meili. "L'ABC des Comics." *La Méthode* (Paris). No. 10, 1963, pp. 5-22.

3266. Clair, René. *Notes sur les Bandes Dessinées*. Paris: Institut de France, 1974.

3267. Collectif. *L'Aventure et l'Image*. Paris: Éd. Vaillant/Gallimard, 1974.

3268. Collectif. "Lecture et Bande Dessinée. Objectif Promo-Durance, Édisud 1977" (Actes du Premier Colloque International Éducation et B.D. Tenu à la Roque d'Anthéron du 15 au 16 Janvier 1977).

3269. Collectif. *Mythes, Histoire, Langage, les Bandes Dessinées*. Bordeaux: Centre Régional de Documentation Pédagogique, 1970.

3270. Combet, Claude. "Succès 1984 et Projets 1985 (B.D.)." *Livres Hebdo*. 7:4 (1985), pp. 85-86, 88-89, 91-94, 97.

3271. "Comics Get Posted." *Comics Journal*. January 1988, p. 18.

3272. Conrad, Didier and Serge St.-Michel. *Le Français et la Bande Dessinée*. Classes de 6e et 5e. Paris: Fernand Nathan, 1972.

3273. Costa, Lorelisa. "Dalla 'Storia a Immagine' Alla Storia dell'Immagine. Appunti Sulla 'Bande Dessinée' d'Espressione Francese." In *Studi e Ricerche di Letteratura e Linguistica Francese. 1. A Cura di Gian Carlo Menichelli e Gian Carlo Roscioni*, pp. 363-401. Naples: Istituto Universitario Orientale, 1980.

3274. Couperie, Pierre. "Aargh!" *Phénix*. No. 17, 1970.

3275. Couperie, Pierre. "Anticipations Réalisées." *Phénix*. No. 14, 1970.

3276. Couperie, Pierre. "BD et Actualité." *Phénix*. No. 18, 1971.

3277. Couperie, Pierre. "Franck Sauvage Revient." *Phénix*. No. 5, 4. Trim., 1967, pp. 16-19.

3278. Couperie, Pierre. *Le Noir et Blanc dans la Bande Dessinée*. Paris: Ed. Serg, 1972.

3279. Couperie, Pierre. "Le Public dans la Bande Dessinée." Catalogue of exposition at the Musée des Arts Décoratifs, Paris, 1967, pp. 147-153.

3280. Couperie, Pierre. "1000.000 de Lieues en Ballon." Catalogue of exposition, Musée des Arts Décoratifs, Paris, 1967, pp. 25-30.

3281. Couperie, Pierre. "100.000.000. de Lieues en Ballon. La Science-Fiction dans la Bande Dessinée." *Phénix*. No. 4, 1967, pp. 31-41.

3282. Couperie, Pierre. "Un Oublié: Bilboquet." *Phénix*. No. 12, 1969.

3283. Covin, Michel. "L'Image Derobee ou Comment le Desir en (Re-) vient a Bande Dessinée." *Communications*. 24 (1976), pp. 197-242.

3284. Cuervo, Javier. "Lauzier, La Misantropia y la Duda." *El Wendigo*. October-December 1987, pp. 26-27.

3285. Darot, Mireille. "Mon Teppaz Est Naze." *Le Français dans le Monde*. April 1986, pp. 30-35.

3286. Decker, Dwight R. "The French Connection." *Amazing Heroes*. August 1, 1984, pp. 51-55, 60.

3287. De Commarmond, P. and C. Duchet. "La Bande Dessinée." In *Racisme et Société*, pp. 259-260. Paris: Maspero, 1969.

3288. De Rambures, Jean-Louis. "Les Don Quichotte de l'Edition." *Réalités* (Paris). No. 260, 1967.

3289. Deruelle, Pierre F. *La Bande Dessinée*. Paris: Hachette, 1972. 192 pp.

3290. "Dessins de RDA." *Mieux Vaut en Rire*. No. 13, 1989, pp. 18-19.

3291. Di Manno, Yves. "D'Univers à l'Autre." *Cahiers Universitaires*. No. 9R, 1970.

3292. Di Manno, Yves. "Le Surréél de l'Absurde dans la RAB." *Cahiers Universitaires*. No. 13, 1971.

3293. "Dix Personnages de Bandes Dessinées." *Magazine Littéraire* (Paris). July-August 1967, pp. 23-27.

3294. Dreyfus, Antoine. "Creation? Vous Avec Dit Création!" *Le Quotidien de Paris*. January 22, 1992, p. x.

3295. Dreyfus, Antoine. "Situation 'Alarmante' en France." *Le Quotidien de Paris*. January 22, 1992, pp. vi-vii.

3296. du Fontbare, Vicky and Philippe Sohet. "Codes Culturels et Logique de Classe dans la Bande Dessinée." *Communications* (Paris). 24 (1976), pp. 62-80.

3297. Dugru, A. "La Saga de Gai-Luron." *Cahiers Universitaires*. No. 13, 1971.

3298. Duranteau, Josanne. "Le Temps et l'Espace." *Les Lettres Françaises*. No. 1138, 1966.

3299. Dutrey, Jacques. "The French Comics Scene." *Comics Journal*. December 1987, pp. 27-34.

3300. Dutrey, Jacques. "The French Comics Scene: Part Two." *Comics Journal*. March 1988, pp. 19-27.

3301. Dutrey, Jacques. "Reviews of New French Releases." *Comics Journal*. January 1988, p. 19.

3302. Eco, Umberto. *Travels in Hyper-reality*. New York: Harcourt, Brace, Jovanovich, 1986.

3303. Enu, Henri J. "Eric Losfeld: 'La Bande Dessinée Intéressante Est Celle Qui Fustige." *La Quinzaine Littéraire* (Paris). August 1973.

3304. Enu, Henri J. "Quatre Créateurs de Bande Dessinée Vous Parlent." *La Quinzaine Littéraire* (Paris). August 1973.

3305. Faur, Jean-Claude. *A la Rencontre de la Bande Dessinée*. Marseilles: Bédésup, 1983. 238 pp.

3306. Faur, Jean-Claude. "Comment J'Ai Failli Devenir 'Maître du Monde.'" *L'Hebdo de la B.D.* (Nice). No. 125, 1992, pp. 3-6.

3307. Faur, Jean-Claude. "Comment J'Ai Trouvé le Moyen de Couler 'l'Hebdo.'" *L'Hebdo de la B.D.* No. 135, 1992, p. 6.

3308. Faur, Jean-Claude. "La Bande Dessinée: la Désinformation des Adultes Comme des Adolescents." Assises (1ères) Internationales de la Désinformation, Nice, 1989, pp. 281-287.

3309. Faur, Jean-Claude. "La B.D. en Région, la Bédé en Questions." *Impressions du Sud* (Aix). Nos. 1-2, 1983, pp. 52-53.

3310. Faur, Jean-Claude. *Lecture et Bande Dessinée: Sondage Auprès de 500 Lecteurs.* Toulouse: Bibliothèque Municipale, n.d. (1972), 10 pp.

3311. Faur, Jean-Claude. "Lecture Publique et Bande Dessinée." *Lecture et Bande Dessinée* (Aix: Édisud) 1977, pp. 65-69.

3312. Faur, Jean-Claude. "Lire des Bandes Dessinées: Un Art Qui N'Est pas Enfantin." *Voies Livres* (Lyon). No. 45, 1991. 28 pp.

3313. Faur, Jean-Claude. *Marseille et la Bande Dessinée.* Marseilles: Bibliothèque Municipale, 1980.

3314. Faur, Jean-Claude. "Voyage en Zines." *Le Français dans le Monde.* April 1986, p. 50.

3315. Fermigier, André. "Un Scoutisme Planétaire." *Le Nouvel Observateur.* No. 127, 1967, pp. 32-33.

3316. Filippini, Henri. "Trinca." *Phénix.* No. 24, 1972.

3317. Forlani, Remo. "Bienvenue Señor Copi." *Giff-Wiff.* No. 14, 1965, p. 10.

3318. Forlani, Remo. "Made in Paris." *Plexus.* No. 14, 1968, pp. 148-149.

3319. *40,000 Bandes Dessinées.* Paris: Ed. Baillant, 1969.

3320. "France Watches the Watchmen." *Comics Journal.* January 1988, p. 17.

3321. François, Edouard. "César, le Mal Nommé." *Phénix.* No. 17, 1970.

3322. François, Edouard. "L'Age d'Or." *Phénix.* SP. 1971.

3323. François, Edouard. "Le Mythe des Terres Lointaines (2)." *Phénix.* No. 23, 1972.

3324. François, Edouard. "Le Père Lacloche." *Phénix.* No. 21, 1971.

3325. François, Edouard and Claude Le Gallo. "A Propos de la Castafiore." *Phénix.* No. 2, 1967, pp. 27-28.

3326. "Frankreich-Paradies der 'Comic-Fans.'" *Bulletin: Jugend + Literatur*. December 1971, p. 11.

3327. Franquin, André and Joseph Gillain. *Comment on Devient Créateur de Bandes Dessinées*. Verviers, Belgique: Marabout, Coll. "Réussir," 1969.

3328. Frémion, Yves. *L'A.B.C. de la B.D.* Paris and Tournai (Belgium): Casterman, 1983.

3329. Frémion, Yves. *Les Nouveaux Petits Miquets*. Paris: Le Citron Hallucinogéne, 1982.

3330. Fresnault-Deruelle, Pierre. "Aspects de la Bande Dessinée en France." In *Comics and Visual Culture: Research Studies from Ten Countries*, edited by Alphons Silbermann and H.-D. Dyroff, pp. 62-78. Munich: K.G. Saur, 1986.

3331. Fresnault-Deruelle, Pierre. *Dessins et Bulles, la B.D.* Paris: Bordas, Coll. "Thèmes et Enquêtes," 1972.

3332. Fresnault-Deruelle, Pierre. *La Chambre à Bulles, Essais sur l'Image du Quotidien dans la B.D.* Paris: Coll. 10/18, 1977.

3333. Fresnault-Deruelle, Pierre. "La Codification de la Couleur dans la Bande Dessinée." *Revue d'Esthétique*. 1972-1973.

3334. Fresnault-Deruelle, Pierre. "Le Casque Tartare." *Phénix*. No. 15, 1970.

3335. Fresnault-Deruelle, Pierre. "Le Prince des Sables." *Phénix*. No. 19, 1971.

3336. Fresnault-Deruelle, Pierre. "Une Unité Commerciale de Narration: la Page de Bande Dessinée." *La Nouvelle Critique*. May 1971, pp. 42-49.

3337. Fronval, George. "Fascicules et Brochures Populaires d'Autrefois." *Phénix*. No. 2, 1967, pp. 24-26.

3338. Fronval, George. "La Dynastie des Offenstadt." *Phénix*. No, 3, 1967, pp. 40-43; No. 5, 4. Trim., 1967, p. 21-26; No. 7, 3. Trim., 1968, p. 13-16.

3339. Furth, Pierre-Pascal. "La Néjour Débile de Phil Actaire." *Le Français dans le Monde*. 200, 1986, pp. 8-11.

3340. "Gallic Comic, Cartoonist Kinnaird's Contes Francais." *Time*. April 12, 1963, p. 86.

3341. Gauthier, Guy. *Graphisme Narratif et Bande Dessinée*. Un Livret et 72 Diapositives. Paris: UFOLEIS, Ligue Française de l'Enseignement et de l'Éducation Permanente, 1975.

3342. Gauthier, Guy. *Les Codes de la Bande Dessinée*. Un Livret et 96 Diapositives. Paris: UFOLEIS, Ligue Française de l'Enseignement et de l'Éducation Permanente, 1972.

3343. Gauthier, Guy and J. Zimmer. "Les Bandes Dessinées." *Image et Son* (Paris). 1968, 20 pp.

3344. Gauthier, Patrice. "Nadal, l'Ironique Imagier." *Giff-Wiff*. No. 16, 1965, p. 23.

3345. Glénat, Jacques. "Les Personnages Secondaires." *Cahiers Universitaires*. No. 17, 1972.

3346. Glénat, Jacques. "Poussy, Chat d'Appartement." *Cahiers Universitaires*. No. 12, 1971.

3347. Goscinny, René. *La Bande Dessinée*. Paris: Planete, 1967.

3348. Goscinny, René. Preface to "Les Chefs-d'Oeuvres de la Bande Dessinée." In *Anthologie Planète*. Paris: Edition Planète, 1967.

3349. Gosset, Philippe. "Les Chevaliers du Ciel Voyagent Beaucoup." *Télémagazine* (Neuilly). No. 656, 1968, pp. 6-9.

3350. "Grâce a San Antonio, Frédéric Dard Bat les Records: 100 Millions d'Exemplaires." *Paris-Match*. No. 1015, 1968.

3351. Grandjean, Raymond. "Souvenirs de l'Âge d'Or." *Giff-Wiff*. No. 9, 1965.

3352. Gre, Monique. *Les Bandes Dessinées*. 2 Vols. Bordeaux: C.R.D.P., 1970-1971.

3353. Guegan, Gerard. "Bandes à Part." *Lui* (Paris). December 1966.

3354. Guth, Paul. "Le Naïf, Edme, et les Bulles." *Giff-Wiff*. No. 23, 1967, pp. 37-38.

3355. Hahn, Otto. "A l'Enseigne des Bandes Dessinées." *L'Express*. No. 747, 1965.

3356. Hartung, Peter. "Paris-Miniguide til Tegneserie Turisten." *Seriejournalen*. September 1990, p. 33.

3357. Held, J.-F. "Les Bons Élèves de la Bande." *Le Nouvel Observateur*. May 24-30, 1976.

3358. Homet, Marcel. *A la Poursuite des Dieux Solaires*. Paris: Ed Planète, Diffusion Denoél, 1972.

3359. Hoog, Armand. "L'Archange à Tête de Chauve-Rosis." *Les Nouvelles Littéraires*. No. 2042, 1966.

3360. Horn, Maurice. "American Comics in France: A Cultural Evaluation." In *For Better or Worse*. Westport, Connecticut: Greenwood Press, 1981.

3361. Horn, Maurice. "Langage et Structure de Bande Dessinée." *Informations et Documents*. No. 344, 1974.

3362. Horn, Maurice. "L'Avènement de la Bande Dessinée." *Opus International*. No. 1, 1967.

3363. Horn, Maurice. "On Reading Comics in Paris, 1939." Program. The International Convention of Comic Art, New York, 1968.

3364. H.R. "'XIII' un Gran Numero." *Le Quotidien de Paris*. January 22, 1992, p. xi.

3365. Igual, A. "Cinq Assertions pour Cinq As." *Cahiers Universitaires*. No. 17, 1972.

3366. *Informations et Documents* (France). May 1, 1967; August 1974. Special issues on comics.

3367. Jannet, Philippe. "La Bande Dessinée dans la Quotidiens." *Presse Actualité* (Paris). 170, 1983, pp. 54-59.

3368. Jennings, Dana. "Will Eisner in France." *Comics Journal*. May 1984, pp. 98-101.

3369. Juin, Hubert. "Au Pays da la Bande Dessinée." *Les Lettres Francaises*. No. 1151, 1966, pp. 5-7.

3370. Juin, Hubert. "Aux Arènes de la Bande Dessinée." *La Dépêche du Midi* (Toulouse). November 6, 1966.

3371. Juin, Hubert. "Le Droit de Rêver." *Les Lettres Française*. No. 1138, 1966.

3372. Klein, Hans. "Eine Witzfigur Erobert Frankreich." *Südanzeiger*. August 15, 1967.

3373. "La Bande Décimée." *Libération*. Supplement Special Angoulême 1992, p. xv.

3374. "La Bande Dessinée Aujourd' hui." *Magazine Littéraire* (Paris). No. 95, 1974. (Issue devoted to comics).

3375. *La Bande Dessinée Depuis* (Comics since 1975). Paris: Editions MA, 1985. 201 pp.

3376. "La BD Fait de la Résistance." Special section of *Quotidien de Paris*. January 22, 1992, 16 pp.

3377. Labesse, Dominique. "A Propos du Racisme." *Cahiers Universitaires*. No. 14, 1971.

3378. Labesse, Dominique. "Galerie de Portraits." *Cahiers Universitaires*. No. 14, 1971.

3379. Labesse, Dominique. "L'Ampleur d'un Succès." *Cahiers Universitaires*. No. 14, 1971.

3380. Labesse, Dominique. "Le Retour Cyclique des Personnages." *Cahiers Universitaires*. No. 14, 1971.

3381. Labesse, Dominique. "Les Régimes Politiques." *Cahiers Universitaires*. No. 14, 1971.

3382. Labesse, Dominique. "Les Voyages et l'Aventure." *Cahiers Universitaires*. No. 14, 1971.

3383. Labesse, Dominique. "Repères Biographiques." *Cahiers Universitaires*. No. 14, 1971.

3384. Lacassin, Francis. "La Bande Dessinée." *Oeuvres Laïques de la Seine*. November-December 1967.

3385. Lacassin, Francis. "L'Age d'Or Devant Nous." *Giff-Wiff*. No. 23, 1967, p. 1.

3386. Lacassin, Francis. "Quand la Bande Dessinée Conteste." *Magazine Littéraire*. 95, 1974, pp. 9-16.

3387. Lacassin, Francis. "Rien n'Est Vrai, Tout Est Permis." *Les Lettres Françaises*. June 30-July 6, 1966.

3388. Lacassin, Francis. "Une Semaine en Ballon." *Midi-Minuit Fantastique* (Paris). No. 6, 1963, p. 88.

3389. Laclos, Michel. "Prolégomènos a Une Étude de la Bande Comique." *Giff-Wiff*. No. 12, 1965, p. 5.

3390. "La Collection des Bandes Dessinées." *L'Obi* (Paris). No. 13, 1967, pp. 10-22.

3391. Lannes, J.M. "Petit Bestiaire Intîme." *Cahiers Universitaires*. No. 13, 1971.

3392. Lanoe, Philippe. "Document." *Bédésup*. 2nd Trim., 1988, pp. 8-10.

3393. Laval, Henri. "Du Coté des Albums." *La Lettre de Bédésup*. No. 58, 1992, p. 3.

3394. Laville, Jean-François. "Fines Bulles." *Figaroscope*. January 22, 1992, pp. 2-3.

3395. Lecigne, Bruno. "Les Critiques au Miroir de Leur Discours." *Le Français dans le Monde*. April 1986, pp. 46-47.

3396. Lecigne, Bruno and Jean-Pierre Tamine. *Fac-Simile. Essai Paratactique sur le Nouveau Réalisme de la Bande Dessinée*. Paris: Futuropolis, 1983.

3397. "Le Dossier." *Bédésup*. Nos. 48/49, 1989, pp. 3-7.

3398. "Le Français et la Bande Dessinée." *Etudes ef Travaux Pratiques pour les Classes de 6 et 5*.

3399. Le Gallo, Claude. "La Marque Jaune." *Phénix*. No. 15, 1970.

3400. Le Gallo, Claude. "Le Mystère de la Grande Pyramide." *Phénix*. No. 2, 1967, pp. 29-30.

3401. Le Gallo, Claude. "Le Piège Diabolique." *Phénix*. No. 16, 1970.

3402. Le Gallo, Claude. "Le Rayon U." *Phénix*. No. 5, 4 Trim., 1967, p. 50.

3403. Le Gallo, Claude. "Q.R.N. sur Bretzelburg." *Phénix*. No. 3, 1967, p. 33.

3404. Le Gallo, Claude. "Vol 714 pour Sidney." *Phénix*. No. 7, 1968, pp. 74-75.

3405. Leguebe, Eric. "L'Amérique à l'Heure des Comics Troupiers." *Arts et Loisirs* (Paris). No. 34, 1966, pp. 3-5.

3406. Leguebe, Eric. *Le Voyage en Balloon*. Paris: *Bédésup*, 1981. 128 pp.

3407. "Le Hit-Parade de Stars de Papier." *Nouveau Candide*. No. 312, 1966, p. 24.

3408. Lentz, Serge. "Il Suffisait de Faire Parler Une Souris." *Candide*. No. 296, 1966, pp. 45-46.

3409. *Les Bandes Dessinées*. 2 Vols. Bordeaux: Centre Régional de Documentation Pédagogique de Bordeaux, 1970.

3410. "Les Bandes Dessinées d'Octobre." *(A Suivre)*. October 1992, p. 122.

3411. "Les Bestsellers Nouveau de Jai Lu B.D." *Bédésup*. 2nd Trim., 1988, p. 3.

3412. *Les Chefs-d'Oeuvre de la Bande Dessinée*. Paris: Ed. Planète, 1968.

3413. *Les Lettres Françaises* (France). June 30, 1966. Special issue on comics.

3414. "Les Nouveaux Scénaristes." *Le Quotidien de Paris*. January 22, 1992, p. ix.

3415. Le Stang, Anne. "Jour de Jeunes au Programme." *Charente Libre*. January 24, 1992, p. 10.

3416. Le Stang, Anne. "Les Mécènes Entrent en Scène." *Charente Libre*. January 23, 1992, p. 10.

3417. Levin, Marc-Albert. "Sans but Lucratif." *Les Lettres Françaises*. No. 1138, 1966.

3418. *Lire la Bande Dessinée* (How To Decipher the Comics). Lyon: Presses Universitaires de Lyon, 1985. 154 pp.

3419. *Livres Hebdo* (France). December 8, 1981. Special issue on comics.

3420. Llobera, L. and Romain Oltra. "La Bande Dessinée." A.F.H.A. *Savoir Dessiner No. 8*. Paris: 1968.

3421. Lob, Jacques. "Au Pays de Comics." *Giff-Wiff*. No. 16, 1965, p. 17.

3422. Lochot, François. "La Bande Dessinée, Une Potion Magique? Faut-Il Scolariser la B.D.?" *Cahiers Pédagogiques*. April 1982, pp. 7-9.

3423. Lo Duca, Joseph-Marie. *Luxure de Luxe*. Paris: Dominique Leroy, 1983.

3424. Marny, Jacques: *Le Monde Étonnant des Bandes Dessinées*. Paris: Le Centurion Science Humaines, 1968. 320 pp.

3425. "Marseille dans la B.D." *Bédésup*. 2nd Trim. 1988, pp. 23-30.

3426. Martínez, Léa. "L'Analyse Structurale des Bandes Dessinées." In *Image et Communication, Sous la Direction de Anne-Marie Thibault-Laulan*. Paris: Éd. Universitaires, 1972.

3427. Masson, Axelle. "Pas si Facile." *Cahiers Pédagogiques*. April 1982, pp. 9-10.

3428. Metken, Günter. "Le Cris de Paris-Lebendige Bilderbogen." *Die Welt* (Hamburg). April 7, 1967.

3429. Metken, Sigrid. "Französische Bilderbogen des 19." *Jahrhunderts* (Baden-Baden). May 1972.

3430. Metz, Christian. "Images et Pédagogie." *Communications* (Paris). No. 15, 1970.

3431. Moliterni, Claude. "Carnet de Voyage à São Paulo." *Phénix*. No. 16, 1970.

3432. Moliterni, Claude. "Jules." *Phénix*. No. 23, 1972.

3433. Morris. "Profession: Dessinateur." *Giff-Wiff*. No. 16, 1965, p. 5.

3434. Neubourg, Cyrille. "Petit Catalogue de Thèmes." *Les Lettres Françaises*. June 30-July 6, 1966.

3435. Neubourg, Cyrille. "Tirage: 26 Millions." *Les Lettres Françaises*. No. 1138, 1966.

3436. Noel, Jean-François. "Laids Band Daissinez...." *Les Lettres Françaises*. No. 1138, 1966.

3437. Nybakken, Scott, ed. "Bande Dessinée: A Panel Discussion About Graphic Novels." *Comics Journal*. March 1992, pp. 66-72, 74-78, 80. (Includes Art Spiegelman, Maurice Horn, Marcel Gutwirth, Robert Hughes, Jules Feiffer, Jerome Charyn, and Jacques de Loustal).

3438. Oltra, Romain and Joseph Llobera. *La Bande Dessinée*. Éd. Alpha, Coll. 'Savoir Dessiner,' 1968.

3439. Pernin, Georges. *Un Monde Étrange: la Bande Dessinée*. Paris: Clédor, 1974.

3440. Pierre, Michel. *La Bande Dessinée*. Paris: Larousse, Coll. "Idéologies et Sociétés," 1976.

3441. Picquenot, Alain. "La Grande Vignette et le Récit." *Communications*. 24 (1976), pp. 177-196.

3442. Pottier, A. *La Presse de Mineurs*. Paris: Cujas, 1956.

3443. Queréel, P. "Anti-Pub et Contre-Bande." *Espaces et Sociétés* (Paris). 22/23, 1977, pp. 65-88.

3444. Rebiére, Michel. "L'Édition BD en Dent de Scie." *Charente Libre*. January 24, 1992, p. 11.

3445. Rebiére, Michel. "Troisième Acte au BD-Musée." *Charente Libre*. January 23, 1992, p. 11.

3446. Renard, Jean-Bruno. *Clefs pour la Bande Dessinée*. Paris: Seghers, 1978. 256 pp.

3447. Rey, Alain. *Les Spectres de la Bande: Essai sur la B.D.* Paris: Les Éditions de Minuit, 1978.

3448. Rivière, François. "Quelques Personnages Diaboliques de la BD." *Cahiers Universitaires*. No. 7, 1970.

3449. Rolin, Gabrielle. "Du Sang, de la Volupté, et de la Mort." *Le Monde*. Supplément. No. 6926, 1967, p. 5.

3450. Rolin, Gabrielle. "La 'Sous-Littérature': le Trois Grands du Circuit Populaire." *Le Monde.* Supplément, No. 6926, 1967, p. 4.

3451. Sadoul, Jacques. "Deux Études Phylacterologiques." *Fiction.* No. 164, 1967, pp. 148-151.

3452. Sadoul, Jacques. "Guide du Collectioneur." *Giff-Wiff.* No. 22, 1966.

3453. Sadoul, Jacques. *L'Enfer des Bulles.* Paris: Pauvert, 1968.

3454. Sadoul, Jacques. *Panorama de la Bande Dessinée.* Paris: Éditions J'ai lu, 1976.

3455. Sadoul, Jacques. "Vie et Mort d'un Prince." *Midi-Minuit Fantastique.* No. 17, 1967, pp. 136-137.

3456. Sadoul, Jacques and Anne. "Panorama du Comicbook." *Giff-Wiff.* No. 14, 1966, p. 22.

3457. Sadoul, Numa. "Johan, la Maison et la Famille." *Cahiers Universitaires.* No. 12, 1971.

3458. Sadoul, Numa. "La RAB ou le Raz de Marée du Rire." *Cahiers Universitaires.* No. 13, 1971.

3459. Sadoul, Numa. "Les Phénomènes Paranormaux." *Cahiers Universitaires.* No. 14, 1971.

3460. Sadoul, Numa. *Portraits à la Plume et au Pinceau.* Grenoble: Glénat, 1976.

3461. Sanders, Alain. *À la Rencontre des Bédéstars.* Marseilles: Bédésup, 1984.

3462. "Slim: La Bande Dessinée." *Jeune Afrique.* No. 504, 1970, pp. 46-47.

3463. "Spotlight on Comics Creators." *Comics Journal.* March 1988, pp. 16-17.

3464. Sullerot, Eveline. "La Presse d'Aujourd' hui." *Blond et Gay* (Paris). 1966.

3465. Tabuche, Bernard. *À la Découverte des Bandes Dessinées Occitanes.* Nîmes: Marpoc, 1987.

3466. Tchernia, Pierre. "Deux Romains en Gaule." *Télé-Magazine.* No. 593, 1967, pp. 86-90.

3467. Tchernia, Pierre. "Un Vieux Copain Tout Jeune." *Giff-Wiff.* No. 19, 1966, pp. 28-29.

3468. Tercinet, Alain. "Deux Gamins au Coeur de l'Afrique." In *CELEG* (Paris). 1964.

3469. "30 Millions des Lecteurs: Du Sang, de la Volupté et de la Mort." *Le Monde*. Supplement to No. 6926, 1967, p. 5.

3470. Thomas, Pascal. "La Littérature en Ballon." *Le Nouveau Candide*. July 25, 1966.

3471. "Tidbits from France." *Comics Journal*. January 1988, p. 19.

3472. Toussaint, Bernard. "Idéographie et Bande Dessinée." *Communications* (Paris). 24 (1976), pp. 81-93.

3473. Trout, Bernard. "La Butte Contre le Dominateur." *Giff-Wiff*. Supplément, No. 22, 1966.

3474. Vidal, Leo. "Pourquoi Cette Folie des Bandes Dessinées?" *Blanc et Noir* (Paris). December 30, 1965, pp. 8-9.

3475. "Vive la BD." *Le Quotidien de Paris*. January 22, 1992, p. xiv.

3476. "Voici Comme Nait Une Bande Dessinée." *Pilote*. No. 283, 1967, pp. 37-42.

3477. Vovelle, Michel. "La Mort et l'Au-delà dans la Dessinée." *L'Histoire* (Paris). 3, 1978, pp. 34-42.

3478. Zanotto, Piero. "I Fumetti in Francia." *Corriere del Giorno*. July 14, 1966.

3479. Zanotto, Piero. "René Clair e la Storia dei Fumetti." *Nazione Sera*. February 28, 1963.

Anthologies

3480. Cazamayou, Philippe (Caza). *Escape from Suburbia*. Stories of the Fantastic, No. 1. New York: Nantier-Beall-Minoustchine, 1987. 64 pp.

3481. Charyn, Jerome and François Boucq. *The Magician's Wife*. New York: Catalan Communications, 1988.

3482. "Dark Horse Announces International Anthology." *Comics Journal*. April 1989, p. 21.

3483. Flaubert, Gustave and Philippe Druillet. *Carthage*. Paris: Dargaud, 1982.

3484. "Livres a Suivre." *(A Suivre)*. October 1992, pp. 142-146.

3485. Loisel, Régis and Serge Le Tendre. *Roxanna and the Search for the Time Bird*. 4 Vols. New York: NBM, 1988-1989.

3486. Macedo. *Psychorock*. New York: Heavy Metal, 1977. 60 pp.

3487. Magnus. *Full Moon in Dendera*. The Specialist, No. 1. New York: Catalan Communications, 1987. 48 pp.

3488. Paringaux, Philippe and Jacques Loustal. *Love Shots*. New York: Catalan Communications, 1988.

3489. Schuiten, François and Benoît Peeters. *The Great Walls of Samaris*. Stories of the Fantastic, No. 2. New York: Nantier-Beall-Minoustchine, 1987. 48 pp.

3490. Sternberg, Jacques, Michel Caen, Jacques Lob. *Les Chefs-d'Oeuvre de la Bande Dessinée*. Paris: Eds. Planète, 1967.

Art, Aesthetics, Architecture

3491. Amiel, Vincent. "Bande Dessinée et Architecture: L'Espace Encadré." *Les Cahiers de la Bande Dessinée*. 69, 1986, pp. 24-25.

3492. André, Jean-Claude. "Esthétique des Bandes Dessinées." *Revue d'Esthétique* (Paris). 18:1 (1965), pp. 49-71.

3493. *Architectures de Bande Dessinée*. Paris: Institut Français d'Architecture, 1985.

3494. Bouret, Jean. "D'Une Esthétique de la Bande Dessinée." *Les Lettres Françaises*. June 30-July 6, 1966.

3495. Bouyer, Sylvain. "Théorie des Symptômes." *Les Cahiers de la Bande Dessinée*. 69, 1986, p. 86-87.

3496. Couperie, Pierre. "Bandes Dessinées et Figuration Narrative." Catalogue of Exposition, Musée des Arts Décoratifs, Paris, 1967.

3497. Couperie, Pierre. *Bande Dessinée et Figuration Narrative*. Paris: Société Civile d'Études et de Recherches des Littératures Dessinées, 1967.

3498. Couperie, Pierre. "Echoes of Modern Art in the Comic Strip. Spiegelungen der Modernen Kunst im Comic Strip. Reflets de l'Art Moderne dans la Bande Dessinée." *Graphis* (Zürich). 28:159 (1972/1973), pp. 14-25.

3499. Couperie, Pierre, Proto De Stefanis, Edouard François, Maurice Horn, Claude Moliterni, and Gérald Gassiot-Talabot. *Bande Dessinée et Figuration Narrative*. Paris: Musee des Arts Decoratifs, Palais du Louvre, 1967.

3500. De Stefanis, Proto. "Bande Dessinée et Figuration Narrative." Catalogue of Exposition, Musée des Arts Décoratifs, Paris, 1967.

3501. Dethier, Jean. "Architecture: du Béton dans les Bulles. (Exposition Architecture de Bande Dessinée)." *Beaux Arts Magazine* (Levallois). 26, 1985, pp. 68-75.

3502. Detowarnicki, Frédéric. "Saga l'Héroine de l'Univers Pop." *L'Express*. No. 862, 1967, p. 44

3503. Duc, B. *L'Art de la BD. Comment Réaliser une BD*. Paris: Eds. Jacques Glénat, 1982.

3504. Duc, B. *L'Art de la BD. T.II.: La Technique du Dessin*. Grenoble: Eds. Jacques Glénat, 1983.

3505. Ecken, Claude. "Paris-New York, Parcours Fléché." *Les Cahiers de la Bande Dessinée*. 63, 1985, pp. 34-36.

3506. "Etude Comparée de l'Art de la Dédicace." *Charente Libre*. January 27, 1992, p. 9.

3507. Faur, Jean-Claude. "La B.D. Est d'Abord un Art du Temps." *Bédésup*. Nos. 48/49, 1989, pp. 40-43.

3508. Faur, Jean-Claude. *L'Esthétique du Cercle dans la Bande Dessinée: Guide Sommaire pour en Faire le Tour*. Toulouse: Union Chrétienne des Jeunes Gens, 1976. 9 pp.

3509. François, Edouard. "Bande Dessinée et Figuration Narrative." Catalogue of Exposition, Musée des Arts Décoratifs, Paris, 1967.

3510. Gassiot-Talabot, Gérald. "Bande Dessinée et Figuration Narrative." Catalogue of Exposition, Musée des Arts Décoratifs, Paris, 1967.

3511. Gassiot-Talabot, Gérald. "La Figuration Narrative dans l'Art Contemporaine." Katalog der Gallerie Creuze, Salle Balzac, Paris, 1966.

3512. Gassiot-Talabot, Gérald. "Le Ballon dans la Figuration Narrative." *Phénix*. No. 3, 1967, pp. 48-51.

3513. Groensteen, Thierry. "Graphic Connection." *Les Cahiers de la Bande Dessinée*. 70, 1986, pp. 87-89.

3514. Groensteen, Thierry. "L'Engeance de l'Art." *Les Cahiers de la Bande Dessinée*. 68, 1986, pp. 88-90.

3515. Groensteen, Thierry. "L'Oeil Pictural." *Les Cahiers de la Bande Dessinée*. 72, 1986, pp. 77-79.

3516. Groensteen, Thierry and Arnaud de la Croix. "Transfuges et Agents Doubles. Quand les Dessinateurs se Mêlent de Peindre." *Les Cahiers de la Bande Dessinée*. 69, 1986, pp. 81-85.

3517. Guichard-Meili, Jean. "La Figuration Narrative Est-Elle le Dictionnaire de Quotidien?" *Arts* (Paris). October 6, 1965, pp. 30-31.

3518. Horn, Maurice. "Bande Dessinée et Figuration Narrative." Catalogue of Exposition, Musée des Arts Décoratifs, Paris, 1967.

3519. Horn, Maurice. "Defense et Illustration de la Pin-up dans la Bande Dessinée." *V-Magazine*. No. 580, 1965.

3520. "La Art de la Bande Dessinée." *Graphis*. (Zurich, Graphis Press). No. 159-160 (Special Edition), 1972.

3521. Lacassin, Francis. "La Bande Dessinée, Art Mineur Réservé aux Mineurs?" *Giff-Wiff*. No. 20, 1966, p. 1.

3522. Lacassin, Francis. "Neuvième Art, au Deux." *Giff-Wiff*. No. 2, 1965.

3523. Lacassin, Francis. *Pour un Neuvième Art: La Bande Dessinée*. Coll. "10-18," Nos. 649-650-651-652. Paris: Plon, 1971.

3524. Metz, Christian. "Image, Enseignement, Culture." *Cahiers Media-Messages* (Paris). No. 1, 1971.

3525. Moliterni, Claude. "Bande Dessinée et Figuration Narrative." Catalogue of Exposition, Musée des Arts Décoratifs, Paris, 1967.

3526. Pascal, David. "Bande Dessinée et Peinture." *S.T.P.: Analyse Critique de la B.D.* (Poitiers). 1, 1978, pp. 39-43.

3527. Prasteau, Jean. "Les Intellectuels Découvrent un Huitième Art: la Bande Dessinée." *Le Figaro Littéraire*. No. 984, 1965, p. 20.

3528. Restany, Pierre. "L'Art pour la Bande." *Arts* (Paris). April 19-25, 1967, pp. 36-38.

3529. Roque, Georges. "Voir la Peinture par la Bande." *Les Cahiers de la Bande Dessinée*. 70, 1986, pp. 84-86.

3530. Roux, Antoine. *La Bande Dessinée. L'Art d'Un Certain Montage. Dossier + 12 Diapositives*. Paris: Ofrateme, 1975.

3531. Roux, Antoine. *La Bande Dessinée. Un Certain Art du Cadrage. Dossier + 12 Diapositives*. Paris: Ofrateme, 1975, 1979.

3532. Sadoul, Jacques. "L'Art du Comic-Book." *Giff-Wiff*. No. 16, 1965, p. 28.

3533. Smolderen, Thierry and Thierry Groensteen. "Tableaux Vivants." *Les Cahiers de la Bande Dessinée*. 68, 1986, pp. 91-97.

3534. Sorel, Philippe. "Autopsie d'Un Voilier." In *Bourgeon à la Hune*, edited by L'Association Clovis, pp. 18-21. Grenoble: Eds. Jacques Glénat, 1986.

3535. Sterckx, Pierre. "BD et Figuration Libre." *Les Cahiers de la Bande Dessinée*. 72, 1986, pp. 74-76.

3536. Virilio, Paul. "L'Architecture dans la Bande Dessinée." *Art et Création* (Paris). 1, 1968, 122-127.

3537. Weaver, Robert. "Experiments in Time-Art. Experimente in Zeit-Kunst. Expériences en Art Séquentiel." *Graphis* (Zürich). 28:160 (1972/1973), pp. 88-95.

Cinema, Theater

3538. Benayoun, Robert. "Comics et Cinéma." *La Méthode* (Paris). No. 10, 1963, pp. 2-4.

3539. Benayoun, Robert. "Filmographie des Comics." *St. Cinéma des Press* (Paris). No. 2, 1950.

3540. Bertieri, Claudio. "Da Louis Forton à Jean-Luc Godard." *Cinema e Teatro* (Genoa). No. 2, 1967.

3541. Beylie, Claude. "Du Septième au Neuvième Art." *Cinéma* (Paris). 159, 1971, pp. 32-35.

3542. Borringo, Heinz-Lothar. "Der Comic—Ein Vergleich zum Film." In *Spannung in Text und Film. Spannung und Suspense als Textverarbeitungskategorien*, edited by Ders, pp. 69-75. Düsseldorf: Pädagogischer Verlag Schwann, 1980.

3543. Bouyer, Sylvain. "Le Théâtre des Alpages." *Les Cahiers de la Bande Dessinée*. 60, 1984, pp. 22-25.

3544. Caen, Michel. "Comic-Strip et Celluloid." *Les Lettres Françaises*. No. 1138, 1968.

3545. Carontini, E. *Le Comique au Cinéma et dans la Bande Dessinée*. Louvain-la-Neuve: Cabay, 1982.

3546. Chateau, René. "Filmographie des Comics." *La Méthode*. No. 10, 1963, pp. 23-53.

3547. *CinémAction*. Summer 1990. Special issue on "Cinéma et Bande Dessinée." 280 pp.

3548. *Cinéma 71* (Paris). September-October 1971. Dossier on "Cinéma et Bande Dessinée" by Claude Beylie, Denis Gifford, Francis Lacassin, and Bernard Trout.

3549. *Cinématographe*. October-November 1976. Dossier on "Cinéma et Bande Dessinée."

3550. De la Croix, Arnaud. "Le Théâtre du Plaisir." *Les Cahiers de la Bande Dessinée*. 65, 1985, pp. 44-45.

3551. De la Croix, Arnaud. "Opéras de Papier." *Les Cahiers de la Bande Dessinée*. 67, 1986, pp. 42-43.

3552. Delperdange, Patrick. "Le Dernier Travelling." *Les Cahiers de la Bande Dessinée*. 57, 1984, pp. 18-21.

3553. "Du Livre à l'Écran: Quand le Cinéma Fait Appel aux Bandes Dessinées." *Pilote*. No. 283, 1967, pp. 6-7.

3554. Groensteen, Thierry. "Bande Dessinée et Théâtre. Ces Héros Qui Ont Pris Vie." *Les Cahiers de la Bande Dessinée*. 67, 1986, pp. 39-41.

3555. Furth, Pierre-Pascal. "Le Sang du Flamboyant ou la Difficulté de Vivre en 'Homme Debout.'" *Les Cahiers de la Bande Dessinée*. 58, 1984, pp. 37-40.

3556. Gauthier, Guy. "Le Langage des Bandes Dessinées." *La Revue du Cinema—Image et Son* (Paris). March 1965, pp. 65-75.

3557. Gauthier, Guy. "Les Codes de la Bande Dessinée." *La Revue du Cinema—Image et Son* (Paris). Numero Special Hors Serie, 1973.

3558. Gautier, G.L. "Nouvelles Catégorisations." *Les Cahiers de la Bande Dessinée*. 67, 1986, pp. 44-46.

3559. Glasser, Jean-Claude. "Bande Dessinée et Théâtre. Une Rencontre Déjà Ancienne." *Les Cahiers de la Bande Dessinée*. 66, 1985, pp. 73-74.

3560. Gola, Guido, Aldo Lombezzi, Yves Froment, and Wilbur Leguébe. *Flashes sur le Comique d'Image dans le Film et la BD*. Louvain-la-Neuve: Cabay, 1983. 280 pp.

3561. Groensteen, Thierry. "L'Amour des Planches: Bande Dessinée et Théâtre." *Les Cahiers de la Bande Dessinée*. 65, 1985, pp. 39-43.

3562. Hangartner, Urs. "Hintergründe zum Vierten Astérix-Zeichentrick-Film." *Comic Forum. Das Magazin für Comicliteratur.* 8:31 (1986), pp. 11-14.

3563. Hurtubise, Jacques. "Les Images Dessinées." *La Revue du Cinema—Image et Son.* June-July 1974.

3564. Lacassin, Francis. "Bande Dessinée et Cinéma." In *Pour un Neuvième Art. La Bande Dessinée*, edited by Francis Lacassin, pp. 331-458. Paris: Slatkine, 1982.

3565. "Le Caméra Fait des Bulles." *Arts* (Paris). No. 21, 1966, p. 7.

3566. *La Méthode.* February 1963. Special number on "Les Comics et le Cinéma" by Robert Benayoun, René Chateau, and Claude Guillot.

3567. *La Revue du Cinéma.* November 1989. Dossier on "BD/Ciné:l'Adaptation."

3568. *L'Avant-Scène Cinéma.* March 1981. Dossier on "BD et Cinéma," by Philippe Mellot.

3569. *L'Image Video.* December 1989. Dossier on "Cassettes, Bulles et Pellicules."

3570. "Lucky Luke. Vorbilder im Kino." *Comic Forum. Das Magazin für Comicliteratur.* 5:21 (1983), pp. 28-31.

3571. *Positif.* July-August 1986. Dossier on "Cinema et BD."

3572. Quinson, René. "Un Cinéma des Bandes Dessinées." *Bulletin Unifrance Film* (Paris). January 22, 1965.

3573. Resnais, Alain. "Films and Comics. Film und Comic Strip. Film et Bande Dessinée." *Graphis* (Zürich). 28:160 (1972/1973), pp. 96-103.

3574. Rolin, Gabrielle. "Bandes Dessinées et Romans-Photos." *Le Monde.* April 19, 1967.

3575. Sadoul, Georges. "Le Cinéma et les Bandes Dessinées." *Les Lettres Françaises.* June 30-July 6, 1966.

3576. Smolderen, Thierry. "Le Medium et les Intervallistes." *Les Cahiers de la Bande Dessinée.* 58, 1984, pp. 94-97.

3577. Tibéri, Jean-Paul. *La Bande Dessinée et le Cinéma.* Paris: Regards, 1981. 264 pp.

Education, Culture

3578. Amutio, Robert, Nadine Bernet, *et al.* (Groupe de Stagiaires). "Boîte à Idées pour l'Exploitation d'une B.D." *Le Français dans le Monde.* 191, 1985, pp. 37-46.

3579. Auvray, Annie. "Utilisation de la Bande Dessinée pour l'Amélioration de l'Expression Orale." *Les Cahiers de l'Enfance Inadaptée* (Paris). 217, 1977, pp. 8-10.

3580. Barrera-Vidal, Albert. "La Bande Dessinée au Service de l'Enseignement des Langues." *Praxis des Neusprachlichen Unterrichts.* (Dortmund). 20, 1973, pp. 288-303.

3581. Baudou, Jacques. *La Bande Dessinée à l'École...* Reims: Centre Régional de Recherche et de Documentation Pédagogiques, 1974.

3582. Bouchard, Gilbert. *La Bande Dessinée à l'École... C'Est Facile.* Marseilles: Bédésup, 1985.

3583. Bourlon, Pierre. "A Comme... Avec une Bande Dessinée Humoristique: Humour et Pédagogie." *Le Français dans le Monde.* 151, 1980, pp. 57-60.

3584. Briquet, Andrée. "Etude d'Une Bande Dessinée en Classe de 5e." *L'Ecole Libératrice* (Paris). 29, 1979, pp. 1297-1300, 1309-1312.

3585. Briquet, Andrée. "Etude d'Une Bande Dessinée en Classe de 5e." *L'École Libératrice* (Paris). 31 (1979), pp. 1385-1388, 1397-1400.

3586. Caput, Jean-Pol. "Pédagogie de l'Expression et Bande Dessinée. Quelques Suggestions." *Etudes de Linguistique Appliquée* (Paris). N.S. 13, 1974, pp. 81-90.

3587. Caré, Jean-Marc. "Enseigner la BD/Enseigner Avec la BD?" *Le Français dans le Monde.* 200, 1986, pp. 60-62.

3588. Carré, Daniel. "La Bande Dessinée Telle Que Nous la Pratiquons. I." *L'Educateur* (Cannes). 9, 1976, pp. 13-36.

3589. Carré, Daniel. "La Bande Dessinée Telle Que Nous la Pratiquons. II." *L'Educateur* (Cannes). 12, 1976, pp. 13-20, 29-36.

3590. Carré, Daniel and Ivan Davy. "Deux Expériences sur la Bande Dessinée." *L'Educateur* (Cannes). 6, 1973, pp. 25-29.

3591. Catteau-Varrasse, Géraldine. *Progression Employée pour Une Meileure Approche de la B.D. Source de Communication.* Marcinelle: Service d'Information aux Enseignants/S.A. Eds. Dupuis, n.d.

3592. Circuel, Francine. "Conversations Écrites." *Le Français dans le Monde.* 167, 1982, pp. 20-27.

3593. "Comics." Special number of *AV-Bulletin. Schweizerische Zeitschrift für Unterrichtstechnologie und Medienpädagogik* (Zürich). 8-9, 1974.

3594. Convard, Didier and Serge Saint-Michel. *Le Français et la Bande Dessinée. Etude et Travaux Pratiques.* (Classes de 6e, 5e). Paris: Nathan, 1972.

3595. Dahlem, J. "L'Enseignement du Français et la Bande Dessinée." *Etudes de Linguistique Appliquée* (Paris). N.S. 13, 1974, pp. 99-109.

3596. Damerment, Martine. "Raconter en Maternelle Avec des BD." *Le Français Aujourd'hui* (Paris). 59, 1982, pp. 69-72.

3597. Deaucourt, Jean-Louis and Bernard Veck. "Une Initiation Littéraire par la Bande Dessinée." *Education et Développement* (Paris). 81, 1972, pp. 44-53.

3598. Dillies, Patrick. "Le Rapport Image—Texte dans la Vignette de B.D. Progression d'Exercises." *Pratiques* (Metz). 18/19, 1978, pp. 21-29.

3599. "Dossier Pédogogique sur la Bande Dessinée." *L'Educateur.* February-April 1976.

3600. Faur, Jean-Claude. "Dossier: La Bande Dessinée." *L'Ecole Ouverte sur le Monde.* No. 94, 1983, pp. 26-34, 41-43, 48-50.

3601. Faur, Jean-Claude. "La Bande Dessinée à l'École: du Refus à la Récupération." Paper presented at Congrès (1er) Français des Sciences de l'Information, Compiègne, April 21-23, 1978.

3602. Fouilhé, Pierre. "Hurrah." *Educateurs* (Paris). No. 51, 1954.

3603. Francart, Emile. *La Bande Dessinée à l'École. Approche Pédagogique d'un Langage.* Marcinelle: Service d'Information aux Enseignants, Jean Dupois, 1982.

3604. Francart, Emile. "La Bande Dessinée pour Apprendre à Lire." *Français 2000.* 105, 1982, pp. 9-16.

3605. Frémion, Yves. *L'A B C de la BD.* Paris: Tournai: Casterman, 1983.

3606. Frémion, Yves. "Réaliser une B.D. en Classe." *Le Français dans le Monde.* 193, 1985, pp. 95-96.

3607. Fresnault-Deruelle, Pierre. *Dessins et Bulles. Cahiers de Travaux Dirigés. (6e).* Paris: Bordas, 1973.

3608. Fresnault-Deruelle, Pierre. *Dessins et Bulles. La Bande Dessinée Comme Moyen d'Expression*. Paris, Brussels, Montreal: Bordas, 1972.

3609. Fresnault-Deruelle, Pierre. "La Langue des Bandes Dessinées et Leur Contenu Culturel." *Le Français dans le Monde*. 13:98, 1973, pp. 14-19.

3610. Gaugeard, Jean. "Une Menace pour la Culture." *Les Lettres Françaises*. June 20-July 6, 1966.

3611. *La Bande Dessinée...* au service de la formation d'une personnalité libre et autonome dans l'enseignement secondaire technique spécial, en première année B et deuxième année professionnelle de l'enseignement secondaire rénové: "morale laïque." Brussels: Ministère de l'Education Nationale et de la Culture Française, 1979.

3612. "Lecture et Bande Dessinée: Actes du Ler Colloque International Education et Bande Dessinée." La Roque d'Anthéron, 15-16 janvier 1977. Aix-en-Provence: Edisud, 1977.

3613. Mahillon, Anita. "B.D. et Enseignement Spécial." *Français 2000*. 105, 1982, pp. 89-92.

3614. Maiffredy, Jean and Jean Moussarie. "Activités Pédagogiques à Partir de la BD Polar." *Le Français dans le Monde*. 187, 1984, p. 51.

3615. Malandain, Jean-Louis. "Une Bande Dessinée pour Apprendre à Argumenter." *Le Français dans le Monde*. 166, 1982, pp. 45-52.

3616. Marsadié, Bernard and Roland Saint-Péron. "Exploitation Pédagogique des Bandes Dessinées de la Presse des Jeunes Français." *Le Français dans le Monde*. 98, 1973, pp. 25-32.

3617. Marsh, Rufus K. "Teaching French with the Comics." *The French Review* (Baltimore). 51:6 (1978), pp. 777-785.

3618. Martin, Michel. "La Bande Dessinée." *Sémiologie de l'Image de Pédagogie. Pour Une Pédagogie de la Recherche*, edited by Ders, pp. 169-218. Paris: Presses Universitaires de France, 1982.

3619. Massart, Pierre, Jean-Luc Nicks, and Jean-Louis Tilleuil. *La Bande Dessinée à l'Université...et Ailleurs*. Louvain: Presses Universitaires de Louvain, 1984.

3620. Masson, Pierre. *Lire la Bande Dessinée*. Lyon: Presses Universitaires de Lyon, 1985.

3621. Meier, Bernhard. "Zeichen in Comics, Vorgestellt an 'Zack', Heft 4/1975. 4. Jahrgangsstufe, Deutsch: Lesen." *Ehrenwirth Grundschulmagazin* (Munich). 2:8 (1975), pp. 25-26.

3622. Meys, Lucien, Rose-Marie Moulins, and Bernard Marinier. *Apprendre l'Allemand par la Bande Dessinée*. Verviers: Marabout, 1976.

3623. Picquenot, Alain. "Enseignement et Bande Dessinée." *Pratiques* (Metz). 7/8, 1975, pp. 47-60.

3624. *Plaisir d'Écrire et de s'Exprimer à Tout Âge par la Bande Dessinée. 3 T.: A 1 Force 1; B 1 Force 2; C 1 Force 3; 1 T.: Le Livre du Maître*. Marcinelle: Service d'Information aux Enseignants, Eds. Jean Dupuis, 1978.

3625. Richardot, J.C. "Enquête sur la Bande Dessinée." *Le Monde de l'Education*. December 1976.

3626. Robin, Christian. *Travaux Dirigés et Bande Dessinée*. Manuel d'Initiation à la Bande Dessinée et d'Apprentissage du Français. Classe de 6e et 5e. Paris: Sudel, 1974.

3627. Rollet, Georges. "La Bande Dessinée Pédagogique Muette. Un Outil Privilégié du Professeur de Français, Langue Étrangère." *Zielsprache Fanzösisch* (Munich). 4, 1979, pp. 168-176.

3628. Rollet, Georges. *Parler et Écrire Avec la Bande Dessinée: Bloc pour 5 Élèves, Matériel Spécialement Conçu pour l'Enseignement du Français*. Paris: Hachette, 1974.

3629. Rosier, Jean-Maurice. "Dossier Pédagogique: la B.D. pour Enseigner." *Français 2000*. 105, 1982, pp. 67-69.

3630. Rosier, Jean-Maurice. "Enseignement et Bande Dessinée." *Français 2000*. 91, 1977, pp. 17-32.

3631. Roux, Antoine. "Bande Dessinée et Pédagogie." *Education 2000*. 21, 1982, pp. 45-52.

3632. Roux, Antoine. *La Bande Dessinée Peut Être Éducative*. Paris: Éditions de l'École, 1970.

3633. Roux, Antoine. *La Bande Dessinée. Références et Suggestions Pédagogiques*. Paris: Centre National de Documentation Pédagogique, 1984.

3634. Sadoux, Jean-Jacques. "Véhiculer par la B.D. les Matières Scolaires: Bande Dessinée: la Fin du Purgatoire?" *Cahiers Pédagogiques*. April 1982, pp. 11-13.

3635. Scher, Hannelore and Philippe Roquigny. "Autour de Carmen." *Le Français dans le Monde*. 200, 1986, pp. 70-71.

3636. Spiraux, Alain. "Petit Playdoyer Illustré (d'exemples) pour l'Utilisation des Bandes Dessinées dans l'Enseignement." *Giff-Wiff*. No. 22, 1966.

3637. Sullerot, Eveline. "Bandes Dessinées et Culture." *Opera Mundi*. May 1966, p. 56.

3638. Sullerot, Eveline. "Les Bandes Dessinées, Réservoir de la Culture." *Giff-Wiff*. No. 15, 1966, p. 15.

3639. Tardif, Michel. *Le Professeur et les Images*. Paris: P.U.F., 1966.

3640. Tisseron, Serge. "Contribution à l'Utilisation de la Bande Dessinée Comme Instrument Pédagogique." Thesis, University of Lyon, 1975.

3641. Van Weyenbergh, Claire, Joséph Gillain, Patrick Moulin, and Félix Packnadel. *Apprendre l'Anglais par la Bande Dessinée*. Verviers: Marabout, 1977.

3642. Zand, Nicole. "Quand les Bandes Dessinées Veulent Entrer à l'Université." *Le Monde*. October 8, 1966, p. 10.

Genres

3643. "Comics Promote Safe Sex." *Comics Journal*. July 1988, pp. 22-23.

3644. Faur, Jean-Claude. "De la Critique B.D. à la Désinformation en Tous Genres." *Bédésup*. Nos. 48/49, 1989, pp. 14-15.

3645. Faur, Jean-Claude. "Les Aventuriers de la B.D." *Enquête sur l'Histoire*. No. 3, 1992, pp. 21-26.

3646. Filippini, Henri. "BD Jeunesse: Pas Morte." *Le Français dans le Monde*. April 1986, pp. 58-59.

3647. "France and Horror Comics." *The Manchester Guardian*. January 20, 1955, p. 5.

3648. "French Giveaway." *The Classics Collector*. February-March 1990, p. 9.

3649. "French Mondial Adventures Update." *The Classics Collector*. February-March 1990, p. 11.

3650. Groensteen, Thierry. "Drôles de Genres." *Les Cahiers de la Bande Dessinée*. 61, 1985, pp. 78-80.

3651. Manjarrez, Froylán C. "Comics: l'École de la Violence." *Révolution*. 12:13 (1964), pp. 42-56.

Animal

3652. Brichant, Christophe. "Entre Chien et Loup." *Les Cahiers de la Bande Dessinée.* 67, 1986, pp. 29-31.

3653. Brunoro, Gianni. "Eloges d'Un Animal Fabuleux Appelé Marsupilami." *Cahiers Universitaires.* No. 10, 1970.

3654. Caré, Jean-Marc. "Les Nouveaux Animaliers." *Le Français dans le Monde.* 176, 1983, pp. 9-11.

3655. Groensteen, Thierry, ed. *Animaux en Cases: Une Histoire Critique de la Bande Dessinée Animalière.* Paris: Futuropolis, 1987.

3656. Rivière, François. "Les Félins de la Bande." *Cahiers Universitaires.* No. 8, 1970.

3657. Sanders, Alain. "Le Cheval dans la B.D." *Bédésup.* 21, 1982, pp. 35-37.

3658. Smolderen, Thierry. "Le Petit Singe Qui Faisait des Manières ou le Récit Délirant." *Les Cahiers de la Bande Dessinée.* 67, 1986, pp. 31-33.

Crime

3659. Caré, Jean-Marc and Jean Maiffredy. "La Bande Dessinée Policière." *Le Français dans le Monde.* August-September 1984, pp. 46-50.

3660. de Pierpont, Jacques. "Amertume et Scepticisme: Ballade en 'Spy Fiction.'" *Les Cahiers de la Bande Dessinée.* 71, 1986, pp. 30-31.

3661. Moliterni, Claude. "Vers Une Définition de la Bande Dessinée Policière." *Giff-Wiff.* No. 10, 1965, p. 9.

3662. Regnier, Michel. "Le Roi de la Police Montée." *Giff-Wiff.* No. 9, 1965.

Erotic, Pornographic

3663. Bourgeois, Michel. *Erotisme et Pornographie dans la B.D.* Grenoble: Eds. Jacques Glénat, 1978, 1980.

3664. Bourgeois, Michel. *L'Oeuvre Érotique de Georges Pichard.* Grenoble: Eds. Jacques Glénat, 1981.

3665. Deans, L. "Move Over Superman—It's Porno." *Macleans.* July 30, 1979, p. 8.

3666. De La Croix, Arnaud. "Eros dans les Cases." *Les Cahiers de la Bande Dessinée.* 57, 1984, pp. 48-50.

3667. De La Croix, Arnaud. "Le Dernier Séducteur Romantique." *Les Cahiers de la Bande Dessinée*. 62, 1985, pp. 20-21.

3668. Dellisse, Luc. "Un Point de Non-Retour." *Les Cahiers de la Bande Dessinée*. 62, 1985, pp. 24-25.

3669. de Pierpont, Jacques. "L'Éternel Enfantin Dure." *Les Cahiers de la Bande Dessinée*. 62, 1985, p. 26.

3670. de Pierpont, Jacques. "Porno BC-BG." *Les Cahiers de la Bande Dessinée*. 57, 1984, pp. 66-67.

3671. "France Threatens To Ban Adult Comics." *Comics Journal*. September 1987, pp. 24-25.

3672. Lo Duca, Joseph-Marie. *Les Triomphes de la Bande Dessinée*. Paris: Eds. Dominique Leroy, 1985.

3673. Lo Duca, Joseph-Marie. *Luxure de Luxe. L'Art Érotique dans la Bande Dessinée de Sandro Botticelli à Roy Lichtenstein*. Paris: Eds. Dominique Leroy, 1983.

3674. Lo Duca, Joseph-Marie. *"Manuel des Confesseurs" et Krafft-Ebing en Bandes Dessinées*. Paris: Eds. Dominique Leroy, 1982. New Ed.

3675. Sadoul, Jacques. *L'Enfer des Bulles (Anthologie de la Bande Dessinée Érotique)*. Paris: J.J. Pauvert, 1968. 254 pp.

3676. Sadoul, Numa. "Une Maison Qui Nous Veut du Bien ou la Bande à Elvifrance." *Schtroumpfanzine*. 16, 1978, pp. 10-14.

Heroes

3677. Bon, Michel. "Mythologie des Super-Héros." *Bédésup*. 22/23, 1982, pp. 35-38.

3678. Caré, François. "Héros en Stock." *Le Français dans le Monde*. April 1986, pp. 40-43.

3679. Courtial, Gérard. *À la Rencontre des Super-Héros*. Marseilles: Bédésup, 1985.

3680. Courtial, Gérard. "À la Rencontre des SUPER-HÉROS." Supplement to *Bédésup*. No. 31, 4th Trim. 1984. 152 pp.

3681. Damelincourt, Benjamin. "Enquête sur la Disparition d'Un Mythe." *Presse Actualité*. 180, 1984, pp. 28-33.

3682. Dellisse, Luc. "L'Enchaînement des Contraires." *Les Cahiers de la Bande Dessinée*. 71, 1986, pp. 28-29.

3683. Dellisse, Luc. "Le Syndrome de l'Éternité." *Les Cahiers de la Bande Dessinée.* 62, 1985, pp. 85-87.

3684. de Pierpont, Jacques. "Figuration sur Mesure." *Les Cahiers de la Bande Dessinée.* 67, 1986, pp. 26-28.

3685. Faur, Jean-Claude. "Aux Origines de la B.D.: les Super-Héros." *Europe.* No. 720, 1989, pp. 9-16.

3686. Gauthier, Guy. "Aventures d'Hier, Héros d'Aujourd 'hui." *Le Français dans le Monde.* April 1986, pp. 21-24.

3687. Herman, Paul. "Rahan a Rencontré Tounga." *Schtroumpf. Les Cahiers de la Bande Dessinée.* 46, 1980, p. 26.

3688. Hugues, Daniel. "Relecture: Hypocrite." *Les Cahiers de la Bande Dessinée.* 61, 1985, pp. 81-83.

3689. Juin, Hubert. "Les Héros de Papier." *Les Lettres Françaises.* No. 1138, 1966.

3690. Lacassin, Francis. "Altération et Transformation du Héros de Bandes Dessinées." Conférence at Deuxième Salon International des Bandes Dessinées, Lucca, September 1966.

3691. Leguébe, Eric. "Métamorphoses d'un Héros." *Arts.* April 13, 1966.

3692. "Le Retour des Heros!" *Le Quotidien de Paris.* January 22, 1992, p. iii.

3693. Lofficier, R.J.M. and Fred Patten. "The Great European Comic Heroes." *Nemo.* October 1985, pp. 50-56.

3694. Serval, Pierre. "Les Héros des Bandes Dessinées." *Parents* (Paris). June 1970.

3695. Thomas, Pascal. "Des Héros à Chaque Page." *Nouveau Candide.* No. 312, 1966.

Parody

3696. Chante, Alain. "La Parodie en Sept Leçons." *Les Cahiers de la Bande Dessinée.* 61, 1985, pp. 73-75.

3697. De La Croix, Arnaud. "Petite Dérive Philosophique." *Les Cahiers de la Bande Dessinée.* 60, 1984, p. 76.

3698. Dellisse, Luc. "L'Optique du Travestissement." *Les Cahiers de la Bande Dessinée.* 60, 1984, pp. 80-82.

3699. Ecken, Claude. "Une Critique Chaude." *Les Cahiers de la Bande Dessinée.* 61, 1985, pp. 76-77.

3700. Groensteen, Thierry. "Essai de Typologie." *Les Cahiers de la Bande Dessinée.* 60, 1984, pp. 77-79.

3701. Hugues, Daniel. "Grandeur et Misère de la Forgerie." *Les Cahiers de la Bande Dessinée.* 61, 1985, pp. 70-72.

3702. Lecigne, Bruno. "Don't Stop the Carnival." *Les Cahiers de la Bande Dessinée.* 60, 1984, pp. 74-75.

Science-Fiction

3703. Auffret, Hélène. "La Bande Dessinée Fantastique en France." *Aspects de la Littérature Populaire* (l'Université de Pau et des Pays de l'Adour, 1977, fasc. 10). 1977, pp. 1-15.

3704. Bouyer, Sylvain. "Prothèses Hallucinées." *Les Cahiers de la Bande Dessinée.* 69, 1986, pp. 26-29.

3705. Chemin, Jean-Paul. "La B.D. Francophone de Science-Fiction." *Français 2000.* 105, 1982, pp. 54-66.

3706. Duveau, Christian and Marc. "Comic-Books et Science-Fiction." *Horizons du Fantastique* (Ed. Ekla, Paris). No. 11, 1970.

3707. Founau, Pierre-Jean. "Bande Dessineé et Littérature Fantastique." *La Nouvelle Revue Français* (Paris). 226, 1971, pp. 173-178.

3708. Frémion, Yves. "Bédé S.F.: Espaces d'Images, Images d'Espaces." *Le Français dans le Monde.* 193, 1985, pp. 72-74.

3709. Gauthier, Guy. *Villes Imaginaires: le Thème de la Ville dans l'Utopie et la Science-Fiction (Littérature, Cinéma, Bande Dessinée).* Paris: CEDIC, 1977.

3710. Hugues, Daniel. "Les Sources du Merveilleux." *Les Cahiers de la Bande Dessinée.* 67, 1986, pp. 23-25.

3711. Renard, Jean-Bruno. "L'Émergence du Surnaturel." *Le Français dans le Monde.* April 1986, pp. 27-29.

3712. Rivière, François and Franquin. "La Galerie des Monstres." *Cahiers Universitaires.* No. 10, 1970.

3713. Sadoul, Jacques. "Fan B.D.S.F." *Magazine Littérature* (Paris). 95, 1974, pp. 23-24.

3714. Sadoul, Jacques. "La Science-Fiction dans le Comic-Book." Catalogue of Exposition, Musée des Arts Décoratifs, Paris, 1967, pp. 31-32.

3715. Smolderen, Thierry. "Histoires en Forme de Planètes, de Villes et de Bateaux." *Les Cahiers de la Bande Dessinée.* 69, 1986, pp. 21-23.

3716. Smolderen, Thierry. "Le Dernier Cri de l'Aventure." *Les Cahiers de la Bande Dessinée.* 56, 1984, pp. 62-65.

3717. Tibéri, J.-P. "Un Pas dans la Science-Fiction." *Schtroumpf. Les Cahiers de la Bande Dessinée.* 31, 1976, p. 29.

Western

3718. Herman, Paul. *Epopée et Mythe du Western dans la Bande Dessinée.* Grenoble: Eds. Jacques Glénat, 1982.

3719. Leguebe, Eric. "Le Mythe du Cow-Boy: C'Était dé jà Reagan!" *L'Astrolabe* (Paris). 1:80 (1985), pp. 27-31.

3720. O'Neil, Patrick D. "The Wild (French) West." *Comics Scene.* No. 9, 1989, pp. 9-12, 68.

Industry

3721. Faur, Jean-Claude. "Publicité et Bande Dessinée: Un Mariage d'Amour!" *Infors Starcs* (Lyon). No. 6, 1989, pp. 5-6.

3722. "French Comics Retrench: Conglomerates Move In." *Comics Journal.* January 1988, p. 17.

3723. "French Marvel Maniacs Can Plug into Info About Comics Via Teletext Net." *Variety.* September 17, 1986, p. 84.

3724. "Glenat 'Americanizes' Production, Concepts." *Comics Journal.* October 1988, pp. 31-32.

3725. "Grenoble Spotlights Kurtzman, Calvo." *Comics Journal.* July 1989, pp. 42-44.

3726. Hansom, Dick and Nigel Curson. "Comics USA Born in the USA." *Speakeasy.* February 1990, pp. 47, 49, 51.

3727. Jaffray, Patricia. "Bande Dessinée: Etat des Lieux." *Livres Hebdo.* 7:4 (1985), pp. 79-83.

3728. Jennequin, Jean-Paul. "Dargaud Sold." *Comics Journal.* March 1989, p. 29.

3729. Jennings, Dana. "Futuropolis: Recreating the Golden Age (in French)." *Comics Journal.* October 1984, pp. 56-57.

3730. "Les Humanoides Associes Buy Dargaud." *Speakeasy*. March 1990, pp. 13, 15.

3731. Miège, Bernard. *The Capitalization of Cultural Production*. Bagnolet, France: International General, 1989. ("The Children's Press," pp. 56, 58, dealing with French comic books).

3732. Monet, Jack. "Gallic Love of Comics Lends Marvel French Licenses a Hand." *Variety*. September 17, 1986, p. 83.

3733. "The Paperback Revolution." *Comics Journal*. July 1988, pp. 21-22.

3734. "Retailer: The Album Shops." *Comics Interview*. No. 73, 1989, pp. 44-65.

Language, Semiotics

3735. Arias Terrón, Horacio. "Aproximación Semiológica al Tebeo." *Messages* (Bordeaux). 3, 1973, pp. 29-38.

3736. Arrouye, Jean. "Espaces Narratifs: Le Lionceau des Sables." *Schtroumpf. Les Cahiers de la Bande Dessinée*. 44, 1980, pp. 18-26.

3737. Baudoux, Vincent. "Les Cases Mémorables de Vincent Baudoux. Case 1: La Mauvaise Tête. Eds. Dupuis, 1956, page 34, case 6. Case 2: La Magique Lanterne Magique. Imagerie d'Epinal, 1983, planc 4." *Les Cahiers de la Bande Dessinée*. 58, 1984, pp. 69-71.

3738. Blanchard, Gérard. "Esartinuloc ou les Alphabets de la Bande Dessinée." *Communication et Langages* (Paris). 26, 1975, pp. 25-45.

3739. Borringo, Heinz-Lothar. "Konkretisierung von Suspensanalysen in Text-verarbeitungsrelationen. 8.1.2.1. Analysebeispiel: Karl May - "Durch die Wüste," 8.1.2.2. Der Resultattext 'Comic.'" In *Spannung in Text und Film*, edited by Ders, pp. 100-123. Düsseldorf: Schwann Verlag, 1980.

3740. Bouyer, Sylvain. "La Transparence Désordonée." *Les Cahiers de la Bande Dessinée*. 65, 1985, pp. 92-97.

3741. Bouyer, Sylvain. "L'Utilisation de la Photographie dans la Bande Dessinée Réaliste: Vers Une Nouvelle Iconographie." *Les Cahiers de la Bande Dessinée*. 58, 1984, pp. 78-81.

3742. Bouyer, Sylvain. "Signal—Éthique." *Les Cahiers de la Bande Dessinée*. 65, 1985, pp. 76-77.

3743. Bremond, Claude. "'Pour un Gestuaire des Bandes Dessinées.'" *Langages* (Paris). 10, 1968, pp. 94-100.

3744. Brichant, Christophe. "Le Masque et la Plume." *Les Cahiers de la Bande Dessinée.* 68, 1986, pp. 24-26.

3745. Brichant, Christophe. "Trois Forces du Rêve et Une Nuit d'Encre." *Les Cahiers de la Bande Dessinée.* 65, 1985, pp. 35-37.

3746. Brunon, Claude-Françoise. "Sens de l'Images et Images du Sens." In Groupe Interdisciplinaire de Recherche Universitaire sur la Bande Dessinée. *A la Rencontre de Jacques Martin*, pp. 9-39. Marseilles: Bédésup, 1985.

3747. Covin, Michel. "Proposition sur la Bande Dessinée." *Communications* (Paris). No. 19, 1972, pp. 138-147.

3748. Darot, Mireille. "Mon Teppaz Est Naze." *Le Français dans le Monde.* 200, 1986, pp. 30-35.

3749. De La Croix, Arnaud. "L'Océan Circulaire." *Les Cahiers de la Bande Dessinée.* 61, 1985, pp. 24-25.

3750. Dellisse, Luc. "L'Absence de Miroir." *Les Cahiers de la Bande Dessinée.* 68, 1986, pp. 27-29.

3751. Dellisse, Luc. "La Peau des Gorilles." *Les Cahiers de la Bande Dessinée.* 61, 1985, pp. 21-23.

3752. Dellisse, Luc. "Une Duplicité Stratégique." *Les Cahiers de la Bande Dessinée.* 57, 1984, pp. 11-13.

3753. Delperdange, Patrick. "Une Comédie de la Métamorphose." *Les Cahiers de la Bande Dessinée.* 62, 1985, pp. 31-32.

3754. Descotes, Dominique. "Le Jeu du Texte et de l'Image dans la Bande Dessinée." *La Nouvelle Revue Françaises* (Paris). 226, 1971, pp. 167-172.

3755. Di Manno, Yves. "Elaboration d'un Épisode. Structure et Découpage." *Schtroumpf. Les Cahiers de la Bande Dessinée.* 22, 1973, pp. 36-37.

3756. Donnadieu, Pierre. "La Bande Dessinée: Un Art du Trait." *Education 2000.* 21, 1982, pp. 29-33.

3757. Ecken, Claude. "C'Est Toujours de la Bande Dessinée." *Les Cahiers de la Bande Dessinée.* 60, 1984, pp. 15-17.

3758. Ecken, Claude. "De l'Excès à la Mesure: Vers Une Mise en Page Efficace." *Les Cahiers de la Bande Dessinée.* 64, 1985, pp. 33-35.

3759. Ecken, Claude. "Les Métamorphoses." *Schtroumpf. Les Cahiers de la Bande Dessinée.* 53, 1982, p. 21.

3760. Everaert-Desmedt, Nicole. *Sémiotique du Récit, Méthode et Applications, Texte Littéraire, Livre pour Enfants, Bande Dessinée, Publicité, Espace.* Louvain-La-Neuve: Cabay, 1981.

3761. Fischer, Hervé. "Ecriture Phonétique et Pictogramme dans les Bandes Dessinées." *Communications* (Sankt Augustin). 9:2/3 (1983), pp. 191-200.

3762. Fouilhé, Pierre. "Le Language de l'Illustré Moderne." *Littérature de Jeunesse* (Paris). No. 68, 1955.

3763. Fresnault-Deruelle, Pierre. "Aux Frontières de la Langue: Quelques Réflexions sur les Onomatopées dans la Bande Dessinée." *Cahiers de Lexicologie* (Paris). 18:1 (1971), pp. 79-88.

3764. Fresnault-Deruelle, Pierre. "De la Vignette à la Page ou de l'Espace Comme Signifiant dans les 'Comics.'" *Messages* (Bordeaux). 5/6, 1974, pp. 13-27.

3765. Fresnault-Deruelle, Pierre. "Du Linéaire du Tabulaire." *Communications* (Paris). 24 (1976), pp. 7-23.

3766. Fresnault-Deruelle, Pierre. *La Bande Dessinée, Essai d'Analyse Sémiotique.* Paris: Hachette, 1972.

3767. Fresnault-Deruelle, Pierre. "La Couleur dans la Bande Dessinée." *Revue d'Esthétique* (Paris). 25 (1972), pp. 443-453.

3768. Fresnault-Deruelle, Pierre. "La Couleur et l'Espace dans les Comics." In *Documents de Travail et Prépublications. Centro Internazionale di Semiotica et di Linguistica* (Universitá di Urbino. Urbino). 40, 1975, pp. 1-18.

3769. Fresnault-Deruelle, Pierre. "Le Personnage de Bande Dessinée et Ses Langages." *Langue Français* (Paris). 7:28 (1975), pp. 101-111.

3770. Fresnault-Deruelle, Pierre. "Le Recit (ou le Scénario-Parenthèses) de Bande Dessinée." *La Nouvelle Critique.* January 1972, pp. 62-65.

3771. Fresnault-Deruelle, Pierre. "Les Instances du Récit dans la Bande Dessinée Réaliste." *Messages* (Bordeaux). 2, 1972, pp. 17-27.

3772. Fresnault-Deruelle, Pierre. "L'Espace Interpersonnel dans les Comics." In *Sémiologie de la Représentation. Théâtre, Télévision, Bande Dessinée,* edited by André Helbo, pp. 129-150. Paris: Presses Universitaires de France, 1977.

3773. Fresnault-Deruelle, Pierre. "L'Étrange et le Discontinu dans la Bande Dessinée." *Critique* (Paris). 28:300 (1972), pp. 460-466.

3774. Fresnault-Deruelle, Pierre. "Le Verbal dans les Bandes Dessinées." *Communications* (Paris). 15, 1970, pp. 145-161.

3775. Fresnault-Deruelle, Pierre. "L'Hexagone." *Zielsprache Französisch* (Munich). 3, 1979, pp. 129-139.

3776. Fresnault-Deruelle, Pierre. *Récits et Discours par la Bande, Essais sur les Comics*. Paris: Hachette, 1977.

3777. Gagnon, Jean Claude. *Lire Une Bande Dessinée*. Montréal: Eds. Ville-Marie, 1983.

3778. Gauthier, Guy. "La Traversée du Signifiant Iconique: Repères pour un Cheminement Pédagogique." *Pratiques* (Metz). 18/19, 1978, pp. 10-20.

3779. Gauthier, R. "Sémiotique et Bande Dessinée." *Annales de l'Université d'Abidjan, Série H: Linguistique* (Abidjan). 8:1 (1975), pp. 69-76.

3780. Gauthier, Guy. "Vingt Leçons sur l'Image et le Sens." Paris: ÉDILIG, 1982.

3781. Groensteen, Thierry. "De Style el d'Histoire(s)..." *Les Cahiers de la Bande Dessinée*. 56, 1984, 30-34.

3782. Groensteen, Thierry. "La Voix off des Gens 'In.'" *Les Cahiers de la Bande Dessinée*. 57, 1984, pp. 27-29.

3783. Groensteen, Thierry. "Les Affiches du Crime." *Les Cahiers de la Bande Dessinée*. 67, 1986, pp. 95-97.

3784. Groensteen, Thierry and Claude Ecken. "Polyphonie et Lisibilité." *Les Cahiers de la Bande Dessinée*. 59, 1984, pp. 91-94.

3785. Guillon, Vincent. "Eléments pour Une Analyse d'Une Bande Dessinée." *Education 2000*. 21, 1982, pp. 53-65.

3786. Heinz, Ludwig. "Zur Handlungsstruktur von Comics und Märchen." *Fabula* (Berlin). 19, 1978, pp. 262-286.

3787. Helbo, André. *Sémiologie de la Représentation. Théâtre, Télévision, Bande Dessinée*. Brussels: Eds. Complexe; Paris: Presses Universitaires de France, 1975.

3788. Hugues, Daniel. "Ce Qu'on Appelle l'Avalanche." *Les Cahiers de la Bande Dessinée*. 57, 1984, pp. 93-96.

3789. Hünig, Wolfgang K. *Strukturen des Comic Strip: Ansätze zu Einer Textlinguistisch-Semiotischen Analyse Narrativer Comics*. Hildesheim, New York: Olms, 1974.

3790. "La Bande Dessinée et Son Discours." *Communications* (Paris). 24, 1976.

3791. Lacassin, Francis. "Etude Comparative des Archétypes de la Litérature Populaire et de la Bande Dessinée." In *Entretiens sur la Paralittérature. Centre Culturel International de Cérisy-la-Salle*, edited by Noël Arnaud *et al.*, pp. 201-220; discussion, pp. 221-227. Paris: Plon, 1970.

3792. Lacassin, Francis. "Etude Comparative des Archétypes de la Litérature Populaire et des Bandes Dessinée." Internationales Colloquium über Literatur und Para-Literatur, Cérisy-la-Salle, September 1967.

3793. Lecigne, Bruno. "Matière et Symbole." *Les Cahiers de la Bande Dessinée*. 57, 1984, pp. 90-92.

3794. Martínez, Léa. "Analyse Structurale des Bandes Dessinées." In *Image et Communication*, edited by Anne-Marie Thibault-Laulan, pp. 171-181. Paris: Eds. Universitaires, 1972.

3795. Massart, Pierre, Jean-Luc Nicks, and Jean-Louis Tilleuil. *La Bande Dessinée à l'Université...et Ailleurs. Etudes Sémiotiques et Bibliographiques*. Louvain-La-Neuve: Presses Universitaires de Louvain, 1984.

3796. Masson, Pierre. *Lire la Bande Dessinée*. Lyon: Presses Universitaires de Lyon, 1985.

3797. Miot, Bernard. *Dictionnaire des Onomatopées. Le Jas du Revest-Saint-Martin*. Basses Alpes: Ed. Robert Morel, 1968.

3798. Moliterni, Claude. "Narrative Technique. Die Erzähltechnik der Comics. La Technique Narrative." *Graphis* (Zürich). 25:159 (1972/1973), pp. 26-43.

3799. Morin, Violette. "Le Dessin Humoristique." *Communications* (Paris). 15, 1970, pp. 110-131.

3800. Neumann, Renate. "L'Art du Montage dans la Bande Dessinée." *Le Nouveau Bédésup*. 32/33, 1985, pp. 79-82.

3801. Peeters, Benoît. "Une Exploration Interrompue." *Les Cahiers de la Bande Dessinée*. 57, 1984, pp. 24-26.

3802. Picquenot, Alain. "La Grande Vignette et le Récit." *Communications* (Paris). 24, 1976, pp. 177-196.

3803. Pinson, Daniel. "Polysémie et Perversion du Sens: le Lecteur Aveuglé." *Les Cahiers de la Bande Dessinée*. 57, 1984, pp. 86-89.

3804. Plécy, Albert. *Grammaire Elémentaire de l'Image*. Paris: Marabout, 1971.

3805. Quella, Didier. "Les Fonctions et l'Évolution du Jeu de Mots." *Bédésup*. 24/25, 1983, pp. 67-70.

3806. Rio, Michel. "Cadre, Plan, Lecture." *Communications*. 24 (1976), pp. 94-107.

3807. Rivière, François. "Un Précieux Chez les Hurons (Suite et Fin)." *Schtroumpf. Les Cahiers de la Bande Dessinée*. 23, 1974, pp. 33-35.

3808. Roux, Antoine. "Lecture Gauche Droite." *Media* (Paris). 49/50, 1973, pp. 63-64.

3809. Roux, Antoine. "Lire les Images." *Le Français Aujourd'hui* (Paris). 61, 1983, pp. 39-44.

3810. Samson, Jacques. "Trou de Mémoire." *Les Cahiers de la Bande Dessinée*. 63, 1985, pp. 18-19.

3811. Saouter Caya, Catherine. "Propos Syntaxique du Langage Sonore dans la Bande Dessinée." *La Nouvelle Barre du Jour* (Outremont, Québec). 110/111, 1982, pp. 19-29.

3812. Smolderen, Thierry. "Les Aventures d'Edith Rabatjoie, ou Le Feuilleton Désenchanté." *Les Cahiers de la Bande Dessinée*. 63, 1985, pp. 23-25.

3813. Spillner, Bernd. "Kontrastive Analysen auf der Grundlage von 'Comic Strips.'" In *Papers from the International Symposium on Applied Contrastive Linguistics; Stuttgart, October 11-13, 1971/ PAKS, Projekt für Angewandte Kontrastive Sprachwissenschaft*, edited by Gerhard Nickel, pp. 27-41. Bielefeld: Cornelsen-Velhagen und Klasing, 1972.

3814. Sterckx, Pierre. "Du Bon Usage de la Coupure." *Les Cahiers de la Bande Dessinée*. 64, 1985, pp. 94-97.

3815. Tamine, Jean-Pierre. "La Bascule à Charlot: Un Délire de Rationalisation." In *A la Rencontre...Jacques Tardi*, edited by Gari, pp. 39-61. Marseilles: Bédésup, 1982.

3816. Tamine, Jean-Pierre. "Pour Une Bande où la Mer Serait Propre et le Saucisson pur Porc." *Les Cahiers de la Bande Dessinée*. 57, 1984, pp. 14-17.

3817. Thibault-Laulan, Anne-Marie. *Image et Communication*. Paris: Eds. Universitaires, 1972.

3818. Tilleuil, Jean-Louis. *Pour Analyser la Bande Dessinée. Propositions Théoriques et Pratiques*. Louvain-La-Neuve: Cabay, 1986.

3819. Toussaint, Bernard. "Idéographie et Bande Dessinée." *Communications* (Paris). 24, 1976, pp. 81-93.

3820. Toussaint, Bernard. "La Bande Dessinée." In *Qu'Est-ce Que la Sémiologie?* edited by Ders, pp. 95-109. Toulouse: Privat, 1978.

3821. Van Belle, Anita. "Caméléon." *Les Cahiers de la Bande Dessinée*. 60, 1984, pp. 90-91.

3822. Van Belle, Anita. "Toujours le Même Homme, Toujours le Même Fleuve." *Les Cahiers de la Bande Dessinée*. 61, 1985, pp. 18-20.

3823. Vanoye, Francis. "L'Expression Verbale dans Ses Rapports Avec les Autres Moyens d'Expression: Langage et Expression Graphique et Picturale: les Mots dans la Bande Dessinée." In *Expression Communication*, edited by Ders, pp. 201-205. Paris: Armand Colin, 1973, 1980.

Legal Aspects

3824. "Contre la Presse de l'Horreur." *Educateurs*. No. 56, 1955, pp. 144-145.

3825. Horn, Maurice. "Défense et Illustration de la Pin-Up dans la Bande Dessinée." *V-Magazine*. No. 580, 1965.

3826. Le Gallo, Claude. "La Grande Ménace." *Phénix*. No. 4, 1967, pp. 18-20.

3827. Limagne, Pierre. "Des Dangers Nouveaux pour la Jeunesse et l'Adolescence." *La Croix*. June 1, 1967.

3828. Trinchero, Sergio. "Away or Not Away, That Is the Question." *Phénix*. No. 6, 1968.

Literature

3829. Compère, Daniel. "Jules Verne et les Bandes Dessinées." *Bulletin de la Société Jules Verne* (Paris). N.S. 22, 1972, pp. 137-139.

3830. Dellisse, Luc. "L'Histoire Énergumène." *Les Cahiers de la Bande Dessinée*. 60, 1984, pp. 28-29.

3831. Gauthier, Guy. "Comment le Dialogue a Profané l'Image." *Le Français Aujourd'hui*. 71, 1985, pp. 80-84.

3832. Kramer, Peter. "Les Anciens et les Modernes? Harpagon Als BD., Emma Bovary Als Roman-Photos." *Französisch Heute* (Frankfurt). 24, 1983, pp. 142-150.

3833. Raymond, François. "Trois Réincarnations de Jules Verne (sur les Cimaises, à la Scène et en Bande Dessinée)." *Bulletin de la Société Jules Verne* (Paris). N.S. 21, 1972, pp. 108-111.

Psychology

3834. Bachand, Denis. "Le Récit Fre(u)dien." *Le Nouvelle Barre du Jour* (Outremont, Québec). 110/111, 1982, pp. 43-50.

3835. Boullet, Jean. "Psychoanalyse des Comics." *Combat* (Paris). June 30, 1949.

3836. Covin, Michel. "La Bande Dessinée Psychédélique." *Critique*. No. 294, 1972, pp. 1018-1025.

3837. Covin, Michel. "L'Image Dérobée ou Comment le Désir en (Re-)vient à la Bande Dessinée." *Communications* (Paris). 24, 1976, pp. 197-242.

3838. Debot-Sevrin, M.-R. and D. Stassart. "Des Situations Émouvantes pour Garçons de Huit Ans." *Enfance* (Paris). 4/5, 1971, pp. 297-331.

3839. Henle, Ilse. "Archetypische Elemente und Reifungssymbolik im Comic-Book." *Wege zum Menschen* (Göttingen). 22:1 (1970), pp. 6-18.

3840. Legman, Gershon. "Psychopathologie des Comics." *Les Temps Modernes* (Paris). No. 43, 1949, pp. 916-933.

3841. Samson, Jacques. "Parenthèse sur la Fascination—BD." *La Nouvelle Barre du Jour* (Outremont, Québec). 110/111, 1982, pp. 9-15.

3842. Smolderen, Thierry. "Bande Dessinée, Feuilleton et Cerveau Droit." *Les Cahiers de la Bande Dessinée*. 70, 1986, pp. 54-58.

3843. Tisseron, Serge. *Psychanalyse de la Bande Dessinée*. Paris: Presses Universitaires de France, 1987.

Religion

3844. Arrouye, Jean. "Histoire(s) de (la) Mort." In *A la Rencontre de... Jacques Tardi*, edited by Gari, pp. 17-30. Marseilles: Bédésup, 1982.

3845. Bouyer, Sylvain. "La Dialectique de la Mort." *Les Cahiers de la Bande Dessinée*. 59, 1984, pp. 32-34.

3846. de la Croix, Arnaud. "Images Pieuses. A Propos de la Bande Dessinée Religieuse." *Les Cahiers de la Bande Dessinée*. 63, 1985, pp. 49-51.

3847. de la Croix, Arnaud. "Le Masque et Ses Profondeurs." *Les Cahiers de la Bande Dessinée*. 60, 1984, pp. 88-89.

3848. de la Croix, Arnaud. "L'Irruption du Divin." *Les Cahiers de la Bande Dessinée*. 60, 1984, pp. 26-27.

3849. Everaert-Desmedt, Nicole. *Dialogue et Bande Dessinée: de l'Utilisation de la Bande Dessinée dans le Cours de Religion*. Louvain-La-Neuve: Cabay, 1981.

3850. Gerlach, Peter. "Comic Als Mythos. Optischer Code und Bildkompetenz." In *Comics und Religion*, edited by Jutta Wermke, pp. 51-79. Munich: Wilhelm Fink Verlag, 1976.

3851. Groeben, Norbert. "Mythos Contra Erklärung. Dimensionen Eines Psychologischen Konflikts. Semantische und Pragmatische Aspekte der Analyse von Comics." In *Comics und Religion*, edited by Jutta Wermke, pp. 137-167. Munich: Wilhelm Fink Verlag, 1976.

3852. Knockaert, André, and Chantal van der Plancke. *Bandes Dessinées Bibliques et Catéchèses*. Brussels: Lumen Vitae, 1979. 171 pp.

3853. Knockaert, André and Chantal van der Plancke. "Bandes Dessinées Bibliques: Pratiques de Lecture." *La Foi et le Temps* (Tournai). 9:3 (1979), pp. 238-254.

3854. Knockaert, André and Chantal van der Plancke. "La Bande Dessinée Saisie par la Religion." *Lumière et Vie*. October-November-December 1981, pp. 35-44.

3855. "Koran Comic Condemned!" *The Classics Collector*. February-March 1990, pp. 9-10.

3856. "Les Marchands des Mythes." *Le Nouveau Candide*. December 25-31, 1967, p. 7.

3857. Maltese, M.-T. and J. Boucard. "Dire la Foi aux Enfants." *Informations Catholiques Internationales* (Paris). 524, 1978, pp. 50-54.

3858. Renard, Jean-Bruno. "L'Idéologie Religieuse dans la Bande Dessinée." *Education 2000*. 21, 1982, pp. 86-95.

3859. Veillet-Lavallée, Bernard. "La B.D. des Mollahs." *Les Nouvelles* (Paris). 1984, pp. 60-61.

Socio-Political

3860. Andrevon, Jean-Pierre. "Le Post-Catastrophisme Prétexte." *Les Cahiers de la Bande Dessinée*. 58, 1984, pp. 20-21.

3861. Arrouye, Jean. "L'Histoire Comme Marge de la Fiction ou l'Architecture en Mal d'Histoires." *Bédésup*. 28, 1984, pp. 13-18.

3862. Barrera-Vidal, Alberto. "La Nouvelle Bande Dessinée d'Expression Française, Vulgaire Produit de Consommation ou Média Réservé à Une Elite?" In *Bildung und Ausbildung in der Romania. Bd.I: Literaturgeschichte und Texttheorie*, edited by Rolf Kloepfer, Arnold Rothe, Henning Krauss, and Thomas Kotschi, pp. 400-407. Munich: Fink, 1979.

3863. Boltanski, Luc. "La Constitution du Champ de la Bande Dessinée." *Actes de la Recherche en Sciences Sociales* (Paris). 1, 1975, pp. 37-59.

3864. Carbonell, Charles-Olivier. *Le Message Politique et Social de la Bande Dessinée.* Toulouse: l'Institut d'Etudes Politiques de Toulouse 8, 1975.

3865. Caré, Jean-Marc. "La BD Rock." *Le Français dans le Monde.* 190, 1985, pp. 17-18.

3866. Chevrier, Jacques and Raphaël Sorin. "La Bande Dessinée Entre la Mythologie et la Politique." *Le Monde.* January 29, 1971, pp. 14-15.

3867. Chombart de Lauwe, Marie-José. "La Transmission des Systèmes de Représentations et de Valeurs Relatifs aux Sexes d'Une Génération à Une Autre." *Revue d'Allemagne* (Paris). 8:3 (1976), pp. 359-368.

3868. "Civilisation de l'Image." *Arthème Fayard* (Paris). 1960.

3869. de la Croix, Arnaud. "Petite Lecture Politique d'Un Grand Romanfleuve." *Les Cahiers de la Bande Dessinée.* 58, 1984, pp. 22-24.

3870. de la Fabegue, H., G. Durandin, and G. Moser. "Bécassine: l'Idéologie, les Structures Sociales et Leur Degré de Transparence." *Bulletin de Psychologie* (Paris). 34:1/4 (1980), pp. 131-135.

3871. du Fontbare, Vicky and Philippe Sohet. "Codes Culturels et Logique de Classe dans la Bande Dessinée." *Communications* (Paris). 24, 1976, pp. 62-80.

3872. Duveau, Marc. "Humour et Bande Dessinée." *Magazine Littéraire* (Paris). 95, 1974, pp. 21-22.

3873. Ecken, Claude. "L'Utopie Post-Atomique." *Les Cahiers de la Bande Dessinée.* 58, 1984, pp. 17-19.

3874. Ecken, Claude. "Scènes de Famille." *Les Cahiers de la Bande Dessinée.* 61, 1985, pp. 28-29.

3875. Eubben, Marie-Claire and Claude Vanderhaegen. "Les Stéréotypes Féminin et Masculin dans la Bande Dessinée pour Enfants et Adolescents d'Expression Française." *Revue de l'Institut de Sociologie* (Brussels). 3/4, 1982, pp. 433-457.

3876. Fermigier, André. "Bande Dessinée et Sociologie." *Le Nouvel Observateur*. April 19, 1967.

3877. Fresnault-Deruelle, Pierre. "Entre l'Ersatz et le Simulacre. La Bande Dessinée." In: *Cahiers du XXéme Siècle* (Paris). 6, 1976, pp. 139-153.

3878. Fresnault-Deruelle, Pierre. "La Bande Dessinée, 'Objet de Civilisation.'" *Le Français dans le Monde*. 173, 1982, pp. 104-111.

3879. Fresnault-Deruelle, Pierre. *La Chambre à Bulles. Essai sur l'Image du Quotidien dans la Bande Dessinée*. Paris: Union Générale d'Éditions, 1977.

3880. Fresnault-Deruelle, Pierre. "Les Clichés dans la Bande Dessinée." *Etudes de Linguistique Appliquée* (Paris). N.S. 17, 1975, pp. 105-114.

3881. Greg, Michel. "La Bande Dessinée, Phénomène Social?" Exhibition catalogue, "Introduction à la Bande Dessinée Belge," Bibliothèque Royale de Belgique, 1968.

3882. Greg, Michel. "La Bande Dessinée, Phénomène Social?" *Phénix*. No. 7, 1968, pp. 70-71.

3883. Groensteen, Thierry. "Allégorie et Politique." *Les Cahiers de la Bande Dessinée*. 65, 1985, pp. 78-79.

3884. Groensteen, Thierry and Christian Marmonnier. "Vous Avez Dit Merchandising?" *Les Cahiers de la Bande Dessinée*. 58, 1984, pp. 46-49.

3885. Lacassin, Francis. "Les Bandes Dessinées, Produit d'Une Civilisation." *Europress-Junior* (Paris). 1966.

3886. Laplaze, Arlette and Huguette Simon. "Une Vision Politique Engagée: La Patrouille des Castors." In *Le Message Politique et Social de la Bande Dessinée*, edited by Charles-Olivier Carbonell, pp. 99-117. Toulouse: Institut d'Etudes Politiques de Toulouse, 1975.

3887. Lecigne, Bruno and Jean-Pierre Tamine. "L'Épique et le Politique." *Les Cahiers de la Bande Dessinée*. 58, 1984, pp. 35-36.

3888. Lettkemann, Gerd. "Clement Moreau. 'Mein Kampf' Gegen Hitler. Comics im Widerstand Gegen den Faschismus." *Comixene. Das Comicfachmagazin*. 8:42 (1981), pp. 14-16.

3889. Loszycer, Charles. "Les Questions Raciales dans Go West." *Schtroumpf. Les Cahiers de la Bande Dessinée*. 50, 1981, pp. 34-35.

3890. Lugadet, Jean Bernard. *et al.* "La Représentation du Tiers Monde dans Quelques Bandes Dessinée set Livres Illustrés pour Enfants." *Le Nouveau Bédésup.* 32/33, 1985, pp. 86-97.

3891. Pennacchioni, Irène. *La Nostalgie en Images. Une Sociologie du Récit Dessinée.* Paris: Librairie des Méridiens, 1982.

3892. Pierre, François. "L'Enfant dans la Bande Dessinée." *B.D. Bulle: Revue du Salon International de la Bande Dessinée* (Angoulême). 5, 1979, pp. 7-9.

3893. Pourprix, Bernard. "Sociologie de la Bande Dessinée." 3 Vols. Thesis, 3e cycle, Université de Grenoble II, 1973.

3894. Renard, Jean-Bruno. "Approche Sociométrique des Communications Entre Personnages d'Une Bande Dessinée." Groupe Interdisciplinaire de Recherche Universitaire sur la Bande Dessinée. *A la Rencontre de Jacques Martin*, pp. 103-140. Marseilles: Bédésup, 1985.

3895. Renard, Jean-Bruno. "La Bande Dessinée Comme Folklore." *Esprit* (Paris). 4, 1980, pp. 116-124.

3896. Renard, Jean-Bruno. "Les Signes Avant Coureurs de Mai 68 dans la B.D." *Imprévue* (Montpellier). 2, 1981, pp. 73-90.

3897. Simon, André. "Anticonformisme et Destruction des Valeurs Bourgeoises." In *A la Rencontre de...Jacques Tardi*, edited by Gari, pp. 67-84. Marseilles: Bédésup, 1982.

3898. Simon, André. "B.D., Folklore et Politique." *Le Nouveau Bédésup.* 31, 1984, pp. 18-20.

3899. Thibault-Laulan, Anne-Marie. "La Bande Dessinée: Un Multi-média." In Dies.: *L'Image dans la Société Contemporaine*, edtied by Dies, pp. 108-123. Paris: Denoël, 1971.

3900. Verstraeten, Jacques. "La Bande Dessinée: Une Société en Images." *Lectures* (Liège). 11, 1983, pp. 28-36.

Technical Aspects

3901. Beaumont, Catherine. *Pour Faire de la BD*. Paris: Ed. Retz, 1984.

3902. Bel, L. "Je Fais de la B.D." *Bédésup.* 20, 1982, p. 18.

3903. Bel, L. "Je Fais de la B.D." *Bédésup.* 21, 1982, p. 7.

3904. Bel, L. "Je Fais de la B.D." *Bédésup*. 22/23, 1982, pp. 21-22.

3905. Bel, L. "Je Fais de la B.D." *Bédésup*. 24/25, 1983, pp. 54-55.

3906. Bouyer, Sylvain. "Bavardage." *Les Cahiers de la Bande Dessinée*. 72, 1986, pp. 94-96.

3907. Bouyer, Sylvain. "Coloriage, Picturalité et Gros Sous." *Les Cahiers de la Bande Dessinée*. 60, 1984, pp. 35-38.

3908. Bouyer, Sylvain. "Inventaire." *Les Cahiers de la Bande Dessinée*. 68, 1986, pp. 20-23.

3909. Bouyer, Sylvain. "Profession: Coloriste." *Les Cahiers de la Bande Dessinée*. 60, 1984, pp. 40-43, 57.

3910. Charlier, Jean-Michel. "Entretien: Autour du Scénario." *Revue de l'Université de Bruxelles*. 1-2, 1986, pp. 49-66.

3911. Dellisse, Luc. "Le Coup de Pouce du Destin." *Les Cahiers de la Bande Dessinée*. 64, 1985, pp. 26-28.

3912. Dellisse, Luc. "Aller-Retour du Scénariste: Autour du Scénario." *Revue de l'Université de Bruxelles*. 1-2, 1986, pp. 89-101.

3913. Derib, Pernin. *L'Aventure d'Une B.D. Ou, Tout Ce Que Vous Avez Toujours Voulu Savoir sur la B.D. Sans Jamais Oser le Demander*. Brussels: Eds. du Lombard, 1981.

3914. Falardeau, Mira. *L'Humour Visuel: Histoire et Technique: Caricature, Bande Dessinée, Dessin Animé*. Québec: Ecole des Arts Visuels, Université Laval, 1976.

3915. Fresnault-Deruelle, Pierre. "Bandes Dessinées ou Histoires Illustrées?" In *A la Rencontre de...Jacques Tardi*, edited by Gari, pp. 133-138. Marseilles: Bédésup, 1982.

3916. Gomez, J. "Je Fais de la B.D." *Bédésup*. 27, 1983, pp. 16-17.

3917. Groensteen, Thierry. "La Cadavre Tombé de Rien ou la Troisième Qualité de Scénariste." *Revue de l'Université de Bruxelles*. 1-2, 1986, pp. 111-118.

3918. Groensteen, Thierry. "L'École de la Simplicité." *Les Cahiers de la Bande Dessinée*. 70, 1986, pp. 30-32.

3919. Groensteen, Thierry. "Ligne de Vie et Trait de Pinceau." *Les Cahiers de la Bande Dessinée*. 68, 1986, pp. 32-35.

3920. Groensteen, Thierry. "Peut-on Enseigner le Scénario?" *Les Cahiers de la Bande Dessinée*. 57, 1984, pp. 82-84.

3921. Herman, Paul. "BD, Un Métier." *La Revue Nouvelle*. 69, 1979, pp. 297-300.

3922. Lecigne, Bruno. "L'Esprit de la Lettre." *Les Cahiers de la Bande Dessinée*. 64, 1985, pp. 87-89.

3923. Llobera, Joseph and Romain Oltra. *La Bande Dessinée. La Dessin Humoristique—La Caricature*. Paris: Eds. Eyrolles, 1982.

3924. Loszycer, Charles. "Histoire Sans Héros: Sans Greg, la Plage!" *Schtroumpf. Les Cahiers de la Bande Dessinée*. 49, 1981, pp. 43-44.

3925. Mayence, Serge and Nathalie Coucke. "Vade-Mecum du Dessinateur Débutant. Comment Faire Publier Votre BD." *Les Cahiers de la Bande Dessinée*. 64, 1985, pp. 39-43.

3926. "Pour la BD, Mieux Voir le Réel." *Livres Hebdo*. 6, 1984, pp. 51-52.

3927. Roux, Antoine. *La Bande Dessinée et les Histoires en Images*. Dossier + 12 Diapositives. Paris: Ofrateme, 1975, 1979.

3928. Roux, Antoine. *Comment on Fait Une Bande Dessinée. Dossier Audiovisuel Comprenant 16 Diapositives, 2 Disques et un Livret d'Accompagnement*. Paris: Oframe, coll. 'Radio-vision,'RV 178, 1976.

3929. Roux, Antoine. *Comment on Fait Une Bande Dessinée. Dossier Radiovision 1975-1976, RV 178, Disque 1 et 2, 16 Diapositives*. Paris: Oframe, 1975, 1979.

3930. Sokal, Benoît. "Pensées: Autour du Scénario." In *Revue de l'Université de Bruxelles*. 1-2, 1986, pp. 15-24.

3931. Tamine, Jean-Pierre. "Un Cinétique Pur." *Les Cahiers de la Bande Dessinée*. 59, 1984, pp. 95-97.

3932. Trenquel, Roger. *Voyage au Pays Perdu*. Carcassonne: Fédération Audoise des Oeuvres Laïques, 1979.

3933. Wurm, Philippe. "Des Volumes et des Plis." *Les Cahiers de la Bande Dessinée*. 63, 1985, pp. 78-79.

3934. Zimmer, Jacques. "La Bande Dessinée. 158 Diapositives et un Livret." Paris: Ligue Française de l'Enseignement et de l'Education Permanente, 1983.

COMIC STRIPS

3935. Barrera-Vidal, Albert. "Clés pour Une Lecture des Frustrés." *Le Français dans le Monde.* April 1986, pp. 36-39.

3936. Beaumatic, Eric. "Des Krostons dans le Chiendent: D l'Être Plat au Personnage." In *Le Personnage en Question*, pp. 343-351. Toulouse: Universite de Toulouse-Le Mirail, 1984. 416 pp.

3937. Caen, Michel. "Comic-Strip et Celluloid." *Les Lettres Française.* June 30, 1966, pp. 17-18.

3938. de la Bigne, Yolaine. "Boucq-Moi un Mouton." *(A Suivre).* October 1992, pp. 120-121.

3939. Du Fontbare, Vicky and Philippe Sohet. "Comic Strip: Social Discourse and Cultural Promotion; Bande Dessinée: Discours Social et Production Culturelle." *Recherches Sociologiques.* May 1975, pp. 186-199.

3940. Frémion, Yves. "Bédé S.F.: Espaces d'Images, Images d'Espaces." *Le Français dans le Monde.* May-June 1985, pp. 72-74.

3941. Horn, Maurice. "Pogo Possum: A French View." *The Okefenokee Star.* No. 3, 1979.

3942. Lieber, Jean-Claude. "La Bande Dessinée Écrite." *Langages.* September 1984, pp. 43-63.

3943. Lindekens, René. "L'Analyse Structurale en Question." *Degrés.* Spring 1983, pp. c1-c12.

3944. McArthur, Tom. "Riders of the Purple Page." *English Today.* October-December 1986, pp. 34-35.

3945. Maré, Thierry. "Comment Faire Passer le Temps en Lisant des Bandes Dessinées." *Poetique.* November 1988, pp. 499-519.

3946. Picquenot, Alain. "La Grande Vignette et le Recit." *Communications.* 24 (1976), pp. 177-196.

3947. Robertson, Nan. "'Peanuts' Bridges a Language Gap and Captivates the French." *New York Times.* March 26, 1975.

3948. "Spécial Vikings." *La Lettre de Bédésup.* No. 58, 1992, p. 1, 8.

3949. Tochon, Maurice. "Dans le Galaxie B.D., *Yoko Tsuno*." *Etudes.* January 1986, pp. 47-56.

3950. Verg, Erik. "Gallier im Vormarsch-Eine Comic-Strip-Figur Begeistert Ganz Frankreich." *Kristall* (Hamburg). December 30, 1966.

Anthologies

3951. Cabu. *Manif de Soutien au Showbiz*. Paris: Albin Michel, 1986.

3952. Geluck, Philippe. "Le Chat." *(A Suivre)*. October 1992, pp. 106-108.

3953. Loup. *Loup: La Vie des Maitres*. Paris: Glénat, 1984.

3954. Sabatier, Roland and Georges Becker. *Le Gratin des Champignons*. Paris: Glénat, 1986. 224 pp.

3955. Thomas, J. *Aidons la Nature!* Paris: Glénat, 1985.

POLITICAL CARTOONS

3956. Adler, Philippe, Robert Mallat, and Jacky Redon. *Drôles d'Oiseaux*. Paris: Éditions Robert Lafont, 1973. 109 pp.

3957. "Barbie." *Mieux Vaut en Rire*. No. 13, 1989, pp. 23-30.

3958. Bordes, G. "La Politique Dessinée." *La Nation Européenne*. September 1967, pp. 30-31.

3959. Chimot, Jean-Philippe. "Sur Une Ideologie en Images." *France Nouvelle*. June 1974, pp. 14-15.

3960. "La Politique Dessinée." *La Nation Européenne*. October 1967, pp. 42-44.

3961. "Le Dossier: Vive le Dessin de Presse!" *Le Nouveau Bédésup*. 1-2 Trim., 1987, pp. 9-13.

3962. Ronge, Peter. "De de Gaulle à Mitterand." *Mieux Vaut en Rire*. No. 13, 1989, pp. 9-15.

3963. Simoën, Jean Claude. *De Gaulle: à Travers la Caricature Internationale*. Paris: Albin Michel, 1969.

3964. Soulas, Philippe. *Dessins Politiques Mai 68-Mai 74*. Paris: Balland, 1974.

3965. Thivolet, Marc. "Le Dessin de Presse (Universalia 1985)." *Mieux Vaut en Rire*. No. 5 (n.d.), pp. 40-42.

3966. "Vive le Dessin de Presse!" *Le Nouveau Bédésup*. Nos. 40-41, 1987, pp. 9-13.

3967. Werly, Richard. "Saint-Just Dessinée la Revolution." *Mieux Vaut en Rire*. No. 12, 1989, pp. 42-43.

4

Country Perspectives—Germany

REFERENCES

3968. Fröhlich, Arnold, Rolf Kämpf, and Ernst Ramseier. *Handbuch zur Medienerziehung. Bd. 2: Comics*. Zurich: Sabe AG, Verlagsinstitut für Lehrmittel, 1983.

3969. *The Grandchildren of Max and Moritz. Comics and Cartoons Made in Germany*. Catalogue of Traveling Exhibition in U.S. Canada, Japan, Korea, 1990. Frankfurt: AuM, 1990. 60 pp.

3970. Hethke, Norbert and Peter Skodzik. *Allgemeiner Deutscher Comic—Preis Katalog*. Schonan, Germany: N. Hethke Verlag. Annual.

3971. Kagelmann, H. Jürgen and Eva Binder, eds. *Comics-Handbuch für Eltern, Lehrer, Erzieher: Grundlagen-Art. zur Verwendung von Comics in Unterrichtsprozessen und zur Beurteilung von Comics; Analysen zu 30 Comic-Periodika; Annotierte Bibliographie von über 300 Neueren Titeln Sekundärliteratur zu den Comics (1973-1976)*. Bonn-Bad Godesberg: Asgard-Verlag Hippe, 1977.

3972. Kaps, Joachim. "Strapazin. 30 x Comic + Art Pur." *Comic Info*. 1/1993, p. 32.

3973. Karrer-Kharberg, Rolf. *Wer Zeichnet Wie? Ein "Who's Who" Einer Anzahl Recht Komischer Künstler von Addams bis Zimnik*. Zurich: Diogenes, 1963. 153 pp.

3974. Kempkes, Wolfgang, ed. *Bibliographie der Internationalen Literatur über Comics*. Munich-Pullach/Berlin: 1971.

3975. Knigge, Andreas C. *Comic Jahrbuch 1987*. Berlin: Ullstein, 1986.

3976. Knigge, Andreas C. *Comic Jahrbuch 1989. Trends, Analysen, Adressen. Dossier: Phantastik und Fantasie im Comic*. Berlin: Ullstein, 1989.

3977. Kolditz, Niels. "Fan-Comics aus Dem in—und Ausland." *Comic Info*. 1/1993, p. 57.

3978. Kolditz, Niels. "Fanszene öder Was Kann Man Mehr (V) Erlangen?" *ICOM*. October 1992, pp. 58-59.

3979. Neuman, Renate. *Bibliographie zur Comic—Sekundärliteratur* (Bibliography of Secondary Literature on Comic Strips). Frankfurt: Peter Lang, 1987. 267 pp.

3980. Reitberger, Reinhold and Wolfgang J. Fuchs. *Comics-Handbuch*. Reinbeck bei Hamburg: Rowolt Taschenbuch Verlag, 1978.

3981. Skodzik, Peter. "Deutsche Comic-Bibliographie für den Zeitraum August 1984 bis September 1985." In *Comic-Jahrbuch 1986*, edited by Martin Compart and Andreas C. Knigge, pp. 319-379. Berlin: Ullstein GmbH, 1986.

3982. Skodzik, Peter. *Deutsche Comic-Bibliographie 1946-1970*. Berlin: Comicaze, 1978.

3983. Skodzik, Peter and Norbert Hethke. *Allgemeiner Deutscher Comic-Preiskatalog 1985*. Schönau: Norbert Hethke Verlag, 1984.

3984. Wansel, Siegmar and Dietmar Stricker, eds. *Illustrierte Deutsche Comic-Geschichte. Der Walter Lehning Verlag. Enzyklopädie in Wort und Bild*. Cologne: Comiczeit, Vol. 1, 1986, 80 pp.; Vol. 2, 1986, 72 pp.; Vol. 3, 1986, 72 pp.; Vol. 4, 1987, 82 pp.; Vol. 5, 1987, 82 pp.; Vol. 6, 1987, 70 pp.; Vol. 7, 1987, 78 pp.; Vol. 8, 1988, 74 pp.; Vol. 9, 1988, 104 pp.; Vol 10, 1988, 88 pp.; Vol. 11, 1989, 88 pp.

3985. Westphal, Heinz and K. Friesicke. *Handbuch der Jugendarbeit und Jugendpresse*. Munich: Juventa-Verlag, 1967.

GENERAL STUDIES

3986. "Festival i Mainz." *Seriejournalen*. September 1992, p. 11.

3987. Granacher, René. "Neues aus Frankfurt. Buchmesse 1989." *ICOM-INFO*. February 1990, pp. 56-57.

3988. Henle, Walter and Peter Richter. "Unter den Augen der Sphinx." *Watcher*. March 1989, pp. 4-18.

3989. Klee, Paul. *Die Zwitscher Maschine*. Berlin: Eulenspiegel-Verlag, 1981.

3990. "Let's Go North! Der 1. Internationale Comic Salon von Hamburg." *Comic Info*. May-June 1993, pp. 58-59.

3991. Ries, Gregor. "1. Mainzer Comic Tage '92. Rhein-Main-Festival der Neunten Kunst." *ICOM*. January 1993, pp. 56-57.

3992. "Satire: Spaß mit Mutter." *Der Spiegel*. No. 5, 1963, pp. 67-69.

3993. Schröder, Peter H. "Unsere Welt im Zerrspiegel." *Die Welt*. June 16-17, 1967.

3994. Silbermann, Alphons. "The Way Toward Visual Culture: Comics and Comic Films." In *Comics and Visual Culture: Research Studies from Ten Countries*, edited by Alphons Silbermann and H.-D. Dyroff, pp. 11-27. Munich: K.G. Saur, 1986.

3995. Søndergaard, Carsten. "Semic Forlagene på Frankfurt Bogmessen 1989." *Serieskaberen*. March 1990, pp. 19-20.

3996. Strelow, Hans. "Das Normale Ist das Absurde." *Frankfurter Allgemeiner Zeitung*. January 10, 1970.

3997. Williams, J.E. "Cartooning Germany." *Christian Science Monitor Magazine*. December 13, 1947, p. 4.

Children's Media

3998. Jensen, Klaus, ed. *Der Medienmarkt für Kinder in der Bundesrepublik*. Tübingen: 1980.

3999. Lettkemann, Gerd. "Ins Neue Leben, die Erste Deutsche Jugendzeitschrift der Nachkriegszeit." *Comixene*. No. 26, 1979, pp. 59-61.

Periodicals

4000. Herbst, Helmut. *Die Illustrationen der "Meggendorfer Blätter." Ein Beitrag zur Erforschung der Illustration im Beginnenden 20. Jahrhundert*. Stuttgart: Apostroph, 1985. 230 pp.

4001. Lettkemann, Gerd. "Oskars Ahnen. Bilddokumentation zur Comicgeschichte der Frankfurter Vorkriegsillustrierten 'Das Illustrierte Blatt.'" *Comixene. Das Comicfachmagazin.* 8:37, pp. 14-16.

4002. Tschernegg, Markus. *Das War Primo.* Vienna: Edition Comic Forum, 1986.

Fliegenden Blätter

4003. Boetticher, G. "Die Münchner 'Fliegenden Blätter' und Ihre Geschichte." *Zeitschrift für Bücherfreunde.* 2:8/9 (1898/1899), p. 146.

4004. Hollweck, Ludwig. *Karikaturen: Von den "Fliegenden Blätter" bis zum "Simplicissimus," 1844-1914.* Munich: Suddeutscher Verlag, 1973.

4005. Schmidt, A.M.R. *Alfred Schmidt Album; Tegninger fra "Fligende Blätter."* Copenhagen: H. Hagerups, 1895.

4006. Wassermann, Henry. "The *Fliegenden Blätter* As a Source for the Social History of German Jewry." *Leo Baeck Year Book.* 28 (1983), pp. 93-138.

Kladderadatsch

4007. Allen, Ann Taylor. *Satire and Society in Wilhelmine Germany: Kladderadatsch and Simplicissimus, 1890-1914.* Lexington, Kentucky: University of Kentucky Press, 1984.

4008. Hartenstein, L., ed. *Facsimile Querschnitt Durch den Kladderadatsch.* Munich, Berlin, Vienna: 1965.

4009. Heinrich-Jost, Ingrid. *Kladderadatsch: Die Geschichte Eines Berliner Witzblattes von 1848 bis Ins Dritte Reich.* Reihe Satire und Macht. Cologne: C.W. Leske, 1982.

4010. Hofmann, Rudolf. *Der Kladderadatsch und Seine Leute 1848-1898: Ein Culturbild.* Berlin: A. Hofmann, 1898.

4011. Ring, Max. *David Kalischs Der Vater des Kladderadatsch und Begründer der Berliner Posse: Ein Erinnerungs-Blatt.* Berlin: Elwin Staude, 1873.

Simplicissimus

4012. Appelbaum, Stanley, comp. *Simplicissimus: 180 Satirical Drawings from the Famous German Weekly.* New York: Dover Publications, 1975. 172 pp.

4013. Christ, Richard. *Simplicissimus 1896-1914.* Berlin: 1972.

4014. Hausenstein, Wilhelm. *Vortrag über der Simplicissimus.* Munich: 1932.

4015. Heller, Steven. "Simplicissimus." *Upper and Lower Case*. December 1981, pp. 14-17.

4016. Reinoss, Herbert. *Bilder aus dem "Simplicissimus."* Hanover: Fackelträger, 1970, 1987. 288 pp.

4017. Rothe, Eugen. *Simplicissimus*. Hanover: Fachkelträger Verlag, 1954.

4018. Wolter, Franz. *Franz von Pocci Als Simplizissimus der Romantik*. Munich: 1925.

Women

4019. Aping, Norbert. "Das Frauenbild in den Deutschen Comicheftserien der 50er Jahre. Blonder Panther und Co." *Comixene. Das Comicfachmagazin*. 6:22 (1979), pp. 48-49.

4020. Boog, Angelo. "Von Frauen und Zwergen." *Fantastrips* (Wuppertal). March 1981.

4021. Brüggemann, Theodor. "Das Bild der Frau in den Comics." *Studien zur Jugendliteratur* (Ratingen). 2:3 (1956), pp. 3-29.

4022. Deutsch, Werner. *Lotte Reiniger*. Berlin: Deutsche Kinemathek/Rainer Verlag, 1969.

4023. Frohner, Karin. "Die Frau in den Bildergeschichten des 19. Jahrhunderts und in den Comics der Gegenwart." Dissertation, Universität Salzburg, 1983.

4024. Fuchs, Eduard. *Die Frau in der Karikatur*. Munich: 1906.

4025. Fuchs, Wolfgang J. "Superheldinnen." *Comixene. Das Comicfachmagazin*. March 1979, pp. 13-14.

4026. Geiger, Elly. "'Junge Liebe'—Comics und Ihre Emanzipationsfeindlichen Tendenzen." *Comixene. Das Comicfachmagazin*. 6:22 (1979), pp. 21-22.

4027. Heidrich, Hanno. "Das Bild der Frau im Comic. Eine Sendung des Bayerischen Rundfunks am 10. November 1975." *Medien + Erziehung* (Leverkusen). 20:1 (1976), pp. 46-52.

4028. Knigge, Andreas C. "Die Frau im Comic." *Comixene. Das Comicfachmagazin*. March 1979, pp. 5-9.

4029. Knigge, Andreas C. and Achim Schnurrer, eds. *Bilderfrauen, Frauenbilder. Eine Kommentierte Bilddokumentation über das Bild der Frau im Comic*. Hanover: Edition Becker und Knigge GmbH, 1980.

4030. "Monica Vitti—Diese Frau Lebt Gefährlich." *Der Stern*. No. 43, 1966.

4031. Neuhardt, Günter. "Das Bild der Frau im Comic. Eine Symbolkundliche Untersuchung mit Schülern." *Zeitschrift für Kunstpädagogik und Ihre Grundlagen* (Ratingen, Kastellaun, Düsseldorf). 4, 1981, pp. 54-58.

4032. "POP Hält Frauen in Atem." *Hamburger Abendecho*. April 30, 1966.

4033. Raddatz, Fritz J. "Die Neuen Heldinnen der Westlichen Welt. Kritisches zu Einigen Verklärten Comicstrips." *Die Zeit*. 22:11 (1967), pp. 17-18.

4034. Strzyz, Klaus. "A Successful Female Cartoonist Looks for Topics in Everyday Life." *WittyWorld*. Autumn 1988, pp. 30-31.

4035. Wolff, Reinhold. "Frauenbilder—Männerträume." *Comixene. Das Comicfachmagazin*. 6:22 (1979), pp. 25-28.

GERMAN DEMOCRATIC REPUBLIC

4036. "Comics-Rezepte für NATO-Söldner." *Neues Deutschland* (Berlin). May 21, 1955.

4037. "Comics-Strips für Kinder." *Der Mittag* (Berlin). November 11, 1954.

4038. Curson, Nigel. "The Berlin Wall—Comics Cross the Border." *Speakeasy*. March 1990, pp. 49-51.

4039. Decker, Dwight R. "Far Away Is Close at Hand in Images of Elsewhere." *Comics Journal*. June 1978, pp. 48-51.

4040. "Der Strom der 'Bunten Hefte' Fließt Nicht Mehr." *Der Bibliothekar* (Berlin). 12, 1961, pp. 1334-1335.

4041. "Ein Art Comic-Strip in der DDR." *Darmstädter Echo*. December 10, 1969.

4042. Eversberg, Gerd. "DDR-Comics. Comics in der DDR—Ohne Zukunft?" *Science Fiction Times* (Bremerhaven). 14:4 (129) (1972), pp. 10-13.

4043. Frohn, Axel. "Summer Palace: A Hot Spot for Cartoon Art." *WittyWorld*. Summer 1987, p. 27.

4044. Gargi, Bahrant. "Comics." *Neues Deutschland* (Berlin). May 24, 1955.

4045. Kaps, Joachim. "Comics und Cartoons Made in Berlin—Teil 2. Interview mit Hansi Kiefersauer und Peter Petri." *ICOM-INFO*. February 1990, pp. 40-47.

4046. *Karikaturen-Ausstellung zum 20. Jahrestag der DDR.* Berlin: 1969.

4047. Kirstein, J. "Comics und Abenteurer-Literatur." *Der Bibliothekar* (Leipzig). 13:5 (1959), pp. 562-564.

4048. Lademann, Norbert. "Bedeutung, Funktionen und Gestaltung von Bildern und Bildgeschichten als Unterrichtsmittel zur Koordinierung von Fernsehkurs und Klassenunterricht im Englischen Grundkurs." Dissertation, Potsdam, 1970.

4049. Lettkemann, Gerd. "Comics in der DDR." In *Fortsetzung Folgt. Comic Kultur in Deutschland*, edited by Andreas Knigge and Gerd Lettkemann, pp. 317-361. Berlin: Ullstein, 1986.

4050. Lettkemann, Gerd. "Comics in der DDR: Mosaik." *Comixene.* No. 16, 1977, pp. 34-36.

4051. Lettkemann, Gerd. "'Die Zukunft Gehört dem Sozialismus!' Aufklärung und Propaganda in den SF-Comics der DDR." *Comixene. Das Comicfachmagazin.* 7:30 (1980), pp. 25, 57.

4052. Meyer, Hans Georg. "Nichts Gegen den Spaß, Jedoch... Was Will das Sein?" *Deutsche Lehrerzeitung* (Berlin). August 3, 1966.

4053. Morrison, Susan S. "The Feminization of the German Democratic Republic in Political Cartoons 1989-90." *Journal of Popular Culture.* Spring 1992, pp. 35-51.

4054. Sandberg, Herbert. *Der Freche Zeichenstift.* Berlin: Eulenspiegel Verlag, 1963.

4055. Schneider, Harriet. "Münchner Bilderbogen in Ihrer Wirkung auf Kinder." Dissertation, Leipzig, 1947.

4056. Thiel, Paul. "Comics in the German Democratic Republic." *Comics Journal.* March 1979, pp. 55-57, 59.

4057. "Zeichner aus Ost-Berlin. BAM. 'Zwischen Not und Nonsen.'" *ICOM-INFO.* February 1990, p. 53.

HISTORICAL ASPECTS

Animation

4058. Kampf, Arthur. "Tiermaske und Charakter: Impressionen des Karikaturisten zur Uraufführung des 'Weber' Filmes." *Berliner Stadtblatt.* May 15, 1927.

4059. Laqua, Carsten. "Micky Maus. Disney Films in Hitler's Germany." *Comics Journal.* April 1990, pp. 100-102.

4060. Seeber, Guido. *Der Trickfilm in Seinen Grundsätzlichen Möglichkeiten*. Berlin: Filmtechnik, 1927.

Caricature

4061. Averanius, Ferdinand. *Das Bild Als Karr. Die Karikatur in der Volferver*. Munich: Georg D.W. Callwey, 1918.

4062. Bartos, Jiri. *Avec la Caricature Contre le Fascisme*. Prague: International Organization of Journalists, n.d.

4063. Borchardt, Georg H. *Die Deutsche Karikatur im 19. Jahrundert*. Velhagen und Klasing, 1901. 132 pp.

4064. Brooks, R.C. "Lèse Majesté in Germany." *Bookman*. September 1914, pp. 68-82.

4065. Demm, Eberhard. *Der Erste Weltkrieg in der Internationalen Karikatur*. Hanover: Fackelträger, 1988. 208 pp.

4066. Ederle, Matthias. *World War I and the Weimar Artists Dix, Grosz, Beckmann, Schlemmer*. New Haven, Connecticut: Yale University Press, 1985. 134 pp.

4067. *Ereignis-Karikaturen. Geschichte in Spottbildern 1600 bis 1930*. Exhibition Catalogue. Münster, 1983.

4068. François, André. *Mit Gestraubten Federn Einteitung von L.G. Bucchein*. Buchhein Verlag, n.d.

4069. Fuchs, Eduard. *Der Weltkrieg in der Karikatur*. Munich: Albert Langen, 1916.

4070. Fuchs, Eduard. *Die Juden in der Karikatur*. Munich: Albert Langen, 1921. 309 pp.

4071. Fuchs, Eduard. *1848 in der Karikatur*. Munich: M. Ernst Verlag, n.d.

4072. Fuchs, Eduard. *Lola Montez in der Karikatur*. Berlin: Ernst Frendsdorff Verlag, n.d.

4073. Fuchs, Eduard and Ernst Kreowski. *Richard Wagner in der Karikatur*. Berlin: B. Behr's Verlag, 1907.

4074. Gessler, Alfred and Karl-Heinz Grahl, eds. *Seine Feinde zu Beißen...*[sic] *Karikaturen aus der Deutschen Bürgerlichen Revolution 1848-1849*. Berlin: Morgen, 1962.

4075. Gonriny, Franz. *Das Deutsche Militar in der Karikatur*. Stuttgart: Herman Schmidt's Verlag, 1907.

4076. Grand-Carteret, John. *Bismarck en Caricatures*. Paris: Perrin et Cie, 1890. 306 pp.

4077. Grand-Carteret, John. *Caricatures et Images de Guerre. Le Kaiser, Le Kromprinz et Cie*. Paris: Librairie Chapelot, n.d.

4078. Grand-Carteret, John. *Crispi, Bismarck et la Triple Alliance en Caricatures*. Paris: Libr. Ch. Delgrave Éd., 1891.

4079. Grand-Carteret, John. *La Femme en Allemagne*. Paris: Louis Westhausser Éditeur, 1887.

4080. Grand-Carteret, John. *Derrière Lui. L'Homosexualité en Allemagne*. Paris: B. Bernard Imprimeur-Éditeur, n.d.

4081. Hanfstaengl, Ernst, ed. *Hitler in der Karikatur der Welt*. Berlin: Carl Reutsch, 1933. 174 pp.

4082. Hanfstaengl, Ernst, ed. *Tat Gegen Tinte, Hitler in der Karikatur der Welt, Neue Folge*. Berlin: Carl Reutsch, 1934.

4083. Hasse, Max. "Spott Mit dem Spott Treiben: Bildzitate in der Karikatur des Ausgehenden 18. Jahrhunderts." *Zeitschrift für Kunstgeschichte*. 47:4 (1984), pp. 523-534.

4084. Hellwag, F. *Die Polizei in der Karikatur*. Berlin: 1926.

4085. Herding, Klaus. "'Inversionen.' Antikenkritik in der Karikatur des 19. Jahrhunderts." In *Nervöse Auffangsorgane des Inneren und Aüsseren Lebens—Karikaturen*, edited by Klaus Herding and Gunter Otto, pp. 131-171. Giessen: 1980.

4086. Hermann, Georg. *Die Deutsche Karikatur*. Leipzig: Verlag von Velhagen und Klafing, 1901.

4087. Hollander, Eugen. *Die Karikatur und Satire in der Medizen*. Stuttgart: Verlag von Ferdinand Enke, 1921.

4088. Klant, Michael. *Der Rote Ballon*. Hanover: Fackelträger, 1988. 240 pp.

4089. Klant, Michael. *Die Literatur in der Karikatur*. Hanover: Fackelträger, 1989. 144 pp.

4090. Klant, Michael. *Die Universität in der Karikatur*. Hanover: Fackelträger, 1984. 232 pp.

4091. Klant, Michael. *SchulSpott. Karikaturen aus 2500 Jahren Pädagogik*. Hanover: Fackelträger, 1985. 192 pp.

4092. Klima, Anton. *Die Technik im Lichte der Karikatur. Eine Analitische Studie von Dr. A. Klima*. Vienna: Bei Franz Malota, 1913.

4093. Klima, Anton. *Tier und Pflanze in der Karikatur*. M. und H. Schaper, 1930. 124 pp.

4094. Kressemeier, Siegfied, ed. *Ereigniskarikaturen: Geschichte in Spottbildern, 1600-1930* (Cartoons in Events: History in Satirical Pictures). Munster: Westfälisches Landesmuseum für Kunst und Külturgeschichted, 1983. 384 pp.

4095. Krüger, H. and W., eds. *Geschichte in Karikaturen. Von 1848 bis zur Gegenwart*. Stuttgart: 1981.

4096. Kunzle, David. "Goethe and Caricature: From Hogarth to Töpffer." *Journal of the Warburg and Courtauld Institute*. 48 (1985), pp. 164-188.

4097. *La Caricature Allemande Pendant la Guerre*. Preface by Fréderic Régamey. Paris: Beyer Leurault Lbrs. Édits., 1921.

4098. Mac Orlan, Pierre. "La Caricature en Allemagne." *Caricatures. Arts et Métiers Graphiques* (Paris). September 15, 1932.

4099. Meyer, R.-A. "La Caricature en Allemagne." *L'Art et les Artistes* (Paris). May 1907.

4100. Olbrich, Harald, ed. *Sozialistische Deutsche Karikaturen 1848-1978*. Berlin: Eulenspiegel-Verlag, 1979.

4101. Ostvald, Hans. *Vom Goldenen Humor in Bild und Wort ein Buch des Lachens und der Freude, Bear Beitel und Herausgeben von Hans Ostvald*. Leipzig: Ernst Wiest Nachf, Verlag, n.d.

4102. Régamy, Frédéric. *La Caricature Allemande Pendant la Guerre*. Paris: Beyer Levrault Librs. Édits., 1921.

4103. Rothe, Eugen. *100 Jahre Humor in der Deutschen Kuust*. Hanover: Fackelträger Verlag, n.d.

4104. Schulze, Friedrich. *Die Deutsche Napoleon Karikatur*. Weimar: Gesellschaft der Bibliophilen, 1916.

4105. Schulz-Besser, E. *Die Karikatur im Weltkrieg*. Leipzig: 1915.

4106. Storck, Karl. *Music und Musiker in Karikatur und Satire*. Berlin: G. Stalling, Verlag, 1910.

4107. Townsend, Mary Lee. *Forbidden Laughter. Popular Humor and the Limits of Repression in Nineteenth-Century Prussia.* Ann Arbor, Michigan: University of Michigan Press, 1992. 258 pp.

4108. Veth, Cornelis. *Der Advokat in der Karikatur.* Berlin: 1927.

4109. Veth, Cornelis. *Der Arzt in der Karikatur.* Berlin: 1927.

4110. Veth, Cornelis. "De Satire in Het Hedendaagsche Duitschland." *Maandblad voor Beeldende Kunsten.* June 1933, pp. 162-173.

4111. Vogt, Helmut. *Medizinische Karikaturen von 1800 bis zur Gegenwart.* Munich: J.F. Lehmann, ca. 1962. 184 pp.

4112. von Pocci, Franz. *Schattenspiel. Originalgetreues Faksimile der Erstausgabe von 1849.* Stuttgart: Klett-Cotta, 1982. 67 pp.

4113. Wathur, K. "Bismarck in German Caricature." *Cartoons Magazine.* June and July 1915, pp. 879-888, 117-124.

4114. Wendell, Friedrich. *Das Neunzehnte Jahrhundert in der Karikatur.* Berlin: J.H.W. Diek Nachfolger, 1925.

4115. Wendell, Friedrich. *Das Schellengeläut; Kulturkritische Karikaturen des 19. Jahrhunderts.* Berlin: "Der Bucherkreis," 1927. 192 pp.

4116. Wendell, Friedrich. *Die Mode in der Karikatur.* Dresden: Paul Aretz Verlag, n.d.

4117. Wendell, Friedrich. *Wilhelm II in der Karikatur.* Dresden: 1928.

4118. Wettich, Hans. *Die Maschine in der Karikatur Ein Buch zum Siege der Technik.* Berlin: Dr. Eysler und Cie, 1920.

4119. Zeman, Zbynek. *Heckling Hitler: Caricatures of the Third Reich.* Hanover and London: University Press of New England, 1984, 1987. 128 pp.

Comics

4120. "Ab Heute Jedes Wochenende: Feuerauge." *Hamburger Morgenpost.* April 12, 1969.

4121. "Artikel über den Comic-Zeichner Aagaard." *Brigitte* (Hamburg). No. 7, 1966.

4122. "Bilder-Hefte Mit Bunten Aufstellfiguren." *Der Neue Vertrieb.* 5:109 (1953), p. 459.

4123. Brück, Axel. *Comics-Weltbekannte Zeichenserien*. Hamburg: Carlsen-Verlag, 1971.

4124. Bunk, Thomas M. "Allemagne." In *Histoire Mondiale de la Bande Dessinée*, edited by Pierre Horay, pp. 12-15. Paris: Pierre Horay Éditeur, 1989.

4125. "Comics." *Eltern* (Munich). No. 4, 1970.

4126. "Comics." *Graphik* (Munich). No. 7, 1966.

4127. "Comics." *Jugendliteratur* (Munich). 1:8 (1955), pp. 349-350.

4128. "Comic Wandlungen." *Bulletin: Jugend + Literatur* (Weinheim). No. 4-5, 1971, p. 18.

4129. Cordt, Willy K. "Neues vom Deutschen 'Bildermarkt.'" *Jugendschriften-Warte* (Frankfurt). N.F., 8, 1956, p. 27.

4130. Cordt, Willy K. "Zur Geschichte der Comics." *Jugendschriften-Warte*. No. 1, 1955, pp. 3-4.

4131. Cordt, Willy K. "Zur Geschichte der Comics." *Schwarzburgbund* (Hamburg). 64:1 (1955), pp. 1-3.

4132. Cordt, Willy K. "Zur Geschichte und Problematik der Modernen Bildserienhefte." *Praxis der Volksschule* (Mannheim). 11, 1954.

4133. Dahrendorf, Malte. "Informationen für den Comics-Interessenten." *Bulletin: Jugend + Literatur*. No. 4, 1972, Kritik 4, pp. 31-32.

4134. Del Buono, Oreste. "Was Alle Diese Damen Betrifft." *Valentina* (Bad Honneff). 1968.

4135. "Den Liebevollen Einfall." *Epoca* (Munich). No. 3, 1966.

4136. "Die Comics." *Deutsche Tagespost* (Würzburg). No. 115, 1954.

4137. Diezemann, Holger. "Die Kunst der Kleinen Leute." *Der Stern*. March 22, 1970, pp. 222-223.

4138. Dolle-Weinkauff, Bernd. *Comics: Geschichte Einer Populären Literaturform in Deutschland Seit 1945* (Comics: History of a Popular Genre in Germany Since 1945). Weinheim: Beltz, 1990. 390 pp.

4139. Drechsel, Wiltrud U. "Über die Politsierbarkeit der Bildergeschichte. Ein Historischer Exkurs." *Kunst und Unterricht*. 10, 1970, pp. 29-31.

4140. Drews, Jörg. "Geschichte der Gargantuesken Slapstick-Komödie." *Süddeutsche Zeitung* (Munich). September 27, 1969.

4141. Ebmeyer, Klaus U. "Cartoons." *Civis* (Cologne). No. 7, 1967, pp. 24-26.

4142. Eichler, Richard W. "Die Tätowierte Muse. Eine Kunstgeschichte in Karikaturen." *blick + bild*. 1965.

4143. "Es Wird Bös' Enden. So Sieht der Satiriker des 'Wecker' die 'Liberale Schule.'" *Hamburger Abendblatt*. December 28/29, 1968, p. 22.

4144. Fuchs, Wolfgang J. "Und Es Gibt Sie Doch! Eine Deutsche Comics-Historie." In *Batman, Beatles, Barbarella. Der Kosmos in der Sprechblase*, edited by Wolfgang J. Fuchs and Thomas Wirsum, pp. 10-23. Ebersberg/Obb: Edition 8/12, Lothar Just, 1985.

4145. "Gegenwärtiger Stand der Heftreihen in der Bundesrepublik." *Jugendliteratur*. 10, 1955, pp. 489-491.

4146. "Geschichte vom Julchen." *Constanze* (Hamburg). No. 51, 1964.

4147. Giehrl, Hans E. "Comic-Books. Eigenart und Geschichte." *Allgem Deutsche Lehrerzeitung* (Frankfurt). 6:3, Beilage, 1954.

4148. Giehrl, Hans E. "Comic-Books. Eigenart und Geschichte." *Jugendschriften-Warte*. 6:1 (1954), p. 3-4; 6:2 (1954), p. 12; 6:3 (1954), pp. 20-21; 6:4 (1954), pp. 30-31.

4149. Handloik, Volker. "Mosaik: Aus der Geschichte Eines Sozialistischen Mythos Oder vom Werdegang Östlicher Knollennasen." *Icom Info*. June 1992, pp. 56-58.

4150. Hemdb, Harald. "Die Mainzelmännchen und Ihr Vater." *Vital* (Munich). 1970, pp. 54-57.

4151. Hespe, Rainer. "Die Belle Epoque der Comics." *Frankfurter Hefte*. 6 (1968), pp. 437-438.

4152. Hürlimann, Bettina. "Die Seifenblasensprache. Zur Entwicklung der Bildgeschichten und Ihren Positiven und Negativen Auswirkungen von Wilhelm Busch bis Walt Disney." *Europäische Kinderbücher in drei Jahrhunderten* (Zürich). 2. erw. Aufl., 1963, pp. 119-132.

4153. Kastner, Klaus. "Familie in der Steinzeit." *Süddeutsche Zeitung* (Munich). July 17, 1969.

4154. Kauka, Rolf. "Comics." Münchener Bilderbogen, Sendung des 1. Deutschen Fernsehprogramms (ARD). December 12, 1971.

4155. Köhler, Otto. "Mächtig Stark." *Der Spiegel*. 23:38 (1969), p. 214.

4156. Kuchenbuch, Thomas. *Bild und Erzählung: Geschichten in Bildern Von Fruhen Comic zum Fernsehfeature*. Munster: Maks Publikationen, 1992. 255 pp.

4157. Lachner, Johann. "Münchener Bilderbogen. Die Comic-Strips von Anno Dazumal." *Lebendige Erziehung* (Munich). 4:15 (1954/1955), pp. 354-355.

4158. Lammel, Gisold. *Karikatur der Goethezeit*. Berlin: Eulenspiegel Verlag, 1992. 433 pp.

4159. Lankheit, Klaus. "Aus der Frühzeit der Weissenburger Bilderfabrik." *Kölner Zschr. für. Soziologie und Sozialpsychologie* (Cologne). 21:3 (1969), pp 585-600.

4160. Lettkemann, Gerd. "Comics im '3. Reich.'" *Comixene. Das Comicfachmagazin*. 6:24 (1979), pp. 49, 52.

4161. Metken, Günter. *Comics*. 2. Vols. Hamburg: Fischer-Taschenbuch, No. 1120, 1970.

4162. Metken, Günter. "Weltgeschichte für Zwei Sous. 'Imagerie Populaire.' Bunte Bilderbogen—Illustrierte der Guten Alten Zeit." *Die Welt*. September 3, 1966.

4163. "Muse, Ganz Frech." *Hamburger Abendecho*. March 19, 1966.

4164. "Nachrichten von Nebenan: Neu-Ruppin." *Bulletin: Jugend + Literatur*. No. 1, 1969/1970, p. 4.

4165. Nilsquist, Lutz. "Comics-Dokumentation." *Underground* (Frankfurt). No. 5, 1970, p. 56-59.

4166. Nolte, Jost. "Comics—Oder Die Brutalität des Bösen." *Die Welt der Literatur* (Hamburg). No. 21, 1970, pp. 12-13.

4167. Nolte, Jost. "Die Geschichte vom Rüssel." *Zeit-magazin*. June 16, 1972, pp. 6-9.

4168. "Nun Sollen die Fahrgäste 'Verkehrsfüchse' Werden." *Hamburger Abendblatt*. October 20, 1967.

4169. Ohff, Heinz. "Die Neue Lust am Trivialen." *Die Neue Barke* (Stuttgart). No. 1, 1971, (Das Buchmagazin), pp. 33-36.

4170. Paulssen, Ernst. "Die Geschichte der Comic Strips." *Archiv für Publizistische Arbeit* (Munzinger-Archiv). Lieferung 37/61. September 16, 1961, 687/8562-8562i.

4171. Pforte, Dietger. "Deutschsprachige Comics." In *Comic Strips: Geschichte, Struktur, Wirkung und Verbreitung der Bildergeschichten, Ausstellungskatalog der Berliner Akademie der Künste, December 13, 1969-January 25, 1970.* pp. 22-27. Berlin.

4172. Pohl, Ulrich. *Von Max und Moritz bis Fix und Foxi.* Wiesbaden: Verlags-Union, 1970.

4173. Pross, Harry. "Von Wilhelm Busch zu Al Capp. Notizen über Bilder-Bogen und Comic Books." *Deutsche Rundschau.* 82e année, No. 8, 1956, pp. 877-881.

4174. Raddatz, Fritz J. "Die Neuen Heldinnen der Westlichen Welt." *Die Zeit.* March 17, 1967, pp. 17-18.

4175. Razumovsky, Andreas. "Im Ringe Mit der Macht." *Frankfurter Allgemeine Zeitung.* March 1, 1968, p. 32.

4176. Reding, Josef. "Geschichte und Wirkkraft der Comic-Strips." *Welt und Wort* (Tübingen). 9:8 (1954), pp 257-258.

4177. Reinecke, Lutz. "Die Wilden Kerle aus Comic-Land." *Underground* 3:2 (1970), pp. 5-10.

4178. Renner, M. "Deutsche Comics." *Der Neue Vertrieb.* October 20, 1953, p. 432.

4179. Riesenberger, Dieter. "Geschichte in Comics." *Geschichte in Wissenschaft und Unterricht* (Seelze; Reprint New York). 25:3 (1974), pp. 162-173.

4180. Riha, Karl. "Groteske, Kommerz, Revolte. Zur Geschichte der Comics-Literatur." In *Comic-Strips: Geschichte, Struktur, Wirkung und Verbreitung der Bildergeschichten, Ausstellungskatalog der Berliner Akademie der Künste, December 13, 1969-January 25, 1970*, pp. 7-10. Berlin.

4181. Riha, Karl. "'Lend Me a Nickel.' Versuch über Comic-Strips." *Diskus* (Frankfurt). 14:6 (1964), pp. 9-10; 14:7 (1964), pp. 8-9.

4182. Rosema, Bernd. "Achtung, die Wilden Männer Kommen!" *Pardon* (Cologne). 9:10 (1970), p. 38.

4183. Sack, Manfred. "Antiheld der Leistungsgesellschaft." *Die Zeit.* January 1, 1971, p. 24.

4184. Salmony, G. "Witzlos ('Unser Thema')." *Süddeutsche Zeitung* (Munich). April 2/3, 1966.

4185. Schmidmaier, Werner. "Kinderheld und Schuhverkäufer. Schwanzlurch Schreiter Rüstig ins 50. Abenteuer." *Werben und Verkaufen* (Munich). January 8, 1971.

4186. Schnurrer, Achim. "10 Jahre ICOM?" *Comic Info*. May-June 1993, p. 57.

4187. Schöler, Franz. "Comics für Erwachsene." *Die Welt der Literatur* (Hamburg). No. 10, 1969, p. 8.

4188. Schulze, Hartmut. "Trashman Ballert für die Unterdrückten. Die Neuen Comics Zwischen Politik und Geschäft." *Konkret* (Hamburg). April 8, 1971, pp. 62-63.

4189. Schwarz, Rainer. "Bilder, Blasen und Banausen." *ER* (Munich). No. 7, 1970, pp. 22-23.

4190. Segebrecht, Dietrich. "Den Comics Eine Gasse." *Frankfurter Allgemeine Zeitung*. November 10, 1970, p. 1-L.

4191. "So Wurde Peggy Geboren." *Hamburger Morgenpost*. No. 110, 1965, p. 14.

4192. Staupendahl, Karin. "Zur Geschichte der Comic-Strips." *Hessische Jugend* (Frankfurt). 22:8 (1970), pp. 4-7.

4193. Strelow, Hans. "Ein Klassiker des Comics." *Die Zeit*. November 24, 1967, p. 19.

4194. Strelow, Hans. "Das Normale Ist das Absurde." *Frankfurter Allgemeine Zeitung*. January 10, 1970.

4195. "Sybille: Ein Unterseeboot Namens Liebe." *Der Stern*. March 23, 1969, p. 15.

4196. Theile, Harold. "Naturgeschichte der Comics." *Deutsche Rundschau*. 77:5 (1951), pp. 447-452.

4197. Weissert, Elisabeth. "Bildergeschichten." *Erziehungskunst* (Stuttgart). 18:11, p. 326.

4198. Wiegand, Wilfried. "Vom Bilderbogen zum Comic-Strip." *Die Welt*. April 26, 1968, p. 15.

4199. Wolf, Ursula. "Jeder ein Pilot." *Publik* (Cologne). No. 15, 1969, p. 23.

4200. Zille, Heinrich. *Das Neue Zille-Buch*. Hanover: Fackelträger, 1988. 436 pp.

Graphic Arts

4201. Coupe, William A. *The German Illustrated Broadsheet in the Seventeenth Century. Historical and Iconographical Studies*. 2 Vols. (Bibliotheca Bibliographica Aureliana XVII, XX). Baden Baden: Verlag Librare Heitz, 1966, 1967.

4202. Dolle-Weinkäuff, Bernd. "From the Pictorial Joke to the Graphik Novel." In *The Grandchildren of Max and Moritz*, pp. 1-6. Frankfurt: AuM, 1990.

4203. Hollstein, F.W.H. *German Engravings, Etchings, and Woodcuts, 1400-1700*. 34 Vols. to date. Amsterdam: Menno Hertzberger, 1959-.

4204. Pniower, O. *Alt-Berliner Humor um 1830*. Potsdam: 1919.

4205. Yenne, Y.P. and K.W. Dills. *German War Art 1939-1945*. Bison Books, 1983. 160 pp.

Political Cartoons

4206. Coupe, W.A. "The German Cartoon and the Revolution of 1848." *Comparative Studies in Society and History*. January 1967, pp. 137-167.

4207. Coupe, W.A. "German Cartoonists and the Peace of Versailles." *History Today*. January 1982, pp. 46-53.

4208. Coupe, W.A. *German Political Satires from the Reformation to the Second World War*. Part II. 1849-1918. White Plains, New York: Kraus International, 1987.

4209. Coupe, W.A. *German Political Satires from the Reformation to the Second World War*. Part III. 1918-1945. White Plains, New York: Kraus International, 1985. Commentary, 298 pp.; Plates, 533 pp.

4210. "Germany's Martial Spirit as Shown in German and Austrian Cartoons." *Review of Reviews*. November 1914, pp. 547-560.

4211. "Japan as Germany Once Saw Her." *New York Times Magazine*. March 29, 1942, p. 29.

4212. Kaps, Joachim. "Aussagerkraft des Bildes Nicht Vertraut. Hitler—der Comic." *ICOM-INFO*. February 1990, pp. 54-55.

4213. Koch, Ursula E. *Der Teufel in Berlin: Von der Märzrevolution bis zu Bismarks Entlassung, Illustrierte Politische Witzblätter Einer Metropole 1848-1890* (The Devil in Berlin: From the March Revolution to Bismarck's Dismissal. Illustrated Political Satire Papers of a Metropolis). Cologne: Leske, 1991. 880 pp.

CARTOONISTS and CARICATURISTS

4214. Alber, Wolfgang. "Interview mit Roswith Krege-Mayer." *Comic Forum. Das Österreichische Fachmagazin für Comicliteratur*. 3:11 (1981), pp. 26-27.

4215. "Als Held Eines Comic-Strip." *Der Spiegel*. No. 44, 1968, p. 180. (Ernst Jünger).

4216. Braun, Alexander. "Hendrik Dorgathen. Vom Gelsenkirchener Barock zum Erlangener Comic-Salon." *ICOM-INFO*. June 1992, pp. 26-29.

4217. Braun, Alexander. "Rache Ist Nicht Suss." *ICOM*. October 1992, pp. 34-39. (Ute Helmbold).

4218. Bunk, Thomas M. *Dose Comics—Zum Abfahren*. Kiel: Semmel, 1984. 144 pp.

4219. Czucha, Kay. *Herr Gott Nochmal*. Kiel: Semmel, 1987. 64 pp.

4220. "David Basler: Comicverlegeraus Leidenschaft." *ICOM*. January 1993, pp. 46-49.

4221. "Der Zeichner R. Dircks." *Die Welt*. April 23, 1968.

4222. Engler-Kellermann, Michael. "Kabelfernsehen im Rhein-Main-Donau-Kanal? Ein Interview mit Jan Gulbransson." *Comic Forum. Das Magazin für Comicliteratur*. 7:28 (1985), pp. 44-45.

4223. "Experiment Wird Grossgeschrieben." *ICOM*. October 1992, pp. 44-46. (Hannes Neubauer).

4224. Fischer, Hans. *Nur zum Spa B*. Berlin: Eulenspiegel, 1957.

4225. Flisak, Jerzy. *Unter uns die Zwerge*. Berlin: Eulenspiegel-Verlag, 1971.

4226. Förster, Gerhard, ed. *Das Große Hansrudi Wäscher-Buch*. Schönau: Hethke, 1987. 146 pp.

4227. Forster-Hahn, Franziska. *Johann Heinrich Ramberg als Karikaturist und Satiriker* (Sonderdruck aus *Hannoverschen Geschichtsblättern*, N.F. Band 17, 1963).

4228. Fuchs, Wolfgang J. "Comic-Studio Comicon. Ein Interview mit Peter Wiechmann und Fred Kipka." *Comixene. Das Comicfachmagazin*. 7:31 (1980), pp. 22-25.

4229. Fuchs, Wolfgang J. "Thema: Roland Kohlsaat. Leben und Werk." *Comixene. Das Comicfachmagazin*. 5:21 (1978), pp. 6-7.

4230. Granacher, René. "Interview: Horst Gotta." *ICOM-INFO*. February 1990, pp. 26-33.

4231. Guratzsch, Herwig. *Karl Arnold—Typen und Figuren der Zwanziger Jahre*. Stuttgart: Hatje, 1989. 164 pp.

4232. Halbritter, Kurt. *Girls, Germanen und Gespenster*. Berlin: Eulenspiegel-Verlag, 1961.

4233. Henniger, Barbara. *Barbaras Praktische Linke.* Berlin: Eulenspiegel-Verlag, 1978.

4234. Hess, Thomas B. *The Art Comics and Satires of Ad Reinhardt.* Düsseldorf: Kunsthalle Düsseldorf, 1975. 58 pp.

4235. "Icom-Zeichnerarchiv." *Comic Info.* 1/1993, pp. 50-51. (Jörg Peter).

4236. "Interview mit Fritz Raab." *Comixene. Das Comicfachmagazin.* 5:21 (1978), pp. 33-36.

4237. Jaeger, Gerd. *Durch Zug der Gladiatoren.* Berlin: Eulenspiegel-Verlag, 1982.

4238. "Kämpfengehörtzum Täglichen Brot." *ICOM INFO.* June 1992, p. 21. (Karl Manfred Fischer).

4239. Kaplan, Anatoli L. *Acht Bunte Blätter.* Berlin: Eulenspiegel-Verlag, 1981.

4240. Kaps, Joachim. "Nordsee-Krimi. Ein Gespräch mit Jens Jeddeloh Über Die Insel Alten Männer." *Comic Info.* May-June 1993, pp. 54-55.

4241. "Keine Zukunft und Eine Dunkle Vergangenheit." *ICOM.* October 1992, pp. 40-42. (Thomas Kühn and Holger Klein).

4242. *Klassiker der Karikatur: No. 1. Thomas Theodor Heine.* Berlin: Eulenspiegel-Verlag, 1968. 168 pp.

4243. *Klassiker der Karikatur: No. 2. Rudolf Wilke.* Berlin: Eulenspiegel-Verlag, 1969.

4244. *Klassiker der Karikatur: No. 11. Bruno Paul.* Berlin: Eulenspiegel-Verlag, 1974.

4245. *Klassiker der Karikatur: No. 14. Josef Lada.* Berlin: Eulenspiegel, 1976.

4246. *Klassiker der Karikatur: No. 15. Albert Weisgerber.* Berlin: Eulenspiegel, 1976.

4247. Kolditz, Niels. "Der Unsichtbare Dritte: Martin Frei." *ICOM INFO.* June 1992, pp. 16-20.

4248. Kunert, Günter. *Acht Bunte Blätter.* Berlin: Eulenspiegel-Verlag, 1979.

4249. Künnemann, Horst. "Ein Großer Fabulierer der Zeichenfeder. Zum Tode Josef Hegenbarths." *Jugendschriften-Warte.* No. 10, 1963, pp. 60-61.

4250. Kurz, Werner. "Christian Jütting und die General Clay Production." *ICOM.* January 1993, pp. 50-51.

4251. Kurz, Werner and Patrick T. Klein. "Klaus Dill." *ICOM INFO.* June 1992, pp. 42-46. (Klaus Dill).

4252. Lettkemann, Gerd. "Fritz Wolf." *Comic Forum. Das Österreichische Fachmagazin für Comicliteratur.* 2:4 (1980), p. 52.

4253. Lettkemann, Gerd. "Markus." *Comic Forum. Das Österreichische Fachmagazin für Comicliteratur.* 1:3 (1979), pp. 36-37. (a.k.a. Jörg Mark-Ingraban von Morgen.).

4254. Mayer, Gyula. *Die Fünf Jahreszeiten.* Berlin: Eulenspiegel-Verlag, 1968.

4255. Merten, Helmut. *Der Busentempel.* Berlin: Eulenspiegel-Verlag, 1979.

4256. Moese, Willy. *Zum Beispiel Fünflinge.* Berlin: Eulenspiegel-Verlag, 1972.

4257. "Neue Comics von Alexey Sagerer, Experimente in 'Pro T.'" *Süddeutsche Zeitung* (Munich). No. 88, 1970, p. 20.

4258. Nieuwendijk, Peter. "Willy Lohmann: 'I Am an Entertainer...I Draw Cartoons.'" *WittyWorld.* Summer 1988, pp. 28-31.

4259. Presber, Rudolf. *Neues Paul Gimmel Ulbum.* Stuttgart: Verlag Heinrich Plesten, 1930's. 200 pp.

4260. Rauch, H.G. *Dessins, L'Oeuvre Grave.* Paris: Les Presses de la Connaissance, 1976.

4261. Reinhardt, Manfred. "Der Zeichner Becker-Kasch." *Comixene. Das Comicfachmagazin.* 7:31 (1980), pp. 19-20.

4262. Riegenring, Wilmar. *Riegenringeleien.* Berlin: Eulenspiegel-Verlag, 1961.

4263. Roehricht, Karl-Hermann. *Acht Bunte Blätter.* Berlin: Eulenspiegel-Verlag, 1977.

4264. Sackmann, Eckart. "Interview mit Reinhold Escher." *Comixene. Das Comicfachmagazin.* 8:36 (1981), pp. 8-9, 14-15.

4265. Schmitt, Erich. *Das Dicke Schmitt-Buch.* Berlin: Eulenspiegel-Verlag, 1968.

4266. Schubert, Wolfgang. *Gullivers Wiederkehr.* Berlin: Eulenspiegel-Verlag, 1973.

4267. Simmel, Paul. *Simmelanten.* Berlin: Eulenspiegel-Verlag, 1964.

4268. Simon, Wolfgang. *Sammelsurium.* Berlin: Eulenspiegel-Verlag, 1976.

4269. Sperzel, Wolfgang. *Kabelbrand im Herzschrittmacher.* Kiel: Semmel, 1989. 48 pp.

4270. Starke, Hans-Jürgen. *Medizynisches.* Berlin: Eulenspiegel-Verlag, 1978.

4271. Strupp, Günther. *Struppzeng*. Berlin: Eulenspiegel-Verlag, 1970.

4272. "Taft und Harper und Cyclobertrand." *ICOM INFO*. June 1992, pp. 30-32. (Martin Pfaender).

4273. Taru, Eugen. *Generalreparatur*. Berlin: Eulenspiegel-Verlag, 1977.

4274. Truck, Walter. "Mitlinks." *ICOM*. January 1993, pp. 38-43. (Anton Atzenhofer).

4275. Truck, Walter. "Vier Stachelköpfe Voll in Fahrt." *ICOM*. October 1992, pp. 52-56. (Michael Schaadt).

4276. Udet, Ernst. *Hals—und Beinbruch, 100 Luftige Karikaturen, Gezeichnet von Ernst Udet*. Berlin: W. Kolk, 1928. 80 pp.

4277. "'Verstärkt Coproductionen!" *Comic Info*. 1/1993, pp. 44-45. (Steffen Boiselle).

4278. Vonderwerth, Klaus. *Cartoonale*. Berlin: Eulenspiegel-Verlag, 1980.

4279. von Kessel-Thöny, Dagmar. *Eduard Thöny*. Munich: Goltz, 1986. 220 pp.

4280. Vontra, Gerhard. *Sehreise Nach Indien*. Berlin: Eulenspiegel-Verlag, 1975.

4281. Vorbeck, Matthias. *Nach Strich und Faden*. Berlin: Eulenspiegel-Verlag, 1983.

4282. "Waldemar Mandzel." *Apropos*. No. 5, 1988, pp. 45-46.

4283. "Walter Neugebauer Ist Tot." *ICOM INFO*. June 1992, p. 11.

4284. Wiessmüller, Michael. "Adolf Kabatek." *Comic Forum. Das Magazin für Comicliteratur*. 8:31 (1986), pp. 21-22.

Becker, Franziska

4285. Becker, Franziska. *Männer*. Cologne: Emma, 1985. 64 pp.

4286. Becker, Franziska. *Mein Feministischer Alltag*. Vols. 1-4. Cologne: Emma, 1981-. 82 pp.

4287. Becker, Franziska. *New York New York*. Cologne: Emma, 1987. 64 pp.

4288. Becker, Franziska and Papan. *Hin und Her*. Cologne: Emma, 1988. 128 pp.

4289. Braun, Alexander. "Franziska Becker." *ICOM*. January 1993, pp. 16-27.

Bengen, Harm

4290. Bengen, Harm. *Harm Bengens Chronik des Wahnsinns*. Kiel: Semmel, 1987. 64 pp.

4291. Kaps, Joachim. "Harm Bengen. Pirat auf Allen Comic-Meeren." *Comic Info*. May-June 1993, pp. 50-53.

Busch, Wilhelm

4292. Arndt, Walter, trans. *The Genius of Wilhelm Busch: Comedy of Frustration*. Berkeley, California: University of California Press, 1982. 264 pp.

4293. Bohne, Friedrich. *Wilhelm Busch: Leben, Werk, Schicksal*. Zurich and Stuttgart: 1958.

4294. Bonati, Peter. *Die Darstellung des Bösen im Werk Wilhelm Buschs*. Francke, 1973. 160 pp.

4295. Brooks, R.C. "Art of Wilhelm Busch." *Bookman*. September 1905, pp. 10-16.

4296. Busch, Wilhelm. *Acht Bunte Blätter*. Berlin: Eulenspiegel-Verlag, 1978.

4297. Busch, Wilhelm. *Band 1 bis 3*. Berlin: Eulenspiegel-Verlag, 1962.

4298. Busch, Wilhelm. *The Bees*. Trans. by Robert Wiemann. New York: 1974.

4299. Busch, Wilhelm. *Brachwert für Alle, Berlin Deutschen Humors*. Berlin: R. Jacobsthal, n.d., Unpaginated.

4300. Busch, Wilhelm. *Das Dioke Busch-Buch*. Berlin: Eulenspiegel-Verlag, 1975.

4301. Busch, Wilhelm. *Das Gesamtwerk des Zeichners und Dichters*. Hanover: Fackelverlag, 1964.

4302. Busch, Wilhelm. *Das Goldene Wilhelm Busch. Album 19*. Hanover: Fackelträger, 1959. 640 pp.

4303. Busch, Wilhelm. *Die Bildergeschichten Zwischen Flugblatt und Cartoon*. Exhibition Catalog, Hanover, 1982.

4304. Busch, Wilhelm. *Dieses War der Erste Streich*. Berlin: Eulenspiegel-Verlag, 1959.

4305. Busch, Wilhelm. *Eins-Twei-Drei im Sanseschritt*. Berlin: Eulenspiegel-Verlag, 1960.

4306. Busch, Wilhelm. *Hypocritical Helena, Plus a Plenty of Other Pleasures.* New York: Dover, 1962. 205 pp.

4307. Busch, Wilhelm. *Kritik des Herzens.* Berlin: Eulenspiegel-Verlag, 1959.

4308. Busch, Wilhelm. *Neues Wilhelm Busch Album.* Berlin: Hermann Klemm, 1912 (?). 488 pp.

4309. Busch, Wilhelm. *Romanze von Ritter Ossa Sepia.* Berlin: Eulenspiegel-Verlag, 1982.

4310. Busch, Wilhelm. *Summa Summarum.* Berlin: Eulenspiegel-Verlag, 1961.

4311. Busch, Wilhelm. *Was Ich Ergötalich Fand.* Munich: F. Bassermann, 1961. 176 pp.

4312. Busch, Wilhelm. *Werke.* Edited by Friedrich Bohne. 4 Vols. Hamburg: 1959.

4313. Busch, Wilhelm. *Wilhelm Busch Album, Ein Heiteres Hausbuch.* Munich: Süd-West Verlags und Vertriebs, [1960's]. 400 pp.

4314. Busch, Wilhelm. *Zu Guter Letzt.* Berlin: Eulenspiegel-Verlag, 1960.

4315. Carano, Ranieri. "I Nipotini di Busch." *Linus.* No. 7, 1965.

4316. Daelen, Edvard. *Über Wilhelm Busch und Seine Bedeutung: Eine Lustige Streitschrift.* Düsseldorf: 1886.

4317. Dangers, Robert. *Wilhelm Busch.* Rembrandt-Verlag, 1937. 127 pp.

4318. Hahne-Braunschweig, Franz. "Vorläufer und Nachahmer Wilhelm Buschs." *Mitteilungen der Wilhelm Busch Gesellschaft.* Nos. 13-14, 1943.

4319. Heuss, Theodor. *Wilhelm Busch.* Bertelsmann, 1959. 21 pp.

4320. Horay, Pierre. *Wilhelm Busch: Histoires Dessinées.* Paris: Pierre Horay Éditeur, n.d. 128 pp.

4321. Just, Harald. "Wilhelm Busch und die Katholiken: Kulturkampfstimmung im Bismarckreich." *Wilhelm-Busch-Jahrbuch.* 40, 1974.

4322. *Klassiker der Karikatur: No. 17. Wilhelm Busch.* Berlin: Eulenspiegel-Verlag, 1978.

4323. Kleeman, Fritz. "Raffs Naturgeschichte für Kinder und die Tiergeschichten Wilhelm Buschs." *Wilhelm-Busch-Jahrbuch.* 38, 1972.

4324. Kunzle, David. *"Busch im Ausland."* Wilhelm-Busch-Jahrbuch. 53, 1987.

4325. Lotze, Dieter. *Wilhelm Busch*. Boston: 1979.

4326. Mihr, Ulrich. *Wilhelm Busch: Der Protestant, der Trotzdem Lacht*. Tübingen: Narr, 1983. 200 pp.

4327. Pietzcker, Frank. *Wilhelm Busch—Schuld und Strafe in Werk und Leben*. Munich: Saur, 1984. 104 pp.

4328. Qualen, Hans Hellmuth. "Politisches bei Wilhelm Busch." *Wilhelm-Busch-Jahrbuch*. 50, 1984.

4329. *Sämtliche Bilderbogen*. Hildesheim: Olms, 1979. 106 pp.

4330. Schmidt, Karl. *The Hollow Tooth. And Other Stories*. Klagenfurt: Heyn, 1980. 60 pp.

4331. Schmidt, Karl. *Six Tales for Nephews and Nieces*. Klagenfurt: Heyn, 1981. 50 pp.

4332. Ueding, Gert. *Wilhelm Busch. Das 19. Jahrhundert en Miniature*. Frankfurt: Insel, 1977. 350 pp.

4333. Vogt, Michael. *Die Boshafte Heiterkeit des Wilhelm Busch*. Bielefeld: Aisthesis, 1988. 199 pp.

4334. "Wilhelm Busch Ausstellung 30 Juli-11 Sept. 1949, Im Helmaus Zurich." 40 pp.

4335. "Wilhelm Busch, the German Caricaturist." *Review of Reviews*. April 1908, pp. 492-494.

Butter, Benno

4336. Butter, Benno. *Herrenpartie Nach Ithaka*. Berlin: Eulenspiegel-Verlag, 1974.

4337. Butter, Benno. *Klamank um Helena*. Berlin: Eulenspiegel-Verlag, 1973.

Büttner, Henry

4338. Büttner, Henry. *Der Mann Mit dem Runden Hut*. Berlin: Eulenspiegel-Verlag, 1973.

4339. Büttner, Henry. *Gesellschaftsspiele*. Berlin: Eulenspiegel-Verlag, n.d.

4340. Büttner, Henry. *Humor aus Linker Hand*. Berlin: Eulenspiegel-Verlag, 1958.

4341. Büttner, Henry. *Mahlzeit!* Berlin: Eulenspiegel-Verlag, 1979.

4342. Büttner, Henry. *Scherzo Curioso.* Berlin: Eulenspiegel-Verlag, 1965.

Canzler, Günter

4343. Canzler, Günter. *Die Schmunzelinsel.* Berlin: Eulenspiegel-Verlag, 1958.

4344. Canzler, Günter. *Er-Sie-Es.* Berlin: Eulenspiegel-Verlag, 1958.

Chodowiecki, Daniel

4345. Focke, R. *Chodowiecki et Lichtenberg. Les Tailles-Douces des Mois.* Leipzig: 1901.

4346. von Oettingen, W. *Daniel Chodowiecki, Ein Berliner Künsterleben in 18ten Jhdt.* Berlin: 1895.

Dittrich, Peter

4347. Dittrich, Peter. *Inventur bei Peter Dittrich.* Berlin: Eulenspiegel-Verlag, 1963.

4348. Dittrich, Peter. *Mensch, Benimm Dir.* Berlin: Eulenspiegel-Verlag, 1956.

Dörbeck, Franz Burchard

4349. Brockerhoff, Kurt. "Die Bilderfolge 'Berliner Redensarten' (1828-1830) von Franz Burchard Dörbeck." In *Beiträge zur Geschichte Berlins,* edited by Felix Hasselberg and Hans Winter. Berlin: Verein für die Geschichte Berlins, 1939.

4350. Dörbeck, Franz Burchard. *Altberliner Typen von Dörbeck.* Ed. by Hans Ludwig. West Berlin: Staneck, 1966.

4351. Dörbeck, Franz Burchard. *Franz Burchard Dörbeck.* Ed. by Hans Ludwig. West Berlin: Stapp, 1979.

4352. Dörbeck, Franz Burchard. *Franz Burchard Dörbeck: Die Eckensteher Nante als Kläger.* Ed. by Gustave Sichelschmidt. West Berlin: Rembrandt, 1971.

4353. *Klassiker der Karikatur: No. 16. Franz Burchard Dörbeck.* Berlin: Eulenspiegel-Verlag, 1978.

4354. Löschburg, Winfried. "Franz Burchard Dörbeck: Zu Seinem 120. Todestag." *Berliner Heimat.* 1955, pp. 38-44.

4355. Löschburg, Winfried. "Ludwig Burger und Franz Burchard Dörbeck." *Berliner Heimat.* 1957, pp. 126-128.

4356. Thieme, Ulrich and Felix Becker, eds. *Allgemeines Lexikon der Bildenden Künstler von der Antike bis zur Gegenwart.* 37 Vols. Leipzig: Wilhelm Engelmann, 1907-1950.

Ernsting, Volker

4357. Sackmann, Eckart. "Interview mit Volker Ernsting." *Comixene. Das Comicfachmagazin.* 8:41 (1981), pp. 19-20.

4358. Sackmann, Eckart. "Volker Ernsting. Karikaturist, Comic-Zeichner und Satiriker." *Comixene. Das Comicfachmagazin.* 8:41 (1981), pp. 16-18.

Fuchs, Eduard

4359. Fuchs, Eduard. *Illustrierte Sittengeschichte.* 6 Vols. Frankfurt: Fischer Verlag, 1985. 1334 pp. (Edited by Thomas Huonker).

4360. Huonker, Thomas. *Revolution, Moral and Kunst. Eduard Fuchs: Leben und Werk.* Zurich: Limmat Verlag, 1985. 595 pp.

Grosz, George (a.k.a. Georg Ehrenfried)

4361. A.B. "Un Grand Dessinateur Populaire: Georges Grosz." *Les Hommes du Jour.* November 1928, pp. 8-9.

4362. Anders, Günther. *George Grosz.* Zurich: Verlag Die Arche, 1961. 56 pp. Reprinted: *Jahresring, 1960-61, Beiträge zur Deutschen Literatur und Kunst der Gegenwart.* Stuttgart: Deutsche Verlags-Anstalt, pp. 313-322.

4363. Apfel, Alfred. "Reichsgericht über George Grosz." *Die Weltbühne.* June 24, 1930, pp. 952-957.

4364. Arcos, René. "Chroniques: À Propos d'un Album. George Grosz et Frans Masereel." *Europe* (Paris). November 15, 1924, pp. 367-370.

4365. Ashton, Dore. "An Interview with George Grosz." *Pen and Brush*. March 1953, pp. 8-9, 12-14.

4366. Avermaete, Roger. *George Grosz*. Paris: Arts et Metiers Graphiques, 1929.

4367. *Bacon a Brera: e Quaranta Desegni di Grosz in Sosta a Milano*. Essays by Carlo Bertelli and Mario De Micheli. Milan: Multipla Edizioni, 1983.

4368. Ballo, Ferdinando, ed. *Grosz*. Milan: Documenti d'Arte Contemporanea, 1946.

4369. Baudy, Nicolas. "George Grosz à Berlin." *Preuves*. August 1961, pp. 37-42.

4370. Baur, John I.H. *George Grosz*. New York: Macmillan Co. for the Whitney Museum of American Art, 1954. 59 pp.

4371. Bazalgette, Leon. *George Grosz: l'Homme et l'Oeuvre*. Paris: Les Écrivains Réunis, 1926. 10 pp.

4372. Bazalgette, Leon. "George Grosz." *Chroniques du Jour*. July 1930, pp. 17-19.

4373. Becher, Ulrich. *Der Grosse Grosz und Eine Grosse Zeit: Rede, Gehalten am 7, Oktober 1962 zur Eröffnung der Grossen Grosz-Ausstellung in der Akademie der Künste, West-Berlin*. Reinbek bei Hamburg: Rowohlt Verlag, 1962.

4374. Becher, Ulrich. "Der Grosse Grosz und Eine Grosse Zeit." *Schweizer Annalen*. No. 11, 1946-1947, pp. 641-655.

4375. Behne, Adolf. "George Grosz." *Die Weltbühne*. 1924, p. 234.

4376. Benson, Emanuel M. "George Grosz, Social Satirist." *Creative Art*. May 1933, pp. 340-347.

4377. Berenson, Ruth and Norbert Mühlen. "George Grosz." *Der Monat*. June 1960, pp. 20-32.

4378. Bergius, Hanne. "Painter and Paster. 'Propagandada' George Grosz" and "'Daum'/'Maud' Eva Grosz." *Das Lachen Dadas: Die Berliner Dadaisten und Ihre Aktionen*. Werkbund Archiv, Vol. 19, pp. 166-175, 176-181. Giessen: Anabas-Verlag, 1989.

4379. Bernier, Jean. "Nos Interviews: Une Neure Avec Georg Grosz." *L'Humanité*. May 20, 1924.

4380. Bittner, Herbert, ed. *George Grosz*. Intro. by Ruth Berenson and Norbert Muhlen. Essay by George Grosz. New York: Arts Inc., 1960. 18 pp. Reprinted: Cologne: DuMont Schauberg, 1961.

4381. Boyer, Richard O. "Profiles, Artist: 1. Demons in the Suburbs." *New Yorker*. November 23, 1943, pp. 32-43.

4382. Boyer, Richard O. "Profiles, Artist: 2. The Saddest Man in All the World." *New Yorker*. December 4, 1943, pp. 39-48.

4383. Boyer, Richard O. "Profiles, Artist: 3. The Yankee from Berlin." *New Yorker*. December 11, 1943, pp. 37-44.

4384. Bradley, Joseph C. "George Grosz: A Study of His Life, Art, and Philosophy." Ph.D. dissertation, University of Wisconsin, 1954.

4385. Brendemühl, Rudolf. "Maler und 'Seelenarzt': Interview Mit dem Heimgekehrten George Grosz." *Berliner Leben*. July 1959, p. 9.

4386. Breuer, Robert. "George Grosz." *Deutsche Republik*. March 28, 1929, pp. 816-817.

4387. Breuer, Robert. "George Grosz." *Die Weltbühne*. February 10, 1921, pp. 164-166.

4388. ten Brook, Joo. "George Grosz." *Der Weg*. 1:8-9 (1919), p. 4.

4389. Brumer, Miriam. "Paradoxes in Style: George Grosz at MOMA." *Arts Magazine*. September/October 1969, pp. 48-50.

4390. Buschbeck, Erhard. "Der Zeichner George Grosz." *Der Friede*. 2 (1918-1919), p. 144.

4391. Coates, Robert M. "George Grosz, Past and Present." *New Yorker*. October 25, 1941, pp. 62-64.

4392. Coellen, Ludwig. "Die Erste George Grosz-Mappe." *Das Kunstblatt*. November 1917, pp. 348-349.

4393. Cooper, Isabel S. "George Grosz—The American Years." M.A. Thesis, Queens College, City University of New York, 1987.

4394. Craven, Thomas. "George Grosz." In *Modern Art: The Men, the Movements, the Meaning*, pp. 204-217. New York: Simon and Schuster, 1934.

4395. "Das Urteil im George Grosz-Prozess." *Die Weltbühne*. May 7, 1929, pp. 708-713.

4396. Däubler, Theodor. "George Grosz." *Das Junge Deutschland.* 2:7 (1919), pp. 175-177.

4397. Däubler, Theodor. "George Grosz." *Das Kunstblatt.* March 1971, pp. 80-82.

4398. Däubler, Theodor. "George Grosz." *Das Kunstblatt.* June 1929, pp. 160-165.

4399. Däubler, Theodor. "Georg Grosz." *Die Weissen Blätter.* October-December 1916, pp. 167-170.

4400. Däubler, Theodor. "George Grosz." *1918: Neue Blätter für Kunst und Dichtung.* November 1918, pp. 153-154. (Issue devoted to Theodor Däubler, including article on him, selections of his poetry, his essay on Grosz, two Grosz poems, and four Grosz drawings).

4401. Dencker, Klaus. ed. *George Grosz: Ach Knallige Welt, du Lunapark. Gesammelte Gedichte.* Munich and Vienna: Carl Hanser Verlag, 1986.

4402. Dolbin, B.F. and Willy Haas. "George Grosz." In *Gesicht Einer Epoche*, pp. 42-44. Munich: A. Langen, 1962.

4403. Dos Passos, John. "Grosz Comes to America." *Esquire.* September 1936, pp. 105, 128, 131.

4404. Dückers, Alexander. *George Grosz. Das Druckgraphische Werk.* Frankfurt: Propyläen Verlag, 1979.

4405. Durus [Alfred Kemeny]. "Künstler des Proletariats (17): George Grosz." *Eulenspiegel.* July 1931, p. 111.

4406. Ehrenburg, Ilja. "George Grosz." *Blätter der Reinhardt-Bühnen.* No. 6, 1929/1930, pp. 9-10. Reprinted from Ehrenburg. *Visum der Zeit.* Leipzig: Paul List Verlag, 1929/1930.

4407. Einstein, Carl. "George Grosz." *Die Kunst der 20. Jahrhunderts.* 2d Ed. Propyläen-Kunstgeschichte, Vol. 16. Berlin: Propyläen Verlag, 1926, pp. 149-153; 2nd Ed., 1928, pp. 162-167; 3rd Ed., 1931, pp. 176-181.

4408. Fels, Florent. "George Grosz." In *Propos d'Artistes*, pp. 75-84. Paris: La Renaissance du Livre, 1925.

4409. Fels, Florent. "Georges Grosz." *Montparnesse.* April 1923, pp. 2-3.

4410. Fels, Florent. "Interviews im Atelier: Grosz." *Die Kustauktion.* August 10, 1930, p. 7; August 17, 1930, p. 9.

4411. Fels, Florent. "Propos d'Artistes: George Grosz." *Les Nouvelles Littéraires.* April 12, 1924, p. 5.

4412. Finkenberg, Liora. "George Grosz' Satiric Work During the Weimar Period 1917-1933." M.A. Thesis, Tel Aviv University, n.d. (Hebrew).

4413. Fischer, Lothar. *George Grosz in Selbstzeugnissen und Biddokumenten.* Reinbek bei Hamburg: Rowohlt Taschenbuch Verlag GmbH, 1976, 1983, 1989.

4414. Flavell, M. Kay. *George Grosz: A Biography.* New Haven and London: Yale University Press, 1988.

4415. Flavell, M. Kay. "*Über Alles die Liebe:* Food, Sex, and Money in the Work of George Grosz." *Journal of European Studies.* 13:51 (1983), pp. 268-288.

4416. Frank, Volker. "Auf der Suche Nach dem Kleinen Ja. Zur Bewertung des Schaffens von George Grosz in den USA von 1932 bis 1959." *Bildende Kunst.* 34:11 (1987), pp. 499-501.

4417. Frei, Bruno. "George Grosz, *Ecce Homo* (Malik Verlag)." *Der Neue Merkur.* Bücher-Anzeiger. December 1922, p. 1.

4418. Friedlaender, Salomo. *Georg Grosz von Mynona.* Rudolf Kaemmerer Verlag, 1922. 96 pp.

4419. Fuchs, Eduard. "George Grosz." In *Die Grossen Meister der Erotik: Ein Beitrag zum Problem des Schöpferischen in der Kunst,* pp. 183-185. Munich: Albert Langen Verlag, 1930.

4420. Gelburd, Gail. *George Grosz: An Artist for 1984.* Hempstead, New York: Emily Lowe Gallery, Hofstra University, 1984.

4421. *George Grosz.* Berlin: Staatliche Museen, Kupferstickkabinett und Sammlung der Zeichnungen, Grosz Kabinett in der Nationalgalerie, GDR, 1977. (Hans Ebert. "Über George Grosz und Sein Frühes Graphisches Werk").

4422. *George Grosz: "Ade, Witboi."* Intro. by Walther G. Oschilweski. Berlin-Grunewald: Arani Verlags GmbH, 1955.

4423. *George Grosz: An Autobiography.* Trans. by Nora Hodges. An Imago Imprint ed. New York: Macmillan Publishing Co., 1983. Reprinted: Milan: SugarCo Edizioni, 1984.

4424. *George Grosz: "A Piece of My World in a World Without Peace, 1914-1946."* New York: Associated American Artists Galleries, October 1946.

4425. *George Grosz: Arbeiten auf Papier/Otto Dix Arbeiten auf Papier.* Hamburg, Madrid, Valencia: Thomas Levy, 1988-1989.

4426. *George Grosz. Deutschland über Alles.* Intro. by Ulrich Becher. Rome: Editori Riuniti, 1963.

4427. *George Grosz. Maler: Leben, Werk und Ihre Zeit*. No. 92. Hamburg: Marshall Cavendish Ltd., 1987.

4428. *George Grosz 1893-1959: Aquarelle Zeichnungen*. Essays by Eila Kokkinen. Munich: Staatliche Graphische Sammlung; Düsseldorf: Städtische Kunsthalle, 1971.

4429. "George Grosz." *A S. Fine Arts Magazine* (Tokyo). 1:1 (1925), pp. 1-30.

4430. "George Grosz." *Current Biography*. April 1942, pp. 19-21.

4431. "George Grosz." *Das Kunstblatt*. October 1925, p. 320.

4432. "George Grosz." *Heute: Eine Illustrierte Zeitschrift*. No. 28, 1927, pp. 18ff.

4433. "George Grosz." *Kunst und Künstler*. 25 (1927), p. 267.

4434. "George Grosz Verurteilt." *Berliner Tageblatt*. February 17, 1924.

4435. "George Grosz Wird Vernommen. Aus dem Stenographischen Protokoll des Gotteslästerungsprozesses." *Das Tagebuch*. December 22, 1928, pp. 2210-2215.

4436. Gettings, Frank. *George Grosz*. Washington, D.C.: Hirshhorn Museum, 1978.

4437. G.G.L. [Gertrude Alexander]. "Herrn John Heartfield und George Grosz." *Die Rote Fahne*. June 9, 1920. Reprinted: Walter Fähnders and Martin Rector, ed. *Literatur im Klassenkampf*, pp. 50-60, 93-95. Munich: 1971.

4438. Goergen, Jeanpaul. "Propaganda Sollte den Gegner Lächerlich Machen: DADA-Filme für den Krieg—Verschollene Arbeiten von George Grosz und John Heartfield." *Der Tagesspiegel*. December 2, 1900.

4439. Goll, Ivan. *"George Grosz."* "900" *Cahiers d'Italie et d'Europe*. Summer 1927, pp. 125-135. Reprinted: *Living Age*. April 1928, pp. 635-638.

4440. Goll, Ivan. "Pittori Europei: George Grosz." *Oggi e Domani*. December 8, 1930, p. 5.

4441. "Gotteslästerung: Der Fall Grosz and Der Fall Hasenclever." *Berichte zur Kultur und Zeitgeschicht*. No. 49-50, 1930.

4442. Grafly, Dorothy. "George Grosz: Painter and Prophet." *American Artist*. March 1949, pp. 20-25, 64-65.

4443. Grohmann, Will. "George Grosz." In *Neue Deutsche Biographie*, pp. 161-162. Berlin: Duncker und Humbolt, 1966.

4444. Grossman, Stefan. "George Grosz." *Das Tagebuch*. November 25, 1922, pp. 1652-1653.

4445. Grosz, George. *Abrechnung Folgt! 57 Politische Zeichnungen*. Kleine Revolutionäre Bibliothek. Vol. 10. Berlin: Malik Verlag, April 1923.

4446. Grosz, George. *A Little Yes and a Big No, the Autobiography of George Grosz*. New York: The Dial Press, 1946; London and New York: Allison and Busby, 1982. Reprinted: *Un Piccolo Si e Un Grande No*. Milan: Longanesi and Co., 1948. 2nd Ed., 1975.

4447. Grosz, George. *Das Neue Gesicht der Herrschenden Klasse*. Berlin: Der Malik Verlag, 1930.

4448. Grosz, George. *The Day of Reckoning*. London: Allison and Busby, 1984. 65 pp. (Cartoons of Soviet Union published in Germany in 1923).

4449. Grosz, George. *The Face of the Ruling Class*. London: Allison and Busby, 1984. 65 pp. (Published in Germany in 1921; satirical look at Weimer Republic).

4450. Grosz, George. *Love Above All*. New York: Allison and Busby, 1985. 77 pp.

4451. Grosz, George. "Moja Žizn [My life]." *Prožektor* (Moscow). April 1, 1928, pp. 16-18. Uwe Schneede, ed. *Die Zwanziger Jahre: Manifeste und Dokumente Deutscher Künstler*, p. 153. Cologne: DuMont Buchverlag, 1979.

4452. Grosz, George. *Mysli i Tvorchestvo* (Thoughts and Life). Ed. by L. Reingardt. Moscow: Progress, 1975.

4453. Grosz, George. "Self-Portrait of the Artist." *Americana*. 1932, pp. 22-23.

4454. Grosz, George. *Über Alles die Liebe*. Berlin: Breno Cassirer Verlag, 1930.

4455. Grosz, George, John Heartfield, and Wieland Herzfelde. *Art Is in Danger!* Art on the Line, 5. Trans. by Paul Gorrell. Willimantic, Connecticut: Curbstone Press, 1987.

4456. "Grosz: Ein Grosses Nein." *Der Spiegel*. June 30, 1954, pp. 26-30.

4457. Hartleb, Renate, ed. *George Grosz. Eintrittsbillett zu Meiner Gehirnzirkus: Erinnerungen, Schriften, Briefe*. Trans. by Herbert Knust and Renate di Pol. Leipzig: Gustav Kiepenheuer Verlag, 1989.

4458. Hecht, Ben. "About Grosz." In *Letters from Bohemia*, pp. 133-154. Garden City, New York: Doubleday, 1964.

4459. Heiberg, Edvard, ed. "George Grosz." In *Social Kunst*, No. 9. Copenhagen and Oslo: Mondes Forlag, 1932.

4460. Herrmann-Neisse, Max. "George Grosz." *Die Neue Bücherschau*. Ser. 2, 4, No. 2, 1923, pp. 67-70.

4461. Herrmann-Neisse, Max. "George Grosz—Ecce Homo." In *Das Querschnittbuch, 1923*, p. 166. Frankfurt: 1923.

4462. Herzfelde, Wieland. "George Grosz—Einst und Heute." *Austro-American Tribune*. February 1945, pp. 9-10.

4463. Herzfelde, Wieland. "George Grosz, John Heartfield und die Zwanziger Jahre." *Die Weltbühne*. July 1, 1964, pp. 846-849.

4464. Herzfelde, Wieland. "Isst George Grosz Wirklich von Goldenen Tellern?" *Aufbau*. 6:1 (1950), pp. 86-88.

4465. Herzfelde, Wieland. "John Heartfield und George Grosz: Zum 75. Geburtstag Meines Bruders." *Die Weltbühne*. June 15, 1966, pp. 745-749.

4466. Herzfelde, Wieland and Hans Marquardt, ed. *Pass Auf! Hier Kommt Grosz: Bilder, Rhythmen und Gesänge 1915-1918*. Leipzig: Verlag Philipp Reclam jun., 1981.

4467. Hess, Hans. *George Grosz*. New York: Macmillan and Studio Vista, 1974. Reprinted: Dresden: VEB Verlag der Kunst, 1982; New Haven, Connecticut: Yale University Press, 1985.

4468. Hielscher, Pieter. "George Grosz in der Turnhalle. Zum Politischen Wandbild in der Weimarer Republik." In *Wem Gehört die Welt: Kunst und Gesellschaft in der Weimarer Republik*, pp. 268-279. Berlin: Neue Gesellschaft für bildende Kunst, 1977.

4469. Hofbauer, Imre, ed. *George Grosz*. Intro. by John Dos Passos. London: Nicholson and Watson, 1948. 103 pp.

4470. Hoffman, Edith. "Scourge of a Tumbling World." *Apollo*. June 1963, pp. 486-491.

4471. Hofmann, Herbert. "Auseinandersetzung mit George Grosz." *Deutsche Kunst und Dekoration*. March 1931, pp. 364-368.

4472. Horst, Jähner. "Grosz Contra Grosz." *Bildende Kunst* (Dresden). 6 (1955), pp. 453, 484-486.

4473. Huder, Walter. "À Propos de George Grosz et de l'Exposition des Archives du Maître." *Gazette des Beaux-Arts*. November 1981, pp. 185-190.

4474. Huder, Walter and Karl Riha, ed. *George Grosz: New York*. Siegen: GFR Machwerk, 1985.

4475. Huelsenbeck, Richard. "Erinnerung an George Grosz." *Neue Zürcher Zeitung*. July 1959. Reprinted: *Phantastische Gebete*, pp. 84-90. Zurich: 1960.

4476. Hütt, Wolfgang. "Die 'Gotteslästerung' des George Grosz." *Bildende Kunst*. 33:8 (1985), pp. 362-364.

4477. Hütt, Wolfgang. "Hintergrund: Gewalt Gegen Kunst und Künstler 1900-1933." *Bildende Kunst, Kunstwissenschaftliche Beiträge*. No. 12, 1979, pp. 6-12.

4478. Kállai, Ernst. "George Grosz." *MA*. July 1924. Reprinted: Kállai. *Vision und Formgesetz: Aufsätze über Kunst und Künstler von 1921 bis 1933*, pp. 55-61. Leipzig and Weimar: Gustav Kiepenheuer Verlag, 1986.

4479. Kane, Martin. *Weimar Germany and the Limits of Political Art: A Study of the Work of George Grosz and Ernst Toller*. Fife, Scotland: Hutton Press, 1987.

4480. Kane, Martin. "The Art and Commitment of George Grosz." *Twentieth Century Studies*. 13-14, 1975, pp. 110-128.

4481. Kane, Martin. "George Grosz: Constructivism Parodied." In *New Studies in Dada: Essays and Documents*, Ed. by Richard Sheppard. Driffield: Hutton Press, 1981.

4482. Kane, Martin. "George Grosz und die Politisierung des Berliner Dada." In *Sinn aus Unsinn: Dada International*, Ed. by Wolfgang Paulsen and Helmut G. Hermann. Berne: Francke, 1982.

4483. Kein, Walter. "A German Caricaturist." *Nation*. February 11, 1931, p. 158.

4484. Kleinfelder, Karen L. "Portrait of the Artist as a Young Man: George Grosz's 'The Lovesick One.'" *Rutgers Art Review*. January 1981, pp. 70-86.

4485. Knauf, Erich. "In der Feuerlinie: George Grosz." *Empörung und Gestaltung. Künstler-Profile von Daumier bis Kollwitz*, pp. 175-184. Berlin: Büchergilde Gutenberg, 1928.

4486. Knoertzer, Cécile. "Livres Nouveaux: Le Dernier Ouvrage de George Grosz." *La Revue Rhenane*. March 1930, pp. 38-40.

4487. Knust, Herbert, ed. *George Grosz: Briefe 1913-1959*. Reinbek bei Hamburg: Rowohlt Verlag GmbH, 1979.

4488. Knust, Herbert. "Exilgespräche: Das Grosz-Archiv als Fundgrube." *Jahrbuch für Internationale Germanistik*. 5, 1979, pp. 112-121.

4489. Knust, Herbert. "George Grosz: Literature and Caricature." *Comparative Literature Studies*. September 1975, pp. 218-247.

4490. Knust, Herbert. "Tucholsky and Grosz: Challenges and Limits of Satire." *Schatzkammer der Deutschen Sprachlehre, Dichtung und Geschichte.* Spring 1988, pp. 60-91.

4491. Kramer, Hilton. "Editorial: The Death of George Grosz." *Arts.* September 1959, p. 13.

4492. Kramer, Hilton. "The Threepenny Artist." *The Reporter.* October 24, 1963, pp. 57-60.

4493. Kusak, Alexej. *George Grosz.* Prague: Státní Nakladatelstvi Krásné Literatury A Umeni, 1965.

4494. Landau, Rom. "George Grosz." *Arts.* December 1927, pp. 295-304.

4495. Lang, Lothar, ed. *George Grosz. Welt der Kunst.* Berlin: Henschelverlag, 1966.

4496. Lang, Lothar, ed. *George Grosz.* Klassiker der Karikatur, 19. Berlin: Eulenspiegel Verlag, 1979.

4497. Lang, Lothar. "Ein Künstler, der den Weg Verfehlte. Gedanken über den Abstieg des Grossen Talents Georg Grosz." *Bildende Kunst,* 11, 1958, pp. 768-771.

4498. Lang, Lothar. "George Grosz Bibliographie." *Marginalien. Zeitschrift für Buchkunst und Bibliophilie, Pirckheimer Gesellschaft.* July 1968, pp. 1-42.

4499. Lasker-Schüler, Else. "Georg Grosz." *Neue Jugend.* August 1916, p. 154.

4500. Lewis, Beth I. *George Grosz: Art and Politics in the Weimar Republic.* Madison, Wisconsin: University of Wisconsin Press, 1971. Reprinted: Milan: Edizioni di Comunità, 1977; Princeton, New Jersey: Princeton University Press, 1991. 342 pp.

4501. Lewis, Beth I. *Grosz/Heartfield: The Artist as Social Critic.* Essays by Sidney Simon and Beth Irwin Lewis. Minneapolis, Minnesota: University Gallery, University of Minnesota, 1980.

4502. Lourie, R. "When To Leave the Country: A Study of George Grosz." *Dissent.* 19:3 (1972), pp. 507-516.

4503. Lowell, Robert. "The Muses of George Grosz." In *Notebook, 1967-1968.* New York: Farrar, Straus and Giroux, 1969.

4504. MacOrlan, Pierre. "George Grosz." *Der Querschnitt.* March-April 1925, pp. 264-265.

4505. MacOrlan, Pierre. "Le Jour—la Nuit: George Grosz." *Paris-Journal.* April 11, 1924, p. 1.

4506. Marcuse, Ludwig. "Grosz und die Beschimpfung Heiliger Gefühle." *Die Weltbühne*. 1930, pp. 914-916.

4507. Mehring, Walter. "George Grosz." *Blätter der Deutschen Theater*. 7:6 (1920-1921), p. 8.

4508. Mehring, Walter. "Gott Contra Grosz." *Das Tagebuch*. April 14, 1928, pp. 621-623.

4509. Mehring, Walter. "Porträt George Grosz." *Das Tagebuch*. February 12, 1927, pp. 276-277.

4510. Melville, Robert and Roger Law. "The Bastard from Berlin." *New York Sunday Times Magazine*. November 4, 1973, pp. 58-72.

4511. Miller, Henry. "Man in the Zoo: George Grosz' *Ecce Homo*." *Evergreen Review*. April 1966, pp. 30-39.

4512. Mollino, Carlo. *36 Disegni di George Grosz*. Turin: Orma, 1945.

4513. Murayama, Tomoyoshi. *Grosz: Social Satire*. Tokyo: Iwasaki Art Co., 1969. 4th Ed., 1976.

4514. Mynona [Salomo Friedländer]. *George Grosz*. Künstler der Gegenwart, Vol. 3. Dresden: Rudolf Kaemmerer Verlag, 1922. 66 pp. Reprinted: Frankfurt: Makol Verlag, n.d.

4515. Naumann, Uwe and Michael Töteberg. "Zanks for your Friendship und für die Kopfhaltung: Ulrich Becher und Seine Freundschaft mit George Grosz." *Exilforschung: Ein Internationales Jahrbuch*. 5 (1987), pp. 150-169.

4516. Naumann, Uwe and Michael Töteberg, ed. *Ulrich Becher/George Grosz: Flaschenpost. Geschichte Einer Freundschaft*. Basel: Lenos Verlag, 1989.

4517. Neugebauer, Rosamunde. "George Grosz und Sein Verhältnis zu Militarismus und Krieg." In *Pazifismus Zwischen den Weltkriegen. Deutsche Schriftsteller und Künstler Gegen Krieg und Militarismus 1918-1933*, edited by Dietrich Harth, D. Schubert, and R.M. Schmidt, pp. 147-162. Heidelberg: 1985.

4518. Neugebauer, Rosamunde. "Was Will, Kann und Darf Satirische Kunst? Die Mappen 'Gott Mit uns,' 'Ecce Homo' und 'Hintergrund' von George Grosz als Beispiel Umstrittener Bildsatire." M.A. Thesis, Ruprecht-Karls-Universität, Heidelberg, 1986.

4519. Niehaus, Kaspar. "Graphisch Werk Door George Grosz." *De Telegraaf*. October 13, 1923, p. 9.

4520. Oeller, Adam C. "Karikatur und Sozialkritik bei George Grosz." In *Beiträge zur Abstrakt-Konkreten und Sozialkritischen Kunst der Zwanziger Jahre*, pp. 50-58. Bonn: 1972.

4521. Panter, Peter (Kurt Tucholsky). "George Grosz in Paris." *Dame*. May 1925, p. 5.

4522. Petermann, Erwin. "Das War Verfemte Kunst: IV. George Grosz." *Aussaat*. 1:3 (1946), pp. 20-24.

4523. Platschek, Hans. "Grosz Oder das Doppelspiel der Satire." *Das Kunstwerk*. June 1978, pp. 30-33.

4524. Pozzati, Concetto. *Dal Suicidio di Grosz*. Bologna: Galleria de' Foscherari, 1972.

4525. Procurator (Robert M.W. Kempner). "Gotteslästerung und Kirchenbeschimpfung von Links und Rechts: Der Fall George Grosz." *Die Justiz*. July 1931, pp. 552-557.

4526. Psychnowskaja, S. "Plakate von Georg Grosz in Moskau." *Bildende Kunst*. 33:8 (1985), pp. 365-366.

4527. Ray, Manuel. *George Grosz*. Paris: Les Éditions Crés et Cie, 1927.

4528. Ray, Marcel. "George Grosz." *Les Cahiers d'Aujourd'hui*. November 1920, pp. 26-33.

4529. "Rebellion Against National Socialism: Dix and Grosz." *Mizui* (Tokyo). 8:811 (1972).

4530. Reimann, Hans. "Monumenta Germaniae: 4. George Grosz." *Das Tagebuch*. August 4, 1923, pp. 1114-1117.

4531. René-Jean. "Le Dessinateur George Grosz." *Comoedia*. September 22, 1927.

4532. Riha, Karl, ed. *George Grosz: Skizzenbuch 1917*. Siegen: Verlag Affholderbach and Strohmann, 1987.

4533. Roditi, Eduard. "George Grosz: An Embittered Romantic." *Arts Magazine*. September 1963, pp. 18-23.

4534. Rothe, Hans. "George Grosz, *Der Grosse Zeitvertreib*." *Der Querschnitt*. January 1933, p. 75.

4535. Sabarsky, Serge. *George Grosz: The Berlin Years*. New York: Rizzoli International Publications, Inc., 1985. Reprinted: Milan: Palazzo Reale, 1986; Vienna: Museum Moderner Kunst, 1986; Berlin: Staatliche Kunsthalle, 1987; Hanover: Kestner Gesellschaft, 1988.

4536. Sahl, Hans, ed. *George Grosz: Heimatliche Gestalten*. Frankfurt: Fischer Bücherei KG., 1966.

4537. Salmony, Alfred. "George Grosz." *Das Kunstblatt*. April 1920, pp. 97-104.

4538. Salpeter, Harry. "Caricature According to Grosz: The Leer of Bitter Faces from Across the Sea." *Ringmaster, the World in Caricature*. July-August 1936, p. 435.

4539. Sándor, Láncz. *George Grosz*. Budapest: Corvina Kiadó, 1971.

4540. Sauvage, Léo. "George Grosz en Amérique." *Preuves*. August 1961, pp. 43-51.

4541. Scheffler, Karl. "Der Künstler als Journalist: George Grosz." *Kunst und Künstler*. 24 (1926), pp. 354-359.

4542. Scheffler, Karl. "George Grosz." *Kunst und Künstler*. 22 (1924), pp. 182-186.

4543. Scheffler, Karl. "George Grosz: Ausstellung von Zeichnungen und Aquarellen im Verlag Bruno Cassirer." *Kunst und Künstler*. 27 (1929), pp. 269-272.

4544. Schlichter, Rudolf. "George Grosz." *Die Kunst und Das Schöne Heim*. September 1949, pp. 221-222.

4545. Schmidt, Paul F. "George Grosz." *Kunst der Zeit*. January 1930, pp. 81-85.

4546. Schmidt, Paul F. "Georg Grosz." *Wiadomoschi Literackie* (Warsaw). April 21, 1929, p. 2.

4547. Schneede, Uwe M. *George Grosz: Der Künstler in Seiner Gesellschaft*. Cologne: Verlag M. DuMont Schauberg, 1975. 2nd Ed. 1977. 216 pp. Reprinted: Woodbury, New York and London: Barrons, 1985.

4548. Schneede, Uwe M. *George Grosz: Leben und Werk*. Stuttgart: Verlag Gerd Hatje, 1975. Reprinted: Milan: Gabriele Mazzota Editore, 1977; Paris: Librairie François Maspero, 1979; New York: Universe, 1979.

4549. Schneede, Uwe M., ed. *George Grosz: Die Welt Ist Ein Lunapark*. Gütersloh: Bertelsmann Reinhard Mohn OHG, 1977.

4550. Schniewind, Carl O. "Review of *George Grosz Drawings*." *Magazine of Art*. April 1954, pp. 154-156.

4551. Schreiner, Helmuth. "Die Hintergrunde des Grosz-Prozesses." *Zeitwende*. 7:1 (1931), pp. 193-206.

4552. S'edin, V. *George Grosz*. Moscow-Leningrad: Ogiz-Izogiz, 1931.

4553. "Seidenschnur Kämpft Gegen George Grosz." *Das Forum*. July 1923, pp. 97-100.

4554. Shapiro, Harriet. "Acid: The Morality of a German Artist—George Grosz." *Intellectual Digest*. March 1973, pp. 69-71.

4555. Sieburg, Friedrich. "Galerie George Grosz." *Die Weltbühne*. December 27, 1923, pp. 668-669.

4556. Simons, Hi. "George Grosz, Artist-Communist." *The Liberator*. July 1922, pp. 28-29.

4557. Tavolato, Italo. *George Grosz*. Rome: Éditions de Valori Plastici, 1924. 9 pp.

4558. Tavolato, Italo. "George Grosz." *Amauta* (Lima). March 1927, pp. 21-23.

4559. Theissing, Heinrich. "George Grosz, die Morde und das Groteske." In *Festschrift für Eduard Trier*, edited by Justus Mueller-Hofstede and Werner Speis, pp. 269-284. Berlin: Gebrüder Mann Verlag, 1981.

4560. Tiljak, Duro. "George Grosz." *Knjizevnik, Hrvatski Knjizevni Mjesecnik* (Zagreb). May 1932, pp. 161-164.

4561. Torres, Domingo Lópes. "Arte Social: George Grosz." *Garera de Arte*. February 1932, p. 2.

4562. Tower, Beeke S. *Envisioning America: Prints, Drawings, and Photographs by George Grosz and his Contemporaries, 1915-1933*. Essay by John Czaplicka. Cambridge, Massachusetts: Harvard University, Busch-Reisinger Museum, 1990.

4563. "Über die Berufsverhandlung in dem George Grosz Prozess." *Die Menschenrechte*. April 20, 1929, pp. 8-11.

4564. "Un Satirique Allemand: George Grosz." *Le Rouge et le Noir* (Brussels). April 27, 1932, p. 3.

4565. "Unterhaltung Zwischen Ohnesorge und George Grosz. Ein Stenographisches Protokoll." *Das Tagebuch*. February 23, 1924, pp. 240-248.

4566. Uschakow, Alexander. "Majakowski und Grosz—Zwei Schicksale." *Sinn und Form*. 20:6 (1968), pp. 1460-1473. Reprinted: *Vladimir Mayakowsky: Innovator*, pp. 181-198. Moscow: Progress Publishers, 1976.

4567. von Waldegg, Joachim. "George Grosz 'Leichenbegängnis. Widmung an Oskar Panizza': Gesellschaftskritische Allegorie als Selbstprojektion." *Pantheon*. 44 (1986), pp. 111-125.

4568. Welblund, Aage. "Samfundsrevseren Georg Grosz." *Social Demokraten*. December 5, 1924.

4569. Werner, Alfred. "Ecce Homo: George Grosz." *American-German Review.* June-July 1967, pp. 33-37.

4570. Wessel, Wilhelm. "Albrecht Dürer—George Grosz? Natürliches und Artfremdes in der Malerei." *Die HJ.* November 16, 1933, p. 4.

4571. West, Richard. "George Grosz. Figures for Yvan Goll's Methusalem." *Bulletin of the Cleveland Museum of Art.* April 1968, pp. 90-94.

4572. Westheim, Paul. "Der Zeichner George Grosz." In *Für und Wider. Kritische Anmerkungen zur Kunst der Gegenwart*, pp. 159-171. Potsdam: Gustav Kiepenheuer Verlag, 1923. Reprinted: *Broom: International Magazine of the Arts* (Berlin). February 1923, pp. 163-169; *Dichtung und Welt* (Beilage zur *Prager Presse*). April 1923; *Die Glocke.* May 14, 1923, pp. 178-184.

4573. Westheim, Paul. "Erinnerungen an George Grosz." *Die Weltkunst.* November 15, 1962, pp. 16-17.

4574. Westheim, Paul. "Zille-Grosz: Der Berliner Humor." In *Helden und Abenteurer. Welt und Leben der Künstler*, pp. 160-166. Berlin: Verlag Hermann Reckendorf, 1931.

4575. Wolfradt, Willi. *George Grosz.* Junge Kunst. Vol 21. Leipzig: Klinkhardt and Biermann Verlag, 1921.

4576. Wolfradt, Willi. "George Grosz-Ausstellung." *Die Literarische Welt.* 3:2 (1927), p. 7.

4577. Wolfradt, Willi. "George Grosz: Der Abenteurer." *Der Ararat.* January 1920, pp. 3-5. (Entire number reissued April/May 1920 as *Der Ararat Erstes Sonderheft, George Grosz Katalog*).

4578. Wrobel, Ignaz (Kurt Tucholsky). "Der Kleine Gessler und der Grosse Grosz." *Freiheit.* October 24, 1920. Reprinted: Kurt Tucholsky. *Gesammelte Werke*, edited by Mary Gerold-Tucholsky and Fritz J. Raddatz. 3 Vols. Vol 1, pp. 751-752. Reinbek bei Hamburg: 1960-1961.

4579. Wrobel, Ignaz (Kurt Tucholsky). "Fratzen von Grosz." *Die Weltbühne.* August 18, 1921, p. 184.

4580. Wrobel, Ignaz (Kurt Tucholsky). "George Grosz als Schriftsteller." *Die Weltbühne.* October 13, 1925, p. 583.

Holtz, Karl

4581. Holtz, Karl. *Acht Bunte Blätter.* Berlin: Eulenspiegel-Verlag, 1977.

4582. Holtz, Karl. *Aus der Holtz-Kiste.* Berlin: Eulenspiegel-Verlag, 1971.

4583. Holtz, Karl. *Holtzkiste.* Berlin: Eulenspiegel-Verlag, 1964.

4584. *Klassiker der Karikatur: No. 21. Karl Holtz.* Berlin: Eulenspiegel-Verlag, 1983.

Hosemann, Theodor

4585. Becker, Ingeborg. "Theodor Hosemann (1807-1875): Ansichten des Berliner Biedermeier." Ph.D. dissertation, Freie Universität Berlin, 1981.

4586. Becker, Ingeborg, ed. *Theodor Hosemann: Illustrator-Graphiker-Maler des Berliner Biedermeier.* Exhibition catalogue, Ausstellung der Staatsbibliothek Preußischer Kulturbesitz mit Beständen der Sammlung Wilfried Göpel, June 1, July 23, 1983. Wiesbaden: Dr. Ludwig Reichert, 1983.

4587. Brieger, Lothar. *Theodor Hosemann: Der Maler des Berliner Volkes.* Munich: Delphin, 1920.

4588. Brieger, Lothar. *Theodor Hosemann: Ein Altmeister Berliner Malerei.* Munich: Delphin, 1920.

4589. Hosemann, Theodor. *Berliner Theater um 1814.* Ed. by W. Klara and R. Badenhausen. Berlin: n.p., 1937.

4590. Hosemann, Theodor. *Druckgraphische Arbeiten von Theodor Hosemann.* Ed. by Wolfram Geister. West Berlin: Haus am Lützowplatz, 1975.

4591. Hosemann, Theodor. *Herr Fischer auf dem Vereinigten Landtage.* 4 Vols. Berlin: C. Reimarus (Gropius), 1847.

4592. *Klassiker der Karikatur: No. 9. Theodor Hosemann.* Berlin: Eulenspiegel-Verlag, 1973.

4593. Knüppel, Juttalis. "Theodor Hosemann, der Maler und Graphiker von Alt-Berlin." *Berliner Heimat.* 1958, pp. 120-127.

4594. Ludwig, Hans, ed. *Theodor Hosemann.* West Berlin: Stapp, 1980.

4595. Mader, Claus P. "Theodor Hosemann zum Gedenken." *Mitteilungen des Vereins für die Geschichte Berlins.* 71 (1975), pp. 81-90.

4596. Weinitz, Franz. "Theodor Hosemann: Eine Kunstgeschichtliche Studie zur Erinnerung an die Neunzigste Wiederkehr des Tages Seiner Geburt." *Schriften des Vereins für die Geschichte Berlins.* 34 (1897), pp. 1-21.

4597. Weinitz, Franz. "Theodor Hosemann Thätigkeit und Bedeutung für den Berliner Verlagsbuchhandel." In *Beiträge zur Kulturgeschichte von Berlin*, edited by Otto Mühlbrecht. Berlin: Korporation der Berliner Buchhändler, 1898.

4598. Winkel, G.G. "Theodor Hosemann and Louis Schneider." 2 parts. *Mittheilungen des Vereins für die Geschichte Berlins*. 15 (1898), pp. 51-54, 65-66.

4599. Wirth, Irmgard. *Theodor Hosemann: Maler und Illustrator im Alten Berlin*. West Berlin: Berlin Museum, 1967.

4600. Wirth, Irmgard, ed. "Unveröffentlichte Briefe von Theodor Hosemann und Eine Erwerbung des Berlin-Museums aus dem Jahre 1968." *Jahrbuch für Brandenburgische Landesgeschichte*. 19 (1968), pp. 45-50.

Immisch, Theo

4601. Immisch, Theo. *Alle Wetter*. Berlin: Eulenspiegel-Verlag, 1982.

4602. Immisch, Theo. *Auto-Biographie*. Berlin: Eulenspiegel-Verlag, 1977.

4603. Immisch, Theo. *Hinans in die Sterne*. Berlin: Eulenspiegel-Verlag, 1975.

4604. Immisch, Theo. *Wohin Mit dem Klavier*. Berlin: Eulenspiegel-Verlag, 1969.

Kellermann, Walter

4605. Förster, Gerhard. "'Rasputin.' Das Aktuelle Interview. Walter Kellermann (1)." *Comic Forum. Das Österreichische Fachmagazin für Comicliteratur*. 1:1 (1979), pp. 28-29.

4606. Förster, Gerhard. "'Rasputin.' Das Aktuelle Interview. Walter Kellermann. (2)." *Comic Forum. Das Österreichische Fachmagazin für Comicliteratur*. 1:2 (1979), pp. 46-50.

Klamann, Kurt

4607. Klamann, Kurt. *Acht Bunte Blätter*. Berlin: Eulenspiegel-Verlag, 1980.

4608. Klamann, Kurt. *Klamanns Puppentheater*. Berlin: Eulenspiegel-Verlag, 1961.

Kley, Heinrich

4609. "Heinrich Kley." *Kayhan Caricature*. April 1993.

4610. Kley, Heinrich. *The Drawings of Heinrich Kley*. 2 Vols. Borden Publishing Co., 1941-1947.

4611. Kley, Heinrich. *More Drawings by....* New York: Dover, 1962. 104 pp.

4612. Kley, Heinrich. *Skissenbuch*. Munich: Albert Langen Verlag, n.d.

Koch-Gotta, Fritz

4613. *Klassiker der Karikatur: No. 6. Fritz Koch-Gotta*. Berlin: Eulenspiegel-Verlag, 1971. 119 pp.

4614. Koch-Gotta, Wilhelm. *Gezeichnetes Leben*. Berlin: Eulenspiegel-Verlag, 1956.

Kollwitz, Käthe

4615. Bittner, Herbert. *Käthe Kollwitz Drawings*. New York: Thomas Yoseloff, 1959.

4616. Zigrosser, Carl. *Prints and Drawings of Käthe Kollwitz*. New York: Dover Publications, 1951.

Kretzschmar, Harald

4617. Kretzschmar, Harald. *Eulen-Leute*. Berlin: Eulenspiegel-Verlag, 1980.

4618. Kretzschmar, Harald. *Fabularium*. Berlin: Eulenspiegel-Verlag, 1973.

Langelotz, Gottfried

4619. Langelotz, Gottfried. *Die Banbude*. Berlin: Eulenspiegel-Verlag, 1981.

4620. Langelotz, Gottfried. *Kunststücke*. Berlin: Eulenspiegel-Verlag, 1971.

Lengren, Zbigniew

4621. Lengren, Zbigniew. *Acht Bunte Blätter*. Berlin: Eulenspiegel-Verlag, 1980.

4622. Lengren, Zbigniew. *Das Dicke Lengren-Buch*. Berlin: Eulenspiegel-Verlag, 1974.

4623. Lengren, Zbigniew. *Die Letzten Abenteuer des Professor Filutek*. Berlin: Eulenspiegel-Verlag, 1962.

4624. Lengren, Zbigniew. *100 Neue Soherze*. Berlin: Eulenspiegel-Verlag, 1967.

4625. Lengren, Zbigniew. *100x Professor Filutek*. Berlin: Eulenspiegel-Verlag, 1958.

4626. Lengren, Zbigniew. *Neues von Professor Filutek*. Berlin: Eulenspiegel-Verlag, 1959.

4627. Lengren, Zbigniew. *Professor Filutek und Sein Hund*. Berlin: Eulenspiegel-Verlag, 1966.

4628. Lengren, Zbigniew. *Ratgeber in Allen Lebenslagen*. Berlin: Eulenspiegel-Verlag, 1964.

Loriot (Viktor von Bülow)

4629. Guratzsch, Herwig. *Loriot*. Stuttgart: Hatje, 1988. 212 pp.

4630. Loriot. *Das Dicke Loriot-Buch*. Berlin: Eulenspiegel-Verlag, 1975.

4631. Loriot. *Loriots Praktische Winke*. Berlin: Eulenspiegel-Verlag, 1976.

4632. *Loriots Dramatische Werke*. Zurich: Diogenes, 1983. 320 pp.

Marcks, Marie

4633. Marcks, Marie. *Autobiographische Autzeichnungen*. Vol. 1: *Marie Es Brennt*. Munich: Frauenbuchvlg., n.d. 96 pp. Vol. 2: *Schwarzweiß und Bunt*. 1989. 104 pp.

4634. Marcks, Marie. *Darf Ich Zwischen Euch?* Zurich: Diogenes, 1982. 120 pp.

4635. Marcks, Marie. *Die Unfähigkeit zu Mauern. Gesammelte Behinderungen der Frau*. Munich: Frauenbuchvlg., n.d. 120 pp.

Oberländer, Adolf

4636. "He Makes Germany Laugh: Adolf Oberländer." *Literary Digest.* May 24, 1913, pp. 1179-1180.

4637. *Klassiker der Karikatur: No. 13. Adolf Oberländer.* Berlin: Eulenspiegel, 1975.

4638. Oberländer. (*Album*) Copenhagen: Ernst Bojesens, Kunstforlag, 1885.

4639. Oberländer, Adolf. *Die Tanzende Dampfmaschine.* Berlin: Eulenspiegel, 1981.

4640. Oberländer, Adolf. *Simplicissimus.* 10 Albums of Selected Drawings from *Simplicissimus.* Munich: Braun und Schneider, n.d.

Otto, Lothar

4641. Otto, Lothar. *Kindereien von 0-70.* Berlin: Eulenspiegel-Verlag, 1975.

4642. Otto, Lothar. *Popogei und Telefant.* Berlin: Eulenspiegel-Verlag, 1980.

Plauen, E.O. (Erich Ohser)

4643. "'I Was Drawing for Germany, Wasn't I?'" *Apropos.* No. 4, 1986, pp. 105-107.

4644. Ohser, Erich. *Vater und Sohn; 50 Lustige Streiche und Abenteuer, Gezeichnet von E.O. Plauen.* Berlin: Ullstein, 1935. Unpaginated.

4645. Plauen, E.O. *Vater und Sohn.* Berlin: Eulenspiegel-Verlag, 1965.

Rauwolf, Louis

4646. Rauwolf, Louis. *Heiter bis Wolkig, Strichweise Schaner.* Berlin: Eulenspiegel-Verlag, 1972.

4647. Rauwolf, Louis. *Witze Mit und Ohne Bart.* Berlin: Eulenspiegel-Verlag, 1960.

Reiche, Volker

4648. Engler-Kellermann, Michael. "Ein Gespräch Mit Volker Reiche." *Comic Forum. Das Magazin für Comicliteratur.* 7:28 (1985), pp. 46-51.

4649. Strzyz, Klaus. "Disney-Zeichner in Europa: (4) Interview mit Volker Reiche." *Comixene. Das Comicfachmagazin.* 8:35 (1981), pp. 48-52.

Sandberg, Herbert

4650. Lang, Lothar. *Herbert Sandberg.* Berlin: Henschel-Verlag, 1977. 212 pp.

4651. Sandberg, Herbert. *Acht Bunte Blätter.* Berlin: Eulenspiegel-Verlag, 1983.

4652. Sandberg, Herbert. *Mit Spitzer Feder.* Berlin: Eulenspiegel-Verlag, 1958.

4653. Sandberg, Herbert. *Sandbergs Satirische Zeitgeschichte.* Berlin: Eulenspiegel-Verlag, 1959.

Schadow, J. Gottfried

4654. Kaiser, K. *Gottfried Schadow als Karikaturist.* Dresden: 1955.

4655. *Klassiker der Karikatur: No. 23. Johann Gottfried Schadow.* Berlin: Eulenspiegel-Verlag, 1987.

Schmidt, Manfred

4656. Becker, Hartmut and Eckart Sackmann. "Interview mit Manfred Schmidt." *Comic Forum. Das Österreichische Fachmagazin für Comicliteratur.* 5:18 (1983), pp. 15-16.

4657. Otto, Ulrich and Axel Koberne. "'Nick Knatterton'—Ein Bundesdeutscher Comic-Strip der 50iger Jahre." *Germanistische Mitteilungen* (Brussels). 10, 1979, pp. 15-51.

4658. Sackmann, Eckart. "Manfred Schmidt—Ein Leben für den Strich." *Comic Forum. Das Österreichische Fachmagazin für Comicliteratur.* 5:18 (1983), pp. 17-20.

Scholz, Wilhelm

4659. Kossak, Ludwig E. *Die Berliner Kunstausstellung im Jahre 1846.* Illus. by Wilhelm Scholz. Berlin: A. Hofmann, 1846.

4660. Kossak, Ludwig E. *Ein Deputirter: Fliegendes Blatt für das Landtags-Album.* Illus. by Wilhelm Scholz. Potsdam: Otto Janke, 1847.

Schrader, Karl

4661. Schrader, Karl. *Acht Bunte Blätter.* Berlin: Eulenspiegel-Verlag, 1976.

4662. Schrader, Karl. *Das Dicke Schrader-Buch.* Berlin: Eulenspiegel-Verlag, 1980.

Schultheiss, Matthias

4663. Handloik, Volker. "Blut Ja—Werbung Nein... Ein Comiczeichner in Hamburg—Matthias Schultheiss." *ICOM INFO.* June 1992, pp. 48-49.

4664. Knigge, Andreas C. "'Mich Faszinieren vor Allem Balladen...' Interview mit Matthias Schultheiss." In *Comic-Jahrbuch 1986,* edited by Martin Compart and Andreas C. Knigge, pp. 77-96. Berlin: Ullstein GmbH, 1986.

Sommer, Manfred

4665. Tschernegg, Markus. "Manfred Sommer." *Comic-Forum. Das Magazin für Comicliteratur.* 7:28 (1985), pp. 26-30.

4666. Wiechmann, Peter and José Canovas. "Eine Reportage über Manfred Sommer Ist das Spiegelbild Seines Helden: Frank Cappa: 'Mut läßt Sich Nicht Befehlen!'" *Comic Forum. Das Österreichische Fachmagazin für Comicliteratur.* 4:16 (1982), pp. 43-48.

Trier, Walter

4667. *Klassiker der Karikatur: No. 4. Walter Trier.* Berlin: Eulenspiegel-Verlag, 1970.

4668. Trier, Walter. *Das Große Trier-Buch.* Berlin: Eulenspiegel-Verlag, 1974.

Zille, Heinrich

4669. *Klassiker der Karikatur: No. 18. Heinrich Zille.* Berlin: Eulenspiegel-Verlag, 1979.

4670. Zille, Heinrich. *Acht Bunte Blätter.* Berlin: Eulenspiegel-Verlag, 1974.

4671. Zille, Heinrich. *Das Dicke Zille-Buch.* Berlin: Eulenspiegel-Verlag, 1971.

4672. Zille, Heinrich. *Das Neue Zille-Buch.* Hanover: Fackelträger, 1988. 436 pp.

4673. Zille, Heinrich. *Sein Milljuh Auswhahl und Text von Werner Schumann.* Hanover: Fackelträger, Verlag, 1952.

4674. Zille, Heinrich. *Zille Sein Milljöh.* Hanover: Fackelträger, 1987. 192 pp.

CHARACTERS and TITLES

4675. "Abenteuer-Serie: Die Fledermaus Geht um." *Der Spiegel.* No. 16, 1966, p. 148.

4676. Atzert, Joachim. *Gewalt und Ordnung. Die Konstruktion der Gerechtigkeit am Beispiel der Comic-Serie BESSY.* Berlin: Volker Spiess, 1982.

4677. Baer, Reto and Joachim Kaps. "Chrigel Farner und Sein Debut-Album *Fliegenpilz.*" *Comic Info.* 1/1993, pp. 27-31.

4678. "Bambino-Bilderhefte." *Der Neue Vertrieb* (Flensburg). 5:106 (1953), p. 394.

4679. Breuer, Hajo. "Daemon: Der Blinde Koenig." *Spinne* (Frankfurt). No. 16, 1983.

4680. "Cisco Ging in den Ruhestand." *Hamburger Abendblatt.* June 10, 1969, p. 18.

4681. "Comic-Figur 'Tupko.'" *Westdeutsche Allgemeine Zeitung* (Essen). No. 69, 1972.

4682. "Comics-Ohne Macke." *Der Spiegel.* No. 44, 1970, p. 256.

4683. "Comic-Zeitschrift 'Tina.'" *Der Spiegel.* No. 24, 1967.

4684. "Cryptogam, der Kühle Bräutigam." *Hamburger Abendblatt.* August 9, 1968, p. 13.

4685. "Das Drachenbuch von W. Schmögner." *Die Welt der Literatur* (Hamburg). No. 21, 1969, p. 68.

4686. "Die Abenteuer des Juan Quinquin." *Der Spiegel.* No. 35, 1971, p. 122.

4687. "Die Abenteuer des Odysseus." *ICOM.* January 1993, p. 63.

4688. "Der Kleine Talisman Brachte Wirklich Glück." *Hamburger Morgenpost.* March 19, 1966.

4689. "Ein Gruß an Willi Wacker." *Offenbach-Post*. December 22, 1967.

4690. "Feminax und Walkürax." *ICOM*. October 1992, p. 60.

4691. *The Gestes of Mak and Morris*. Heidelberg: Winter, 1981. 64 pp.

4692. "Gnom von Gallien." *Der Spiegel*. No. 47, 1966, p. 154.

4693. "Hier Ist Alfred." *Hamburger Morgenpost*. September 21, 1970, p. 11.

4694. Kempkes, Wolfgang. "Wetterfrosch Willi." *Bulletin: Jugend + Literatur*. No. 6, 1970, p. 6.

4695. "Mini-Männchen Suchen Mini-Mädchen." *Funk-Uhr* (Hamburg). No. 29, 1969.

4696. Peterson, Dave. "Superman in Germany: The Man of Steel's Other Life." *Comics Buyer's Guide*. October 28, 1983, p. 20.

4697. "Quick und Quack." *Die Zeit*. No. 4, 1967.

4698. Schnurrer, Achim. "Jimmy das Gummipferd. Ein Plädoyer für die Phantasie." *Comixene. Das Comicfachmagazin*. 5:21 (1978), pp. 9-10, 12.

4699. "Sophie und Bruno im Lande des Atoms." *UNESCO-Kurier* (Cologne). 9:8 (1968), pp. 28-34.

4700. Stelly, Gisela. "Tick, Trick und Track Geben Anti-Unterricht." *Die Zeit*. April 25, 1969, p. 68.

4701. "Styx: Zym Jagt Dr. Fu." *Die Zeit*. November 10, 1967, p. 16.

4702. Van Belle, Anita. "Hans: un Futur Malléable." *Les Cahiers de la Bande Dessinée*. 70, 1986, pp. 28-29.

4703. Watzke, Oswald. "Wir Lesen Eine Funny Strip 'Der Kleine Wolf' und Einen Adventure Strip 'Supergoof' (4. Schuljahr)." In *Umgang mit Texten in der Primarstufe. Eine Einführung Anhand von Unterrichtsmodellen*, edited by Oswald Watzke *et al.*, pp. 205-222. Munich: List, 3 Überarbeitete und Erweiterte Auflage, 1979.

4704. "Witzbildchen." *ICOM*. January 1993, p. 63.

"Andy Morgan" ("Bernard Prince")

4705. Knigge, Andreas C. "Serie: Die Abenteurer: (1). Andy Morgan." *Comixene. Das Comicfachmagazin*. 7:29 (1980), pp. 20-25.

4706. Tschernegg, Markus. "Andy Morgan. Der Weltenbummler. Jugurth." *Comic Forum. Das Magazin für Comicliteratur.* 5:19 (1983), pp. 19-23.

"Die Abenteuer der Phoebe-Zeitgeist"

4707. Flemming, Hanns Th. "Phoebe Zeitgeist und die Folgen. Internationale Comics im Kunsthaus." *Die Welt* (Hamburg). July 2, 1971.

4708. Lefevre, Gaston. "Phoebe Zeit-Geist, Strictement pour Adultes." *Rantanplan.* No. 12, 1968, pp. 30-32.

4709. O'Donoghue, Michael and Frank Springer. *Die Abenteuer der Phoebe-Zeitgeist.* Hamburg: Konkret-Buchverlag, 1970.

4710. O'Donoghue, Michael and Frank Springer. *The Adventures of Phoebe Zeit-Geist.* Park Forest, Illinois: K. Pierce, 1986. 77 pp.

4711. Schöler, Franz. "Mischung aus Schneewittchen und Gesellschaftsbiene (Phoebe-Zeitgeist)." *Die Welt der Literatur* (Hamburg). No. 1, 1969, p. 7.

"Evarella"

4712. "Evarella Darf nie Mehr als drei Worte Sagen...." *Welt am Sonntag* (Hamburg). July 14, 1968, p. 34.

4713. "Evarella 68." *Hör Zu* (Hamburg). No. 52, 1968, p. 12.

4714. Rehder, Mathes. "Jenseits der Vierten Milchstraße. In Hamburg Ensteht: Grassmanns Comic-Strip-Film 'Evarella.'" *Hamburger Abendblatt.* July 27-28, 1968, p. 21.

4715. "Stern am Brüstchen (Evarella)." *Der Spiegel.* No. 49, 1968.

"Familie Feuerstein" (Flintstones)

4716. "Familientratsch-Familie Feuerstein." *Der Spiegel.* No. 36, 1971, p. 17.

4717. "Wiedersehen mit 'Familie Feuerstein.'" *Hör Zu.* No. 38, 1969, p. 147.

4718. "Yabba-Dabba-Doo!" *ICOM.* January 1993, p. 10.

4719. "Zeitschriften: Familie Feuerstein." *Der Spiegel.* No. 34, 1971, p. 82.

"Fix und Foxi"

4720. Kaps, Joachim. "Zeichnen für Fuxholzen. Ein Interview mit Fix und Foxi-Chefzeichner Helmut Murek." *Comic Info.* May-June 1993, pp. 48-49.

4721. Kauka, Rolf. "Fix und Foxi. Eine Qualitative Leserschaftsuntersuchung." Unveröffentlichte Untersuchung, Munich. 1965.

4722. Kauka, Rolf. "Fix und Foxi. Leseranalyse." Unveröffentlichte Untersuchung, Munich. 1967.

4723. Kauka, Rolf. "Fix und Foxi. Leserhaushalte und Deren Demographische Zusammensetzung." Unveröffentlichte Untersuchung, Munich. 1965.

4724. Kempkes, Wolfgang. "Comics: Nachträgliche Beinerkungen zur 'Fix und Foxi'—Weihnachtsausgabe 1969." *Bulletin: Jugend + Literatur.* No. 2, 1970, pp. 13-14.

4725. Köhler, Rosemarie. "Fix und Foxi Schaffen Es: Die Wiedervereinigung." *Blickpunkt.* No. 184/185, 1969, pp. 46-47.

4726. "Wie Fix und Foxi Millionäre Wurden." *Welt am Sonntag* (Hamburg). March 5, 1972.

4727. Zschocke, Fee. "Mit Fix und Foxi Gegen Micky Maus." *Der Stern.* No. 44, 1972, pp. 124-125, 127, 129, 131.

"Helene"

4728. Bohne, Friedrich, ed. *Die Fromme Helene: Faksimile der Handschrift.* Hanover: 1972.

4729. Cornioley, Hans. "Die Sexual-Symbolik in der Frommen Helene von Wilhelm Busch." *Die Psychanalytische Bewegung.* 1929. (Offprint in Wilhelm Busch Museum, Hanover).

4730. "Die Fromme Helen." *Der Stern.* No. 39, 1965.

4731. "Die Leibhaftige Helene." *Hamburger Morgenpost.* August 6, 1965.

"Max und Moritz"

4732. Busch, Wilhelm. *Max and Moritz.* New York: Dover, 1962. 216 pp.

4733. Schmidt, Karl. *Max and Maurice. A Story of Two Mischievous Boys in Seven Tricks.* Klagenfurt: Heyn, 1980. 58 pp.

4734. "So Wurden Max und Moritz Geboren." *Das Neue Blatt.* November 14, 1964.

"Mecki"

4735. Sackmann, Eckart. "Mecki. Die Abenteuer Eines Redaktionsigels." *Comixene. Das Comicfachmagazin.* 8:36 (1981), pp. 4-7.

4736. Sackmann, Eckart. *Mecki: Maskottchen und Mythos.* Hamburg: Comicplus +, Verlag Eckart Sackmann, 1984.

"Nick Knatterton"

4737. Schmidt, Manfred. "Meine 10 Jahre mit Nick Knatterton." *Quick.* 23:3 (1970), pp. 24-25.

4738. Schmidt, Manfred. *Nick Knatterton.* Oldenburg: Lappan, 1983. 192 pp.

"Perry Rhodan"

4739. Leiner, Friedrich. "Perry Rhodan—Eine Untersuchung über Wesen, Wirkung und Wert der Science-Fiction-Literatur." *Blätter für den Deutschlehrer* (Frankfurt). No. 3, 1968.

4740. "Perry Rhodan." *Hör Zu* (Hamburg). No. 12, 1969.

4741. "Perry Rhodan, der Groschenheld aus dem Weltall." Monitor, 1. Deutsches Fernsehen (ARD), February 24, 1969, Cologne.

4742. "Perry Rhodan-SOS Gefahr aus dem Weltraum." 1. Deutsches Fernsehen (ARD), October 16, 1971, Hamburg.

"Robinson"

4743. Aping, Norbert. "Die Abenteurer (3): Robinson." *Comixene. Das Comicfachmagazin.* 7:33 (1980), pp. 58-60.

4744. Herr, Alfred. "Robinson in Comic-Sicht." *Jugendschriften-Warte* (Frankfurt). 9:7/8 (1957), pp. 52-53.

4745. Mickethier, Knut. "Robinson und Robinsonaden in den Literarischen Medien—Nachahmung, Adaptation, Literarische Verwertung." In *Literatur in den Massenmedien—Demontage von Dichtung?*, edited by Friedrich Knilli, Knut Hickethier, and Wolf Dieter Lützen, pp. 61-88. Munich: Hanser, 1976.

"Schmutz und Schund"

4746. Becker, Walter. *Wie Schützen Wir Unsere Jugend vor Schmutz und Schund?* Gütersloh: Mohn-Verlag, 1959.

4747. Cordt, Willy K. "Bilderserienhefteunter die Lupe Genommen." *Unsere Schule.* 11, 1954, pp. 690-694.

4748. Dolle-Weinkauff, Bernd. "Die Wissenschaft von Schmutz und Schund. Jugendliteraturforschung und Comics in der Bundesrepublik." In *Comic-Jahrbuch 1986*, edited by Martin Compart and Andreas C. Knigge, pp. 97-106. Berlin: Ullstein GmbH, 1985.

4749. Fissen, Gebhard. "Schmutz und Schund." "Abend für Junge Hörer," Norddeutscher Rundfunk, 1. Hörfunkprogramm, September 4, 1966, Hamburg.

4750. Hesse, Kurt W. *Schmutz und Schund unter der Lupe*, pp. 21-23, Frankfurt: dipa-Verlag, 1955.

4751. Krüger, Anna. "Der Schmutz Geht—der Schund Bleibt." *Leben und Erziehen* (Aachen). 10, 1965, p. 20.

4752. Lange, Fritz. "Schmutz und Schundein Teil Imperialistischer Psychologischer Kriegführung." Tägliche Rundschau, May 18, 1955, Berlin (East).

4753. Langfeldt, Johannes. "Die Ausländischen Gesetze zur Bekämpfung von Schmutz und Schund." *Bücherei und Bildung* (Frankfurt). 8, 1956, pp. 199-208.

4754. Langfeldt, Johannes. "Schmutz und Schund unter der Lupe." *Bücherei und Bildung* (Frankfurt). 11, 1955, pp. 391-393.

4755. Reinhardt, Helmut. *Schmutz-und Schundliteratur im Volksschulalter.* Ratingen: 1957.

"Struwelpeter"

4756. Hoffmann, Heinrich. *Der Struwelpeter*. Frankfurt: Insel, n.d. 50 pp.

4757. "Struwelpeter-Hilfe von Oben." *Der Spiegel*. No. 17, 1969, p. 205.

4758. "Struwelpeter-Karikatur." *Der Spiegel*. No. 32, 1969, p. 115.

"Till Eulenspiegel"

4759. "'Eine Neue Jungendzeischrift'...oder Till Eulenspiegels 'Comic-Streiche.'" *Deutsche Jugend*. 1:3 (1953), p. 41.

4760. "'Till Eulenspiegel' Eine Deutsche Bilderzeitschrift." *Der Neue Vertrieb*. 5:98 (1953), p. 177.

4761. Yoseloff, Thomas, ed. *The Further Adventures of Eulenspiegl*. New York: Yoseloff, 1957. 122 pp.

"Tim und Struppi"

4762. "Aus Hergés Kinderstube." *ICOM*. October 1992, pp. 62-63.

4763. Kempkes, Wolfgang. "Tim und Struppi." *Bulletin: Jugend + Literatur*. No. 6, 1970, p. 13.

4764. Knigge, Andreas C. "50 Jahre Tim und Struppi. Die Schule Hergé." *Comixene. Das Comicfachmagazin*. 6:23 (1979), pp. 7-11.

4765. Künnemann, Horst. "Comics—Tim und Struppi." *Bulletin: Jugend + Literatur*. No. 10, 1972, Kritik 4, p. 73.

4766. Ostertag, Hansjörg. "Tim und Struppi—Eine Erfreuliche Comicserie." *Schweizerische Lehrerzeitung* (Zurich). October 26, 1972, pp. 1659-1665.

4767. "Tim und Struppi in Aktion." *Bulletin: Jugend + Literatur*. No. 10, 1972, Kritik 4, pp. 74-75.

"Vater und Sohn"

4768. Plauen, E.O. *Vater und Sohn*. Berlin: Verlag Ullstein, 1936. 50 pp.

4769. Plauen, E.O. *Vater und Sohn. Gesamtausgabe.* Constance: Südvlg, 1982. 309 pp.

"Werner"

4770. Brösel (Rötger Feldmann). *Werner—Alles Klar?* Kiel: Semmel, 1982. 144 pp.

4771. Brösel. *Werner—Besser Is Das!* Kiel: Semmel, 1989. 144 pp.

4772. Brösel. *Werner—Eiskalt!* Kiel: Semmel, 1985. 144 pp.

4773. Brösel. *Werner Hat Durst.* Kiel: Semmel, 1984.

4774. Brösel. *Werner im Schnellimbiß.* Kiel: Semmel, 1984.

4775. Brösel. *Werner Is Schlecht.* Kiel: Semmel, 1984.

4776. Brösel. *Werner Macht Faxen.* Kiel: Semmel, 1984.

4777. Brösel. *Werner—Normal Ja!* Kiel: Semmel, 1987. 144 pp.

4778. Brösel. *Werner—Oder Was?* Kiel: Semmel, 1981. 144 pp.

4779. Brösel. *Werner—Wer Sonst?* Kiel: Semmel, 1983. 144 pp.

4780. Brösel. *Werner Winzig.* Vols. 1-8. Kiel: Semmel, 1983-1986. 32 pp.

4781. Brösel (Rötger Feldmann)/Bartnick/Feldmann. *Werner—Das Rennen.* Kiel: Semmel, 1988. 144 pp.

4782. Feldmann, Ursula, ed. *Alles Über Werner.* Kiel: Semmel, 1986. 144 pp.

4783. "Werner Oder Wer?" *ICOM.* October 1992, pp. 30-33.

"Zack"

4784. Knigge, Andreas C. "Das Ende Einer Ära." *Comixene. Das Comicfachmagazin.* 7:32 (1980), pp. 58-59.

4785. "ZACK - da Lacht die Koralle." *Der Spiegel.* No. 38, 1972, pp. 62-63, 65.

4786. "ZACK Dumm...." *Spontan* (Munich). No. 9, 1972.

4787. "Zwischendurch Spaghetti mit Tomatensauce." *Der Stern.* No. 46, 1967, p. 221.

"Zok Roarr Wumm"

4788. Forster, Peter. "Mph Stöhn Ächz Roarr Zisch Päng." *Hamburger Morgenpost.* June 24, 1971, p. 14.

4789. Marcks, Michael. "Roarr! Millionen Lesen Comic-Hefte." *Lübecker Nachrichten.* June 27, 1971, p. 37.

4790. Riha, Karl. *Zok Roarr Wumm. Zur Geschichte der Comics-Literatur.* Steinbach: Anabas—Verlag Kämpf, 1970. 141 pp.

ANIMATION

4791. "Ausgezeichnete Animation." *Comic Info.* 1/1993, p. 10.

4792. Dosch, Andreas. "Westwärts Zieht die Maus." *ICOM INFO.* June 1992, pp. 40-41.

4793. Hansen, Eric. "Rise of Features Favors German Tooners." *Variety.* September 1992, p. 70.

4794. Kindred, Jack. "Cartoon Studios Are Animated in Germany." *Variety.* May 27, 1991, p. 48.

4795. Kindred, Jack. "Germans Drawing as Fast as They Can." *Variety.* November 5, 1990, p. 58.

4796. Kindred, Jack. "Germans Finding U.S. Too Big in Kiddie Kultur." *Variety.* September 10, 1990, pp. 39, 43.

4797. Lieb, Rebecca. "Animated Cat in Jugendfilm Bag." *Variety.* July 29, 1991, p. 29.

4798. Schmidmaier, Werner. "Animation für den Konsum." *Graphik* (Munich). No. 10, 1970, pp. 42-44.

4799. Swain, Bob. "Star Rises for German Toonsters." *Variety.* June 7, 1993, p. 37.

4800. Truck, Walter. "Gut Gebrüllt, Maus!" *Comic Info.* 1/1993, pp. 54-55.

CARICATURE

4801. *Bild als Waffe. Mittel und Motive der Karikatur in Funf Jahrhuderten.* Munich: Prestel-Verlag, 1984.

4802. Boeck, W. *Die Bolognesischen Meister des Karikaturenbandes der Münchner Graphischen Sammlung.* 3. Folge, Bd. 5. Munich: 1954.

4803. Conring, F. *Das Deutsche Militär in der Karikatur.* Stuttgart, n.d.

4804. Dollinger, Hans. *Lachen Streng Verboten!* (die Geschichte der Deutschen im Spiegel der Karikatur.) Munich: Sudwest Verlag, 1972.

4805. Haese, Klaus. "Unsere Wirklichkeit und Unsere Karikaturen" (Our Reality and Our Caricature). *Neue Deutsche Presse.* No. 18, 1977, pp. 1-8.

4806. Heine, Th. *Der Zeichner Gelcitwort.* Freiburg in Breisgan: H. Klemm, 1955.

4807. Herding, Klaus and Gunter Ott, eds. *Karikaturen.* Giessen: Anabas-Verlag, 1980.

4808. Hofmann, Werner. "Bemerkungen zur Karikatur." *Merkur.* 7, 1953, pp. 949-950.

4809. Konrad. *Sprach die Frau Manin. Adenauer in der Karikatur.* Hamburg: Gerhard Staling Verlag, 1955.

4810. Mac Orlan, Pierre. "La Caricature en Allemagne." *Arts et Métiers Graphiques.* September 15, 1932, pp. 5-20.

4811. Ramseger, Georg. *Duell mit der Geschichte. Deutsche Karikaturen der Gegenwart.* Hamburg: Gerhard Salattury, Verlag, 1955.

4812. Ronge, Peter. "De de Gaulle à Mitterrand." *Mieux Vaut en Rire.* No. 13, 1989, pp. 9-15.

4813. Seeberg, Hans-Adolf. "Die Karikatur der Neuen Welt." 1. Deutsches Fernsehen (ARD), November 3, 1969, Frankfurt.

4814. Szewezuk, Misko. *Stars und Sterne.* Hamburg: Rowohlt Taschenbuch Verlag, 1955.

4815. "Theologie in Karikaturen, Hrsg. SMD." *Dynamics* (Marburg). June 20, 1967.

4816. Troll, T., ed. *Der Deutsche in Seiner Karikatur.* Stuttgart, n.d.

4817. Wiechert, Karl. "Wie aus Kortums Jobsiade Eine Buschiade Wurde." *Wilhelm-Busch-Jahrbuch.* 34, 1968.

4818. Wiechert, Karl. "Vor Allen Dingen... 'Der Geburtstag Oder die Partikularisten.'" *Wilhelm-Busch-Jahrbuch.* 36, 1970.

4819. Woile, Hans-Peter. *Karikaturen.* Reutlingen: Zukunft, 1947. Unpaginated.

CARTOONS

4820. Arnold, Karl. *Der Mensch Ist Gut*. Hamburg: Hans Dalk Verlag, 1952.

4821. Bauer, Dietrich. *Teufel, Teufel*. Berlin: Eulenspiegel-Verlag, 1983.

4822. Bauer, Peter. *Cartoons*. Berlin: Eulenspiegel-Verlag, 1981.

4823. Behling, Heinz. *Blätter die Welt Bedenteln*. Berlin: Eulenspiegel-Verlag, 1979.

4824. Beier-Red, Alfred. *Ins Schwarze Getroffen*. Berlin: Eulenspiegel-Verlag, 1970.

4825. Blank, Hajo. *Kleines Bilderbuch der Mode*. Berlin: Eulenspiegel-Verlag, 1983.

4826. Bofinger, Manfred. *Schwarze Ärmel-Weiße Westen*. Berlin: Eulenspiegel-Verlag, 1978.

4827. Burnett, Hugh. *Lachender Himmel: Cartoons Um Fröhliche Mönche*. Munich: Roven, 1964. Unpaginated.

4828. "Cartoons." *Hör-Zu*. No. 12, 1969.

4829. *Cartoon 62, 63, 64*. Zurich: Diogenes, 1961, 1962, 1963. 88, 72, 106 pp.

4830. *Das Waren Zeiten*. Munich: Süddt. Vlg., 1989. 192 pp.

4831. Gross, Horst-Eckart and Rainer Hachfeld. *Peacemakers*. Cologne: Weitkreis, 1987.

4832. *Hundert Deutsche Bilderbogen*. Hildesheim: Olms, 1978. 106 pp.

4833. Rauch, Hans-Georg. *Battle Lines*. New York: Charles Scribner's Sons, 1977. Unpaginated.

COMIC BOOKS

4834. Arfort-Cochey, Edith. "Comics Contra Schriftsteller." *Der Schriftsteller* (Frankfurt). 6:10 (1953), p. 221.

4835. "Auch Marylin Liebt Comic-Helden." *Hamburger Morgenpost*. No. 210, 1969, p. 1.

4836. "Auf den Kopf." *Der Spiegel*. No. 33, 1967, pp. 85-86.

4837. "Ausgeschaltete Phantasie." *Frankfurter Allgemeine Zeitung*. March 18, 1967.

4838. "Averty-Verdrehtes Gehirn." *Der Spiegel*. No. 48, 1968.

4839. "Balduin Ist Da!" *St. Pauli Nachrichten* (Hamburg). No. 112, 1970, p. 20.

4840. Bamberger, Richard. "Das Kind vor der Bilderflut des Alltags." *Das Kind in Unserer Zeit* (Stuttgart). 1948, pp. 135-150.

4841. Baumann, Max. "Comics-Gefahr Oder Positiver Beginn? Die Wiedergeburt des Bildes." *Der Schriftsteller*. 6:10 (1953), p. 218.

4842. Baumgärtner, Alfred. "Comics in Deutschland." In *Handbuch der Pulizistik*, Vol. 2, edited by Emil Dovifat, pp. 127-132. Berlin: Walter de Gruyter und Co., 1969.

4843. Baumgärtner, Alfred C. "Comics-Ewige Mythen Oder Esperanto der Analphabeten?" *Radius* (Stuttgart-Bad Cannstatt). 1, 1968, pp. 42-44.

4844. Baumgärtner, Alfred C. "Das Weltbild der Comics." *Vortrag im Deutschland-funk* (Cologne). June 3, 1970.

4845. Baumgärtner, Alfred C. "Die Bildergeschichte Damals und Heute. Zum Problem der 'Comics.'" *Jugend und Buch*. 15:1 (1966), pp. 11-15.

4846. Baumgärtner, Alfred C. *Die Welt der Comics. Probleme Einer Primitiven Literaturform*. Bochum: 1965.

4847. Becker, Hartmut and Andreas C. Knigge. "Comicland Bastei." *Comicszene*. No. 28, 1980.

4848. Bézard, Clemens. "Mainzelmännchens Drehbuch." *Funk-Uhr* (Hamburg). No. 35, 1967.

4849. "Bildfolge." *Der Spiegel*. No. 40, 1968.

4850. Bogdon, Klaus, ed. *Bromics*. Dormagen: Ed. Quasimodo, 1988. 48 pp.

4851. Bollinger, Mike. "Der Fledermausmann Hat Geburtstag." *Abendzeitung* (Munich). January 11-12, 1967.

4852. "Bremer Inszenierung mit Comics." *Frankfurter Allgemeine Zeitung*. March 12, 1966.

4853. Breuer, Hajo. "Die Neuen Inhalte der Comics." *Comicstars* (Frankfurt). No. 17, 1983.

4854. Breuer, Hajo. "Helden im Wandel der Zeit." *Comicstars* (Frankfurt). No. 7, 1981.

4855. Brinkmann, G. "Der Giftstrom der Comic-Books." *Der Katholische Erzieher* (Bochum). 8:2 (1955), pp. 68-69.

4856. Brück, Axel. "Zur Theorie der Comics." *Katalog der Comics*-Ausstellung im Hamburger Kunsthaus, July 1971, pp. X-XV. Hamburg.

4857. Brüggemann, H.A. "Mainzelmännchen Dürfen Nicht Durch Schweizer Käse Kriechen." *Westdeutsche Allgemeine Zeitung* (Essen). December 24, 1965.

4858. Buhl, Wolfgang. "Für Sechzig Pfennig Zärtlichkeit." *Die Welt.* No. 38, 1961.

4859. "Bumskopp." *Abendpost* (Nachtausgabe). June 21, 1967.

4860. "Charlies Schwester." *Underground (Frankfurt).* No. 4, 1970, p. 4.

4861. Colly, Axel. "Comics." *General-Anzeiger* (Cologne). December 8, 1955.

4862. "Comic-Ausstellung in Berlin." *Börsenblatt für den Deutschen Buchhandel* (Frankfurt). No. 4, 1970.

4863. "Comic-Ausstellung in Hamburg." "Magazine der Woche." 1. Deutsches Fernsehen (ARD), July 25, 1971, Hamburg.

4864. "Comic-Blasen, Eine 'Abfallgrube' und die Dichterseele." *Der Schriftsteller.* 9, 1956, pp. 81-82.

4865. "Comic-Buch." *Der Spiegel.* No. 25, 1972, p. 119.

4866. "Comic-Bücher." *Bulletin: Jugend + Literatur.* No. 2, 1972, Kritik 4, p. 15.

4867. "Comic-Charts Deutschland." *Comic Info.* 1/1993, p. 13.

4868. "Comicland." *Underground.* No. 3, 1970, p. 4.

4869. "Comics." *Abendpost* (Nachtausgabe). June 28, 1967.

4870. "Comics." *Bulletin: Jugend + Literatur.* No. 8, 1972; Übersichten 6, p. 13.

4871. "Comics." *Der Spiegel.* No. 18, 1968.

4872. "Comics." *Die Welt.* April 23, 1968.

4873. "Comics." *Frankfurter Allgemeine Zeitung.* January 10, 1966.

4874. "Comics." *Hör Zu.* No. 25, 1969.

4875. "Comics." *Jugendliteratur* (Munich). 1, 1955.

4876. "Comics." *Jugendliteratur* (Munich). 1:2 (1955), p. 285; 1:6 (1955), p. 285; 1:8 (1955), pp. 381-382; 1:7 (1956), pp. 349-350.

4877. "Comics-Bücher." *Bulletin: Jugend + Literatur.* No. 6, 1972; Kritik 4, p. 42.

4878. "Comics-Ernst Genommen." *Zeitschrift für Jugendliteratur.* 1:8 (1967), pp. 504-505.

4879. "Comics-Flucht vom Stuhl." *Der Spiegel.* No. 41, 1966, p. 148.

4880. "Comics Galore in Germany." *Variety.* June 10, 1987, p. 92.

4881. "Comics-Informationen." *Bulletin: Jugend + Literatur.* No. 8, 1971, p. 18.

4882. "Comics in Kürze." *Zeitschrift für Jugendliteratur.* 1:1 (1967), pp. 52, 54.

4883. "Comics-Materialien zu Einer Literarischen Zeiterscheinung." *Pegasus.* No. 3, 1972.

4884. "Comics 1966: Kennen Sie Jena, das Höllenweib? *Twen* (Munich). January 1967, p. 64.

4885. "Comics Oder die Züchtung des Unpolitischen Arbeitsmenschen." *Die Weltbühne* (Berlin). 10, 1955, pp. 1006-1009.

4886. "Comics-Schundhefte." *Zentralblatt für Jugendrecht und Jugendwohlfahrt* (Cologne). 41, 1954, pp. 242-243.

4887. "Comics: Stichwortartikel." In *Brockhaus-Enzyklopädie*, Vol. 4, p. 125. Wiesbaden: Brockhaus, 1968.

4888. "Comics-Szene." *Bulletin: Jugend + Literatur.* No. 6, 1972; Kritik 4, p. 44.

4889. Cordt, Willy K. "Der Rückfall ins Primitive." *Westermanns Pädagogische Beiträge* (Braunschweig). 6:4 (1954), pp. 161-181.

4890. Couperie, Pierre. "Keine Arbeiter—Keine Neger. Die Manipulierte Thematik der Comics." *Tendenzen* (Munich). 1. Sonderheft, No. 53, 1968, pp. 184-186.

4891. Czernich, Michael. "Czernichs Comic Corner." *Spontan* (Munich). No. 2, 1972.

4892. Dagen, Philippe. "Dessins d' Allemagne." *Mieux Vaut en Rire.* No. 13, 1989, pp. 20-21.

4893. "Der Mann Mit der Tüte auf dem Kopf." *ICOM INFO.* June 1992, pp. 50-53.

4894. "Der Mensch der Serie." *Die Welt der Literatur* (Hamburg). February 3, 1966.

4895. Derouet, Paul. "Allemagne: Le Réveil Se Confirme." *Les Cahiers de la Bande Dessinée*. 63, 1985, pp. 46-48.

4896. Derouet, Paul. "Les Allemands Vont Faire des Bulles!" *Les Cahiers de la Bande Dessinée*. 57, 1984, pp. 44-45.

4897. "Deutsche Comics." *Der Neue Vertrieb* (Flensburg). 5:110 (1953), p. 464.

4898. *Deutsche Comics*. Begleitheft zur Ausstellung Einer Arbeitsgruppe von Volkskundlern der Universität Freiburg. Freiburg/Breisgau: Arbeitsgruppe von Volkskundlern der Universität, 1979.

4899. "Die Comics." *Allgemeine Deutsche Lehrerzeitung* (Frankfurt). 11:6 (1959), pp. 60-62.

4900. "Die Flut der Minderwertigen Bunten Hefte." *Südkurier* (Constance). July 23, 1952.

4901. "Die Gefährlichkeit der Comics." *Die Wahrheit* (Berlin). January 29-31, 1970.

4902. "Die Jagd Nach dem Atomgeheimnis." *Der Neue Vertrieb* (Flensburg). 5:108 (1953), p. 434.

4903. "Die Monstersinger." *Time*. November 6, 1950, pp. 72-78.

4904. Döring, Karl-Heinz. "Comics. Ein Überblick Über die Bisherigen Veröffentlichungen." *Bücherei und Bildung* (Reutlingen). 9, 1957, pp. 237-242.

4905. "Edelmann: Garten der Lüste." *Der Spiegel*. No. 31, 1968, p. 86.

4906. "Ein Hund Gegen Richthoven." *Der Stern*. No. 24, 1967.

4907. "Ein Hund Macht Millionen." *Der Stern*. No. 11, 1970, p. 200.

4908. "Ein Roman Wird Verschrottet." *Frankfurter Allgemeine Zeitung*. January 29, 1966.

4909. Ell, Ernst. "Der Jammer mit den Bildheften." *Leben und Erziehen* (Aachen). 10:11 (1961), pp. 408-409; *Die Mitarbeiterin* (Düsseldorf). 12:4 (1961), pp. 116-119.

4910. "Eltern-Comic-Test." *Eltern* (Munich). No. 4, 1970, pp. 26-29.

4911. "Emanzipation." *Der Spiegel*. No. 45, 1972, p. 161.

4912. Engelhardt, Victor. "Versteppung des Geistes." *Dien Neue Ordnung* (Cologne). 9, 1955, pp. 30-37, 92-100.

4913. Frenzel, Martin. "Comicolympiade. Festival der Pannen und Peinlichkeiten." *Comic Forum. Das Magazin für Comicliteratur.* 7:29 (1985), pp. 21-23.

4914. Fuchs, Wolfgang J., ed. *Comics—im Medienmarkt, Comics in der Analyse, Comics im Unterricht.* Opladen: 1977.

4915. Fuchs, Wolfgang J. "Eine Zensur Findet Nicht Statt. Jugendmedienschutz in der Bundesrepublik Deutschland." In *Batman, Beatles, Barbarella. Der Kosmos in der Sprechblase,* edited by Wolfgang J. Fuchs and Thomas Wirsum, pp. 24-29. Ebersberg/Obb: Editions 8 1/2, Lothar Just, 1985.

4916. Fuchs, Wolfgang J. "Prominenz in Comics." In *Batman, Beatles, Barbarella. Der Kosmos in der Sprechblase,* edited by Wolfgang J. Fuchs and Thomas Wirsum, pp. 44-91. Edersberg/Obb: Editions 8 1/2, Lothar Just, 1985.

4917. Fuchs, Wolfgang J. "Trends in den Comics." *Jugend-Film-Fernsehen* (Munich). 16:2 (1972), pp. 6-13.

4918. Funhoff, Jörg. "Comics." *INCOS-Nachrichten* (Berlin). June 15, 1972.

4919. Funhoff, Jörg. "Panel-Comics." *INCOS-Nachrichten.* June 15, 1972.

4920. Furian, Martin, ed. *Phänomen Comics-Transparent Gemacht.* Fellbach: 1978.

4921. Galweit, George M. "Das Medium Mit Eigenen Gesetzen. Die Hamburger Comic-Ausstellung." *Weserkurier* (Bremen). June 29, 1971.

4922. "Gebremster Schaum." *Der Spiegel.* No. 24, 1967.

4923. "Gefährliche Spur." *Der Spiegel.* No. 53, 1969, p. 83.

4924. Geisler, Jürgen. "Der Löwe Leo Mit dem Sanften Blick." *Abendzeitung* (Munich). November 12-13, 1966.

4925. "Gepeinigte Nerven." *Der Spiegel.* No. 4, 1972, pp. 104-105.

4926. "Gestiefelter Mythos." *Der Spiegel.* No. 52, 1968, pp. 145-146.

4927. Giachi, Arianna. "Aus Lauter Gier...." *Bücherei und Bildung* (Reutlingen). 6:4/5 (1954), p. 362; *Gegenwart* (Cologne). 6, 1954, p. 179.

4928. "Gibt Es Gute Comics? Eine Entgegnung." *Jugendliteratur.* 5:11 (1959), pp. 258-259.

4929. Glietenberg, Ilse. "Die Comics. Wesen und Wirkung." Dissertation, Munich, July 9, 1956.

4930. Görlich, Ernst J. "Comic-Books." *Erziehung und Unterricht* (Hamburg). 10, 1957, pp. 584-587.

4931. Grossmann, Johannes F. "Übermensch/Untermensch." *Die Welt*. February 1966.

4932. "Gruß an Neufundland." *Der Spiegel*. No. 36, 1972, pp. 110, 113.

4933. Gubern, Román and Claude Moliterni. *Comics—Kunst und Konsum der Bildergeschichte*. Reinbek B. Hamburg: 1978.

4934. Guhert, Georg. "Schmunzeln und Gänsehaut." *Der Dom* (Cologne). No. 24, 1966.

4935. "HB Gegen BH." *Der Spiegel*. No. 39, 1966, p. 173.

4936. Helger, Walter. "Überschwemmung Mit Bilderserien." *Lebendige Schule* (Munich). 7, 1952, pp. 503-506.

4937. Hell, L. "Comics." *Jugendschriften-Warte* (Frankfurt). 24:5 (1972), p. 19.

4938. Hembus, Joe. "Intellektuelle Dürfen Lachen." *Twen* (Munich). No. 8, 1965.

4939. Herburger, Günter. "Dreck als Reim." *Der Spiegel*. May 29, 1972, p. 138.

4940. Herms, Uwe. "Schneller, Leichter, Mehr Verbieten." *Konkret* (Hamburg). July 28, 1969, pp. 46-47.

4941. "Heute Stimmen Wir Ab." *Frankfurter Rundschau*. February 26, 1966.

4942. "Hockney: Comic Mit Gretchen." *Der Spiegel*. No. 47, 1968, p. 188.

4943. Hoffmann, Detlef and Sabine Rauch. *Comics. Materialien zur Analyse Eines Massenmediums*. Frankfurt: Diesterweg, 1975. 109 pp.

4944. Hoffmann, Michael. "Geschäft Mit dem Glück." *Kunst und Unterricht*. 10, 1970, pp. 22-24.

4945. Höhn, Hans. "Im Jahre 40000 Liebt Man Anders." *Westdeutsche Allgemeine Zeitung*. September 2, 1967.

4946. Holtz, Christina. *Comics—Ihre Entwicklung und Bedeutung*. Munich, New York, London, Paris: 1980.

4947. Hon, Walter. "Die Bildersprache der Comics." *Welt und Wort* (Cologne). 11:4 (1956), p. 108.

4948. Hoppe, Edda. "Die Comics." *Frankfurter Nachtausgabe*. November 27, 1954.

4949. Hoppe, Wilhelm. "Der 'Bild-Idiotismus' Triumphiert." *Bücherei und Bildung* (Reutlinger). 7:11 (1955), pp. 381-386; *Freundliches Begegnen* (Düsseldorf). 6:5 (1956), pp. 1-6.

4950. Hoyer, Franz. "Bilderbücher-Comics." *Hessische Hefte*. 5:10 (1955), pp. 389-391.

4951. "ICOM-Zeichnerarchiv." *Comic Info*. May-June 1993, pp. 62-63.

4952. Illg, Renate. "Untersuchungen zur Trivialliteratur. Typen der Comics. Zulassungsarbeit zur 1. Dienstprüfung fur das Lehramt an Grund-und Hauptschulen." Ludwigsburg: 1969.

4953. "Im Bann von Technik und Magie." *ICOM INFO*. June 1992, pp. 54-55.

4954. "In Bonn Tickt Eine Bombe." *Der Stern*. No. 14, 1968.

4955. Isani, Claudio. "Oh, Du Meine Blase!" *Der Abend* (Berlin). December 4, 1972.

4956. "Jubel auf Zehen—Comic-Sängerin." *Der Spiegel*. No. 35, 1971, pp. 110-111.

4957. "Jünger-Strip-Detail." *Der Spiegel*. No. 47, 1968.

4958. "Käferliebe." *Gute Fahrt* (Munich). No. 3, 1969, p. 10.

4959. Kagelmann, H. Jürgen. *Comics—Aspekte zu Inhalt und Wirkung*. Bad Heilbrunn/Obb: J. Klinkhardt, 1976. 144 pp.

4960. Kampel, Herbert. "Der Friseur im Comic." *Comic Forum. Das Magazin für Comicliteratur*. 8:31 (1986), pp. 24-29.

4961. Kempkes, Wolfgang. "Comic-Dokumentation: Schweizer Urteilen Über Comics." *Bulletin: Jugend + Literatur*. No. 8, 1970, p. 7.

4962. Kempkes, Wolfgang. "Comics im Weltall." *Bulletin: Jugend + Literatur*. No. 2, 1970, p. 10.

4963. Kempkes, Wolfgang. "UNESCO-Comics." *Bulletin: Jugend + Literatur*. No. 4, 1970, p. 12.

4964. Klausnack, Hartmut. "Comics." *Bulletin: Jugend + Literatur*. No. 7/71, 1971, p. 12.

4965. "Kleine Bilder für Millionen." *Berliner Telegraf*. May 4, 1952.

4966. "Kleine Henker-Comics und Spielzeug." *Der Spiegel*. No. 29, 1971, p. 120.

4967. Klie, Barbara. "Das Elend Mit den 'Comics.'" *Der Tagesspiegel*. November 13, 1954.

4968. Klönne, Arno. "Analphabetentum Unserer Zeit: Die Comics." *Druck und Papier* (Stuttgart). 8, 1956, p. 59.

4969. Knehr, Edeltraud. "Western und Comics Kommen Mir Nicht Über Meine Schwelle!" *Eltern*. 7:9 (1966), pp. 31-33.

4970. Knigge, Andreas C. and Gerd Lettkemann. *Fortsetzung Folgt. Comic Kultur in Deutschland. Mit Einem Beitrag Über die Comics in der DDR*. Frankfurt, Berlin: Ullstein, 1986.

4971. Knigge, Andreas C., Raoul O'Hara, *et al*. "Der Comic-Markt September 1984 bis August 1985. In *Comic-Jahrbuch 1986*, edited by Martin Compart and Andreas C. Knigge, pp. 171-227. Berlin: Ullstein GmbH, 1985.

4972. Knigge, Andreas C., Raoul O'Hara, Heinz Remus, *et al*. "Die 30 Wichtigsten Comic-Neuerscheinungen." In *Comic-Jahrbuch 1986*, edited by Martin Compart and Andreas C. Knigge, pp. 130-165. Berlin: Ullstein GmbH, 1985.

4973. Knilli, Friedrich, Clemens Schwender, Erwin Gundelsheimer, and Elke Weisser. "Aspekte der Entwicklung zu Einer Visuellen Kultur am Beispiel des Comics: Der Stand der Comicforschung in der Bundesrepublik." *Communication* (Sankt Augustin). 9 (1984), pp. 149-190.

4974. Knilli, Friedrich *et al*. "Some Aspects of the Development Toward a Visual Culture. The Example of Comics." In *Comics and Visual Culture: Research Studies from Ten Countries*, edited by Alphons Silbermann and H.-D. Dyroff, pp. 109-143. Munich: K.G. Saur, 1986.

4975. Köhlert, Adolf. "Bilderbücher?" *Jugendschriften-Warte* (Frankfurt). 1954.

4976. Köhlert, Adolf. "Weiter Mit den Comics?" *Jugendschriften-Warte*. No. 1, 1971, pp. 2-3.

4977. Kotschenreuther, Hellmut. "Crash! Boing! Woumm!!!" *Stuttgarter Zeitung*. December 17, 1969.

4978. Kumlin, Gunnar D. "Luxustraum der Armen." *Rheinischer Merkur* (Düsseldorf). July 3, 1953.

4979. Künnemann, Horst. "Comics, Comiciasten und Comicologen." *Die Zeit*. No. 29, 1971, p. 13.

4980. Künnemann, Horst. "Comics in der Bundesrepublik. Eine Einführung, Übersicht und Anregung zum Kennenlernen." *Medien + Erziehung* (Leverkusen). 20:1 (1976), pp. 4-15.

4981. Lakner, Petra. "Designer-Comics: Neue Akzente aus der Edition Rossi Schreiber?" *ICOM INFO*. June 1992, p. 33.

4982. Langosch, K. "Die Comics." In *Bücher-Wegbereiter fürs Leben, Aufsatzreihe*, pp. 40-55. Ratingen: Verlag Henn, 1956.

4983. Leier, Manfred. "Grober Raster Wirklichkeit." *Die Welt*. April 4, 1969, p. 31.

4984. Leipziger, Walter. "Die Comics und die Märchen." *Freundliches Begegnen*. 6:5 (1956), p. 7.

4985. Lettkemann, Gerd. "Ins Neue Leben." *Comixene. Das Comicfachmagazin*. 6:26 (1979), pp. 59-61.

4986. "Liebe auf der Milchstraße." *Der Stern*. No. 34, 1967.

4987. Löschenkohl, Anneliese. "Die Helden der Serie 'Comics' Erobern die Welt." *Sonntagsblatt* (Hamburg). 6:6 (1953), p. 7.

4988. Lucas, Robert. "Pophelden Siegten Über Seehelden." *Die Zeit*. No. 25, 1968.

4989. Luft, F. "Comics." *Der Neue Vertrieb* (Flensburg). 54, 1951, p. 262.

4990. "Machen Sie Mit Beim Fragespiel des HVV." *Welt am Sonntag* (Hamburg). November 5, 1967.

4991. Mai, Karl F. "Weltreise des Seepferdchens." *Hamburger Abendecho*. March 21, 1966.

4992. Maier, Karl-Ernst. *Comics*. Bad Heilbrunn: Klinkhardt, 1976. 144 pp.

4993. "Mainzelmännchen." *Hör Zu*. No. 7, 1969, p. 8.

4994. Markwart, Helmut. "Armes Schweinchen Dick." *Gong* (Munich). No. 45, 1972, p. 3.

4995. Martineau, P.D. "Artikel Über Eine Comic-Leseranalyse." *Werbe-Rundschau*. 1. Sommerheft, No. 81, 1967.

4996. "Mit Einfällchen." *Der Spiegel*. No. 30, 1969, p. 111.

4997. "Mit Gebrabbel." *Der Spiegel*. No. 30, 1969, p. 111.

4998. "Mit Xram Gegen das Baarzel." *Der Spiegel*. No. 25, 1972, pp. 121-122.

4999. Moeller, Michael. "Publizierte Träume." *Kunst und Unterricht*. 10, 1970, pp. 27-29.

5000. "Mond-Bücher: Rasante Niederkunft." *Der Spiegel*. No. 30, 1969, p. 116.

5001. "Mordgeschichten." *Der Spiegel*. No. 29, 1971, p. 129.

5002. "Ms. -Zeitschrift." *Der Spiegel*. No. 31, 1972, p. 91.

5003. Müller, Hans-Georg. "Wir Sprechen Mit Bildern." *Hamburger Lehrerzeitung*. No. 18, 1972, p. 621.

5004. "Nächtlicher Diskurs-Die Fröhliche Wissenschaft." *Der Spiegel*. No. 28, 1969, p. 117.

5005. Nagel, Wolfgang. "Comics." *Neue Deutsche Hefte*. 17:4 (1970), pp. 206-208.

5006. "Neues Comic-Buch." *Bulletin: Jugend + Literatur*. No. 12, 1972; Nachrichten-Inland 2, p. 38.

5007. "Nicht zu Bremsen." *Der Spiegel*. No. 17, 1972, pp. 179-180.

5008. Nicolaus, K.N. "Der Triumpf der Blasenmenschen." *Die Zeit*. 8:22 (1953).

5009. "Oh Gegenwelt." *Der Spiegel*. No. 18, 1969, p. 183.

5010. Pachnicke, Peter. "Für Analphabeten?" *Sonntag*. 23:49 (1969), p. 5.

5011. Peeters, Benoît. "Une Pratique Insituable." In *Revue d l'Université de Bruxelles*. 1-2, 1986, pp. 5-14.

5012. Pforte, Dietger. "Deutschsprachige Comics." In *Vom Geist der Superhelden. Comic Strips. Zur Theorie der Bildergeschichte*, edited by Hans Dieter Zimmermann, pp. 54-63. Munich: Deutscher Taschenbuch Verlag, 1975.

5013. Pirich, H. "Comics—Das Können Wir Besser." *Kölnische Rundschau*. June 20, 1953.

5014. Pleuß, Alfred. *Bildergeschichten und Comics. Grundlegende Informationen und Literaturhinweise für Eltern*. Bad Honnef: Bock + Herchen, 1983. 292 pp.

5015. Preisendanz, Wolfgang. "Zum Vorrang des Komischen bei der Darstellung von Geschichtserfahrung in Deutschen Romanen Unserer Zeit." *Deutschunterricht*. June 1975, pp. 44-54.

5016. Preußler, Ottfried. "Die Reise ins Märchenland Findet Nicht Statt." *Jugendliteratur*. 4:7 (1958), pp. 326-329.

5017. Radbruch, Wolfgang. "Arbeitstagung der Landesgruppe Schleswig-Holstein." *Bücherei und Bildung*. 8, 1956, pp. 290-291.

5018. Reitberger, Reinhold C. and Wolfgang J. Fuchs. *Comics—Anatomie Eines Massenmediums*. Munich: 1971.

5019. Reitberger, Reinhold C., ed. *Comics—Katalog der Ausstellung im Münchner Stadtmuseum*. Munich: 1974.

5020. "Richard und Kolumbus Sollen Bleiben." *Frankfurter Rundschau*. March 12, 1966.

5021. Richter, Hans P. "Die Verteufelten Comics." *Bulletin: Jugend + Literatur*. No. 2/71, 1971, pp. 23-24.

5022. Riha, Karl. "Die Blase im Kopf." In *Trivialliteratur-Aufsätze*, pp. 176-191. Berlin: Verlag Litterarisches Colloquium, 1964.

5023. "Rote Affen." *Neuer Vorwärts*, (Hanover). November 1952.

5024. Rudloff, Diether. "Comics." *Die Kommenden* (Freiburg). 25:15 (1971), pp. 15-17.

5025. Sanders, Rino. "Romane aus Bildern und Blasen (Photoromanzi)." *Die Zeit*. July 9, 1971, p. 15.

5026. Santucci, Luigi. *Das Kind—Sein Mythos und Sein Märchen*, pp. 150-153, 194-195, 208-217. Hanover: Schroedel-Verlag, 1964.

5027. Schaaf, Ernst-Ludwig. "Die Lust Am Irrationalen: Ein Bericht Über Comics." Rundfunkvortag, 1. Programm, December 27, 1968. Hamburg.

5028. Schaller, Horst. "Die Welt der Comics (Buchbesprechung)." *Zschr. für Jugendliteratur*. 1:2 (1967), pp. 115-117.

5029. "Schatz für den Scheich." *Der Spiegel*. No. 44, 1966, p. 184.

5030. Scheerer, Friedrich. "Eine Lanze für die Comics." *Zeitnahe Schularbeit*. 22:4/5 (1969), pp. 146-167.

5031. Schelduk, Burkhardt. "Comics für Spezialisten." *Bulletin: Jugend + Literatur*. No. 2, 1972; Kritik 4, p. 13.

5032. Schmidmaier, Werner. "Der Zoom zum Verständnis." *Graphik*. No. 8, 1971, pp. 48-49.

5033. Schmidmaier, Werner. "Neuer Boom Beim Publikum." *Graphik*. No. 7, 1971, pp. 34-38.

5034. Schöler, Franz. "Wo Helden Noch Helden Sind." *Die Welt*. July 17, 1965.

5035. Scholl, Robert. "Die Comic-Hefte." *Unsere Jugend*. 8:8 (1956), pp. 363-364.

5036. Schröder, Peter H. "Unsere Welt im Zerrspiegel." *Die Welt*. June 16-17, 1967.

5037. "Schüler Wollen Liebe in Turnhalle." *Streit-Zeitschrift* (Frankfurt). 7/1 (1969).

5038. Schwarz, Rainer. "Auf dem Wege zu Einer Comicforschung." *Jugend-Film-Fernsehen*. 16:2 (1972), pp. 3-6.

5039. Schwarz, Rainer. "Zur Zeitkommunikativen Bedeutung der Comics." Munich: Magisterarbeit, 1969.

5040. "Schwarzkopf." *Lady-International* (Munich). No. 11, 1969, p. 26.

5041. Siebenschön, Leona. "Wo Steckt der Räuber? Eh... Raaah... Hepp!" *Die Zeit*. No. 32, 1972, p. 38.

5042. "Sind Es Wirklich Comic-Books?" *Die Muschel* (Lübeck). No. 2, 1949, pp. 46-47.

5043. Sonnergaard, Jørgensen and Werner Wejp-Olsen, eds. *Comics 2. Weltbekannte Zeichenserien*. Reinbek: 1972.

5044. Spitta, Theodor. "Die Bildersprache der Comics." *Jugendliteratur*. 10 (1955), pp. 460-468; *Welt und Wort*. 4 (1956), pp. 108-110.

5045. Spranger, Eduard. "Das Geheimnis des Lesens." *Darmstädter Echo*. May 9, 1959, p. 5.

5046. "Ständig Amüsiert." *Der Spiegel*. No. 16, 1969.

5047. "Sterne Sinken." *Der Spiegel*. No. 16, 1967.

5048. Strzyz, Klaus. "Das Gesetz der Serie." *Fantastische Vier* (Vilbel). No. 9, 1983.

5049. Suchan, Eric. "Das Tier im Comic. 1. Teil." *Comic Forum. Das Österreichische Fachmagazin für Comicliteratur*. 2:6 (1980), pp. 34-37.

5050. Suchan, Eric. "Das Tier im Comic. 2. Teil." *Comic Forum. Das Österreichische Fachmagazin für Comicliteratur*. 2:7/8 (1980), pp 58-61.

5051. "Super-Bürgermeister." *Der Spiegel*. No. 53, 1970, p. 92.

5052. Toll, Claudia. "Alle Comics auf den Müll?" *Spielen und Lernen* (Hanover). No. 8, 1971, pp. 14-17.

5053. "Unglückliche Liebe." *Der Spiegel*. No. 29, 1972, pp. 98-99.

5054. Usko, Hans-Jürgen. "Für Ein Paar Groschen Blut und Eisen." *Die Welt*. No. 140, 1960.

5055. "Verdummung Durch Comics." *Jugendschriften-Warte*. 8:4 (1956), p. 26.

5056. "Verliebt in Die Tödliche Lady." *Hamburger Abendecho*. March 18, 1966.

5057. "Viel Blut um Schiller." *Der Stern*. No. 18, 1966.

5058. von Zitzewitz, Monika. "Carmen, das Gammlerliebchen." *Die Welt*. February 8, 1967.

5059. "Vorkriegs-Comics in Deutschland." *Comixene*. Nos. 12, 13, 14, 1977.

5060. Voß, Herbert. "Charlie Ist Besser." *Hamburger Morgenpost*. No. 210, 1969, p. 27.

5061. "Waffen Gegen Viren." *Der Spiegel*. No. 48, 1968, p. 195.

5062. "Wasservögel." *Der Spiegel*. No. 44, 1970, p. 25.

5063. "Wer Lacht Da?" *Der Spiegel*. No. 39, 1968, pp. 190-191.

5064. Wermke, Jutta. *Wozu Comics Gut Sind?!* Kronsberg/Ts: 1973.

5065. Wermke, Jutta. *Kerygma in Comic-Form*. Munich: W. Fink, 1979. 214 pp.

5066. "Wie Butter an der Sonne." *Süddeutsche Zeitung* (Munich). December 11, 1967, p. 14.

5067. Wirsum, Thomas. "Verlage, Studios, Agenturen. Einblicke in den Deutschen Comic-Kosmos." In *Batman, Beatles, Barbarella, Der Kosmos in der Sprechblase*, edited by Wolfgang J. Fuchs and Thomas Wirsum, pp. 92-109. Ebersberg/Obb: Edition 8 1/2, Lothar Just, 1985.

5068. Wolfradt, Willi. "Der Killer und die Hexen." *Der Schriftsteller*. 6:10 (1953), p. 224.

5069. "Wortblasen." *Die Welt*. January 27, 1966.

5070. "Zeichentrick." *Der Spiegel*. No. 16, 1972, p. 153.

5071. Zeiger, Ivo A. "Comic-Books." *Stimmen der Zeit* (Freiburg). 77:7 (1952), pp. 64-67.

5072. Zimmer, Dieter F. "Niemand Schläft Sehr Schlecht." *Die Zeit*. No. 51, 1972, p. 23.

5073. "Zipzip-Zipzip." *Der Spiegel*. No. 52, 1966, pp. 98-99.

5074. "Zyniker auf der Hundehütte." *Der Spiegel*. No. 45, 1972, p. 186.

Art

5075. Bongard, Willi. "Pop, Op et cetera und die Folgen." *Die Zeit*. December 26, 1969-January 2, 1970, pp. 28-29.

5076. "Comic-Ausstellung im Hamburger Kunsthaus." June 24-July 25, 1971. Hamburg.

5077. *Comic Strips: Geschichte, Struktur, Wirkung und Verbreitung der Bildgeschichten.* Ausstellungskatalog der Berliner Akademie der Künste, December 13, 1969-January 25, 1970. Berlin.

5078. "Comics-Zwischen Kunst und Konsum." 2. Deutsches Fernsehen (ZDF), June 27, 1969. Mainz.

5079. Frank, Tom. "ZONK! Die Comic-Kunst Ist Da." *Hamburger Abendecho*. May 21, 1966, p. 16.

5080. Galweit, George M. "Sind 'Bildergeschichten' Kunst? Im Hamburger Kunsthaus Wird Größte Comic-Ausstellung der Welt Gezeigt." *Lübecker Nachrichten*. June 1971.

5081. Galweit, George M. "Sind Comics Kunst? In Hamburg: Größte Comic-Ausstellung der Welt." *Schleswig-Holsteinische Landeszeitung*. June 1971.

5082. Hofmann, Will. "Comic-Subkultur: Eine Lehrreiche Ausstellung im Hamburger Kunsthaus." *Hamburger Anzeiger und Nachrichten*. June 26, 1971.

5083. Kempkes, Wolfgang. "Comics an der Berliner. 'Akademie der Künste.'" *Bulletin: Jugend + Literatur*. No. 5, 1970, pp. 27-28.

5084. Metken, Günter. "Das Gesetz der Serie-Wie Künstler Comics Benützen." *Das Kunstwerk* (Stuttgart). 24:5 (1971), pp. 29-35.

5085. Olbricht, Klaus-Hartmut." Comic-Strips. Revolutionierung Traditioneller Kunstformen." *Die Kunst und das Schöne Heim* (Munich). 67:1 (1969), p. 20.

5086. Piwitt, Hermann. "Pop-Mariners, Plastik-Nacken." *Konkret* (Hamburg). August 25, 1969, pp. 40-41.

5087. Schauer, Lucie. "Comics-Kunst für Kleine Leute?" *Die Welt*. January 27, 1970, p. 23.

5088. Schlocker, Georg. "Die Neue Kunst der Comic-Strips. Anmerkung zu Einer Pariser Ausstellung." *Deutsches Allgemeines Sonntagsblatt* (Cologne). June 18, 1967.

5089. Schmalenbach, Werner. "Die Kunst vom Montag Ist Am Dienstag Vergessen." *Der Spiegel.* November 1967, pp. 202, 204.

5090. Schmidmaier, Werner. "Comication Art." *Graphik* (Munich). No. 9, 1971, pp. 51-54.

5091. Schmidmaier, Werner. "Der Kick im Media-Mix." *Graphik.* No. 10, 1971, pp. 49-51.

5092. Schmidmaier, Werner. "Sproing! Macht die Werbung-Ein Neuer Stil Kommt aus den Comics." *Graphik.* No. 12, 1968, pp. 22-23.

5093. Schmidmaier, Werner. "Werber als Comic-Strip-Akteure." *Graphik.* No. 7, 1970, p. 37.

5094. Schmidmaier, Werner. "Witze Über Reklame und Werbung." *Graphik.* No. 2, 1970, pp. 32-34.

5095. Schmidt, Jürgen. "Comics Über Comics im Kunsthaus." *Aachener Nachtrichten.* July 28, 1971.

5096. Schober, Siegfried. "Ein Versuch in Multi-Media, Heinz v. Cramer auf der POP-Welle." *Die Zeit.* November 29, 1968.

5097. Spies, Werner. "Auf den Strip Gekommen.... Comics im Louvre." *Frankfurter Allgemeine Zeitung.* June 13, 1967, p. 18.

5098. "UNESCO-Diapositive Über Moderne Architektur und Angewandte Graphik." *UNESCO-Dienst* (Cologne). 16:24 (1969), pp. 1-2.

Children

5099. Andres, Stefan. "Die Komics. Eine Neue Art des Lesens." *Jugendliteratur* (Munich). 1:2 (1955), pp. 63-64; *Jugendschriften-Warte* (Frankfurt). N.F., 7:3 (1955), pp. 17-18; *Mitteilungen der Bundesprüfstelle* (Bad Godesberg). No. 4, 1954, 5 pp.

5100. Autorenkollektiv. *Wir Machen Unsere Comics Selber: Erfahrungen Mit Comics an der Grundschule.* Berlin: Basis Verlag, 1974.

5101. Backus, Dana. "Comics." *Jugendschriften-Warte* (Frankfurt). 10 (1959), pp. 60-62.

5102. Bamberger, Richard. *Dein Kind und Seine Bücher*. Vienna: 1957.

5103. Bamberger, Richard. "Die Verführung der Unschuldigen." *Jugendliteratur*. 3:10 (1957), pp. 478-479.

5104. Bamberger, Richard. "Erfolge im Kampfe Gegen die Comics." *Jugendliteratur*. 4:1 (1958), pp. 43-44.

5105. Bamberger, Richard. *Jugendlektüre*. Bonn/Vienna: 1955.

5106. Bamberger, Richard. "Zum Literarischen Kleingut." *Jugendliteratur*. 3:7 (1957). pp. 305-308.

5107. Baumgärtner, Alfred C. *Perspektiven der Jugendlektüre*. Weinheim: Beltz-Verlag, 1969.

5108. Beer, Ulrich. *Geheime Miterzieher der Jugend*. Düsseldorf: Verlag Walter Rau, 1960.

5109. "Bildhefte-Große Gefahr für die Jugend." *Katholisches Sonntagsblatt*. 103:35 (1955), p. 3f.

5110. Bossert, A. "Zur Frage der Comics." *Jugendliteratur*. 1955, p. 381.

5111. Brauer, J. "Auswertung Einer Schülerbefragung Über Gute und Schlechte Heftreihen." *Jugendschriften-Warte*. 1954, p. 71; *Die Situation* (Cologne). No. 6/7, 1954.

5112. Bunk, Hans. *Beziehung Jugendlicher zu Film und Bildserie*. Cologne-Klettenberg: 1955.

5113. Bunk, Hans. "Einfluß der Comics auf Schulkinder." *Jugendschriften-Warte*. 1955, p. 11.

5114. Burkholz, G. "Bildserien-Jugendzeitschriften, Gefahr für Dein Kind." In *Die Schul-Familie*. Munich: 1954.

5115. Calmes, M. "Die Comics und das Kind. Verbildung Durch Verbilderung." *Kinderheim*. 34:2 (1956), pp. 64-68.

5116. "Comic-Books Verantwortlich? Verrohung der Jugend—Ein Internationales Problem." *Ruf ins Volk*. No. 11, 1954, p. 84.

5117. "Comics." *Zentralblatt für Jugendrecht und Jugendwohlfahrt* (Cologne). 43 (1956), pp. 29-31.

5118. "Comics-Blöd und Jugendgefährdend." *Unser Kind* (Essen). 5:11 (1954), p. 3.

5119. "Comics—Opium der Kinderstube." *Der Spiegel.* No. 12, 1951, pp. 39-41.

5120. Cordt, Willy K. "Für und Wider die Comics." *Jugendschriften-Warte.* 8:4 (1956), pp. 69-70.

5121. Cordt, Willy K. "Lesen Ihre Kinder Auch Comic-Books?" *Unser Kind.* 5:1 (1954), pp. 4-5.

5122. Cordt, Willy K. "Warum Werden die Comics-Books von den Jugendlichen Bevorzugt?" *Blätter für Lehrerfortbildung* (Nurenberg). 7:5 (1954/1955), pp. 178-180.

5123. Dahrendorf, Malte. "Comics—Immer Noch Streitobjekt?" *Jugendschriften-Warte.* 23:5-71 (1971), pp. 19-20.

5124. Diehl, Hildegard. "Untersuchungen Über die Einstellungen Lernbehinderter Kinder zu Verschiedenen Comic-Serien." *Hausarbeit für die 1. Staatsprüfung für das Lehramt an Sonderschulen.* May 12, 1971.

5125. Doetsch, Marietheres. *Comics und Ihre Jugendlichen Leser.* Meisenheim am Glau: A. Hain, 1958. 144 pp.

5126. Ecker, Hans. "Der König Ist Tot, Es Lebe der König (Comics und Des-illusionierung)." *Jugend und Buch.* 13:1 (1964), pp. 16-19.

5127. Ell, Ernst. "Der Jammer Mit den Bildheften. Bilderidiotismus Oder Bildungsgut? Erlauben Oder Verbieten?" *Jugendwohl* (Freiburg i. Br.). 42:2 (1961), pp. 75-80.

5128. Gatzweiler, Richard. *Verbrecher-Comics Gefährden die Jugend.* Cologne: Volkswartbund, 1954.

5129. "Gefährdung der Jugend Durch Comics." *Hygieia.* 1950.

5130. Giffhorn, Hans. "Comics als Lesestoff von Kindern und als Gegenstand Politischer Erziehung." In *Die Heimlichen Erzieher: Kinderbucher und Politisches Lerner,* edited by Dieter Richter and Jochen Vogt, pp. 142-160. Hamburg: Rowohlt, 1974.

5131. Giffhorn, Hans. *Seh-und Lesegewohnheiten von Kindern in Bezug auf Comics, Leitstudie-Sonderdruck.* Berlin: Neue Gesellschaft für Bildende Kunst e.V., 1971.

5132. Glade, Dieter. "Massen-Jugendliteratur." *Mitteilungen des Vereins für Niedersächsisches Volkstum* (Hanover). 40:75 (1965), pp. 44-50.

5133. Grünewald, Dietrich. "Kinder in den Comics. 1. Teil." *Comixene. Das Comicfachmagazin.* 6:26 (1979), pp. 17-20, 24-26.

5134. Grünewald, Dietrich. "Kinder in den Comics. 2. Teil." *Comixene. Das Comicfachmagazin.* 6:27 (1979), pp. 19-22, 24-25.

5135. Grünewald, Dietrich. *Wie Kinder Comics Lesen. Eine Untersuchung zum Prinzip Bildgeschichte, Seinem Angebot und Seinen Rezeptionsanforderungen Sowie dem Diesbezüglichen Lesevermögen und Leseinteresse von Kindern.* Frankfurt: dipa Verlag, 1984.

5136. Herr, Giesela. "Die Wirkungen der Comics auf Kinder. Hausarbeit für die 1. Staatsprüfung für das Lehramt an Volks-und Realschulen." Hamburg: 1957.

5137. Hintz-Vonthron, Erna. "Comic-Books: Verderben der Jugend." *Frau und Frieden* (Wattensheid). No. 8, 1955, p. 8.

5138. Hübner, Gerd. *Gute Heftreihen—Eine Hilfe im Kampf Gegen Jugendgefährdende Schriften.* Cologne-Klettenberg: Volkswartbund, 1957.

5139. Ipfling, Heinz-Jürgen. *Jugend und Illustrierte.* Osnabrück: Fromm-Verlag, 1965.

5140. Jansen, Hans. "Comics—Opium fürs Kind." *Westdeutsche Allgemeine Zeitung* (Essen). Pfingsten 1965.

5141. "Jugendgefährdung Durch Comics." *Katholische Zeitschrift für Kinder- und Jugendfürsorge* (Freiburg). 35, 1954, pp. 362-363.

5142. Kempkes, Wolfgang *et al.* "Die 'Komik' der Comics." In *Humor in der Kinder- und Jugendliteratur*, pp. 117-119. Insel Mainau: Angelos-Verlag, 1970.

5143. Kiefer, Elfriede. "Untersuchungen Über das Sinnverständnis von Comics bei Lernbehinderten Kindern." *Hausarbeit zur 1. Lehreprüfung für Sonderschulen.* May 1971.

5144. *Kinder—Der Neu Entdeckte Markt.* Stuttgart: Ehapa Verlag, 1973.

5145. "Kinden Sollen Speedy Retten." *Gong* (Munich). No. 45, 1972, p. 22.

5146. Klug, Maria. "Comics, Eine Sittliche Gefahr für Unsere Jugend." *Katholische Frauenbildung* (Paderborn). 56, 1955, pp. 195-198.

5147. Koch, Renate. "Der Zusammenhang von Leserfertigkeit und Comic-Konsum bei 11-12 Ährigen Volksschülern." Hausarbeit für die 1. Staatsprüfung für das Lehramt an Volks- und Realschulen (Hamburg). June 1970.

5148. "Koch-Comic für Kinder." *Eltern.* No. 10, 1972, pp. 166-167.

5149. Köhl, R. "Förderung Guter Jugendhefte Durch Eine Umtauschaktion." In *Börsenblatt für den Deutschen Buchhandel*, pp. 290-295. Frankfurt: 1956.

5150. Köhlert, Adolf. "Hefte Gegen Hefte." *Jugendschriften-Warte*. 8:7/8 (1956), p. 52-53.

5151. "Kohlhaas: Sind Comics Jugendgefährdend?" *Unsere Jugend* (Munich). 7:10 (1955), pp. 450-457.

5152. Künnemann, Horst. "Comics: Ikonen für Kinder?" *Zeit-magazin*. December 31, 1971, pp. 8-13.

5153. Künnemann, Horst. *Kinder und Kulturkonsum*. Weinheim: Beltz, 1972. 163 pp.

5154. Langfeldt, Johannes. "Man Kann den Schund Nur Mit der Jugend Bekämpfen." *Bücherei und Bildung* (Reutlingen). 8, 1956, pp. 292-293.

5155. Lenz, Heinrich. "Comics-Reißer-Jugendlust." *Die Bayerische Schule* (Munich). 9:1-2 (1956), pp. 4-6.

5156. "Leseinteressen der Kinder, Umfrage der Hamburger Bücherhallen." Hamburg. May-June 1965.

5157. Lissner, Erich. "Müssen Wir die Kinder vor Comics Schützen?" *Frankfurter Rundschau*. August 18, 1955.

5158. Maier, Karl-Ernst. *Jugendschrifttum*. Bad Heilbrunn: Verlag Klinckhardt, 1969.

5159. "Marsyas: Revolution in der Kinderstube?" *Jugendschriften-Warte*. 5:11 (1953), p. 73.

5160. *Medium Comic, Kunst, Kommerz, Kinderkram?* Ausstellung vom 14. 10.- 22.11.78, Galerie im Ideal Haus. Berlin: 1979.

5161. Metzen, Gabriele. "Über die Verbreitung und Wirkung von Comics bei Kindern des 3. und 4. Schuljahres." *Hausarbeit zur 1. Lehrerprüfung für Volksschulen*. Trier. 1970.

5162. Mosse, Hilde L. *Die Bedeutung der Massenmedien für die Entstehung Kindlicher Neurosen (Gefährliche Comics)*. Cologne-Klettenberg: Verlag Volkswartbund, 1955.

5163. Mosse, Hilde L. "Die Bedeutung der Massenmedien für die Entstehung Kindlicher Neurosen." *Monatsschrift für Kinderheilkunde*. 113:2, pp. 85-91.

5164. Mosse, Hilde L. "Die Comics und die Kinder." *Frankfurter Allgemeine Zeitung*. January 7, 1956.

5165. Nothmann, K.H. "Looping the Loop!" *Jugendschriften-Warte*. No. 2, 1952, p. 61f.

5166. Oerter, R. "Kognitive Dissonanz und Erzieherliche Beeinflussung (Zur Wirkung Überredender Kommunikation bei Jugendlichen)." *Psychologie und Praxis* (Cologne). 8:3 (1964), pp. 108-118.

5167. Richter, Dieter, ed. *Das Politische Kinderbuch: Eine Aktuelle Historische Dokumentation.* Darmstadt: Luchterhand, 1973.

5168. Römhild, Wolfgang. "Comic-Strips und Derartige Bildergeschichten für Kinder?" *Westdeutsche Schulzeitung* (Speyer). 73, 1964, pp. 27-28.

5169. Sarcander, Alice. "Untersuchungen Über die Wirkungen von Comics auf Kinder." *Hausarbeit für das 1. Staatsexamen für das Lehramt an Volks- und Realschulen.* Hamburg. 1955.

5170. Scheibe, Wolfgang. "Jugendzeitschriftenkritisch Gesehen!" *Recht der Jugend* (Cologne). 4:17 (1956), pp. 258-260.

5171. Scherf, Walter. "Gibt Es Gute Comics?" *Jugendliteratur.* 9:9 (1959), pp. 406-411, 528-529.

5172. Schilling, Robert. "Aus der Arbeit der Bundesprüfstelle für Jugendgefährdende Schriften." *Recht der Jugend.* 12, 1956, p. 59.

5173. Schilling, Robert. *Literarischer Jugendschutz.* Berlin: Luchterhand, 1959.

5174. Schilling, Robert. "Zum Jahresbericht der Bundesprüfstelle für Jugendge Fährdende Schriften." *Recht der Jugend.* 20, 1955.

5175. Schmidt, Heiner. "Jugend und Buch in der Gefährdung von Comics und Kitsch." *Unsere Volksschule* (Frankfurt). September 1961, pp. 260-264.

5176. Schneider, Harriet. "Müncher Bilderbogen in Ihrer Wirkung auf Kinder (Literaturhinweis)." *Jugendschriften-Warte.* 6:1 (1954), p. 2.

5177. Schnurrer, Achim and Hartmut Becker. *Die Kinder des Fliegenden Robert. Beiträge zur Archäologie der Deutschen Bildergeschichtentradition: Katalogbuch zur Gleichnamigen Ausstellung.* Hanover: Ed. Becker und Knigge, 1979.

5178. Schückler, Georg. *Jugendgefährdung Durch Comics.* Cologne-Klettenberg: Verlag. Volkswartbund, 1955.

5179. Schückler, Georg. "Verbrecher-Comics-Jugendgefährdend. Eine Bedeutsame Entdeckung des Bundesgerichtshofs." *Ruf ins Volk.* 10, 1955.

5180. Söhlmann, Fritz. "Welche Situation Findet das Gesetz Über die Verbreitung Jugendgefährdender Schriften vor?" *Recht der Jugend.* 1:4 (1953), pp. 57-58.

5181. "Sucht den Kindern die Comics aus!" *Jugendschriften-Warte.* 6:11 (1954), p. 79.

5182. Teichmann, Alfred. "Betrachtung Nach Einer Umtauschaktion von Schundheften." *Jugendschutz* (Darmstadt). 1:11 (1956), pp. 18-20.

5183. "Was Ist Gegen die Jugendgefährdung Durch die Comic-Books zu Tun?" *Kommunalpolitische Blätter* (Recklinghausen). 7, 1955, pp. 84-86.

5184. Weise, Gerhard. "Warum Kaufen Kinder Immer Wieder Schundliteratur?" *Jugendschriften-Warte*. 18:3 (1966), p. 10.

5185. Wellnhoener, Axel. "Mass Media As a Socialization Factor: The Influence of Comics on Children. Massenmedien als Sozialisationsfaktor. Der Einfluss von Comics auf Kinder." *Soziologenkorrespondenz*. 7 (1980), pp. 135-156.

5186. Wichmann, Jürgen. "Wie Lange Noch Jugendgefährdung Durch Comics?" *Die Neue Ordnung* (Paderborn). 9:3 (1955), pp. 172-175.

5187. Wiegand, Wilfried. "Böse Kinder, Sadistische Enten." *Die Welt*. No. 283, 1969, p. 9.

Cinema, Television, Theater

5188. Bentlin, Dirk. "Comic-Bilderwelten auf dem Neuen ARTE-TV-Kanal." *ICOM INFO*. June 1992, p. 3.

5189. Borringo, Heinz-Lothar. *Spannung in Text und Film*. Düsseldorf: 1980.

5190. Braune, Heinrich. "Mandra als Film." *Hamburger Morgenpost*. July 19, 1965.

5191. Bunk, Hans. *Beziehung Jugendlicher zu Film und Bildserie*. Cologne-Klettenberg: Verlag Volkswartbund, 1955.

5192. "Comic-Fernsehfilme." *Hör Zu*. No. 15, 1970, p. 147.

5193. Dahrendorf, Malte and Wolfgang Kempkes. "Comics Heute." *Jugend-Film-Fernsehen* (Munich). 16:4 (1972), pp. 14-19.

5194. Doelker-Tobler, Verena. "Zeichentrickfilm und Comics aus Medien-Pädagogischer Sicht." In *Comics and Visual Culture: Research Studies from Ten Countries*, edited by Alphons Silbermann and H.-D. Dyroff, pp. 248-253. Munich: K.G. Saur, 1986.

5195. Doelker-Tobler, Verena. "Zeichentrickfilm und Comics aus Medien-Pädagogischer Sicht." *Communications* (Sankt Augustin). 9:2/3 (1983), pp. 221-226.

5196. "Film und Comics." *Comic Forum. Das Österreichische Fachmagazin für Comicliteratur.* 5:18 (1983), pp. 65-66.

5197. Freisewinkel, Ernst L. "Comics—Die Lustigen Streifen." 1. Deutsches Fernsehen (ARD), March 17, 1969. Cologne.

5198. Fuchs, Wolfgang J. "Comics, Film und Fernsehen." In *Batman, Beatles, Barbarella*, edited by Wolfgang J. Fuchs and Thomas Wirsum, pp. 30-43. Edersberg/Obb: Edition 8 1/2, Lothar Just, 1985.

5199. Ihme, Burkhard. "Montage im Film und im Comic." *Comic Info.* May-June 1993, pp. 37-40.

5200. Kempkes, Wolfgang. "Comic-Film." *Bulletin: Jugend + Literatur.* No. 4, 1970, p. 12.

5201. Kempkes, Wolfgang. "Comics und Fernsehen." *Bulletin: Jugend + Literatur.* No. 9, 1970, pp. 13-14.

5202. Kempkes, Wolfgang. "Comics und Film. Ein Vergleich." In *Comic Strips: Geschichte, Struktur, Wirkung und Verbreitung der Bildergeschichten. Ausstellungskatalog der Berliner Akademie der Künste, 13.12. 1969-25.1.1970,* pp. 32-35. Berlin.

5203. Kempkes, Wolfgang. "Comic-Zeichentrickfilme." *Bulletin: Jugend + Literatur.* No. 6, 1970, p. 6.

5204. Kluwe, Sigbert. "Gewalt in Comics." *Jugend-Film-Fernsehen.* 16:2 (1972), pp. 20-28.

5205. "Mainzelmännchen Kapriolen; Beilage: RTV-Radio und Television, das Illustrierte Programm." *Hamburger Abendecho.* April 24, 1966.

5206. "Radio-Strip." *Die Welt.* March 15, 1967.

5207. von Praunheim, Rosa. *Oh Muvie.* Frankfurt: Heinrich-Heine-Verlag, 1969. 168 pp.

Education, Culture

5208. Andersch, Lothar. "Comics im Englischunterricht. Eine Unterrichtseinheit für die Sekundarstufe I." *Englisch-Amerikanische Studien* (Cologne). 3, 1981, pp. 234-255.

5209. Apelt, Hans-Peter. "Bildergeschichten im Sprachunterricht." *Zielsprache Deutsch* (Munich). 3, 1978, pp. 21-28.

5210. Bamberg, Michael and Walter Henning. "Comics im Unterricht. Zwei Modelle für die Klassen 9 und 13." *Diskussion Deutsch* (Frankfurt, Berlin, Munich). 14, 1973, pp. 379-397.

5211. Barrera-Vidal, Albert. "Comics, Fumetti, Bande Dessinée—Semiotik und Didaktik Eines Massenmediums." *Neusprachliche Mitteilungen aus Wissenschaft und Praxis* (Berlin). 39:3 (1986), pp. 166-173.

5212. Bauer, Hans. *Die Moderne Schule im Kampf Gegen Schmöker, Plund und Schund.* Kulmbach: E.C. Baumann, 1957.

5213. Baumgärtner, Alfred C. "Comics, Pädagogisch Gesehen. Zum Gegenwärtigen Stand der Diskussion." *Sprache im Technischen Zeitalter* (Berlin). 44, 1972, pp. 327-331.

5214. Baumgärtner, Alfred C. "Die Welt der Comics." *Kamps Pädagogische Taschenbücher* (Bochum). No. 26, 4. Aufl., 1971.

5215. Baumgärtner, Maja, Roberto Braun, Christian Doelker, *et al. Comics: Unterrichtsvorschläge für das 1. - 3. Schuljahr und die Vorschule.* Zug: Klett und Balmer, 1982.

5216. Baur, Elisabeth Katrin. *Der Comic: Strukturen-Vermarktung-Unterricht.* Düsseldorf: Schwann Verlag, 1977. 96 pp.

5217. Beinlich, H. *Handbuch des Deutschunterrichts.* Stuttgart: 1964. Vol. 2, pp. 800-801, 804, 824-825, 869.

5218. Blau, Arno. "Comic-Books—Und Was Sagt der Taubstrummenlehrer Dazu?" *Neue Blätter für Taubstummenbildung* (Heidelberg). 9:3/4 (1955), pp. 101-103.

5219. Börner, Elisabeth. "Eine Bilderfibel als. Weltkundliches Unterrichtsmittel." Hamburg: Hausarbeit für das 1. Staatsexamen für das Lehramt an Volks- und Realschulen, 1962.

5220. Bosshard, Rosmarie, Roberto Braun, Christian Doelker, *et al. Comics: Unterrichtsvorschläge für das 4.-6. Schuljahr.* Zug: Klett und Balmer, 1981.

5221. Brawand, Leo. "Wer Niemals Eine Schraube Sah...." *Der Spiegel.* No. 43, 1967, p. 118.

5222. Brück, Axel. "Comics in der Schule?" *Jugendschriften-Warte.* N.F., 23:3 (1971), p. 11.

5223. Buck, Siegfried. "Comics und Fernsehsendungen im Lernbereich 'Texte Verstehen.'" In Hans-Joachim Neumann. *Der Deutschunterricht in der Grundschule. 3 Bde*, Vol. 2, pp. 83-95. Freiburg/Breisgau: Herder, 1976.

5224. Burgdorf, Paul. *Comics im Unterricht*. Weinheim, Basel: Julius Beltz Verlag, 1976.

5225. Buschmann, Christel. "Verachtet, Aber Höchst Lebendig. Comics Zwischen Propaganda und Protest." *Die Zeit*. October 16, 1970, p. 28.

5226. Bußmann, M. "Die Wirkung von Comic-Books auf 11-14 jährige Kinder." Bonn: Hausarbeit zur 1. Lehrerprüfung, 1964.

5227. "Comics." *Bayerische Schule* (Munich). September 20, 1952.

5228. "Comics." *Neue Deutsche Schule* (Essen). 22, 1954.

5229. "Comics im Arbeitsprozeß." *Berufspädagogische Zeitschrift* (Frankfurt). 2/3, 1960, p. 34.

5230. Conrady,   Peter.   "Bildergeschichten-Schüler-Unterricht."   *Muttersprache* (Wiesbaden). 88:5 (1978), pp. 291-295.

5231. Cordt, Willy K. "Neues von den Comics." *Westermanns Pädagogische Beiträge* (Braunschweig). 7:9 (1955), pp. 462-469.

5232. Dahrendorf, Malte. "Comics in der Schule. Ein Unterrichtsmodell." In *Comics im Medienmarkt, in der Analyse, im Unterricht*, edited by Wolfgang C. Fuchs, pp. 149-162. Opladen: Leske und Budrich, 1977.

5233. Dahrendorf, Malte. "Vorüberlegungen zu Einer Didaktik der Comic Strips." *Jugendschriften-Warte*. 23:12-71 (1971), pp. 42-43.

5234. "Der Vertrag in Bildern." *Hamburger Abendblatt*. September 26/27, 1970, p. 2.

5235. Dilthey, Helga. "Ausgewählte Comics in Einer R7. Hinführung zum Kritischen, Bewußten Lesen." Hamburg: Hausarbeit für die 2. Lehrerprüfung, March 1972.

5236. Eckart, Walter. "Was Ist Es um die Comics?" *Die Scholle* (Hanover). 27:4 (1959), pp. 215-216.

5237. Eversberg, Gerd. "Comics im Unterricht. Ein Literaturbericht." *Medien und Sexualpädagogik* (Bonn-Bad Godesberg). 3:2 (1975), pp. 15-25.

5238. Faust, Wolfgang. "Über das 'Lesen' von Comics." In *Comics Strips: Geschichte, Struktur, Wirkung und Verbreitung der Bildergeschichten, Ausstellungskatalog der Berliner Akademie der Künste, 13.12.1969-25.1.1970*, pp. 28-31, Berlin.

5239. Fischer, Gert. "Die Außerschulischen Leseinteressen der Kinder des 7. und 8. Schuljahres und Möglichkeiten der Lenkung Durch die Schule." Hamburg: Hausarbeit zur 2.Lehrerprüfung, 1965, pp. 5-8, 10-17.

5240. Flacke, Walter. "Information Oder Instruktion?" *Jugendschriften-Warte* (Frankfurt). 23:6 (1971), p. 23.

5241. "Fortschritt Durch Comic-Books." *Velhagen u. Klasings Monatshefte* (Bielefeld). 61:10 (1953), p. 895.

5242. Forytta, Claus. "Sprache in den Comics. Anmerkungen zu Einem Unterrichtsversuch im 4. Schuljahr." In *Deutschunterricht in der Grundschule*, edited by Sönke Zander, pp. 215-229. Bad Heilbrunn: Klinkhardt, 1977.

5243. Frings, Udo. "Comics im Lateinunterricht?" *Gymnasium* (Heidelberg). 85:1 (1978), pp 47-54.

5244. Fuchs, Wolfgang J. "Anwendungsgebiete und Einsatzmöglichkeiten von Comics." *Medien + Erziehung*. (Leverkusen). 20:1 (1976), pp. 16-23.

5245. Fuchs, Wolfgang J., ed. *Comics im Medienmarkt—Comics in der Analyse—Comics im Unterricht*. Leverkusen: Leske and Budrich, 1977. 160 pp.

5246. Funhoff, Jörg. "Comics im Unterricht." *Kunst und Unterricht*. 10, 1970, p. 17.

5247. Funhoff, Jörg. "Dynamik und Aggression in den Comics." *Kunst und Unterricht*. 10, 1970, pp. 25-26.

5248. Fusshöller, Wolfgang and Eugen Schröter. "'Der Frosch.' Ein Gedicht von Wilhelm Busch als Anlaß für Erste Reflexionen Über Comics in Klasse 3." *Kunst + Unterricht* (Velber bei Hanover). 27, 1974, pp. 24-26.

5249. Gaupp, Berthold, Ute Jürgens, Bernhard Link, and Achim Schnurrer. *Phänomen Comics Transparent Gemacht. Programme, Anleitungen und Vorschläge für die Erzieherische Praxis in Hort, Heim, Freizeiten und Seminaren*. Fellbach: Adolf Bonz, 1978.

5250. "Gefechtsmäßig Gelächelt." *Informationen für die Truppe* (Cologne). No. 9, 1966, p. 638.

5251. Geist, Hans-Friedrich. "Inflation der Bilder. Eine Betrachtung zur Erziehungssituation der Gegenwart." *Lebendige Erziehung*. (Hamburg). 5:6 (1956), pp. 131, 134.

5252. Geitel, Klaus. "Traumlieferant Oder Kulturvermittler?" *Die Welt*. No. 59, 1962.

5253. Gerstenlauer, Wolfgang. "Birne Ist Kein Helferlein Oder: Warum Daniel Düsentrieb Daniel Herburger Nicht das Wasser Reichen Kann." *Der Deutschunterricht*. 34:4 (1982), pp. 64-71.

5254. Giffhorn, Hans. *Seh-und Lesegewohnheiten von Kindern in Bezug auf Comics: Eine Leitstudie*. Berlin: Neue Gesellschaft für Bildende Kunst, 1971.

5255. Glaubitz, Joachim. "Kommunistische Moralpredigten in Comic Books." *Die Zeit*. August 19, 1966, p. 26.

5256. Gonnermann, Elke. "Versuch Einer Kritischen Auseinandersetzung Mit Comic-Books im Unterricht Einer 6. Klasse." Hamburg: Hausarbeit für das 1. Staatsexamen für das Lehramt an Volks- und Realschulen, 1969.

5257. Greiner, Rudolf, ed. *Comics—Arbeitstexte für den Unterricht*. Stuttgart: 1977.

5258. Greiner, Rudolf, ed. *Comics: für die Sekundarstufe*. Stuttgart: Reclam Verlag, 1983.

5259. Groß, Heinrich. "Untersuchungen zur Privaten Lektüre von Schülern der Oberstufe der Sonderschule für Lernbehinderte." Mainz: Hausarbeit für die 1. Lehrerprüfung an Sonderschulen, 1969.

5260. Grünewald, Dietrich. "Bildgeschichten und Comics." *Kunst + Unterricht* (Hanover). Sonderheft, 1982, pp. 93-105.

5261. Grünewald, Dietrich. *Comics—Kitsch Oder Kunst? Die Bildgeschichte in Analyse und Unterricht. Ein Handbuch zur Comic-Didaktik*. Weinheim: Beltz, 1982. 208 pp.

5262. Grünewald, Dietrich. "Die Comic-Story im Unterricht. Zur Analyse von Comics." *Praxis Deutsch: Kunst + Unterricht* (Hanover). Sonderheft, 1978, pp. 96-97.

5263. Grünewald, Dietrich. *Karikatur im Unterricht: Geschichte, Analysen, Schulpraxis*. Weinheim, Basel: Beltz, 1979.

5264. Gulnar, Duve, ed. *Wir Machen Unsere Comics Selber: Erfahrungen Mit Comics an der Grundschule*. Berlin: Basis Verlag, 1974.

5265. Habermann, Hilke. "Comic-Hefte als Lektüre 11-15 Jähriger Volksschüler." Hamburg: Hausarbeit zur 1. Lehrerprüfung an Volks- und Realschulen, May 1968.

5266. Hahn, Ronald M. "Comics Auch Mit Klassenkampf." *General-Anzeiger* (Wuppertal). December 30, 1971.

5267. Hennings, Hermann. "Comics-Lesestoff für Gehörlose?" *Jugendschutz* (Darmstadt). 7:4 (1962), pp. 200-202.

5268. Hensel-Johne, Christiane. "Ein Comic Entsteht im Lateinunterricht." *Der Altsprachliche Unterricht*. 26:1 (1983), pp. 75-77.

5269. Herr, Alfred. "Comic-Sucht im Frühen Grundschulalter." *Westdeutsche Schulzeitung* (Speyer). 73, 1964, pp. 26-27.

5270. Herr, Alfred. "Grenzfall—Comics im Frühen Grundschulalter." *Hamburger Lehrerzeitung*. 17:15 (1964), pp. 516-519.

5271. Herr, Alfred. "Verbreitung der Comics bei Zehnjährigen." *Die Schule* (Bielefeld). 35:6 (1959), p. 28.

5272. Hinninger, Volker. "Comic-Schemata Abändern. Unterricht in Klasse 5." *Kunst + Unterricht* (Velber bei Hanover). 24, 1974, pp. 25-28.

5273. Hoffmann, Bärbel and Hans Hoffmann. "Kunstunterricht und Comics." *Kunst und Unterricht*. 10, 1970, pp. 21-22.

5274. Hoffmann, Ludger. "Comics: Geschichte, Struktur und Didaktik." *Massenmedien im Deutschunterricht. Lernbereiche und Didaktische Perspektiven*, edited by Hans-Dieter Kübler, pp. 238-262. Frankfurt: Haag + Herchen, 1981.

5275. Hoffmann, Michael. "Was Schüler Durch Comic Strips 'Lernen.'" *Westermanns Pädagogische Beiträge*. 22:10 (1970), pp. 497-507.

5276. Hoppe, Wilhelm. "Schluß Mit den Comics." *Kulturarbeit*. 8:5 (1956), pp. 96-100.

5277. Hühnken, Renate. "Wie Werden Comics Gelesen? Untersuchungen am Verhalten von Schülern 5. Klassen." Hamburg: Hausarbeit für die 1. Prüfung für das Lehramt an Volks- und Realschulen, October 1970.

5278. Jeske, Uwe, ed. *2-4-6-8 Wird Hier Ein Freßsack Angebracht? (Antiautoritäre Comic-Geschichte)*. Cologne: Jeske-Verlag, 1970.

5279. Jöckel, Frauke. "Unterrichtseinheit: Les Aventures d'Idéfix in der 9. Klasse Einer Integrierten Gesamtschule." *Französisch Heute* (Frankfurt). 4,1974, pp. 177-191.

5280. "Keine 'Comics' Mehr Unter Schulbänken!" *Neue Zeit* (Cologne). January 13, 1955.

5281. Kempkes, Wolfgang. "Comics im Schulunterricht." *Bulletin: Jugend + Literatur*. No. 8, 1970, p. 6.

5282. Kempkes, Wolfgang. "Comics im Schulunterricht in Hessen." *Bulletin: Jugend + Literatur*. No. 3, 1970, p. 25.

5283. Kempkes, Wolfgang. "Comics im Unterricht—Stundenprotokolle." *Jugendschriften-Warte* (Essen—Stadtwald). 3, 1972, pp. 9-11.

5284. Kempkes, Wolfgang. "Comics im Unterricht: Stundenprotokoll I-II." *Jugendschriften-Warte*. 24:1,3 (1972), pp. 2-4, 9-11.

5285. Kempkes, Wolfgang. "Der Zweite Weltkrieg: Comic-Artig?" *Bulletin: Jugend + Literatur*. No. 4, 1970, pp. 28-29.

5286. Kempkes, Wolfgang. "Märchen-Comics." *Bulletin: Jugend + Literatur*. No. 7, 1970, p. 12.

5287. Kempkes, Wolfgang. "Studenten Lesen Comics." *Bulletin: Jugend + Literatur*. No. 9, 1970, p. 14.

5288. Kerkhoff, Ingrid. *Literaturunterricht. Didaktik und Theorie am Beispiel der Comics*. Gießen: Anabas-Verlag, 1975.

5289. Klose, Werner. "Alles Lesen, Alles Sehen, Alles Hören." *Die Zeit*. December 24, 1971, pp. 42-43.

5290. Köhlert, Adolf. "Schule und Comics." *Jugendschriften-Warte*. 6:10 (1954), pp. 35-36.

5291. Köhlert, Adolf and L. Hell. "Comics in der Schule?" *Jugendschriften-Warte*. 22:10-70 (1970), pp. 33-34.

5292. Köther, Hermann. "Analyse Eines Werbecomics. Ein Unterrichtsversuch in Einer Quarta." *Zeitschrift für Kunstpädagogik* (Ratingen). 1, 1975, pp. 35-38.

5293. Kraus, Gerda. "Comics im Unterricht, Aber Wie?" *Die Grundschule* (Braunschweig). 7:7 (1975), pp. 364-369.

5294. Krause, Ursula. "Comic-Books als Lektüre von Volksschülern. Untersuchungen an Einer Hamburger Schule." Hamburg: Hausarbeit für das 1. Staatsexamen für das Lehramt an Volks- und Realschulen, May 1962.

5295. Kronenberg, Martin. *Comics und Bildergeschichten. Lehrerinformation. Schülerheft*. Wolfenbüttel: Kallmeyer, 1985.

5296. Kühl, Marlene. "Kritisches Lesen von Comics. Theorie und Praxis Eines Unterrichts auf der Sekundarstufe." Kiel: Hausarbeit für das 1. Lehrerexamen, 1972.

5297. Kuhlmay, Egbert. "Wir Gestalten Eine Bildergeschichte in Einen Comic um. 5. Jahrgangsstufe: Deutsch: Sprachgebrauch." *Ehrenwirth Hauptschulmagazin* (Munich). 7:11 (1982), pp. 31-32, 37-38, 63.

5298. Lecke, Bodo. "Comics als Vorschule." In *Projekt Deutschunterricht 5. Massenmedien und Trivialliteratur*, edited by Heinz Ide and Bremer Kollektiv, pp. 105-155. Stuttgart: J.B. Metzler Verlag, 1973/1977.

5299. Lehmann, Bernd. "Leseinteressen und Lesegewohnheiten 3-15 Jähriger Schüler." *Zeitnahe Schularbeit* (Frankfurt). 22:4/5 (1969), pp. 107-126.

5300. Leipziger, Walter. "Das Spiel Mit dem Feuer." *Elternhaus und Schule* (Cologne). 22:1 (1956), pp. 2-6.

5301. Löffler, Renate. "Über Bild und Rolle zum Sprachhandeln: Überlegungen und Praktische Beispiele zur Arbeit Arbeit Mit Rollenspiel und Bildergeschichte im Deutschunterricht Mit Ausländischen Studenten." *Zielsprache Deutsch* (Munich). 2, 1979, pp. 23-33.

5302. Menzel, Wolfgang. "Einen Streich Erzählen. 3./4. Schuljahr." *Praxis Deutsch* (Velber bei Hanover). 11:65 (1984), pp. 25-26.

5303. Merdian, Franz. "Die Sprechblase—Was Verbinden Jüngere Kinder Damit? Untersuchung zum Bedeutungserwerb Eines Comic-Zeichens." *Kodikas/Code* (Tübingen). 6:1/2 (1983), pp. 85-102.

5304. Metzer, H. *Trivialliteratur 2: Comics und Triviales Jugendbuch in der Sekundarstufe I*. Munich: 1974.

5305. Minte-König, Bianka. "Comics im Unterricht der Sekundarstufe II." *Lehrmittel Aktuell* (Braunschweig). 1, 1977, pp. 16-23.

5306. Missfeldt, Wulf. *Comics zur Analyse Lateinischer Sätze*. Paderborn: Schöningh, 1976.

5307. Modellversuchsgruppe Kunst/ Visuelle Kommunikation. *Comics, die Presse der 2. Etage der Schulbänke*. Wiesbaden: Hessisches Institut für Bildungsplanung und Schulentwicklung, 1976.

5308. Nellen-Piské, Jutta. *Erziehung zum Lesen im Unterricht*, pp. 28-31, 48-53. Hamburg: Verlag für Buchmarktforschung, 1966.

5309. Niggemaier, Friedhelm and Edeltraud Schumacher-Gerdes. "Comics—in Deutsch und Kunst (5. Schuljahr)." *Kunst + Unterricht* (Velber bei Hanover). 30, 1975, pp. 30-33.

5310. Oberst, Helmut. *Comics als Gestaltungsmittel im Altsprachlichen Unterricht. Aus dem Sammelband der Referate des Paderborner Werkstattgesprächs. Visualisation von Informationen in Lernprogrammen*. Paderborn: FEoLL, 1978.

5311. Oberst, Helmut. *Plautus in Comics. Die Gespenstergeschichte (Mostellaria)*. Zurich, Munich: Artemis Verlag, 1971, 1973.

5312. Oberst, Helmut. *Terenz, Die Brüder: Mit Ausführlichem Wörterverzeichnis*. Munich: Heimerman, 1975.

5313. Otto, Renate and Karl-Heinz Otto. "Bewegung und Handlung. Schüler Zeichnen Comics." *Kunst und Unterricht*. 10, 1970, pp. 18-20.

5314. Pantel, Volker. *Comics. Arbeitsheft für den Deutsch-und Kunstunterricht ab dem 5. Schuljahr und Lehrerbegleitheft zum Arbeitsheft für den Deutsch-und Kunstunterricht ab dem 5. Schuljahr.* Munich: List, 1980.

5315. Pforte, Dietger, ed. *Comics im Ästhetischen Unterricht.* Frankfurt: Athenäum Fischer Taschenbuch Verlag, 1974.

5316. Pforte, Dietger. "Comics im Ästhetischen Unterricht." *Sprache im Technischen Zeitalter* (Berlin). No. 44, 1972, pp. 332-341.

5317. Rauch, Sabine. "Untersuchung von Comics im Unterricht." *Diskussion Deutsch* (Frankfurt). No. 6, 1971, pp. 351-371.

5318. Saxer, Robert. "Comics." In *Deutschunterricht in der Diskussion. Forschungsberichte,* edited by Dietrich Boueke, Vol. 1, pp. 403, 409; Vol. 2, pp. 362-391. Paderborn: Schöningh, 1979.

5319. Saxer, Robert. "Die Verschulung der Comics." *Informationen zur Deutschdidaktik* (Hanover). 8:1 (1983), pp. 6-9.

5320. Schappacher, D. "Comics im Unterricht." *Zeitschrift für Kunstpädagogik und Ihre Grundlagen* (Ratingen). 3, 1972, pp. 129-138.

5321. Scheckel, Rainer. *Bildgeleitete Sprachspiele. Theorie und Praxis Produktiver Bildverwendung im Sprachunterricht der Grundschule.* Tübingen: Niemeyer, 1981. 191 pp.

5322. Schmidmaier, Werner. "Verkehrser-Ziehung für Alfonso." *Graphik.* No. 12, 1971.

5323. Schmidt-Rogge, C.H. "Die Comics und die Phantasie. Inflation der Bilder und Visueller Dadaismus." In *Schule und Leben* (Cologne). 9:12 (1958), p. 469-470; *Polizei, Polizeipraxis* (Cologne). 49, 1958, pp. 170-171.

5324. Schnurrer, Achim. "Abriß zur Vermittlung Sozialen Verhaltens Durch Comics. Ansprüche und Beispiele." *Comixene. Das Comicfachmagazin.* 6:23 (1979), pp. 15-16.

5325. Schwadtke, Brita. "Comics als Unterrichtsmedien im Sexualunterricht." *Westermanns Pädagogische Beiträge* (Braunschweig). 27:4 (1975), pp. 215-222.

5326. Siegert, Babette. "Die Bildreihe im Erstaufsatzunterricht." Hamburg: Hausarbeit für das 1. Staatsexamen für das Lehramt an Volks- und Realschulen, 1966.

5327. "Sind Sie Konsequent?" *Brigitte* (Hamburg). December 31, 1968, pp. 78-79.

5328. Slama, Elke. *Comics im 4. Schuljahr. Ein Beitrag zur Medienerziehung.* Düsseldorf: Bagel, 1976.

5329. Streit, Jakob and Elisabeth Klein. *Comics Oder Märchen? Gift Oder Nahrung für die Seelen Unserer Kinder.* Bad Liebenzell/Ul.: Verein für Ein Erweitertes Heilwesen; Dornach: Auslieferung für die Schweiz: Verein für Ein Anthroposophisch Erweitertes Heilwesen, 1981.

5330. Strich, Wolfgang. "Stoffplan für das Fach 'Form und Farbe' an der Walter-Gropius-Schule in Berlin." *Gesamtschule* (Braunschweig). 3:2 (1971), pp. 10-13.

5331. Szyszkowitz, Peter. "Comics und Bildgeschichten—Untersuchung Eines Massenmediums für die Unterrichtbarkeit im Fach Bildnerische Erziehung." In *Der Mensch im Spannungsfeld Zeitgenössischer Künstlerischer Bestrebungen. Bericht Uber die Gesamtösterreichische Arbeitstagung für Lehrer an Allgemeinbildenden Höheren Schulen in Graz im September 1974*, edited by Erich Benedikt, pp. 75-79. Vienna: Österreichischer Bundesverlag, 1977.

5332. Sulzbach, Peter. "Politische Bildung für die Kleinen." *Pardon.* No. 6, 1965.

5333. Vogel, Harald. "Comics im Deutschunterricht. Von der Behandlung als Triviale Jugendlektüre zur Semiotischen Analyse Eines Massenmediums." *Der Deutschunterricht.* 27:1 (1975), pp. 6-33.

5334. Vogel, Klaus. "Comics. 6. Jahrgangsstufe. Deutsch: Arbeit Mit Texten." *Ehrenwirth Hauptschulmagazin* (Munich). 3:11 (1978), pp. 35-38.

5335. von Ziegesar, Detlef. "Die Behandlung Fremdsprachlicher Comics in den Oberklassen der Hauptschule." *Englisch* (Berlin). 10:2 (1975), pp. 53-59.

5336. Wasem, Erich. *Der Audio-Visuelle Wohlstand. Didaktik und Interpretationsmedien.* Munich: Ehrenwirth, 1968.

5337. Wasem, Erich. *Presse, Rundfunk, Fernsehen, Reklame, Pädagogisch Gesehen.* Munich: 1959.

5338. Watzke, Oswald. "Comics." In Oswald Watzke, Reiner Friedrichs, and Wolfgang Babucke. *Umgang mit Texten in der Sekundarstufe 1. Eine Einführung Anhand von Unterrichtsmodellen*, pp. 229-237. Munich: List, 1975.

5339. Watzke, Oswald, ed. *Bildergeschichten und Comics in der Grundschule.* Donauwörth: Auer, 1982. 144 pp.

5340. Watzke, Oswald. *Bildergeschichten und Comics in der Sekundarstufe I.* Donauwörth: Auer, 1981. 184 pp.

5341. Weber, Erich. "Die Pädagogische Auseinandersetzung der Eltern und Lehrer mit den Geheimen Miterziehern." *Welt der Schule.* 19:10 (1966), pp. 433-439.

5342. Welke, Manfred. *Die Sprache der Comics.* Frankfurt: 1956.

5343. Wenz, Gustav. "Die Kunst des Lesens und die Comics." *Unsere Volksschule.* 12:8 (1961), pp. 385-388.

5344. Werlich, Egon. *Comics and Cartoons. Translating Visual Elements into Language.* Dortmund: Lensing, 1980.

5345. Wermke, Jutta. "Der 'Tiefere Sinn' in den Comics. Comics im Kreuzfeuer der Kritik." In *Massenmedium Comics,* edited by Dieter Golombek and Reinhold Lehmann, pp. 9-13. Bonn: Bundeszentrale für Politische Bildung, 1976.

5346. Wermke, Jutta. *Wozu Comics Gut Sind?! Unterschiedliche Meinungen zur Beurteilung des Mediums und Seiner Verwendung im Deutschunterricht.* Kronberg: Scriptor Verlag, 1979.

5347. Wermke, Jutta. "Zur Behandlung von Comics im Literaturunterricht." *Zeitschrift für Literaturwissenschaft und Linguistik* (Frankfurt). 2:6 (1972), pp. 65-77.

5348. Wienhöfer, Friederike. "Comics als Gegenstand Literatur—und Kunstdidaktischen Bemühens. Eine Kritische Bestandsaufnahme." *Zeitschrift für Kunstpädagogik und Ihre Grundlagen* (Ratingen). 3:3 (1974), pp. 171-174.

5349. "Wieso Taugen 'Comic'—Märchen Nicht?" *Die Schule.* 37:7 (1961), pp. 38-39.

5350. Willeke, O. *Über Audio-Visuellen Unterricht, Methodische Hinweise.* Paris: Verlag Didier, 1965.

5351. "Witziges und Aberwitziges." *Der Spiegel.* No. 45, 1972, p. 16.

5352. Zimdahl, Gudrun. "Untersuchung des Urteilsvermögens 11-13 jähriger Schüler in Bezug auf Comics." Hamburg: Hausarbeit für das 1. Staatsexamen für das Lehramt an Volks- und Realschulen, May 1971.

Effects Debate

5353. Barclay, Dorothy. "Zur Frage der Comic-Books." *Jugendliteratur.* 1:6 (1955), pp. 280-282.

5354. Blaich, Ute. "Ein Wenig Terror Muß Dabei Sein; Polit-Comics für Kinder." *Deutsches Allgemeines Sonntagsblatt* (Cologne). November 8, 1970, p. 1

5355. Certain, Friedrich. "Verbrecher-Comics Unter der Lupe." *Blätter für Wohlfahrtspflege* (Stuttgart). 103, 1956, pp. 104-109.

5356. "Comic-Strip. Sieg Heil." *Der Spiegel.* No. 1-2, 1966, p. 74.

5357. Coulter, Leonárd. "Freiwillige Selbstzensur." *Englische Rundschau* (Cologne). November 5, 1954, p. 611.

5358. Dahrendorf, Malte. "Die Dauersieger, Comics, Kinder, Kriminelle." *Christ und Welt*. February 25, 1966.

5359. Demisch, Heinz. "Auswirkungen der Comic-Books." *Erziehungskunst*. 20:2 (1956), pp. 53-57.

5360. Demisch, Heinz. "Sind die Comics Harmloser Geworden?" *Blätter für Wohlfahrtspflege* (Stuttgart). 103, 1956, pp. 105-107.

5361. "Der Kampf Gegen die Comic-Strips." *Freundliches Begegnen* (Düsseldorf). 6:5 (1956), pp. 13-15.

5362. "Die Bundesprüfstelle." *Hamburger Abendecho*. September 5, 1966.

5363. Dorfmann, Ariel and Armand Mattelart. *Walt Disney's "Dritte Welt"—Massenkommunikation und Kolonialismus bei Micky Maus und Donald Duck*. Berlin: 1977.

5364. Drechsel, Wiltrud Ulrike, Jörg Funhoff, and Michael Hoffmann. *Massenzeichenware—Die Gesellschaftliche und Ideologische Funktion der Comics*. Frankfurt: 1975.

5365. "Entsetzlicher Knall." *Der Spiegel*. No. 11, 1972.

5366. Feld, Friedrich. "Comics—Immer Brutaler." *Zschr. für Jugendliteratur*. 1:8 (1967), p. 505.

5367. Gong, W. "Muskelmann Mordet aus Langeweile." *Süddeutsche Zeitung* (Munich). September 16, 1954.

5368. "Greuel-Comics." *Verlags-Praxis* (Darmstadt). 2, 1955, p. 31.

5369. "Heftumtausch in Regensburg." *Jugendschriften-Warte*. 8:4 (1956), p. 63.

5370. Hensel, Georg. "Bilderbogen und Bilderdrogen: Zum Problem der Comic-Strips." *Jugendschriften-Warte*. 8:4 (1956), pp. 25-26.

5371. Hesse, Kurt W. "Die Freiwillige Selbst-Kontrolle für Serienbilder." *Der Neue Vertrieg* (Flensburg). 7, 1955, pp. 618-619.

5372. "Kioske Gegen Comics?" *Soziale Arbeit* (Berlin). 4, 1955, pp. 309-310.

5373. Köhlert, Adolf. "Comics-Probleme." *Börsenblatt für den Deutschen Buchhandel*. 13:62 (1957), pp. 1062-1063.

5374. Kühne, Paul. "Verführung der Unschuldigen." *Der Tagesspiegel.* July 8, 1955, p. 3.

5375. "Luxemburger: Gutachten Über Bildstreifenhefte." *Mitteilungen der Bundesprüfstelle für Jugendgefährdende Schriften* (Bad Godesberg). August 1954.

5376. Merkelbach, Heinz J. "Mr. Babbitt und die Comics." *Deutsche Zeitung und Wirtschaftszeitung* (Stuttgart). 12:73 (1957), p. 20.

5377. "Mit Gebrochenen Armen...." *Constanze.* No. 24, 1966.

5378. Mühlen, Norbert. "Säuberung und Selbst-Kontrolle der Comic-Books." *Die Neue Zeitung.* 4, 1955, p. 4.

5379. Péus, Gunter. "Bilderstreifen als Symbole der Masse." *Christ und Welt.* February 10, 1961, p. 9.

5380. Pfannkuch-Wachtel, H. "Gangster in der Kinderstube." *Der Lehrerrundbrief* (Frankfurt). 7, 1952, pp. 120-122.

5381. Pol, Heinz. "Jugendkriminalität Durch Comics?" *Neue Ruhr Zeitung* (Essen). May 27, 1955.

5382. "Rechtsstreit: Ferkelei im Zitat." *Der Spiegel.* No. 29, 1969, p. 124.

5383. Reinecke, Lutz. "Sind Comics Gefährlich?" *Underground.* No. 4, 1970, pp. 16-17.

5384. Rest, W. "Die Pest der Comic-Books." *Die Kirche in der Welt.* 7, 1954, Lieferung 3, pp. 313-316.

5385. "Saubere Presse." *Die Zeit.* January 15, 1971, p. 2.

5386. Schilling, Robert. "Der Bundesgerichtshof Über Comics, Händlerische Prüfungspflicht und Andere Einschlägige Fragen." *Der Neue Vertrieb.* 7:153 (1955), pp. 482-493.

5387. Schmidt-Rogge, C.H. "Die Comics und die Phantasie. Inflation der Bilder und Visueller Dadaismus." *Welt der Schule* (Frankfurt). 12, 1959, pp. 425-426.

5388. "Schmökergrabaktion Gegen Comics." *Herner Zeitung.* May 16, 1956.

5389. "Schmutzflut Wird Eingedämmt. Auch das Englische Volk Wehrt Sich Gegen die Amerikanischen 'Comics.'" *National-Zeitung* (Cologne). July 26, 1952.

5390. "Selbstkontrolle für Comicstrips." *Main-Echo.* October 30, 1954.

5391. "Selbstzensur für Comics." *Börsenblatt für den Deutschen Buchhandel* (Frankfurt). 11:12 (1955), p. 90.

5392. Specht, Fritz. "Stars und Strips. Zum Problem der Comics." *Jugendschriften-Warte*. 1954, p. 29.

5393. Stoss, Irma. "Vom Kampf Gegen die 'Comics.'" *Mädchenbildung und Frauenschaffen* (Hamburg). 5:7 (1955), pp. 331-333.

5394. Tröger, Walter. "Wie Schädlich Ist das Chaos? Comics und Politisches Verhalten." *Süddeutsche Zeitung* (Munich). June 15, 1966.

5395. Ulshöfer, Robert. "Bekämpfung der Comics." *Der Deutschunterricht*. 13:6 (1961), pp. 31-41.

5396. "Umtausch von Schundheften?" *Jugendschriften-Warte*. 8:7/8 (1956).

5397. "Verbot der Comic-Strips Gefordert." *Die Evangelische Elternschaft* (Bethel). No. 2, 1956.

5398. "Vom Comic-Leser zum Mörder." *Neue Zeit*. October 26, 1955.

5399. von Uexküll, Gösta. "Opium fürs Kind. USA und England im Kampf Gegen Greuelserien." *Die Zeit*. No. 9, 1955, p. 1.

5400. Weise, Gerhard. "Machen Comics Kinder zur Kriminellen?" *Stuttgart Zeitung*. January 3, 1966, p. 3.

5401. Wertham, Frederic. "Lektüre für die Unschuldigen." *Jugendliteratur*. 7, 1956, pp. 325-328.

5402. Wetterling, Horst. "Sind die Comicstrips Gefährlich?" *Der Stern*. No. 33, 1967, pp. 58-59.

5403. Wichmann, Jürgen. "Comics, die Bunte Jugendpest." *Echo der Zeit* (Münster). December 9, 1954, p. 3.

5404. Wirsing, Giselher. "Geschäft Mit dem Schrecken. Man Muß den Comics zu Leibe Gehen. Wir Sind Alle Angeklagt." *Christ und Welt*. March 3, 1955, p. 3.

Komischen Streifen

5405. "Comics-Kaum Komisch." *Zeitschrift für Jugendliteratur*. 1:5 (1967), p. 315.

5406. "Comics Sind Nicht Komisch." *Münchner Illustrierte*. June 14, 1952.

5407. "Die Komischen Streifen." *Der Spiegel*. No. 12, 1969, p. 190.

5408. "Die Komischen Streifen." *Hör Zu.* No. 11, 1969.

5409. "Die Komischen Streifen." *Hör Zu.* No. 14, 1969.

5410. Giehrl, Hans E. "Comic-Books-Komische Bücher?" *Welt der Schule.* 6:4 (1953), pp. 130-133.

5411. Groezinger, Wolfgang. "Die Komischen Streifen." *Süddeutsche Zeitung* (Munich). May 27, 1953.

5412. Guhert, Georg. "Comics Sind oft Gar Nicht Komisch." *Neue Ruhr Zeitung* (Essen). June 19, 1966.

5413. Rosiny, Tony. "Comics Sind Nicht Komisch." *Aachener Volkszeitung.* November 20, 1954.

5414. "Sind Comics Komisch?" *Rheinischer Merkur* (Cologne). May 1955.

5415. Vater, Theo. "Das Komische und der Humor." *Der Deutschunterricht* (Frankfurt). 5, 1962, pp. 61-105.

Genres

5416. "Antifaschismus-Cartoons." *Comic Info.* May-June 1993, p. 10.

5417. Brück, Axel. "Sex und Horror in den Comics." *Katalog der Comics-Ausstellung im Hamburger Kunsthaus, Juni-Juli 1971*, 90 pp. Hamburg.

5418. Künnemann, Horst. "Sex und Horror, Crime und Comics." In *Katalog der Comics—Ausstellung im Hamburger Kunsthaus, Juni-Juli 1971*, pp. I-IX. Hamburg.

5419. Schad, Renate. "Gangster, Grafen, Superhelden. Realität und Wunschwelt der Trivialliteratur." In *Sozialkundebriefe für Jugend und Schule.* Wiesbaden: G/14, 1967.

5420. Weichert, Helga. "Gangster, Grafen, Superhelden. Wunschwelten der Trivialliteratur." *Deutschliteratur, Hessischer Rundfunk, Schulfunkheft* (Frankfurt). 23, 1968, pp. 46-47.

Adventure

5421. "Abenteuer der Weltgeschichte in Bildern." *Der Neue Vertrieb.* 5:112 (1953), p. 519.

5422. Baumgärtner, Alfred C. *Die Welt der Abenteuer-Comics und Andere Beitrage zu Einem Massenmedium.* Bochum: Kamp, 1979.

5423. "Eine Mode Voller Abenteuer." *Welt am Sonntag* (Hamburg). April 23, 1967.

5424. Hare, Peter. "Abenteuergeschichten Fast Ohne Worte." *Englische Rundschau.* June 18, 1954, p. 343.

5425. Kuhlmay, Egbert. "Wir Lesen Abenteuer-Comics. 6. Jahrgangsstufe; Deutsch: Umgang Mit Texten." *Ehrenwirth Hauptschulmagazin* (Munich). 9:9 (1984), pp. 37-40.

5426. Löffler, Angelika. "Aggressionsdarstellung und Aggressionsbewältigung am Beispiel von Adventure-Comics." *Ehrenwirth Hauptschulmagazin.* 5:9 (1980), pp. 51-54.

5427. Maier, Karl Ernst. "Gute und Schlechte Abenteuergeschichten." *Der Deutschunterricht* (Stuttgart). 13:6 (1961), pp. 5-13.

5428. Tschernegg, Markus. "Das Große Abenteuer. Die Stille Revolution—Comic Klassiker der Achtziger Jahre. 1. Teil. Eine Kurzanalayse." *Comic Forum. Das Magazin für Comicliteratur.* 7:30 (1985), pp. 28-32.

5429. Watzke, Oswald. "Gute and Böse Figuren in Abenteuer-Comics. Ein Beitrag zur Didaktik der Comicsliteratur in der Förderstufe." In *Kinder-und Jugendlektüre im Unterricht. Bd. 2: Sekundarstufe,* edited by Theodor Karst, pp. 204-221. Bad Heilbrunn/Obb.: Klinkhardt, 1979.

Alternative, Underground

5430. Dahrendorf, Malte. "Comic und Bucheine Alternative?" *Jugendschriften-Warte.* 22:9-70 (1970), p. 29.

5431. "Eine Literarische Untergrundbewegung." *Überblick* (Munich). December 10, 1949.

5432. Fuchs, Wolfgang J. "Ein Interview aus dem Deutschen Comix-Underground." *Comixene. Das Comicfachmagazin.* 6:25 (1979), pp. 19-23.

5433. Hahn, Roland M. "Untergrund-Comix." *Science Fiction Times* (Bremerhaven). 14:4 (1972), pp. 4-10.

5434. Knigge, Andreas C. "Die Geschichte der Underground-Comics." *Comixene. Das Comicfachmagazin.* 6:25 (1979), pp. 4-11.

5435. Knigge, Andreas C. "Underground Comix in Deutschland." *Comixene.* No. 25, 1979, p. 11.

5436. Truck, Walter. "U-Comix. Vom Underground Zum Overground." *ICOM*. January 1993, pp. 44-45.

Education

5437. "Hamlet aus Comic-Blasen." *Lehrer-Korrespondenz* (Frankfurt). 12, 1955.

5438. Herr, Giesela. "Shakespeares Hamlet—als Comic Zerstümmelt." *Jugendliteratur*. 2, 1957, pp. 86-87.

5439. Kempkes, Wolfgang. "Comics für den Sexualkunde-Unterricht." *Bulletin: Jugend + Literatur*. No. 8, 1970, p. 6.

5440. Kempkes, Wolfgang. "Die Educational Comics und Möglichkeiten Ihrer Verwertung im Unterricht." Hamburg: Hausarbeit für die 1. Staatsprüfung für das Lehramt an Volks-und Realschulen, May 8, 1970.

5441. Kempkes, Wolfgang. "Informationen Über Comics, Educational Comics und Ihre Schulische Verwendung." *Jugendschriften-Warte*. 23:3 and 5 (1971), pp. 10-11; pp. 17-19.

5442. Kempkes, Wolfgang. "Informative Comics." *Bulletin: Jugend + Literatur*. No. 9, 1970, p. 13.

Erotic, Pornographic

5443. Bourgeois, Michel. *Erotik und Pornographie im Comic Strip*. Linden: 1981.

5444. Buch, Hans Christoph. "Sex-Revolte im Comic-Strip." *Pardon*. No. 12, 1966, p. 15ff.

5445. "Comic-Sex-Figur." *Der Spiegel*. No. 31, 1972, p. 106.

5446. Knigge, Andreas C. *Sex im Comic*. Frankfurt, Berlin: Ullstein GmbH, 1985.

5447. Strzyz, Klaus. "Alle Zeigen Immer Nur das Eine... Die Welt der Hard Core-Porno Comics." *Comic Forum. Das Magazin für Comicliteratur*. 24, 1984, pp. 48-56.

5448. Truck, Walter. "Süsse Sünder in Blau-Weiss." *ICOM INFO*. June 1992, pp. 22-25.

Heroes, Superheroes

5449. Decker, Dwight. "Stahlman—The Man of Steel." *Comics Journal*. Winter 1980, pp. 122-128.

5450. Hausmanninger, Thomas. *Superman: Eine Comic und Sein Ethos.* Frankfurt: Suhrkamp, 1988. 250 pp.

5451. Thielke, Adolf. "Superhelden-Comics. Ein Unterrichtsprogramm für die 6. Oder 7. Jahrgangsstufe." *Kunst + Unterricht* (Velber bei Hanover). 32, 1975, pp. 33-38.

5452. Trabant, Jürgen. "Superman—Das Image Eines Comic-Helden." In *Visuelle Kommunikation,* edited by H.K. Ehmer, pp. 251-276. Cologne: Verlag Du Mont Aktuell, 1971.

5453. *Vom Geist der Superhelden.* Berlin: Akademie der Künste, 1971.

5454. von Doetinchem, Dagmar and Klaus Hartung. "Die Verhinderung der Phantasiearbeit in Superheldencomics." In *Massenkommunikationsforschung: 3. Produktanalysen,* edited by Dieter Prokop, pp. 327 ff. Frankfurt: Fischer, 1977.

5455. von Doetinchem, Dagmar and Klaus Hartung. *Zum Thema Gewalt in Superhelden-Comics.* Berlin: Basis Verlag, 1974.

5456. Wiener, Oswald. "Der Geist der Superhelden." In *Vom Geist der Superhelden Comic Strips. Zur Theorie der Bildergeschichte,* edited by Hans Dieter Zimmermann, pp. 126-141. Munich: Deutscher Taschenbuch Verlag, 1975.

5457. Wiener, Oswald. "Der Geist der Superhelden." *Süddeutsche Zeitung.* February 18-March 1, 1970.

5458. Zimmermann, Hans Dieter. *Vom Geist der Superhelden. Comic Strips. Colloquium zur Theorie der Bildergeschichte, Schriftenreihe der Akademie der Künste.* Vol. 8. Berlin: Mann-Verlag, 1970. 128 pp.

5459. Zimmermann, Hans Dieter. *Vom Geist der Superhelden. Zur Theorie der Bildergeschichte.* Munich: Deutscher Taschenbuch Verlag, 1970.

Horror

5460. Cummings, A.J. "Horror Comics Verbieten." *Englische Rundschau.* November 5, 1954, p. 611.

5461. Schilling, Robert. "Die Comics-Verbreitung, Horror-Comics und Allgemein." *Literarischer Jugendschutz.* Berlin-Darmstadt: Luchterhand, 1959.

5462. von Zitzewitz, Monika. "Einspruch Gegen Sex und Horror." *Die Welt.* January 17, 1967.

Science Fiction

5463. Couperie, Pierre. "100 Millionen Meilen im Ballon. Science Fiction im Comic-Strip." In *Katalog der "Science-Fiction"*—Ausstellung in der Kunsthalle, 1968. Düsseldorf.

5464. Golowin, S. "Das Abenteuer der Mythologie von Morgen." In *Ausstellungskatalog der Science-Fiction-Austellung*, Kunsthalle Bern, Bern, July 8-July 17, 1967, p. 2.

5465. Gutsch, J. and Fr. Leiner. *Science Fiction. Materialien und Hinweise.* Frankfurt: Salle Verlag, 1971. 80 pp.

5466. Knigge, Andreas C. "Deutschlands Griff Nach den Sternen. Eine Entwicklungsgeschichte der SF-Comics in der BRD." *Comixene. Das Comicfachmagazin.* 7:30 (1980), pp. 20-24.

5467. Knigge, Andreas C. "Die Entwicklungsgeschichte der SF-Comics in der BRD." *Comixene.* No. 30, 1980, pp. 20-24.

5468. Lettkemann, Gerd. "Aufklärung und Propaganda in den SF-Comics der DDR." *Comixene.* No. 30, 1980, pp. 25, 57.

5469. Schmidmaier, Werner. "Werbung Mit Zukunft-Science-Fiction-Appeal in der Werbung." *Graphik.* No. 1, 1970, pp. 26-27.

5470. Schröder, Horst. *Bildwelten und Weltbilder. Science-Fiction-Comics in den USA, in Deutschland, England und Frankreich.* Reinbek bei Hamburg: Carlsen Verlag, 1982.

Industry

5471. "Auch die 'Piccolos' Bringen Geld." *Der Neue Vertrieb* (Flensburg). 5:100 (1953), p. 235.

5472. Becker, Hartmut, Andreas C. Knigge, and Rainer Clodius. "Comicland Bastei. Ein Interviewportrait." *Comixene. Das Comicfachmagazin.* 7:28 (1980), pp. 4-8.

5473. Bungardt, Karl. "Kennen Sie Bulls Pressedienst." *Allgemeine Deutsche Lehrerzeitung* (Frankfurt). No. 18, 1952, pp. 147-248.

5474. "Comic-Charts Deutschland." *Comic Info.* May-June 1993, p. 13.

5475. "Comics-Auflagen." *Kunst und Unterricht.* 10, 1970, p. 32.

5476. "Comic-Strips." *Dipa-Information für Jugendarbeit und Erziehungswesen* (Frankfurt). 6:14 (1954), p. 12.

5477. Couperie, Pierre. "Männer, Mächte, Monopole—Der Apparat der Comics." *Tendenzen.* 1: 53 (1968), pp. 168, 173-174.

5478. Donner, Wolf. "Rückschritte in den Fortschritt." *Die Zeit.* August 28, 1970, p. 20.

5479. "ECA Denies Granting Credits for Comics in Germany." *Publisher's Weekly.* December 11, 1948, p. 2346.

5480. Göllner, Lutz and Dirk Rehm. "Harte Zeiten—Harte Comics. Die Neue Berliner Comic-Scene." *Comic Info.* May-June 1993, p. 56.

5481. Guhert, Georg. "Der Siegeszug der Comics." *Ruf ins Volk.* No. 12, 1965, pp. 93-94.

5482. Hack, Berthold. "Einige Comic-Probleme." *Börsenblatt für den Deutschen Buchhandel* (Frankfurt). 11:80 (1955), pp. 646-647.

5483. Hagen, Jens. "Das Goldkind der POP-Szene (A. Aldridge)." *Underground.* No. 5, 1970, pp. 32-35.

5484. Helger, Walter. "Bildserien als Jugendschrifttum in Millionenauflage." *Schola-Lebendige Schule.* 8:10 (1953), pp. 708-710.

5485. Herbert, Alan. "Report from Germany: Comics Are Thriving, and So Is Asterix." *Comics Buyer's Guide.* June 16, 1989, p. 34.

5486. "Jährlich 300,000 Dollars." *Pfälzer Tageblatt* (Landau). May 13, 1954.

5487. Kleffel, Walther. "Die Neue 'Weltmacht' Comics." *Der Neue Vertrieb* (Flensburg). 5:107 (1953), pp. 404-407.

5488. Kraatz, Birgit. "Doktorhut für Fumetti." *Rheinischer Merkur* (Cologne). December 2, 1966.

5489. Krafft, Ulrich. *Comics Lesen. Untersuchungen zur Textualität von Comics.* Stuttgart: Klett-Cotta, 1978. 205 pp.

5490. Künnemann, Horst. "Comics-Weiter im Vormarsch." *Bulletin: Jugend und Literatur.* No. 6, 1972, p. 1.

5491. "Lizenz für Hampelmänner." *Der Spiegel.* No. 31, 1967, p. 100.

5492. Metzger, Juliane. "Von Bilderbögen und Zugabeheften." *Jugendliteratur.* 3:7 (1957), pp. 300-304.

5493. "Neu in Deutschland (Comic-Bücher)." *Der Spiegel*. No. 41, 1970, pp. 242, 245-246.

5494. Ruloff, Ernst. "Comics Werden zu Kunst-Objekten." *Weser-Kurier* (Bremen). September 8, 1972.

5495. Schmidmaier, Werner. "Der Wumm im Umsatz." *Graphik*. No. 12, 1971.

5496. Schmidmaier, Werner. "Ruckzuck zum Konsum." *Graphik*. No. 11, 1971.

5497. Setterblad, Svante. "Vom Künstler zum Leser. Die Internationale Produktion und Distribution von Comics." *Communications*. 1:3 (1984), pp. 129-137.

5498. "Spielzeug-Profit in der Röhre." *Der Spiegel*. No. 49, 1967, pp. 108, 110.

5499. "Stürmische Nachfrage Nach den 'Piccolos.'" *Der Neue Vertrieb*, 5:103 (1953), p. 304.

5500. Witter, Ben. "Ein Preuße, der Jault und Bellt." *Die Zeit*. No. 46, 1972, p. 80.

5501. "Zeitschriften 'Panel.'" *Der Spiegel*. No. 15, 1972, p. 148.

Carlsen-Verlag

5502. Alber, Wolfgang and Markus Tschernegg. "Der Carlsen-Verlag. Ein Portrait." *Comic Forum. Das Österreichische Fachmagazin für Comicliteratur*. 3:9 (1981), pp. 52-54.

5503. Borchert, Karlheinz. "Carlsen—Qualität und Sorgfalt Als Programm. Ein Interview mit Carlsen—Redakteur Eckart Sackmann." *Comic Forum. Das Magazin für Comicliteratur*. 7:27 (1985), pp. 40-45.

5504. Knigge, Andreas and Helmut Becker. "25 Jahre Carlsen-Verlag in Deutschland. Ein Interview mit Mitarbeitern des Carlsen-Verlages." *Comixene. Das Comicfachmagazin*. 6:23 (1979), pp. 4-6.

Ehapa-Verlag

5505. Alber, Wolfgang. "Portrait Ehapa-Verlag." *Comic Forum. Das Österreichische Fachmagazin für Comicliteratur*. 3:11 (1981), pp. 23-25.

5506. Uderzo, Albert. *Biographische Notizen des Ehapa-Verlages*. Cologne: Ehapa-Verlag, 1971.

Kauka-Comics

5507. Becker, Hartmut and Andreas C. Knigge. "Interview mit Rolf Kauka." *Comixene. Das Comicfachmagazin*. 7:31 (1980), pp. 4-5.

5508. Becker, Hartmut and Andreas C. Knigge. "Zur Chronologie der Kauka-Comics 1953-1980." *Comixene. Das Comicfachmagazin.* 7:31 (1980), pp. 6-15.

5509. Granacher, René. "40 Jahre Kauka-Comics. Eine Kurze Geschichte der Langlebigsten Deutschen Comic-Produktion." *Comic Info.* May-June 1993, pp. 46-47.

5510. Pohl, Ulrich. "Kauka-Comics." *Bulletin: Jugend + Literatur.* No. 3, 1971, pp. 9-10.

Advertising

5511. Kagelmann, H. Jürgen and Rosi Zimmermann. "Comics und Werbung." *Medien und Sexualpädagogik* (Bonn-Bad Godesberg). 3:2 (1975), pp. 33-36.

5512. Kempkes, Wolfgang. "Werbungs-Comics." *Bulletin: Jugend + Literatur.* No. 7, 1970, pp. 12-13.

5513. Moeller, Michael L. "Comics und Ihre Konsumenten." *Vortrag, Deutschlandfunk* (Cologne). June 4, 1970.

5514. Riha, Karl. "Comics und Werbung. Comics als Werbung. Comics-Elemente in der Werbung." *Sprache im Technischen Zeitalter* (Berlin). 42, 1972, pp. 153-165.

5515. Schnurrer, Achim. "Comics und Merchandising." In *Comics and Visual Culture: Research Studies from Ten Countries*, edited by Alphons Silbermann and H.-D. Dyroff, pp. 234-246. Munich: K.G. Saur, 1986.

5516. Schnurrer, Achim. "Comics und Merchandising. Intermediale Dependenzen. Strategie der Wirkungsverstärkung." *Communications* (Sankt Augustin). 9:2/3 (1983), pp. 201-220.

5517. von Stillfried, Christoph. "Comics in der Werbung." *Graphik.* 27:7 (1974), pp. 20-26.

Literature

5518. "Balzac und Puschkin." *Frankfurter Allgemeine Zeitung.* November 16/17, 1966.

5519. Beuche, Jürgen. "Literatur des Großstadtkindes und Ihr Einfluß auf das Spiel." *Jugendschriften-Warte.* 7:2 (1955), pp. 12-13.

5520. Bondy, Barbara. "Tun Sie, Was Sie Lesen? Eine Kritische Betrachung zur Schundliteratur und Comic-Strips." *Vortrag im Frauenfunk* (Cologne). April 18, 1955.

5521. Brück, Axel. "Sekundärliteratur zum Thema Comics." *Bulletin: Jugend + Literatur.* No. 4-5, 1971, pp. 27-28.

5522. "Buchmarkt." *Der Spiegel.* No. 34, 1972, p. 98.

5523. Dahrendorf, Malte. "Die Comics-Stiefkind der Literatur." *Bulletin: Jugend + Literatur.* No. 9, 1970, pp. 33-34.

5524. "Das Jüngste Kind der Literatur—und Ein Neues Zeitungsressort." *Die Deutsche Zeitung.* November 1949, pp. 14-15.

5525. Fischer, Helmut. "Das Außerschulische Leseverhalten von Hauptschülern." In *Literaturdidaktik-Ansichten + Aufgaben,* edited by Jochen Vogt, pp. 207-231. Düsseldorf: Bertelsmann, 1972.

5526. Freitag, Günther. "Die Literarischen Interessen von Schülern und Schülerinen Einer Nöheren Lehranstalt." *Psychologische Beiträge.* 1:2 (1953/1954), pp. 264-311.

5527. "'Julius Caesar' und 'Hamlet' in Bildern." *Deutsche Schule.* 5:14/15 (1953), p. 223.

5528. Kempkes, Wolfgang. "Comic-Seminar an der Universität Hamburg." *Bulletin: Jugend + Literatur.* No. 6, 1970, p. 6.

5529. "Klassische Comics." *Börsenblatt für den Deutschen Buchhandel* (Frankfurt). 12:94 (1956), pp. 1732-1733.

5530. Laub, Gabriel. "Die Karriere Einer Zeitschrift." *Die Zeit.* March 21, 1969, p. 28.

5531. "Romanheft Mit Bilderserie." *Der Neue Vertrieb.* 5:100 (1953), p. 235.

Psychology

5532. Biscamp, Helmut. "Was Liest die Jugend der Großstadt? Eine Psychologische Untersuchung an Einem Realgymnasium der Stadt Frankfurt a.M." *Jugendschriften-Warte.* 9:1 (1957), pp. 1-3.

5533. Demisch, Heinz. "Psychiatrie und Comicbooks: Eine Amerikanische Untersuchung." *Frankfurter Allgemeine Zeitung.* June 21, 1955; *Pegasus.* No. 3, 1955, pp. 19-21.

5534. Gans, Frobian (Michael M. Lzernich, Carl Ludwig Reichert, Ludwig Moos). *Die Ducks. Psychogramm Einer Sippe.* Reinbek b. Hamburg: 1972.

5535. Gehring, Bernhard. "Psychologisch-Pädagogische Studie Über das Comic-Lesen der Kinder." Hamburg: Hausarbeit für das 1. Staatsexamen für das Lehramt an Volks-und Realschulen, 1962.

5536. Kagelmann, Hans Jürgen. *Forschungsbericht—Sozialisationspsychologische Aspekte der Comics.* Regensburg: 1974.

5537. Kagelmann, Hans Jürgen. "Guten Tag! Wer von Ihnen Ist Napoleon? Psychologen, Psychiater und 'Irre' in Comics." In *Comics in Medienmarkt, in der Analyse, im Unterricht,* edited by Wolfgang J. Fuchs, pp. 94-104. Opladen: Leske und Budrich, 1977.

5538. Kantelhardt, Arnhild. *Die "Komik" der Comics in Psychologischer und Pädagogischer Analyse. Arbeit für das 1.* Hamburg: Staatsexamen für Volks-und Realschullehrer, 1969.

5539. Maletzke, Gerhard. *Psychologie der Massenkommunikation.* Hamburg: Bredow-Institut, 1963, pp. 247-248.

5540. Moeller, Michael Lukas. "Zur Primären Wirklichkeit in Künstlerischen Comics. Ein Psychoanalytischer Beitrag." In *Vom Geist der Superhelden,* edited by Hans Dieter Zimmermann, pp. 112-125. Munich: Deutscher Taschenbuch Verlag, 1975.

5541. Orban, Peter. "Zur Sozialpsychologie der Comics Über die Dritte Welt." *Comixene. Das Comicfachmagazin.* 7:29 (1980), pp. 15-17.

5542. Trescher, H.-G. "Narzißmus und Comic." *Kindheit* (Wiesbaden). 1:1 (1979), pp. 87-104.

5543. Von Hänisch, Ingrid. *Reich-Stark-Mächtig: Die Phantasiehelden Unserer Kinder.* Fellbach: Verlag Adolf Bonz, 1982.

5544. Wermke, Jutta. "Comics." In *Medienpsychologie. Ein Handbuch in Schlüsselbegriffen,* edited by Hans Jürgen Kagelmann and Gerd Wenninger, pp. 9-17. Munich: Urban und Schwarzenburg, 1982.

Religion

5545. "Die Bibel als Comic." *Jugendschriften-Warte.* 8:4 (1956), p. 63.

5546. Güttgemanns, Erhardt. "Strukturen des Mythos in Comic-Form." In *Comics und Religion. Eine Interdisziplinäre Diskussion,* edited by Jutta Wermke, pp. 33-50. Munich: Wilhelm Fink Verlag, 1976.

5547. Halbfas, Hubertus. "Die Bibel in Comics. Anmerkungen zur Unterrichtlichen Auseinandersetzung." In *Kinderund Jugendlektüre im Unterricht. Bd. 1: Primärstufe*, edited by Theodor Karst, pp. 186-193. Bad Heilbrunn/Obb.: Klinkhardt, 1978.

5548. Hartung, Rudolf. "Mit Rauchwölkchen... Bibel in 'Comic-Strips.'" *Neue Deutsche Hefte*. 56, 1959, p. 1125.

5549. Hauser, Linus. "Religiöse Comics aus der Sicht der Narrativen Theologie." In *Religiöse Comics*, edited by Johannes Horstmann, pp. 137-179. Schwerte: Katholische Akademie, 1981.

5550. Horstmann, Johannes, ed. *Religiöse Comics: Aum Pastoralen Einsatz von "Bibel-Comics" und von "Allgemeinen Religiosen Comics."* Schwerte: Katholische Akademie Schwerte, 1981. 243 pp.

5551. Kempkes, Wolfgang. "Allgemeine Religiöse Comics: Ihre Inhalte, Formen und Möglichkeiten Ihrer Praktischen Nutzung." In *Religiöse Comics*, edited by Johannes Horstmann, pp. 101-136. Schwerte: Katholische Akademie, 1981.

5552. Kempkes, Wolfgang. "Bibel-Comics: Gattungsüberblick und Erfahrungen aus Ihrem Einsatz." In *Religiöse Comics*, edited by Johannes Horstmann, pp. 33-100. Schwerte: Katholische Akademie, 1981.

5553. Knigge, Andreas C. "Sekten und Ihre Comics." *Comixene. Das Comicfachmagazin*. 6:24 (1979), pp. 47-48.

5554. Krege-Mayer, Roswith. "Gründe fur und Gegen Bibel-Comics aus Verlegerischer Sicht." In *Religiöse Comics*, edited by Johannes Horstmann, pp. 221-228. Schwerte: Katholische Adademie, 1981.

5555. Lange, Günter. "Wie Sind Bibelcomics zu Beurteilen?" *Religionsunterricht an Höheren Schulen* (Düsseldorf). 2, 1978, pp. 66-74.

5556. Lange, Günter and Rolf Wertz. "Ist die Bibel Comic-Able?" *Katechetische Blätter* (Munich). 1976, pp. 174-191.

5557. Müller, Josef. "Allgemeine Religiöse Comics aus Pastoraler Sicht." In *Religiöse Comics*, edited by Johannes Horstmann, pp. 200-220. Schwerte: Katholische Akademie, 1981.

5558. Nübel, Hans Ulrich. "Comics Fordern den Religionspädagogen Heraus." *Der Evangelische Erzieher* (Frankfurt). 32:1 (1980), pp. 38-58.

5559. Ohlig, Karl-Heinz. "Comics und Religiöse Mythen. Oder: Was Religion und Unterhaltungsliteratur Nicht Gemeinsam Haben." In *Comics und Religion. Eine Interdisziplinäre Diskussion*, edited by Jutta Wermke, pp. 121-136. Munich: Wilhelm Fink Verlag, 1976.

5560. "Pino Zac Will die Bibel als Comic Herausbringen." *Kristall* (Hamburg). No. 10, 1966.

5561. Poeplau, Wolfgang. "Religiöse Comics in der Kirchenzeitung. Ein Werkstattbericht." In *Religiöse Comics*, edited by Johannes Horstmann, pp. 229-242. Schwerte: Katholische Akademie, 1981.

5562. Scholl, Norbert. "Comics im Religionsunterricht." *Lehrmittel Aktuell* (Braunschweig). 1, 1977, pp. 24-27.

5563. Scholl, Norbert. *Gleichnisse als Comics—Comics als Gleichnisse. Arbeitshilfen für den Religionsunterricht Mit Zeichnungen von Jan Enderlin, Thomas Hebgen und Rolf Wertz.* Freiburg: Herder Verlag, 1980.

5564. Stahl, August. "Comics und Mythenkritik." *Fabula* (Berlin). 19, 1978, pp. 241-251.

5565. Stahl, August. "Die Mythologie der Comics." In *Comics und Religion. Eine Interdisziplinäre Diskussion*, edited by Jutta Wermke, pp. 18-32. Munich: Wilhelm Fink Verlag, 1976.

5566. Veit, Reinhard. "Anforderungen an Bibel-Comics und Deren Verwendung aus Pastoraler Sicht." In *Religiöse Comics*, edited by Johannes Horstmann, pp. 180-199. Schwerte: Katholische Akademie, 1981.

5567. Wermke, Jutta. *Comics und Religion. Eine Interdisziplinäre Diskussion.* Munich: Wilhelm Fink Verlag, 1976. 186 pp.

5568. Wermke, Jutta, ed. *Kerygma in Comic-Form.* Munich: Wilhelm Fink Verlag, 1979.

5569. Wermke, Jutta, ed. *Moderne Mythen und Mythenkritik. Arbeitsbuch für den Deutschunterricht.* Frankfurt: Diesterweg, 1977.

Semiotics, Language

5570. Ballweg, Joachim. "Iznogoud, Dilat Lahrat, Saussures 'Assoziative Relationen' und das Problem der Übersetzung." In *Festschrift für Rupprecht Rohr zum 60. Geburtstag: Gewidmet von Seinen Kollegen, Schülern und Mitarbeitern*, edited by Wolfgang Bergerfurth *et al.*, pp. 1-12. Heidelberg: Groos, 1979.

5571. Baumgärtner, Alfred C. "Die Welt der Comics als Semiologisches System. Ansätze zur Decodierung Eines Mythos." In *Vom Geist der Superhelden*, edited by Hans Dieter Zimmermann, pp. 98-111. Munich: Deutscher Taschenbuch Verlag, 1975.

5572. Brüggemann, Theodor. "Eine Klasse Urteilt Über Comics." *Pädagogische Rundschau*, 11:6 (1956/57), pp. 226-230.

5573. Ell, Ernst. "Comics Strips." *Lexikon der Pädagogik* (Freiberg). 5, 1964, Spalte 134.

5574. "Esperanto der Analphabeten." *Christ und Welt*. November 1953.

5575. Havlik, Ernst. *Lexikon der Onomatopöien. Die Lautimitierenden Wörter im Comic*. Frankfurt: Fricke, 1981. 264 pp.

5576. Klöckner, Klaus. "Die Sprache der Comics." *Hessische Jugend*. 22:8 (1970), pp. 14-16.

5577. Kloepfer, Rolf. "Komplementarität von Sprache und Bild. Am Beispiel von Comic, Karikatur und Reklame." *Sprache im Technischen Zeitalter* (Berlin). 57, (1976), pp. 42-56.

5578. Knigge, Andreas C. *Comic-Lexikon*. Berlin: Ullstein, n.d.

5579. Krafft, Ulrich. *Comics Lesen. Untersuchungen zur Textualität von Comics*. Stuttgart: Klett-Cotta, 1978.

5580. Müller, Monika. "Visualisierungs-und Verbalisierungsmechanismen in Comics." Doctoral dissertation, Philosophischen Fakultät, Universität Salzburg, 1979.

5581. Oberlindober, Hans. "Sprache und Bild in den Comics." *Westermanns Pädagogische Beiträge*. No. 2, 1971, p. 102.

5582. Paetel, Karl O. "Der Siegeszug der Phonetik. Randbemerkungen zu den Comics." *Recht der Jugend*. 4:17 (1956), p. 1; September-Heft, pp. 257-258.

5583. Riha, Karl. "Die Blase im Kopf." In *Trivialliteratur. Aufsätze*, edited by Gerhard Schmidt-Henkel *et al.*, pp. 176-191. Berlin: Literarisches Colloquium, 1964.

5584. Schnackertz, Hermann J. *Form und Funktion Medialen Erzählens: Narrativität in Bildsequenz und Comicstrip*. Munich: Fink, 1980.

5585. Seeliger, Rolf. "Comics, Esperanto der Analphabeten." *Junge Gemeinschaft*. 10:10 (1958), p. 5.

5586. Spillner, Bernd. "Semantisch und Pragmatisch Bedingte Ambiguität. Analysen am Beispiel von Französischen Comics." In *Literatur im Fremdsprachenunterricht. Beiträge zur Theorie des Literaturunterrichts und zur Praxis der Literaturvermittlung im Fremdsprachenunterricht*, edited by Konrad Schröder and Franz-Rudolf Weller, pp. 185-210. Frankfurt: Verlag Moritz Diesterweg, 1977.

5587. Urban, Dieter. "Comics als Gestaltungsmittel." *Novum* (Munich). 50:10 (1979), pp. 19-28.

5588. Welke, Manfred. *Die Sprache der Comics* Frankfurt: Verlag dipa, 1956.

5589. Welke, Manfred. *Die Sprache der Comics. Eine Untersuchung.* Frankfurt: dipa Verlag, 1958, 1974.

5590. Welke, Manfred. "Die Sprache der Comics." *Börsenblatt für den Deutschen Buchhandel* (Frankfurt). 16:97 (1960), p. 2073.

5591. Wienhöfer, Friederike. "Untersuchungen zur Semiotischen Ästhetik des Comic Strip Unter der Besonderen Berücksichtigung von Onomatopoese und Typographie. Zur Grundlage Einer Comic-Didaktik." Doctoral dissertation, Doktors der Erziehungswissenschaft der Pädagogischen Hochschule Ruhr Dortmund, 1979.

Socio-Political

5592. Clodius, Rainer. "'Ich Will den Ganzen Leidensweg der Indianer Darstellen,' Hans Kresses Indianercomics." *Comixene. Das Comicfachmagazin.* 6:23 (1979), pp. 49-50.

5593. Couperie, Pierre. "Mit Comics Leben. Zur Soziologie der Comics." *Tendenzen* (Munich). 1. Sonderheft, No. 53, 1968, pp. 179-180.

5594. Davidson, Steef. *Bildersturm—Politische Comics. Entwicklung des Politischen Comics von 1965 bis Heute.* Berlin: Karin Kramer Verlag, 1978.

5595. Drechsel, Wiltrud Ulrike, Jörg Funhoff and Michael Hoffmann. *Massenzeichenware, die Gesellschaftliche und Ideologische Funktion der Comics.* Frankfurt: Edition Suhrkamp 501, Suhrkamp Verlag, 1975.

5596. Erckenbrecht, Ulrich. *Politische Sprache Marx, Rossi-Landi, Agitation, Kindersprache, Eulenspiegel, Comics.* Giessen/Lollar: Andreas Achenbach, 1975.

5597. Fuchs, Wolfgang J. "Trends in den Comics." *Jugend, Film, Fernsehen.* 16:2 (1972), pp. 6-13.

5598. Fuchs, Wolfgang J. "Comics und Politik." In *Massenmedium Comics,* edited by Dieter Golombek and Reinhold Lehmann, pp. 46-50. Bonn: Bundeszentrale für Politische Bildung, 1976.

5599. Fuchs, Wolfgang J. "Wo Sind All die Krieger Hin?" In *Comic-Jahrbuch 1986,* edited by Martin Compart and Andreas C. Knigge, pp. 44-51. Berlin: Ullstein GmbH, 1985.

5600. Hesse-Quack, Otto. "Der Comic-Strip als Soziales und Soziologisches Phänomen." *Kölner Zeitschrift für Soziologie und Sozial-Psychologie* (Cologne). 21:3 (1969), pp. 680-703.

5601. Hesse-Quack, Otto. "Die Soziale und Soziologische Bedeutsamkeit der Comic Strips." In *Vom Geist der Superhelden*, edited by Hans Dieter Zimmermann, pp. 82-97. Munich: Deutscher Taschenbuch Verlag, 1975.

5602. Holtz, Christina. "Comics, von der Medien-und Wirkungsforschung Vernachlässigt." *Media-Perspektiven* (Frankfurt). 8, 1978, pp. 572-579.

5603. Honsza, Norbert. "Die Comics: Literatur als Symptom der Zeit." *Universitas* (Stuttgart). 34 (1979), pp. 405-410.

5604. Kagelmann, Hans Jürgen. *Comics: Aspekte zu Inhalt und Wirkung*. Bad Heilbrunn/Obb.: J. Klinkhardt, 1976.

5605. Kagelmann, Hans Jürgen and Rosi Zimmermann. "Behinderte im Comic (1)." *Comixene. Das Comicfachmagazin*. 7:32 (1980), pp. 18-21.

5606. Kagelmann, Hans Jürgen and Rosi Zimmermann. "Behinderte im Comic (2)." *Comixene. Das Comicfachmagazin*. 7:33 (1980), pp. 14-18.

5607. Kagelmann, Hans Jürgen, Rosi Zimmermann, and Franz Eich. "Zur Diskussion um die Wirkung Aggressiver Szenen in den Comics." *Medien + Erziehung* (Leverkusen). 20:1 (1976), pp. 24-34.

5608. Kluwe, Sigbert. "Gewalt in Comics. Versuch Einer Analyse Deutschsprachiger Comics." *Jugend, Film, Fernsehen*. 16:2 (1972), pp. 20-28.

5609. Knigge, Andreas C. "Nach der Bombe." In *Comic-Jahrbuch 1986*, edited by Martin Compart and Andreas C. Knigge, pp. 51-65. Frankfurt: Ullstein GmbH, 1985.

5610. Kutsch, Thomas. "Comics—Soziologisch Betrachtet." *Communications* (St. Augustin). 6:1 (1980), pp. 43-57.

5611. Lehmann, Reinhold. "Eine Welt Mit Festen Spielregeln und Gags. 90 Prozent Aller Kinder Lesen Comics. Ein Medium, das Gesellschaftsfähig Wurde." In *Massenmedium Comics*, edited by Dieter Golombek and Reinhold Lehmann, pp. 3-8. Bonn: Bundeszentrale für Politische Bildung, 1976.

5612. Marcel, René. "Comics auf der Anklagebank. Fördert das Massenmedium Comics Aggressives Verhalten?" In *Massenmedium Comics*, edited by Dieter Golombek and Reinhold Lehmann, pp. 24-29. Bonn: Bundeszentrale für Politische Bildung, 1976.

5613. Orban, Peter. "Untertanen und Schurken." *Comixene. Das Comicfachmagazin.* 7:29 (1980), pp. 12-15.

5614. Roggatz, Detlef and Adolf Thielke. "Möglichkeiten der Analyse und Praktischen Arbeit zum Thema 'Comic als Vehikel von Ideologien.'" In *Politische Erziehung im Ästhetischen Bereich*, edited by Hans Giffhorn, pp. 17-36. Hanover: Friedrich Verlag, 1971.

5615. Schober, Otto. "Zur Körpersprache von Mädchen und Jungen." *Praxis Deutsch* (Velber bei Hanover). 12:73 (1985), pp. 53-57.

5616. Schröder, Horst. "Politik und Comics in der 'Dritten Welt.'" *Comixene. Das Comicfachmagazin.* 7:29 (1980), pp. 4-8.

5617. Schwarz, Rainer *et al. Comics und Medienpädagogik.* Munich: Arbeitszentrum Jugend, Film Fernsehen, 1972.

Technical Aspects

5618. Acevedo, Juan. *Wie Man Comix Macht. Aus dem Spanischen Übersetzt von Klaus Schübbe und Andreas Baumgart.* Munich: AG-SPAK-Publ, 1982.

5619. Krafft, Ulrich. *Comics Lesen: Untersuchungen zer Textualiät von Comics.* Stuttgart: Klett-Cotta, 1978.

5620. Strzyz, Klaus. "The Future Has Just Begun for Computer Comics." *WittyWorld.* Winter/Spring 1990, pp. 82-83.

5621. Strzyz, Klaus and Jari P. Cuypers. *Comic-Zeichen-Buch. Zeichne deine eigenen Comics!* Berlin: Gerald Leue, 1987. 128 pp.

COMIC STRIPS

5622. Akademie der Kunste, Berlin. *Comic Strips.* 1969. 103 pp.

5623. Blechen, Camilla. "Hühner Sind Auch Enten. Das Kolloquium Über Comic-Strips in Berlin." *Frankfurter Allgemeine Zeitung.* January 22, 1970, p. 15.

5624. Bohne, Friedrich, ed. *Sämtliche Briefe.* 2 Vols. Hanover: 1968.

5625. "Bonns Ostpolitik als Comic-Strip." *Der Spiegel.* No. 40, 1970, p. 26.

5626. Brüggemann, Theodor. "Comic Strips." In *Lexikon der Pädagogik.* Vol. 1, pp. 69-70. Freiburg: Neue Ausgabe, Herder Verlag, 1970.

5627. Brüggemann, Theodor. "Comic Strips." In *Lexikon der Pädagogik*, pp. 255-256. Freiberg: Herder, 1972.

5628. "Comic Strip als Farbholzschnitt." *Frankfurter Allgemeine Zeitung*. September 30, 1969, p. 2.

5629. "Comic Strip-Nackt im All." *Der Spiegel*. No. 33, 1965, p. 80.

5630. "Comic-Strips." *Der Spiegel*. No. 46, 1965.

5631. "Comic Strips." *Hör Zu*. No. 5, 1969, p. 22.

5632. "Comic Strips." *Petra* (Hamburg). No. 12, 1969, p. 153.

5633. "Comic Strips." *Zentralblatt für Jugendrecht und Jugendwohlfahrt*. 41, 1954, pp. 168-169.

5634. "Comic-Strips, Bilder Unserer Zeit." *Welt-Stimmen* (Stuttgart). 25:12 (1956), pp. 534-538.

5635. "Comic Strips: Pow, Wap, Bang." *Der Spiegel*. No. 18, 1968, p. 157f.

5636. "Comic Strips Sind Komische Segnungen für die Jugend." *Wiesbadener Kurier*. July 25, 1952.

5637. Couperie, Pierre. "Comic Strips à Berlin." *Phénix*. No. 12, 1969.

5638. Dangerfield, George. "Über die 'Funnies.'" *Die Amerikanische Rundschau*. January 1947.

5639. Ditzen, Lore. "Die Sprechblase im Kopf. Die Berliner Ausstellung Über 'Comic Strips.'" *Mainzer Tageszeitung*. December 1970, pp. 22-23; *Süddeutsche Zeitung*. December 29, 1969.

5640. Engelsing, Rolf. "Comic Strips." *Börsenblatt für den Deutschen Buchhandel*. 26:4 (1970), pp. 52-55.

5641. "Germany's Merry Elves." *Newsweek*. May 6, 1968, p. 88.

5642. Grassegger, Hans. "Wortspiel und Übersetzung." In *Sprache, Kultur und Gesellschaft*, edited by Wolfgang Kühlwein, pp. 81-83. Tübingen: Narr., 1984. 166 pp.

5643. Grolms, Maximilian. "Comic Strips für Anfänger und Fortgeschrittene." *Hannoversche Allgemeine Zeitung*. June 26, 1971.

5644. Hafner, Georg. "Comic-Strips, Kunsterziehlich Gesehen." *Jugendliteratur*. 9, 1957, pp. 389-391.

5645. Herold, Heidrun. "Zum Lesen von Comic-Strips. Untersuchungen an Volksschülern Verschiedener Altersstufen." Hausarbeit für die 1. Lehrerprüfung für das Lehramt an Volks-und Realschlen, Fall 1968. Hamburg.

5646. Hiepe, Richard. "Comic-Strip—Wesen und Wirkung Einer Optischen Ware." *Tendenzen.* 1. Sonderheft, No. 53, 1968, pp. 159-160, 164, 166.

5647. Hofmann, Werner. "Die Kunst der Comic-Strips." *Merkur.* 23:3 (1969), pp. 251-262.

5648. Hoidal, J. "Das Übel der Comic-Strips." *Industriekurier* (Düsseldorf). 7:87 (1954), p. 9; *Ludswigburger Kreiszeitung.* May 29, 1954, p. 10.

5649. Hünig, Wolfgang K. *Strukturen des Comic Strip: Anätze zu Einer Textlinguistisch-Semiotishen Analyse Narrativer Comics.* Hildesheim: Georg Olms Verlag, 1974. 343 pp.

5650. Kaps, Joachim. "Cartoon: Fetziger Auftakt." *Comic Info.* 1/1993, p. 56.

5651. Klie, Barbara. "Die Barbarei der Comic-Strips." *Die Schule.* 32:2 (1956), p. 16.

5652. Künnemann, Horst. "Literatur zu Comic Strips—Schund und Schmutz-Trivial-Literatur und Kitsch." *Internationale Jugendbibliothek.* Munich: 1956. 11 pp.

5653. Lachner, Johann. "Münchener Bilderbogen-die Comic-Strips von Anno Dazumal." *Lebendige Erziehung.* 4ᶜ année, 1954-1955, pp. 354-355.

5654. "Lesen Sie Auch Comic-Strips?" *Hamburger Abendblatt.* No. 64, 1969, p. 12.

5655. Mackscheidt, Elisabeth. "Mitmenschen-Comic-Strips-für und Wider." Vortrag, 2. Rundfunkprogramm, August 25, 1970. Cologne.

5656. "Modernes Leben: Comic Strips vom Minister." *Hamburger Morgenpost.* November 7, 1967, p. 6.

5657. Nafziger, Ralph O. "Die Entwicklung der Comic-Strips." *Publizistik.* 1:3 (1956), pp. 158-164.

5658. Nöhbauer, Hans F. "Comic-Strips und Literatur." *EPOCA* (Munich). No. 9, 1966.

5659. Panskus, Hartmut. "Kritische Marginalien zum Comic-Strip." *ASTA-Quartal* (Berlin). 12, 1967, pp. 283-285.

5660. Pehlke, Michael. "Die Zukunft der Comic-Strips." In *Comic Strips: Geschichte, Struktur, Wirkung und Verbreitung der Bildergeschichten, Ausstellungskatalog der Berliner Akademie der Künste, 13.12.1969-25.1.1970,* pp. 50-57, Berlin.

5661. Pforte, Dietger. "Deutscheprachige Comics." In *Comics Strips, Geschichte, Struktur, Wirkung und Verbreitung der Bildergeschichte*, exhibition catalogue, Akademie der Künste. (Berlin, 1970).

5662. Ropohl, Hanna. "Made in USA, Wider die Invasion der Comic-Strips." *Die Kommenden* (Freiburg). 14:4 (1969), p. 7.

5663. Sama, Dominic. "West German Salute to Comic-Strip Imps." *Philadelphia Inquirer*. April 8, 1990, p. 7K.

5664. Sautermeister, Gert. "...Meisterlicher Anwalt der Pietätlosigkeit." *Wilhelm-Busch-Jahrbuch*. 36, 1970.

5665. Schnackertz, Hermann J. *Form und Funktion Medialen Erzählens. Narrativität in Bildesquenz und Comicstrip*. Munich: W. Fink, 1980. 139 pp.

5666. Schneider, Helmut. "Struktur und Schablone: Ein Aufschlussreiches Beispiel für Aspekte der Sogenannten Trivialliteratur in der Prosa H.C. Artmanns." *Literatur und Kritik*. November-December 1984, pp. 189-190, 482-499.

5667. Sello, Katrin. "Zuunterst Wir Selbst! 'Zur Theorie der Comic-Strips'; Colloquium in der Akademie." *Der Tagesspiegel*. January 22, 1970.

5668. Sickert, Walter. "Diez, Busch and Oberländer." *Burlington Magazine*. October 1922, pp. 180-188.

5669. Smith, Norman. "Was Macht die 'Comic-Strips' So Popular?" *Spandauer Volksblatt*. November 3, 1963.

5670. Spillmann, Klaus. "4th Congress of German D.O.N.A.L.D." *The Barks Collector*. July 1981, pp. 1-4.

5671. Strobel, Ricarda. *Die "Peanuts"—Verbreitung und Ästhetische Formen. Ein Comic-Bestseller im Medienverbund*. Heidelberg: Winter, 1987. 251 pp.

5672. Voss, Frantz. "Comic-Strips." *Süddeutsche Zeitung*. April 20, 1967.

5673. "Warnung vor Biblischen Comic-Strips." *Weg und Wahrheit* (Frankfurt). March 28, 1954.

5674. "Was Macht die Comic-Strips So Popular?" *Gewerkschaftliche Rundschau für die Bergbau-und Energiewirtschaft*. 17, 1964, pp. 41-42.

5675. Weber, Gerhard W. "Malerei im Rohzustand. Comic-Strips und Werke von Geisteskranken." *Die Welt*. April 21, 1967.

5676. Wetterling, Horst. "Das Menschenbild in den Comic-Strips." *Zeitwende*. 31:10 (1960), pp. 691-695.

5677. Wills, Franz H. "Immer Gesellschaftsfähig—Der Comic-Strip in der Werbung-Gern Konsumierte Trivialkunst." *Absatzwirtschaft* (Frankfurt). 18/70, 1970, pp. 51-52.

5678. Zimmermann, Hans Dieter, ed. *Comic Strips. Geschichte, Struktur, Wirkung und Verbreitung der Bildergeschichten*. Berlin: Ausstellung in der Akademie der Künste, 1970.

POLITICAL CARTOONS

5679. Gross, Arnold. "Millionen Mögen Ihn Schon Zum Frühstück." *Rhein-Main-Presse*. December 14, 1991, p. A-2.

5680. Schaber, Will. *B.F. Dolbin: der Zeichner als Reporter*. Munich: Verlag Dokumentation, 1976. 177 pp.

5681. Sokkari, Hosam. "German Unification in Terms of the Banana." *WittyWorld*. Winter/Spring 1991, pp. 28-29.

5

Country Perspectives—Great Britain

REFERENCES

Catalogues, Collections

5682. Austin, Alan, Justin Ebbs, and Gary Fox. *The Comic Guide for Great Britain.* London: Fantasy Unlimited Publication, 1983.

5683. British Museums. *Catalog of Print and Drawings of the British Museum, Division I: Political and Personal Satire,* 11 Vols. 1-4, edited by F.G. Stephens; Vols. 5-11, edited by M. Dorothy George. London: Issued periodically between 1870 and 1954.

5684. George, Mary Dorothy, ed. *Catalogue of Political and Personal Satires Preserved in the Department of Prints and Drawings in the British Museum, Vols. 5-11.* London: British Museums Publications, Ltd., 1935-1954.

5685. Gifford, Denis. *The British Comic Catalogue 1874-1974.* London: Mansell; Westport, Connecticut: Greenwood, 1975. 210 pp.

5686. Gifford, Denis. *Christmas Comic Posters—A Denis Gifford Collection.* London: Blossom—The Greenwood Publishing Co., 1991.

5687. Gifford, Denis. *The Complete Catalogue of British Comics, Including Price Guide.* Exeter, England: Webb and Bower, 1985. 224 pp.

5688. Huxley, David. *Twenty-Two Comic Artists, an Exhibition*. Manchester, England: Manchester Polytechnic Library, 1975. 26 pp.

5689. Krumbhaav, E.B. *Isaac Cruikshank: A Catalogue Raisonné with a Sketch of His Life and Work*. Philadelphia: University of Pennsylvania Press, 1966. 177 pp.

5690. Lofts, W.O.G. and D.J. Adley. *Old Boys Books. A Complete Catalogue*. London: Lofts and Adley, 1970.

5691. Stevens, F.G., ed. *Catalogue of Prints and Drawings in the British Museum, Div. 1: Political and Personal Satires*. Vols. 1-4. London: British Museum, 1870-1873.

5692. Watson, Alex N. "Christmas Comic Posters—A Denis Gifford Collection." *The Jester*. April 1992, p. 7.

Dictionaries, Directories, Encyclopedias

5693. Cartoonists' Club of Great Britain. *Members' Handbook 1992/93*. Foreword by Clive Collins. London: Cartoonists' Club of Great Britain, 1992. 115 pp.

5694. Coe, Dale. "'Zines Across the Ocean." *Amazing Heroes*. August 1, 1984, pp. 48-49.

5695. Doyle, Brian. *Who's Who of Boys' Writers and Illustrators*. London: Doyle-Verlag, 1964.

5696. Gifford, Denis. *The British Comics and Story Paper Price Guide*. London: Association of Comics Enthusiasts, 1982.

5697. Gifford, Denis. *The International Book of Comics*. New York: Crescent Books, 1984.

5698. Houfe, Simon. *The Dictionary of British Book Illustrators and Caricaturists, 1800-1914*. Woodbridge, Suffolk and London: The Antique Collectors' Club, 1978.

5699. Scott, K.J., ed. *British Cartoonist Year Book 1964*. London: Anthony Gibbs [ca. 1963]. 138 pp.

GENERAL STUDIES

5700. Albert, A. *What Shall We Read?* London: Collins, 1930.

5701. Alderson, Frederick. *The Comic Postcard in English Life*. London: David and Charles, 1970.

5702. Barker, Martin. "Dennis Rules OK! Gnashee!" *New Society*. November 13, 1990, pp. 332-333.

5703. Bate, Jonathan. "Hal and the Regent." *Shakespeare Survey*. 38, 1985, pp. 69-75.

5704. Beckett, Francis. "Sex, Hard Cash and Rock-'n'-Roll." *The Independent*. May 31, 1989, p. 17.

5705. Bing, Roger. "Following in the Footsteps of Thurber and Co." *The Jester*. February 1993, p. 2.

5706. "British MP Blasts St. Swithin's Day." *Comics Journal*. October 1990, p. 25.

5707. "Cartoons of Di Disrobing Blamed on Yank." *Comics Journal*. April 1993, p. 35.

5708. "A Comic Cure." *The Sun*. February 12, 1989.

5709. Cummings, Michael. "Masters of the Art of Fun." *The Jester*. November 1992, p. 13. Reprinted from *Daily Mail*. September 19, 1992.

5710. Curtis, Manny. "Freelancing in England." *Cartoonist PROfiles*. September 1977, pp. 70-73.

5711. Davies, R. "Just a Smile at Twilight." *Times Literary Supplement*. September 24, 1976, p. 1203.

5712. Forbes, A. "Bretonnes with Flair." *The Times Literary Supplement*. May 6, 1977, p. 546.

5713. Fraydas, S. *Graphic Humor*. Reinhold, 1961.

5714. Gifford, Denis. "Are You a Youth at Heart?" *Guest and Host*. 1979.

5715. Gifford, Denis. "British Cartoonists Invade New York." *Graphics World*. (London). February 1980.

5716. Gifford, Denis. "Cartoon Aid." *WittyWorld*. Autumn 1987, p. 29.

5717. Gifford, Denis. "Cartoonists of the Kingdom Unite!" *Rex* (London). 1972.

5718. Gifford, Denis. "Comical Teddy Bears." *In Praise of Teddy Bears*. London: Souvenir Press, 1980.

5719. Gifford, Denis. "The Funny Wonders." *Art and Artists*. February 1971.

5720. Gifford, Denis. "A Laughtime of Comics." In *Cartoon Aid*. Letchworth: Cartoon Aid, April 1987.

5721. "Great Britain." *FECO News*. No. 3, 1987, p. 10.

5722. Griggs, Barbara. "Today's Thrills." *The Sunday Times*. June 28, 1981.

5723. Hardman, Paul. "Working in Advertising." *Jester 186*. July 1988, pp. 11-12.

5724. Harley, Gill. "Finding Strength in Adversity on a Trip out of the Spiral Cage." *Sunday Times* (London). August 20, 1989.

5725. Ivins, William M., jr. *Prints and Visual Communication*. London: Routledge and Kegan Paul, 1935. Reprinted: Cambridge, Massachusetts: The M.I.T. Press.

5726. Lilley, Les. "The Brits Christmas Visit—1991." *Cartoonist PROfiles*. December 1992, pp. 60-63.

5727. Lilley, Les. "Jubilee and Competition in the British Isles." *WittyWorld*. Spring 1988, pp. 20-21.

5728. Lilley, Les. "The State of the Art of Cartoon in Great Britain." *FECO News*. No. 5, 1987, p. 6.

5729. Lilley, Les. "The State of the Art of Cartoon in Great Britain." *WittyWorld*. Autumn 1987, pp. 28-29.

5730. Mackenzie, Keith. "Not by Appointment." *Cartoonist PROfiles*. September 1978, pp. 76-81.

5731. Mellini, Peter. "Gabriel's Message." *History Today*. February 1990, pp. 46-52.

5732. "Mischievous Literature." *The Bookseller*. July 1, 1868, pp. 445-449.

5733. Overy, Paul. "Pinpricks with Impunity: The Cartoonist's Job." *Communicator*. January 1976, pp. 25-26.

5734. "Politics in Comics." *Comics Journal*. May 1989, pp. 27-29.

5735. Reid, Arthur. "The FECO Edinburgh International Cartoon Festival 1990." *WittyWorld*. Summer/Autumn 1991, pp. 12-13.

5736. Richardson, John. "Cartooning in England." *Cartoonist PROfiles*. December 1986, pp. 26-31.

5737. Ryan, Rob. "The Comic Conspiracy." *Midweek*. June 16, 1988.

5738. Seymour-Ure, Colin. "Cartoon Follies." *The Times Higher Education Supplement*. March 23, 1990, p. 16.

5739. Shadwell, Wendy. "Brittania in Distress." *American Book Collector*. January 1986, pp. 3-12.

5740. Steadman, Ralph. "Cartooning As an Art." *Modern Painters*. Spring 1989.

5741. Stickler, Eve. "A School for Cartoonists That Isn't Just for Laughs." *WittyWorld*. Summer/Autumn 1991, pp. 32-33.

5742. Thompson, Ben. "Cor, It's a Big One." *Midweek Media*. July 6, 1989, pp. 11-12.

5743. Turner, E.S. *Boys Will Be Boys*. London: Penguin, 1948, 1976.

5744. Turner, Martyn. "Great Cartooning Disasters." *WittyWorld*. Winter/Spring 1989, p. 21.

5745. "UK News." *Speakeasy*. August 1988, pp. 20, 23, 27, 33.

5746. Walmsley, Janice. "Hold the Front Page, Kids." London *Daily Mail*. May 20, 1988.

5747. Wood, Art. "Pilgrimage to Canterbury." *Cartoonist PROfiles*. December 1990, pp. 76-79.

5748. Wood, J.M. "Artist Makes Britons Look Like Peculiar Birds." *Life*. April 12, 1948, pp. 16-18.

5749. "Work's No Fun If It's for Peanuts." *The Jester*. November 1992, p. 12.

Anthologies

5750. Armengol, M.H. *Those Three*. Foreword by J.M. Batista Roca. London: George Harrap and Co., n.d.

5751. *British Cartoonist Club Album*. London: Anthony Gibbs, 1962. 128 pp.

5752. *Cartoon 58. The Best Cartoons of 1957*. London: Hanison, 1957. Unpaginated.

5753. Cowper, Francis. *Topolski's Legal London*. London: The Lawyer, 1961. 76 pp.

5754. Findler, Gerald. *Lightning Cartoons*. London: Foulsham, n.d. 64 pp.

5755. Ffolkes, Michael. *Ffanfare!* London: Faber and Faber, n.d.

5756. Gabriel, pseud. *Cartoons*. Commentary by Philip Bolsover. London: *Daily Worker*, n.d.

5757. Graham, Alex. *Daughter in the House*. Brattleboro, Vermont: Stephen Greene Press. 1971, 64 pp.

5758. Grosvenor, Peter. *We Are Amused*. London: The Bodley Head, 1978. 126 pp.

5759. Hillier, Bevis. *Cartoons and Caricatures*. London: Studio Vista and Dutton Paperback, 1970.

5760. Hogarth, Paul. *America Observed*. Text by Stephen Spender. London: Clarkson N. Potter, Inc., 1979. 128 pp.

5761. Huggett, Frank E. *Cartoonists at War*. Leicester: Windward, 1981.

5762. Jones, Michael W., ed. *The Cartoon History of Britain*. London: Tom Stacey; New York: Macmillan, 1971.

5763. Jones, Michael W., ed. *A Cartoon History of the Monarchy*. London: Macmillan, 1978.

5764. Langdon, David. *Home Front Lines*. London: Methuen and Co., 1942. 88 pp.

5765. Lowell, J. *Dumb Belles-Lettres-Lallapaloozas from the Morning Mail*. New York: Simon and Schuster, 1933. 127 pp.

5766. Madden, Tim. *How's the Family? Cartoons from the Catholic Herald*. London: Burns and Oates, n.d.

5767. *Neb, Lee, Moon, Gittins, Illingworth, 400 Famous Cartoons by 5 Famous Cartoonists*. London: Associated Newspapers Ltd., n.d.

5768. *New Scientist. Spin-off: A Selection of Cartoons*. London: Harrap, [ca. 1965].

5769. Oistros. *Truffle-Eater, Pretty Stories and Funny Pictures*. London: Arthur Barker, n.d., ca. 1933.

5770. Parkes, Terence. *Man in Motion*. Brattleboro, Vermont: The Stephen Greene Press, 1971. 64 pp.

5771. Peynet, Raymond. *The Lover's Travelogue*. Intro. by Kay Webb. London: Perpetua Book, 1958. Unpaginated.

5772. Read, Herbert. *Art and Society*. London: Faber and Faber, 1945.

5773. Taylor, Richard. *Wrong Bag*. London: Hamish Hamilton, 1961. 96 pp.

5774. Ullyett, Roy. *Sports Cartoons*... 6th, 7th, 8th and 9th Series. London: Beaverbrook Newspapers, n.d.

5775. Walker, Martin. *Daily Sketches, A Cartoon History of British Twentieth-Century Politics*. London, 1978.

5776. Webster, Tom. *Annual. 1924, '25, '26, '27. Cartoons from the Daily Mail, Evening News and Weekly Dispatch*. London: Associated Newspapers, 1923. 112 pp.

5777. Wilkinson, Gilbert. *What a War!* London: Odhams Press, n.d.

5778. W.S.C. (Winston Churchill). *A Cartoon Biography*. Compiled by Fred Urguhart; foreword by Harold Nicholson. London: Cassel and Comp., 1955.

Children

5779. Dixon, Bob. *Catching Them Young*. London: Pluto Press, 1977. Vol. 1, "Sex, Race and Class in Children's Fiction"; Vol. 2, "Political Ideas in Children's Fiction."

5780. Fenwick, Geoff. "Comics and Education." *Bookmark*. No. 9, 1982, pp. 2-9.

5781. Gosling, Kenneth. "Children's Cartoon Heroes To Be Banned from Appearing in Television Advertising." *London Times*. September 9, 1975, p. 1.

5782. Laing, A. "Children's Comics." *Researches and Studies* (The University of Leeds, Institute of Education). May 1955, pp. 5-17.

5783. Legman, Gershon. "Introduction." In *Children's Humor*, by Sandra McCosh. London: Panther, 1976.

5784. Mauger, Peter. "Children's Reading." In "The U.S.A. Threat to British Culture," special issue, *Arena* (London). June-July 1951, pp. 45 ff.

5785. Morgan, Vanessa. "Children of the World to Kidz International—Still Drawing the World Together." *WittyWorld*. Summer/Autumn 1991, pp. 68-71.

5786. O'Connell, Judith. "Sexist Images in Children's Comics and Television." B.Ed. dissertation, University of Sheffield, 1982.

5787. O'Connell, Judith. "Sexist Images in Children's Comics and Television Programmes." *University of Sheffield: Faculty of Educational Studies*. April 1982. Abstracted: *Sheffield Educational Research: Current Highlights*. April 1982.

5788. Whitehead, Frank. *Children and the Books*. London: Macmillan, 1977.

5789. Whitehead, Frank *et al. Children's Reading Interests*. London: Evans/Methuen, 1975.

Professionalism

5790. "Britain's First School of Cartooning Moves to New Permanent Premises." *Comics Journal*. May 1989, p. 30.

5791. "Britain's Largest Con: UKCAC '88." *Comics Journal*. May 1989, pp. 25-27.

5792. "Cartoon Centre Appeal." *Speakeasy*. December 1990-January 1991, p. 13.

5793. "Cartoonists' Club of Great Britain." *Cartoonist PROfiles*. March 1980, pp. 55-63.

5794. "Cartoons Become an Important Research Tool in England!" *Cartoonist PROfiles*. March 1983, pp. 18-23.

5795. "Comics Creators Guild." *The Jester*. February 1993, p. 6.

5796. "Comics-Fair in London." *Illustrated London News*. November 20, 1954.

5797. "Conventional Wisdom." *Speakeasy*. February 1989, pp. 40, 42, 44.

5798. Curson, Nigel. "Angoulême 1990—The Brits Abroad." *Speakeasy*. March 1990, pp. 38-39, 41.

5799. "Exhibit of English Cartoons." *Cartoonist PROfiles*. December 1979, pp. 36-37.

5800. Green, Stuart. "The London Cartoon Centre." *Speakeasy*. June 1990, p. 53.

5801. Green, Stuart. "Speakeasy Award Winner 1990—The Untold Story." *Speakeasy*. May 1990, pp. 40-41, 43.

5802. "International Cartoon Festival at Margate." *FECO News*. No. 7, 1989, pp. 3-4.

5803. Lilley, Les. "The British FECO Exhibition at Lisse, Are You Amused?" *FECO News*. No. 3, 1987, p. 8.

5804. Lilley, Les. "Cartoonist Hotel." *WittyWorld*. Spring 1988, p. 15.

5805. Lilley, Les. "The Edinburgh Festival." *Inkspot*. Autumn 1993, pp. 25-28.

5806. Lilley, Les. "FECO Report from Great Britain." *FECO News*. No. 1, 1986, p. 7.

5807. Lilley, Les. "FECO UK—The First Four Years." *FECO News*. Special Edition, 1989.

5808. Lilley, Les. "Margate (Great Britain), A Home Away from Home in England." *FECO News*. No. 6, 1988, p. 15.

5809. Lilley, Les. "A New British Festival?" *WittyWorld*. Autumn, 1988, p. 29.

5810. Lilley, Les. "Report from Great Britain." *FECO News*. No. 2, 1986, p. 4.

5811. Lilley, Les. "We've Got the Key Of the Door Dept., Twenty-One Years at the Cartoonist!" *The Jester*. October 1992, pp. 8-9.

5812. "UK Cartoonists' Association Renamed." *Comics Journal*. February 1993, p. 20.

5813. "Waddington's International Cartoon Festival at Margate 1989." *FECO News*. No. 8, 1989, pp. 3-4.

Technical Aspects

5814. Farrow, Will. *Practical Cartooning for Profit*. London: Hurst and Blackett, n.d.

5815. Ffolkes, Michael. *Drawing Cartoons*. London: Watson-Guptill, 1963.

5816. Maddocks, Peter. *Caricature and the Cartoonist. Drawings of the Famous by the Famous*. London: Elm Tree Books, 1989.

5817. Reading, Bryan. *Drawing Cartoons and Caricature*. London: Armanda Original, 1987.

5818. Thompson and Hewison. *How To Draw and Sell Cartoons*. London: Apple Press, 1985.

Television, Film, Radio

5819. "*Brought to Life* and Other Comics Featured on British Television." *Comics Journal*. May 1989, pp. 30-31.

5820. "Comics on British TV." *Comics Journal*. June 1988, p. 32.

5821. "Denis Gifford's British TV Game Show." *Cartoonist PROfiles*. September 1981, pp. 70-72.

5822. Gifford, Denis. "Comic Strip Radio." *The Listener* (London). January 7, 1971.

5823. Gifford, Denis. "The First Television Comic." *Collectors' Fayre*. November 1986.

5824. Gifford, Denis. "Radio Fun: Secret Weapon." *The Guardian* (London). December 30, 1978.

5825. Heller, Steven. "Spitting Images (Britain's Most Biting TV Revue)." *Print*. May/June 1986, pp. 98-105+.

5826. Lanihorne, Ruan. "New Weekly British TV Comic Begins." *Comics Buyer's Guide*. April 5, 1985, p. 3.

5827. Lewis, Peter and Corinne Pearlman. *Media and Power: From Marconi to Murdoch*. London: Camden Press, 1986.

5828. Verity, Edward. "Bunter on TV? A Fat Chance, Says the BBC." *The Jester*. October 1992, p. 12. Reprinted from *Daily Mail*. September 9, 1992.

Women

5829. Bennett, Carol. "What Do Women Want?" *Speakeasy*. November 1990, pp. 30-31.

5830. Clayton, Ellen. *English Female Artists*. London: 1876, pp. 331-333.

5831. Fenwick, L. "Periodicals and Adolescent Girls." *Studies in Education*. 2:1 (1953).

5832. Gifford, Denis. "British Girls." *Glamour International* (Florence, Italy). No. 7, 1983.

5833. Hasted, Nick. "British Market Frustrating for Women Cartoonists." *Comics Journal*. February 1992, pp. 33-36.

5834. Hollings, Julie. "The Portrayal of Women in Romance Comic Strips 1964-84." BA dissertation, University of Reading, 1985.

5835. Hollowood, Bernard. *The Women of Punch*. London: Arthur Barker, 1961. 166 pp.

5836. Hughes, Dave. "Sex for Sale." *Speakeasy*. November 1990, pp. 53, 55.

5837. Kunzle, David. "Marie Duval: A Caricaturist Rediscovered." *Woman's Art Journal*. Spring/Summer 1986, pp. 26-31.

5838. Layard, George Somes. *A Great "Punch" Editor: Being the Life, Letters, and Diaries of Shirley Brooks*. London: Pitman, 1907.

5839. Stonier, G.W. *Girls, Girls*. London: Penguin Book, 1963.

HISTORICAL ASPECTS

Animation

5840. "Animation—It Goes Back to the Roots of the Movies." *Variety*. November 5, 1990, pp. 62, 70.

5841. Brunel, Adrian. *Nice Work: The Story of Thirty Years in British Film Production*. London: Forbes Robertson, 1949.

5842. Clark, Ken. "Anson Dyer." Program notes, Cambridge (England) Animation Festival, 1979.

5843. Clark, Ken. "Early Pioneers." Program notes, Cambridge Animation Festival, 1979.

5844. Gifford, Denis. *British Animated Films, 1895-1985. A Filmography*. Jefferson City, North Carolina: McFarland and Co., 1987. 352 pp.

5845. Givens, Bill. "With Acknowledgments to Raymond Briggs." *Animation*. Winter 1989, pp. 67-69.

5846. Low, Rachel. *The History of the British Film, 1914-1918*. London: Allen and Unwin, 1971.

5847. Low, Rachel. *The History of the British Film, 1918-1929*. London: Allen and Unwin, 1971.

5848. Low, Rachel and Roger Manvell. *The History of the British Film, 1896-1906*. London: Unwin, 1948.

5849. Pilling, Jayne, ed. *That's Not All Folks!* London: British Film Institute, 1985. 38 pp.

Caricature and Cartoons

5850. Adhémar, Jean. *Graphic Art of the 18th Century*. London: Thames and Hudson, 1964.

5851. *The Age of Horace Walpole in Caricature: An Exhibition of Satirical Prints and Drawings from the Collection of W.S. Lewis*, Sterling Memorial Library, Yale University, 1973. Catalogue by John C. Riely.

5852. Alexander, David and Richard T. Godfrey. *Painters and Engraving: The Reproductive Print from Hogarth to Wilkie*. New Haven, Connecticut: Yale Center for British Art, 1980.

5853. "Animals in Caricature." *Spectator*. August 10, 1895, pp. 174-175.

5854. Ashbee, C.R. *Caricature*. London: Chapman and Hall, Ltd., 1928.

5855. Ashton, J. *English Caricature and Satire on Napoleon, 1*. Vol. 1. London: 1884.

5856. Atherton, H.M. "Mob in Eighteenth-Century English Caricature." Eighteenth Century Studies. Fall 1978, pp. 47-54 +.

5857. Beerbohm, Max. *Rossetti and His Circle*. New Haven, Connecticut: Yale University Press, 1987.

5858. Bradshaw, Percy V. *They Make Us Smile*. London: 1942.

5859. "British Statesmen in Caricature." *Living Age*. October 15, 1926, pp. 170-171.

5860. "The Caricature History." *Kayhan Caricature*. May 1992, pp. 29-31.

5861. *Cartoon and Caricature from Hogarth to Hoffnung*. Intro. by Draper Hill. London: Arts Council, 1962.

5862. "Cartoon Critic: London Caricaturist Finds American Colleagues Lack Originality." *Literary Digest*. November 21, 1936, pp. 31-32.

5863. "A Century of English Laughter." *Picture Post* (London). July 16, 1949.

5864. Churchill, Winston. "Cartoons and Cartoonists." *Strand Magazine*. June 1931, pp. 583-584.

5865. Curtis, Lewis P., jr. *Apes and Angels: The Irishman in Victorian Caricature*. Newton Abbot: David and Charles; Washington, D.C.: Smithsonian, 1971.

5866. Davies, Randall. *Caricature of Today*. London: The Studio Ltd., 1928.

5867. Davies, Randall. *Caricatures et Moeurs Anglaises. 1750-1850*. Catalogue de l'Éxposition des Arts Décoratifs. Association Franco-Britannique Art et Tourisme. Paris, February-March 1938.

5868. de Haswell, James. *Napoleon III from the Popular Caricatures of the Last Thirty Years*. London: James Camden, n.d., [ca. 1874].

5869. de Maré, Eric. *The Victorian Woodblock Illustrators*. London: Gordon Fraser, 1980.

5870. Donald, Diana. "Mr. Deputy Dumpling and Family: Satirical Images of the City Merchant in Eighteenth-Century England." *Burlington Magazine*. November 1989, pp. 755-763.

5871. Duff, Charles. "Os Caricaturistas Inglêses." *Vamos Ler!* (Rio de Janeiro). November 19, 1942.

5872. Duffy, Michael, ed. *The English Satirical Print, 1600-1832*. London: Chadwyck-Healey, 1986.

5873. Dukelskaja, L.A. *Die Englische Gesellschaftskarikatur in der 2. Hälfte des 18. Jahrhunderts*. Leningrad: n.d.

5874. "English Caricature 1620 to the Present (Victoria & Albert Museum, London)." *Art and Artists*. August 1985, p. 34.

5875. Espoir [pseud.] *Communist Cartoons*. London: Executive Committee of the Communist Party of Great Britain, 1922. 44 pp.

5876. Everitt, Graham. *English Caricaturists and Graphic Humourists of the Nineteenth Century*. London: Swann Sonnerschein and Co., 1885; Le Bas and Lowrey, 1886; 1885. Reissued. Freeport, New York: Books for Libraries Press, 1972. 427 pp.

5877. Everitt, Graham. *English Caricaturists from Cruikshank to Leech*. London: Swann Sonnerschein, 1886.

5878. Filon, Augustin. *La Caricature en Angleterre*. Paris: Libr. Hachette, 1902.

5879. Frewin, Anthony. *One Hundred Years of Science Fiction Illustration*. London: Bloomsbury Books, 1988. 128 pp.

5880. George, M. Dorothy. *English Political Caricature, 1793-1832. A Study of Opinion and Propaganda*. Oxford: Clarendon Press, 1959. 275 pp.

5881. George, M. Dorothy. *English Political Caricature to 1792: A Study of Opinion and Propaganda*. Oxford: Clarendon Press, 1959. 237 pp.

5882. George, M. Dorothy. *Hogarth to Cruikshank: Social Change in Graphic Satire*. New York: 1967.

5883. Gibson-Cowan, Ialeen. "Smile Please." *Creative Camera*. April 1985, pp. 24-28. (19th Century Photographic Cartoons).

5884. Gifford, Denis. "Flavour of the Month: The Spice of Life." *Films and Filming*. November 1984, p. 6. (R. Lindup caricatures).

5885. Gifford, Denis. "The Time for Kidding Mr. Hitler." *The Guardian* (London). October 20, 1979.

5886. Gifford, Denis. "You Had To Laugh Even in Wartime." *The Joker* (London). 1975.

5887. Godfrey, Richard. *English Caricature, 1620 to the Present: Caricaturists and Satirists, Their Art, Their Purpose and Influence*. Exhibition Catalogue. London: Victoria and Albert Museum, 1984. 144 pp.

5888. "Gott Straffe England!" Munich: *Simplicissimus* Verlag, Albert Langen Verlag, n.d. (Caricatures about England in *Simplicissimus*).

5889. Gould, Ann. "La Gravure Politique de Hogarth à Cruikshank." In *Revue de l'Art*. No. 30. *Aspects de l'Art Anglais*. Paris: Editions C.N.R.S., 1975.

5890. Gould, Ann, J. Jensen, and F. Whitford. "Politics in Cartoon and Caricature." In *Twentieth-Century Studies*. No. 13/14. Canterbury: University of Kent, Scottish Academic Press, 1975.

5891. Gould, Francis. *Political Caricatures*. London: *Westminster Gazette*. Annual volume of caricatures, 1895-1906.

5892. Grand-Carteret, John. *John Bull sur la Sallette. Le Livre Bleu en Images*. Paris: Libr. J. Strauss, n.d.

5893. Grand-Carteret, John. *Napoléon en Images. Estampes Anglaises. Portraits et Caricatures*. Paris: Librairie de Firmin Didot, 1895.

5894. Grego, Joseph. "The Exhibition of Humorists in Art." *Magazine of Art*. 12 (1889), pp. 334 +.

5895. Grose, Francis. *Rules for Drawing Caricatures with an Essay on Comic Painting*. London: Samuel Bagster, 1791. Also in *The Antiquarian Repository*. New Ed., Vol. 1, 1807.

5896. Halsey, R.T.H. "'Impolitical Prints': The American Revolution As Pictured by Contemporary English Caricaturists. An Exhibition." *Bulletin of the New York Public Library*. 43 (1939), pp. 795-829.

5897. Holme, Geoffrey, ed. *Caricature of To-day*. Intro. by Randall Davies. London: The Studio, 1928. 136 plates.

5898. Jackson, Holbrook. *The Eighteen Nineties*. Harmonsworth Middlesex: Penguin Book, 1939.

5899. Jean-Aubry, G. "Caricature Anglaise." *Arts et Métiers Graphiques*. September 15, 1932, pp. 21-46.

5900. Jean-Aubry, G. "Las Orígines de la Caricatura Inglesa." *La Prensa* (Buenos Aires). October 16, 1932.

5901. "John Bull, Seen by an Anthropologist." *Literary Digest.* December 11, 1926, p. 24.

5902. Jouve, Michel. *L'Âge D'Or de la Caricature Anglaise.* Paris: Presses de la Foundation Nationale des Sciences Politiques, 1983.

5903. Jouve, Michel. "L'Image du Sansculotte dans la Caricature Politique Anglaise: Création d'un Stéréotype Pictural." *Gazette des Beaux-Arts.* 91 (1978), pp. 187-196.

5904. Judy. *The Right Hon. W.E. Gladstone from Judy's Point of View.* London: The Judy Office, 1880.

5905. Knox, E.V. "British Humour Is Still Unrationed." *New York Times Magazine.* March 15, 1942.

5906. Knox, E.V. "From Queen Victoria to Hitler." *New York Times Magazine.* January 23, 1944.

5907. Koenig, Thilo, Robert Ohrt, and Christian Troster. "Die Stecher von London: Englische Politische Karikatur Unter dem Einfluss der Französischen Revolution." In *Karikaturen*, edited by Klaus Herding and Gunter Ott. Giessen: Anabas-Verlag, 1980.

5908. Kris, Ernst and E.H. Gombrich. "The Principles of Caricature." *British Journal of Medical Psychology.* 17 (1938), pp. 319-342.

5909. Kunzle, David. "Between Broadsheet Caricature and 'Punch': Cheap Newspaper Cuts for the Lower Classes in the 1830s." *Art Journal.* Winter 1983, pp. 339-346.

5910. Lambert, Susan. *The Franco-Prussian War and the Commune in Caricature, 1870-1871.* Exhibition Catalogue. London: Victoria and Albert Museum, 1971.

5911. *Laughs on the Home Front.* Compiled and Published by S. Evelyn Thomas. St. Albans: "Rathcoole," 1943.

5912. Lemann, Bernard. "English Caricature." *American Magazine of Art.* September 1935, pp. 548-555.

5913. Lynch, Bohun. *A History of Caricature.* London: Faber and Gwyer, 1926. 126 pp.

5914. Malcolm, J.P. *An Historical Sketch of the Art of Caricaturing, with Graphic Illustrations*. London: Printed for Longman, Hurst, Rees, Orme, and Brown, 1813.

5915. Maurois, André. "Caricatures et Moeurs Anglaises." In *L'Amour de l'Art*. Paris: Éditions Hyperion, March 1938, No. 2.

5916. Mellini, Peter and Roy T. Matthews. "John Bull's Family Arises." *History Today*. May 1987, pp. 17-23.

5917. "Old-Time Caricatures—No. 3." *Twinkles*. February 7, 1897, p. 13.

5918. "Old-Time Caricatures—No. 5." *Twinkles*. February 21, 1897, p. 13.

5919. "Old-Time Caricatures—No. 6." *Twinkles*. February 28, 1897, p. 13.

5920. "Old-Time Caricatures—No. 9." *Twinkles*. March 27, 1897, p. 13.

5921. Paston, George [pseud.]. *Social Caricature in the Eighteenth Century*. London: Methuen and Company, 1906; Reissued: New York: Benjamin Blom, 1968.

5922. Patten, Robert L. "Conventions of Georgian Caricature." *Art Journal*. Winter 1983, pp. 331-338.

5923. Penn, A. *The Growth of Caricature*. London: The Critic. 1882.

5924. Randolph, H. *Life of General Sir Robert Wilson*. London, 1862. Vol. 1 (B. Wilson, pp. 20-22).

5925. Reisner, M.E. "Effigies of Power: Pitt and Fox as Canterbury Pilgrims." *Eighteenth Century Studies*. Summer 1979, pp. 481-508.

5926. Rosner, Charles. *The Writing on the Wall. 1813-1943*. London, Nicholson and Watson, 1943.

5927. Stonach, George. *The Gladstone Almanack, 1885*. London: William Blackwood and Sons, 1885.

5928. Strachan, P. "Days of Shovel-Scoop Hats; Caricatures of the 18th and Early 19th Centuries in England." *Christian Science Monitor Magazine*. December 6, 1947, p. 13.

5929. Sutton, Denys. "The Satiric Spirit in British Art (English Caricature 1620 to the Present) (Library of Congress, Washington, D.C.; traveling exhibit)." *Apollo* (London). November 1984, pp. 304-311.

5930. Veth, Cornelius. *Comic Art in England*. London: Edward Goldstein, 1930.

5931. Wardroper, John. *Kings, Lords, and Wicked Libellers. Satire and Protest 1760-1837.* London: Murray, 1973.

5932. Webster, Tom. *Annual.* 1924, 1925, 1926, 1927. Cartoons from the *Daily Mail, Evening News* and *Weekly Dispatch.* London: Associated Newspapers, 1923. 112 pp.

5933. *Wellington in Caricature.* London: Victoria and Albert Museum, 1965. Catalogue by John Physick.

5934. Westwood, H.R. *Modern Caricaturists.* Foreword by David Low. London: Lovat Dickson Ltd., 1932.

5935. Wilenski, R.H. "Caricature and Comment." In *English Painting.* London: Faber and Faber, 1933.

5936. Wright, Thomas. *Caricature History of the Georges.* New York and London: Benjamin Blom, 1968. 639 pp. First published: London, 1868.

Comic Books

5937. Carpenter, Kevin. *Penny Dreadfuls and Comics.* London: Victoria and Albert Museum, 1983. 124 pp.

5938. Carpenter, Kevin. "Vom Penny Dreadful zum Comic. Englische Jugendzeitschriften, Heftchen und Comics von 1855 bis zur Gegenwart. Eine Ausstellung im Rahmen der 7. Oldenburger Kinder-und Jugendbuchmesse aus den Beständen der Universitätsbibliothek und aus Privatbesitz. November 7-22, 1981, Stadtmuseum Oldenburg." Oldenburg: Bis, 1981.

5939. "*Dandy* and *Beano* at 50." *Comics Journal.* June 1988, pp. 32-33.

5940. Fiore, R. "Funnybook Roulette." *Comics Journal.* June 1988, pp. 41-44.

5941. Gifford, Denis. "Biff! Gosh! Wow! 50 Years of Cow Pie." *London Daily News.* April 23, 1987; May 4, 1987.

5942. Gifford, Denis. "British Comics Pull Duty During the War." *WittyWorld.* Winter/Spring 1989, pp. 84-86.

5943. Gifford, Denis. "Caper Source: 100 Years of Comics." *The Guardian* (London). December 18, 1974.

5944. Gifford, Denis. "A Century of Comics." *Antiquarian Book Monthly Review.* November 1975.

5945. Gifford, Denis. "The Comic Kids Who Never Grow Up." *Liverpool Echo*. July 25, 1975.

5946. Gifford, Denis. "Comics in Great Britain." *Histoire Mondiale des Comics*. Paris: Pierre Horay, 1980.

5947. Gifford, Denis. *Comics 101 Souvenir Book*. London: Gifford, 1976.

5948. Gifford, Denis. "Evolucion de las Revistas Britanicas Hasta los Años 80." *Historia de los Comics* (Spain). No. 40, 1983.

5949. Gifford, Denis. "Evolution of the British Comic." *History Today* (London). May 1971.

5950. Gifford, Denis. "The First British Comic Book." *Collectors' Fayre*. May 1987.

5951. Gifford, Denis. "A Ghost of Christmas Past." *Observer Colour Magazine* (London). December 19, 1971.

5952. Gifford, Denis. "A Golden Age of Comics." *Penrose Graphic Arts Annual* (London). No. 65. December 1972.

5953. Gifford, Denis. "Golden Pennyworths (Independent Penny Comics: Part 2)." *Collector's Fayre*. February 1987.

5954. Gifford, Denis. "Grande-Bretagne." In *Histoire Mondiale de la Bande Dessinée*, edited by Pierre Horay, pp. 128-153. Paris: Pierre Horay Éditeur, 1989.

5955. Gifford, Denis. *Happy Days: A Century of Comics*. London: Jupiter Books, 1975, and Bloomsbury Books, 1988. 128 pp.

5956. Gifford, Denis. "He Put Men into Space 36 Years Ago." *Observer Colour Magazine* (London). January 28, 1972.

5957. Gifford, Denis. "How Rockfist Rogan and 100 Heroes Beat the Baddies." *Mayfair*. August 1971.

5958. Gifford, Denis. "Look Back and Chuckle at Your Little Chums." *Mayfair* (London). July 1971.

5959. Gifford, Denis. "Los Centenarios Comics Britanicos." *Historia de los Comics* (Spain). No. 13, 1983.

5960. Gifford, Denis. "Los Heroes de los Comics de Aventuras en Gran Bretano." *Historia de los Comics* (Spain). No. 19, 1983.

5961. Gifford, Denis. "Mansfield's Monster (Independent Penny Comics: Part 1)." *Collectors' Fayre*. January 1987.

5962. Gifford, Denis. *Penny Comics of the Thirties*. London: New English Library, 1975.

5963. Gifford, Denis. *Run Adolf Run, the World War Two Fun Book*. London: Corgi, 1975.

5964. Gifford, Denis. *Six Comics of World War One*. London: Peter Way, 1972.

5965. Gifford, Denis. *Test Your N.Q. (Nostalgia Quotient)*. London: New English Library, 1972.

5966. Gifford, Denis. *Victorian Comics*. London: George Allen and Unwin, 1976. 144 pp.

5967. Gifford, Denis. "The War Laughs of a Nation." *Collectors' Fayre*. June 1987.

5968. Gifford, Denis and Marcus Morris. *The Best of Eagle*. London: Michael Joseph/Ebury, 1977.

5969. Packman, Leonard. "Those Comic Papers of Yesterday." *Collectors Digest* (Surrey). Annual, 1967.

5970. Perry, George and Alan Aldridge. *The Penguin Book of Comics: A Slight History*. London: Penguin Books, 1967. Rev. Eds., 1971, 1989. 272 pp.

5971. Stringer, Lew. "A History of British Comics." *Comics Journal*. June 1988, pp. 57-67.

5972. Woollcombe, Alan. "Traildust and Saddle Leather." *Speakeasy*. November 1989, pp. 42-43.

Comic Strips

5973. Gifford, Denis. *The Comic Art of Charlie Chaplin*. London: Hawk Books, 1989. 128 pp.

5974. Gifford, Denis. "Comic Cuts That Brought the Stars to Life." *T.V. Times* (London). December 13, 1979.

5975. Gifford, Denis. *Stap Me! The British Newspaper Strip*. Tring: Shire Publications, 1971. 96 pp. Reissued as *The History of the British Newspaper Strip*.

5976. Gifford, Denis. *Stop Me! A History Covering Newspapers Strips by British Artists from 1900-1971*. London: Shire Publications, 1971.

5977. Gifford, Denis. "Uncle Oojah." *Collectors' Fayre*. July 1987.

5978. MacKenzie, Keith. "Pop." *Cartoonist PROfiles*. December 1975, pp. 20-24.

Political Cartoons

5979. Baker, Rosemary. "Satirical Prints As a Source of English Social History." *Quarterly Journal of the Library of Congress*. Summer 1982.

5980. Broadley, A.M. "The Evolution of John Bull." *Pearson's Magazine*. 1909, pp. 543-551.

5981. Buss, R.W. *English Graphic Satire*. London, 1874.

5982. Churchill, Winston. "Cartoons and Cartoonists." In *Thoughts and Adventures*, pp. 19-20. London: Thornton and Butterwood Ltd., 1933.

5983. Connolly, Joseph. "Drawings for Low Tastes." *The Jester*. February 1992, p. 2. Reprinted from *Daily Telegraph* (London). January 6, 1993.

5984. Crane, Walter. *Cartoons for the Cause, 1886-1896*. London: The Twentieth Century Press, 1896.

5985. "Gad, Sir, He Had to Die; Colonel Blimp." *Time*. June 21, 1943, p. 31.

5986. George, M. Dorothy. *Hogarth to Cruikshank: Social Change in Graphic Satire*. New York: Walker and Co., 1967. 224 pp.

5987. Helfand, William H. "John Bull and His Doctors." *Veröffentlichungen der Internationalen Gesellschaft für Geschicht der Pharmazie*. 28, 1966, p. 131 +.

5988. Helfand, William H. "Medicine and Pharmacy in British Political Prints—The Example of Lord Sidmouth." *Medical History*. 29, 1985, pp. 375-385.

5989. Hughes, Catherine. "Imperialism, Illustration and the *Daily News*, 1896-1904." In *The Press in English Society from the Seventeenth to Nineteenth Centuries*, edited by Michael Harris and Alan Lee, pp. 187-200. London: Associated University Presses, 1986.

5990. Middleton, L. "Chamberlain's Bumbershoot; British Cannot Lampoon Officials but the Law Is Silent About Umbrellas." *Current History*. April 1939, pp. 30-31.

5991. Paulson, Ronald. "Political Cartoons and Comic Strips." *Eighteenth Century Studies*. Summer 1975, pp. 479-489.

5992. Press, Charles. "The Georgian Political Cartoon and Democratic Government." *Comparative Studies in Society and History*. 19, 1977, pp. 216-238.

5993. *The Rake's Progress and Other Political Cartoons Reprinted from St. Stephen's Review*. London: The Conservative Press Co. Ltd., 1884.

5994. Rickwood, Edgell. *Radical Squibs and Loyal Ripostes. Satirical Pamphlets 1819-21*. Bath: Adams and Dart, 1971.

5995. Walker, Martin. *Daily Sketches, A History of British Twentieth Century Politics*. London: Paladin Granada Books, 1978.

CARTOONISTS and CARICATURISTS

5996. "A.B.C. Warriors." *Speakeasy*. No. 81, 1987, pp. 7-9.

5997. à Beckett, Arthur W. "Pen-Humorists of England." *Harper's Weekly*. August 15, 1903, p. 1336.

5998. à Beckett, Arthur W. *Recollections of a Humorist: Grave and Gay*. London: Pitman, 1907.

5999. Appleby, Steven. "Still with Us—John Ryan." *The Jester*. June 1992, p. 17.

6000. "Arnold Lerner—Cartoonist, Illustrator." *FECO News*. No. 10, 1990, p. 13.

6001. "Arthur Reid." *FECO News*. No. 5, 1987, p. 17.

6002. Ball, Ian. "Once Upon a Monstruous Time...the Man Who Drew Fester." *Daily Telegraph Magazine* (London). No. 157, 1967, pp. 24-35.

6003. Brockbank, R. *The Brockbank Omnibus*. New York: G.P. Putnam's Sons, 1958.

6004. Brooks, Bradi. "Frank Bellamy." *Comics Journal*. September 1989, pp. 13-14.

6005. Buckland, Elfreda. *The World of Donald McGill*. London: Blandford, 1990. 128 pp.

6006. Campbell, Peter. "Homages." *The Listener* (London). January 7, 1971.

6007. "Carruthers Gould, Veteran British Cartoonist." *Review of Reviews*. March 1925, pp. 311-312.

6008. Clark, Alan. *The Comic Art of Reg Parlett: 60 Years of Comics*. Tunbridge Wells, Kent: Golden Fun Publishing, 1986. 128 pp.

6009. Clark, Alan and David Ashford. *The Comic Art of Roy Wilson*. Tunbridge Wells, Kent: Midas Books; New York: Hippocrene Books, Inc., 1983. 128 pp.

6010. Collins, Clive. "Griffin." *WittyWorld*. Winter/Spring 1989, pp. 72-76.

6011. Collins, Mark and Eli and Dave Friedmann. "The Studio. 2: Barry Windsor-Smith." *Comixene. Das Comicfachmagazin*. 7:29 (1980), pp. 52-55.

6012. Crown, Patricia. "E.F. Burney: An Historical Study in British Romantic Art." Ph.D. dissertation, University of California, 1977.

6013. "Curly and Co., Mike Atkinson." *Cartoonist PROfiles*. June 1978, pp. 64-65.

6014. Dalziel, Edward and George Dalziel. *The Brothers Dalziel: A Record of Fifty Years Work 1840-1890*. London: Methuen, 1901.

6015. "Dave Gibbons." *Comics Interview*. October 1984, pp. 51-65.

6016. De Suinn, Colin. "Bryan Talbot: Luther in the Sky with Diamonds." *Speakeasy*. February 1990, pp. 33-35, 37.

6017. De Suinn, Colin. "Down Among the Bat Mites." *Speakeasy*. February 1991, pp. 47-49. (Norm Breyfogle).

6018. "Dez Skinn Leaves Marvel U.K." *Comics Journal*. March 1980, p. 15.

6019. Ellis, Warren. "Steve Pugh: Fear and Loathing and Process White." *Speakeasy*. May 1990, pp. 54-55.

6020. "Excalibur." *Speakeasy*. No. 81, 1987, pp. 12-13.

6021. Fernández, Norman. "Pat Mills: El Rey de los Celtas." *El Wendigo*. No. 53, 1991, pp. 34-35.

6022. Florez, Florentino and Faustino Arbesú. "Brian Bolland, Un Autor Entrañable." *El Wendigo*. February-April 1988, pp. 11-13.

6023. "Frank Humphris Rides Off into the Sunset." *Comics Journal*. May 1993, p. 31.

6024. Furniss, Harry. *The Confession of a Caricaturist*. 2 Vols. London: T. Fisher Unwin, 1901.

6025. "Future Shocks." *Speakeasy*. December 1990-January 1991, pp. 14-15, 17.

6026. "Future Toxic: A Knightly Pursuit." *Speakeasy*. June 1990, pp. 33, 35, 37.

6027. George, Hardy. "Aspects of Prevalent Forms. The Works of Andrew Greaves and Roderic Stokes." *Unit*. (University of Keele, London). No. 11, 1968.

6028. Gifford, Denis. "Frozen Smiles." *WittyWorld*. Summer 1987, pp. 44-45.

6029. Gifford, Denis. *The Great Cartoon Stars*. London: Jupiter, 1979.

6030. Gifford, Denis. "Obituary: Mr. William Bunter." *The Guardian* (London). October 30, 1976.

6031. Gifford, Denis. "Walter Bell." *Graphics World* (London). 1976.

6032. Goldkind, Igor. "The Fire Sermon." *Speakeasy*. February 1991, pp. 50-51, 53.

6033. Hansom, Dick. "Grime and Punishment." *Speakeasy*. February 1991, pp. 33-34. (Klaus Janson).

6034. Hardman, Robert. "Telegraph's Matt Made Cartoonist of Year." *The Jester*. April 1992, p. 14. Reprinted from *Daily Telegraph*. February 21, 1992.

6035. Hetherington, John A. *Norman Lindsay*. Oxford, London: Oxford University Press, 1973. 272 pp.

6036. Hodnett, Edward. *Francis Barlow: First Master of English Book Illustration*. London: 1978.

6037. Hollowood, Bernard. *Pont, the Life and Work of the Great Punch Artist*. London: 1969.

6038. Hudson, D. *Charles Keene*. London: 1947.

6039. "The Industry: Nick Landau and Mike Lake." *Comics Interview*. No. 7, 1983, pp. 49-57.

6040. "Interview: Mark Buckingham." *Fantazia*. No. 4, 1990, pp. 21-24.

6041. Ivey, Jim. "Abu of the London Observer." *The World of Comic Art*. 1:4 (1967), pp. 12-13.

6042. Jay, Bill. "Cuthbert Bede." *British Journal of Photography*. January 10, 1986, pp. 37-39.

6043. Jensen, J. "'Curious! I Seem To Hear a Child Weeping!' Will Dyson 1880-1938." *Twentieth Century Studies*. No. 13/14, 1975.

6044. Kemnitz, Thomas M. "Matt Morgan of 'Tomahawk' and English Cartooning, 1867-1870." *Victorian Studies*. September 1975, pp. 5-34.

6045. Knox, E.V. "From Queen Victoria to Hitler; Partridge of *Punch* Has Pictured in His Cartoons the Pageant of Forty Years of Europe." *New York Times Magazine*. January 23, 1944, pp. 14-15 +.

6046. Kraft, David A. "Steve MacManus and Alan McKenzie." *Comics Interview*. No. 58, 1988, pp. 18-23, 26-29, 31, 33-35, 37.

6047. Lambourne, Lionel. *Ernest Griset, Fantasies of a Victorian Illustrator*. London: 1979.

6048. Lambourne, Lionel. "Paradox and Significance in Burne-Jones's Caricatures." *Apollo*. November 1975, pp. 125-133.

6049. "Les Barton, England." *FECO News*. No. 8, 1989, p. 19.

6050. Lilley, Les. "Albert Saunders (Alby)." *The Jester*. February 1993, p. 5.

6051. Littlefield, Andrew. "Mike McMahon." *Comics Journal*. June 1988, pp. 81-85.

6052. Low, David. *British Cartoonists, Caricaturists and Comic Artists*. London: William Collins, 1942, 1947.

6053. MacKenzie, Keith. "Dame Rebecca West." *Cartoonist PROfiles*. No. 31, 1976, pp. 38-42.

6054. MacKenzie, Vic. "JAK and MAC: The Demon Drawers of Fleet Street." *Target*. Autumn 1984, pp. 16-20.

6055. "Make 'Em Laugh Is Roy's Advice." *Jester 186*. July 1988, p. 9.

6056. Matthews, Roy. "Spy" (Sir Leslie Ward). *British History Illustrated*. June-July 1976, pp. 50-57.

6057. "Mel Calman Talks to Himself." *Cartoonist PROfiles*. September 1978, pp. 82-83.

6058. "Morrison and Yeowell in Cut Controversy." *Comics Journal*. September 1989, p. 11.

6059. Nicholls, Stan. "The Shakespeare of Gore." *Speakeasy*. February 1991, pp. 29, 31. (Shaun Hutson).

6060. O'Gara, Noreen. "Retrospective... Charles J. Connick." *Stained Glass Quarterly*. Spring 1987, pp. 44-49 +. (Closing of Connick Associates).

6061. Oldham, Stephen. "Joe Colquhoun." *Comics Interview*. November 1984, pp. 37-43.

6062. O'Neill, Dan. "Top Drawer—25 Years of...Gren." *The Jester*. February 1993, pp. 10-11. (Grenfell Jones).

6063. *O Rare Hoffnung. A Memorial Garland*. London: Putnam, 1960. 223 pp. (Gerard Hoffnung).

6064. Ormond, L. *George Du Maurier*. London: 1969.

6065. Pennell, Joseph. *The Work of Charles Keene*. New York: R.H. Russell; London: T. Fisher Unwin and Bradbury, Agnew and Co., 1897. 289 pp.

6066. Plowright, Frank. "John Wagner and Alan Grant." *Comics Journal*. June 1988, pp. 69-80.

6067. Plowright, Frank. "Kevin O'Neill." *Comics Journal*. June 1988, pp. 86-105.

6068. Pressley, William. *The Life and Art of James Barry*. New Haven, Connecticut, and London: Yale University Press, 1981.

6069. Rennie, Gordon. "Delano." *Speakeasy*. October 1990, pp. 31-34.

6070. Rennie, Gordon. "Mark Millar: Apocalypse Now!" *Speakeasy*. April 1990, pp. 55, 57.

6071. Rodríguez, Carlota. "Jerry Ordway: la Modernizacion de un Estilo Preterito." *El Wendigo*. No. 45, 1989, pp. 12-13.

6072. Rose, Dennis. *Life, Times and Recorded Works of Robert Dighton (1752-1814). Actor, Artist and Printseller and Three of His Artist Sons*. Sussex: W.E. Baxter, 1981. 95 pp.

6073. "Sally Artz." *Cartoonist PROfiles*. June 1980, pp. 46-51.

6074. Schaffer, Bernhard. "Interview mit Peter O'Donnell." *Comic Forum. Das Österreichische Fachmagazin für Comicliteratur*. 3:11 (1981), pp. 37-39.

6075. Siepmann, M.H. *Montage: John Heartfield*. Berlin: Elefanten Press Galerie, 1977.

6076. Smolderen, Thierry. "Relecture. L'Empire de Trigan." *Les Cahiers de la Bande Dessinée*. 57, 1984, pp. 72-75. (Don Lawrence).

6077. Starke, Leslie. *Starke and Unashamed*. London: Max Reinhardt, 1953.

6078. Sutton, Denys. "The Roman Caricatures of Reynolds." *Country Life Annual*. 1965, pp. 113-116.

6079. Thorpe, James. "A Great Comic Draughtsman." *Print Collector's Quarterly*. 1938, pp. 59-79. (W.G. Baxter).

6080. Tisdall, Caroline. "(George) Melly, More Than a Flook." *The Guardian* (London). April 1, 1971.

6081. "Toni Goffe." *Cartoonist PROfiles*. December 1975, pp. 41-45.

6082. Trevelyan, G.M. *The Seven Years of William IV, A Reign Cartooned by John Doyle*. London: Avalon Press and William Heinemann, 1952.

6083. Vince, Alan. "Ron Embleton (1930-1988): The Artist and the Man." *Society of Strip Illustration Newsletter*. March 1988, pp. 5-6, 12.

6084. Wallace, R.W. "Joseph Goupy's Satire of George Frederic Handel." *Apollo*. February 1983.

6085. Whitaker, Steve. "Stanley White." *Society of Strip Illustrators Newsletter*. December 1988, pp. 7-8.

6086. Zec, Donald. "The Fosdyke Saga (Bill Tidy)." *Daily Mirror* (London). February 26, 1971.

Anderson, J. Martin (Cynicus)

6087. Anderson, J. Martin (Cynicus). *The Humours of Cynicus*. London: Cynicus Studio, 1891.

6088. Anderson, J. Martin (Cynicus). *The Satires of Cynicus*. London: Cynicus Studio, 1892.

Bairnsfather, Bruce

6089. Bairnsfather, Bruce, ed. *The Best of Fragments from France*. London: Tonie and Valmai Holt, 1978.

6090. Bairnsfather, Bruce. *The Collected Drawings of Bruce Bairnsfather*. New York: W.C. Leigh, 1931. 160 pp.

6091. Bairnsfather, Bruce. *Fragments from France*. New York: G.P. Putnam's, n.d. Unpaginated.

6092. Bairnsfather, Bruce. *Jeeps and Jests. Containing about 100 Cartoons*. New York: G.P. Putnam's Sons, 1943. Unpaginated.

6093. Bairnsfather, Bruce. *Laughing Through the Orient with "Old Bill" and Bruce Bairnsfather*. New York: The Viking Press, 1932. 68 pp.

Bateman, H.M.

6094. Bateman, H.M. "An Humourist with a Sense of Humour? An Interview with H.M. Bateman by Roger Wimbush." *Windsor* (London). January 1938.

6095. Bateman, Michel. *Funny Way To Earn a Living*. London: Leslie Frewin, 1965.

6096. Bateman, Michel. *The Man Who Drew the Twentieth Century*. London: 1969.

Baxendale, Leo

6097. Baxendale, Leo. *A Very Funny Business*. London: Duckworth, 1978. 136 pp.

6098. Baxendale, Leo. *On Comedy: The Beano and Ideology*. London: Reaper Books, 1988.

6099. "Baxendale Claim Settled." *Comics Journal*. September 1987, p. 26.

Beerbohm, Max

6100. Beerbohm, Max. *Fifty Caricatures*. London: William Heinemann, 1913. 56 pp.

6101. Beerbohm, Max. *Max Beerbohm and Arthur Conan Doyle*. Hanover, New Hampshire: J. Peter Williamson, 1969. 20 pp.

6102. Beerbohm, Max. "Max Beerbohm's Edwardyssey." *Times Literary Supplement*. August 22, 1975, pp. 944-945.

6103. Beerbohm, Max. *Max's Nineties. Drawings 1892-1899*. Intro. by Osbert Lancaster. Philadelphia, Pennsylvania, and New York: Lippincott; London: Rupert Hart-Davis, 1958. 10 pp., 46 plates.

6104. Beerbohm, Max. *Observations*. London: William Heinemann, 1925. 56 pp.

6105. Beerbohm, Max. *The Poet's Corner*. London: The King Press, Penguin Books, 1943.

6106. Beerbohm, Max. *The Second Childhood of John Bull*. London: Stephen Swift and Co., 1901.

6107. Beerbohm, Max. *A Survey*. New York: Doubleday, 1921. 8 pp.

6108. Beerbohm, Max. "Tales of Three Nations; a Series of Historical Cartoons of the Relations of England, France, and Germany Since the Time of Napoleon." *Yale Review*. January 1924, suppl., p. 11.

6109. Hall, N.J. "A Genre of His Own: Max Beerbohm's Title-Page Caricatures." *English Literature in Transition 1880-1920*. 27:4 (1984), pp. 270-288.

6110. Hart-Davis, Rupert. *A Catalogue of the Caricatures of Max Beerbohm*. Cambridge, Massachusetts: Harvard University Press, 1972. 258 pp.

6111. Hart-Davis, Rupert, ed. *Letters to Max Beerbohm 1892-1956*. London: John Murray, 1988. 244 pp.

6112. Holbrook, Jackson. "The Incomparable Max." In *The Eighteen Nineties*. Harmonsworth Middlesex: Penguin Books, 1939.

6113. Lewis, R. "The Child and the Man in Max Beerbohm." *English in Transition 1880-1920*. 27:4 (1984), pp. 296-303.

6114. Littell, P. "Exhibition at the Leicester Galleries in London, of Mr. Max Beerbohm's Newest Caricatures." *New Republic*. July 7, 1921, p. 170.

6115. Lynch, Bohun. "Mr. Beerbohm's Caricatures." *Fortune*. June 1925, pp. 794-803.

6116. "Max Makes an Exhibition of His Contemporaries." *Living Age*. June 6, 1925, pp. 553-554.

6117. Nadel, I.B. "The Smallest Genius and 'The Wittiest Mind'; Max Beerbohm and Lytton Strachey." *English Literature in Transition 1880-1920*. 27:4 (1984), pp. 289-295.

6118. Riewald, J.G. *Beerbohm's Literary Caricature from Homer to Huxley*. New York: Archon Books, 1977. 295 pp.

6119. Swinnerton, Frank. "Max Beerbohm Caricatures." In *A London Bookman*. London: Martin Secker, 1928.

Bolton, John

6120. Dakin, John. "John Bolton: Britain's Foremost Fantasy Artist, from Dracula to the Bionic Woman." *Comics Journal*. April 1980, pp. 54-62.

6121. Nicholls, Stan. "The Yattering and John: John Bolton and Clive Barker." *Speakeasy*. February 1991, pp. 37-38, 41, 43, 45.

6122. "Sketchbook: John Bolton." *Comics Interview*. June 1988, pp. 135-137.

Boxer, Mark

6123. Boxer, Mark. *The Times We Live In*. London: 1978.

6124. Boxer, Mark. *The Trendy Ape*. London: 1968.

Bunbury, Henry W.

6125. "Henry William Bunbury." Exhibition Catalogue, Gainsborough's House, London. 1983. Essay by John Riely.

6126. Riely, John C. "Horace Walpole and 'The Second Hogarth.'" *Eighteenth Century Studies*. Autumn 1975, pp. 28-44.

Campbell, Eddie

6127. Gravett, Paul. "Il Était Une Fois en Grande-Bretagne...Eddie Campbell." *Les Cahiers de la Bande Dessinée*. 68, 1986, pp. 54-55.

6128. Hansom, Dick. "The Complete Eddie (Campbell)." *Speakeasy*. June 1990, pp. 38-39, 41, 43.

6129. Yang, Sam. "A Load of Bread, A Jug of Wine and Eddie Campbell." *Comics Journal*. October 1991, pp. 59-87.

Collins, Clive

6130. "Clive Collins." *Cartoonist PROfiles*. September 1982, pp. 52-59.

6131. Collins, Clive. *The International Pavilion of Humor of Montreal Presents Clive Collins 1985 Cartoonist of the Year*. Montreal: 1985.

6132. "Grand Prix Skopje, Clive Collins, Great Britain: Everything Is Cabaret." *FECO News*. No. 3, 1987, p. 16.

Cruikshank, George

6133. Buchanan-Brown, John. *The Book Illustrations of George Cruikshank*. London: David and Charles, and Rutland, Vermont: Charles E. Tuttle Company, 1980. 256 pp.

6134.   Chesson, W.H. *George Cruikshank*. London: Duckworth and Co., n.d.

6135.   Cohen, Jane. "All-of-a-Twist: The Relationship of George Cruikshank and Charles Dickens." *Harvard Library Bulletin*. April 1969, pp. 109-194; July 1969, pp. 320-342.

6136.   Cohn, Albert M. *George Cruikshank: A Catalogue Raisonné of the Work Executed during the Years 1806-1877*. London: "Bookman's Journal," 1924. 375 pp.

6137.   Cruikshank, Percy R. "George Cruikshank, with Some Account of His Brother, Robert Cruikshank." Princeton, New Jersey: Princeton University Library, ca. 1879. Unpublished memoir.

6138.   Evans, Hilary and Mary Evans. *The Life and Art of George Cruikshank, 1792-1878: The Man Who Drew the Drunkard's Daughter*. New York: S.G. Phillips, 1978. 192 pp.

6139.   *George Cruikshank*. London: Arts Council, 1974. Catalogue and notes by William Feaver.

6140.   Griffin, M.S. "Cruikshank." *Golden Book*. December 1930, pp. 58-61.

6141.   Jerrold, Blanchard. *The Life of George Cruikshank in Two Epochs*. London: Chatto and Windus Publishers, 1882. New Ed., 1894.

6142.   Jones, Michael W. *George Cruikshank, His Life and London*. London: 1978.

6143.   *Klassiker der Karikatur: No. 8. George Cruikshank*. Berlin: Eulenspiegel, 1972.

6144.   Kunzle, David. "Mr. Lambkin: Cruikshank's Strike for Independence." In *George Cruikshank: A Revaluation*, edited by Robert Patten. *Princeton University Library Chronicle*. 35 (1974), pp. 169-187.

6145.   Layard, George S. "George Cruikshank." *Blackwood's Edinburgh Magazine*. July 1823, pp. 18-26.

6146.   Lockhart, John G. "Lectures on the Fine Arts, No. 1. On George Cruikshank." *Blackwood's Magazine*. July 1823, p. 23.

6147.   McGreal, Dorothy. "The Inimitable George." *The World of Comic Art*. June 1966, pp. 34-40.

6148.   "Old-Time Caricatures—No. 1." *Twinkles*. January 24, 1897, p. 13.

6149.   "Old-Time Caricatures—No. 4." *Twinkles*. February 14, 1897, p. 13.

6150.   "Old-Time Caricatures—No. 7." *Twinkles*. March 13, 1897, p. 13.

6151. "Old-Time Caricatures—No. 13." *Twinkles*. April 24, 1897, p. 13.

6152. Patten, Robert L., ed. *George Cruikshank. A Revaluation*. Princeton, New Jersey: Princeton University Library, 1974. 258 pp. Originally in *The Princeton University Library Chronicle*. Autumn, Winter 1973-1974.

6153. Reid, G.W. *Descriptive Catalogue of the Works of George Cruikshank*. London: 1871.

6154. Steig, M. "Chapter of Noses: George Cruikshank's Psychonography of the Nose." *Criticism*. Fall 1975, pp. 308-325.

6155. Thackeray, William Makepeace. *An Essay on the Genius of George Cruikshank*, edited by W.E. Church. London: [1840] 1884.

6156. Vogler, Richard. "Cruikshank and Dickens: A Reassessment of the Role of Artist and Author." In *George Cruikshank: A Revaluation*, edited by Robert Patten. *Princeton University Library Chronicle*. 35 (1974), pp. 61-92.

6157. Vogler, Richard, ed. *Graphic Works of George Cruikshank*. New York: 1979.

6158. Wardroper, John. *The Caricatures of George Cruikshank*. London: Gordon Fraser; New York: David R. Godine, 1977.

Emett, Rowland

6159. Emett, Rowland. *The Forgotten Tramcar*. London: Faber and Faber, Ltd., 1952.

6160. "Emett of Punch." *Time*. August 2, 1943, p. 50.

6161. "Rowland Emett's Cartoons Are Favorites of the English." *Life*. August 2, 1943, pp. 6-8.

Ennis, Garth

6162. Bellamy, Frank. *The Daily Mirror Book of Garth*. London: IPC Magazines, 1974.

6163. Ennis, Garth. "Garth Ennis." *Society of Strip Illustration Newsletter*. June 1989, pp. 16-17.

6164. Ennis, Warren. "If I Should Fall from Grace with God...." *Speakeasy*. December-January 1990-1991, pp. 53-55.

6165. Schaffer, Bernhard. "Kontroversen um Garth. Eine Dokumentation aus Unserer Reihe Über Zeitungsstrips." *Comic Forum. Das Österreichische Fachmagazin für Comicliteratur.* 4:14 (1982), pp. 21-22.

Fawkes, Wally (Trog)

6166. Fawkes, Wally. *The International Pavilion of Humor of Montreal Presents Wally "Trog" Fawkes. 1976 Cartoonist of the Year.* Montreal: 1976. Unpaginated.

6167. *Trog. Forty Graphic Years: The Art of Wally Fawkes.* Intro. by Frank Whitford. London: Fourth Estate, 1987. 191 pp.

6168. *The World of Trog.* Intro. by James Cameron. London: 1977.

Fiddy, Roland

6169. Nieuwendijk, Peter. "Roland Fiddy." *WittyWorld.* Summer 1987, pp. 16-17.

6170. "Roland Fiddy, England." *FECO News.* No. 5, 1987, p. 9.

6171. "Roland Fiddy: 'The Crazy World of the Handyman.'" *FECO News.* No. 7, 1989, pp. 8-9.

Giles, Carl Ronald

6172. Barber, Lynn. "Funny Man's Express Delivery." *The Jester.* December 1992/January 1993, p. 12. Reprinted from *The Independent.* November 1, 1992.

6173. Cummings, Michael. "Master Mirthmaker." *The Jester.* December 1992/January 1993, p. 13. Reprinted from *Sunday Express* (London). November 1, 1992.

6174. *Giles Sunday Express and Daily Express Cartoons.* Thirty-Seventh Series, London: Express Newspapers Ltd., 1983. Annual.

6175. Giles, F.T. *Open Court.* London: Cassell, 1964, 202 pp.

6176. Tory, Peter. *Giles: A Life in Cartoons.* London: Headline, 1992.

Gillray, James

6177. Alvarus (Álvaro Cotrim). "J. Gillray, um dos Grandes Caricaturistas Inglêses do Passado." *Vamos Ler!* (Rio de Janeiro). September 24, 1942.

6178. Bate, Jonathan. "Shakespearean Allusion in English Caricature in the Age of Gillray." *Journal of the Warburg and Courtauld Institutes.* 49 (1986), pp. 196-210.

6179. "Cartoon of 1808: James Gillray's Napoleon in the Valley of the Shadow of Death." *The Bookman.* July 1916, pp. 542-544.

6180. Gillray, James. *Fashionable Contrasts. Caricatures by James Gillray.* Intro. and annotations by Draper Hill. London: Phaidon Press, 1966. 184 pp.

6181. Hill, Draper. *Mr. Gillray, the Caricaturist.* London: Phaidon Publishers, 1965. 266 pp.

6182. Hill, Draper, ed. *The Satirical Etchings of James Gillray.* New York: Dover, 1976. 142 pp.

6183. Jackson, W.S. "Wanted—a Gillray." *Nineteenth Century.* September 1910, pp. 522-531.

6184. Kennedy, Jean-Louis. "J. Gillray, um dos Grandes Caricaturistas Inglêses do Passado." *Vamos Ler!* (Rio de Janiero). September 24, 1942.

6185. *Klassiker der Karikatur: No. 3. James Gillray.* Berlin: Eulenspiegel-Verlag, 1970.

6186. Piltz, Georg. *James Gillray.* Berlin: 1970.

6187. *The Works of James Gillray from the Original Plates with the Addition of Many Subjects Not Before Collected.* London: Printed for Henry G. Bohn by Charles Whiting, 1968.

6188. "World Caricature History: Gillray." *Kayhan Caricature.* May 1993.

6189. Wright, Thomas. *The Works of James Gillray. The Caricaturist. With the Story of His Life and Times.* London: Chatto and Windus Publishers, 1873.

6190. Wright, Thomas and R.H. Evans. *Historical and Descriptive Account of the Caricatures of James Gillray.* New York, London: Benjamin Blom, 1851, 1968. 495 pp.

Halas, John and Joy Batchelor

6191. Canemaker, John. "Halas and Batchelor, A Visit with England's Leading Producers of Animated Film." *Funnyworld*. Spring 1983, pp. 3-12.

6192. Moliterni, Claude. "Halas and Batchelor." *Phénix* (Paris). No. 21, 1971.

6193. Thompson, Bill. "Talking with Halas and Batchelor." *The Thousand Eyes Magazine*. February 1976, pp. 5-6, 19, 21.

Hogarth, William

6194. Antal, Frederick. *Hogarth and His Place in European Art*. London: Routledge and Kegan Paul, 1962.

6195. Antral, Louis. *William Hogarth*. Coll. "Maîtres de l'Art Ancien." Paris: Les Éditions Rieder, 1931.

6196. Atherton, Herbert M. *Political Prints in the Age of Hogarth: A Study of the Ideographic Representation of Politics*. London: Oxford University Press, 1974; New York: Clarendon, 1974.

6197. Barton, Stuart and R.A. Curtis. *The Genius of William Hogarth*. Worthing, Sussex: Lyle Publications, 1972.

6198. Benoit, François. *Hogarth*. Coll. "Les Grands Artistes." Paris: Henri Laurens, Édit., n.d.

6199. Bindman, D. *Hogarth*. London: 1981.

6200. Blum, André. *Hogarth. Art et Esthétique*. Paris: Libr. Félix Alcan, 1922.

6201. Brown, B.G. *William Hogarth*. London: Walter Scott Publishing Co.; New York: Charles Scribner's Sons, 1905. 217 pp.

6202. Burke, J., ed. *Hogarth, The Analysis of Beauty*. Oxford: Oxford University Press, 1955.

6203. Busch, Werner. *Nachahmung als Bürgerliches Kunstprinzip: Ikonographische Zitate bei Hogarth und in Seiner Nachfolge*. Hildesheim and New York: 1977.

6204. "Caricature History: William Hogarth." *Kayhan Caricature*. June 1992.

6205. Craven, Thomas. *Hogarth*. New York: Simon and Schuster, 1940.

6206. Crown, Patricia. "Visual Music: E.F. Burney and a Hogarth Revival." *Bulletin of Research in the Humanities*. Winter 1980, pp. 435-472.

6207. Cruikshanks, Eveline. *Hogarth's England. A Selection of the Engravings with Descriptive Text*. London: Folio Society, 1957.

6208. Defferre, Gaston and Maurice Horn. *Hogarth*. Marseilles: Bibliotheque Municipals de Marseille, 1985.

6209. Dobson, Austin. *Hogarth*. London: Sampson Low, Marston, Searle, and Rivington, 1883. 128 pp.

6210. Dobson, Austin. *William Hogarth*. London: 1907.

6211. Florisone, Michel. "Hogarth." *Vamos Ler!* (Rio de Janeiro). November 26, 1942.

6212. Girard, Richard. "Hogarth." *Vamos Ler!* (Rio de Janeiro). December 17, 1942.

6213. Gordon, Jan. "Hogarth and English Caricature." *The Studio* (London). December 1943.

6214. Hogarth, William. *Marriage a la Mode and Other Engravings*. New York: Lear, 1947.

6215. Hogarth, William. *The Works of William Hogarth in a Series of Engravings with Description and a Comment on Their Moral Tendency by the Rev. John Trusler and Others*, 2 Vols. London-New York: The London Printingland Publisher Company Ltd., ca. 1850.

6216. *Hogarth*. Tate Gallery, 1972. Notes and essays by Lawrence Gowing and Ronald Paulson.

6217. Ireland, Samuel. *Graphic Illustrations of Hogarth from Pictures, Drawings and Scarce Prints in the Possession of Samuel Ireland, Author of This Work*. London: Published by R. Faulder, 1794.

6218. *Klassiker der Karikatur: No. 22. William Hogarth*. Berlin: Eulenspiegel-Verlag, 1983.

6219. Klingender, F.D. *Hogarth and English Caricature*. London: Transatlantic Books, 1944.

6220. Kromm, Jane E. "Hogarth's Madmen." *Journal of the Warburg and Courtauld Institutes*. 48 (1985), pp. 238-242.

6221. Kunzle, David. "Plagiaries by Memory of *The Rake's Progress* and the Genesis of Hogarth's Second Picture Story." *Journal of the Warburg and Courtauld Institutes*. 29 (1966), pp. 311-348.

6222. Kurz, Hilde. "Italian Models of Hogarth's Picture Stories." *Journal of the Warburg and Courtauld Institutes.* 15 (1952), pp. 136-168.

6223. "Lichtenberg, (G.C.) Sämmtliche Werke: Ausführliche Erklärung Hogarth's Kupferstiche." *Foreign Quarterly Review.* 16 (1836), pp. 279-303.

6224. Nichols, John. *Biographical Anecdotes of William Hogarth and a Catalogue of His Works....* London: 1781.

6225. Oppé, A.P. *The Drawings of William Hogarth.* London: Phaidon Press, 1948. 65 pp. + plates.

6226. Paulson, Ronald. *Hogarth: His Life, Art and Times.* 2 Vols. New Haven, Connecticut: Yale University Press, 1971.

6227. Paulson, Ronald. *Hogarth's Graphic Works.* 2 Vols. New Haven, Connecticut: Yale University Press, 1970.

6228. Paulson, Ronald. *Popular and Polite Art in the Age of Hogarth and Fielding.* South Bend, Indiana: University of Notre Dame Press, 1979.

6229. Read, Herbert. "William Hogarth." In *Art and Society.* London: Faber and Faber, 1945.

6230. Sala, George A. *William Hogarth.* London: 1866.

6231. Strinati, Pierre. "Les Animaux Vus par Hogarth." *Giff-Wiff.* No. 18, 1966.

6232. Trusler, John. *Hogarth Moralized, Being a Complete Edition of Hogarth's Works.* London: 1768.

6233. Wind, Edgar. "'Borrowed Attitudes' in Reynolds and Hogarth." *Journal of the Warburg and Courtauld Institutes.* 2 (1938/1939), pp. 184 +.

Illingworth, L.G.

6234. Hill, Draper. *Illingworth: On Target.* Boston: Boston Public Library, 1970.

6235. *Pett's Annual.* Guest Artist, Illingworth. Birmingham: Thomas' Publications, 1944. 80 pp.

Jones, "Jon"

6236. Bryant, Mark. "Jon—An Appreciation." *The Jester.* August 1992, pp. 10-11.

6237. "Obituaries: 'Jon' Jones." *The Jester.* August 1992, p. 11. Reprinted from *Daily Telegraph.* July 2, 1992.

Lancaster, Osbert

6238. Boston, Richard. *Osbert: A Portrait of Osbert Lancaster.* London: Collins, 1989. 265 pp.

6239. Lancaster, Osbert. *The Alarms and Excursions of Lady Littlehampton.* Boston: Houghton Mifflin Co., 1952. 77 pp.

6240. Lancaster, Osbert. *Assorted Sizes.* London: John Murray, 1944. 48 pp.

6241. Lancaster, Osbert. *Drayneflete Revealed.* London: John Murray, 1949. 70 pp.

6242. Lancaster, Osbert. *A Few Quick Tricks.* London: John Murray, 1965. 64 pp.

6243. Lancaster, Osbert. *Graffiti.* London: John Murray, 1964. 64 pp.

6244. Lancaster, Osbert. *Here, Of All Places.* Boston: Houghton, 1958. 189 pp.

6245. Lancaster, Osbert. *Mixed Notices.* London: John Murray, 1963. Unpaginated.

6246. Lancaster, Osbert. *A Pocketful of Cartoons.* London: Gryphon, 1949. 64 pp.

6247. Lancaster, Osbert. *The Saracen's Head.* London: John Murray, 1948. 67 pp.

6248. Lancaster, Osbert. *Signs of the Times.* Boston: Houghton Mifflin, 1961. 144 pp.

6249. Lancaster, Osbert. *The Year of the Comet.* London: Gryphon, 1957. 64 pp.

Leech, John

6250. *Catalogue of an Exhibition of Works by John Leech (1817-1864).* Held at the Grolier Club from January 22 Until March 8, 1914. New York: The Grolier Club, 1914. 187 pp.

6251. Frith, William P. *John Leech: His Life and Work.* London: Richard Bentley and Son, 1891. Vol. 1, 268 pp.; Vol. 2, 306 pp.

6252. Houfe, Simon. *John Leech and the Victorian Scene.* London: Antique Collector's Club, 1984. 265 pp.

6253. Leech, John. *Four Hundred Humorous Illustrations*. London: Simpkin, Marshall, Hamilton, Kent and Co., n.d. 416 pp.

6254. "Old-Time Caricatures—No. 14." *Twinkles*. May 1, 1897, p. 13.

6255. Rose, June. *The Drawings of John Leech*. London: Art and Technics, 1950. 96 pp.

6256. Saint-Gaudens, H. "John Leech." *Critic*. October 1905, pp. 358-367.

Low, David

6257. Brown, J.M. "Saluting Colonel Blimp." *Saturday Review of Literature*. April 21, 1945, pp. 22-23.

6258. Campbell, Gordon. "Low—Arise! And Follow Me in the Fight Against Barbarism!" *Cartoonist PROfiles*. June 1981, pp. 20-25.

6259. "Cartoons from For Readers Only, Drawn by Low." *Library Journal*. May 15, 1937, p. 421.

6260. Chamberlain, J. "Low, Jack and the Game." *New Republic*. August 23, 1939, pp. 80-81.

6261. Da Costa, R. "David Low on Art and Propaganda." *The Listener* (London). February 15, 1940.

6262. Da Costa, R. "Low, the Cartoonist Who Makes Fun of His Boss." *Books to Come* (London). April 1949.

6263. "A David Low Album—Selected by Low." *New York Times Magazine*. September 29, 1963, pp. 24-25.

6264. (David Low Comments). *Literary Digest*. November 12, 1936, pp. 31-32.

6265. "David Low; Nuisance Dedicated to Sanity." *Time*. July 3, 1939, pp. 21-22.

6266. Fleming, Peter. *The Flying Visit*. Drawings by David Low. New York: Charles Scribner's Sons, 1940. 128 pp.

6267. Grattan, C. Hartley. "'Funny Pictures' Man with a Mind." *New York Times Magazine*. August 18, 1946.

6268. Hauser, E.O. "Gad, Sir, Here's Col. Blimp's Creator! D. Low." *Saturday Evening Post*. November 17, 1945, pp. 14-15 +.

6269. Innes, Guy. "Mighty Mr. Low." *New York Times Magazine*. November 30, 1941, pp. 6-7.

6270. Kirby, R. "Low and His Cartoons." *American Mercury*. May 1945, pp. 606-612.

6271. Lima, Herman. "O Poderoso Senhor Low." *Rio Magazine* (Rio de Janeiro). April 1951.

6272. Low, David. *A Cartoon History of Our Times*. New York: Simon and Schuster, 1939.

6273. Low, David. "The Cartoonist at War." *Liliput* (London). May 1940.

6274. Low, David. "Cartoonist's Job in Wartime." *Living Age*. January 1940, pp. 408-409.

6275. Low, David. *Europe at War*. London: Penguin Books, 1941.

6276. Low, David. *The Fearful Fifties*. New York: Simon and Schuster, 1960.

6277. Low, David. "Gad, Sir, Col. Blimp Is Very Much Alive." *New York Times Magazine*. March 7, 1943, pp. 8-9 +.

6278. Low, David. *Low on the War. A Cartoon Commentary of the Years 1939-1941*. New York: Simon and Schuster, 1941. 157 pp.

6279. Low, David. "Low Reports on his Fellowmen." *New York Times Magazine*. June 1, 1941.

6280. Low, David. *Low's Autobiography*. London: Michael Joseph, 1956; New York: Simon and Schuster, 1957.

6281. Low, David. *Low's Cartoon History 1945-1953*. New York: Simon and Schuster, 1953. 159 pp.

6282. Low, David. *Low's Company*. London: Methuen, 1952. 108 pp.

6283. Low, David. *Low's Political Parade with Colonel Blimp*. London: The Cresset Press, 1936.

6284. Low, David. *Low's Visibility. A Cartoon History, 1945-1953*. London: Collins, 1953.

6285. Low, David. *Low's War Cartoons*. London: Cresset, 1941.

6286. Low, David. *The Modern "Rake's Progress."* London: Hutchinson and Co., 1934. 128 pp.

6287. Low, David. "A Plea for 'the Cult of Personality.'" *New York Times Magazine*. December 2, 1956.

6288. Low, David. "Round-Up of Recent Drawings." *The Nation*. January 22, 1949, pp. 98-99.

6289. Low, David. "Streamlining the Cartoon for the Airplane Age." *New York Times Magazine*. February 7, 1937, pp. 10-11.

6290. Low, David. "The World and Colonel Blimp." In *David Low's Political Parade*. London: The Cresset Press, 1936.

6291. Low, David. *Years of Wrath. A Cartoon History: 1931-1945*. New York: Simon and Schuster, 1946; London: Victor Gollancz, 1949.

6292. Low, David. *Ye Madde Designer*. London: The Studio Limited, 1935.

6293. "Low on Beaverbrook." *Time*. July 27, 1936, pp. 21-22.

6294. "Low on Chamberlain." *Time*. July 11, 1938, p. 21.

6295. "Low's Forebears." *Time*. April 10, 1939, p. 57.

6296. "The Man Who Fought Hitler with His Pen." *Picture Post* (London). October 14, 1939.

6297. Mellini, Peter. "Colonel Blimp's England." *History Today*. October 1984, pp. 30-37.

6298. "Mr. Low and Mr. High." *New York Times Magazine*. March 16, 1947, p. 57.

6299. Separman, Leonardo. "La Aventura de un Caricaturista Político." *La Nación* (Buenos Aires). November 15, 1936.

6300. Seymour-Ure, Colin and Jim Schoff. *David Low*. London: Secker and Warburg, 1985. 179 pp.

6301. Smith, A. "Low and Lord Beaverbrook: The Cartoonist and the Newspaper Proprietor." *Encounter*. December 1985, pp. 7-24.

6302. Streicher, L.H. "David Low and the Sociology of Caricature." *Comparative Studies in Society and History*. October 1965, pp. 1-23.

6303. Swinnerton, Frank. "David Low." In *A London Bookman*. London: Martin Secker, 1928.

6304. van Gelder, Robert. "The Powerful Satire of David Low." *New York Times Magazine*. August 10, 1941.

6305. Whitaker, Steve. "David Low." *Comics Journal.* August 1988, p. 21.

Moore, Alan

6306. Groth, Gary. "Big Words: Alan Moore." *Comics Journal.* October 1990, pp. 56-95.

6307. Stangroom, Howard. "Captain Britain Gets Own Comic: Alan Moore Discusses Marvelman." *Comics Buyer's Guide.* June 29, 1984, pp. 42, 44, 54, 56.

Mortimer, John

6308. Lilley, Les. "John Mortimer 1930-1992: An Appreciation." *The Jester.* November 1992, pp. 2, 5.

6309. Took, Barry. "Johnnie Mortimer: Leaving Them Laughing." *The Jester.* November 1992, p. 20. Reprinted from *The Guardian.* September 8, 1992.

Robinson, Heath

6310. Beare, Geoffrey. *Heath Robinson Advertising.* London: Bellew Publishing, 1991.

6311. Lewis, John N.C. *Heath Robinson, Artist and Comic Genius.* New York: Barnes and Noble, 1973. 223 pp.

6312. Robinson, Heath. *Heath Robinson at War.* London: Methuen and Co., 1942.

Rowlandson, Thomas

6313. Alvarus (Álvaro Cotrim). "Rowlandson o Maior Caricaturista de Costumes do Seu Tempo." *Noite* (Rio de Janeiro). July 7, 1957.

6314. Alvarus (Álvaro Cotrim). "Thomas Rowlandson." *Vamos Ler!* (Rio de Janeiro). October 8, 1942.

6315. *The Amorous Illustrations of Thomas Rowlandson.* Intro. by William G. Smith. London: Bibliophile Books, 1983. 41 pp.

6316. Baum, Richard M. "A Rowlandson Chronology." *Art Bulletin.* 20 (1938), pp. 237-250.

6317. Bury, Adrian. *Rowlandson Drawings*. London: Avalon Press, 1949.

6318. Falk, Bernard. *Thomas Rowlandson, His Life and Art*. New York and London: Hutchinson, 1949.

6319. *Gentleman's Magazine*. XCVII, Pt. 1 (1827), pp. 564-565. (Obituary of Thomas Rowlandson).

6320. Grego, Joseph. *Rowlandson the Caricaturist: A Selection of His Works*. 2 Vols. London: Chatto and Windus, 1880; Reissued. New York: Collectors Editions, n.d. (ca. 1972).

6321. Hayes, J. *Rowlandson: Watercolours and Drawings*. London, 1972.

6322. Heintzelman, Arthur W. *The Watercolor Drawings of Thomas Rowlandson from the Albert H. Wiggin Collection in the Boston Public Library*. New York: Watson-Guptill, 1947.

6323. Kennedy, Jean-Louis. "Th. Rowlandson." *Vamos Ler!* (Rio de Janeiro). October 5, 1942.

6324. Lima, Herman. "Um Gênio do Grotesco." *Diário de Notícias* (Rio de Janeiro). August 20, 1950.

6325. Oppé, A. Paul. *Thomas Rowlandson: His Drawings and Watercolours*. London: 1923.

6326. Paulson, Ronald. *Rowlandson: A New Interpretation*. London: Studio Vista, 1972.

6327. "Ribald Rowly; England's 18th Century Master of Caricature." *Time*. September 20, 1943, p. 70.

6328. Roe, F. Gordon. *Rowlandson: The Life and Art of a British Genius*. Leigh-on-Sea, England: F. Lewis, 1947.

6329. Rowlandson, Thomas. *Rowlandson's Drawings for a Tour in a Post Chaise*. Intro. and notes by Robert R. Wark. San Marino, California: The Huntington Library, 1963. 150 pp.

6330. Schiff, Gert. *The Amorous Illustrations of Thomas Rowlandson*. London: Cytherd Press, 1969.

6331. Sitwell, Osbert. *Rowlandson. Famous Water-Colour Painters*. London: *The Studio*, 1929.

6332. Stuart, Dorothy M. "Rowlandson and His England." *Illustrated London News*. Christmas Number, 1930.

6333. Wark, Robert R., ed. *Rowlandson's Drawings for the English Dance*. San Marino, California: Huntington Library, 1966.

6334. Wolf, Edward C.J. *Rowlandson and His Illustrations of Eighteenth Century English Literature*. Copenhagen: 1945.

6335. "World Caricature History: Rowlandson." *Kayhan Caricature*. June 1993.

6336. Young, Art. *Thomas Rowlandson*. New York: Willey Book Co., 1938. 54 pp.

Scarfe, Gerald

6337. Kallaugher, Kevin. "Pressing the Limits—Gerald Scarfe." *Target*. Autumn 1984, pp. 4-12.

6338. Scarfe, Gerald. *Gerald Scarfe*. New York: Thames and Hudson, 1982. 168 pp.

Searle, Ronald

6339. Bertieri, Claudio. "Un Giannino Albionico di Ronald Searle." *Il Lavoro* (Genoa). March 31, 1967.

6340. Cavallone, Bruno. "Ronald Searle." *Linus*. No. 20, 1966.

6341. Davies, Russell. *Ronald Searle: A Biography*. London: Sinclair-Stevenson, 1990. 192 pp.

6342. *I Disegni di Ronald Searle*. Milan: Garzanti Editore, 1973.

6343. Pojarlieva, Marjorie, trans. "Ronald Searle." *Apropos*. No. 5, 1988, pp. 86-98.

6344. Raspe, R.E. *The Adventures of Baron Munchausen*. Profusely illustrated by Ronald Searle. Intro. by S.J. Perelman. New York: Pantheon Books, 1969. 139 pp.

6345. Searle, Ronald. *The Addict: a Terrible Tale*. London: Dobson, 1971; Greene, 1971.

6346. Searle, Ronald. *Ah Yes, I Remember It Well... Paris 1961-1975*. Englewood Cliffs, New Jersey: Pavilion, 1987; Salem House, 1988.

6347. Searle, Ronald. *Anatomie Eines Adlers: Ein Deutschlandbuch*. With Heinz Huber. (Desch, 1966; as *Haven't We Met Before Somewhere?*, trans. by Constantine FitzGibbon). New York: Heinemann, 1966; Viking, 1966.

6348. Searle, Ronald. *Back to the Slaughterhouse and Other Ugly Moments*. London: Macdonald, 1951.

6349. Searle, Ronald, with Alex Atkinson. *The Big City; or, The New Mayhew*. New York: Perpetua, 1958; Braziller, 1959.

6350. Searle, Ronald. *The Compleet Molesworth*, with Geoffrey Willans. London: Parrish, 1958; reprinted, Englewood Cliffs, New Jersey: Pavilion, 1984.

6351. Searle, Ronald. *Dick Deadeye*. New York: Harcourt Brace Jovanovich, 1975.

6352. Searle, Ronald. *The Dog's Ear Book: with Four Lugubrious Verses*, with Geoffrey Willans. London: Parrish, 1958; Crowell, 1960.

6353. Searle, Ronald. *Down with Skool!*, with Geoffrey Willans. London: Parrish, 1953; Vanguard, 1954.

6354. Searle, Ronald. *Escape from the Amazon!*, with Alex Atkinson. New York: Perpetua, 1964.

6355. Searle, Ronald. *The Female Approach. The Belle of St. Trinian's and Other Cartoons*. New York: Alfred A. Knopf, 1954. 147 pp.

6356. Searle, Ronald. *The Female Approach, with Masculine Sidelights*. London: Macdonald, 1949.

6357. Searle, Ronald. *Filles de Hambourg* (Jean-Jacques Pauvert Editeur, 1969). As *Secret Sketchbooks: The Back Streets of Hamburg*. London: Weidenfeld and Nicolson, 1970.

6358. Searle, Ronald. *Forty Drawings*. London: Cambridge University Press, 1946; New York: Macmillan, 1947.

6359. Searle, Ronald. *45 Ans de Dessins*. Paris: Denoël, 1983. 224 pp.

6360. Searle, Ronald. *From Frozen North to Filthy Lucre*. New York: Viking; London: Heinemann, 1964. 112 pp.

6361. Searle, Ronald. *Gilbert & Sullivan: A Selection from Ronald Searle's Original Drawings from the Animated Feature Film 'Dick Deadeye.'* London: Entercom Productions, 1975.

6362. Searle, Ronald. *The Great Fur Opera: Annals of the Hudson's Bay Company, 1670-1970*, with Kildare Dobbs. Toronto: McClelland and Stewart, 1970; Brattleboro, Vermont: Greene, 1970.

6363. Searle, Ronald. *Hello—Where Did All the People Go?* London: Weidenfeld and Nicolson, 1969; Brattleboro, Vermont: Greene, 1970. As *Tiens! Il n'y a Personne?* Paris: Jean-Jacques Pauvert, editor, 1969.

6364. Searle, Ronald. *Hommage à Toulouse-Lautrec.* Paris: Editions Empreinte, 1969. As *The Second Coming of Toulouse-Lautrec.* London: Weidenfeld and Nicolson, 1970.

6365. Searle, Ronald. *How to be Topp*, with Geoffrey Willans. London: Parrish, 1954; Vanguard, 1955.

6366. Searle, Ronald. *Hurrah for St. Trinians! and Other Lapses.* London: Macdonald, 1948.

6367. Searle, Ronald. *The Illustrated Winespeak: Ronald Searle's Wicked World of Winetasting.* London: Souvenir Press, 1983; New York: Harper, 1984.

6368. Searle, Ronald. *La Caricature: Art et Manifeste. Du XVIᵉ Siècle à Nos Jours.* Paris: Editions Skira, 1974.

6369. Searle, Ronald. *The King of Beasts and Other Creatures.* London: Allen Lane, 1980. As *The Situation Is Hopeless.* New York: Viking, 1981.

6370. Searle, Ronald. *Le Nouveau Ballet Anglais.* Paris: Editions Montbrun, 1946.

6371. Searle, Ronald. *Looking at London, and People Worth Meeting*, with Kaye Webb. London: News Chronicle Publications, 1953.

6372. Searle, Ronald. *Médisances. Les Meilleurs Dessins Humoristiques.* Paris: *Revue Neuf*, 1953.

6373. Searle, Ronald. *Merry England.* London: Perpetua Books, 1956; New York: Knopf, 1957.

6374. Searle, Ronald. "The Missing 'Reuben.'" *Cartoonist PROfiles.* No. 22, 1974, pp. 32-33.

6375. Searle, Ronald. *More Cats.* London: Dobson, 1975; Greene, 1976.

6376. Searle, Ronald. *Pardong, M'sieur: Paris et Autres.* Paris: Denoël, 1965.

6377. Searle, Ronald. "Paris in the Summer." *Holiday.* September 1960, pp. 48-51.

6378. Searle, Ronald. *Paris! Paris!*, with Irwin Shaw. New York: Harcourt, Brace, Jovanovich, 1977; London: Weidenfeld and Nicolson, 1977.

6379. Searle, Ronald, with Kate Webb. *Paris Sketchbook.* New York: Saturn Press, 1950; Braziller, 1958; Rev. Ed. London: Perpetua, 1967. 120 pp.

6380. Searle, Ronald. *Patrick Campbell's Omnibus*. London: Hulton Press, 1954.

6381. Searle, Ronald. *The Penguin Ronald Searle*. London: Penguin Books, 1960. 124 pp.

6382. Searle, Ronald. *The Rake's Progress*. London: Perpetua, 1955; New Ed. as *The Rake's Progress: Some Immoral Tales*. Dobson, 1968.

6383. Searle, Ronald, with Kate Webb. *Refugees, 1960*. New York: Penguin, 1960.

6384. Searle, Ronald. *Ronald Searle*. Berlin: Rowohlt, 1978; Berlin: Deutsch, 1978; Mayflower Books, 1979.

6385. Searle, Ronald. *Ronald Searle in Perspective*. London: New English Library; Boston Massachusetts: Atlantic Monthly Press, 1984. 224 pp.

6386. Searle, Ronald. *Ronald Searle's Big Fat Cat Book*. New York: Macmillan, 1982; Boston: Little, Brown, 1982.

6387. Searle, Ronald. *Ronald Searle's Golden Oldies 1941-1961*. London: Pavilion Books, 1985. 144 pp.

6388. Searle, Ronald. *Ronald Searle's Non-Sexist Dictionary*. London: Souvenir Press, 1988; Berkeley, California: Ten Speed Press, 1989.

6389. Searle, Ronald. *Ronald Searle, with an Introduction by Henning Bock and an Essay by Pierre Dehaye*. London: 1978.

6390. Searle, Ronald. "Ronald Searle Writes from France." *Cartoonist PROfiles*. Fall 1969, pp. 16-23.

6391. Searle, Ronald. *Back in the Jug Agane*, with Geoffrey Willans. London: Parrish, 1959; As *Molesworth Back in the Jug Agane*. London: Vanguard, 1960.

6392. Searle, Ronald. *Russia for Beginners*, with Alex Atkinson. London: Perpetua, 1960; As *By Rocking-Chair Across Russia*. New York: World Publishing, 1960.

6393. Searle, Ronald. *Searle in the Sixties*. New York: Penguin, 1964.

6394. Searle, Ronald. *Searle's Cats*. Brattleboro, Vermont: Stephen Greene Press, 1968. Unpaginated. Editions in 1967 by Dobson; 1987, London: Souvenir Press.

6395. Searle, Ronald. *Searle's Zodiac*. Dobson, 1977; As *Zoodiac*. New York: Pantheon, 1978.

6396. Searle, Ronald. "Seeing the Light Side of the Campaign." *Life*. October 31, 1960, pp. 76-81.

6397. Searle, Ronald. *Slightly Foxed—But Still Desirable: Ronald Searle's Wicked World of Book Collecting.* London: Souvenir Press, 1989.

6398. Searle, Ronald. *Something in the Cellar: Ronald Searle's Wonderful World of Wine.* London: Souvenir Press, 1986; Berkeley, California: Ten Speed Press, 1988.

6399. Searle, Ronald. *Souls in Torment.* New York: Perpetua, 1953.

6400. Searle, Ronald. "Sound Off!" *Cartoonist PROfiles.* Summer 1969, p. 3.

6401. Searle, Ronald. *The Square Egg.* London: Weidenfeld and Nicolson, 1968; Brattleboro, Vermont: Greene, 1968.

6402. Searle, Ronald. *The St. Trinian's Story and the Pick of the Searle Cartoons.* London: Penguin Books, 1961. pp. Unpaginated.

6403. Searle, Ronald. *The St. Trinian's Story*: The Whole Ghastly Dossier, compiled by Kaye Webb. London: Perpetua, 1959.

6404. Searle, Ronald. *Take One Toad: A Book of Ancient Remedies.* London: Dobson, 1968.

6405. Searle, Ronald. *The Terror of St. Trinian's; or Angela's Prince Charming*, with 'Timothy Shy', alias D.B. Wyndham Lewis. London: Parrish, 1952; reprinted, Ian Henry Publications, 1976.

6406. Searle, Ronald. *Too Many Songs by Tom Lehrer: With Not Enough Drawings by Ronald Searle.* New York: Pantheon, 1981; Eyre Methuen, 1981.

6407. Searle, Ronald. *To the Kwai—and Back. War Drawings 1939-1945.* Boston, Massachusetts: Atlantic Monthly Press; London: Collins, 1986. 192 pp.

6408. Searle, Ronald. *USA for Beginners*, with Alex Atkinson. New York: Perpetua, 1959; As *By Rocking-Chair Across America.* New York: Funk, 1959.

6409. Searle, Ronald. *Von Katzen und Anderen Menschen.* Berlin: Eulenspiegel, 1980.

6410. Searle, Ronald. *Weil Noch das Lämpchen Glüht.* Diogenes, 1952.

6411. Searle, Ronald. *Which Way Did He Go?* New York: Perpetua, 1961; World Publishing, 1962.

6412. Searle, Ronald. *Whizz for Atomms*, with Geoffrey Willans. London: Parrish, 1956; As *Molesworth's Guide to the Atomic Age.* London: Vanguard, 1957.

6413. Webb, Kay. "Once Upon a Time." Prologue to *The Saint Trinian's Story.* London: Penguin Book, 1963.

Seymour, Robert

6414. Seymour, Robert. *Seymour's Comic Album*. London: W. Kidd, n.d. 203 pp.

6415. Seymour, Robert. *Seymour's Humorous Sketches*. London: F. Bentley, n.d.

Smythe, Reg

6416. Gristwood, Sarah. "Meet Reg the Andy Man." *Society of Strip Illustration Newsletter*. March 1988, p. 10. Reprinted from *Radio Times*. February 6-12, 1988.

6417. Ruth, Jim and Gerry. "A Visit with Smythe and Andy Capp." *Cartoonist PROfiles*. November 1970, pp. 7-16.

6418. Smythe, Reg, with Les Lilley. *The World of Andy Capp*. London: Titan Books, 1990. 160 pp.

Stampa, G.L.

6419. Gruss, Flavia Stampa, ed. *The Last Bohemian: G.L. Stampa of Punch*. London: Bellew Publishing, Cartoon Library, 1992.

6420. Stampa, G.L. *Ragamuffins*. London: Duckworth, 1906. 48 pp.

6421. Watson, Alex N. "Book Review: 'The Last Bohemian.'" *The Jester*. October 1992, pp. 6-7.

Steadman, Ralph

6422. "Cartoonist's Wonderland: An Evening with Ralph Steadman." *Comics Journal*. March 1989, pp. 79-86.

6423. Groth, Gary. "Ralph Steadman: Into the Gentle Darkness." *Comics Journal*. September 1989, pp. 40-91.

6424. Kallaugher, Kevin and Richard S. West. "Ralph Steadman: Fear and Loathing at the Drawing Board." *Target*. Spring 1983, pp. 11-18.

6425. "Slaves of Fashion." *Kayhan Caricature*. August 1992.

6426. Steadman, Ralph. *America*. New York: Straight Arrow, 1974.

6427. Steadman, Ralph. *Between the Eyes*. London: Jonathan Cape, 1984. 239 pp.

6428. Steadman, Ralph. *I, Leonardo*. New York: Summit Books, 1983. 128 pp.

6429. Steadman, Ralph. "Ralph Steadman Introduces a Special Issue." *Observer Magazine*. December 1992, p. 7.

6430. Steadman, Ralph. *Scar Strangled Banger*. Topsfield, Massachusetts: Salem House; London: Harrap Ltd., 1987.

6431. Steadman, Ralph. *Sigmund Freud*. New York: Paddington Press, 1979.

6432. Steadman, Ralph. *Still Life with Raspberry*. London: Rapp and Whiting, 1969.

6433. "Theo, di Ralph Steadman." *Linus*. No. 29, 1967, p. 37.

6434. Steadman, Ralph. "Wrapping Wonderland." *HOW*. January 1989.

Stephen

6435. Stephen. *Divided They Fall*. London: John Murray, 1943.

6436. Stephen. *My Patience Is Exhausted... 62 Political Cartoons*. Preface by Jan Masaryk. London: John Murray, 1942.

Strube, Sidney

6437. Brookes, Rod. "Everything in the Garden Is Lovely: The Representation of National Identity in Sidney Strube's Daily Express Cartoons in the 1930s." *Oxford Art Journal*. 13:2 (1990), pp. 31-43.

6438. Brookes, Rod. "The Little Man and the Slump: Sidney Strube's Cartoons and the Politics of Unemployment 1929-1931." *Oxford Art Journal*. 8:1 (1985), pp. 49-61.

6439. Strube, Sidney. *Cartoons from the Daily Express*. London: *London Express*, annual paperback series, 1927-1933.

Tenniel, John

6440. Burnand, F.C. "Sir John Tenniel." Supplement to *Punch*. March 4, 1914, pp. 3, 11.

6441. "Death of Sir John Tenniel." *Daily Telegraph* (London). February 27, 1914, p. 11.

6442. "Fine Art Gossip." *Athenaeum*. March 7, 1914, p. 349.

6443. "Historian in Cartoon: Sir John Tenniel." *Literary Digest*. March 28, 1914, p. 700.

6444. Morris, Frankie. "Tenniel's Cartoons: 'The Pride of Mr. Punch.'" *Journal of Newspaper and Periodical History*. 7:2 (1991), pp. 67-72.

6445. "Mr. Tenniel's Lalla Rookh." *London Times*. October 31, 1860, p. 9.

6446. Sarzano, Frances. *Sir John Tenniel, English Masters of Black and White*. London: Art and Technics, New York: Pellegrini and Cudahy, 1948.

6447. Simpson, Roger. *Sir John Tenniel*. Rutherford, New Jersey: Fairleigh-Dickinson University, forthcoming.

6448. "Sir John Tenniel's Fifty Years on Punch." *Review of Reviews*. January 1901, pp. 31-36.

6449. Spielmann, H.M. "Sir John Tenniel: An Appreciation." *London Daily Graphic*. January 5, 1901, p. 13.

6450. Stack, Frank. "Through the Looking Glass, Darkly. Sir John Tenniel: Alice's White Knight." *Comics Journal*. January 1993, pp. 85-87.

6451. Tenniel, John. *Cartoons* (from "Punch"). 2nd Series. London: Bradbury, Evans, n.d.

6452. Weitenkampf, Frank. "Sir John Tenniel—Cartoonist." *Scribner's*. 55 (1914), pp. 794 +.

Townshend, George

6453. Atherton, Herbert M. "George Townshend, Caricaturist." *Eighteenth-Century Studies*. Summer 1971, pp. 437-446.

6454. Atherton, Herbert M. "George Townshend Revisited: The Politician As Caricaturist." *Oxford Art Journal*. 8:1 (1985), pp. 3-19.

6455. Donald, Diana. "'Calumny and Caricatura': Eighteenth-Century Political Prints and the Case of George Townshend." *Art History*. March 1983, pp. 44-66.

6456. Grundy, C. Reginald. "An XVIIIth Century Caricaturist: George 1st Marquess Townshend." *The Conoisseur*. 94, pp. 94-97.

6457. Ketton-Cremer, R.W. "An Early Political Caricaturist." *Country Life*. January 10, 1964, pp. 214-216.

6458. *The Townshend Album*. London: National Portrait Gallery, 1974. Catalogue by Eileen Harris.

Vicky (Victor Weisz)

6459. Cameron, James, ed. *Vicky, A Memorial Volume*. London: Allen Lane, Penguin Press, 1968.

6460. Davies, Russell and Liz Ottaway. *Vicky*. London: Secker and Warberg, 1988.

6461. Searle, Ronald. "Vicky." *S.I.A. Journal* (London). March 1966.

6462. Vicky. *Home and Abroad—Vicky Cartoons from the Evening Standard*. Foreword by Osbert Lancaster. London: n.d. (1964).

6463. Vicky. *Stabs in the Back*. London: Max Reinhardt, 1952.

6464. Vicky. *Vicky Must Go—A Selection of Vicky Cartoons from the Evening Standard*. Foreword by Lord Butler. London: n.d. (1960).

6465. Weisz, Victor. *Twists: Vicky Cartoons from the Evening Standard*. London: Beaverbrook Newspapers, 1962.

CHARACTERS and TITLES

6466. Ball, Murray. *Bruce the Barbarian*. London: Quartet Books, 1973.

6467. Baxendale, Leo. "Minnie the Minx—More Than a Match for the Boys." *Guardian*. October 13, 1982. (Strip).

6468. "Blue Comet Crosses the Atlantic." *Comics Journal*. May 1993, p. 29.

6469. "*Buddies* Returns to Publication." *Comics Journal*. February 1993, p. 20.

6470. Burns, John M. and Richard O'Neill. *Danielle*. First American Edition Series. Park Forest, Illinois: K. Pierce, 1984. 72 pp.

6471. Dakin, John. "AXA Invades England." *Comics Journal*. May 1979, pp. 54, 56-57. (Strip).

6472. Dodd, Maurice and Dennis Collins. *The Perishers Omnibus*. London: Mirror Books, 1984. 192 pp.

6473. "'Dr. Who' Under Stethoscope." *Variety*. September 17, 1986, p. 88.

6474. Egran, Charles. "The British Chuckle Over Their 'Emetts.'" *New York Times Magazine*. September 28, 1947. (Strip).

6475. Featherstone, Mike and Mike Hepworth. "The Midlifestyle of 'George and Lynne': Notes on a Popular Strip." *Theory, Culture and Society*. 1:3 (1983), pp. 85-92. (Strip).

6476. Gaiman, Neil. "Thumper Comics and the Ghetto." *Society of Strip Illustration Newsletter*. December 1987, pp. 8-11.

6477. Green, Stuart. "Revolver: Mad, Bad and User-Friendly." *Speakeasy*. May 1990, pp. 31, 33, 35.

6478. Holdaway, Jim and Peter O'Donnell. *Romeo Brown, the Arabian Knight*. Daily strips, No. 2. London: J. Dakin, 1979. 18 pp.

6479. "*Hot Box*: The Wrong Time, the Wrong Place." *Gauntlet*. No. 2, 1991, pp. 217-225.

6480. Jackson, Cath. *Nurse Nightshade*. Basingstoke, Hants: Nursing Times, 1984. 32 pp.

6481. Littlefield, Andrew. "Paradax: A Preview of England's Coolest Import." *Amazing Heroes*. June 15, 1987, pp. 49-52.

6482. "Little Guy; Louie." *Time*. April 21, 1947, p. 49. (Strip).

6483. Mackenzie, Keith. "Carol Day." *Cartoonist PROfiles*. March 1982, pp. 64-69. (Strip).

6484. Mackenzie, Keith. "Matt Marriott." *Cartoonist PROfiles*. March 1977, pp. 56-61. (Strip).

6485. Mullally, Frederic. *Amanda*. First American Edition Series. Park Forest, Illinois: K. Pierce, 1984. 64 pp.

6486. Pett, Norman and Don Freeman. *Jane at War*. London: Wolfe, 1976. 480 pp.

6487. Ruth, Jim and Gerry. "Clive and Augusta by Angus McGill." *Cartoonist PROfiles*. No. 13, 1972, pp. 70-74. (Strip).

6488. Tidy, Bill. *The Cloggies*. London: Andre Deutsch, 1973. 64 pp.

6489. Tidy, Bill. *Fosdyke Saga*. London: Mirror Books, 1972?-.

6490. "Übungen Mit Charles: Britischer Prinz als Liebestolle Strip-Figur." *Der Stern*. No. 12, 1967.

"Ally Sloper"

6491. Bailey, Peter. "Ally Sloper's Half-Holiday: Comic Art in the 1880s." *History Workshop*. Autumn 1983, pp. 4-31.

6492. Gifford, Denis. "Ally Sloper." *Book and Magazine Collector* (London). May 1984.

6493. Kunzle, David. "The First Ally Sloper: The Earliest Political Cartoon Character As a Satire on the Victorian Work Ethic." *Oxford Art Journal*. 8:1 (1985), pp. 40-48.

"Andy Capp"

6494. Capp, Al. "Other Capp: R. Smythe's Andy Capp." *Saturday Evening Post*. March 1993, pp. 47-49.

6495. Cosulich, Oscar. "Arancia Meccanica? Meglio Andy Capp." *Comic Art*. No. 46, 1988, pp. 48-49.

6496. "'Es Luv'ly (Andy Capp)." *Time*. November 1, 1963, p. 71.

6497. Fresnault-Deruelle, Pierre. "Comic-Strips: Comique et Strips." *Cahier Comique Communication*. 1, 1983, pp. 40-47.

6498. MacGeachy, Pat. *The Gospel According to Andy Capp*. Richmond, Virginia: John Knox Press, 1973.

6499. Reese, Mary A. "Andy Capp Is No 'andicap." *Stars and Stripes*. January 24, 1971, pp. IV-V.

6500. Smythe, Reg. *Andy Capp*. London: Mirror Books, 1960?-. (Series of paperback reprintings; Vols. 22-41 dated 1969-1978).

6501. Smythe, Reg. *Andy Capp*. London: Fleetway, 1962. 96 pp.

6502. Smythe, Reg. *Andy Capp*. London: Daily Mirror Publications, ca. 1964. 96 pp.

6503. Smythe, Reg. *Andy Capp Picks His Favourite*. London: *Daily Mirror*, 1963. 96 pp.

6504. Smythe, Reg. *What Next Andy Capp*; *Hats Off, Andy Capp*; *You Tell 'em Andy Capp*; *In Your Eye: Andy Capp*; *What A Break, It's Andy Capp*; *None of Your Lip, Andy Capp*; *You Were Saying, Andy Capp*; *The Undisputed Andy Capp*; *Rise and Shine Andy Capp*; *You're Some Hero, Andy Capp*; *Quiet Please! It's Andy Capp*; *Andy Capp Strikes Back*; *Watch Your Step, Andy Capp*; *Meet Andy Capp*; *You're The Boss, Andy Capp*; *Andy Capp, Man of the Hour*. Greenwich, Connecticut: Fawcett Gold Medal Books.

6505. Smythe, Reg. *The Flippin' Rest of Andy Capp*. New York: Doubleday and Co., 1970. 156 pp.

6506. Smythe, Reg. *Hurray for Andy Capp*. Greenwich, Connecticut: Fawcett, 1967.

6507. Smythe, Reg. *Laugh Again with Andy Capp*. London: Hamlyn, 1968.

"Beano"

6508. Dewhurst, Keith. "In Beano Veritas." *The Guardian*. July 22, 1970.

6509. Gifford, Denis. "The Beano's Fortieth Birthday." *The Guardian* (London). July 31, 1978.

6510. Moonie, George. "Comical Warfare." *Radio Times*. January 4-15, 1988.

6511. Wan A. Hulaimi. "Beano, Folks Is 40 This Week." *New Straits Times* (Kuala Lumpur). August 4, 1978.

"Bristow"

6512. Bertieri, Claudio. "Bristow, the Rebel." *Photographia Italiana*. No. 150, 1970.

6513. Bertieri, Claudio. "The Employed of the Devil." *Il Lavoro*. July 12, 1968.

6514. Zanotto, Piero. "In Volume le Proteste del Mezzemaniche Bristow." *La Nuova Sardegna* (Sassari). August 3, 1967; *Il Piccolo* (Trieste). August 20, 1967.

"Dan Dare"

6515. Crompton, Alastair. *The Man Who Drew Tomorrow.* Bournemouth, Dorset, England: Who Dares Publishing, 1985. 216 pp.

6516. Curson, Nigel. "Daring Future: The Sad Fate of Dan Dare." *Speakeasy.* May 1990, pp. 26-27, 29.

6517. "Eagle Relaunch on Dan Dare's 40th Birthday." *Speakeasy.* May 1990, p. 19.

6518. Gifford, Denis. "Dan Dare's Diary." *Illustrators* (London). August 1977.

6519. Hampson, Frank. *Dan Dare, Pilot of the Future in Rogue Planet.* Hendrik-Ido-Ambacht, The Netherlands: Dragon's Dream, 1980. 101 pp.

6520. Midgley, Carol. "Dan Dare Zooms Back to the Front." *The Jester.* September 1992, p. 12. Reprinted from *Daily Mail* (London). July 30, 1992.

6521. Taylor, Ken. "Dan Stages a Desperate Fight-Back." *ACE Newsletter.* May 1987.

6522. Woolcombe, Alan. "Dan Dare: Pilot of the Past." *Speakeasy.* May 1990, pp. 46-47, 49.

"Dandy"

6523. Curson, Nigel. "The Dandy: Still Slapstick After All These Years." *Speakeasy.* April 1990, pp. 52-53.

6524. Gifford, Denis. "Fifty Years of Fun." *Society of Strip Illustration Newsletter.* March 1988, pp. 7-8.

6525. Gifford, Denis. "Fifty Years of Fun! Britain's Oldest Comic, The Dandy, Celebrates Its Half-Century." *WittyWorld.* Spring 1988, pp. 35-36.

6526. Stangroom, Howard W. "'Dandy' Is 50." *Comics Buyer's Guide.* March 25, 1988, p. 38.

"Escape"

6527. Clarke, Theo, *et al.* "And Then Nothing Happened—*The Escape* Interview." *Comics Journal.* June 1988, pp. 107-124.

6528. "*Escape* Captured." *Comics Journal.* September 1987, p. 27.

"Fred Basset"

6529. Graham, Alex. *Fred Basset*. London: Harmsworth, 1966?-

6530. Graham, Alex. *Fred Basset, No. 3*. London: Associated Newspapers, n.d.

6531. Graham, Alex. *Fred Basset the Hound That's Almost Human!* London: Associated Newspapers, n.d.

6532. Mackenzie, Keith. "Alex Graham's Fred Basset." *Cartoonist PROfiles*. No. 30, 1976, pp. 60-65.

6533. Mackenzie, Keith. "Dogs and People." *Cartoonist PROfiles*. December 1977, pp. 50-52.

"Garth"

6534. Edgar, Jim and Martin Asbury. *Garth: Mr. Rubio Calls*. London: J. Dakin, 1981. 20 pp.

6535. Edgar, Jim and Frank Bellamy. *Garth: Bride of Jenghiz Khan*. Daily Strips, No. 1. London: J. Dakin, 1979. 20 pp.

6536. Edgar, Jim and Frank Bellamy. *Garth: The Cloud of Balthus*. London: Titan Books, 1985. 96 pp.

6537. Edgar, Jim, Frank Bellamy, and John Allard. *Garth: The Doomsmen*. Daily Strips, No. 7. London: J. Dakin, 1981. 20 pp.

6538. Edgar, Jim, Frank Bellamy, and John Allard. *Garth: The Spanish Lady*. Daily Strips, No. 3. London: J. Dakin, 1979. 20 pp.

"Jackie"

6539. Frazer, Elizabeth. "Teenage Girls Reading *Jackie*." *Media, Culture and Society*. 9 (1987), pp. 407-425.

6540. Hebron, Sandra. "*Jackie* and *Woman's Own*: Ideological Work and the Social Construction of Gender Identity." BA thesis, Sheffield City Polytechnic, 1983. Published as *Occasional Paper*. May 1983.

6541. McRobbie, Angela. "*Jackie*: An Ideology of Adolescent Femininity." Birmingham: Occasional Paper, Centre for Contemporary Cultural Studies, University of Birmingham, 1978.

6542. McRobbie, Angela and Trisha McCabe. *Feminism for Girls: An Adventure Story.* London: Routledge and Kegan Paul, 1981. (See "Just Like a *Jackie* Story").

"James Bond"

6543. Lawrence, Jim and Yaroslav Horak. *James Bond, the Living Daylights.* Great British Newspaper Strips. London: Titan Books, 1987. 71 pp.

6544. McLusky, John and Henry Gammidge. *The Illustrated James Bond, 007.* Bronxville, New York: James Bond 007 Fan Club, 1981. 90 pp.

"Jeff Hawke"

6545. Patterson, Willie and Sydney Jordan. *Jeff Hawke, Overlord.* Great British Newspaper Strips. London: Titan Books, 1986. 88 pp.

6546. Schaffer, Bernhard. *Die Jeff Hawke-Story.* Zusammengestellt Nach Einem Interview aus COMIC MEDIA 11 (1974) und Primärmaterial." *Comic Forum. Das Magazin für Comicliteratur.* 7:30 (1985), pp. 58-64.

6547. Zanotto, Piero. "Il Terrestre Jeff Hawke Pedina di un Gioco Cosmico." *Il Gazzettino.* July 24, 1967.

"Judge Dredd"

6548. "Batman V Dredd, Dredd Monthly." *Speakeasy.* May 1990, pp. 12-13.

6549. "Judge Dredd: I Am the Law." *Fantazia.* No. 4, 1992, pp. 58-59.

6550. Keenan, Bob. "The History of Judge Dredd." *Comics Buyer's Guide.* April 19, 1991, pp. 24, 28.

6551. Keenan, Bob. "Judge Dredd: The MegaZine." *Comics Buyer's Guide.* April 19, 1991, pp. 40, 42.

6552. Littlefield, Andrew. "Dredd Reckoning." *Amazing Heroes.* August 1, 1984, pp. 29-32, 34-38, 40.

6553. "The Long Walk." *Speakeasy.* September 1990, pp. 34-35, 37, 39.

6554. Milligan, Pete, Brett Ewins and Jim McCarthy. *Bad Company. The Best of 2000 AD.* No. 31. London: Titan Books, 1987. 63 pp.

6555. Mills, Pat, Mike McMahon, and Brian Bolland. *Cursed Earth*. The Chronicles of Judge Dredd, Nos. 2-3. 2 Vols. London: Titan Books, 1982.

6556. "Tegneserier i England: 'Crisis' og 'Judge Dredd' Fra Fleetway." *Seriejournalen*. September 1990, p. 14.

6557. Wagner, John and Brian Bolland. *Judge Death*. The Chronicles of Judge Dredd, No. 7. London: Titan Books, 1982. 62 pp.

6558. Wagner, John, Brian Bolland, and Mike McMahon. *Judge Caligula*. The Chronicles of Judge Dredd, No. 4-5. 2 Vols. London: Titan Books, 1982-1983.

6559. Wagner, John and Alan Grant. *City of the Damned*. The Chronicles of Judge Dredd, No. 24. London: Titan Books, 1986. 96 pp.

6560. Wagner, John, Alan Grant, and Carlos Ezquerra. *Apocalypse War*. The Chronicles of Judge Dredd, No. 13-14. 2 Vols. London: Titan Books, 1984.

6561. Wagner, John and Mike McMahon. *The Streets of Mega-City*. Judge Dredd Colour Series, No. 1. London: Titan Books, 1982. 48 pp.

6562. Wagner, John, Mike McMahon, and Ron Smith. *Block Mania*. The Chronicles of Judge Dredd, No. 12. London: Titan Books, 1984. 63 pp.

6563. Wagner, John, Mike McMahon, and Ron Smith. *Judge Child*. The Chronicles of Judge Dredd, No. 8-10. 3 Vols. London: Titan Books, 1983-1984.

6564. Wagner, John, Ron Smith, and Alan Grant. *The Judge Dredd Collection*. 2 Vols. London: IPC Magazines, 1985-1986.

6565. Wagner, John, *et al. Judge Dredd*. The Chronicles of Judge Dredd. London: Titan Books, 1981-.

6566. Wheelock, Jim. "Judge Dredd." *Comics Scene*. March 1982, pp. 20-22.

"Lord Snooty"

6567. "Comic Cuts Call on Naughty Lord Snooty." *Evening Tribune* (Wolverhampton). September 7, 1985, p. 1.

6568. "Lord Snooty in the News." *Comics Journal*. October 1992, p. 34.

6569. Prescott, Michael and Tim Rayment. "Lord Snooty Bids Farewell After 54 Toffee-Nosed Years." *The Jester*. August 1992, p. 16. Reprinted from *Sunday Times*. July 12, 1992.

"Modesty Blaise"

6570. O'Donnell, Peter and Jim Holdaway. *Modesty Blaise, Mister Sun.* Great British Newspaper Strips. London: Titan Books, 1985. 80 pp.

6571. O'Donnell, Peter and Jim Holdaway. *Modesty Blaise, the Gabriel Set-Up.* Great British Newspaper Strips. London: Titan Books, 1985. 96 pp.

6572. O'Donnell, Peter and Jim Holdaway. *Modesty Blaise, the Hell-Makers.* Great British Newspaper Strips. London: Titan Books, 1986. 96 pp.

6573. O'Donnell, Peter, Jim Holdaway, and Neville Colvin. *Modesty Blaise.* First American Edition Series. 8 Vols. Park Forest, Illinois: K. Pierce, 1981-1986.

6574. O'Donnell, Peter, Jim Holdaway, and Enrique Romero. *The Warlords of Phoenix.* Great British Newspaper Strips. London: Titan Books, 1987. 96 pp.

"Roy of the Rovers"

6575. "*Roy* To Rove No More." *Comics Journal.* April 1993, p. 34.

6576. Verity, Edward. "Roy of the Savers! TSB Puts Its Shirt on Comic-Strip Star." *The Jester.* September 1992, p. 12. *Daily Mail* (London). July 30, 1992.

"Rupert"

6577. *The New Adventures of Rupert.* London: Express Newspapers, 1985. 123 pp.

6578. Perry, George and Alfred Bestall. *Rupert, a Bear's Life.* London: Pavilion, 1985. 169 pp.

PERIODICALS

6579. Ingrams, Richard, ed. *The Life and Times of Private Eye, 1961-1971.* London: Allen Lane, Penguin Books, 1971.

6580. Mellini, Peter and Roy Matthews. *In Vanity Fair.* London: Scolar Press, 1981.

6581. "New Humor Paper Makes U.K. Debut." *Comics Journal.* May 1993, pp. 29-30.

6582. "Oink!" *Speakeasy.* No. 81, 1987, pp. 10-11.

6583. Morris, Marcus, ed. *The Best of "Eagle."* London: 1977.

6584. Robinson, Dane, ed. *Twenty Five Years of British Mad.* London: Suron International Publications, 1984.

Punch

6585. à Beckett, Arthur William. *The à Becketts of "Punch."* New York: Dutton, 1903.

6586. Abraham, Abu. "Mr. Punch in Old Age." *Vidura* (New Delhi). July-October 1991, pp. 17, 19.

6587. Altick, Richard. *"Punch's* First Ten Years: The Ingredients of Success." *Journal of Newspaper and Periodical History.* 7:2 (1991), pp. 5-16.

6588. *America Laughs at "Punch."* London: Thames and Hudson, 1953.

6589. *The Best Cartoons from "Punch."* New York: Simon and Schuster, 1952.

6590. Briggs, Susan and Asa Briggs, eds. *Cap and Bell, Punch's Chronicle of English History in the Making, 1841-1861.* London: Macdonald, 1972.

6591. Burnand, F.C. "Mr. Punch—Some Precursors and Competitors." *Pall Mall Gazette.* January-April 1903.

6592. *The Cartoon Connection: the Art of Personal Humour.* London: Hamish Hamilton, 1978.

6593. *Cartoons from Punch.* 4 Vols. London: Bradbury and Agnew, 1906.

6594. *A Century of "Punch" Cartoons. 1000 Humourous and Nostalgic Drawings from 100 Years of England's Famous Weekly.* Edited by R.E. Williams; foreword by Malcolm Maggeridge. New York: Simon and Schuster, 1955.

6595. Cole, William. *A Big Bowl of Punch.* New York: Simon and Schuster, 1964. 336 pp.

6596. Coren, Alan. "The Passing of Punch." *The Jester.* June 1992, p. 5. Reprinted from *Time.* April 20, 1992.

6597. Daris, W., ed. *Punch and the Monarchy.* London: Hutchinson, 1977.

6598. Donald, James M. *"Punch* and All Carry on." *New York Times Magazine.* December 29, 1940.

6599. Doran, Amanda-Jane. "The Development of the Full-Page Wood Engraving in *Punch.*" *Journal of Newspaper and Periodical History.* 7:2 (1991), pp. 48-63.

6600. "Drawing Cartoons for Punch." *Review of Reviews.* May 1904, pp. 617-618.

6601. Dry Point (Henry Stacy Marks). "The Art of 'Punch'—Second Notice." *Spectator.* September 21, 1861.

6602. Fogarty, Kevin. "After 150 Years, British *Punch* To Close Doors." *Magazine Week.* April 13, 1992, p. 5.

6603. Foster, R.E. "Mr. Punch and the Iron Duke." *History Today.* May 1984, pp. 36-42.

6604. Foster, R.F. "Paddy and Mr. Punch." *Journal of Newspaper and Periodical History.* 7:2 (1991), pp. 33-47.

6605. Feuillet, Octave. *The Story of Mr. Punch.* New York: Dutton, 1929. 139 pp.

6606. Graves, C.L. *Mr. Punch's History of England.* London: 1922.

6607. Heller, Steven. "The History of Punch." *Upper and Lower Case.* June 1981, pp. 22-27.

6608. Knox, E.V. "Punch's Best in '48." *New York Times Magazine.* December 26, 1948, pp. 10-11.

6609. "MacBeth or Local Thane Makes Good; Reproduced from *Punch.*" *Saturday Review of Literature.* December 2, 1950, pp. 13-14.

6610. "The Moral of Punch." *Apropos.* No. 5, 1988, pp. 123-125.

6611. *Mr. Punch's Irish Humour in Picture and Story.* London: Carmelite House, n.d.

6612. *Mr. Punch's Scottish Humor.* London: The Amalgamated Press, n.d.

6613. "Portrait by Punch of Herr Hitler." *New York Times Magazine.* December 14, 1941, pp. 16-17.

6614. Price, Clair. "Mr. Punch, Centenarian." *New York Times Magazine.* July 13, 1941, pp. 14-15 +.

6615. Price, Richard G.G. *A History of "Punch."* London: Collins, 1957.

6616. *Punch and the War.* Garden City, New York: Blue Ribbon Books, 1941. 120 pp.

6617. *Punch Library of Humour.* Edited by J.A. Hammerton. London: Amalgamated Press, n.d. (18 Vols. of contents including, *Mr. Punch in the Hunting Field*; *Golf*

Stories; In Bohemian; In the Highlands; Life in London; At the Play; In Wig & Gown; After Dinner Stories; Book of Love; With the Children; Mr. Punch at Home; Mr. Punch on Tour; On the Warpath; Mr. Punch Awheel; Country Life; Irish Humour; With the Rod & Gun. II series: *The Fun Library.* Edited by J.A. Hammerton. London: Educational Book Co. Ltd., n.d. 10 Vols.: *Courtship & Matrimony; The Family Circle; Society & Clubland; Holidays & Travel; Sports & Pastimes; Round the Town; Our Country Cousins; Stage, Study & Studio; In Animal Land; Things in General).*

6618. "Punch Looks at Television." *New York Times Magazine.* May 9, 1948, p. 61.

6619. "Punch on Nationalization." *New York Times Magazine.* February 27, 1949, pp. 52-53.

6620. "*Punch* To End 151-Year History." *Comics Journal.* March 1992, p. 14.

6621. Rosenberg, Marvin and William Cole, eds. *The Best Cartoons from Punch.* New York: Simon and Schuster, 1952.

6622. Sanders, Andrew. "Thackeray and *Punch,* 1842-1847." *Journal of Newspaper and Periodical History.* 7:2 (1991), pp. 17-24.

6623. Sillince, W.A. *Combined Observations; More Pictures from Punch.* London: Collins, 1944. 96 pp.

6624. Sillince, W.A. *Minor Relaxations; Further Pictures from Punch.* London: Collins, 1945. 96 pp.

6625. Slater, Michael. "Douglas Jerrold: *Punch*'s First Star Writer." *Journal of Newspaper and Periodical History.* 7:2 (1991), pp. 25-32.

6626. Spielmann, Marion H. *The History of "Punch."* London: Cassell and Co., 1895; New York: Greenwood, 1969.

6627. Spielmann, Marion H. "The *Punch* Dinner—The Diners and Their Labours." *Magazine of Art.* 18 (1895), p. 93.

6628. Sprod, George. "My Life with Mr. Punch." *Inkspot.* Winter 1992, pp. 23-24.

6629. Story, D. "Cockney's Calendar: Punch." *Munsey.* December 1902, pp. 357-367.

6630. Thackeray, William Makepeace. *The Book of Snobs and Other Contributions to "Punch."* London: Smith, Elder and Co., 1887.

6631. Townsend, F.H. *"Punch" Drawings.* London: Cassell, 1921. 225 pp.

6632. "Twenty Religious Cartoons Selected from the Pages of the British Humor Magazine, Punch." *Critic.* Spring 1978, pp. 54-60.

6633. "Unrationed Humor; Cartoons Selected from Punch." *New York Times Magazine*. November 22, 1942, p. 18.

6634. Walkley, Christina. *The Way to Wear 'Em. One Hundred Fifty Years of "Punch" on Fashion*. London: Peter Owen, 1985.

6635. Walsh, William S. *Abraham Lincoln and the London Punch*. New York: Moffat, Yard and Co., 1909.

6636. "When the British Can't Laugh." *Kayhan Caricature*. August 1992.

6637. Williams, R.E., ed. *A Century of Punch Cartoons*. New York: Simon and Schuster, 1955. 340 pp.

Viz

6638. Donald, Chris, *et al.*, eds. *Viz Comic, the Big Hard One*. London: Virgin Books, 1985? 93 pp.

6639. "The Fine Art of Viz." *Speakeasy*. December 1990-January 1991, p. 13.

6640. "Viz, Ten Years Down the Drain." *Speakeasy*. December-January 1989-1990, pp. 27-29.

6641. Von Busack, Richard. "Britain's 'Mad' about *Viz*." *Comics Journal*. July 1991, pp. 52-54.

ANIMATION

6642. Andersson, Max. "01 Med Film." *Story Board*. No. 7, 1988, p. 24.

6643. Barker, Martin. "How Nasty Are the Nasties?" *New Society*. November 10, 1983, pp. 231-233.

6644. "Brit Animator Irked at BBC's Foreign Pickup." *Variety*. April 27, 1988, p. 114.

6645. "Brits Adjust to New World Order." *Variety*. September 21, 1992, pp. 61, 64.

6646. Coopman, Jeremy. "Bart Conquers U.K." *Variety*. March 4, 1991, p. 67.

6647. Coopman, Jeremy. "Brit Cartoonists Ride a Hot Streak." *Variety*. May 27, 1991, pp. 60, 71.

6648. Coopman, Jeremy. "Brit Sats Boost Kidvid." *Variety*. November 5, 1990, p. 60.

6649. Coopman, Jeremy. "Welsh-Lingo Web Spurs Prod Boom." *Variety*. January 21, 1991, pp. 71, 74.

6650. Davis, Brian. "Oscar the Grouch." *Advertising Age*. September 3, 1990, pp. 28-29, 37.

6651. Edera, Bruno. and John Halas, eds. *Full-Length Animated Feature Films*. London: Focal Press, 1977.

6652. Fitzgerald, Theresa. "How'd They Do That?—Tricks of the Trade." *Variety*. November 5, 1990, p. 68.

6653. Gifford, Denis. *The Enchanted Drawing*. London: British Cartoonist Association and National Film Archive, n.d.

6654. Gifford, Denis. "Is There Still Life after Animation?" *The Guardian* (London). March 29, 1980.

6655. "A Heavy Bet on Bart Pays Off." *Variety*. November 5, 1990, p. 60.

6656. Pitman, Jack. "Latest Star Lying Low in Britain." *Variety*. May 27, 1991, p. 69.

6657. Pitman, Jack. "A Long Time in Dreaming, a Feature Gets Its Cash." *Variety*. November 5, 1990, p. 66.

6658. Solomon, Charles. "Fun with Animation: In Great Britain, Commercials Are Different." *Emmy*. September/October 1985.

6659. Stephenson, R. *The Animated Film*. London: Tantivy, 1973.

6660. Wober, J.M. *Children's Tastes in TV Cartoons: A Brief Note*. London: Independent Broadcasting Authority, 1989.

CARICATURE

6661. Allodoli, Ettore. *La Caricature Inglese*. Firenze: Novissima Enciclopedia Monografica Illustrada, n.d.

6662. Baker, Steve. *Picturing the Beast. Animals, Identity and Representation*. Manchester: Manchester University Press, 1993. 242 pp.

6663. Cimarróno. *Inglaterra Partida por "El Eje."* Buenos Aires: Editorial "La Mazorca," n.d.

6664. Cunningham, Hugh. "Will the Real John Bull Stand Up, Please." *Times Higher Education Supplement.* February 19, 1982.

6665. *Getting Them in Line.* An Exhibition of Caricature in Cartoon, University of Kent at Canterbury, 1975. Essays by Colin Seymour-Ure and Stephen Bann.

6666. Gombrich, E.H. "The Cartoonist's Armory." In *Meditations on a Hobby Horse.* London: Phaidon, 1963.

6667. Gombrich, E.H. *The Experiment of Caricature in Art and Illusion.* London: Phaidon, 1960.

6668. Gombrich, E.H. *Meditations on a Hobby Horse.* London: Phaidon, 1963; Reprinted 1965.

6669. Gombrich, E.H. and Ernst Kris. *Caricature.* Harmondsworth: Penguin Books, 1940.

6670. Herbert, W.A.S. *Caricatures and How To Draw Them.* London: Pitman, 1951.

6671. Lambourne, Lionel. *An Introduction to Caricature.* London: Her Majesty's Stationery Office; Owings Mills, Maryland: Stemmer House, 1983. 48 pp.

6672. Longden, Alfred A. *Cartoon Wit and Caricature in Britain.* London: Print Collectors' Club, 1944. 62 pp.

6673. Magnan, Henry. "Humour Brittanique." *Le Monde Illustré* (Paris). December 18, 1948.

6674. Matthews, Roy T. and Peter Mellini. *In "Vanity Fair."* Berkeley, California: University of California Press, 1982. 275 pp.

6675. Munby, A.N.L. *Some Caricatures of Book-Collectors. An Essay.* London: Printed for private circulation by William H. Robinson Ltd., Christmas, 1948.

6676. *New Readings of Old Authors. Shakespeare.* London: E. Wilson, n.d.

6677. Nicolson, Harold. "Churchill in Caricature." *New York Times Magazine.* April 3, 1955.

6678. Physick, John. *The Duke of Wellington in Caricature* (esp. W.H. Heath—"Peter Pry"). London: Her Majesty's Stationary Office, 1965.

6679. Russell, John. "Caricatures That Still Draw Blood." *New York Times.* October 14, 1984.

6680. Searle, Ronald, Claude Roy, and Bernd Bornemann. *La Caricature: Art et Manifeste.* Geneva: Editions d'Art Skira, 1974.

6681. Tremain, Ruthven. *The Animal's Who's Who*. London: Routledge and Kegan Paul, Ltd., 1982.

6682. Tylee, Claire M. "Virginia Woolf and the Art of Caricature." In *Literary and Linguistic Aspects of Humour*, pp. 257-264. Barcelona: University of Barcelona Department of Languages, 1984.

COMIC BOOKS

6683. "Aaargh! Comics at the ICA." *Time Out* (London). December 26, 1970.

6684. "A Case of Taking the Mickey." *The Guardian* (London). February 2, 1971.

6685. Aldridge, Alan and George Perry. *The Penguin Book of Comics*. London: Penguin, 1967, 256 pp.

6686. Andersen, Verner E. "England Intet U-land." *Seriejournalen*. December 1991, pp. 48-49.

6687. Anglo, Michael. *Penny Dreadfuls*. London: Jupiter Books, 1977.

6688. "Anyone for a Sleezy Night?" *Fantazia*. No. 4, 1990, p. 9.

6689. Ashford, Richard. "Timemasters—Back to the Future." *Speakeasy*. November 1989, pp. 46-47.

6690. Barker, Martin. *Comics, Ideology, Power and the Critics*. Manchester: Manchester University Press, 1989. 320 pp.

6691. Bonner, Michael. "The Doctor's Adventures." *Speakeasy*. November 1989, pp. 26-27, 29.

6692. "Boys Don't Cry." *Speakeasy*. November 1990, pp. 27-28.

6693. Brown, Ray. "An Analysis of Comics in Britain and Their Possible Contribution to a Visual Culture." In *Comics and Visual Culture: Research Studies from Ten Countries*, edited by Alphons Silbermann and H.-D. Dyroff, pp. 79-95. Munich: K.G. Saur, 1986.

6694. "Charts." *Speakeasy*. February 1990, p. 7; April 1990, p. 7; May 1990, p. 7.

6695. "Comic Release." *Society of Strip Illustration Newsletter*. March 1988, pp. 12-13.

6696. "The Comics." *The Times Literary Supplement* (London). February 25, 1955.

6697. "Comics in England." *Library Journal*. April 1, 1953, p. 580.

6698. "Comics That Can 'Lead to Murder.'" *London Daily Mail*. October 23, 1970.

6699. Dawson, Paul. "The Comic Comes of Age." *Society of Strip Illustration Newsletter*. May 1989, p. 6.

6700. Dellino, Clare. "Comics That Set a Bad Example." *Sunday Times* (London). February 15, 1981, p. 19.

6701. De Suinn, Colin. "Let Me Take You Down 'Cause I'm Going To...." *Speakeasy*. November 1990, pp. 48-49, 51.

6702. "Find the Cost of Freedom." *Fantazia*. No. 4, 1990, p. 4.

6703. Gaskell, Jane. "Pow, Zap, Aaargh!" *Daily Sketch* (London). January 1, 1971.

6704. Giacardi, David. "Collecting Comics in the Fifties." *Comics Unlimited* (London). 52, 1982.

6705. Gifford, Denis. "The American Influence on the British Comic." In *Federation of Children's Book Groups Yearbook*. No. 65. London: Lund Humphries, 1972.

6706. Gifford, Denis. "Bertie's Bag." *The Guardian* (London). May 25, 1972.

6707. Gifford, Denis. *Discovering Comics*. Tring, Herts.: Shire Publications, 1971. 64 pp.

6708. Gifford, Denis. "Fun Filled Fantasy." *The Newsagent* (London). November 28, 1985.

6709. Gifford, Denis. "The Fun of Chasing Comics." *Everything Has a Value*. February 1981.

6710. Gifford, Denis. "Have a Comic Christmas Chums!" *Collectors' Fayre*. December 1986.

6711. Gifford, Denis. "It's Number One and Full of Fun." *Aaargh! Catalogue of Institute of Contemporary Arts Exhibition*, London, December 1970.

6712. Gifford, Denis. "It's Number One and Full of Fun!" *Collectors' Fayre*. October 1986.

6713. Gifford, Denis. "It's Super Duper!" *Collectors' Fayre*. April 1987.

6714. Gifford, Denis. "The Last Rover." *The Guardian* (London). January 28, 1973.

6715. Gifford, Denis. "La Tradizione Ultrasecolare del Compassato Fumetto Brittanico." In *6 Convengno Internazionale del Fumetto*. (Prato, Italy). February 1983.

6716. Gifford, Denis. "My Funny Frankenstein." *The Frankenstein File* (London). 1977.

6717. Gifford, Denis. "The Mystery of the Multiplying Marvels." *Rex* (London). 1972.

6718. Gifford, Denis. "A Penn'orth of Chips." *Collectors' Fayre*. March 1987.

6719. Gifford, Denis. "Pow! Splat! Make Way for a New Super Hero." *T.V. Times* (London). June 8, 1978.

6720. Gifford, Denis. *Quick on the Draw*. London: ITV/Arrow, 1978.

6721. Gifford, Denis. "Tuppenny Coloureds." *The Saturday Book*. No. 31. London: Hutchinson, December 1971.

6722. Gifford, Denis. "Tuppenny Heroes." *The Saturday Book*. No. 32. London: Hutchinson, 1972.

6723. Gosling, Nigel. "Comic Culture." *The Observer* (London). January 3, 1971.

6724. Gravett, Paul. "Correspondance d'Angleterre." *Les Cahiers de la Bande Dessinée* (Grenoble). 58, 1984, pp. 50-52; 63, 1985, pp. 44-45.

6725. Green, Stuart. "Savoy." *Speakeasy*. December-January 1989-1990, pp. 56-57.

6726. Green, Stuart. "A Walk on the Downside." *Speakeasy*. May 1989, pp. 47, 49.

6727. Green, Stuart. "Wow! Sheer Carnage!" *Speakeasy*. September 1990, pp. 20-21, 23, 25.

6728. Griffith, Walter D. "An Adventure in Pedagogy." *Journal of Adult Education* (London). 6:4 (1964), pp. 404-407.

6729. Hildick, E.W. *A Close Look at Comics and Magazines*. London: Faber and Faber, 1966.

6730. Hildick, E.W. "Satirising the Comics." *Journal of Education*. January 1956, pp. 18-19.

6731. Hillier, Bevis. "Penny Plain and Twopence Lurid." *Sunday Times* (London). January 3, 1971.

6732. Hogan, Peter. "Im Media." *Society of Strip Illustration Newsletter*. June 1989, pp. 24-25.

6733. "How the Greatest Comic Paper in the World Is Produced." *Comic Cuts*. February 2, 1892.

6734. Hunt, Leon. "Destination: Planet Thatcher." *Comics Journal*. October 1990, pp. 45-52.

6735. James, Louis. *Fiction for the Working Man*. Harmondsworth: Penguin, 1974. (Penny dreadfuls).

6736. Kaveney, Roz. "Grid-Locked Soliloquies: A New Wave of Comic Books." *Society of Strip Illustration Newsletter*. April 1989, p. 17. Reprinted from London *Sunday Times*. March 26, 1989, pp. G-8-9.

6737. Kidson, Mike, *et al*. "Rule, Brittanica." *Comics Journal*. April 1993, pp. 5-9.

6738. Laishley, Jennie. "Can Comics Join the Multi-Racial Society?" *London Times Educational Supplement*. November 24, 1972.

6739. Langley, Charles. "Comics That Are No Laughing Matter." *Weekend*. March 16-22, 1988, pp. 4-5.

6740. Lister, David. "Traditional Novel 'in Danger' As Teenagers Turn to Comics." *The Independent*. September 9, 1989.

6741. Love, Philip H. *Phil Love Talks of the Comics*. London: Metropolitan Sunday Newspaper Inc., 1970.

6742. Mathiasen, Paw. "Tegneserier i England." *Seriejournalen*. March 1991, pp. 17-20.

6743. Midgley, Dominic. "Our Comic Culture Is Killing the Book." *The Jester*. July 1992, p. 16. Reprinted from *Today*. May 15, 1992.

6744. Mitchell, Adrian. "Nostalgia Now 3d Off!" Souvenir Catalogue, Institute of Contemporary Arts, December 1970, London.

6745. "New Bite from British Marvel." *Comics Journal*. June 1988, p. 31.

6746. "The New Speakeasy." *Speakeasy*. February 1990, pp. 21-22.

6747. *Penny Dreadfuls and Comics. English Periodicals for Children from Victorian Times to the Present Day*. A Loan Exhibition from the Library of Oldenburg University, West Germany at the Bethnal Green Museum of Childhood, 2 June - 2 October 1983. London: Printed by Victoria and Albert Museum, 1983. 124 pp.

6748. Pickard, P.M., ed. *British Comics—An Appraisal*. London: Comics Campaign Council, 1955.

6749. Plowright, Frank. "And As Ye Reap Shall Ye Sow." *Comics Journal*. June 1988, p. 11.

6750. Plowright, Frank. "Rule Britannia." *Amazing Heroes*. August 1, 1984, pp. 43-47.

6751. "Precinct." *Speakeasy*. February 1990, p. 5; April 1990 (by Gordon Rennie), p. 5; May 1990 (by Adrian Dungworth), p. 5.

6752. Pritchett, Oliver. "Age No Bar to Comics." *The Guardian* (London). February 3, 1971.

6753. "A Reverse British Invasion. *Comics Journal*. October 1991, p. 19.

6754. Ridout, Cefn. "Knockabout Confessions." *Speakeasy*. May 1989, pp. 39, 41, 43, 45.

6755. Rodi, Rob. "Cruel Britannia." *Comics Journal*. June 1991, pp. 41-47.

6756. Rodríguez Arbesú, Faustino. "El Señor del Dia." *El Wendigo*. February-April 1988, pp. 31-34.

6757. Rose, Cynthia. "A BOOM of One's Own." *Society of Strip Illustration Newsletter*. May 1989, pp. 7-9.

6758. Rosie, George. "The Land of Ooer, Erk and Aargh!" *New Society* (London). November 19, 1970.

6759. Shapiro, Pat. "Do Comic Book Covers Make the Grade?" *Four Color Magazine*. March 1987, pp. 50-55.

6760. Shaw, F.H. *The Golden Book of Comics*. London: Odhams Press, 1950. 320 pp.

6761. Sherwood, Martin. "Aaargh!" *New Scientist* (London). February 4, 1971.

6762. Skidmore, Martin. "Trident Comics: The Hype Article." *FA*. March 1989, pp. 24-27.

6763. Stangroom, Howard. "Comics News from British Isles." *Comics Buyer's Guide*. June 22, 1984, pp. 34-35.

6764. Stangroom, Howard. "A Delayed Look at British Comics." *Comics Buyer's Guide*. December 7, 1984, pp. 56, 58.

6765. Stangroom, Howard. "News from England." *Comics Buyer's Guide*. March 30, 1984, pp. 1, 3.

6766. "Super Trip." *The Guardian* (London). February 6, 1971.

6767. "Third World War Crisis." *Speakeasy*. August 1988, pp. 12-14.

6768. Thomas, Steve and Neil Hansen. "The British Invasion." *Comics Values Monthly*. November 1992, pp. 9-13.

6769. Thompson, Kim. "The British Invasion." *Amazing Heroes*. August 1, 1984, pp. 27-28.

6770. Thorpe, Dave. "Speakout." *Speakeasy*. April 1990, p. 27.

6771. "TSR UK Is 10." *Fantazia*. No. 4, 1990, p. 9.

6772. "UK Creator Rights Panel Argues the Kirby-Marvel Dispute." *Comics Journal*. February 1987, pp. 23-24.

6773. "UK News." *Speakeasy*. February 1989, pp. 16, 18; December-January 1989-1990, pp. 21, 23.

6774. "Vadim in Space." *Continental* (London). December 1967.

6775. Vulliamy, Ed. "Comic Opera Returns to Covent Garden." *Guardian*. November 28, 1987.

6776. Wagner, Geoffrey. *Parade of Pleasure*. London: Derek Verschoyle, 1954.

6777. Warman, Christopher. "A Nostalgia for Comics." *The Times* (London). January 1, 1971.

6778. Wells, Dominic. "Comics: Astounding Tales." *Time Out*. August 17-24, 1988.

6779. "Zoning in on L.E.M." *Fantazia*. No. 4, 1990, p. 7.

Anthologies

6780. Bellamy, Frank and Clifford Makins. *High Command*. Hendrik-Ido-Ambacht, The Netherlands: Dragon's Dream, 1981. 93 pp.

6781. Birch, Paul H. and Sheldon Bayley. "Comics Reviews." *Fantazia*. No. 4, 1990, p. 11.

6782. Brooks, Brad. *"A1*: A New Beginning for Anthology Comics?" *Comics Journal*. December 1989, pp. 27-28.

6783. Finley-Day, Gerry, *et al. Rogue Trooper*. The Best of 2000 AD, No. 9, 14, 16, 18, 23. 5 Vols. London: Titan Books, 1984-1986.

6784. Finley-Day, Gerry, *et al. The VC's*. The Best of 2000 AD, No. 28. London: Titan Books, 1987-.

6785. Lawrence, Don. *The Trigan Empire*. London: Hamlyn, 1978. 189 pp.

6786. Mills, Pat. *The A.B.C. Warriors*. The Best of 2000 AD, No. 3-4. 2 Vols. London: Titan Books, 1983.

6787. Mills, Pat and Joe Colquhoun. *Charley's War*. The Best of Battle, Vols. 1-2. 2 Vols. London: Titan Books, 1983-1986.

6788. Mills, Pat and Mike McMahon. *Slaine*. The Best of 2000 AD, No. 15. London: Titan Books, 1986. 64 pp.

6789. Mills, Pat, Kevin O'Neill, and Bryan Talbot. *Nemesis the Warlock*. The Best of 2000 AD, Nos. 5, 8, 13, 17, 27. 5 Vols. London: Titan Books, 1985-1987.

6790. Mills, Pat, *et al*. *Ro-busters*. The Best of 2000 AD, No. 6-7. 2 Vols. London: Titan Books, 1983.

6791. Moore, Alan. *Shocking Futures*. The Best of 2000 AD, No. 24. London: Titan Books, 1986. 72 pp.

6792. Moore, Alan and Alan Davis. *D.R. and Quinch's Totally Awesome Guide to Life*. The Best of 2000 AD, No. 22. London: Titan Books, 1986. 96 pp.

6793. Moore, Alan and Ian Gibson. *The Ballad of Halo Jones*. The Best of 2000 AD, No. 19-21. 3 Vols. London: Titan Books, 1986.

6794. Morris, Marcus. *The Best of Eagle*. London: Michael Joseph, 1977. 192 pp.

6795. Rooum, Donald. "Review of *On Comedy*." *Society of Strip Illustration Newsletter*. June 1989, p. 22.

6796. Wagner, John and Carlos Ezquerra. *Strontium Dog*. London: Titan Books, 1987. 63 pp.

6797. Wagner, John and Ian Gibson. *Robohunter*. The Best of 2000 AD, No. 1-2, 1-11. 4 Vols. London: Titan Books, 1982-1985.

Anti-Comics Campaign, 1949-1955

6798. Allaway, Jeremy. "The Ideology of the Comics Campaign: 1949-55." Special Study, BA Humanities, Bristol Polytechnic, 1982.

6799. Anderson, Paul and Gordon Watkins. "Horror Comics—Is This the End?" *Picture Post*. November 20, 1954.

6800. "Auch in England Hält die Debatte um die Comics An." *Jugendliteratur* (Munich). 1:1 (1955), p. 43.

6801. Barker, Martin. *A Haunt of Fears: The Strange History of the British Horror Comics Campaign*. London: Pluto Press, 1984. 228 pp.

6802. Brooks, Brad and Stuart Green. "A Haunt of Fears." *Speakeasy*. November 1990, pp. 58-59.

6803. "Comics Campaign Is Anti-US Move." *Hampstead and Highgate Express*. March 7, 1952.

6804. "Comics Sind Nicht Komisch. England Wehrt Sich Gegen die Invasion der Amerikanischen Bildstreifen." *Münchner Illustrierte*. 1955.

6805. "Comics—the 'Horrors' and the 'Harmless.'" *Sunday Observer*. November 14, 1954.

6806. Edelman, M. "More Complaints About Comics." *Publishers Circular and Booksellers Report* (London). 166:4511 (1952), p. 1680.

6807. "England und die Horror-Comics." *dipa-Information* (Frankfurt). 13, 1955, pp. 12-18.

6808. Hewett, R.P. "These Comics Are Not Funny." *Schoolmaster*. March 28, 1952.

6809. Hill, Roland. "Horror-Comics in England." *Katholische Orientierung* (Zurich). 19, 1955, pp. 70-71.

6810. Hollbrook, David. "Inoffensive Comics?" *Journal of Education* (London). 88:1045 (1956), pp. 348-352.

6811. "'Horror Comics,' Action of the Home Secretary." *British Medical Journal*. No. 4895, 1954, pp. 1038-1042.

6812. "Horror Comics in Parliament." *Lancelot* (London). 1:10 (1955), pp. 493, 505.

6813. "Inoffensive Comics?" *Journal of Education*. October 1956, p. 437.

6814. Lamont, Duncan. "Is This the Kind of Comic Your Child Is Reading?" *Daily Record*. September 27, 1954.

6815. MacDougall, George. "USA-Comics in England Verboten." *Neues Deutschland* (East Berlin). April 21, 1955.

6816. McGlashan, Alan. "Comic-Strips: A New Fantasia of the Unconscious." *Lancet* (London). 264:6753 (1953), p. 238.

6817. Mauger, Peter. "The Cult of Violence Persists." *Picture Post.* November 20, 1954.

6818. Pumphrey, George. *Children's Comics—A Guide for Parents and Teachers.* London: Epworth Press, 1956.

6819. Pumphrey, George. "The Children Tell...." *Daily Herald* (London). August 26, 1953.

6820. Pumphrey, George. "Classifying Comics." *Head Teachers Review.* 1953.

6821. Pumphrey, George. "Comics." *School Librarian.* July 1953, pp. 310-318.

6822. Pumphrey, George. "Comics and 'Moral Disarmament.'" *Schoolmaster.* October 8, 1954, pp. 476-477, 486.

6823. Pumphrey, George. *Comics and Your Children.* London: Comics Campaign Council, 1954.

6824. Pumphrey, George. "Difficulty of Defining Harmful Comics." *Schoolmaster.* February 18, 1955, p. 285.

6825. Pumphrey, George. "Viciousness of Comics—A Recent Example." *Times Educational Supplement.* September 17, 1954.

6826. Pumphrey, George. *What Children Think of Their Comics.* London: The Epworth Press, 1956.

6827. "Schauer-Comics in England und Indien Verboten." *Welt der Arbeit.* August 5, 1955.

6828. Sumner, Ed. "The Comics Code—Twenty Years of Self-Strangulation." *Inside Comics.* Part 1, Vol. 1, No. 3, 1974; Part 2, Vol. 1, No. 4, 1974-1975.

6829. Wertham, Frederic. *The Guide of the Guilt.* London: Dennis Dobson Ed., 1953. 211 pp.

6830. Williams, W.T. "Possible Actions Against Vulgar Comics." *Publishers Circular and Booksellers Report.* 166:4483 (1952), p. 717.

Censorship

6831. "The Anti-Censorship Update." *Big O Magazine* (Singapore). January 1991, p. 12.

6832. "Bible Fury." *Speakeasy.* No. 81, 1987, p. 1.

6833. "The Censor Strikes!" *Speakeasy*. June 1990, pp. 11-12.

6834. Coles, Joanna. "Foreign Office Finds Cartoonists' EC Offerings No Laughing Matter." *The Jester*. September 1992, p. 7.

6835. "Crisis of Faith." *Big O Magazine* (Singapore). March 1991, p. 78.

6836. "Comic Retailer Takes Police Advice." *Speakeasy*. October 1990, p. 11.

6837. "Crumb Book Banned in Britain." *Comics Journal*. June 1991, p. 12.

6838. "Gosh! Comics Raided by Customs." *The Jester*. February 1993, p. 12.

6839. "London Comic Shop Raided." *Speakeasy*. September 1990, pp. 10-11.

6840. "London Editions Cancel Adult Comics But Announce Another." *Speakeasy*. February 1991, p. 7.

6841. "*Lord Horror* Author Jailed." *Comics Journal*. July 1993, p. 23.

6842. "More Imports Seized." *Comics Journal*. September 1987, p. 26.

6843. Plowright, Frank. "Last Gasp Titles Seized by British Customs." *Comics Journal*. July 1987, p. 129.

6844. "Savoy Raided." *Speakeasy*. November 1989, p. 9.

6845. "Should US Comics Be Banned?" *Picture Post*. May 17, 1952.

6846. "Strange British Customs." *Comics Journal*. January 1993, pp. 17-19.

6847. Tucker, Nicholas. "What Was All the Fuss About?" *Times Educational Supplement* (London). August 22, 1980.

6848. "U.K. Customs Seizes Underground Comix." *Comics Buyer's Guide*. November 13, 1987, pp. 1, 3.

Effects Debate

6849. Bacon, Edward. "Oath of the B.O.P." *Illustrated London News*. January 21, 1967, p. 25.

6850. Chesterton, G.K. "A Defence of Penny Dreadfuls." *The Defendant* (London). 1901, p. 17.

6851. Dyer, Christopher. "Language for Action, Case for Defense." *Times Educational Supplement* (London). February 5, 1971.

6852. Fleming, G. "The Didactic Organization of Pictorial Reality in the New Language Teaching Media." *Praxis* (London). April 1967, pp. 163-166.

6853. Gale, George. "Violent and Deformed, the Prosecution Case." *Times Educational Supplement* (London). February 5, 1971.

6854. Green, Stuart. "Strip Search: Comics in the Real World. Shock Horror Exposé." *Speakeasy*. March 1990, pp. 52-53, 55.

6855. Holbrook, David. "Seduction of the Innocent." *Sunday Times* (London). January 3, 1983.

6856. Holbrow, Bob. "Violence in Comics—Will it Cease?" *Retail Management*. October 2, 1976, p. 7.

6857. Jestico, Thorn. "Soon We Are Over a City?" *Architectural Association Quarterly* (London). Autumn 1970.

6858. Pickard, P.M. *I Could a Tale Unfold, Violence, Horror and Sensationalism in Stories for Children*. London: Tavistock Publications, 1967.

Genres

6859. Alderson, Connie. *Magazines Teenagers Read*. London: Pergamon Press, 1968.

6860. "British Thriller Comics Update." *The Classics Collector*. February-March 1990, p. 10.

6861. "Cartoon 'Macbeth' with Lots of Gore." *Near Mint*. October 1982, pp. 42-43.

6862. Conroy, Mike. "Britain's Other Comics." *Comics Scene*. January 1981, pp. 40-41.

6863. Denholm, Jane. "Love and Comics." *NSM*. 1989, pp. 12-13.

6864. Heeley, John. "Boys' Comics: Violence Rules." *Sunday Times* (London). February 27, 1983.

6865. Johnson, Nicholas. "What Do Children Learn from War Comics?" *New Society* (London). July 7, 1966.

6866. "Mature Comics Struggle To Survive in Britain." *Comics Journal*. April 1991, p. 19.

6867. Orwell, George. "Boys' Weeklies." In *The Collected Essays, Journalism and Letters: Vol. 1, 1920-40.* Harmondsworth: Penguin, 1970.

Industry

6868. "All Change at Fleetway." *Comics Journal.* July 1989, pp. 44-45.

6869. "Artists Criticize Book's Print Quality." *Comics Journal.* October 1991, pp. 20-21.

6870. "Britain's Biggest Publisher IPC Sold." *Comics Journal.* September 1987, p. 13.

6871. Coopman, Jeremy. "Sales of Marvel Comics Move Up Fast in Britain." *Variety.* September 17, 1986, p. 83.

6872. "*Crisis* Folds; Fleetway Merges." *Comics Journal.* November 1991, pp. 22-23.

6873. "Crisis Management." *Speakeasy.* December 1988, pp. 39-40, 42.

6874. Dakin, John. "'Marvel Revolution' in England." *Comics Journal.* March 1979, p. 14.

6875. "Fleetway Pulls 'Skin' from *Crisis.*" *Comics Journal.* December 1989, pp. 25-26.

6876. "Glenat Launches US Invasion." *Speakeasy.* August 1988, p. 18.

6877. "'Marvel Revolution' in England." *Comics Journal.* March 1979, p. 14.

6878. "Marvel UK Introduces New Frontier." *Comics Journal.* April 1993, p. 35.

6879. "New British Comic Company." *Comics Feature.* No. 25, 1983, p. 11.

6880. Plowright, Frank. "British Black-and-Whites After Market Collapse." *Comics Journal.* July 1987, p. 131.

6881. Plowright, Frank. "Rumors of IPC Sale Denied." *Comics Journal.* July 1987, p. 131.

6882. Thompson, Don. "British Comics Foresee Bleak Future, Unending Wars." *Comics Buyer's Guide.* July 8, 1983, pp. 34, 36.

6883. "U.K. Copyright Dispute Resolved." *Comics Journal.* April 1993, p. 34.

Underground

6884. Emerson, Hunt. *The Big Book of Everything*. London: Knockabout Comics, 1983. 96 pp.

6885. Gifford, Denis. "Alternative Comics." *Brainstorm*. December 1976.

6886. Jerome, Fiona. "Notes from the Underground (Revisited)." *Speakeasy*. October 1990, pp. 49-51.

6887. "Notes from the Underground." *Before I Get Old* (Singapore). January 1987, pp. 31-34.

6888. Oldfield, Andy. "Going Underground." *Talking Turkey*. 1:1 (1991), pp. 34-35.

6889. Sherman, Bill. "A Glimpse at British Undergrounds." *Comics Journal*. Summer 1979, pp. 122-124.

6890. Wallis, James. "From Russell with Love." *Speakeasy*. February 1991, pp. 60-61.

COMIC STRIPS

6891. "Aesthetics and the Strip Cartoon." *Continental* (London). December 1967.

6892. Ames, Winslow. "Caricature and Cartoon, II.D.C.Strips, III. Comic-Strip-Techniques." In *Encyclopaedia Brittannica*. Vol. 4. London: 1960.

6893. "Comic Strip Hooligans." *Daily Mail* (London). September 17, 1976, p. 27.

6894. "Direct Contact (How Energy Can Go Straight Through to Power and Create Light)." *Society of Strip Illustration Newsletter*. December 1987, pp. 5-6.

6895. Gifford, Denis. "The Funny Wonders." *Art and Artists* (London). February 1971.

6896. Gifford, Denis. "Los Comics en la Prensa Britanica de Joy a Jane." *Historia de los Comics* (Spain). No. 15, 1983.

6897. Hawthorne, Mike. "The Serious Art of Comic Strips." *Artist's and Illustrator's Magazine*. June 1988, pp. 9-10, 42-43.

6898. Lilley, Les. "More New Comic Strip Trends in Britain!" *WittyWorld*. Summer/Autumn 1991, p. 28.

6899. Lilley, Les. "New Trends for the Comic Strip in Britain." *WittyWorld*. Winter/Spring 1990, pp. 92-93.

6900. McNay, Michael. "Strip Joint." *The Guardian* (London). January 1, 1971.

6901. Muggeridge, Malcolm. "The Art of Comic-Strips." *New Statesman and Nation* (London). 59:1510 (1960), pp. 250-253.

6902. O'Hara, Frank. "Living in the City." *Society of Strip Illustration Newsletter*. December 1988, pp. 5-7.

6903. Quennell, Peter. "The Comic Strips in England; Future Folklorists Will Find in Them the Mythology of the Present Day." *Living Age*. March 1941, pp. 21-23.

6904. "Such Language; *London Daily Express* Trial Run of Steve Canyon." *Time*. August 25, 1947, p. 54.

6905. Thomson, Ross and Bill Hewison. *How to Draw and Sell Cartoons*. Cincinnati, Ohio: North Light, 1985. 143 pp.

6906. Tiner, Ron. "Whatever Happened to Bristol Board?" *Society of Strip Illustration Newsletter*. March 1988, pp. 14-15.

6907. Wheatcroft, Geoffrey. "Tearing Comic Strips Off the Opera." *Telegraph* (London). November 27, 1987.

6908. Zimmermann, Hans D. "Comic Strip As Popular Art Form." *Architectural Association Quarterly*. Autumn 1970.

POLITICAL CARTOONS

6909. Atherton, H.M. "The British Defend Their Constitution in Political Cartoons and Literature." *Studies in Eighteenth Century Culture*. 2 (1982).

6910. "Birth of a Cartoon." *Picture Post* (London). October 22, 1938, pp. 7-11.

6911. Brookes, Peter. "The Political Cartoonist and Illustrator." *IFRA Newspaper Techniques*. March 1984, pp. 18, 20.

6912. Cummings, Michael. *The Uproarious Years, a Pictorial Post War History*. London: MacGibbon and Kee, 1954.

6913. *Daily Sketch* (London). *Cartoon Book No. 4*. London: *Daily Sketch*, n.d. 80 pp.

6914. Dyson, Will. *Cartoons*. London: *Daily Herald*, 1913.

6915. Gabriel. *Cartoons*. Commentary by Philip Bolsover. London: *Daily Worker*, n.d. Unpaginated.

6916. Garland, Nicholas. "Cartoonist's-Eye View." *National Review.* September 1, 1989, pp. 32-33.

6917. Gaskell, John. "Mastering the Art of Poking Fun." *The Jester.* March 1993, p. 8.

6918. Higgins, Ria. "At the Sharp End." *The Jester.* November 1992, pp. 10-11.

6919. Horsey, David R. "Visions of the Bear, Western Perceptions of the Soviet Union, 1947 to 1980, As Evidenced by British and North American Political Cartoons." MA thesis, University of Kent at Canterbury, 1986.

6920. Kallaugher, Kevin. "British Drawing Board." *Target.* Summer 1982, pp. 24-25; Autumn 1982, pp. 30-31; Winter 1982, pp. 29-30; Spring 1983, pp. 30-31; Summer 1983, p. 31; Autumn 1983, pp. 30-31; Spring 1984, pp. 28-29; Summer 1984, p. 30; Autumn 1984, p. 30; Winter 1984, pp. 24-26; Spring 1985, p. 33; Summer 1985, pp. 33-35; Autumn 1985, pp. 30-31; Winter 1985, pp. 32-33; Spring 1986, p. 30-31; Summer 1986, pp. 28-29; Autumn 1986, p. 29; Spring 1987, pp. 30-31.

6921. Kem. *Toy Titans, Political Cartoons and Socio-Caricatures.* London: Arthur Barker, 1937.

6922. Linton, David. "...While a 'British' Cartoonist Draws Them." *IPI Report.* January 1988, p. 16.

6923. McEnroe, Colin. "Drawing the Political Lines." *The Jester.* February 1993, pp. 14-15. Reprinted from *Hartford* (Connecticut) *Courant.*

6924. "1992—the Year in Cartoons." *Observer Magazine.* December 1992, pp. 12-18, 19-22, 25-28, 30, 32-35.

6925. "A One-Man Crusade." *Newsweek.* September 14, 1959, pp. 114-115.

6926. "The Other Cruikshank." *The World of Comic Art.* Fall 1966, pp. 24-25.

6927. Regan, C., S. Sinclair, and M. Turner. *Thin Black Lines: Political Cartoons and Development Education.* Birmingham, England: Development Education Centre, Selly Oak College, 1988.

6928. Whiting, R. "'It's on the Cards.'" *History Today.* July 1988, p. 61.

6

Country Perspectives—Greece, Hungary, Ireland

GREECE

General Studies

6929. Apostolidi, Tasos and George Akokalidi. *The Comedies of Aristophanes in Comics. Nefeles (Clouds)*. Thessalaniki: Nasé A.E., 1988. 51 pp.

6930. "Arkas" (The Rooster). *No Way Out*. 5th Album. Athens: Ars Longa, 1986. 79 pp.

6931. "Greek International Cartoon Exhibition." *Cartoonist PROfiles*. June 1978, pp. 76-79.

6932. Ioannov, John. *The End of an Era*. Athens: Kastanioti, 1989. 159 pp.

6933. Stavropoulos, Stathi. *The Inner Strength (Superman) of Stathi*. 2nd Ed. Athens: Kastanioti, 1985. 142 pp.

6934. Zhechev, Marin. "*Romios* and the Satirical Panorama of Greece." *Apropos*. No. 6, pp. 124-125.

Caricature

6935. Bailey, D.M. "Caricature of Socrates." *American Journal of Archaeology*. October 1974, p. 427.

6936. Brown, E.L. "Cleon Caricatured on a Corinthian Cup." *Journal of Hellenic Studies*. 94 (1974), pp. 166-170.

6937. Pavlidis, Vangelis. *Caricatures*. Athens: Kaktoz, 1987.

Comic Books

6938. "Classical Comics; Excerpts tr. from Greek Comic Books." *Horizon*. Summer 1966, pp. 116-120.

6939. Martinidis, Petros. *Comics: The Skill and Technique of Illustration*. Thessaloniki: Nasé A.E., 1990. 185 pp.

6940. Rodi, Rob. "Those Greeks Are Crazy." *Comics Journal*. October 1990, pp. 39-43.

6941. Tenan, Brad. "Little Lulu Comics in Greece." *The Hollywood Eclectern*. August 1993, pp. 6-7.

HUNGARY

General Studies

6942. "Cartoon-Stamps Issued in Hungary." *WittyWorld*. Summer/Autumn 1991, p. 82.

6943. Lajos, Gellert. *Egy Cigány Egy Kiraty...* Budapest: Weiss L. Es., 1928.

6944. Lent, John A. and Joseph G. Szabo. "3800 Entries from 72 Countries—Budapest Festival Hailed a Success." *WittyWorld*. Summer/Autumn 1991, pp. 76-79.

6945. Osgyani, Csaba. "'Batman' Flies into Record Number of Hungarian Cinemas." *Variety*. January 3, 1990, p. 5.

6946. Weber, John. "Budapest: Scatalogical or Satirical?" *WittyWorld*. Summer/Autumn 1991, pp. 80-81.

Cartoonists

6947. "The Art and Mind of Ernö Toth: The Venturesome Carry the Day." *Apropos*. No. 7, 1991, pp. 58-62.

6948. Dallos, Jenö. *Eva und Adam*. Berlin: Eulenspiegel-Verlag, 1978.

6949. "Laszlo Dluhopolszky, Hungary." *FECO News*. No. 7, 1989, pp. 26-27.

6950. Paleveda, Gloria Sipes. "Hungarian Political Cartoonist Finds U.S. a Better Climate for Craft." *Philadelphia Inquirer*. June 23, 1985, pp. 1-W, 4-W.

6951. Szabo, Joseph G. "The Master of Piercing Irony." *WittyWorld*. Autumn 1988, pp. 43-45. (Tamás Császár).

Animation

6952. Natwick, Grim. "Tissa." *Cartoonist PROfiles*. March 1977, pp. 14-17.

6953. Patten, Frederick. "Much Animation Sprouts from Hungary's Pannonia Film Studio." *WittyWorld*. Winter/Spring 1990, pp. 76-80.

Cartoons, Comics

6954. Lacassin, Francis. "La Réprésentation de la Parole et des Sons dans les Bandes Dessinées." Vortrag. Internationale Konferenz der UNESCO, September 1966, Budapest.

6955. Máriamak, Ember. "Mit Szabad a Szatfrának?" *Beszélö*. August 25, 1990, pp. 28-29.

Political Cartoons

6956. Buzinkay, Géza. "Borsszem Jankó—The Classic of Hungarian Humorous Political Newspapers." *Apropos*. No. 7, 1991, pp. 124-126.

6957. Szabo, Joseph George. "Never Pointing a Different Way: Cartooning in Hungary." *Target*. Autumn 1985, pp. 12-14.

IRELAND

General Studies

6958. "Cartoons by the Irish Cartoonists." *FECO News*. No. 13, 1992, p. 21.

6959. Fitzgerald, Anne. "Breaking Through to Joy." *Guideposts*. July 1988, pp. 10-13.

6960. Ungerer, Tomi. *Grenouillades*. Paris: Herscher, 1984.

Animation

6961. Fitzgerald, Theresa. "Irish Toonsters Not Smiling as Pair Fight Bankruptcy." *Variety*. September 21, 1992, p. 64.

6962. Tierney, Jim. "With Mickey Past 60, Dublin Becomes Animated." *Variety*. March 4, 1991, pp. 49, 51.

Comics

6963. "Gaelic CI." *The Classics Collector*. February-March 1990, p. 8.

6964. "A Short History of Northern Irish Comics." *Society of Strip Illustration Newsletter*. June 1989, pp. 14-15.

Political Cartoons

6965. DeVeau, Vincent. "Drawing Blood." *FECO News*. No. 13, 1992, pp. 3-6.

6966. Friers, Rowell. *Pig in the Parlor*. Belfast: Blackstaff Press, 1973.

6967. Friers, Rowell. *Riotous Living*. Belfast: Blackstaff Press, 1971.

6968. Holohan, Renagh. "Manager Darts in and Removes a Turner." *The Irish Times*. November 3, 1988, p. 1.

6969. Turner, Martyn. "A Cartoonist Comes Out." *The Irish Times*. December 29, 1988.

6970. Turner, Martyn. *Fistful of Dailers: Political Cartoons 1983-87*. Dublin: Gill and Macmillan, 1987.

6971. Turner, Martyn. "Great Cartooning Disasters." *WittyWorld*. Summer 1988, p. 32.

6972. Turner, Martyn. "Notes from Ireland." *WittyWorld*. Autumn 1987, pp. 16-17.

7

Country Perspectives—Italy

REFERENCES and RESOURCES

6973. Bertieri, Claudio. "An Italien 'Fanzine.'" *Il Lavoro*. September 27, 1968.

6974. Bertieri, Claudio. "Portraits of 42 Comic-Series and Comic-Artists." *Enciclopedia dei Fumetti*. Florence: Ed. "Sansoni," 1970.

6975. del Buono, Oreste, ed. *Enciclopedia dei Fumetto: I*. Milan: Milano Libri, 1969.

6976. Gerosa, Ambrogio. "Il Museo Internazionale della Caricatura." *Il Fumetto*. September 1973, p. 63.

6977. Groensteen, Thierry. "Bibliothèque Italienne." *Les Cahiers de la Bande Dessinée*. 71, 1986, pp. 78-79.

6978. *Guida Alla Mostra Internazionale dei Cartoonists*. Rapallo: Associazione Italiana Cartoonists e Animatori, 1973. 76 pp. (Includes Mort Walker, "Aside from the Money," p. 1; Carlo Chendi, "Come Nascono i Fumetti," p. 4; Piero Zanotto, "Guido Moroni Celsi e la 'Scuda' Italiana Degli Anni Trenta," p. 11; Luciano Bottaro, "Il Mestiere del Cartoonist," p. 17; Carlo della Corte," Un Louvre Piu' Fantasioso," p. 25; Umberto Eco, Il Linguaggio del Fumetto," pp. 42-43; Giancarlo Berardi, "Fumetto e Neocapitalismo," p. 46; Ranieri Carano, "Tempi Duri Per La Satira," pp. 50-52; "Un Giornalino Divertente," pp. 60-61).

6979. Strazzulla, Gaetano, ed. *Enciclopedia dei Fumetti*. Florence: Sansoni, 1970.

GENERAL STUDIES

6980. Bertarelli, Achille. *L'Imagerie Populaire Italienne*. Duchartre und Van Buggenhoudt, 1929. 105 pp.

6981. Biamonte, S.G. "Che Ne è di Diana Palmesi?" *Linus*. No. 25, 1966, pp. 1-9.

6982. Caradec, François. *I Primi Eroi*. Milan: Garzanti, 1962.

6983. Cuesta, Fernando. "Martin Mystere: Entre Jimenez del Oso e Indiana Jones." *El Wendigo*. January 1984, pp. 36-38.

6984. Eco, Umberto. *Apocalittici e Intergrati: Comunicazioni di Massa e Teoria della Cultura di Massa* (Attitudes of the Doomsayers and the Well-Adjusted Toward Mass Culture). Milan: Bompiani, 1965; Barcelona: Lumen, 1977.

6985. Eco, Umberto. *Il Superuomo di Massa*. Milan: Bompiani, 1978.

6986. Faeti, Antonio. "In Ricordo dell' Unomofanciullo." *Comic Art*. No. 46, 1988, p. 30.

6987. Flórez, Florentino. "Fuego de Paja." *El Wendigo*. Verano 1990, pp. 9-10.

6988. Fossati, Franco and Roberto DiVanni. *Guida al "Giallo."* Milan: Gammalibri, 1979.

6989. Gianeri, Enrico. *Storia del Cartone Annato*. Milan: Editrice Omnia, 1960.

6990. Pascal, David. "Our Man in Italy." *Newsletter*. May 1965, p. 16.

6991. Valle, Bruno. "News aus Italien." *Watcher of the Unknown*. October 1988, pp. 31-34.

Children and Youth

6992. Ajello, Nello. "La Stampa Infantile in Italia." *Nord e Sud* (Milan). 1959.

6993. Battistelli, V. *La Letteratura Infantile Moderna*. Firenze: Vallecchi, 1923.

6994. Buzzatti, Dino. "Fumetti 1952, Tomba della Fantasia Infantile." In *Atti del Congresso Internazionale Sulla Stampa Periodica, Cinematographica e Radio per Ragazzi*. Milan: Giuffré, 1954.

6995. Cuesta, U. "Problemi Attuali della Lettura Infantile e Giovanile." In *Atti del Congresso del Sindicato Nazionale de Autori e Scrittori*. Rome: 1940.

6996. Del Buono, Oreste. "Il Ritorno del Primi Eroi della Nostra Infanzia." *L'Europeo* (Rome). No. 46, 1965, pp. 34-37.

6997. Del Buono, Oreste. "Il Ritorno del Primi Eroi della Nostra Infanzia." *L'Europeo*. No. 58, 1967.

6998. Massari, G. "I Compagni dell'Infanzia." *Il Mondo* (Milan). February 24, 1963.

6999. Miotto, Antonio. "Imagination Enfantine et Presse Enfantine." Actes du Congrès International sur la Presse Périodique, 1952, Milan.

7000. Petrini, Enzo. "L'Illustration dans le Monde de la Jeunesse." *Il Centro*. October-November 1955.

7001. Volpicelli, Luigi. "Dall' Infanzia all'Adolescenza." *La Scuola* (Brescia). 1952.

Festivals

7002. Bernardi, Luigi. "Si è Aperto à Lucca il Salone dei Comics." *Il Telegrafo* (Milan). September 25, 1966.

7003. Bertieri, Claudio. "Appointment at Lucca." *Il Lavoro*. November 8, 1968.

7004. Bertieri, Claudio. "The Discussed Exhibition." *Il Lavoro*. November 23, 1968.

7005. Bertieri, Claudio. "Kirk a Lucca." *Il Lavoro*. September 13, 1966.

7006. Bertieri, Claudio. "Lucca 5." *Photographia Italiana* (Milan). No. 147, 1970.

7007. Bertieri, Claudio. "Tebeo, Western e i Gracchi di Lucca." *Il Lavoro*. September 29, 1967.

7008. Bertieri, Claudio. "Un Salone per i Comics." *Il Lavoro*. January 30, 1965.

7009. Brunoro, Gianni. "Lucca 5." *Phénix*. No. 12, 1969.

7010. Couperie, Pierre. "Lucca—The World's Most Famous Comics Congress!" *Cartoonist PROfiles*. September 1982, pp. 26-32.

7011. Couperie, Pierre and Claude Moliterni. "Lucca 6." *Phénix*. No. 15, 1970.

7012. De Angelis, Marco. "Bordighera." *WittyWorld*. Spring 1988, pp. 26-28.

7013. Frere, Claude. "Le Congrès de Lucca." *Giff-Wiff*. No. 22, 1966.

7014. "Fumetti a Lucca." *Linus*. No. 20, 1966.

7015. Ghirotti, Gigi. "Pedagoghi e Filosofi Reuniti a Bordighera per Discutere su Paperino e Mandrake." *La Stampa*. February 23, 1965.

7016. Halas, John. "20 Years of Comics at Lucca." *Novum Gebrauchsgraphik*. June 1987, pp. 46-51.

7017. Lefevre, Gaston. "2e. Salon International des Bandes Dessinées à Lucca." *Rantanplan*. No. 4, 1966/January 1967, p. 1.

7018. Listri, Francesco. "E'Finito il Congresso dei Fumetti." *La Nazione* (Firenze). September 26, 1966.

7019. Marschall, Richard. "Lucca: The Greatest Comics Convention in the World." *Comics Journal*. October 1982, pp. 71-74.

7020. Moliterni, Claude. "Lucca 7." *Phénix*. No. 19, 1971.

7021. Natoli, Dario. "Il Secondo Salone Internazionale di Lucca." *L'Unità* (Milan). 43:258 (1966).

7022. Natoli, Dario. "Lucca Diverrà la Venezia dei Comics." *L'Unità* (Milan). September 18, 1966.

7023. Origa, Graziano. "Lucca Exhibition Is *Un Grande Successo*." *Comics Journal*. February 1993, p. 14.

7024. Rondolino, Gianni. "Il Festival Internazionale di Mamaia." *Linus*. No. 18, 1966, pp. 27-30.

7025. "Si Apre Questa Mattina al Teatro del Giglio il Secondo Salone Internazionale dei 'Comics.'" *La Nazione*. September 24, 1966, p. 5.

7026. "Stamani: Lavori al Salone 'Comics.'" *Il Telegrafo* (Milan). 90:217 (1966).

7027. Trinchero, Sergio. "La Guerra a Lucca." *Hobby* (Milan). No. 5, 1967.

7028. Trinchero, Sergio. "Libro Bianco Sul Salone di Lucca." *Eureka*. No. 15, 1969.

7029. Trinchero, Sergio. "Squallida Retrospettiva al Salone di Lucca." *Hobby* (Milan). No. 1, 1966.

7030. Walker, Mort. "Viva Il Popeye." *Cartoonist PROfiles*. December 1972, pp. 54-55.

7031. Zanotto, Piero. "I Maestri del Fumetto al Festival di Lucca." *Il Gazzettino* (Venice). July 2, 1967.

7032. Zanotto, Piero. "La Guerra nei Fumetti a Lucca." *Il Gazzettino* (Venice). July 3, 1967.

7033. Zanotto, Piero. "La Venezia delle Strisce." *Sgt. Kirk*. No. 16, 1968, pp. 96-99.

7034. Zanotto, Piero. "Lucca: 2e. Salone Internazionale dei Comics." *Sipradue* (Torino). No. 11, 1966.

7035. Zanotto, Piero. "Lucca: 3e. Convegno Internazionale dei Comics." *Sipradue* (Torino). No. 6, 1967.

7036. Zanotto, Piero. "Si Inauguro Oggi a Lucca il 3e. Salone dei Fumetti." *Il Gazzettino* (Venice). June 30, 1967.

Women

7037. Casarotti Sacchi, Marica. "Rapporto fra l'Immagine Femminile Presentata della Letteratura Fumettistica e l'Immagine Che la Donna ha di se Stessa." *Ikon* (Milan). 23:84 (1973), pp. 79-118.

7038. Costa, Lorelisa. *Da Becassine a "Casque d'Ore."* Naples: Liguori Editore, 1979.

7039. Imbasciati, Antonio. "'Alika': Il Fumetto e la Satira Sociopolitica." *Ikon* (Milan). 23:85 (1973), pp. 23-47.

7040. Laterza, Rossella and Marisa Vinella. *Le Donne di Carta. Personaggi Femminili Nella Storia del Fumetto*. Bari: Dedalo, 1980.

7041. Spinazzola, Vittorio. "Donne e Fumetti." *Linus*. No. 37, 1968, pp. 1-5.

7042. Traverson, Giovanni, ed. *Official Catalog for Women in the Comics Exposition for the 5th International Comic Art Convention*. Genoa: Club Anni Trenta, 1982.

HISTORICAL ASPECTS

Caricature

7043. Blunt, A. and E. Croft-Murray. "Consul Smith's Album of Caricatures." *Venetian Drawings of the XVII and XVIII Centuries...at Windsor Castle*. London: Phaidon, 1957.

7044. Bouvy, Eugéne. "Notes sur la Caricature Italienne." *Arts et Métiers Graphiques*. September 15, 1932, pp. 115-122.

7045. Cima, Otto. *Mezzo Secolo di Caricatura Milanesa (1860-1910)*. Milan: Stabilimento Arte Grafiche Bertarelli, 1928.

7046. "Como se Ridi. Breve Storia della Caricatura." *La Domenica del Corriere* (Rome). 52:18.

7047. Croft-Murray, E. "Venetian Caricatures." In *Venetian Drawings of the XVII and XVIII Centuries in the Collection of Her Majesty the Queen, at Windsor Castle.* London: Phaidon, 1957.

7048. [Leonardo da Vinci Reproductions: (Untitled: Caricatures): Pen and Ink, ca. 1480]. *Connaissance des Arts.* June 1984, p. 42.

7049. G.E.C. *D'Annunzio nella Caricatura.* Milan: Garzante, Editore, 1941.

7050. G.E.C. *Gli Avvocatti nella Caricatura, "Tocchi e Toghe."* Torino: Grandi Edizioni Vega, n.d.

7051. G.E.C. *Il Cesare di Cartapesta. Mussolini nella Caricatura.* Torino: Grandi Edizioni Vega, n.d.

7052. G.E.C. *La Donna, la Moda, l'Amore in Tre Secoli di Caricatura.* Milan: Garzante, Editore, 1942.

7053. G.E.C. "La Storia dei Nostri Giorni in Quindice Anni de Caricatura. I—La Donna Conquista il Potere." *L'Europeo* (Rome). November 2, 1958; II—"Il Sesso Forte Depone le Armi." *L'Europeo*, November 9, 1958; III—"Il Piú Comico Colonello del Mondo." *L'Europeo.* November 16, 1958; IV—"Segnorine e Vecchi Ministri." *L'Europeo.* November 23, 1958.

7054. G.E.C. *La Vita é Dura Ma é Comica. 1890-1915.* Milan: Garzante, Editore, 1940.

7055. "Sessante Anni di Cinema nella Caricatura. I—Dammi una Sigaretta." *L'Europeo.* January 8, 1959; II—"Il Figli—delle Ombre." *L'Europeo.* January 15 1959.

7056. Gianeri, Enrico. *Storia della Caricatura.* Milan: 1959.

7057. Musacchio, C. *Come Li Ho Visti. Ritratti de Contemporanei Disegnati da C. Musacchio.* Preface by Diego Angeli. Rome: Edizione Musacchio, 1913-1914.

7058. Musacchio, C. *"Contemporanei," (1915-1921) Caricature e Ritratti Disegnati dal Vero da Musacchio.* Rome: Fratelli, Palombi, 1922. 167 pp.

7059. Novello, Giuseppe. *Che Cosa Dirá la Gente?* Milan: A. Mondadori, 1937.

7060. Petrucci, Carlo Alberto. *La Caricatura Italiana dell'Ottocento.* Rome: 1954.

7061. Teall, G.C. "Italian As a Caricaturist." *The Bookman.* July 1908, pp. 477-484.

7062. Teja (Casimiro). *Caricature di Teja dal "Pasquino." (1856-1897).* Annotated by Augusto Ferrero. Torino: Roux e Viarengo Editori, 1900.

Comics

7063. Abbà, A. and F. Rossi. "I Fumetti. Indagine Comparativa Sulle Letture dei Ragazzi." In *Società Umanitaria, Lettura Giovanile e Cultura Populare in Italia.* Florence: 1962.

7064. Bargellini, P. "Fumetti e Fumetti." *Indice d'Oro* (Siena). October 1952.

7065. Barilla, Giuseppe. "Il Fumetto Sta Conquistando la Nuova Generazione di Narratori." *Il Messaggero* (Rome). January 16, 1967.

7066. Becciu, Leonardo. *Il Fumetto in Italia.* Florence: Sansoni, 1971. 356 pp.

7067. Bertieri, Claudio. "Anhole in the Desert." *Photographia Italiana.* No. 156, 1970.

7068. Bertieri, Claudio. "Banda Stagnata e Banda Disegnata." *Finsider* (Rome). No. 6, 1967.

7069. Bertieri, Claudio. *Gli Eroi dei Tempo-Libero.* Padua: Ed. "Radar," 1968.

7070. Bertieri, Claudio. "Il Delatore Degli Anni 60." *Il Lavoro Nuovo.* June 24, 1965.

7071. Bertieri, Claudio. "I Quadretti della Rivoluzione d'Ottobre." *Il Lavoro.* November 3, 1967.

7072. Bertieri, Claudio. "Italie." In *Histoire Mondiale de la Bande Dessinée,* edited by Pierre Horay, pp. 102-127. Paris: Pierre Horay Éditeur, 1989.

7073. Bertieri, Claudio. "L'Invasione Degli Ultracorpi." *Il Lavoro.* June 22, 1963.

7074. Bertieri, Claudio. "L'Uomo Vestito di Grigio." *Il Lavoro.* August 11, 1967.

7075. Bertieri, Claudio. "Moonday." *Sgt. Kirk.* No. 27, 1969.

7076. Bertieri, Claudio. "Novità per l'Estate." *Il Lavoro.* 1966.

7077. Bertieri, Claudio. "A Ondate Successive." *Il Lavoro.* December 1, 1967.

7078. Bertieri, Claudio. "Tempo di Posters." *Il Lavoro.* January 26, 1968.

7079. Bertieri, Claudio. "Un Principe Spericolato alla Corte di Re Artú." *Il Lavoro Nuovo*. July 24, 1965.

7080. Bertieri, Claudio. "Un Radar per i Giovanni." *Il Lavoro*. January 12, 1968.

7081. Bertieri, Claudio. "We Are Comin' with Spirit of Peace." *Comics* (Lucca). 1969.

7082. Biamonte, S.G. "I Fumetti Cantano." *Sgt. Kirk*. No. 11-12, 1968, pp. 14-18.

7083. Biamonte, S.G. "La Folk Cronaca dei Cantastorie." *Linus*. No. 37, 1968, pp. 69-72.

7084. Biamonte, S.G. "S.O.S. Svalbard." *Sgt. Kirk*. No. 5, 1967, pp. 1-3.

7085. Bono, Giani. "The Great Comic Book Heroes." *Comics World*. No. 1, 1968.

7086. Brunoro, Gianni. "I Periodici Giovanili Non a Fumetti (II)." *Sgt. Kirk*. No. 9, 1968, pp. 25-28.

7087. Brunoro, Gianni. "Periodici Illustrati Non a Fumetti." *Sgt. Kirk*. No. 8, 1968, pp. 1-5.

7088. Cuccinelli. "Fumetti e Fumettismo." *Studi Cattolici* (Rome). September 1959, pp. 62-64.

7089. Cupisti, Claudio. "Il Calcio Ilustrato." *Il Fumetto*. September 1973, p. 59.

7090. Di Giacomo, Franco. "I Fumetti Inglesi Dagli Inizi al' 30." *I Fumetti, Instituto della Pedagogia dell' Università di Roma*. June 1967, pp. 127-134.

7091. Della Corte, Carlos. "Anche Gli Eroi (Gualche Volta) Muoiono." *Eureka*. No. 5, 1968, pp. 1-4.

7092. Della Corte, Carlos. "I Comics in Italia, Oggi." *Almanacco Letterario Bompiani*. 1963.

7093. Della Corte, Carlos. "I Generosi Eroi Chifanno Amare la Vita." *Oggi Ilustrato*. August 30, 1964.

7094. Della Corte, Carlos. "Nuovi Eroi del Fumetto." *Avanti*. August 23, 1955.

7095. Della Corte, Carlos. "Una Bella Coppia." *Eureka*. No. 2, 1967, pp. 1-4.

7096. Ferraro, Ezio. "La Storia del Giornalismo Italiano." *Sgt. Kirk*. No. 11-12, 1968, pp. 53-67.

7097. "Filmografia Essenziale Sonora Dei Comics (1931-1967)." *Teatro e Cinema*. April-September 1967, pp. 43-59.

7098. Gasca, Luis. "Giulietta Degli Fumetti." *Film Ideal* (Rome). No. 186, 1965.

7099. Gazzarri, Michele and Piero Carpi. *Un Eroe Degli Anni Trenta.* 1967.

7100. "Gli Eroi del Nostro Tempo." *Le Ore.* January 6, 1966, p. 36.

7101. "L'Eleganza di Sto." *Linus.* No. 42, 1968, pp. 1-5.

7102. Martinori, Nato. "Fumetti Che Passione! I Vecchi Fumetti Degli Anni Trenta Tornano nelle Edicole in Una Serie de Ristampe." *Vita* (Rome). No. 442, 1967, pp. 36-37.

7103. Mosca, Benedetto. "Anche i Fumetti Hanno la Loro Storia." *L'Europeo.* March 10-24, 1957.

7104. Pezzangora, Luigi. *160 Cronologie del Fumetto Italiano dal 1945 al 1960.* Padova: Fumetto Club, 1980.

7105. Riha, Karl. "I Problemi dei Fumetti." *I Problemi della Pedagogia* (Rome). 13:4-5 (1967), pp. 696-710.

7106. Traini, Rinaldo. "La Tecnica dei 'Comics' Italiani dal 1930 al 1943." *I Fumetti* (Rome). No. 9, 1967, pp. 115-122.

7107. Traini, Rinaldo and Sergio Trinchero. "Ils Sont Fous Ces Romains." *Hobby.* No. 4, 1967.

7108. Trinchero, Sergio. "Abbecedario dei Fumetti 1A, 2A, 3B, 4B, 5B, 6B, 7B, 8B, 9C, 10C, 11C, 12C, 13C, 14C, 15C, 16C." *Ciccio e Franco.* No. 1-16, 1967-1968.

7109. Trinchero, Sergio. "Bella Copia." *Hobby.* No. 3, 1967.

7110. Trinchero, Sergio. "Breve Cronistoria di un Personaggio Intramontabile." *L'Uomo Mascherato, Albi Fratelli Spada.* No. 22, 1962.

7111. Trinchero, Sergio. "Cronaca e Fumetti." *Sgt. Kirk.* No. 27, 1969.

7112. Trinchero, Sergio. "Il Fumetto Nero." *Hobby.* November 1966.

7113. Trinchero, Sergio. "Il Re del Mare." *Eureka-Natale* (Genoa). December 1968.

7114. Trinchero, Sergio. "L'Abbecedario dei Fumetti (A1, A2, A3)." *Gli Sdragoli* (Genoa). No. 1-3, 1968-1969.

7115. Trinchero, Sergio. "L'Abbecedario dei Fumetti (A1)-Ripetizione." *Gli Sdragoli* (Genoa). No. 4, 1969.

7116. Trinchero, Sergio. "L'Ultimo Signore della Foresta." *Sgt. Kirk.* No. 29, 1969.

7117. Trinchero, Sergio. "Mini-Notizie." *Hobby.* November 1966.

7118. Trinchero, Sergio. "Notizie, Notizie, Notizie." *Supplemento: Super Albo.* No. 66, 1964.

7119. Trinchero, Sergio. "Nuovi e Vecchi Eroi." *Sgt. Kirk.* No. 30, 1969.

7120. Trinchero, Sergio. "Ritorno alla Caverna." *Momento-Sera.* August 29, 1965.

7121. Trinchero, Sergio. "Ritorno a Mun...." *Il Cavernicolo Uup.* July 1965.

7122. Trinchero, Sergio. "Un Cavernicolo en Turist." *Comic Art in Paper Back.* No. 3, 1966.

7123. Trinchero, Sergio. "Un Italiano a Cartoonland." *Sgt. Kirk.* No. 16, 1968, pp. 49-51.

7124. Trinchero, Sergio and Giorgio Salvucci. *I Giornaletti* (Rome). Edizione "Revival," 1971.

7125. Trinchero, Sergio and Giorgio Salvucci. "I Periodici Italiani a Fumetti." *Comics, Archivio Italiano della Stampa a Fumetti* (Rome). September 1966, pp. 28-30.

7126. Zanotto, Piero. "Due Serials Degli Anni Trenta." *La Biennale.* No. 61, 1967.

7127. Zanotto, Piero. "I Fantacomics." *Sgt. Kirk.* No. 3, 1967, pp. 1-3.

7128. Zanotto, Piero. "La Storia del Fumetto Italiano del Cattivo Ribo a Neutron." *Il Gazzettino.* November 21, 1967.

7129. Zanotto, Piero. "Ritornano Altri Eroi del Fumetto." *Nazione Sera* (Florence). November 22, 1966.

7130. Zanotto, Piero. "Sulle Nuvole delle Storie a Fumetti, le Testoline dei Fanciulli d'Oggi." *Gazzettino Sera.* March 6, 1958.

7131. Zanotto, Piero. "Sulle Nuvole delle Storie a Fumetti, le Testoline dei Fanciulli d'Oggi." *Sicilia del Popolo* (Palermo). March 8, 1958.

7132. Zolla, Elémire. "Storia del Fumetto." *Gazzetta del Popolo.* December 1, 1960.

LEGAL ASPECTS

7133. Albertarelli, Rino. "La Questione del Fumetto." *Uomini e Idea* (Milan). No. 2, 1966.

7134. Alessi-Conte, Andrea. "I Fumetti Neri e la Legge." *Fantascienza Minore* (Milan). Special number, 1967, pp. 57-60.

7135. Carpi, Piero and Michele Gazzarri. *Libertà di Fumetti.* 1967.

7136. Colella, D. "Orrori Assortiti per Fumetti Neri." *Nuovi Orizzonti* (Milan). No. 9, 1966.

7137. Conte, Francesco P. "Si o No alla Censura Sui Fumetti?" *I Fumetti* (Rome). No. 9, 1967, pp. 19-26.

7138. Cosimini, Eliana. "Piu Forte di Ercole nei Fumetti une Scanzonato Nipote di Maciste." *Gazzetta del Popolo del Lunedi* (Genoa). February 22, 1965.

7139. Cuccolini, Giulio. "Ordinaria Amministrazione." *Comic Art.* No. 46, 1988, p. 75.

7140. Della Corte, Carlos. "I Fumetti in Purgatorio." *Ulisse* (Rome). July 1961.

7141. Franciosa, Massimo. "Le Nuvole Sotto Controllo." *Lavoro Illustrato.* March 1952.

7142. "Fumetti Neri." *Corriere della Sera* (Milan). Fall 1966.

7143. "Fumetti Neri." *Vita* (Rome). Fall 1966.

7144. Gazzarri, Michele. *Libertà di Fumetto.* Milan: 1967.

7145. Grimaldi, Patricia. "Considerazioni su un Campione di Ragazzi Dichiaratisi Non Lettori di 'Comics.'" *I Fumetti* (Rome). No. 9, 1967, pp. 81-86.

7146. "Il Governo é Andato Nello Spazio." *Epoca* (Milan). May 22, 1966.

7147. "La Stampa Periodica Vuole Difendere la Sua Independenza." *Epoca* (Milan). October 22, 1967, p. 35.

7148. Ormezzano, Gianpaolo. "L'Italie a le Mal du Sexe." *Plexus* (Paris). No. 14, 1968, pp. 140-144.

7149. Pompi, G.B. "Fumetti Seconda Cartella." *Indice d'Oro.* March, 1950.

7150. Rava, Enzo. "Fallito il Tentativo di Mettere ai Fumetti la Museruola della Censura." *Paese Sera* (Milan). September 26, 1966.

7151. Sansoni, Gino. "C'è Nero e Nero." *I Fumetti*. No. 9, 1967, pp. 27-34.

7152. Traini, Rinaldo. "Il Copyrights." *Sgt. Kirk*. No. 9, 1968, pp. 55-65.

7153. Zanotto, Piero. "In Mr. Spaghetti i Difetti Degli Italiani." *Il Gazzettino* (Venice). January 11, 1966.

CARTOONISTS and CARICATURISTS

7154. Bernazzali, Nino. "Artisti Italiani Aurelio Galleppini." *Comics World* (Genoa). No. 1, 1968.

7155. Caradec, François, ed. *I Primi Eroi*. Presentazione di René Clair. Milan: Garzanti, 1962, 1965.

7156. Coco, Giuseppe. *C'Est Grave, Docteur?* Grenoble: Glénat, 1984.

7157. Coco, Giuseppe. *Coco. VIP. Costumi e Scostumi*. Milan: Rizzoli, 1987. 91 pp.

7158. Doeller, Stefan. "Franco Caprioli. Comickunst aus Italien." *Comixene. Das Comicfachmagazin*. 6:23 (1979), pp. 52-53.

7159. Groensteen, Thierry. "Entretien avec Silvio Cadelo." *Les Cahiers de la Bande Dessinée* (Grenoble). 71, 1986, pp. 70-73.

7160. Groensteen, Thierry. "Magnus. Les Deux Visages de Raviola." *Les Cahiers de la Bande Dessinée* (Grenoble). 72, 1986, pp. 81-84. (a.k.a. Roberto Raviola).

7161. "Intervista per...Lettera con Vincenzo Baggioli, lo Scrittore de Fulmine." *Collana Anni Trenta*. August 1, 1967.

7162. Kaps, Joachim. "Mattotti Seit Feuer." *Comic Info*. May-June 1993, pp. 19-27. (Lorenzo Mattotti).

7163. "Liviano Riva, Italy." *FECO News*. No. 7, 1989, p. 11.

7164. "Marco Lupoi." *Comics Interview*. No. 60, 1988, pp. 38-53.

7165. "Maria Assunta Toti-Buratti." *Apropos*. No. 5, 1988, pp. 78-80.

7166. Moretto, Mauro. "Portfolio." *La Borsa del Fumetto*. No. 1, 1979, pp. 7-18.

7167. Niffle, Frédéric. "Entretien avec Liberatore." *Les Cahiers de la Bande Dessinée* (Grenoble). 71, 1986, pp. 46-49. (Gaetano Liberatore).

7168. "Paolozzi: Geschichte vom Nichts." *Der Spiegel*. No. 8, 1969, p. 131.

7169. Pedrocchi, Carlo. "Federico Pedrocchi." *Linus*. No. 39, 1968, pp. 1-8.

7170. "Portfolio: Romano Garofalo." *La Borsa del Fumetto*. March 1980, pp. 5-28.

7171. "Portfolio Terenghi." *La Borsa del Fumetto*. September 1979, pp. 9-25. (Antonio Terenghi).

7172. Sisci, Francesco. "Je Me Souviens de Valvoline." *Les Cahiers de la Bande Dessinée* (Grenoble). 71, 1986, pp. 50-53. (Roberto Baldazzini, Daniele Brolli, Charles Burns, Giorgio Carpinteri, Massimo Giacon, Igort (alias Igor Tuveri), Marcello Jori, Massimo Mattioli, Lorenzo Mattotti).

7173. Trinchero, Sergio. "Hanno Detto de.... L'Uomo Mascherato: Carlo Della Corte." *L'Uomo Mascherato*. No. 51, 1963. Fratelli Spada.

7174. Zanotto, Piero. "Almanacco Linus con Bibi Cianuro." *Tribuna del Mezzogiorno* (Messina). February 25, 1966.

7175. Zanotto, Piero. *Il Mito dei Mari del Sud nel Fumetto di Cappioli a Pratt*. Galliano: Vallagarina, 1976.

7176. Zanotto, Piero. "I Pagot Brothers." *Linus*. 4:34 (1968), pp. 1-5.

7177. Zanotto, Piero. "René Clair Presenta: I Primi Eroi." *Tribuna del Mezzogiorno* (Messina). February 18, 1963.

7178. Zapperi, Roberto. "I Ritratti di Antonio Carracci." *Paragone*. July 1987, pp. 3-22.

Battaglia, Dino

7179. "Battaglia par Lui-Même." *Les Cahiers de la Bande Dessinée* (Grenoble). 57, 1984, p. 38.

7180. Delperdange, Patrick. "Battaglia et Maupassant: Les Deux Amis." *Les Cahiers de la Bande Dessinée*. 57, 1984, p. 39.

7181. "Lire Battaglia." *Les Cahiers de la Bande Dessinée*. 57, 1984, p. 40.

7182. Mollica, Vincenzo, ed. *Dino Battaglia*. Montepulciano (Siena): Editori del Grifo, 1981.

7183. Van Belle, Anita. "Battaglia le Méconnu." *Les Cahiers de la Bande Dessinée*. 57, 1984, pp. 37-38.

Buzzatti, Dino

7184. Buzzatti, Dino. *Orphi und Eura*. Berlin: Propyläen-Verlag, 1970.

7185. "Buzzatti: Strip von Orfi." *Der Spiegel*. No. 49, 1969, pp. 192-194.

Crepax, Guido

7186. Alber, Wolfgang. "Guido Crepax." *Comic Forum. Das Österreichische Fachmagazin für Comicliteratur*. 3:9 (1981), pp. 33-35.

7187. Augusto, Sergio. "A Revolucao de Guido Crepax." *Jornal do Brasil*. August 25, 1967.

7188. Bletter, Diana K. "Interview mit Guido Crepax." *Comic Forum. Das Österreichische Fachmagazin für Comicliteratur*. 3:10 (1981), pp. 41-43.

7189. Buschmann, Christel. "Valentina von Guido Crepax." *Die Zeit*. May 7, 1971, p. 22.

7190. Champarnaud, François. "La Justine de Sade, Vue par la Bande Dessinée." *Critique* (Paris). 38:425 (1982), pp. 871-875.

7191. Crepax, Guido. *The Man from Harlem*. New York: Catalan Communications, 1987. 52 pp.

7192. Grange, Dominique. "Traduire...Dit-Elle." *Schtroumpf. Les Cahiers de la Bande Dessinée*. 52, 1982, pp. 43-45.

7193. Groensteen, Thierry. "Entretien avec Guido Crepax." *Schtroumpf. Les Cahiers de la Bande Dessinée*. 52, 1982, pp. 9-20.

7194. Kockerbeck, Christoph. "Guido Crepax. Zur Entwicklung Seines Zeichenstils." *Comic Forum. Das Österreichische Fachmagazin für Comicliteratur*. 3:10 (1981), pp. 33-39.

7195. Lefevre, Gaston. "Neutron di Guido Crepax." *Rantanplan*. No. 6, 1967, pp. 7-9.

7196. Longatti, Alberto. "Fumetti di Guido Crepax." In *Ausstellungskatalog*, La Colonna, 1968. Como.

7197. Mollica, Vincenzo and Mauro Paganelli. *Guido Crepax. Aus dem Italienischen Ubersetzt von Dorian Ling*. Munich: BAHIA Verlag, 1981.

7198. Natoli, Dario. "Fra' Salmastro di Lenari ed i Pirati Spaziali di Crepax." *Fantascienza Minore*. Special number, 1967, pp. 22-24.

7199. Natoli, Dario. "Fra' Salmastro di Lenari ed i Pirati Spaziali di Crepax." *L'Unità*. February 9, 1967.

7200. Roux, Antoine. "Histoires de Pirates." *Schtroumpf. Les Cahiers de la Bande Dessinée*. 52, 1982, pp. 37-40.

7201. Rusconi, Marisa. "Il Dottor Crepax, Suppongo...." *Linus*. No. 44, 1968, pp. 1-9.

7202. Tamine, Jean-Pierre. "Un Nouveau Jeu des Images." *Schtroumpf. Les Cahiers de la Bande Dessinée*. 52, 1982, pp. 25-28.

7203. Van Cauwenbergh, Franz. "Bibliographie." *Schtroumpf. Les Cahiers de la Bande Dessinée*. 52, 1982, pp. 47-48.

7204. Zanotto, Piero. "Brasse e Crepax col Cuore in Gola." *Sgt. Kirk*. No. 5, 1967, pp. 42-45.

Ghezzi, Pier L.

7205. Bodart, Didier. "Disegni Giovanili Inediti di P.L. Ghezzi Nella Biblioteca Vaticana." *Palatino*. April-June 1967, pp. 141-154.

7206. Bodart, Didier. "Pier Leone Ghezzi, the Draftsman." *Print Collector*. March-April 1976, pp. 12-31.

7207. Clark, A.M. "Pier Leone Ghezzi's Portraits." *Paragone*. September 1963, pp. 11-21.

7208. Ferrero, Augusto. *Caricature di Teja (Casimiro) dal "Pasquino" (1856-1897)*. Torino: Roux e Viarengo Editori, 1900.

7209. "Ghezzi, Pier Leone: 1674-1755. Caricatures of Vandieres, Marigny, le Blanc, Soufflot and Cochin." *The Art Bulletin*. March 1990, p. 81.

7210. Olszewski, Edward J. "The New World of Pier Leone Ghezzi." *Art Journal*. Winter 1983, pp. 325-330.

Giardino, Vittorio

7211. "Bibliographie de Vittorio Giardino." *Les Cahiers de la Bande Dessinée*. 71, 1986, p. 36.

7212. Giardino, Vittorio. *Hungarian Rhapsody*. The Adventures of Max Friedman, No. 1. New York: Catalan Communications, 1986. 96 pp.

7213. Giardino, Vittorio. *Orient Gateway*. The Adventures of Max Friedman, No. 2. New York: Catalan Communications, 1987. 64 pp.

7214. Groensteen, Thierry. "Entretien avec Vittorio Giardino." *Les Cahiers de la Bande Dessinée*. 71, 1986, pp. 8-14.

Giovannetti, Pericle L.

7215. Giovannetti, Max. *Max*. Paris: L'École des Loisirs, 1978.

7216. Giovannetti, Pericle Luigi. *Beware of the Dog*. New York: Macmillan, 1958.

7217. Giovannetti, Pericle Luigi. *Birds Without Words*. New York: Macmillan, 1961. Unpaginated.

7218. Giovannetti, Pericle Luigi. *Nothing But Max*. New York: Macmillan, 1959. 85 pp.

7219. Giovannetti, Pericle Luigi. *The Penguin Max*. London: Penguin, 1962. Unpaginated.

Manara, Maurillo (Milo)

7220. Dellisse, Luc. "Avec Machines, Moi Machin." *Les Cahiers de la Bande Dessinée*. 64, 1985, pp. 84-86.

7221. Groensteen, Thierry. "Manara." *Les Cahiers de la Bande Dessinée*. 64, 1985, p. 74.

7222. Lecigne, Bruno and Jean-Pierre Tamine. "Un Manuel du Vide." *Les Cahiers de la Bande Dessinée*. 64, 1985, pp. 80-83.

7223. Legaristi, Francisco. "Monocomics (Manara)." *Trix*. No. 3 (n.d.), p. 35.

7224. Manara, Milo. *Click!* New York: Catalan Communications, 1985. 56 pp.

7225. Manara, Milo. *The Paper Man*. New York: Catalan Communications, 1986. 54 pp.

7226. Manara, Milo and Silverio Pisu. *The Ape*. New York: Catalan Communications, 1986. 86 pp.

7227. Manara, Milo and Hugo Pratt. *Indian Summer*. New York: Catalan Communications, 1986. 151 pp.

7228. Mollica, Vincenzo. *Manara*. Hounoux: SEDLI, Jacky Goupil, 1983.

7229. "Monocomics: Maurillo (Milo) Manara." *Trix*. No. 3, p. 26.

7230. Paganelli, Mauro and Patrizia Zanotti, eds. *Milo Manara*. Munich: Verlag Schreiber und Leser, 1986.

7231. Tschernegg, Markus. "Milo Manara. Das Große Abenteuer. Übersetzt von R. Schreiber." *Comic Forum. Das Österreichische Fachmagazin für Comicliteratur*. 2:7/8 (1980), pp. 88-91.

Pericoli, Tullio

7232. *Furti ad Arte: Italo Calvino e Tullio Pericoli*. Milan: Edizioni della Galleria Il Milione, 1980. (Catalogue).

7233. Heller, Steven. "Tullio Pericoli and the Power of Gesture." *U and l.c.* Summer 1990, pp. 38-41.

7234. Pericoli, Tullio. *Contessa Che è Mai la Vita*. Milan: 1970.

7235. Pericoli, Tullio. *Fogli di Vita*. Turin: 1976.

7236. Pericoli, Tullio. *I Mostri Descritti da Pintor e Disegnati da Pericoli*. Rome: 1976.

7237. Pericoli, Tullio. *Le Gioie dell'Occhio*. Milan: 1981.

7238. Pericoli, Tullio, with Emanuele Pirella. *Cronache di Palazzo*. Milan: 1979.

7239. Pericoli, Tullio, with Emanuele Pirella. *Falsetto*. Milan: 1982.

7240. Pericoli, Tullio, with Emanuele Pirella. *Identikit di Illustri Sconosciuti*. Milan: 1974.

7241. Pericoli, Tullio, with Emanuele Pirella. *Il Centro Sinistra Biodegradato*. Florence: 1975.

7242. Pericoli, Tullio, with Emanuele Pirella. *Il Dottor Rigolo*. Milan: 1976.

7243. Pericoli, Tullio, with Emanuele Pirella. *Tutti da Fulvia*. Milan: 1987.

7244. Pericoli, Tullio, with Emanuele Pirella. *Tutti da Fulvia Sabato Sera*. Milan: 1978.

7245. *Pericoli-Pirella*. Milan: Centro di Studi e Archivo della Comunicazione, Università di Parma, 1978. (Catalogue).

7246. Ramseger, Georg. "Tullio Pericoli." *Graphis*. March/April 1989, pp. 82-89.

7247. *Tullio Pericoli, Disegni per Robinson, Paesaggi e Personaggi*. Texts by Umberto Eco, Tullio Pericoli, Francesco Poli. Milan: 1985. (Catalogue).

7248. *Tullio Pericoli, Geologie dell'Io*. Milan: Istituto di Storia dell'Arte, Università di Parma, 1972. (Catalogue).

7249. *Tullio Pericoli, Le Copertine di Repubblica*. Rome: Galleria Il Segno, 1986. (Catalogue).

7250. *Tullio Pericoli, Paesaggio Italiano*. Text by Giulio Carlo Argan. Milan: Studio Marconi, 1982. (Catalogue).

7251. *Tullio Pericoli, Quarantanove Ritratti*. Texts by Francesco Poli, Enrico Castelnuovo. *L'Indice*, 1987. (Catalogue).

Pratt, Hugo

7252. Alber, Wolfgang and Markus Tschernegg. "Gespräch Mit Hugo Pratt." *Comic Forum. Das Österreichische Fachmagazin für Comicliteratur*. 4:14 (1982), pp. 62-67.

7253. Arbesú, Faustino R. "Lo Que Nunca se Dijo Sobre Hugo Pratt." *El Wendigo*. No. 57, 1992, pp. 7-9.

7254. Arrouye, Jean. "Images Aveugles Chez... Pratt." *Bédésup*. 17, 1981, pp. 11-13.

7255. Arrouye, Jean. "Images Aveugles Chez Pratt." In *A la Rencontre de... Hugo Pratt*, edited by Collectif, pp. 73-77. Marseilles: Bédésup, 1983.

7256. Centre d'Etude et de Documentation sur l'Image de la Bibliothèque Municipale de Marseille. "Bibliographie." In *A la Rencontre de... Hugo Pratt*, edited by Collectif, pp. 134-136. Marseilles: Bédésup, 1983.

7257. Chante, Alain. "Les Héros de Pratt: Spectateurs ou Acteurs." *Bédésup*. 17, 1981, pp. 19-22.

7258. Collectif. *A la Rencontre de... Hugo Pratt*. Marseilles: Bédésup, 1983.

7259. de Blas, Juan Antonio. "Du Soleil, du Sable et de la Mort." In *A la Rencontre de... Hugo Pratt*, edited by Collectif, pp. 103-110. Marseilles: Bédésup, 1983.

7260. Delafuente, Francisco. "Ugo Pratt." *U.N. Special*. No. 222, 1968.

7261. Faur, Jean-Claude. "Comment Je Suis Devenu l'Éditeur d'Hugo Pratt." *L'Hebdo de la B.D.* No. 12, 1992, pp. 1-6.

7262. Fossati, Franco. "Incontro con Ugo Pratt." *Comics World*. No. 1, 1968.

7263. Grande Loge de France. "Les Symboles Maçonniques dans 'Fables de Venise.'" In *A la Rencontre de... Hugo Pratt*, edited by Collectif, pp. 43-49. Marseilles: Bédésup, 1983.

7264. Jongue, Serge. "Hugo Pratt: Visages de l'Aventure et Silences de la Narration." *La Nouvelle Barre du Jour* (Quebec). February 1982, pp. 71-77.

7265. Magoni, Andreas, Mauro Marcheselli, Spiri and Giorgio Zambotto. "Entrevue avec Hugo Pratt." In *A la Rencontre de... Hugo Pratt*, edited by Collectif, pp. 111-131. Marseilles: Bédésup, 1983.

7266. Moliterni, Claude. "H. Pratt Parle de Corto Maltese." *Phénix*. No. 14, 1970.

7267. Mollica, Vincenzo and Mauro Paganelli. *Hugo Pratt*. Montepulciano: Editori del Grifo, 1980.

7268. Mollica, Vincenzo and Mauro Paganelli. *Pratt*. Hounoux: SEDLI, Jacky Goupil, 1984.

7269. Pohl, Peter. "Hugo Pratt + Comicographie." *Comic Forum*. 8:32 (1986), pp. 22-24.

7270. Pohl, Peter. "Von Wheeling nach Doumera." *Comic Forum*. 8:32 (1986), pp. 19-20.

7271. Pratt, Hugo. "Hugo Pratt." *Sgt. Kirk*. No. 6, 1967, pp. 89-91.

7272. Pratt, Hugo. *Univers de Hugo Pratt*. Neuilly-sur-Seine: Dargaud, 1984.

7273. Roux, Antoine. "Hugo Qui ne Dit Mots... Qu'on Sent..." *Bédésup*. 17, 1981, pp. 28-30; 18/19, 1981, pp. 38-44.

7274. Saint-Michel, Serge. "Néo-Réalisme et Baroque Contemporain Chez Hugo Pratt." In *A la Rencontre de... Hugo Pratt*, edited by Collectif, pp. 69-71. Marseilles: Bédésup, 1983.

7275. Sanders, Alain. "Hugo Pratt, Ce Vieux Facho Honteux." In *A la Rencontre de... Hugo Pratt*, edited by Collectif, pp. 27-31. Marseilles: Bédésup, 1983.

7276. Tamine, Jean-Pierre. "Hugo Pratt et la Gnose." In *A la Rencontre de.. Hugo Pratt*, edited by Collectif, pp. 39-41. Marseilles: Bédésup, 1983.

7277. Tschernegg, Markus. "Hugo Pratt. Ein Comiczeichner der Weltklasse. (Einleitung zu): Corto Maltese. Entstehungsgeschichte." *Comic Forum*. 1:1 (1979), pp. 12-16.

Rubino, Antonio

7278. Albertarelli, Rino. "Antonio Rubino." *Linus*. No. 1, 1965.

7279. Albertarelli, Rino. "Antonio Rubino." *Phénix*. No, 3, 1967, pp. 34-36.

7280. Bertieri, Claudio. "I Personaggi di Antonio Rubino." *Il Lavoro* (Genoa). May 29, 1965.

7281. Bertieri, Claudio. "L'Universo Dementicato di Antonio Rubino." *Il Lavoro Nuovo*. March 14, 1965.

7282. Caldiron, Orio. "Rubino Liberty." *Sgt. Kirk*. No. 16, 1968, pp. 72-75.

CHARACTERS and TITLES

7283. Bertieri, Claudio. "Flipper Tutt o Beat." *Il Lavoro*. June 16, 1967.

7284. Bertieri, Claudio. "La Squadra Tumo." *Il Lavoro*. April 14, 1967.

7285. Bertieri, Claudio. "Trent Anni Dopo: il 'Bertoldo.'" *Il Lavoro*. August 25, 1967.

7286. Bertieri, Claudio. "Virus: the Sorcerer of the Dead Forest." *Sgt. Kirk*. April 1969. ("Virus, il Mago della Foresta Morta").

7287. Bono, Giani. "La Pipa." *Comics World*. No. 2, Special number, 1968.

7288. Bono, Giani. "Piccolo Re." *Sgt. Kirk*. No. 15, 1968, p. 67.

7289. Calisi, Romano. "Annibale Alle Porte." *Linus*. No. 3, 1965.

7290. Castelli, Alfredo. "Carnet di Tarzan." *Comics Club*. No. 1, 1967, pp. 45-56.

7291. De Giacomo, Franco, Ezio Ferraro and Georgio Salvucci. "L'Audace." *Linus*. No. 15, 1966, pp. 1-7.

7292. Fabrizzi, Paolo, Sergio Trinchero, and Rinaldo Traini. "Cirillino." *Mondo Domani*. August 25, 1968.

7293. Fenzo, Stellio. "Kiwi il Figlio della Jungla." *Sgt. Kirk*. No. 5, 1967, pp. 104-105.

7294. Ferrari, Giorgio. *Sturmtruppen. Il Fumetto di Satira Antimilitarista*. Milan: Gammalibri, 1983.

7295. Ferraro, Ezio. "Buck il Primo." *Sgt. Kirk*. No. 8, 1968, pp. 26-31.

7296. Fossati, Franco. "Magnas." *Fantasy*. November-December 1966.

7297. La Polla, Franco. "A Note on *Marcovaldo*." *The Review of Contemporary Fiction*. Summer 1986, pp. 38-41.

7298. Lecigne, Bruno. "Relecture: Zorry Kid. Une Esthétique un Remplissage." *Les Cahiers de la Bande Dessinée*. 62, 1985, pp. 72-75.

7299. Mariani, Enzo. "Thunder Agents." *Fantascienza Minore*. Special number, 1967, pp. 55-56.

7300. Naviglio, L. "Selene." *Nuovi Orizzanti*. No. 4, 1967. ("Il Cinque della Selena").

7301. Prever, Giorgio. "Alfy il Robot. La Coscienza Critica e le Sue Transformazioni." *Sgt. Kirk*. No. 6, 1967, p. 49.

7302. "Romanità, Sesso e Fumetto." *L'Europeo*. January 27, 1966.

7303. Rusconi, Marisa. "L'Amico Licantropo." *Settimana Incom*. No. 44, 1965, pp. 44-47.

7304. Seal, Basil. "L' Inimitable George." *Linus*. 4:45 (1968), pp. 1-10.

7305. Traini, Rinaldo. "Indian River." *Sgt. Kirk*. No. 3, 1967, p. 31.

7306. Trinchero, Sergio. "Bonghy Bo Contro Gli Ononoes." *Hobby*. No. 4, 1967.

7307. Trinchero, Sergio. "La Balma Chiamata Goliath." *La Tribuna Italiana*. No. 16, 1970.

7308. Trinchero, Sergio. "Quattro Chiacchiere su Johnny Azzardo." *Gli Eroi dell' Avventura*. No. 17, 1963, Vita Editore. ("Johnny Hazard").

7309. Trinchero, Sergio. "I Saturniani e Barbra." *Sgt. Kirk*. No. 25, 1969.

7310. Zanotto, Piero. "Beppe, Cucciolo, Tiramolla Nuovi Idoli dei Più Piceini." *Corriere di Trieste*. March 18, 1958.

7311. Zanotto, Piero. "Chi Vuole Uccidere Jessie?" *Linus* (Milan). No. 19, 1966; *Planeta*. No. 13, 1966.

7312. Zanotto, Piero. "Il Complesso Facile di Bernard e Dorothy." *Sgt. Kirk*. No. 7, 1968, pp. 73-76.

"Archibaldo e Petronilla" ("Bringing Up Father")

7313. Del Buono, Oreste. "Archibaldo e Petronilla." *Garzanti*. 1966.

7314. Fabrizzi, Paolo, Sergio Trinchero, and Rinaldo Traini. "Arcibaldo e Petronilla." *Mondo Domani*. September 22, 1968.

"Asso di Picche"

7315. Castelli, Alfredo. "Phantom Made in Italy. L'Asso di Picche." *Comics*. April 1966, pp. 14-15.

7316. Faustinelli, Mario. "Davide Uno dell' Asso." *Sgt. Kirk*. No. 16, 1968, pp. 2-3.

7317. Ongaro, Alberto. "L'Asso di Picche." *Sgt. Kirk*. No. 6, 1967, pp. 72-74.

A-Z Comics

7318. Bertieri, Claudio. *A-Z Comics*. Genoa: Ed. "E.K.," 1969.

7319. Zanotto, Piero. "A-Z Comics." *Archivio Stampa a Fumetti*. October 1969.

"Bibi e Bibó"

7320. Bono, Giani. "Bibi e Bibó." *Sgt. Kirk*. No. 15, 1968, p. 66.

7321. Fabrizzi, Paolo, Sergio Trinchero, and Rinaldo Traini. "Bibi é Bibò" *Mondo Domani*. June 2, 1968.

"Bonaventura"

7322. Bertoluzzi, Attilio. "Bonaventura." Milan: Garzanti, 1964.

7323. Fabrizzi, Paolo and Sergio Trinchero. "Il Signor Bonaventura." *Mondo Domani*. October 20, 1968.

"Braccio di Ferro" ("Popeye")

7324. Banas, Pietro. "Omaggio a Braccio di Ferro." *Linus*. No. 40, 1968, pp. 1-7.

7325. Del Buono, Oreste. *Braccio di Ferro*. Milan: Garzanti, 1965.

"Corrierino"

7326. Bertieri, Claudio. "The New 'Corrierino.'" *Il Lavoro*. March 22, 1968.

7327. Vercelloni, Isa. "Il Vecchio Corrierino." *Linus*. No. 23, 1967, pp. 1-14.

"Corto Maltese"

7328. Brunoro, Gianni. "Corto Come un Romanzo." Illazioni su Corto Maltese, Ultimo Eroe Romantico. Presentazione di F. Quilici. Bari: Dedalo, 1984.

7329. "Corto Maltese." *La Borsa del Fumetto*. September 1979, pp. 4-5.

7330. de Blas, Jean Paul. "El Mundo Mágico de Corto Maltés." *SNIF: El Mitín del Nuevo Cómic* (México). September 1980, pp. 2-8.

7331. Fossati, Franco. "Corto Maltese ou le Signe du Succès." In *A la Rencontre de... Hugo Pratt*, edited by Collectif, pp. 7-12. Marseilles: Bédésup, 1983.

7332. Lofficier, R.J.M. and Fred Patten. "The Great European Comic Heroes. Corto Maltese." *Nemo*. December 1985, pp. 47-50.

7333. Pratt, Hugo. *Corto Maltese*. 4 Vols. New York: Nantier-Beall-Minoustchine, 1986-1987.

7334. Pratt, Hugo. *Corto Maltese, the Lagoon of Beautiful Dreams*. Paris: Publicness, 1972? 20 pp.

7335. Strzyz, Klaus. "Serie: Die Abenteurer (4): Corto Maltese." *Comixene. Das Comicfachmagazin*. 8:35 (1981), pp. 5-9.

7336. Thompson, Kim. "Corto Maltese." *Comics Journal*. May 1986, pp. 43-56.

"Diabolik"

7337. Albertarelli, Rino. "Diabolika Contestazione." *Linus*. 5:46 (1969), p. 34.

7338. Bertieri, Claudio. "Doolittle e Diabolik." *Il Lavoro*. February 23, 1968, p. 3.

7339. "Deux Institutrices Enfoncent James Bond/Elles Inventent Diabolik, un Superman, et en Font un Héros de Cinéma." *Paris-Match*. May 4, 1968.

7340. Goimard, Jacques. "Danger, Diabolik." *Fiction* (Paris). No. 175, 1968, pp. 143-144.

7341. Latona, Robert. "Diabolik." *Vanguard*. No. 2, 1968, pp. 16-17.

7342. Marini, A. "...Che Cosa Avete Contro Diabolik?" *Linus*. No. 15, 1966.

7343. Pottar, O. "Diabolik et Satanik, ou le Conformisme du Sexe." *Arts* (Paris). August 10, 1966.

7344. Tortora, Enzo. "I Figli di 007, Sadik, Diabolik, Magik, Kriminal." *La Nazione*. May 12, 1965.

7345. Tornabuoni, Lietta. "Diabolik Protesta: Finalment si Fa il Film Sull'Eroe dei Fumetti Neri." *L'Europeo*. July 13, 1967, pp. 56-61.

"Dick Fulmine"

7346. Alessandrini, Ferruccio. "Il Mistero di Fulmine." *Collana Anni Trenta*. August 15, 1967.

7347. Cannata, Nino. "A Suon di Pugni Arriva Fulmine." *Avanti* (Milan). June 10, 1967.

7348. Della Corte, Carlos. "Il Favoloso Dick Fulmine." *Collana Anni Trenta*. No. 1, 1967, p. 4.

7349. De Turris, Gianfranco and S. Fusco. "Gli Anni di Dick Fulmine." *Linus*. No. 26, 1967, pp. 1-5.

7350. "Il Ritorno di Dick Fulmine." *L'Europeo*. July 13, 1967, p. 82.

7351. Zanotto, Piero. "Fu Fascista in Camicia Bianca il Forzutissima Dick Fulmine?" *Il Gazzettino* (Venice). November 11, 1967.

"Fortunello" ("Happy Hooligan")

7352. Bertoluzzi, Attilio. "Fortunello e la Cecca." Milan: Garzanti, 1965.

7353. Fabrizzi, Paolo, Sergio Trinchero and Rinaldo Traini. "Fortunello." *Mondo Domani.* June 30, 1968.

7354. Zanotto, Piero. "Il Ritorno di Fortunello." *Nazione Sera* (Florence). November 13, 1965.

"Il Cavernicolo Uup"

7355. Bertieri, Claudio. "Un Tempio per il Cavernicolo Uup." *Comics Almanacco, Salone Internazionale dei Comics*, Rome. June 1967, p. 60.

7356. Bertieri, Claudio. "Va a Zonzo per la Foresta Uup-Uup Candido Cavernicolo." *Il Lavoro Nuovo.* August 3, 1966.

7357. Natoli, Dario. "Arriva Uup." *L'Unità.* September 11, 1965.

7358. Zanotto, Piero. "Il Cavernicolo Uup." *Corriere del Giorno.* October 25, 1966.

"Kriminal" and "Satanik"

7359. Navire, Louis. "Horreur sur l'Écran: Kriminal." *Wampir*, edition Francés (Milan). No. 1, 1967, pp. 189-194.

7360. Patania, Luigi. "Satanik, Kriminal e C.: i Valori Se Ne Vanno in Fumetto." *L'Azione Giovanile.* April 13, 1965.

7361. Quarantotto, Claudio. "Satanik, Kriminal, Fantax e Co." *Il Borghese.* March 25, 1965.

"La Rivolta dei Racchi"

7362. Bologna, Mario. "La Rivolta dei Racchi." *Comics Almanacco* (Rome). June 1967, pp. 4-5.

7363. Natoli, Dario. "Guido Buzzelli Si Rivolta." *Sgt. Kirk.* No. 7, 1968, pp. 29-31.

7364. Trinchero, Sergio. "La 'Rivolta' di Buzzelli." *Psyco* (Milan). No. 6, 1970.

"Linus"

7365. Bertieri, Claudio. "Linus, Anno Primo, Numero Uno." *Il Lavoro Nuovo*. May 1, 1965.

7366. "Our Hero (Linus)." *Linus*. 5:49 (1969), pp. 1-8.

"Marmittone"

7367. Del Buono, Oreste. "Marmittone Va Alla Guera." *Linus*. 5:48 (1969), pp. 1-14.

7368. Trinchero, Sergio. "Marmittone nel Vietnam." *Hobby*. No. 3, 1967.

"Nembo Kid"

7369. Fossati, Franco. "Nembo Kid in Arlecchinata." *Fantascienza Minore*. January 1966.

7370. Gerosa, Guido. "Diventerano Tutti Nembo Kid?" *ABC*. June 28, 1964.

"Pecos Bill"

7371. Griego, Giuseppe. "Assolti con Formula Piena Pecos Bill e Compagni." *Il Corriere d'Informazione*. June 30, 1955.

7372. "Nun Auch 'Pecos Bill.'" *Der Neue Vertrieb* (Flensburg). 5:98 (1953), pp. 176-177.

7373. Piccoli, Giuliano. "La Colpa Non e di Pecos Bill." *Cronache* (Milan). October 5, 1954.

"Pinocchio e Romolo"

7374. Trinchero, Sergio. "Scompare l'Autore di Pinocchio e Romolo." *Hobby* (Milan). No. 1, 1966.

7375. Zanotto, Piero. "Un Pinocchio a Fumetti." *Il Gazzettino* (Venice). January 24, 1968.

"RanXerox"

7376. Liberatore, Tanino and Stefano Tamburini. *RanXerox. Happy Birthday Lubna.* New York: Catalan Communications, 1985. 50 pp.

7377. Liberatore, Tanino and Stefano Tamburini. *RanXerox in New York.* New York: Catalan Communications, 1984. 56 pp.

7378. Sterckx, Pierre. "Liberatore-Ranxerox-Ranxerox (…) Ranxerox-Ranxerox-Liberatore." *Les Cahiers de la Bande Dessinée.* 71, 1986, pp. 43-45.

7379. Tuten, F. "Ranxerox." *Artforum.* November 1983, pp. 69-71; December 1983, pp. 70-71.

"Sam Pezzo"

7380. Glasser, Jean-Claude. "Une Pièce de Choix: Sam Pezzo." *Les Cahiers de la Bande Dessinée.* 71, 1986, pp. 19-21.

7381. Saouter. Caya, Catherine and Philippe Sohet. "De Pezzo à Fridman, les Réajustements de Giardino." *Les Cahiers de la Bande Dessinée.* 71, 1986, pp. 22-24.

"Sergente Kirk"

7382. Bertieri, Claudio. "Il Sergente Kirk di Hugo Pratt." *Il Lavoro* (Genoa). July 14, 1967.

7383. Della Corte, Carlos. "Sergente Kirk." *Sgt. Kirk.* No. 1, 1967, p. 70.

"Tex"

7384. Bertieri, Claudio. "Il Semper Giovanne Tex." *Il Lavoro.* September 22, 1967, p. 3.

7385. Carpi, Piero and Michele Gazzarri. "Dice no al Cinema il Vecchio Tex." *Il Giorno* (Genoa). September 29, 1966.

"Topolino"

7386. Bernardi, Luigi. "Gli Intellettuali alle Prese con Topolino e Paperino." *Il Telegrafo* (Milan). June 30, 1967.

7387. Bertieri, Claudio. "Ampia Discussione a Lucca Sulle Variazioni di Topolino." *Il Lavoro Nuovo* (Genoa). November 5, 1966.

7388. Bertieri, Claudio. "Il Ritorno di Topolino." *Il Lavoro Nuovo* (Genoa). February 10, 1967.

7389. Castelli, Alfredo. "I Giganti del Fumetto Topolino." *Eureka*. No. 5, 1968, pp. 53-54.

7390. Castelli, Alfredo. "I Walt Disney Italiani." *Guida a Topolino*. November 1966, pp. 35-39.

7391. Castelli, Alfredo and Franco De Giacomo. "La Produzione a Fumetti." *Guida a Topolino*. November 1966, pp. 11-12.

7392. De Giacomo, Franco. "Topolino." *Linus*. No. 9, 1965.

7393. Gentilini, Mario. "Io Topolino." *Mondadori*. 1970.

7394. "Guida a Topolino." *Comics Club*. November 1966.

7395. Laura, Ernesto G. "Topolino Negli Anni Trenta." *Comics Almanacco* (Rome). June 1967, p. 52.

7396. Oppo, Cipriano E. "Origine di Topolino." *L'Ore*. September 3, 1944.

7397. Traini, Rinaldo. "Topolino e l'Uomo Nuvola." *Hobby* (Rome). No. 1, 1966.

7398. Traini, Rinaldo and Sergio Trinchero. "Topolino Contro Bond." *I Miei Fumetti*. 1967.

7399. Traini, Rinaldo and Sergio Trinchero. "Topolino Contro James Bond." *Hobby*. October 1966.

7400. Trinchero, Sergio. "Cronache di Topolina." *Sgt. Kirk*. No. 24, 1969.

7401. Trinchero, Sergio. "Quando Topolino Doveva Guadagnarsi da Vivere." *Almanacco Comics* (Milan). October 1968.

7402. Trinchero, Sergio. "Topolino e Paperino." *Mondo Domani*. No. 51, 1968.

7403. Zanotto, Piero. "Il Ritorno di Topolino Anni 30." *Nazione Sera* (Florence). September 27, 1966.

7404. Zanotto, Piero. "Quando Topolino, Strizza l'Occhio a Verne." *Il Gazzettino* (Venice). March 20, 1967.

"Valentina"

7405. de la Croix, Arnaud. "J'Aimerais Vous Voir Complètement Nue, Valentina." *Les Cahiers de la Bande Dessinée*. 71, 1986, pp. 74-77.

7406. Groensteen, Thierry. "Si Valentina M'Était Contée..." *Schtroumpf. Les Cahiers de la Bande Dessinée*. 52, 1982, pp. 29-34.

ANIMATION

7407. Alberti, Walter. *Il Cinema di Animazione, 1832-1956*. Turin: Edizione Radio Italiani, 1957. 223 pp.

7408. Bastiancich, Alfio. "Il Cinema d'Animazione in Italia." *Corto Circuito*. April 1992, pp. 49-51.

7409. Bendazzi, Giannalberto. *Il Cinema d'Animazione 1888-1988*. Reviewed by Lorenzo Pellizzari in *Domus*. March 1989, p. x.

7410. Clark, Jennifer. "Italy Devours Cartoons, but Savors Imports." *Variety*. September 21, 1992, p. 65.

7411. Cosulich, Oscar. "E l'Ouest Si Scopre a Zagabria." *Comic Art*. No. 46, 1988, pp. 49-50.

7412. Gianeri, Enrico. *Storia del Cartone Animato*. Milan: Omnia, 1960.

7413. Giromini, Ferruccio. "Sullo Schermo Trevigiano." *Comic Art*. No. 46, 1988, pp. 50-51.

7414. "Italian Animators Finding Yank Firms Unreceptive." *Variety*. April 19-25, 1989, p. 186.

7415. "Italy's New Ad Ban Clouds Bambino TV." *Variety*. September 10, 1990, p. 39.

7416. Robinson, David. "Pordenone Scores with Borzage, Disney Works." *Variety*. November 2, 1992, p. 35.

7417. Rondolino, Gianni. *Storia del Cinema d'Animazione*. Turin: Einaudi, 1974.

7418. Zanotto, Piero. "I Disegni Animati." In *Radar. Enciclopedia del Tempo Libero.* Padua: 1968. 62 pp.

CARICATURE

7419. Novello, Giuseppe. *Dunque Dicevamo... 100 Disegni.* Milan: Arnoldo Mondadori, Editore, 1950.

7420. Novello, Giuseppe. *Il Signore di Buona Famiglia.* 100 Disegni. Milan: Arnaldo Mondadori, 1945.

7421. Novello, Giuseppe. *La Guerra é Bella Ma é Scomoda.* Preface by Paolo Monelli, Rome: Aldo Gazanti Editore, 1951.

7422. Rubiu, Vittorio. *La Caricatura.* Florence: 1973.

7423. Trinchero, Sergio. "I Caratteristi." *Sgt. Kirk.* No. 3, 1967, pp. 60-61.

COMIC BOOKS

7424. Albertarelli, Rino. "La Civiltà del Cavallo." *Linus.* 2:18 (1966), pp. 1-5.

7425. Alessandrini, Ferruccio. "Una Perfida Macchia Nera!" *Comix. Il Giornale dei Fumetti.* No. 18, 1992, p. 1.

7426. Aspesi, Natalia. "Giallo, Sesso, Brivido Siamo Bravi. Nelle Risate, Poco." *Il Giorno* (Genoa). September 26, 1966.

7427. Battistelli, V. "Il Libro del Fanciullo." *La Nuova Italia* (Florence). 1948.

7428. Becciu, Leonardo. *Il Fumetto in Italia.* Florence: Sansoni, 1971.

7429. Bertieri, Claudio. "Banda Stagnata e Banda Disegnata." *Finsider.* October 1967.

7430. Bertieri, Claudio. "Contestation." *Sgt. Kirk.* No. 19, 1969.

7431. Bertieri, Claudio. "E' Tempo di Supereroi." *Il Lavoro.* October 4, 1966.

7432. Bertieri, Claudio. "Fumetto e Costume." *Il Lavoro.* June 22, 1963.

7433. Bertieri, Claudio. "Gli Eroi Giovani." *Il Lavoro.* August 2, 1968.

7434. Bertieri, Claudio. "Gli Eroi Senza Tempo." *Il Lavoro.* February 7, 1965.

7435. Bertieri, Claudio. "Immagine, Segno del Nostro Tempo." *Cinema 60* (Rome). No. 52, 1965.

7436. Bertieri, Claudio. "I Ragazzi dell'Avorio." *Il Lavoro*. October 20, 1967.

7437. Bertieri, Claudio. "La Famiglie déi Mostri." *Il Lavoro*. May 26, 1965.

7438. Bertieri, Claudio. "La Massa e la Communicazione." *Il Lavoro Nuovo*. February 15, 1964.

7439. Bertieri, Claudio. "La Società Che Consuma e Immagini Publicitarie." *Il Lavoro*. October 6, 1967.

7440. Bertieri, Claudio. "Un Prosit Disincantato." *Il Lavoro*. February 3, 1968.

7441. Biagi, E. "La Fantasia d'Oro." *L'Europeo*. December 29, 1966.

7442. Bocca, Giorgio. "La Posta delle Anime Morte." *Il Giorno*. January 25, 1968.

7443. Bocca, Giorgio. "Risposte ai Difensori della Stampa Cochonne." *Il Giorno*. January 27, 1968.

7444. Brolli, Daniele, ed. *Il Crepuscolo Degli Eroi*. Bologna: Telemaco Communicazioni Editorial Bologna, 1992.

7445. Brunoro, Gianni. "La BD Italienne Sous le Signe de la Crise." *Les Cahiers de la Bande Dessinée*. 65, 1985, pp. 46-48.

7446. Brunoro, Gianni. "La BD Italienne, un Paysage pour les Années 80." *Les Cahiers de la Bande Dessinée*. 59, 1984, pp. 52-53.

7447. Brunoro, Gianni. *Quel Fantastico Mondo. Padri, Figli, Padrini, Padroni e Padreterni del Fumetto Italiano*. Bari: Dedalo, 1984.

7448. Brunoro, Gianni. "Terra di Santi...." *Sgt. Kirk*. No. 11-12, 1968, pp. 92-95.

7449. Camerino, Aldo. *Fumetti*. Padua: Il Salotto Giallo, 1958.

7450. Carano, Ranieri. "America the Beautiful." *Linus*. No. 42, 1968, p. 50.

7451. Carano, Ranieri. "Comics in Italy." In *Comics and Visual Culture: Research Studies from Ten Countries*, edited by Alphons Silbermann and H.-D. Dyroff, pp. 96-108. Munich: K.G. Saur, 1986.

7452. Carpi, Piero and Michele Gazzarri. *Il Giallo a Fumetti*. 1967.

7453. Carpi, Piero and Michele Gazzarri. *Il Lettore Diventa Spettatore*. 1967.

7454. Carpi, Piero and Michele Gazzarri. *Pappagone un Occasione Mancata*. 1967.

7455. Carpi, Piero and Michele Gazzarri. *Una Satira Sterilizzata*. 1967.

7456. Castelli, Alfredo. "No al Lutulento Marasma Ovvero Senti Chi Parla!" *Comics*. No. 4, 1966, p. 25.

7457. Cavallone, Franco. "Il Teatro Fatto in Casa." *Linus*. 4:34 (1968), p. 26.

7458. Cavallone, Franco. "Il Topo Amoroso." *Linus*. No. 22, 1967, p. 33.

7459. Cavallone, Franco. "L'Impiegato del Diavolo." *Linus*. No. 27, 1967, pp. 1-5.

7460. Cavallone, Franco. "Toporama." *Linus*. No. 38, 1968, pp. 1-7.

7461. Cremaschi, I. "Diavolacci Ma Cosi, all'Ingrosso." *Corriere d'Informazione* (Milan). May 6-7, 1965.

7462. Cuccolini, Giulio. "Pax Tibi, Augustine." *Comic Art*. No. 46, 1988, p. 75.

7463. "Cunsolo: Libri e Fumetti." *Vita e Pensiero* (Milan). January 1954, pp. 720-723.

7464. "Dal Fumetto alla Pittura." *L'Europeo*. February 10, 1966.

7465. De Giacomo, Franco. "Como Restaurare Vecchi Giornalini." *Linus*. October 1967, p. 79.

7466. Del Bianco, Berto. "Gente Che Va Gent Che Viene nei Fumetti di Paese Sera." *Paese Sera* (Milan). October 25, 1960.

7467. Del Buono, Oreste. "La Nube Purpurea." *Linus*. No. 41, 1968, p. 58.

7468. Della Corte, Carlo. "Allegri é Natale." *Eureka*. No. 2, Supplement, 1967, pp. 1-2.

7469. Della Corte, Carlo. "Appunti in Margine." *Eureka*. No. 6, 1968, pp. 1-2.

7470. Della Corte, Carlo. "Fumetti a Peso d'Oro." *Avanti*. February 3, 1950.

7471. Della Corte, Carlo. "I Comics in Italia, Oggi." *Almanacco Letterario Bompiani*. 1963.

7472. Della Corte, Carlo. *I Fumetti*. Milan: Mondadori, 1961.

7473. Della Corte, Carlo. "I Nostri Amici di Carta." *Bella* (Milan). February 13, 1966.

7474. Della Corte, Carlo. "L'Olimpio in Quadricomia." *La Lettura del Medico* (Milan). August 1958.

7475. Della Corte, Carlo. "Meritano Diffusione i Fumetti Intelligenti." *Paese Sera* (Milan). September 3, 1959.

7476. "Due Superuomini di Carta Conquistano l'America." *Panorama* (Milan). No. 47, 1966.

7477. Eco, Umberto. *Apocalittici e Integrati*. Milan: Bompiani, 1956.

7478. "Faust: I Rumori Disegnati." *La Domenica del Corriere* (Milan). April 19, 1959.

7479. Ferro, Marise. "Ragazzi, Libri e Fumetti." *Stampa Sera* (Milan). November 9, 1960.

7480. Forte, Gioacchino. "Allegretto, Lettera ai Dotti." *Sagittarius* (Milan). December 1965, p. 3.

7481. Fossati, Franco. *I Fumetti in 100 Personaggi*. Milan: Longanesi and C., 1977. 235 pp.

7482. Fossati, Franco. "Italien." In *Comic-Jahrbuch* 1986, edited by Martin Compart and Andreas C. Knigge, pp. 262-271. Berlin: Ullstein GmbH, 1985.

7483. "Fumetti del Rinascimento." *Selearte* (Milan). March-April 1953.

7484. *Fumetto fra Arte e Impegno*. Grafiche B.G., n.d. 30 pp.

7485. Gallini, Clara. "Arabesque-Images of a Myth; Arabesque. Immagini di un Mito." *Clinica Sociologica*. April-June 1989, pp. 98-104.

7486. Gandini, Giovanni. "Il Sogni nel Fumetto." *Settegioni* (Rome). 2:41 (1968).

7487. Gasca, Luis. "Bandes Dessinées et Publicité." *I Fumetti* (Rome). No. 9, 1967, pp. 71-79.

7488. Ghirotti, Gigi. "Uno Svago di Prendersi con Misura." *La Stampa* (Milan). No. 269, 1965.

7489. Giammanco, Roberto. *Il Sortilegio a Fumetti*. Milan: Mondadori, 1965.

7490. Groensteen, Thierry. "Le Monde Paradoxal des Fumetti." *Les Cahiers de la Bande Dessinée*. 71, 1986, pp. 37-42.

7491. "Il Fumetto in Mano ai Politicanti." *Dick Fulmine* (Milan). No. 9, 1967.

7492. "I Polli non Hanno Sedie." *La Fiera Letteraria* (Rome). May 30, 1968.

7493. Lamberti-Bocconi, Maria R. "Inchiesta Sui Fumetti." *I Problemi della Pedagogia*. No. 3, 1960, pp. 592-600.

7494. Laura, Ernesto G. "Che Cosa Accadrá Ora Che il Mago di Burbank Non C'É Più?" *Sgt. Kirk*. No. 6, 1967, pp. 3-9.

7495. Leydi, Roberto. "Il Trionfo del Supercretino." *L'Europeo*. April 14, 1966.

7496. Listri, Francesco. "Fumetti Senza Poesia." *La Nazione*. July 1, 1967.

7497. Maglietto, William. "Giustizia Per i Fumetti." *Cinquedue* (Milan). November 1957.

7498. Mannucci, Cesare. "Un Diluvio di Fumetti." *Corriente della Sera* (Milan). March 24, 1965.

7499. Monaco, Steve. "Slow, Acquired Taste." *Four Color Magazine*. March 1987, p. 64.

7500. Müller, Elsa. "Il Corsario Salgariano." *Sgt. Kirk*. No. 10, 1968, pp. 20-24.

7501. Occhiuzzi, Franco. "La Leggenda di Pinkerton." *Domenica del Corriere* (Milan). December 12, 1967, pp. 58-63.

7502. Paderni, S. "L'Immagine." *Gazzetta di Modena*. February 2, 1953.

7503. Pivano, Fernanda. "I Fumetti Hanno Sessent'Anni." *Il Giorno* (Milan). September 13-17, 1957.

7504. Prezzolini, Giuseppe. "Non c'e Figura Più Popolare Degli Eroi dei Fumetti Americani." *Il Tempo* (Milan). January 31, 1965.

7505. Quilici, Folco. "La Verde Batalla." *Sgt. Kirk*. No. 9, 1968, p. 1.

7506. Resnais, Alain. "La Disturba il Fumetto?" *L'Europeo*. August 25, 1966.

7507. Rubino, Antonio. "Tavole a Quadretti." *Paperino*. August 18, 1938.

7508. Sach, Anne. "Nostalgia del Vecchio Fumetto." *Sipra Uno* (Torino). No. 1, 1965, pp. 113-120.

7509. Sala, Paolo. "Rassegna del Número Uno." *Comics Club*. No. 1, 1967, pp. 5-17.

7510. Sambonet-Bernacchi, Luisa. "I Comics dei Consumi." *Sgt. Kirk*. No. 4, 1967, pp. 49-52.

7511. Serafini, Don Luigi. "Su, Vitt, Coraggio!" *Linus*. No. 22, 1967, p. 6.

7512. Simpson, Howard. "The Italian Difference." *Comics Scene*. July 1983, pp. 41-44.

7513. Spinazzola, Vittorio. "Comic di Protesta e Fumetti d'Apprendice." *Linus*. No. 27, 1967, pp. 63-64.

7514. Spirito, S. "In Margine Alla Polemica Sulla Stampa a Fumetti." *Nuova Rivista Pedagogica* (Rome). No. 4-5-6, 1967, pp. 52-56.

7515. Strazzulla, Gaetano. *I Fumetti*. Florence: Sansoni, 1970.

7516. *Strisce d'Africa. Colonialismo e Anticolonialismo nel Fumetto d'Ambiente Africano*. Rome. l'Istituto Italo Africano di Roma, 1985. (Articles by Maurice Horn, Piercarlo Longo, Carlo Della Corte, Piero Zanotto, Stelio Millo, Alberto Ongaro, Carlo Chendi, François Corteggiani, Francisco de la Fuente).

7517. Traini, Rinaldo. "I Prodotto Comics, Primera Parte." *Sgt. Kirk*. No. 2, 1967.

7518. Traini, Rinaldo. "I Prodotto Comics, Segunda Parte." *Sgt. Kirk*. No. 6, 1967.

7519. Traini, Rinaldo and Sergio Trinchero. "I Fumetti." *Enciclopedia del Tempo Libero*. Padua: Ed. Radar, May 1968. 62 pp.

7520. Trevisani, Giuseppe. "Il Giorno in Cui Mòri de Amicis." *Le Ore* (Milan). 1964.

7521. Trinchero, Sergio. "Away or Not Away." *Sgt. Kirk*. No. 8, 1968, pp. 101-103.

7522. Trinchero, Sergio. "Galassia Che Vai." *Psyco* (Milan). No. 1, 1970.

7523. Trinchero, Sergio. "I Cattivi." *Super Albo* (Milan). January 24, 1965.

7524. Trinchero, Sergio. "Il Lettore di Comics: Un'Anima Angosciata." *Hobby*. No. 5, 1967.

7525. Trinchero, Sergio. "Il Mio Amico...." *Horror*. No. 8, 1970.

7526. Trinchero, Sergio. "Il Nazamore." *Horror*. No. 4, 1970.

7527. Trinchero, Sergio. "Il Piffero Magico." *Comics* (Milan). November 1969.

7528. Trinchero, Sergio. "Il Tempo della Nonna." *Sgt. Kirk*. No. 4, 1967, pp. 82-83.

7529. Trinchero, Sergio. "I Miei Fumetti." Padua: Edizioni Comic Art. Ed. Radar, 1967, 126 pp.

7530. Trinchero, Sergio. "Indovina Chi Viene a Cena." *Sgt. Kirk*. No. 14, 1968.

7531. Trinchero, Sergio. "La Banda Disegnata Sposa la Banda Stagnata." *Italsider* (Milan). September 22, 1967.

7532. Trinchero, Sergio. "La Nuova Frontiera." *Hobby*. No. 0, 1966.

7533. Trinchero, Sergio. "La Poesia a Fumetti." *Hobby*. November 1966.

7534. Trinchero, Sergio. "L'Eredità della Vecchia Guardia." *Sgt. Kirk*. No. 13, 1968, pp. 96-98.

7535. Trinchero, Sergio. "Ma l'Amore che Fa Fà." *Hobby*. No. 6, 1967.

7536. Trinchero, Sergio. "Occasione Mancata." *Hobby*. No. 0, 1966.

7537. Trinchero, Sergio. "Preistoria Per Tutti." *Sagittarius*. No. 9, 1965.

7538. Trinchero, Sergio. "Proponiamo." *Comic Art in Paper Back* (Milan). No. 1, 1966.

7539. Trinchero, Sergio. "Raquel Emula di Dora." *Hobby*. No. 2, 1967.

7540. Trinchero, Sergio. "Ridere, Ridere, Ridere." *Sgt. Kirk*. No. 10, 1968, pp. 1-5.

7541. Trinchero, Sergio. "Trenta Mila Pagine dei Fumetti." *Comic Art in Paper Back*. No. 4, 1967; "I. Fumetti." No. 9, 1967, pp. 57-70.

7542. Trinchero, Sergio. "Ultime Notizie." *Hobby*. No. 2, 1967.

7543. Trinchero, Sergio. "Una Rassegna Significativa." *Avanti* (Milan). No. 68, 1970.

7544. Valeri, M. "La Gabbia dei Fumetti." *Puer* (Siena). 1, 1951, pp. 21-23.

7545. Valle, Bruno. "Italienische Magazine." *Watcher of the Unknown*. October 1988, pp. 20-22.

7546. Venantino, Gianni. "I Vip." *Sgt. Kirk*. No. 15, 1968, pp. 2-4.

7547. Volpicelli, Luigi. "I Fumetti, Spettaculo e Lettura." *Lo Spettacolo* (Rome). April-May 1965, pp. 3-39.

7548. Volpicelli, Luigi. "Lettera a Piero Bargellini Sui Fumetti." *Puer* (Siena). 3:2 (1953).

7549. Zanotto, Piero. "Combattiamo con i Dadi la Battaglia di Waterloo." *Nazione Sera*. February 15, 1966.

7550. Zanotto, Piero. "Fumetti Amorosi e Ragazze d'Oggi." *Il Lavoro*. May 26, 1958.

7551. Zanotto, Piero. "I Comics Esistano." *Corriere del Giorno*. August 13, 1966.

7552. Zanotto, Piero. "I Miei Fumetti, di S. Trinchero." *Carlino Sera* (Bologna). June 24, 1967.

7553. Zanotto, Piero. "La Civiltà dell'Immagini è Fatta Anche di Questi Fumetti." *La Nueva Sardegna*. January 2, 1966.

7554. Zanotto, Piero. "La Magica Arcivenice del Prof. Lambicchi." *Corriere del Trieste*. June 20, 1967.

7555. Zanotto, Piero. "La Società a Fumetti." *Corriere del Ticino*. January 11, 1966.

7556. Zanotto, Piero. "La Vetrina dell'Insolito." *Nazione Sera*. July 30, 1966.

7557. Zanotto, Piero. "L'Età d'Oro del Fumetto: Quadratino e Amici." *Nazione Sera*. December 8, 1967; *La Nuova Sardegna*. December 13, 1967.

7558. Zanotto, Piero. "Libri. I Miei Fumetti, di S. Trinchero." *Il Piccolo* (Trieste). June 9, 1967.

7559. Zanotto, Piero. "Parliamo Ancora di Me, o Zavattini Contro la Terra." *Linus*. No. 43, 1968, pp. 1-10.

7560. Zanotto, Piero. "Planète Rappresenta i Fumetti-Capolavoro." *Il Piccolo*. May 9, 1967; *Carlino Sera* (Bologna). May 13, 1967.

7561. Zanotto, Piero. "Questi Benedetti Fumetti." *Il Lavoro* (Genoa). April 18, 1958; *Enciclopedia Motta* (Milan). September 23, 1958.

7562. Zanotto, Piero. "Ribolle de Iniziative il Calderone dei Fumetti." *Nazione Sera*. June 17, 1967.

7563. Zanotto, Piero. "Ritornano i Primi Eroi di Carta." *Il Lavoro*. January 5, 1966.

7564. Zanotto, Piero. "Sulle Tavole delle Storie a Fumetti le Testoline dei Fanciulli d'Oggi." *Gazzettino Sera* (Venice). March 6, 1958.

7565. Zanotto, Piero. "Tornano Gli Eroi di Carta." *Tribuna del Mezzogiorno* (Venice). November 12, 1965.

7566. Zanotto, Piero. "Tra le Nuvole dei Fumetti le Testoline dei Fanciulli d'Oggi." *La Nuova Sardegna* (Sassari). March 19, 1958.

7567. Zanotto, Piero. "Una Breve Inchiesta Sui Fumetti." *Il Paese* (Rome). March 23, 1958.

7568. "Zorzi: Discorso Sui Fumetti." *Fiera Letteraria* (Siena). May 25, 1952.

7569. Zucconi, Guglielmo. "Ragazzini e Signore-Bene Divorano i Fumetti dell'Orido." *La Domenica dell Corriere* (Milan). 1965.

Anthologies

7570. Liberatore, Tanino, *et al. Video Clips.* New York: Catalan Communications, 1985. 67 pp.

7571. Mattioli, Massimo. *Squeak the Mouse.* Paris: A. Michel, 1984. 48 pp.

Cinema, Television, Theater

7572. Alessi-Conte, Andrea and Franco Fossati. "Filmografia (Fantascienza nei Comics)." *Fantascienza Minore* (Milan). Special number, 1967, pp. 63-65.

7573. Bertieri, Claudio. "Ballata per un Pezzo da Novanta." *Il Lavoro.* November 13, 1966.

7574. Bertieri, Claudio. "Cinema e Comics." *Il Lavoro.* March 2, 1965.

7575. Bertieri, Claudio. "Cinema e Fumetti." *Comics* (Bordighera). 1965.

7576. Bertieri, Claudio. "Comics, Cinema and Photoromances." *Il Lavoro* (Genoa). February 15, 1965.

7577. Bertieri, Claudio. "Comics, Fotoromanzi e Cinema Alla Sbarra." *Il Lavoro Nuovo.* April 15, 1964.

7578. Bertieri, Claudio. "Comics e Video." *Linus.* April 1966, pp. 29-32.

7579. Bertieri, Claudio. *Film di Carta. Ottanta Anni di Fumetto Sullo Schermo et di Cinema Nei Fumetti.* Firenze: Vallecchi, 1979.

7580. Bertieri, Claudio. "I Baloons Nel Video." *Linus.* No. 25, 1967.

7581. Bertieri, Claudio. "Immagine in Poltrona." *Cinema 60.* No. 57, 1965.

7582. Bertieri, Claudio. "I Promessi Sposi della TV." *Il Lavoro.* March 17, 1967.

7583. Caen, Michel. "Fellini und die Comics." *Film.* No. 2/66, 1966.

7584. Caen, Michel and Francis Lacassin. "Fellini et les Fumetti." *Cahiers du Cinéma.* No. 172, 1965.

7585. Caen, Michel and Francis Lacassin. "L'Esperienza di Federico Fellini." *Comics Archivio Italiano dell Stampa a Fumetti* (Rome). No. 1, 1966.

7586. Caen, Michel and Francis Lacassin. "Los Comics y Federico Fellini." *Cuto* (San Sebastian). No. 4-6, 1968, pp. 5-9.

7587. Carpi, Piero and Michele Gazzarri. *Il Fumetto in Teatro*. Milan: 1967.

7588. Cavallina, P. "Como Si è Arrivati all'Attuale Boom dei Comics e dei Fotoromanzi." *Gazzetta del Popolo* (Milan). October 18, 1964.

7589. Del Buono, Oreste. "Copi: il Teatro a Fumetti." *Linus*. No. 27, 1967, pp. 1-5.

7590. Della Corte, Carlo. "Si Mordano la Coda Fumetto e Cinema." *Cinema* (Milan). May 16, 1956.

7591. Eco, Umberto. "Verso una Civiltà dell'Immagine." *Televisione e Cultura*. Milan: Bompiani, 1961.

7592. "Esplode in Sicilia il Mito di Fenomenal." *Film-TV-Spettacolo*. May 10, 1968.

7593. "Fellini and Comics." *Film*. February 1966, pp. 24 ff.

7594. Fossati, Franco. "Dai Fumetti al Cinema." *Fantascienza Minore* (Milan). Special number, 1967, pp. 3-7.

7595. Lhassa, Gian and Michele Lequeux. *Seul au Monde dans le Western Italien: Une Poignée de Thèmes*. Mariembourg (Belgium): Grand Angle, 1983.

7596. Mollica, Vincenzo. "Le Rêve du Maestro." *(A Suivre)*. October 1992, pp. 4-7.

7597. Moscati, Massimo. *Comics nel Cinema: Gli Eroi di Carta nel Regno della Celluloide*. Milan: Studio Metropolis, 1982.

7598. Rossi, Annabella. "Coi Fotoromanzi dei Santi a Cacchia di Anime Perdute." *Paese Sera* (Milan). January 25, 1968.

7599. Surchi, Sergio. "Roger Vadim Gira il Film Sul Futuro." *La Nazione*. June 30, 1967, p. 10.

7600. Tosi, Franco. "Fumetti e Cinema Preavvisano la Liberazione della Donna?" Milan: August 1966.

7601. Trinchero, Sergio. "Cinema e Comics." *Sgt. Kirk*. No. 7, 1968.

7602. Trinchero, Sergio. "King Louis." *Sgt. Kirk*. No. 26, 1969.

7603. Zanotto, Piero. "Fumetti e Cinema." *La Bienale* (Venice). No. 57-58, 1965.

7604. Zanotto, Piero. "Fumetto e Cinema si Mordono la Coda." *Il Gazzettino* (Venice). November 14, 1965.

7605. Zanotto, Piero. "I Beatles a Locarno." *Linus*. No. 44, 1968, pp. 46-47.

7606. Zanotto, Piero. "Les Pieds Nickeles Ritornano in un Film." *Il Gazzettino* (Venice). November 10, 1964.

7607. Zanotto, Piero. "Ritorna Zazie Camuffata da Comics." *Nazione Sera*. December 24, 1966; *Il Piccolo* (Trieste). June 1, 1967.

7608. Zanotto, Piero. "Vita Rigogliosa dei Fotoromanzi." *Il Paese* (Rome). May 23, 1958.

Collecting, Fandom

7609. Castelli, Alfredo. "Il Fandom Americano." *Linus*. No. 19, 1966; *Fantascienza Minore*. Numero speciale, 1967, pp. 48-51.

7610. Cavallina, P. "Dal Mondo dei Fans a Quello Degli Studiosi." *Il Quotidiano* (Milan). November 10, 1964.

7611. De Giacomo, Franco. "Fumetti e Collezionisti." *Linus*. No. 29, 1967, pp. 4-5.

Commercial Aspects

7612. Del Buono, Oreste. "A Proposito di Tutte Quelle Signore." *Valentina* (Milan). 1968.

7613. Del Buono, Oreste. "Due Scuole di Narratori a Fumetti." *Pesci Rossi* (Milan). July 1947.

7614. Della Corte, Carlo. "Almanaccando." *Eureka*. Supplemento, February 1968, pp. 1-2.

7615. Fallaci, Oriana. "Ho Speso Miliardi." *L'Europeo*. June 9, 1966.

7616. Giani, Renato. "I Fumetti e il Fumettismo." *Communità* (Milan). April 1955.

7617. Polimeni, I. "Problemi Economici dell'Editoria." *L'Osservatore di Borsa* (Milan). June 1967.

7618. "'Spider-Man' Departs Web of Italian Newsstands As Chief Shareholder Exits." *Variety*. September 17, 1986, p. 84.

7619. Stuart, Jay. "Italian Comic World Follows the Credo 'Let It All Hang Out.'" *Variety*. September 17, 1986, p. 82.

7620. Traini, Rinaldo. "Un Italiano a Cartoonland." *Sgt. Kirk*. No. 15, 1968, pp. 29-31.

7621. Trinchero, Sergio. "Fogli di Notes: Poli, Raymond, F. Vichi." *Sgt. Kirk*. No. 23, 1969.

7622. Trinchero, Sergio. "I Disegnatori dell' Uomo Mascherato." *Classici dell'Avventura* (Milan). Fratelli Spada, 1967.

7623. Trinchero, Sergio. "I Fumetti Influenzano Monicelli." *Hobby*. No. 1, 1966.

7624. Trinchero, Sergio. "Statuto del Club dell'Uomo Mascherato." *L'Uomo Mascherato*. No. 121, 1965.

Culture and Society

7625. Bertieri, Claudio. "Comics Como Specchio della Società." *Il Lavoro*. March 9, 1965.

7626. Bertieri, Claudio. "I Comics dei Consumi." *Il Lavoro*. October 6, 1967.

7627. Bertieri, Claudio. "The Religion and the Comics." *Il Lavoro*. April 5, 1968.

7628. Bertieri, Claudio. "Un Fenómeno Contemporaneo Come Specchio della Società." *Il Lavoro Nuovo*. March 2, 1965.

7629. Biamonte, S.G. "I Fumetti dell'Inconscio." *Il Giornale d'Italia* (Milan). February 18, 1965.

7630. Calisi, Romano. "Stampa a Fumetti, Cultura di Massa, Società Contemporanea." *Quaderni di Communicazioni di Massa*. No. 1, 1965, pp. 9-15.

7631. Chiaromonte, N. "Fumetti e Cultura." *Il Mondo* (Milan). August 11, 1964.

7632. Forte, Gioacchino. "La Persuasione a Fumetti." *Nord e Sud* (Milan). April 1965.

7633. Garroni, Emilio. "Fumetti e Cultura di Massa." *Sapere* (Milan). April 1965.

7634. Guglielmo, Salvatore. "Fumetti e Società." *Rassegna di Pedagogia* (Padua). No. 6, 1951.

7635. "I Bimbi, i Fumetti e la Moda." *La Stampa* (Milan). March 21, 1968.

7636. Mannucci, Cesare. "Sociologia del Fumetto." *Il Mondo*. January 12, 1965.

7637. Mei, Francesco. "Patologia del Fumetto." *Opera Aperta* (Rome). No. 4, 1965.

7638. Ossicini, A. "Primi Rilievi su Una Inchiesta Sull'Influenza del Cinema e dei Fumetti." *Rivista Psicopatologia e Neuropsicologia* (Milan). 20, 1952, p. 33.

7639. Paderni, S. "I Fumetti Come Fenomeno Culturale." *Gazzetta di Modena*. July 13, 1953.

7640. Pellegrino, Alberto. *Il Mondo a Strisce. Fumetti e Società*. Firenze: Bulgarini, 1973.

7641. Sullerot, Eveline. "Bandes Dessinées et Culture." *Quaderni di Communicazioni di Massa* (Rome). No. 1, 1965, pp. 43-51.

7642. Valentini, E. "Influenza dei Fumetti." *Civiltà Cattolica* (Rome). September 6, 1952.

7643. Zanotto, Piero. "Anche Gli Uomini di Cultura Sono Influenzati dai Fumetti." *Il Gazzettino* (Venice). September 25, 1966.

Education

7644. Bertin, Giovanni M. *Stampa, Spettacolo ed Educazione*. Milan: Marzorati, 1956.

7645. Biamonte, Salvatore G. "I Disidattati nei Fumetti." *Il Giornale d'Italia* (Milan). September 9, 1965.

7646. Bocca, Giorgio. "La Bibbia a Fumetti." *L'Europeo*. March 1, 1959.

7647. Canziani, Fabio. "Nuove Esperienze Sulla Comprensione del Linguaggio dei Fumetti in Soggetti di 3-10 Anni." *Ikon* (Milan). 18:64 (1968), pp. 79-101.

7648. Canziani, Fabio. "Sulla Comprensione di Alcuni Elementi del Linguaggio Fumettistico in Soggetti Tra i Sei e i Dieci Anni." *Ikon* (Milan). 54, 1965, pp. 15-88.

7649. Carpi, Piero and Michele Gazzarri. *Il Fumetto a Scuola?* Milan: 1967.

7650. Chiappano, N. "Di Un Uso Didattico dei Fumetti." *Cultura Popolare* (Milan). February 1954.

7651. Chiappano, N. "Uso Didattico dei Fumetti." *La Cultura Popolare* (Milan). 1954, pp. 37f.

7652. Cianfarra, C.M. "Comics Work for the ECA in Italy." *New York Times Magazine*. August 21, 1949, p. 20.

7653. Dallari, Marco and Roberto Farné. *Scuola e Fumetto. Proposte per l'Introduzione nella Scuola del Linguaggio dei Comics*. Milan: Emme Edizioni, 1977.

7654. Detti, Ermanno. *Il Fumetto Fra Cultura e Scuola*. Firenze: La Nuova Italia, 1984.

7655. Donizetti, Pino. "Diagnostica Medica e Fumetto." *Quaderni di Communicazioni di Massa* (Rome). No. 6, 1965.

7656. Faeti, Antonio. *Dacci Questo Veleno! Fiabe Fumetti Feuilletons Bambine*. Milan: Emme, 1980.

7657. Foresti, Renato. "I Giornali a Fumetti e le Letture Educative per la Gioventù." *Puer* (Siena). No. 1, 1951.

7658. Franchini, Rolando. "Fumetti e Didattica Nella Scuola Moderna." *Quaderni di Communicazioni di Massa* (Rome). No. 6, 1965.

7659. Genovesi, Giovanni. "Limiti e Valore del Fumetto." *I Problemi della Pedagogia* (Rome). 11:1 and 5/6 (1965).

7660. "La Scuola Inglese." *Linus*. No. 14, 1966, p. 1.

7661. Listri, Francesco. "Facciamo Entrare i Fumetti a Scuola." *La Nazione*. July 2, 1967.

7662. Ossicini, A. "Cinema, Letture e Rendimento Scolastico." *Inf. Anorm* (Milan). 14, 1953, p. 473.

7663. "Processo alla Terra, Experimental Comics." *Sergente Kirk*. No. 11-12, 1968, p. 97.

7664. Quadrio, Assunto. "I Fumetti Nella Cultura del Preadolescente." *Ikon* (Milan). 17:61 (1967), pp. 9-52.

7665. Quadrio, Assunto. "La Letteratura dei 'Comics' Quale Fattore di Integrazione Nella Pre-Adoleszenza." *I Fumetti* (Rome). No. 9, 1967, pp. 11-18.

7666. Radice, Lucio L. "Vigili e Ipnotizzati." *Riforma della Scuola* (Rome). No. 5-6, 1965.

7667. Santucci, Luigi. "I Fumetti." *L'Educatore Italiano* (Milan). December 20, 1957.

7668. Scotti, Pietro. "Fumetti e Catechesi." *Quaderni di Communicazioni di Massa* (Rome). No. 6, 1965.

7669. Valentini, E. *I Fumetti, Archivio Didattivo*. Serie 2, No. 20. Rome: 1964.

7670. Volpi, Domenico. *Didattica dei Fumetti*. Brescia: La Scuola, 1983.

7671. Volpi, Domenico. "La Ricerca dei Valori Educativi nei 'Conduct.'" *I Fumetti* (Rome). No. 9, 1967, pp. 5-9.

7672. Volpicelli, Luigi. "Aspetto Psico-Pedagogico della Stampa Periodica per Ragazzi." Congresso Internationale sulla Stampa Periodica, la Cinematografia e la Radio per Ragazzi, Milan, 1952.

7673. Zavalloni, Roberto and M. Luisa Bertolini. *La Metodologia dei Fumetti Applicata Ai Subnormali*. Brescia: La Scuola, 1973.

Fascism

7674. Carabra, Claudio. *Il Fascismo a Fumetti*. Florence: Guaraldi, 1973.

7675. Eco, Umberto. "Fascio e Fumetto." *Espresso-Colore*. March 28, 1971.

7676. Laura, Ernesto G. "La Stampa Italiana a Fumetti nel Periodo Fascista." *I Fumetti* (Rome). No. 9, 1967, pp. 87-113.

7677. Millo, Stelio. "Appunti sul Fumetto Fascista." *Linus*. No. 10, 1966.

7678. Natoli, Dario. "Fascismo e Antifascismo in 10 Anni di Fumetto Italiano." *L'Unità*. September 28, 1966.

7679. Zanotto, Piero. "30 Years of Social and Custom Satire in the Italian Comics." In *Guida Alla Mostra Internazionale dei Cartoonists*, edited by Luciano Bottaro and Carlo Chendi, pp. 36-40. Rapallo: Officine Grafiche Canessa, 1978.

Genres

7680. Strinati, Pierre. "Bandes Dessinées et Surréalisme." *Quaderni di Communicazioni di Massa* (Rome). No. 6, 1965.

7681. Trinchero, Sergio. "Gli Animali nei Comics." *Super Albo*. No. 44, Supplemento, December 1964.

Adventure

7682. Ajello, Nello. "Gli Album d'Avventura." *Il Mulino* (Bologna). April 1953.

7683. Castelli, Alfredo. "I Fumetti Avventurosi Sono Figli del Feuilleton." *Eureka* (Milan). No. 1, 1967, pp. 59-60.

7684. Castelli, Alfredo. "L'Avventuroso." *Eureka*. No. 6, 1968, pp. 53-54.

7685. Della Corte, Carlo. "Dall' Avventuroso a Eureka." *Eureka*. No. 1, 1967, pp. 1-2.

7686. Della Corte, Carlo. "L'Avventura, Gli Eroi." *Smack*. No. 1, 1968, pp. 1-2.

7687. De Vita, Giuseppe. "L'Aventuroso." *Il Fumetto*. September 1973, pp. 64-67.

7688. Trinchero, Sergio. "La Nascità dei Comics Avventurosi." *Il Lavoro*. 1967.

Crime

7689. Ferraro, Ezio and Giani Bono. "Bob Star il Poliziotto dai Capelli Rossi." *Comics World* (Genoa). No. 1, 1968.

7690. Lavezzolo, Andrea. "Petrosino, il Grande Polizotto Italo-Americano." *Sgt. Kirk*. No. 15, 1968, pp. 59-61.

7691. Zanotto, Piero. *Il Giallo a Fumetti*. Preface of Carlo della Corte. Milan: Milano Libri, 1976.

Erotic, Pornographic

7692. Barbiani, Laura and Alberto Abruzzese. *Pornograffiti*. Da Jacula a Oltretomba, da Cappucetto Rotto a Mercenari. Trame e Figure del Fumetto Italiano per Adulti. Rome: R. Napoleone, 1980.

7693. Bertieri, Claudio. "Nude with Balloons." *Photographia Italiana*. No. 133, 1968.

7694. Caputo, T. "Serso e Pazzia nel Fumetto per Adulti." *L'Osservatore di Borsa* (Milan). January 1967.

7695. Cavallina, P. "Un Passatempo per Ragazzi Che Piace Agli Adulti." *Il Quotidiano* (Milan). October 18, 1964.

7696. de la Croix, Arnaud. "Déclic Mortel." *Les Cahiers de la Bande Dessinée*. 64, 1985, pp. 77-79.

7697. de la Croix, Arnaud. "Douce à Regarder, Douces à Entendre." *Les Cahiers de la Bande Dessinée*. 71, 1986, pp. 32-35.

7698. Ghiringhelli, Zeno. *Erotismo and Fumetti*. Milan: 1969.

7699. Imbasciati, Antonio. "I Fumetti Neri." *Ikon* (Milan). 20:75 (1970), pp. 9-45.

7700. Lecigne, Bruno. Une Esthétique de la Jouissance." *Schtroumpf. Les Cahiers de la Bande Dessinée*. 52, 1982, pp. 21-24.

7701. Lüthje, Heinz. "Italien Hart am Rande des Porno." *Hamburger Morgenpost.* September 16, 1970, p. 4.

7702. "Ma Cos' è la Pornografia?" *L'Espresso.* November 19, 1967.

7703. Maraini, Dacia. "Una Falsa Spregiudica—Tezza al Servizio della Morale, Corente: Non Sempre Erotismo Significa Libertà." *Paese Sera* (Milan). December 16, 1967.

7704. Schnurrer, Achim. "Sex und Gewalt. Eine Kommentierte Bildmonografie zu Italienischen Comictaschenbuchserien." *Comixene. Das Comicfachmagazin.* 6:22 (1979), pp. 10-12.

7705. Trinchero, Sergio. "Sexy Comics." *Hobby.* No. 1, 1966.

Fantasy

7706. Bertieri, Claudio. "L'Occulata Saggezza di Un Mago, Uno dei Primi Persuasori Occulti." *Il Lavoro.* December 17, 1966.

7707. Della Corte, Carlo. "Fantascienza a Strisce." *Smack* (Milan). No. 3, 1968, pp. 1-2.

7708. De Rossignoli, Emilio. "La Stampa per Ragazzi Prepara Una Generazione Senza Fantasia." *La Tribuna* (Milan). January 5, 1958.

7709. Fossati, Franco. "Appunti Sulla Considdetta Fantascienza Minore." *Nuovi Orizzonti* (Milan). No. 9, 1966.

7710. Fossati, Franco. "Introduzione." *Fantascienza Minore* (Milan). Numero speciale, 1967, pp. 1-2.

7711. Trinchero, Sergio. "I Comics, Un'Offerta di Differenziata Fantasia." *Comics Club* (Milan). No. 1, 1967, pp. 1-3.

7712. Trinchero, Sergio. "Ieri Fantasia, Domani Realtà?" *Sgt. Kirk.* No. 5, 1967, pp. 78-80.

7713. Zanotto, Piero. "Cartoons e Fantascienza." *Fantascienza Minore.* Special number, 1967, pp. 12-16.

7714. Zanotto, Piero. "La BB della Fantascienza." *Nazione Sera.* April 1, 1965.

7715. Zanotto, Piero. "La Fantascienza." In *I Radar.* Serie 9, No. 13. Padova: Editrice Radar, 1967. 64 pp.

7716. Zanotto, Piero. "Ritorna il Nonno dei Comics di Fantascienza." *Nazione Sera.* December 13, 1966; *La Nuova Sardegna.* December 20, 1966.

7717. Zorzoli, G.B. "Fantascienza Minorenne." *Linus*. No. 2, 1965.

Horror

7718. Bertieri, Claudio. "Attinge All'orrore la Seduzione Spettacolare." *Il Lavoro Nuovo*. April 17, 1965.

7719. Bertieri, Claudio. "The Families of the Monsters." *Il Lavoro*. May 26, 1967.

7720. Mennella, Francesco. "Italy Reports Boom in Horror Comics." *Syracuse (New York) Herald*. November 21, 1965.

7721. Pellegrini, Giuseppe and Gianni Rodari. "Il Processo ai Fumetti dell'Orrore." *Tribuna Illustrata* (Rome). 76:40 (1966), pp. 10-13.

7722. Trinchero, Sergio. "E Dio...." *Horror*. No. 5, 1970.

7723. Trinchero, Sergio. "Horror Gourmet." *Horror*. No. 7, 1970.

7724. Trinchero, Sergio. "Il Caro Estinto." *Horror*. No. 7, 1970.

7725. Trinchero, Sergio. "Tartarughe d'Abord." *Horror*. No. 6, 1970.

Humor

7726. "Umorismo e Fumetti." *Sgt. Kirk*. No. 16, 1968, pp. 52-53.

7727. Zanotto, Piero. "Un Umorista Ha Ideato la Scritura a Fumetti." *Il Paese* (Genoa). May 12, 1959.

New Wave, Underground

7728. Branzaglia, Carlo. "Comics of the Italian New Wave." *Comics Journal*. February 1993, pp. 33-39.

7729. De Luca, Michele. "Il Secondo Underground Italiano." *Comics*. May 1973.

Science Fiction

7730. Bertieri, Claudio. "Viaggio Nella Fantasia." *Il Lavoro*. December 29, 1967.

7731. De Turris, Gianfranco and Sebastiano Fusco. "Les Bandes Dessinées de Science-Fiction en Italie." *Mercury* (Paris). No. 13, 1967, pp. 67-74; No. 14, 1967, pp. 65-73.

7732. Minuzzo, Nerio. "La Fidanzata del Robot." *L'Europeo*. July 6, 1967, pp. 34-39.

7733. Traini, Rinaldo and Sergio Trinchero. "Il Risveglio del Dinosauro." *Filatelia Italiana* (Milan). No. 10, 1965.

7734. Zanotto, Piero. "I Fumetti Nella Science-Fiction: Si Rimova il Mito dil Atlantide." *Il Gazzettino* (Venice). June 22, 1967.

Superhero

7735. Eco, Umberto. "Il Mito di Superman e la Dissoluzione del Tempo." *Archivio di Filosofia*. 1-2, 1962.

7736. Lacassin, Francis. "Alteration et Transformation du Héros de Bandes Dessinées." *I Fumetti*. June 1967, pp. 41-51.

7737. Sala, Paolo and Alfredo Castelli. "Amok, il Gigante Mascherato." *L'Asso di Picche*. June 1966, p. 15.

7738. Trinchero, Sergio. "Batmania: il Morbo Non Attacca." *Hobby*. No. 2, 1967.

7739. Trinchero, Sergio. "I Cattivi e la Eroine dei Fumetti." *Fichel Club* (Milan). No. 8-9, 1967.

7740. Trinchero, Sergio. "Le Eroine." *Super Albo*. No. 131, Fratelli Spada, April 4, 1965.

War

7741. Bono, Giani. *Appunti sul Fumetto Italiano del Dopoguerra*. Genoa: Gli Amici del Fumetto, 1972.

7742. Del Buono, Oreste. "Guerra e Fumetti: Ma'chi Si Rivede?" *Linus*. No. 29, 1967, p. 62.

7743. Ferraro, Ezio. "I Fumetti nel Dopoguerra." *Comicsrama* (Milan). No. 4, 1968, p. 21.

7744. Forte, Gioacchino. "I Fumetti della Guerra Fredda." *Quaderni di Communicazioni di Massa*. No. 1, 1965, pp. 103-110.

7745. Rubino, Antonio. "Salgari a Fumetto nel Dopoguerra." *L'Asso di Picche* (Milan). Numero speciale, June 1966, pp. 12-14.

7746. Trinchero, Sergio. "Appunti Sui Fumetti di Guerra." *Dick Fulmine*. Collana Anni Trenta. September 26, 1967.

Western

7747. Castelli, Alfredo. "Il Western all'Italiana è Nato dai Fumetti." *Eureka*. No. 2, 1967, pp. 65-66.

7748. Fossati, Franco. "L'Histoire de l'Ouest." In *Histoire et Bande Dessinée: Actes du 2e Colloque International Éducation et Bande Dessinée*, pp. 79-85. La Roque d'Anthéron: Objectif Promo Durance, 1979.

7749. Groensteen, Thierry. "Ken Parker ou l'Ouest à Visage Humain." *Les Cahiers de la Bande Dessinée*. 71, 1986, pp. 65-69.

7750. Trinchero, Sergio. "Un Cowboy e Due Sottomarini." *Sgt. Kirk*. No. 28, 1969.

Psychology

7751. Bertieri, Claudio. "Un Giallo Psicologico." *Il Lavoro*. May 12, 1967.

7752. Imbasciati, Antonio and Carlo Castelli. "Effetti dei Fumetti Neri Rilevati Mediante Tests di Personalità." *Ikon* (Milan). 24:90 (1974), pp. 7-99.

7753. Imbasciati, Antonio and Carlo Castelli. *Psicologia del Fumetto*. Rimini, Firenze: Guaraldi, 1975. 293 pp.

7754. Leoni, Paola. "Il Ruolo dei Personaggi dei Fumetti Nella Dinamica della Proiezione Ostile." *Ikon* (Milan). 20:75 (1970), pp. 57-75.

7755. Origlia, Dino. "Psicologia del Fumetto." *Illustrazione Scientifica*. October 1950.

7756. Valentini, E. "Aspetti Psico-Pedagogici dei Fumetti." *Civiltà Catolica* (Rome). March 1952, p. 500.

Structure

7757. Aspesi, Natalia. "Hanno Invaso Con le K, il Mondo dei Fumetti." *Il Giorno*. September 25, 1966.

7758. Biamonte, S.G. "Follia dei Fumetti." *Le Ore*. January 6, 1966, pp. 38-41.

7759. Boatto, Alberto. "Il Fumetto al Microscopio." *Fantazaria* (Rome). No. 2, 1967.

7760. Caradec, François. *I Primi Eroi*. Milan: Garzanti, 1962.

7761. Carpi, Piero and Michele Gazzarri. "Como Nasce un Fumetto." *Il Giorno*. July 21, 1965.

7762. Casccia, A. "Eroi e Miti in Fumo." *Atlanta*. No. 16, 1966.

7763. Castelli, Alfredo. "Il Mondo dei Comics." *Collana Oceano*. No. 4, 1966, p. 25.

7764. Clair, René. *I Primi Eroi*. Milan: Garzanti, 1962. 478 pp.

7765. Cozzi, Luigi. "AAAHHH! EEEE-YAHHH!" *Sgt. Kirk*. No. 11-12, 1968, pp. 41-47.

7766. Della Corte, Carlo. "L'Età d'Oro in Mito?" *Eureka*. No. 3, 1968, pp. 1-3.

7767. Eco, Umberto. *Die Formen des Inhalts*. Milan: Bompiani, 1971.

7768. Eco, Umberto. "La Struttura Iterativa nei Fumetti." *Quaderni di Communicazioni di Massa*. No. 1, 1965, pp. 30-34.

7769. Forte, Gioacchino. "Gli Eroi di Carta." In *Edizioni Scientifiche Italiane*. Naples: 1965.

7770. Giammanco, Roberto. "I Comics, Metodologia o Merceologia?" *Opera Aperto*. March-April 1965.

7771. Giuntoli, Ilio. "Giustificazione e Piscologia del Fumetto." *Quaderni di Communicazioni di Massa* (Rome). No. 6, 1965.

7772. "Gli Eroi del Nostro Tempo." *Le Ore*. January 6, 1966, p. 36.

7773. Lamberti-Bocconi, Maria R. "La Narrativa a Fumetti." *I Problemi della Pedagogia* (Rome). No. 6, 1956, pp. 462-480; No. 1, 1957, pp. 189-197.

7774. Leydi, Roberto. "L'Autore Smascherato." *L'Europeo*. March 1965.

7775. Pagliaro, Antonio. "La Parola e l'Immagine." *Edizioni Scientifiche Italiane*. Naples: 1957.

7776. Rava, Enzo. "I Personaggi e Noi." *Noi Donne* (Rome). No. 22-23, 1966.

7777. Speciale, Liberio. "I Personaggi dei Fumetti Stanno Invadendo lo Schermo." *Momento Sera*. August 28, 1965.

7778. Strinati, Pierre. "Le Thème de la Grotte dans les Bandes Dessinées." *I Fumetti*. No. 9, 1967, pp. 53-56.

7779. Trevisani, Giuseppe. "Il Mondo a Quadretti." *Il Politecnico* (Rome). October 6, 1945.

7780. Trinchero, Sergio. "Civiltà e Anticonformismo." *Comic Art in Paper Back*. No. 2, 1966.

7781. Trinchero, Sergio. "La Mitologia." *Comic Art in Paper Back*. No. 4, 1967.

7782. Volpicelli, Luigi. "Il Linguaggio dei Fumetti." *Quaderni di Communicazioni di Massa*. No. 1, 1965, pp. 17-29.

7783. Zanotto, Piero. "Esplorano il Nostro Mondo i Moderni Poeti del Fumetto." *Il Gazzettino*. September 16, 1967.

Technical Aspects

7784. Bruschini, Saverio and Pietro di Vita. *Come Disegnare i Fumetti*. Milan: Il Castello, 1977.

7785. Calligaro, Renato. "Les Aventures de la Forme." *Les Cahiers de la Bande Dessinée*. 71, 1986, pp. 62-64.

7786. Groensteen, Thierry. "Réalisme et Virtuosité." *Les Cahiers de la Bande Dessinée*. 64, 1985, pp. 16-18, 75-76.

7787. Groensteen, Thierry. "Une Transparence Ambiguë." *Les Cahiers de la Bande Dessinée*. 71, 1986, pp. 16-18.

COMIC STRIPS

7788. Bertieri, Claudio. "Orpheus in Strips." *Photographia Italiana*. No. 148, 1970.

7789. Cosulich, Oscar. "Amare Napoli (a Fumetti)." *Comic Art*. No. 46, 1988, p. 49.

7790. "Craxi Furious Over L'Unita Cartoon Strip." *IPI Report*. February 1989, p. 12.

7791. Hofmann, Paul. "Comic-Strip Version of Bible Is Fought in Italy As Profane." *New York Times*. February 20, 1959.

7792. Mattioli, Massimo. *Squeak the Mouse*. Paris: Éditions Albin Michel, 1984. 49 pp.

7793. "New Cartoon Treat for Italian Kids." *IPI Report*. October 1987, p. 9.

7794. Possati, Franco. "Dalle Comic Strips Allo Schermo." *Oltre il Cielo* (Rome). No. 145, 1967, pp. 108-110.

7795. Schiaffino, Gualtierno. [Italian Comic Strips]. In *Guida Alla Mostra Internazionale dei Cartoonists*, edited by Luciano Bottaro and Carlo Chendi, pp. 74-74. Rapallo: Officine Grafiche Canessa, 1978.

7796. Tamagnini, Luciano. "Il Cowboy." *Il Fumetto*. September 1973, pp. 17-.

POLITICAL CARTOONS

7797. Chiesa, Adolfo. *La Satira Politica in Italia*. Rome: Editori Laterza, 1990. 330 pp.

7798. Della Sala, Modestino. *Aspetti della Satira Politica in Irpinia*. Rome: Bulzoni Editore, 1988. 79 pp.

7799. Flaiano, E. *La Solitudine del Satiro*. Milan: Rizzoli, 1973.

7800. Fossati, Franco. *Guida al Fumetto Satirico e Politico*. Milan: Gammalibri, 1979.

7801. Istituto Nazionale per la Documentazione sull' Imagine. *Centro Anni di Satira Politica in Italia*. Firenze: Guaraldi, 1976. 38 pp.

7802. Ratano, F. *La Satira Italiana nel Dopoguerra*. Firenze: D'Anna, 1976.

7803. Universale Economica Feltrinelli. *Cuor da Cuore. Un Anno di Satira Sinistra*. Milan: Feltrinelli, 1990. 208 pp.

7804. Vené, Gian Franco. *La Satira Politica*. Milan: 1976.

8

Country Perspectives—Luxembourg to Yugoslavia

LUXEMBOURG

Animation

7805. "Animation de Lux." *Story Board*. No. 6, p. 20.

MACEDONIA

General Studies

7806. [Ane Vasilevski]. *Kayhan Caricature*. November 1992.

7807. "Ane Vasilevski, Jugoslavia." *FECO News*. No. 5, 1987, p. 3.

7808. "Dmitar Ćudo, Jugoslavia." *FECO News*. No. 5, 1987, p. 10.

World Cartoon Gallery

7809. *XV World Cartoon Gallery, Skopje, 1983. Tomorrow*. Skopje: NIP Nova Macedonia, 1984. 72 pp.

7810. *V World Cartoon Gallery, Skopje, 1973. Today's Myth*. Skopje: Novo Macedonia, 1974.

7811. *4th World Cartoon Gallery, Skopje, 1972. Why?* Skopje: Novo Macedonia, 1973.

7812. Lent, John A. "Born Out of a Catastrophe, Osten Gallery Becomes One of World's Most Important Exhibitions." *WittyWorld*. Winter/Spring 1992, p. 37.

7813. *II World Cartoon Gallery, Skopje—70. Man and City*. Skopje: Novo Macedonia, 1971.

7814. *IIIrd World Cartoon Gallery—Skopje 1971*. Skopje: Novo Macedonia, 1972.

7815. "23 World Cartoon Gallery Skopje 91." *Kayhan Caricature*. May 1992, pp. 37-38.

7816. Vasilevski, Ane. *24 World Cartoon Gallery Skopje 92 "My Theme."* Catalogue. Skopje: Nova Macedonia, 1992.

7817. Vasilevski, Ane. *23 World Cartoon Gallery Skopje 91 "My Theme."* Skopje: Nova Macedonia, 1991.

7818. World Cartoon Gallery. *C'Est la Vie. Skopje, 1979*. Skopje: Nova Macedonia, 1980.

7819. *World Cartoon Gallery Skopje. How Are You?* Skopje: Novo Macedonia, 1989.

7820. *World Cartoon Gallery Skopje. Joke*. Skopje: Novo Macedonia, 1990.

7821. *World Cartoon Gallery Skopje, '78*. Skopje: Novo Macedonia, 1979.

NETHERLANDS

General Studies

7822. Breed, Kees. "Humor in Hilversum 1991." *Sick*. 22/23 (1991), p. 22.

7823. "Comics-Bibliographie." *Volks-Opvoeding* (Amsterdam). 19:9/10 (1970).

7824. Dros, Rick Lorenzo. "Het Stenen Tijdperk." *Sick*. 22/23 (1991), pp. 16-17.

7825. "The Fifth Dutch Cartoonfestival." *FECO News*. No. 5, 1987, p. 13.

7826. "Lambiek Celebrates 15th Anniversary." *Comics Journal*. April 1993, p. 33.

7827. Munnik, Len. "De Onzekerheid Blijft." *Sick*. 22/23 (1991), p. 36.

7828. Nieuwendijk, Peter. "The 7th Dutch Cartoonfestival Amsterdam." *FECO News*. No. 12, 1991, pp. 18-19.

7829. Pit, Johan. "Met Pit op Pad." *Sick.* 22/23 (1991), p. 24.

7830. "Sabam." *Kever.* September 1988, pp. 3-5.

7831. Van den Hanenberg, Patrick. "Baas in Eigen Brik." *Sick.* 22/23 (1991), pp. 30-31.

7832. Van Gogh, Theo. "Computerhumor—Sympathieke Achterlijkheid." *Sick.* 22/23 (1991), pp. 20-21.

7833. Van Kuyk, J. *Oude Politiche Spotprenten.* Graavenhage: Martinus Nijhoff, 1940.

Cartoonists

7834. Berghs, B. "Bob Vincke." *Sick.* 22/23 (1991), pp. 26-27.

7835. "Bert Witte, Holland." *FECO News.* No. 7, 1989, p. 22.

7836. "Braakensiek, Holland's Famous Cartoonist." *Review of Reviews.* August 1925, pp. 211-212.

7837. De Laet, D. "Hans Kresse, où l'Homme Qui Se Perdit au Nord." *Phénix.* No. 12, 1969.

7838. Friedman, Rick. "Dutch Cartoonist Wim Calls Riviera Home." *Editor and Publisher.* April 25, 1964, pp. 74, 76.

7839. Gilroy, Harry. "As Behrendt Sees It." *New York Times Magazine.* March 11, 1962, pp. 18-21.

7840. Lammertink, Harry (Yrrah). *Yrrah. Deadline.* Amsterdam: Em. Querido's Uitgeverij b.v., 1987.

7841. Landwehr, John. *Romeyn de Hooghe the Etcher.* Leiden: A.W. Sitjhoff; Dobbs Ferry, New York: Oceana, 1973.

7842. Nieuwendijk, Peter. "'I Am an Entertainer...I Draw Cartoons.'" *WittyWorld.* Summer 1988, pp. 28-31.

7843. Schifferstein, Mat and Peter Kuipers. "Il Était Une Fois aux Pays-Bas... Hanco Kolk & Peter de Wit." *Les Cahiers de la Bande Dessinée.* 68, 1986, pp. 52-53.

7844. Schuh, Alfred. "Wil Raymakers und Thijs Wilms: Paradies der Tiere. Eine Bestandsaufnahme des Animalen im Niederländischen Zeitungsstrip." *Comic Forum. Das Magazin für Comicliteratur.* 8:33 (1986), pp. 32-34.

7845. Spaanstra-Polak, Bettina. "Albert Hahn en Zijn Inspiratiebronnen." *Nederlands Kunsthistorisch Jaarboek*. 38 (1987), pp. 331-341.

7846. "Ton Smits Penning." *FECO News*. No. 3, 1987, p. 5.

7847. Van den Hanenberg, Patrick. "Len Munnik." *Sick*. 22/23 (1991), pp. 18-19.

7848. "Willy Lohmann—A Famous Dutch Cartoonist." *FECO News*. No. 9, 1990, p. 12.

Raemakers, Louis

7849. Fragoso, Augusto. "Um Caricaturista Holandês Que a França na Guerra Passada Condecorou com a Legião de Honra." *Vamos Ler!* (Rio de Janeiro). January 14, 1943.

7850. Raemakers, Louis. *America in the War*. New York: The Century Club, 1918.

7851. Raemakers, Louis. *Kultur in Cartoons*. New York: The Century Co., 1917.

7852. Raemakers, Louis. *Raemakers' Cartoon History of the War*. New York: Century, 1918.

7853. Raemakers, Louis. *Raemakers' Cartoons*. New York: Doubleday, Page and Co., 1916.

7854. Snabilié. "Les Dessins d'un Neutre." *L'Illustration Française* (Paris). June 12, 1915.

Swarte, Joost

7855. Glasser, Jean-Claude. "Swarte Hors Hergé." *Les Cahiers de la Bande Dessinée*. 64, 1985, pp. 90-93.

7856. Mutterer, François and Martine Van. "Strictement Absurde." *L'Architecture d'Aujourd'Hui* (Paris). 257 (1988), pp. 35-37.

Animation

7857. Edmunds, Marlene. "Dutch Animators Want To Do It Their Way." *Variety*. September 21, 1992, p. 68.

7858. "En Kort Historik over Hollandsk Animation." *Story Board*. No. 2, pp. 23-26.

7859. Ribe, Göran and Fred Milton. "Disney-Zeichner in Europa. (1) Interview mit Daan Jippes (Holland). Übersetzt und Bearbeitet von Klaus Strzyz." *Comixene. Das Comicfachmagazin.* 7:32 (1980), pp. 4-8.

Caricature

7860. Raam, Van X. "La Caricature dan les Flandres et en Hollande." *Arts et Métiers Graphiques.* September 15, 1932, pp. 129-134.

7861. Veth, C. *Geschiedenes van de Nederlandsche Caricatuur.* Leiden: 1921.

Comic Books

7862. Baur, Elisabeth K. *La Historieta Como Experiencia Didáctica (The Comics as Educational Experience).* Translated by Pablo Kein. México: Editorial Nueva Imagen, 1978.

7863. Milton, Fred. "'Albums' and a Dutch Donald Duck." *Funnyworld.* Spring 1983, pp. 28-33.

7864. Smulders, René, Mat Schifferstein, and Fred Wald. "Radiographie du Marché Hollandais." *Les Cahiers de la Bande Dessinée.* 62, 1985, pp. 43-45.

7865. Swarte, Joost. *Kultur & Technik,* Aus dem Niederländischen von Caterina von Beers, Hendrick Venebrügge, und Ebi Wilke. Osnabrück: Neunte Kunst, 1993. 52 pp.

7866. Van den Boom, Hans. "Holland." In *Comic-Jahrbuch 1986,* edited by Martin Compart and Andreas C. Knigge, pp. 252-255. Berlin: Ullstein GmbH, 1985.

7867. Van Gool, C. "Pays-Bas." In *Histoire Mondiale de la Bande Dessinée,* edited by Pierre Horay, pp. 170-173. Paris: Pierre Horay Éditeur, 1989.

Comic Strips

7868. Bouckaert-Ghesquiere, Rita. "Stripverhalen Waarheen?" *Dietsche Warande en Belfort.* May 1984, pp. 271-278.

7869. de Leon, Clark. "Comics: Call Him Henkie." *Philadelphia Inquirer.* May 4, 1989, p. 2B.

7870. den Dulk, Cor. "Benôt van Innis." *Sick.* 22/23 (1991), p. 3.

7871. Ghesquiere, Rita. "Stripverhalen en Kinderboeken aan de Universiteit, Kan Dat?" *Ons Erfdeel: Algemeen-Nederlands Tweemaandelijks Cultureel Tijdschrift*. November-December 1984, pp. 670-683.

7872. Kousemaker, Kees and Maria Willems. *Strip voor Strip*. Amsterdam: 1970, 152 pp.

7873. Kruis, Jan. *Jack, Jacky and the Juniors*. No. 2. Kockengen, The Netherlands: Joop Wiggers, 1979. 46 pp.

7874. *Strip-3-daagse 1986. De Stripmaatschappij, 19, 20 en 21 September 1986, Het Turfschip, Breda*. Het Stripschap, 1986. n.p.

7875. Ten Berge, Domien. "De Voorvaderen van Panda en Heer Bommel of: De Romantische Middeleeuwen van Marten Toonder." *Stripschrift*. No. 70, October 1974.

7876. Toonder, Marten. "Strip als Randgebied van de Literatuur, of Literatuur als Randgebied van de Strip." *Dietsche Warande en Belfort*. May 1984, pp. 279-284.

NORWAY

General Studies

7877. Andreasen, Mogens Wenzel, Forlaget Artia. "Se til Norge Om Biblioteksafgiften." *Politiken*. 3. July 1989.

7878. Bjorklid, Finn. "Bør Strupentil Inger Bentzrud Rives Opp Med Motorsag?" *TEGN*. No. 3 (13), 1989, pp. 4-5.

7879. "Fra TEGNs Aner:—Det Startet Med Henrik Ibsen." *TEGN*. 1, 1990, p. 19.

7880. Hartung, Peter. "Semic I Norge Mixer Unge Talenter." *Serieskaberen*. June 1990, p. 7.

7881. "Norwegian Cartoonist Association." *FECO News*. No. 13, 1992, p. 24.

7882. Sandberg, Tor. "Gule Pantere og Knøtt i Forsikrings-Selskapenes Tjeneste." *TEGN*. No. 3 (13), 1989, p. 43.

Gulbransson, Olaf

7883. Gulbransson, Olaf. *Ach Wüsstest du Sprüche und Wahrheiten Gezeichnet von Olaf Gulbransson*. Hanover: Fackelträger, Verlag, 1956.

7884. Gulbransson, Olaf. *Es War Einmal*. Munich: Piper Verlag, 1934.

7885. Gulbransson, Olaf. *50 Jahre Humor*. Hanover: Fackelträger Verlag, 1955.

7886. Gulbransson, Olaf. *Franziska Bilek/Lieber Olaf/Liebe Franziska*. Hamburg: Hans Dulk, 1950.

7887. Gulbransson, Olaf. *Und So Weiter*. Munich: Piper Verlag, 1954.

7888. Gulbransson-Björnson, Dagny. *Das Olaf Gulbransson Buch*. Berlin: Langen Müller, 1977. 382 pp.

7889. Gulbransson-Björnson, Dagny. *Olaf Gulbransson*. Neske, 1967. 303 pp.

7890. "Olaf Gulbransson. Zum 85. Geburtstag." *Simplicissimus*. May 31, 1938. (Number dedicated to 85th anniversary of Gulbransson).

Animation

7891. "Nordisken Animerade Asgudar." *Story Board*. No. 6, p. 7.

Comic Books

7892. Atterbom, Daniel. "Tre Dage i Oslo Som Fornyede Nordiske Serier." *Seriejournalen*. June 1992, pp. 20-21.

7893. Braaten, Oyvind. "TEGN—Now Also a Publisher." *Nordic Comics Revue International*. Autumn 1992, pp. 5-6.

7894. Braaten, Oyvind. "Tegneserieutstilling i Sarp." *TEGN*. 1, 1990, p. 39.

7895. "Censur og Tegneserier." *Serieskaberen*. March 1990, p. 10.

7896. "Comic Artist Get [sic] Sponsors." *Nordic Comics Revue*. April 1992, p. 13.

7897. Eide, Knut and Stig Kjelling. *Norsk Tegneserie Index*. Bodo, Norway: NTI. Biennial.

7898. Haxthausen, Toerk. *Opdragelse til Terror*. Oslo: Forlaget Fremad, 1955.

7899. Hegna, Tor Arne. "Norwegian Comics Is *Python!*" *Nordic Comics Revue*. Winter 1992-1993, pp. 11-12.

7900. Hegna, Tor Arne. "Renaissance = Relevance—Meeting Eirik Ihldal, Writer." *Nordic Comics Revue International*. Autumn 1992, pp. 3-5.

7901. Hegna, Tor Arne. "Smørbukk—The True Norwegian Hero!" *Nordic Comics Revue International*. Autumn 1992, p. 6.

7902. Hegna, Tor Arne. "Storytellers Gift." *Nordic Comics Revue*. Winter 1992-1993, p. 12.

7903. Hegna, Tor Arne. "TEGN Celebrates Its Fifth Birthday." *Nordic Comics Revue International*. Autumn 1992, p. 5.

7904. "Import of Serier Presser Markedet i Bund." *Seriejournalen*. December 1991, p. 12.

7905. Kidde, Rune. "Nordisk Samar Bejde." *Seriejournalen*. September 1992, pp. 18-19.

7906. "Kristina." *Nordic Comics Revue International*. Autumn 1992, pp. 8-9.

7907. "Kristina of Tunsberg." *Nordic Comics Revue*. April 1992, p. 13.

7908. Larson, Lorentz. "Children and Comic Books." *Norsk Pedagogisk Tedsskritt*. 38 (1954), pp. 25-32.

7909. Madsen, Frank. "Tor Bomann-Larsen—en Oversigt." *Serieskaberen*. December 1989, pp. 25-29.

7910. "News from Norway." *Nordic Comics Revue International*. Autumn 1992, p. 7.

7911. Nordlund, Eva. *Studie Über die Comics*. Oslo: 1972.

7912. "Norsk Album—Priser." *Seriejournalen*. March 1992, p. 7.

7913. "Norsk Pyton Omtegner Kiddes 'Klassikere.'" *Seriejournalen*. December 1991, p. 6.

7914. "Norsk Tegneserie Forum Fylder 10 År." *Seriejournalen*. September 1990, p. 10.

7915. "Norsk Tegneserieforums Pris til Christopher Nielsen." *Serieskaberen*. March 1990, pp. 9-10.

7916. "Pia Zawa." *Nordic Comics Revue*. April 1992, p. 12.

7917. "Proffer Kontra Freaks." *Seriejournalen*. December 1991, pp. 4-5.

7918. "Profile: Tore Knutsen—Not Bored Yet...." *Nordic Comics Revue*. April 1992, p. 12.

7919. "TEGN." *Serieskaberen*. December 1989, p. 8.

7920. "TEGN 1/90." *Serieskaberen*. June 1990, p. 8.

7921. "Training Course in Graphic Storytelling." *Nordic Comics Revue*. Winter 1992-1993, p. 12.

Comic Strips

7922. "Dansk Udgave af Solruns Saga ud Konkurrerer Norsk Udgave—I Norge." *Serieskaberen*. March 1990, p. 9.

7923. Rosendahl, Peter J. *Han Ola og Han Per: A Norwegian American Comic Strip*. Oslo: Universitetsforlaget, 1984. 165.

7924. Skirbekk, Gunnar. "Donald Duck og den Norske Barnesjel." *Samtiden*. 93:4 (1984), pp. 25-26.

POLAND

General Studies

7925. Bojko, Simon. "Polish Humor and Satirical Drawing." *Arts and Artists*. September 1976.

7926. "Convention." *Comics News Service from Poland*. July-September 1992, pp. 1, 3-6.

7927. "'Fan' Is in Rearganization [sic]." *Comics News Service from Poland*. October-December 1991, p. 1.

7928. Januszewski, Zygmunt. "Warsaw Cartoon Museum Formed When Caricaturist's Home Overflows." *WittyWorld*. Autumn 1988, pp. 26-27.

7929. "Satire Awards." *IPI Report*. October 1987, p. 5.

Animation

7930. "Kiddie Cartoon Earns Big Money for Polish Films." *Variety*. May 18, 1976, p. 434.

7931. Kramer, Hilde. "Skisser Fra Polen." *Story Board*. 1, 1989, pp. 10-11.

7932. "Polish Animation Cinema." *Kayhan Caricature*. January 1993.

Cartoons

7933. Grudzinska-Gross, Irena. "The Art of Solidarity." *International Popular Culture.* 3 (1985), pp. 1-124.

7934. Januszewski, Zygmunt. "Polish Contemporary Cartoon." *WittyWorld.* Autumn 1987, pp. 16-17.

7935. "Slawomir Mrožek." *Apropos.* No. 7, 1991, pp. 84-85.

7936. W.T. "Stalin i Komiksy." *Glos Wielkopolski Siodemka.* Sierpnia 1, 1991, p. 6.

Comic Books and Strips

7937. "Big Changes in 'Komiks.'" *Comics News Service from Poland.* April-June 1992, p. 2.

7938. "Comics Strips in Polish Newspapers." *Comics News Service from Poland.* January-March 1993, p. 2.

7939. "First Comics Shop in Krakow, Not in Warszawa." *Comics News Service from Poland.* July-September 1992, p. 7.

7940. "'Gazeta Wyborcza' and Comics." *Comics News Service from Poland.* July-September 1992, p. 2.

7941. "Grand Prix for Krzysztof Gawronkiewicz." *Comics News Service from Poland.* July-September 1992, p. 3.

7942. "Kloss Still Alive." *Comics News Service from Poland.* July-September 1992, p. 2.

7943. "'Komiks' Nr 10." *Comics News Service from Poland.* July-August 1991, p. 2.

7944. "Lech Walesa a Comics Star Again." *Nordic Comics Revue International.* Autumn 1992, p. 26.

7945. "Lech Walesa Is a Comics Star Again." *Comics News Service from Poland.* April-June 1992, p. 2.

7946. "Manara in Polish." *Comics News Service from Poland.* September 1991, p. 1.

7947. Marciniak, Tomasz. "Erotocomics." *Comics News Service from Poland.* January-March 1993, p. 4.

7948. Mathiasen, Paw. "Polens Mr. Comic." *Seriejournalen*. March 1992, pp. 38-39. (Witold Tkaczyk).

7949. Mathiasen, Paw. "Polske Pirater." *Seriejournalen*. December 1991, p. 15.

7950. "New Comics Magazine." *Comics News Service from Poland*. January-March 1993, p. 1.

7951. "New Comics Projects in Kraków." *Comics News Service from Poland*. January-March 1993, p. 2.

7952. "New Magazine." *Comics News Service from Poland*. September 1991, p. 2.

7953. "New, Regular Hard-Cover Albums." *Comics News Service from Poland*. October-December 1991, p. 1.

7954. "News from Poland: Comics Convention." *Nordic Comics Revue*. Winter 1992-1993, p. 15.

7955. "New Underground Magazine 'Inny Komix.'" *Comics News Service from Poland*. September 1991, p. 1.

7956. "Old Christa in New Edition." *Comics News Service from Poland*. September 1991, p. 2.

7957. "Poles, Protest About 'Mary Worth' Strip." *Menomonee Falls Gazette*. December 15, 1977, p. 4. Reprinted from *Milwaukee Journal*. November 13, 1977.

7958. "Polish Comics Industry Tries To Rebuild." *Comics Journal*. August 1993, pp. 38-39.

7959. "The Prize Winners." *Comics News Service from Poland*. July-September 1992, p. 5.

7960. Skarzynski, Jerzy. "Pologne." In *Histoire Mondiale de la Bande Dessinée*, edited by Pierre Horay, pp. 206-208. Paris: Pierre Horay Éditeur, 1989.

7961. Stopczyk, Stanislaw K. "Edward Lutczyn." *Projekt*. 4/91/199, pp. 8-11.

7962. "Swede Opens Polands [sic] First Comics Store." *Nordic Comics Revue International*. Autumn 1992, p. 26.

7963. Tkaczyk, Witold. "Is Polish Comics Already Dead?" *Comics News Service from Poland*. April-June 1992, p. 4.

7964. Tkaczyk, Witold. "Polish Comics Promotion and Information Presents Jacek Michalski." *Comics News Service from Poland*. July-September 1992, pp. 6 A, B.

7965. Tkaczyk, Witold. "Tegneserier i Polen." *Seriejournalen.* March 1991, pp. 22-25.

7966. Tkaczyk, Witold. "What Comics Do We Need?" *Comics News Service from Poland.* January-March 1993, p. 1.

7967. "Ustabilt Marked." *Seriejournalen.* December 1991, p. 14.

7968. "Where Is 'Yes' + O.K.?" *Comics News Service from Poland.* July-September 1992, p. 7.

7969. "Whole Polish Comics in Lódź." *Comics News Service from Poland.* July-September 1992, p. 4.

7970. "'Wiedźmin' Back for Correct." *Comics News Service from Poland.* January-March 1993, p. 3.

"Awantura"

7971. "'Awantura' Nr 2/3/91." *Comics News Service from Poland.* July-August 1991, pp. 1-2.

7972. "'Fan' and 'Awantura' in Crisis." *Comics News Service from Poland.* September 1991, p. 2.

7973. Janicki, Andrzej. "All the Truth About 'Awantura.'" *Comics News Service from Poland.* July-September 1992, p. 8.

"Boom"

7974. "'Boom'—Two Pages of Polish Comics Every Week in Gdánsk Weekly." *Comics News Service from Poland.* April-June 1992, p. 1.

7975. "Wrong Distribution Plan Killed 'Boom' from Poznán." *Comics News Service from Poland.* July-September 1992, p. 7.

Rosinski, Grzegorz

7976. Groensteen, Thierry. "Entretien avec Grzegorz Rosinski." *Les Cahiers de la Bande Dessinée.* 70, 1986, pp. 9-13.

7977. Szylak, Jerzy. "Grzegorz Rosinski." *Nordic Comics Revue International.* Autumn 1992, pp. 24-25.

7978. Szylak, Jerzy. "Komiksy Grzegorza/Grzegorz Rosiński's Comic Strips." *Projekt.* 4/91/199, pp. 1-2.

7979. Van Cauwenbergh, Franz. "Fiche Bibliographique de Rosinski." *Les Cahiers de la Bande Dessinée.* 70, 1986, p. 36.

Wroblewski, Jerzy

7980. "Jerzy Wróblewski Died." *Comics News Service from Poland.* September 1991, p. 2.

7981. "Jerzy Wróblewski in 'Nordic Comics Revue International.'" *Comics News Service from Poland.* April-June 1992, p. 3.

Political Cartoons

7982. Avas. *Proverbs Illustrated. Polish Political Cartoons.* London: P.S. King and Staples, n.d.

7983. Glodowski, Wlodzimierz. "Karykatura Polityczna Jako Forma Komunikowania W Badaniach Amerykanskich." *Zeszyty Prasoznawcze.* 29:3 (1988), pp. 29-44.

7984. Szyk, Arthur. *The New Order.* New York: G.P. Putnam's Sons, 1941.

PORTUGAL

General Studies

7985. de Matos-Cruz, José. "Portugal: Filmes de Animaçao." *Corto Circuito.* April 1992, pp. 22-23. (Animation).

7986. de Sousa, Osvaldo. "From Bordalo Pinheiro to Manta: The Tortuous Route of Portugal's Humorous Art." *WittyWorld.* Summer/Autumn 1989, pp. 36-38.

7987. "Portfolio: Antonio Moriera Antunes." *Target.* Autumn 1984, pp. 26-27. (Political Cartoons).

Caricature

7988. Boaventura, Armando. "De Rafael Bordalo Pinheiro a Leal da Câmara." *Voz de Portugal* (Rio de Janeiro). October 7, 1948.

7989. Boaventura, Armando. "Ramos Lobão." *Voz de Portugal* (Rio de Janeiro). November 7, 1948.

7990. "Da Caricatura. Seu Moderno Significado." *Águia* (Lisbon). January-June 1919.

7991. Dom Fuas. *12 Desenhos.* Pranchas Sôltas. Pôrto: Impr. Portuguêsa, 1945.

7992. Lima, Herman. "Lápis Portuguêses no Brasil." *Rio Magazine* (Rio de Janeiro). March 1950.

7993. Lima, Herman. *A Caricatura nas Letras e nas Artes de Portugal*. 20.ª aula do 10.º ano letivo do Instituto de Estudos Portuguêses Afrânio Peixoto, Rio de Janeiro. *Jornal do Brasil*. September 14, 1952.

7994. Martins, Rocha. "A Caricatura em Portugal. Do Tempo dos Franceses a El-Rei Dom Fernando." *Serões* (Lisbon). No. 51.

7995. Ressano, Arnaldo. *Álbum de Caricaturas*. Lisbon: Author, 1935.

7996. Valença, Francisco. *Varões Assinalados*. Lisbon: Author, 1909-1911.

7997. Valença, Francisco and Carlos Simões. *Catálogo Cômico da Exposição de Belas-Artes, de 1914, 1915, 1916, 1923 e 1924*. Lisbon: Edição, Comp. e Impressão Franco & Cia, 1914. Edição da Papelaria Áurea, 1915 e 1916. Depositária Livraria Portugália, 1923 e 1924.

Leal da Câmara

7998. da Câmara, Leal. *Miren Ustedes. Portugal Visto de Espanha*. Pôrto: Livraria Chardron, 1917.

7999. Frances, José. "Leal da Câmara." *Vamos Ler!* (Rio de Janeiro). December 31, 1942.

8000. Lago, Silvio. "Leal da Câmara." *La Esfera* (Madrid). February 5, 1916.

8001. Ribeiro, Aquilino. *Leal da Câmara. Vida e Obra*. Lisbon: Livraria Bertrand, 1951.

Pinheiro, Rafael Bordalo

8002. Brandão, Raul. "Rafael Bordalo Pinheiro." In *Memórias*, Vol. 1. Lisbon, Paris: Livrarias Aillaud and Bertrand, 1925.

8003. Chaves, Luís. *A Inspiração Folclórica na Obra de Rafael Bordalo Pinheiro*. Lisbon: Edições José Fernandes Jr., 1937.

8004. Dantas, Júlio. "Rafael Bordalo Pinheiro." In *Figuras d'Ontem e de Hoje*. Pôrto: Livraria Chardron, 1924.

8005. D'Almeida, Fialho. "Pequena Romaria à Fábrica de Faiança de Bordalo, nas Caldas da Rainha." In *Os Gatos*. 6th Vol., New Ed. Lisbon: Livraria Clássica Editôra, n.d.

8006. D'Almeida, Fialho. "Rafael Bordalo Pinheiro." In *À Esquina*. 4th Ed. Lisbon: Livraria Clássica Editôra, 1920.

8007. de Carvalho, Maria Amália Vaz. "Rafael Bordalo Pinheiro." In *Páginas Escolhidas*. Lisbon: Portugal-Brasil Ltda., 1920.

8008. Ferrão, Julieta. *Monografia do Museu Rafael Bordalo Pinheiro*. Lisbon: Museu R.B. Pinheiro, n.d.

8009. Ferrão, Julieta. *Rafael Bordalo Pinheiro e a Crítica*. Coimbra: Imprensa da Universidade, 1924.

8010. França, José Augusto. *Raphael Bordallo Pinheiro—O Português tal e Qual*. Lisbon: 1981.

8011. Gill, Ruben. "O Século Boêmio." In *Dom Casmurro* (Rio de Janiero). December 4, 1943.

8012. Gill, Ruben. "Rafael Bordalo Pinheiro." *O Século Boêmio* (Rio de Janeiro). March 9, 1948.

8013. Guimarães, Ângela. "At Home and Abroad. Anglo-Portuguese Colonial Rivalries and Their Domestic Impact in the Work of Raphael Bordallo Pinheiro." *Oxford Art Journal*. 8:1 (1985), pp. 29-39.

8014. *Inspiração Folclórica na Obra de Rafael Bordalo Pinheiro*. Lisbon: Edições José Fernandes Jr., 1937.

8015. Leitão, Joaquim. *O Poco Que Ri. Conferência*. Lisbon: Editor, 1926.

8016. Lima, Herman. "Rafael Bordalo Pinheiro." *Vitrina* (Rio de Janeiro). May 1943.

8017. Lima, Herman. "Rafael Bordalo Pinheiro. Os Mestres do Lápis Brasileiro." *O Jornal* (Rio de Janeiro). December 2, 1951.

8018. Lima, Herman. "Um Grande Caricaturista Português no Brasil." *Revista Municipal* (Lisbon). Nos. 24, 25, 1st and 2nd Trims. 1945.

8019. Machado, J. Saavedra. *O Desenho e as Mulheres no Labor Artístico de Rafael Bordalo*. Preface by Arlindo Camilo Monteiro. Coimbra: Imprensa da Universidade, 1934.

8020. Maglhães, Cruz. *Rafael Bordalo Pinheiro. Moralizador Político-Social*. Seguido de *O Museu Bordalo Pinheiro*. Coimbra: Imprensa da Universidade, 1925.

8021. Ortigão, Ramalho. "Rafael Bordalo Pinheiro e o *Antônio Maria*." In *As Farpas*. Seleção. Vol. 2. Rio de Janeiro: Edições Dois Mundos Ltda., 1943.

8022. Pinheiro, Rafael Bordalo. *Álbum das Glórias*. Lisbon: n. ind. editor, March 1880-January 1883.

8023. Pinheiro, Rafael Bordalo. Álbum de Caricaturas. Frases e Anexins da Língua Portuguêsa. Preface by Júlio César Machado. Lisbon: Livraria Editôra de Matos Moreira e Cia, 1876.

8024. Pinheiro, Rafael Bordalo. *Almanaque de Caricaturas*. Lisbon: 1874, 1875, 1882, 1883 and 1884.

8025. Pinheiro, Rafael Bordalo. *A Paródia* (Lisbon). January 17, 1900 to December 25, 1901.

8026. Pinheiro, Rafael Bordalo. *No Lazareto de Lisboa*. Lisbon: Emp. Literaria Luso-Brasileira Editôra, 1881.

8027. Pinheiro, Rafael Bordalo. *O Antônio Maria* (Lisbon). June 12, 1879 to December 25, 1894.

8028. Pinheiro, Rafael Bordalo. *O Besouro* (Rio de Janeiro). April 6, 1878 to March 8, 1879.

8029. Pinheiro, Rafael Bordalo. *O Calcanhar de Aquiles*. Lisbon: n.ind. editor, 1870.

8030. Pinheiro, Rafael Bordalo. *O Mosquito* (Rio de Janeiro). September 11, 1875 to May 26, 1877.

8031. Pinheiro, Rafael Bordalo. *Pontos Nos ii* (Lisbon). May 7, 1885 to December 29, 1887.

8032. Pinheiro, Rafael Bordalo. *Psit!* (Rio de Janeiro). September 15, 1877 to November 17, 1877.

8033. Pinto, Manuel de Sousa. *Rafael Bordalo Pinheiro. O Caricaturista*. Lisbon: Livraria Pereira, n.d.

Comic Books

8034. "Ainda as Historias em Quadrinhos, Uma Realidade e Varios Niveis de Analise e Critica." *Républica* (Lisbon). July 19, 1967, pp. 4-7.

8035. "Banda Desenhada: Primado da Violencia?" *Diario de Lisboa*. August 1, 1968, p. 8.

8036. Batoreo, Manuel L. "Vamos Desenhar Historias sem Ilustrar Palavras." *A Capital* (Lisbon). November 28, 1968.

8037. Gasca, Luis and Vasco Granja. "Diccionario da Banda Desenhada." In *Jornal do Fundao* (Lisbon). Supplement to "E Etc." 1968.

8038. Gassiot-Talabot, Gérald. "Pintura e Banda Desenhada." *A Semana*. Supplement to *A Capital* (Lisbon). October 11, 1968, pp. 6-8.

8039. Granja, Vasco. "A Banda Desenhada Expressao Artistica do Nosso Tempo." *A Semana*. Supplement to *A Capital* (Lisbon). October 11, 1968, p. 6.

8040. Granja, Vasco. "A Banda Desenhada na Universidade." *A Capital* (Lisbon). November 28, 1968.

8041. Granja, Vasco. "Alain Resnais e a Banda Desenhada." *A Capital* (Lisbon). October 11, 1978, p. 6.

8042. Granja, Vasco. "Bienal Mundial da Banda Desenhada." *Républica* (Lisbon). May 23, 1968, p. 4.

8043. Granja, Vasco. "Defesa da Banda Desenhada." *Républica* (Lisbon). January 18, 1967, p. 3.

8044. Granja, Vasco. "The Great Comic-Book Heroes." *Républica*. July 19, 1967, p. 7.

8045. Granja, Vasco. "Historía da Banda Desenhada." *Jornal do Fundao* (Lisbon). Supplement to *E Etc* (Lisbon). November 26, 1967.

8046. Lacassin, Francis. "Alain Resnais e As Bandas Desenhadas." *Républica* (Lisbon). January 18, 1967, p. 3.

8047. Lucchetti, Rubens Fr. "As Historias em Quadrinhos Criam o Hábito da Leitura." *Républica* (Lisbon). April 12, 1967.

8048. Lucchetti, Rubens Fr. "Historias em Quadrinhos, Expressao do Nosso Século." *Républica* (Lisbon). July 12, 1967, pp. 3-4.

8049. McColvin, Lionel M. "Os Servicos de Leitura Publica Para Criancas." *Seara Nova* (Lisbon). No. 1466, 1967.

8050. Mesquita, Victor. "Portugal." In *Histoire Mondiale de la Bande Dessinée*, edited by Pierre Horay, pp. 192-196. Paris: Pierre Horay Éditeur, 1989.

8051. Quintas Alves, Emma. "Escollia de Livros Para Criancas." *Sera Nova* (Lisbon). No. 1466, 1967, pp. 381-384.

8052. Sadoul, Georges. "A Banda Desenhada e o Cinema." *Républica*. April 5, 1967, pp. 3-4.

8053. "Serieskaberen Rosende Omtalt i Portugisisk Ugeavis." *Serieskaberen*. March 1990, p. 11.

ROMANIA

General Studies

8054. Arapu, Mircea. "Roumanie." In *Histoire Mondiale de la Bande Dessinée*, edited by Pierre Horay, pp. 296-299. Paris: Pierre Horay Éditeur, 1989.

8055. *Din Haz in Haz. Circa 300 Desene*. Bucharest: Arta Grafica, 1986.

8056. "Magazine of Roumania." *FECO News*. No. 10, 1990, p. 17.

8057. *Mai Mare Hazul. 200 Desene*. Bucharest: Uniunea Artistilor Plastici din R.S. Romania, n.d.

8058. "Moldoveanu Nicolae." *FECO News*. No. 6, 1988, p. 13.

RUSSIA (SOVIET UNION)

General Studies

8059. Babuchkina, A.P. *I Storia Russkoy Dietskoy Literatury*. Moscow: 1948.

8060. Filipovsky, Nikolai I. "Emblems of Perestroika." *Apollo* (London). January 1990, pp. 12-13.

8061. "Ha Ha Habitat." *FECO News*. No. 8, 1989, pp. 10-11.

8062. "Jokes with a Purpose." *Parade Magazine*. November 27, 1955.

8063. King, David and Cathy Porter. *Images of Revolution*. New York: Pantheon Books, 1983. 128 pp.

8064. "The Kremlin Wall Will Never Be the Same!" *Cartoonist PROfiles*. June 1977, pp. 64-67.

8065. Martin, Donna. "Soviet Humor: Funny Business in the USSR." *Cartoonist PROfiles*. September 1989, pp. 54-59.

8066. Ostrander, Sheila and Lynn Schroeder. "From Russia with Laughs." *The World of Comic Art*. Winter 1966/1967, pp. 48-52.

8067. Schmidt, W. *Russische Graphik des XIX. und XX. Jahrhunderts*. Leipzig: 1967.

8068. Sykalin, S. and I. Kremenskaia. *Sovetskaya Satireskaya Pechat': 1917-1963*. Moscow: 1963.

Latvia

8069. *Latvijas PSR Karikatúristu Darbu Krajums*. Zvaigzne, 1969. 79 pp.

8070. "Sergey Mosienko." *FECO News*. No. 13, 1992, p. 8.

Cartoonists

8071. Dangulov, S. "People's Artist Efimov and His Portraits of Soviet Writers." *Soviet Literature*. No. 12, 1974, pp. 163-168.

8072. Deneroff, Harvey. "Feodor Khitruk: The Gentle Master of Animation." *Animation*. Winter 1989, pp. 43-44.

8073. "Gali Mirgasim, U.S.S.R." *FECO News*. No. 6, 1988, p. 1.

8074. "Garif Bassirov." *Apropos*. No. 5, 1988, pp. 69-72.

8075. "Kazanevsky." *WittyWorld*. Summer/Autumn 1991, pp. 62-65.

8076. *Klassiker der Karikatur: No. 10. Dmitri Moor*. Berlin: Eulenspiegel-Verlag, 1973. (a.k.a. Dimitry Stakhiyevich Orlov).

8077. Krnstev, Todor. "Andrei Nekrassov's Two Faces." *Apropos*. No. 6, pp. 17-18.

8078. Rifas, Leonard. "Soviet Cartoonist Finishes Sentence." *Comics Buyer's Guide*. April 26, 1985, p. 62.

8079. "Sergei Tunin." *Apropos*. No. 5, 1988, pp. 36-37.

8080. "Victor Bogorad." *Apropos*. No. 7, 1991, p. 39.

Kukriniksi

8081. "The Cartoons of Koukriniksi." *Apropos*. No. 1, 1983, pp. 144-147.

8082. Kamenskii, Aleksandr A. *Kukryniksy*. Moscow: Sovetskii Khudozhnik, 1973.

8083. "Kukriniksi: Collectivized Caricaturists, Mikhail Kuprianoff, Porfiri Kriloff, and Nikolai Sokoloff." *Newsweek*. September 27, 1943, pp. 80 +.

8084. Kukryniksy. *Karikaturen*. Berlin: Eulenspiegel-Verlag, 1977.

Sysoyev

8085. "How Sysoyev Became a Non-Conformist." *Index on Censorship*. October 1984.

8086. Rifas, Leonard. "Sysoyev: The Plight of a Soviet Cartoonist." *Comics Journal*. September 1986, pp. 105-108.

Animation

8087. "Animation Is So Popular, Paying Its Own Way Should Be a Breeze." *Variety*. July 1, 1987, p. 70.

8088. Fraser, Hugh. "Bard Project Spans the Globe." *Variety*. August 17, 1992, p. 31.

8089. "Mickey Mouse in Russian." *Comics Buyer's Guide*. March 8, 1991, p. 62.

8090. Petrucci, Noberto P. "El Dibujo Animado en la URSS." *Dibujantes* (Buenos Aires). No. 16, 1955, pp. 4-6.

8091. Samu, Charles. "Soviet Animation: A Brief History." *Animation*. Winter 1989, pp. 42-43.

8092. Strom, Gunnar. "Moskva: Nordmenn i Sovjet." *Story Board*. No. 7, 1988, pp. 22-23.

Caricature

8093. Beckmann, Oda. *Freund und Feind im Spiegel der Sowjetischen Karikature*. Howacht-Verlag, 1977. 168 pp.

8094. Grand-Carteret, John. *Musée Pittoresque du Voyage du Tzar*. Paris: Eugène Fasquelle Éd., 1897.

8095. Nir, Yeshayahu. *The Israeli-Arab Conflict in Soviet Caricatures, 1967-1973*. Tel Aviv: Tcherikover Publishers, 1976.

8096. Nir, Yeshayahu. "U.S. Involvement in the Middle East Conflict in Soviet Caricatures." *Journalism Quarterly*. Winter 1977, pp. 697-702, 726.

8097. Roger-Marx, Claude. *La Caricature Étrangére. Russie et Europe Central*. No. 3. Paris: Laboratoires Le Brun et Mictasol, n.d.

8098. "Soviet Freedom for Caricaturists." *Literary Digest*. January 28, 1933, p. 17.

8099. Varschavski, L.R. "A Caricatura Russa." *Vamos Ler!* (Rio de Janeiro). June 17, 1943.

8100. Varschavski, L.R. "Aperçu Historique de la Caricature Russe." *Arts et Métiers Graphiques*. September 15, 1932, pp. 122-128.

8101. Verechagin, B.A. *Russkaia Caricatura*. St. Petersburg: 1911.

Cartoons

8102. "As Russia Portrays Us; Cartoons from the Soviet Press." *New York Times Magazine*. October 5, 1947, pp. 8-9.

8103. Bostrup, Lise. "Tegneserier i Sovjet." *Seriejournalen*. March 1991, p. 21.

8104. Kourtev, Krassimir. "Cartoons." *Thalia: Studies in Literary Humor*. 11:1 (1989), pp. 52-60.

8105. Misyuchenko, Vladimir. "Soviet Cartoons." *Cartoonist PROfiles*. November 1970, pp. 18-25.

8106. Prodshivalov, Ivan. "Soviet Cartoons: From an Aesopian Language to the Language of Satire." *Democratic Journalist*. July 1989, pp. 14-18.

8107. Rifas, Leonard. "Cartooning in the Soviet Union." *Comics Journal*. September 1986, pp. 106-107.

8108. Schwartz, Harry. "Russia Itself Reveals Russian Weaknesses." *New York Times Magazine*. April 25, 1948, pp. 12-13.

8109. "Some Russian Cartoons." *Asia*. June 1919, pp. 578-579.

8110. *Spirit of the Soviet Union; Anti-Nazi Cartoons and Posters*. London: The Pilot Press, 1942. 48 pp.

Comic Books

8111. Mansurov, N.S. "Children's Publications in the Soviet Union." In *Comics and Visual Culture: Research Studies from Ten Countries*, edited by Alphons Silbermann and H.-D. Dyroff, pp. 144-158. Munich: K.G. Saur, 1986.

8112. Rifas, Leonard. "Gorbachev in Comics: From Tyrant to Democrat." *Reflex* (Seattle). July/August 1990.

Political Cartoons

8113. Evans, E. "Soviet Satirists." *Asia*. June 1933, pp. 362-367.

8114. Kunzle, David. "Gustave Doré's History of Holy Russia: Anti Russian Propaganda from the Crimean War to the Cold War." *Russian Review*. July 1983, pp. 271-299.

8115. Mattern, Kendall, jr. "Political Cartooning in the Soviet Union: Toeing the Line." *Target*. Autumn 1984, pp. 13-15.

8116. Peltzer, Marina. "Imagerie Populaire et Caricature: La Graphique Politique Antinapoleonienne en Russia et Ses Antecedents Petroviens." *Journal of the Warburg and Courtauld Institutes*. 48 (1985), pp. 189-221.

8117. "Russian Cartoons of Nazis Are Savage." *Life*. March 29, 1943, pp. 4 ff.

Krokodil

8118. "Krokodil Criticisms." *New York Times Magazine*. October 28, 1962, pp. 30-31.

8119. Lo Bello, Nino. "The *Krokodil* That Bites Russians." *Parade*. November 13, 1969, p. 6.

8120. Markham, James W. *Voices of the Red Giants*. Ames: Iowa State University Press, 1967. 513 pp.

8121. Nelson, William, ed. *Out of the Crocodile's Mouth: Russian Cartoons About the United States from "Krokodil," Moscow's Humor Magazine*. Washington, D.C.: Public Affairs Press, 1949.

8122. Pehowski, Marian. "*Krokodil* Magazine: Laughter in the Soviet Union." Presented at Association for Education in Journalism, College Park, Maryland: July 1976. 10 pp.

8123. Pehowski, Marian. "*Krokodil*—Satire for the Soviets." *Journalism Quarterly*. Winter 1978, pp. 726-731.

8124. Shabad, Theodore. "Behind the Smile on Krokodil." *New York Times Magazine*. June 7, 1964, pp. 22-24, 85-87.

8125. *Soviet Humor: The Best of Krokodil*. Kansas City, Missouri: Andrews and McMeel, and London: Sidgwick and Jackson, 1989. 192 pp.

8126. Swearingen, Rodger. *What's So Funny, Comrade? 152 Cartoons from Krokodil.* New York: Praeger, 1961. 156 pp.

8127. Tempest, Peter. *Soviet Humour: Stories and Cartoons from Crocodile.* London: The Society for Cultural Relations with the U.S.S.R., n.d.

Pravda

8128. Gordey, Michel. "Pour la Première Fois, une Bande Dessinée dans la Pravda." *France-Soir.* October 10, 1967, p. 4.

8129. Ladiges, P.M. "Pravda-Heroine der Comics." *Deutsches Allgemeines Sonntagsblatt* (Cologne). June 15, 1969.

8130. Milenkovitch, Michael M. *The View from Red Square: A Critique of Cartoons from Pravda and Izvestia, 1947-1964.* New York: Hobbs, Dorman, and Co., 1966.

8131. Schober, Siegfried. "Pravda." *Die Zeit.* March 14, 1969, p. 31.

SPAIN

References

8132. Delhom, J.M. *Catalogo del Tebeo en España, 1865-1980.* Barcelona: Circulo del Comic y del Coleccionismo, 1989.

8133. Delhom, J.M. and J. Navarro. "Catálogo del Tebeo en España, 1915-1965." Barcelona: Club Amigos de la Historieta, 1980.

8134. Faur, Jean-Claude. "El Cedoci. Centro de Estudios y de Documentación Sobre la Imagen en la Biblioteca Municipal de Marsella." *Neuróptica* (Zaragoza). 2, 1984, pp. 134-140.

8135. Gasca, Luis. "Bibliografia Mundial del 'Comic.'" *Revista Española de la Opinión Pública* (Madrid). 14, 1968, pp. 365-380; No. 17, 1969, pp. 431-576.

8136. "Los 100 Mejores: 50 Numeros y 16 Años. Hay Quien de Mas?" *El Wendigo.* No. 50, 1990, pp. 31-33.

8137. Pérez, Ramón F. "50 Numeros 50. Wendigo: los Años Heroicos." *El Wendigo.* No. 50, 1990, pp. 37-39.

General Studies

8138. Alemán Sainz, Francisco. *Las Literaturas de Kiosco*. Barcelona: Planeta, 1975.

8139. Arbesú, Faustino. "Al Otro Lado del Espejo." *El Wendigo*. October-December 1987, pp. 4-7.

8140. Arbesú, Faustino R. "Asi Nos Luce el Pelo." *El Wendigo*. 14:43 (1988), pp. 4-5.

8141. Arbesú, Faustino R. "'Comic Arte-Nuevo Comic': Un Comic de Vanguardia?" *El Wendigo*. No. 22, pp. 30-34.

8142. Arbesú, Faustino R. "Lo Que Nunca se Dijo Sobre." *El Wendigo*. March 1979, pp. 15-18.

8143. Arbesú, Faustino R. "Totem por el Buen Camino." *El Wendigo*. October 1978, pp. 11-15.

8144. Battaglia, Roberto C. "Sentida Gráfico y Humanidad Son la Base del Dibujo Humoristico." *Dibujantes* (Buenos Aires). No. 2, 1953.

8145. Bermeosolo, Francisco. "El Origen del Periodismo Amarillo." *Rialp* (Madrid). 1962.

8146. Cebrian, Julio. "La Nueva Frontera del Humor Español." *La Actualidad Española*. No. 729. 1965.

8147. Cuervo, Javier. "Intracairo y Extravibora." *El Wendigo*. May-June 1985, pp. 27-28.

8148. Cuervo, Javier. "1984 x 50 = 2." *El Wendigo*. May 1983, pp. 2-5.

8149. Cuervo, Javier. "Un Año en el Cairo." *El Wendigo*. February 1983, pp. 1-4.

8150. Cuervo, Javier and Faustino Rodríguez. "Que Esta Pasando?" *El Wendigo*. November 1981, pp. 6-9.

8151. Cuervo, Javier, Faustino Rodríguez and Gonzalo Lorenzo." En Frecuencia No Moderada." *El Wendigo*. August 1982, pp. 29-34.

8152. Cuesta Fernández, Fernando. "El Viaje de los Condenados." *El Wendigo*. February-April 1988, pp. 36-39.

8153. Cuesta Fernández, Fernando. "Giardino: Un Humorista Rumbo a Oriente." *El Wendigo*. October-December 1987, pp. 34-38.

8154. de Liñares, Antonio S. "El Humorismo ante la Guerra." *La Esfera* (Madrid). July 31, 1915.

8155. "El del Establishment." *El Wendigo.* March 1979, pp. 3-5.

8156. Escobar. "Humor Grafico." In *Curso de Dibujo Humoristico por Correspondencia.* Barcelona: 1965.

8157. Fermín Pérez, Ramón. "Al Dia Siguiente...." *El Wendigo.* May 1984, pp. 12-16.

8158. Fermín Pérez, Ramón. "Algo Mas Que Nostalgia." *El Wendigo.* December 1984-January 1985, pp. 57-59.

8159. Fermín Pérez, Ramón. "Asignatura Pendiente." *El Wendigo.* December 1985, p. 26.

8160. Fermín Pérez, Ramón. "El Tren de la Historia." *El Wendigo.* October-December 1987, pp. 11-14.

8161. Fermín Pérez, Ramón. "La Noche de los Encantos." *El Wendigo.* May-June 1985, pp. 17-20.

8162. Fermín Pérez, Ramón. "Las Jornadas Catalanas." *El Wendigo.* January 1984, pp. 52-53.

8163. Fermín Pérez, Ramón. "No Todo son Golpisas y Batacazos." *El Wendigo.* March-April 1987, p. 14.

8164. Flórez, Florentino. "Vida en Este Planeta." *El Wendigo.* October-December 1987, pp. 16-19.

8165. Gasca, Luis. *Los Héroes de Papel.* Barcelona: Editorial Táber, 1969.

8166. Gubern, Román. *Literatura de la Imagen* (Pictorial Literature). Barcelona: Salvat, 1973.

8167. Mingote. *Humor 1953-55.* Prologue by Edgar Neville. Madrid: Editorial Prensa Española, 1956.

8168. Paniceres, Ruben. "Custer/Dr. Mabuse: Las dos Caras de la Cinefilia." *El Wendigo.* October-December 1987, pp. 28-31.

8169. Parramón, José M. *El Arte de la Ilustración.* Madrid: Instituto Parramón, 1965.

8170. Tarin-Iglesias, José. "Cu-Cut y El Bé Negre." *Gaceta de la Prensa Española.* January 15, 1968.

8171. Waldmann, Emil. *Arte del Realismo y Impresionismo en el Siglo XIX. Historia del Arte Labor.* Vol. 15. Barcelona: Editorial Labor, 1937.

Children's Press

8172. Altabella, José. "Las Publicaciones Infantiles en Su Desarollo Histórico." In *Curso de Prensa Infantil*. Madrid: Escuela Oficial de Periodismo, 1964.

8173. Barriales Ardura, Andrés. *El Héroe en la Prensa Infantil y Juvenil*. Pamplona: Instituto de Periodismo, 1964.

8174. Beneyto, Juan. "Publicaciones Infantiles y Juveniles en el Cuadro de las Communicaciones Sociales." In *Curso de Prensa Infantil*. Madrid: Escuela Oficial de Periodismo, 1964.

8175. Bouvard, Maria L. "La Prensa Para Adolescentes en España." *Gaceta de la Prensa Española* (Madrid). No. 111, 1957, pp. 40-57.

8176. Bravo-Villasante, Carmen. "Historia de la Literatura Infantil Española." In *Revista del Occidente*. Madrid: 1959. 270 pp.

8177. Castillo, José C. *Aptitudes Politicas en la Prensa Juvenil*. Madrid: 1962.

8178. De Laiglesia, Juan A. "El Guión Gráfico Ilustrado. Sus Problemas y Peculiariades." In *Curso de Prensa Infantil*. p. 203. Madrid: Escuela Oficial de Periodismo, 1964.

8179. De Laiglesia, Juan A. "El Humor en las Revistas de Niños." In *Curso de Prensa Infantil*, p. 193. Madrid: Escuela Ofical de Periodismo, 1964.

8180. Fernández Larrondo, Pacho. "Cuarenta Años de Censura Infantil." *Ciudadano*. June 1976.

8181. Gil Roesset, C. "La Pedagogía en la Prensa Infantil." In *Escuela Social*. Madrid: 1947.

8182. Grimalt, Manuel. *Los Niños y los Libros*. Barcelona: 1962.

8183. Hazard, Paul. *Los Libros, los Niños y los Hombres*. Barcelona: 1965.

8184. Magaña, Fuensanta. "La Información en la Prensa Infantil." Madrid: Escuela de Periodismo de la Iglesia, 1964.

8185. Maillo, Adolfo. "Aspectos Educativos de la Prensa Infantil." In *Curso de Prensa Infantil*. Madrid: Escuela Oficial de Periodismo, 1964.

8186. Manent, A. "La Revista Infantil en Barcelona." *ABC* (Madrid). February 16, 1965.

8187. Martín, Antonio. "Alienación y Prensa Infantil." *Claustro* (Valencia). January 1962; *La Estafeta Literaria* (Madrid). August 14/18, 1965.

8188. Martín, Antonio. "Notas Para una Ideología de la Prensa Juvenil." *Marzo* (Madrid). No. 31, 1965.

8189. Nadal Gaya, C. "Temática de la Actual Prensa Infantil Española." *Gaceta de la Prensa Española* (Madrid). No. 130, 1960.

8190. Paya, Maria R. "El Mundo Profesional a Través de la Prensa Infantil y Juvenil." In *Curso de Prensa Infantil*, p. 211. Madrid: Escuela Oficial de Periodismo, 1964.

8191. Pericas, Juana. "El Héroe y el Personaje." In *Curso de Prensa Infantil*, p. 183. Madrid: Escuela Oficial de Periodismo, 1964.

8192. Perucho, Juan. "Una Revista Infantil: Cavallo Fort." *Destino* (Barcelona). No. 1479, 1965.

8193. Reyna Domenech, Consuelo. "Prensa Juvenil, Tesis Fin de Carrera." Madrid: Escuela Oficial de Periodismo, 1963.

8194. Rovira, M. Theresa. "La Revista Infantil en Barcelona." In *Disputación de Barcelona*. Barcelona: 1965.

8195. Saladrigas, Roberto. "Los Niños y la Literatura Que No Tienen." *Siglo XX* (Madrid). No. 30, 1965.

8196. Sánchez Brito, Margarita. "Prensa Infantil." *Gaceta de la Prensa Española* (Madrid). No. 124, 1959.

8197. Toral, Carolina. *Literatura Infantil Española*. Madrid: Editora Coculsa, 1957.

8198. Vazquez, Jésus. "Decontología del Periodista en Publicaciones Infantiles y Juveniles." In *Curso de Prensa Infantil*, p. 295. Madrid: 1964.

8199. Vazquez, Jésus. *La Prensa Infantil en España*. Madrid: Doncel, 1963.

8200. Vazquez, Jésus. "La Prensa Infantil y Juvenil en España." *Gaceta de la Prensa Española*. No. 59-60, 1964.

8201. Vazquez, Jésus. "Panorama de las Publicaciones Infantiles en España." In *Curso de Prensa Infantil*. Madrid: 1964.

8202. Vazquez, Jésus. "Sociologia Infantil. Encuesta Sobre la Lectura de los Niños en un Sector de Madrid." *Revista Educación* (Madrid). No. 67, 1957, pp. 41-48.

8203. Volpi, Domenico. "Panorama Internacional de la Prensa Infantil." In *Curso de la Prensa Infatil*, p. 285. Madrid: 1964.

Salons   ·

8204. "A la Cuarta Va la Vencida, Salon del Comic Ciudad de Oviedo." *El Wendigo*. February-April 1988, pp. 4-7.

8205. Arbesú, Faustino R. "Con Frecuencia, la 'Vista' Engaña." *El Wendigo*. No. 58, 1993, pp. 33-35.

8206. Arbesú, Faustino R. "Haxtur." *El Wendigo*. November 1981, pp. 18-24.

8207. "Cita en Oviedo: Sexto Salon del Comic." *El Wendigo*. Autumn/Winter 1989-1990, pp. 37-41.

8208. "Comic: Año VI." Program of Caja de Ahorros de Asturias, Oviedo, Spain, November 1989, p. 45.

8209. Cuervo, Javier. "Ventura y Nieto en el Salón del Cómic." *El Wendigo*. No. 58, 1993, p. 36.

8210. Cuesta, Fernando. "V Salon del Comic 'Ciudad de Oviedo' No Hay Quinto Malo, Pero Este Fue Mejor." *El Wendigo*. Winter 1988-1989, pp. 37-42.

8211. Cuesta, Fernando. "XVI Salón Internacional del Comic del Principado de Asturias: El Salón de España." *El Wendigo*. No. 58, 1993, pp. 40-42.

8212. Fermín Pérez, Ramón. "Hubo Salón!!... y van XIV." *El Wendigo*. No. 51, 1991, pp. 36-38.

8213. Fermín Pérez, Ramón. "Premios Haxtur III Salon del Comic Ciudad de Oviedo." *El Wendigo*. March-April 1987, pp. 15-16.

8214. Fernández Mieres, Gonzalo. "Introducción Entrega Premios HAXTUR (XV Salón Internacional del Cómic)." *El Wendigo*. No. 54, 1991, p. 3.

8215. "XV Salón Internacional del Comic del Principado de Asturias. El Salón del Norte." *El Wendigo*. No. 54, 1991, pp. 13-15.

8216. Flórez Fernández, Florentino. "Color y Aventura en Domingo." *El Wendigo*. No. 59, 1993, pp. 14-15.

8217. Giménez, Carlos. "Oviedo, Sí." *El Wendigo*. March-May 1986, pp. 44-45.

8218. Lago, Silvio. "El Primer Salon de Humoristas de Barcelona." *La Esfera* (Madrid). February 26, 1916.

8219. "Los Premios 'Haxtur.'" *El Wendigo*. No. 54, 1991, p. 43.

8220. "100.000 til Festival i Barcelona." *Seriejournalen*. September 1990, p. 18.

8221. Paniceres, Ruben. "V Salon del Comic 'Ciudad de Oviedo.'" Program of Centro Cultural Campoamor, Oviedo. November 1988, pp. 26-28.

Cartoonists

8222. Arbesú, Faustino R. "Coma, y Sus Desprecios Cuando no Como." *El Wendigo*. No. 50, 1990, p. 8.

8223. Arbesú, Faustino R. "Un Pionero: Alfredo Truan." *El Wendigo*. May-June 1985, pp. 5-10.

8224. Auad, Manuel. "Victor de la Fuente." *Cartoonist PROfiles*. No. 32, 1976, pp. 77-82.

8225. Beck, C.C. "Picasso Was a Cartoonist." *Comics Journal*. January 1986, p. 7.

8226. Bergdoll, Udo. "Der Charmante Aufklärer. Die Politischen Comics des Zeichners José María Peridis." *Süddeutsche Zeitung* (Münich). January 1983, p. 66.

8227. Coma, Javier. "Spain's Figueras Switches from Good John to Perverse Mr. Hyde." *WittyWorld*. Winter/Spring 1989, pp. 64-65.

8228. Cuervo, Javier. "Berardi y Milazzo: 'los Historietistas Somos Artesanos y a Veces Artistas." *El Wendigo*. No. 45, 1989, pp. 4-5.

8229. Cuesta, Fernando. "Miguelanxo Prado: Desde Galicia con Humor Negro." *El Wendigo*. No. 54, 1991, pp. 8-9.

8230. Cuesta, Fernando and José Ramón Matilla. "Roberto Alcazar... y Pedrín." *El Wendigo*. October 1978, pp. 29-31.

8231. Cuesta Fernández, Fernando. "Freddy Lombard: Juventud (Postmoderna) a la Intemperie." *El Wendigo*. March-April 1987, pp. 4-6.

8232. Davis, Bruce. "Pier Francesco Mola's Autobiographical Caricatures: A Postscript." *Master Drawings*. Spring 1991, pp. 48-51.

8233. de Pierpont, Jacques. "Muñoz. La N'Est pas une BD, Baby." *Les Cahiers de la Bande Dessinée*. 59, 1984, pp. 88-90.

8234. Fermín Pérez, Ramón. "Gaspar Meana: Un Narrador Nato." *El Wendigo*. No. 58, 1993, pp. 10-11.

8235. Fernández, Norman. "José Luis García López: La Elegancia Hecha Historietista." *El Wendigo*. No. 50, 1990, pp. 9-11.

8236. Galindo, Federico. *Galindadas: Caricaturas de Galindo*. Madrid: Lifesa, 1957. 286 pp.

8237. "Gente de Comic: J.B. Artés." *Comicguia*. No. 19, 1990, p. 9.

8238. Green, Stuart. "José Muñoz, Sinner Unrepentant." *Speakeasy*. February 1990, pp. 38-39, 40, 43, 45.

8239. Lago, Silvio. "Luis Bagaria." *La Esfera* (Madrid). October 21, 1916.

8240. "Martínez, El Gran Comodin." *Comicguia*. No. 19, 1990, pp. 2-8.

8241. Martínez Peñaranda, Enrique. "¿Roald Dahl en S.O.S. (1951)?" *Comicguia*. Verano 1992, pp. 46-47.

8242. Navarro, Joan. "Il Était une Fois en Espagne... Roger." *Les Cahiers de la Bande Dessinée*. 69, 1986, pp. 58-59.

8243. Tadeo Juan, Francisco. "Falleció Federico Amorós, Acuarelista y Escritor." *Comicguia*. No. 22, 1991, p. 38.

8244. Tadeo Juan, Francisco. "Necrologia: Miguel Gonzalez Casquel." *Comicguia*. No. 21, 1991, p. 22.

8245. Tadeo Juan, Francisco. "Vicente Ibañez, El Gran Ausente." *Comicguia*. No. 20, 1990/1991, pp. 29-30.

Alfonso

8246. Avello, Manuel F. "Recuerdo de Alfonso." Program of Centro Cultural Campoamor, Oviedo, December 1988, pp. 12-13.

8247. Cuervo, Javier. "Alfonso, un Fenomeno Sociologico y Singular." *El Wendigo*. No. 42, 1988, pp. 15-18.

8248. Fermín Pérez, Ramón. "Alfonso." Program of Centro Cultural Campoamor, Oviedo, November 1988, pp. 42-44.

Ambrós, Miguel

8249. Tadeo Juan, Francisco. "Ambrós, Antes Que Mito, Ídolo; Amigo y Genio Siempre." *Comicguia*. No. 24, 1992/1993, pp. 4-47.

8250. Tadeo Juan, Francisco. "Ambrós, Antes Que Mito, Ídolo, Amigo y Genio Siempre." *El Wendigo*. No. 58, 1993, p. 32.

8251. Tadeo Juan, Francisco. "Miguel Ambrosio, Ambrós, el Ultimo Clasico." *El Wendigo*. March-April 1987, pp. 39-42.

Beltran, Mique

8252. Arbesú, Faustino. "Nacio Para Ser Historietista: Mique Beltran." *El Wendigo*. 14:43 (1988), p. 9.

8253. Cuesta, Fernando. "Mique Beltran: A la Rica Paella!" Program of Centro Cultural Campoamor, Oviedo, November 1988, pp. 29-30.

8254. Pérez, Ramón F. "Mique Beltran. ¡Deprisa, Deprisa!" *El Wendigo*. September-October 1984, pp. 29-34.

Darnis, Francisco

8255. Darnis, Silvio. "Francisco Darnis Dibujante." *Comicguia*. No. 21, 1991, pp. 4-8.

8256. Tadeo Juan, Francisco. "Francisco Darnis, Un Recuerdo." *Comicguia*. No. 21, 1991, p. 3.

Giménez, Carlos

8257. "Carlos Giménez: Una Obra...." *El Wendigo*. December 1984-January 1985, pp. 63-67.

8258. Coma, Javier. "Spain's Unknown Cartoonist: Carlos Giménez." *WittyWorld*. Autumn 1987, pp. 10-11.

8259. Monfort Cañellas, Blas. "Interview mit Carlos Giménez." *Comixene. Das Comicfachmagazin*. 7:32 (1980), pp. 22-26.

Giner, Eugenio

8260. Cuesta, Fernando. "Eugenio Giner: Misterio a la Orden." Program of Centro Cultural Campoamor, Oviedo, November 1988, p. 31.

8261. "Giner: 'Esta Es Mi Vida.'" *Comicguia*. No. 20, 1990/1991, p. 5.

8262. Ledesma, Gonzalez. "El Inspector Dan de la Patrulla Volante." *Comicguia*. No. 20, 1990/1991, p. 4.

8263. Martínez Peñaranda, Enrique. "El Inspector Dan, de la Patrulla Volante Documentacion." *Comicguia*. No. 20, 1990/1991, pp. 6-16.

8264. Tadeo Juan, Francisco. "El Inspector Dan, Giner y Nosotros." *Comicguia*. No. 20, 1990/1991, pp. 2-3.

Goya, Francisco

8265. Andioc, René. "Al Margen de los *Caprichos*: Las 'Explicaciones' Manuscritas." *Nueva Revista de Filología Hispánica*. 33 (1984), pp. 257-284.

8266. Askew, Mary. "The 'Caprichos' of Francisco Goya." Ph.D. dissertation, Stanford University, 1988.

8267. Bareau, Juliet W. *Goya's Prints: The Tomás Harris Collection in the British Museum*. London: British Museum, 1981.

8268. de Beruete y Moret, Aureliano. *Goya, Grabador*. Madrid: 1918.

8269. de Salas, Xavier. "Light on the Origin of Los Caprichos." *Burlington Magazine*. 121 (1979), pp. 711-716.

8270. Gassier, Pierre. *Les Dessins de Goya: Les Albums*. Fribourg: 1973.

8271. Gassier, Pierre and Juliet Wilson. *The Life and Complete Work of Francisco Goya*. Trans. by Christine Hauch and Juliet Wilson. New York: 1971.

8272. Glendenning, Nigel. "Goya and England in the Nineteenth Century." *Burlington Magazine*. 116 (1964), pp. 4-14.

8273. Glendenning, Nigel. "The Monk and Soldier in Plate 58 of Goya's *Caprichos*." *Journal of the Warburg and Courtauld Institutes*. 24 (1961), pp. 115-120.

8274. *Goya and the Satirical Print in England and on the Continent, 1730-1800*. Boston: David R. Godine, 1991. 110 pp.

8275. Harris, Enriqueta. "A Contemporary View of Goya's 'Caprichos.'" *Burlington Magazine*. 106 (1964), pp. 38-43.

8276. Hofmann, Werner. *Goya: Das Zeitalter der Revolutionen, 1789-1830*. Munich: Prestel Verlag: Hamburger Kunsthalle, 1980.

8277. Lefort, Paul. *Francisco Goya: Étude Biographique et Critique Suivie de l'Essai d'un Catalogue Raisonné de Son Oeuvre Gravé de Lithographié*. Paris: 1877.

8278. López-Rey, José. *Goya's Caprichos: Beauty, Reason and Caricature*. 2 Vols. Princeton, New Jersey: Princeton University Press, 1953.

8279. Martínez Ripoll, Antonio. "Un Dibujo Inédito de Goya con Cabezas Caricaturescas." *Goya*. 177 (1983), pp. 110-115.

8280. Moralejo Alvarez, María R. "Un Ejemplar de la Primera Edición de los *Caprichos*, de Goya, con Comentarios Manuscritos, en la Biblioteca de la Facultad de Filosofía y Letras de la Universidad de Zaragoza." *Boletin del Museo e Instituto "Camón Aznar."* 4 (1981), pp. 5-22.

8281. Sánchez Cantón, Francisco J. *Los Caprichos de Goya y Sus Dibujos Preparatorios*. Barcelona: 1949.

8282. Soubeyroux, Jacques. "Ordre Social et Subversion d'Ordre dan les Caprices de Goya (Essai d'Approche Sémiologique)." *Imprévue*. 2 (1981), pp. 107-137.

8283. Tomlinson, Janis A. *Francisco Goya: The Tapestry Cartoons and Early Career at the Court of Madrid*. Cambridge: 1989.

8284. Tomlinson, Janis A. "Francisco Goya: The Tapestry Cartoons and Early Career at the Court of Madrid." Reviewed by Yves Bottineau-Fuchs. *Gazette des Beaux-Arts*. September 1990, pp. 20-21; Reviewed by Jutta Held. The *Burlington Magazine*. February 1991, p. 124.

Ortiz, José

8285. Conde Martín, Luis. "José Ortiz, el Más 'Americano' de los Dibujantes 'Valencianos.'" *Comicguia*. Verano 1992, pp. 8-40.

8286. Tadeo Juan, Francisco. "José Ortiz, Un Clasico con Inquietudes." *Comicguia*. Verano 1992, pp. 1-7.

Palacios, Antonio Hernandez

8287. Tschernegg, Markus. "Palacios. Von Manos Kelly bis MacCay. Palacios-Comicographie." *Comic Forum. Das Magazin für Comicliteratur*. 5:22 (1983), pp. 45-48.

8288. Wiechmann, Peter and José Canovas. "Antonio Hernandez Palacios." *Comic Forum. Das Magazin für Comicliteratur*. 5:22 (1983), pp. 23-28.

Ribera, Julio

8289. Filippini, Henri. "Bibliographie." *Schtroumpf. Les Cahiers de la Bande Dessinée*. 41, 1979, pp. 45-48.

8290. Gilloud, André. "Julio Ribera, ou la Longue Route d'Une Jeune Vedette de la B.D." *Schtroumpf. Les Cahiers de la Bande Dessinée*. 41, 1979, pp. 30-32.

8291. Léturgie, Jean. "Entretien avec Julio Ribera." *Schtroumpf. Les Cahiers de la Bande Dessinée*. 41, 1979, pp. 7-25.

Ripoll G., M.

8292. Conde, Luis. "El Desconocido y Fascinante Ripoll G." *Comicguia*. No. 22, 1991, pp. 5-11.

8293. "Cronologia de las Obras de Ripoll G." *Comicguia*. No. 22, 1991, pp. 17-36.

8294. Martínez Peñaranda, Enrique. "M. Ripoll G.: Un Maestro de la Historieta Española Entre el Expresionismo y el Realismo." *Comicguia*. No. 22, 1991, pp. 12-18.

Sió, Enric

8295. Flórez, Florentino. "Enric Sió, No." *El Wendigo*. No. 42, 1988, p. 32.

8296. Léturgie, Jean and Maria Smirnof. "Entretien avec Enric Sió." *Schtroumpfanzine* (Grenoble). 31, 1979, pp. 11-17.

8297. Paramio, Ludolfo. "Comic: Enric Sió y la Crisis de Un Lenguaje." *Cuadernos Hispanoamericanos* (Madrid). 86:256 (1971), pp. 146-153.

Torres, Daniel

8298. Arbesú, Faustino R. and Javier Cuervo. "Daniel Torres: Tejedor de Géneros y Estéticas." *El Wendigo*. March-May 1986, pp. 4-9.

8299. Juanamartí, Jordi and Javier Riva. "Daniel Torres, el Cuentacuentos." *El Wendigo*. No. 57, 1992, pp. 40-41.

Vibora

8300. Cuervo, Javier. "Hay Mucho Vibora." *El Wendigo*. 14:43 (1988), pp. 37-40.

8301. Cuervo, Javier and Faustino Arbesú. "Los Majos de Vibora." *El Wendigo*. November 1982, pp. 13-16.

Characters and Titles

8302. Alvarez Villar, Alfonso. "Superman Prohibido en España." *Cuto*. No. 2-3, 1967, pp. 41-48.

8303. Arbesú, Faustino R. "'Chiqui,' Baron de Munchausen." Program of Centro Cultural Campoamor, Oviedo, November 1988, pp. 44-45.

8304. Coma, Javier. *Del Gato Félix al Gato Fritz: Historia de los Cómics*. Barcelona: Editorial Gustavo Gili, 1979.

8305. Conde Martín, Luis. "'Pinín,' Asturias y Yo Notas, a Contrapelo, Sobre una Devoción Antigua." *El Wendigo*. March-May 1986, pp. 41-42.

8306. Cuervo, Javier. "Papel Vivo." *El Wendigo*. January 1982, pp. 25-26.

8307. Cuesta, Fernando. "'La Pandilla Cu-Cux-Plaf': Un Clásico Atípico e Ignorado." *El Wendigo*. No. 53, 1991, pp. 12-13.

8308. Cuesta Fernández, Fernando. "Apache King: Un Heroe Mestizo Para un Western Valenciano." *El Wendigo*. September-October 1984, pp. 35-.

8309. Cuesta Fernández, Fernando. "El Cosaco Verde: Un Heroe de la Estepas." *El Wendigo*. January 1984, pp. 20-22.

8310. Cuesta Fernández, Fernando. "Mosquetero Azul. Un Emmascarado Mas." *El Wendigo*. May 1984, pp. 17-18.

8311. Fermín Pérez, Ramón. "La Cronica Chunga." Program of Centro Cultural Campoamor, Oviedo, November 1988, pp. 32-33.

8312. Fermín Pérez, Ramón. "Max: Un Celta Atipico." *El Wendigo*. Winter 1988-1989, pp. 4-7.

8313. Fernández, Fernando. *Zora and the Hibernauts*. New York: Catalan Communications, 1984. 110 pp.

8314. Giménez, Juan. *A Matter of Time*. New York: Catalan Communications, 1985. 62 pp.

8315. Lorenzo, Gonzalo. "Tardi, o el Culto al Serial de Misterio." *El Wendigo*. 22, pp. 27-28.

8316. Martín, Antonio. "Rip Kirby en España." *Cuto*. May 1967, pp. 6-7.

8317. Martínez Peñaranda, Enrique. "El Inspector Dan. Un Coloso de la Historieta Gráfico Española." *Comics Camp Comics In*. August 1972.

8318. Mingote. *Pequeno Planeta*. Madrid: Taurus Ediciones, 1957.

8319. Moreno, Pepe. *Rebel*. New York: Catalan Communications, 1986. 70 pp.

8320. Navarro, Joan. "Nouvelles d'Espagne." *Les Cahiers de la Bande Dessinée*. 57, 1984, pp. 46-47.

8321. Navarro, Joan. "Nouvelles d'Espagne." *Les Cahiers de la Bande Dessinée*. 61, 1985, pp. 48-49.

8322. Nazario. *Anarcoma*. New York: Catalan Communications, 1983. 62 pp.

8323. Parra, Sylvio. "Benitin y Emeas—Mutt and Jeff." *Cartoonist PROfiles*. No. 7, 1970, pp. 66-69.

8324. Ramírez, Juan Antonio. "Dos Versiones de la Historia de Don Crispin: Un Estudio Comparado (Consideraciones Sobre el Lenguaje Estético de las Aleluyas)." *Cuadernos Hispanoamericanos* (Madrid). 277/278, 1973, pp. 272-288.

8325. Riera, Marti. *The Cabbie*. New York: Catalan Communications, 1987. 79 pp.

8326. Sayrem, Joel. "Rintintin Triunfa Otra Vez." *Selecciones del Reader's Digest*. January 1956, pp. 67-75.

8327. Segalá, V.L. "El Jabato: Una Historia Rio." Boletín Informativo *Bang!* September-October 1972.

8328. Segrelles, V. *The Mercenary*. 3 Vols. New York: Nantier-Beall-Minoustchine, 1985-1986.

8329. Torres, Daniel. *Opium*. London: Knockabout Publications, 1986. 55 pp.

8330. Torres, Daniel. *Triton*. The Adventures of Rocco Vargas. New York: Catalan Communications, 1986. 48 pp.

"Cimoc"

8331. Fernández, Norman. "100 Numeros de 'Cimoc.'" *El Wendigo*. Autumn/Winter 1989-1990, pp. 30-31.

8332. Pérez, Ramón F. "Cimoc." *El Wendigo*. November 1981, pp. 25-29.

8333. Tschernegg, Markus. "Die Großen Europäischen Comic-Magazine. Eine Neue Comic-Forum-Serie." *Comic Forum. Das Magazin für Comicliteratur*. 7:30 (1985), p. 21.

"Diego Valor"

8334. Arbesú, Faustino R. "Algo Mas Que 'Diego Valor.'" *El Wendigo*. June-August 1987, pp. 11-13.

8335. Moreno Santabárbara, F. "Diego Valor en Historietas." *Bang!* Nos. 7/8, 1972.

"Dr. Niebla"

8336. Cuesta, Fernando. "El Doctor Niebla: Un Breve Clasico entre los Clasicos." *El Wendigo*. No. 42, 1988, pp. 36-38.

8337. Martínez-Peñaranda, Enrique. "Dr. Niebla." *Comics Camp Comics In.* No. 8, October 1973.

"El Capitán Trueno"

8338. Martínez Peñaranda, Enrique. "Almanaques y Extraordinarios de 'El Capitán Trueno.'" *Comicguia.* No. 19, 1990, pp. 11-12.

8339. Segalá, V.L. "Minidossier Capitán Trueno." *Bang!* No. 5, April 1971.

"El Guerrero del Antifaz"

8340. Arbesú, Faustino R. "El Guerrero del Antifaz. Crónica de la dé Cada de los Cuarentas." *Comics Camp Comics In.* March 1974.

8341. Lara, Antonio. "El Guerrero del Antifaz." *Bang!* No. 1, 1st Trim., 1969.

"Perramus"

8342. Coma, Javier. "Perramus, Un Poème sur l'Aventure Humaine." *Les Cahiers de la Bande Dessinée.* 62, 1985, pp. 91-93.

8343. Sasturain, Juan and Alberto Breccia. *Perramus. Grafischer Roman.* Hamburg: Carlsen Verlag, 1993. 178 pp.

"Torpedo"

8344. Cuervo, Javier. "Un Billete de Vuelta Llamado 'Torpedo.'" *El Wendigo.* February 1983, pp. 12-14.

8345. Sanchez Abuli, Enrique, Alex Toth and Jordi Bernet. *Torpedo 1936.* New York: Catalan Communications, 1984-.

8346. "*Torpedo* Creators in Dispute with Ex-Publisher." *Comics Journal.* November 1991, pp. 24-25.

"Xuasús"

8347. Cuervo, Javier. "Xuasús, el Asturiano Que Dibuja 'Las Tortugas Ninja.'" *El Wendigo.* No. 53, 1991, p. 42.

8348. García Alvarez, Jesús. "Xuasús: Por el Buen Camino." *El Wendigo.* No. 53, 1991, pp. 5-6.

Animation

8349. "BRB, D'ocon Up the Ante in Animation." *Variety*. September 23, 1991, pp. 68, 70.

8350. Cuenca, Carlos Fernandéz. *Segundo de Chomón, Maestro de la Fantasia y de la Tecnica (1871-1929)*. Madrid: Editora Nacional, 1972.

8351. de la Rosa, Emilio and Hipólito Vivar. "Animación por Ordenador en España." *Corto Circuito*. April 1992, pp. 26-29.

8352. Goméz-Mesa, L. *Los Films de Dibujos Animados*. Madrid: 1929.

8353. Moore, Linda. "Spanich Toonsters Have Lotsa Work but Little Cash." *Variety*. September 21, 1992, p. 62.

8354. Ramírez, Juan Antonio. "The Structure and Ideology of Television Adventures in Postwar Spain." *Cuadernos de Realidades Sociales*. May 1977, pp. 27-46.

8355. "Spanish Animation Is Moving with the Times." *Variety*. September 23, 1991, p. 68.

8356. "Tube Demand Keeping Animation Studios Busy." *Variety*. September 24, 1990, pp. 58, 63.

Caricature

8357. "A Caricatura." *Nôvo Mundo* (New York). September 23, 1874.

8358. Benet, Rafael. *Xavier Nogués. Caricaturista y Pintor*. Barcelona: Ediciones Omega S.A., 1949.

8359. Bréal, Auguste. "La Caricature en Espagne." *Arts et Métiers Graphiques*. September 15, 1932, pp. 47-56.

8360. Fiol, E. Gonzalez. "La Caricatura en los Libros de Devoción." *La Esfera* (Madrid). March 25, 1916.

8361. Gamonal Torres, Miguel Angel. *La Illustración Gráfica y la Caricatura en la Prensa Granadina del Siglo xix* (Graphic Illustration and Caricature in the Granada Press of the Nineteenth Century). Granada: Excelentisima Diputación Provincial de Granada, 1983. 249 pp.

8362. Garrido. *Madrileños en Serie*. Prologue by Marino Rodrigues de Rivas. Madrid: Author, 1940.

8363. Lago, Silvio. "El Humorismo Espanol y la Guerra." *La Esfera* (Madrid). July 24, 1915.

8364. Lago, Silvio. "Exposición de Caricaturas." *La Esfera* (Madrid). December 19, 1914.

8365. Lago, Silvio. "La Caricatura Española y la Guerra." *La Esfera* (Madrid). March 6, 1915.

8366. Lago, Silvio. "El Caricaturista Sirio." *La Esfera* (Madrid). June 9, 1917.

8367. Teja, [Casimiro]. *Caricature dal Pasquino 1856-1897.* Edited by A. Ferrero. Torino: 1900.

Cartoons

8368. Bozal, Valeriano. *La Ilustración Gráfica del Siglo XIX en España. Comunicación.* Madrid: Alberto Corazón, 1979.

8369. Bozal, Valeriano. *La Ilustración Gráfica del Siglo XIX en España. Comunicación.* Madrid: Editorial Cambio 16, 1977.

8370. Conde Martín, Luis. "Hazañas Bélicas." *Bang!* No. 13, 1974.

8371. Figueras, Alfons. *Un Beau Petit Diable.* Paris: Le Vaisseau d'Argent Éditeur, 1988.

8372. Gila, Miguel. *Gila y Sus Gentes.* Madrid: Taurus Ediciones, 1957.

8373. Lago, Silvio. "El Humorismo y la Guerra." *La Esfera* (Madrid). October 19, 1913.

8374. Lago, Silvio. "El Humorismo Frances." *La Esfera* (Madrid). June 21, 1914.

8375. Lago, Silvio. "La Guerra y el Humorismo." *La Esfera* (Madrid). November 14, 1914.

Comics

8376. Acevedo, Juan. *Para Hacer Historietas* (How To Make Comic Books). Madrid: Editorial Popular, 1981, 1984. 192 pp.

8377. Arbesú, Faustino R. *Asturias y la Historieta.* Gijon: Servicio Publicaciones, 1985. 67 pp.

8378. Arbesú, Faustino R. "Cuando los Heroes Eran Miopes." *El Wendigo*. August 1982, pp. 1-4.

8379. Arbesú, Faustino R. "Dreadstar: La Eternidad Narrada en Doce Paginas." *El Wendigo*. March/April 1987, pp. 17-20.

8380. Arbesú, Faustino R. "El Barón de la Historieta Asturiana." *El Wendigo*. No. 58, 1993, pp. 29-31.

8381. Arbesú, Faustino R. "Requiem por un Madrileño." *El Wendigo*. No. 57, 1992, pp. 38-39.

8382. Arbesú, Faustino R. "Un Caballo de Carreras Cojo, Taimado y Tuerto." *El Wendigo*. No. 58, 1993, p. 37.

8383. Arbesú, Faustino R. and Javier Cuervo. "'El Comic al Desnudo.'" *El Wendigo*. November 1982, pp. 1-3.

8384. Arbesú, Faustino R. and Javier Cuervo. "La 'Linea Clara'... Que No Esta Tan Clara." *El Wendigo*. September-October 1984, pp. 4-12.

8385. Arbesú, Faustino R. and Ramón Fermín Pérez. "Dos Comics Futuristas para el Futuro." *El Wendigo*. December 1985, pp. 17-23.

8386. Beneyto, Juan. "Sobre el Repertorio Instrumental de la Propaganda." *Revista Española de la Opinion Publica*. April-September 1975, pp. 23-30.

8387. Cañellas, Blas-Monfort. "Spanien." In *Comic-Jahrbuch 1986*, edited by Martin Compart and Andreas C. Knigge, pp. 271-275. Berlin: Ullstein GmbH, 1985.

8388. "Chronique d'Espagne. 1980 - ." *Bédésup*. No. 18/19, 1981.

8389. Coma, Javier. "'Comics' Clásicos y Modernos." *El País*. November 15, 1987 through May 1, 1988. (25 installments of 16 pages each of Spanish and U.S. comic art).

8390. Coma, Javier. *El Ocaso de los Héroes en los Comics de Autor*. Barcelona: Peninsula, 1984.

8391. Coma, Javier. *El Espiritu de los Comics*. Barcelona: Toutain Editor, 1981.

8392. Coma, Javier. *Los Comics: Un Arte del Siglo XX*. Barcelona: Ediciones Guadarramo Colección, Universitaria de Bolsillo, Punta Omega, 1978. 204 pp.

8393. Coma, Javier. *Y Nos Fuimos a Hacer Viñetas*. Madrid: Penthalon Ediciones, 1981. 229 pp.

8394. "Comentarios en Voz Alta." *El Wendigo*. No. 51, 1991, p. 31; No. 54, 1991, pp. 31-32; No. 58, 1993, p. 39.

8395. Conde Martín, Luis. "Boxicar: El Maestro de la Trama." *Comicguia*. No. 24, 1992/1993, pp. 50-52.

8396. Cuervo, Javier. "El Largo Verano Indio." *El Wendigo*. June-August 1987, pp. 33-35.

8397. Cuervo, Javier and Fernando Cuesta. "Dieter Lumpen Aventuras de un Canalla." *El Wendigo*. October 1986, pp. 27-29.

8398. Cuesta, Fernando. "Fantasia 'Camp' Española." Program of Centro Cultural Campoamor, Oviedo, December 1988, pp. 1-5.

8399. Cuesta, Fernando. "Martin Mystere Cabalga de Nuevo." *El Wendigo*. No. 57, 1992, pp. 36-37.

8400. Cuesta Fernández, Fernando. "El Último Héroe." *El Wendigo*. March-May 1986, pp. 52-59.

8401. Cuesta Fernández, Fernando. "Para Vidas Ejemplares las de Antes." *El Wendigo*. June-August 1987, pp. 36-38.

8402. "Deadlier Than the Male." *Escapada* (Madrid). March 1967, pp. 28-31.

8403. De Laiglesia, Juan A. *El Arte de la Historieta*. Madrid: Doncel, 1964.

8404. Del Pozo, Mariano. "El Comic y las Peliculas." *La Actualidad Española* (Madrid). November 28, 1968.

8405. Diaz, Lorenzo. "Un Super Heroe Espresionista." *El Wendigo*. May 1983, pp. 7-10.

8406. *Dirty Comics*. Barcelona: Ediciones Cupula, 1980.

8407. Fermín Pérez, Ramón. "Bruguera: El Ocaso de los Dioses." *El Wendigo*. August 1982, pp. 6-9.

8408. Fermín Pérez, Ramón. "La Ballena Varada." *El Wendigo*. No. 52, 1991, pp. 6-7.

8409. Fermín Pérez, Ramón. "Polvo, Sudor y Tinta." Program of Centro Cultural Campoamor, Oviedo, November 1988, pp. 33-34.

8410. Fernández, Juan José and Luis Vigil, eds. *El Comix Marginal Español* (Spain's Under-Ground Comix). Barcelona: Producciones Editoriales, 1976.

8411. Fernández, Norman. "El Felino Vegetariano." *El Wendigo*. No. 52, 1991, p. 10.

8412. Fernández, Norman. "El Invierno del Payaso." *El Wendigo*. No. 57, 1992, pp. 10-11.

8413. Fernández, Norman. "El Penúltimo Aventurero." *El Wendigo*. Verano 1990, pp. 4-5.

8414. Fernández, Norman. "La Loba y el 3 de Agosto." *El Wendigo*. No. 53, 1991, pp. 7-9.

8415. Fernández, Norman. "Más Claro Que Oscuro." *El Wendigo*. Verano 1990, pp. 30-38.

8416. Fernández, Norman. "Un Par de Granujas." *El Wendigo*. No. 52, 1991, pp. 32-33.

8417. Fernández, Norman and Faustino R. Arbesú. "La Ley de la Menta." *El Wendigo*. No. 53, 1991, pp. 10-11.

8418. Gasca, Luis. "Del Marqués al Comic, Passando por la Condesa." *Film Ideal* (San Sebastian). November 1, 1965.

8419. Gasca, Luis. "El Llanero Solitario." *Unidad* (Madrid). May 8, 1964.

8420. Gasca, Luis. "Elogio del Tebeo." *Véteres* (Madrid). December 1, 1962.

8421. Gasca, Luis. "Imagen y Ciencia Ficción." "Festival International del Cine," San Sebastian, 1966.

8422. Gasca, Luis. *Los Comics en España*. Barcelona: Editorial Lumen, 1969.

8423. Gasca, Luis. *Los Comics en la Pantalla*. San Sebastian: Festival International del Cine, 1965. 359 pp.

8424. Gasca, Luis. *Mujeres Fantásticas*. Barcelona: Editorial Taber and Editorial Lumen, 1969.

8425. Gasca, Luis. "Storia dei Fumetti Alla Spagna." *Quaderni di Communicazioni di Massa*. No. 6, 1965.

8426. Gasca, Luis. *Tebeo y Cultural de Masas* (Comics and Mass Culture). Madrid: Editorial Prensa Española, 1966. 249 pp.

8427. Gasca, Luis. "Un Arte Menor." *La Voz de España* (Madrid). November 12, 1963.

8428. Gimferrer, Pedro. "El Fabuloso Mundo de los Comics." *Destino* (Barcelona). August 28, 1965, p. 19.

8429. Gubern, Román. *El Lenguaje de los Cómics*. Barcelona: Península, 1972.

8430. Lara, Antonio. *El Apasionante Mundo del Tebeo*. Madrid: Editorial Cuadernos para el Diálogo, 1968.

8431. Lebrato, Jaime R. "Los Comics." *Prensa Infantil*. Palma de Mallorca: Diario de Mallorca, December 1965.

8432. "Le Comic Espagnol et Son Engagement." *B.D. Bulle: Revue du Salon International de la Bande Dessinée* (Angoulême). 3, 1978, pp. 13-17.

8433. "Levante-EMV Lanza la 'Historia del Tebeo Valenciano.'" *Comicguia*. Verano 1992, pp. 41-42.

8434. Liobera, José and Romain Oltra. *La Bande Dessinée*. Spain: Ed. Alpha, Coll. "Savoir Dessiner/Savoir Peindre," 1968.

8435. Liobera, José. *Dibujo de Historietas*. Barcelona: Edición Afha, 1961.

8436. "Los Premios Historieta Diario de Avisos de 1990." *Comicguia*. No. 21, 1991, p. 2.

8437. Mannucci, Cesare. "Sociología del Fumetto." *El Mundo* (Madrid). January 12, 1965.

8438. Martín, Antonio. "El Arte LSD." *Arriba* (Madrid). January 15, 1967.

8439. Martín, Antonio. "El Comic Norteamericano en España." *Gaceta de la Prensa Española* (Madrid). September 1965, pp. 37-47.

8440. Martín, Antonio. "Los Comics." *Triunfo* (Madrid). No. 148, 1965, pp. 66-71.

8441. Martín, Sabas. "Alternativas del 'Comic' y del Cine Español." *Cuadernos Hispanoamericanos* (Madrid). 103:309, 1976, pp. 376-385.

8442. Martínez Peñaranda, Enrique. "El Espadachín Enmascarado." *Comicguia*. Verano 1993, pp. 27-40.

8443. Mathiasen, Paw. "På Skolebaenken i Barcelona." *Seriejournalen*. June 1992, pp. 46-47.

8444. Mathiasen, Paw. "Rejsebrev fra Barcelona." *Seriejournalen*. December 1991, p. 16.

8445. Menéndez, Germán. "El Libro de Estilo Ataca de Nuevo." *El Wendigo*. No. 51, 1991, p. 7.

8446. Menéndez, Germán and Norman Fernández. "Una Semana en Otra Ciudad." *El Wendigo*. No. 54, 1991, pp. 10-12.

8447. Minuzzo, Nerio. "La Prometida del Robot." *Gaceta Illustrada* (Madrid). No. 569, 1967, pp. 42-43.

8448. Mira, J. Eduard. "Notes on a Comparative Analysis of American and Spanish Comic Books." *Journal of Popular Culture*. Summer 1971, pp. 203-220.

8449. Moix, Ramón-Terenci. "El Fabuloso Mundo de los Comics." *Destino* (Barcelona). August 28, 1965, p. 19.

8450. Moix, Ramón-Terenci. *Los "Comics": Arte Para el Consumo y Formas "Pop."* Barcelona: Libres de Sinera, 1968.

8451. Montañes, Luis. "La Publicación de Cuadernos de Historietas Gráficas." *Bibliografía Hispánica* (Madrid). No. 6, 1945.

8452. Moreno, Federico. "La Diffusion des Schtroumpfs en Espagne." *Bédésup*. 22/23, 1982, pp. 13-17.

8453. Paniceres, Ruben. "Beroy." Program of Centro Cultural Campoamor, Oviedo, November 1988, pp. 30-31.

8454. Paniceres, Ruben. "La Noche de Pons." *El Wendigo*. June-August 1987, pp. 29-31.

8455. Parramón, José Maria and Jesús Blasco. *Cómo Dibujar Historietas*. Madrid: Ediciones Instituto Parramón, 1966; Barcelona, 1971.

8456. Pastecca. *Dibujando Chistes*. Barcelona: Ediciones CEAC, 1969.

8457. Pérez, Ramón. "Asturias y la Historieta." *El Wendigo*. December 1985, p. 30.

8458. Puig, Miguel. *Ilustración de Historietas y Cuentas*. Barcelona: E. Meseguer, 1965.

8459. Ramírez, Juan Antonio. *El 'Comic' Feminino en España: Arte Sub y Anulación* (The Woman's Comic in Spain...). Madrid: Editorial Cuadernos para el Diálogo, 1975.

8460. Resnais, Alain. "A. Resnais Entrevista al Padre del Hombre Enmascerado." *Cuto*. No. 4-6, 1968, pp. 12-19.

8461. Rodríguez Diéguez, José Luis. "El Cómic Como Instrumento de Enseñanza." In *Las Funciones de la Imagen en la Enseñanza*. Barcelona: Gustavo Gili, 1977.

8462. Ruppert, C.H. "'Tebeo, Historieta, Comic, Fotonovela' im Spanischunterricht." *Zielsprache Spanisch* (Munich). 2, 1975, pp. 6-13.

8463. Sempere, Pedro. *Semiología del Infortunio; Lenguaje e Ideología de la Fotonovela.* Madrid: Felmar, 1976.

8464. Sempronio. "Aquel Patufet." *Tele-Express* (Barcelona). September 2, 1968.

8465. Serafini, Horacio and Roberto Bardin. "La Inocencia de la Historieta." *Cambio.* 1976, pp. 49-53.

8466. Tadeo Juan, Francisco. "Juan Escandell, Otro Dibujante para la Exportacion." *Comicguia.* Verano 1993, pp. 25-26.

8467. Thompson, Don. "Spanish Publisher Compiles World History of the Comics." *Comics Buyer's Guide.* July 8, 1983, pp. 1, 3.

8468. Traini, Rinaldo and Sergio Trinchero. "Un Fumetto Indovinato, Saturnino Farandola." *Hobby.* No. 3, 1967.

8469. Tubau, Iván. *Dibujando Historietas.* Barcelona: Ediciones CEAC, 1969.

8470. Vilabella Guardiola, José Manuel. *Los Historistas.* Barcelona: Ediciones Amaika, 1975. 304 pp.

Cinema

8471. Bertieri, Claudio. "Sobre la Relación Cine y Comics." *Cuto.* No. 4-6, 1968, pp. 35-47.

8472. Gasca, Luis. "Cine y Comic Hablan el Mismo Lenguaje." *Film Ideal* (San Sebastian). September 1, 1965.

8473. Gasca, Luis. "Cuando el Cine se Inspira en el Comic." Festival International del Cine, San Sebastian, June 4, 1965.

8474. Lacassin, Francis. "De Marienbad a Diego. Resnais Dibuja Comics con la Camèra." *Cuto.* No. 4-6, 1968, pp. 25-31.

8475. "Los Comics, Cine Dibujado." *SP* (Madrid). February 13, 1966.

8476. Moix, Ramón. "A la Búsqueda se Un Pop-Cinema." *Film Ideal* (San Sebastian). May 1, 1965, pp. 295-299.

8477. Tuduri, José L. "Del 6 a 20 de Junio, la Exposición Mundial del Comics en el Cine y la TV." *Diario Vasco* (San Sebastian). 1965.

Effects

8478. Alvarez Villar, Alfonso. "Función Formativa de los Tebeos en las Mentes Infantiles." *Hoja del Lunes* (Madrid). September 20, 1965.

8479. Alvarez Villar, Alfonso. "La Literatura Infantil en la Luz de la Psicología." *La Voz de España* (Madrid). January 1966.

8480. Alvarez Villar, Alfonso. "Psicología y Cuentos de Hadas." *La Voz de España* (Madrid). January 11, 1966.

8481. "El Problema de los Tebeos." *Mundo Cristiano* (Madrid). No. 30, 1958, p. 8.

8482. Mouerris, Alejandro G. "La Literatura No Es Para Mayores." *La Estafeta Literaria* (Madrid). May 5, 1956.

8483. Perucho, Juan. "El Poder de los Comics." *Destino* (Barcelona). April 16, 1966.

8484. Romero Marín, Anselmo. "La Psicologia Infantil y Juvenil en Relación con la Información." In *Curso de Prensa Infantil*. Madrid: Escuela Oficial de Periodismo, 1964.

8485. Sarto, Maria M. "Caracter Activo de la Prensa Infantil." In *Curso de Prensa Infantil*, p. 219. Madrid: Escuela Oficial de Periodismo, 1964.

History

8486. Barrier, Michael, Bill Blackbeard, Javier Coma and others. *Historia de los Comics*. 4 Vols. Barcelona: Toutain Editor, 1982.

8487. Gasca, Luis. "Historia y Anécdota del Tebeo en España." In *Disputación de Zaragoza*. Zaragoza: 1965. Manuscript.

8488. Gasca, Luis. "Elogio del Tebeo." *Véteres*. December 1, 1962.

8489. Gasca, Luis and Edouard François. "Espagne." In *Histoire Mondiale de la Bande Dessinée*, edited by Pierre Horay, pp. 174-191. Paris: Pierre Horay Éditeur, 1989.

8490. Hoveyda, Foreydon. "Historia de la Novela Policiaca." In *El Libro del Bolsillo*. Madrid: Alianza Editorial, 1967. 266 pp.

8491. Martín, Antonio. "Apuntes para una Historia de los Tebeos. I. Los Periódicos Para la Infancia (1833-1917)." *Revista de Educación*. December 1967.

8492. Martín, Antonio. "Apuntes para una Historia de los Tebeos. II. La Civilización de la Imagen." *Revista de Educación*. January 1968.

8493. Martín, Antonio. *Historia del Comic Español: 1875-1939.* Barcelona: Editorial Gustavo Gill, 1978. 245 pp.

8494. Mingote. *Historia de la Gente.* Madrid: Taurus Ediciones, 1955.

8495. Ramírez-Domínguez, Juan Antonio. "Estructura e Ideología del Tebeo de Aventuras en la España de Post-Guerra." *Cuadernos de Realidades Sociales.* May 1977, pp. 27-46.

8496. Ramírez-Domínguez, Juan Antonio. "Grupos Temáticos del Tebeo de Aventuras en la España de la Post-Guerra: Notas para una Historia Iconográfica e Ideológica (I)." *Cuadernos de Realidades Sociales.* September 1975, pp. 81-120.

8497. Ramírez-Domínguez, Juan Antonio. *La Historieta Cómica de Post Guerra* (The Post-War Comics). Madrid: Editorial Cuadernos para el Diálogo, 1975.

8498. Ramírez-Domínguez, Juan Antonio. "Thematic Grouping of Adventure Comics in Postwar Spain: Notes Toward an Iconographic and Ideological History (II)." *RS, Cuadernos de Realidades Sociales.* January 1976, pp. 87-150.

8499. Rodrigo, Antonina. "Las Aleluyas, Precursoras de los 'Cómics.'" *Cuadernos Hispanoamericanos: Revista Mensual de Cultural Hispanica.* December 1988, pp. 137-143.

8500. Rollet, Georges. "Les Formes Multiples de la Résistance Espagnole Sous l'Occupation Napoléonienne." In *Histoire et Bande Dessinée: Actes du 2e Colloque International Éducation et Bande Dessinée,* pp. 59-70. Lo Roque d'Anthéron: Objectif Promo-Durance, 1979.

8501. Vásquez de Parga, Salvador. *Los Comics del Franquismo.* Barcelona: Editorial Planeta, 1980. 264 pp.

Political Cartoons

8502. "Cartoon Lands Journalists in Trouble." *IPI Report.* February 1988, p. 7.

8503. Martin, Wayne R. "'Peridis' and Political Cartoons in Post-Franco Spain." *Journal of Popular Culture.* Spring 1987, pp. 159-173.

8504. Roca, Javier and Santiago Ferrer. *Humor Politico en la España Contemporánea.* Madrid: Editorial Cambio 16, 1977.

SWEDEN

General Studies

8505. Allwood, Martin S. *The Impact of the Comics*. Mullsjó, Sweden: Institute of Social Research, 1956.

8506. Andersson, Per A.J. "Sverige—Storebror og Lillebror i Tegneserieverdenen." *TEGN*. No. 3 (13), 1989, pp. 36-41.

8507. Bejerot, Nils. "Barn, Serier, Samhälle." Stockholm: Folkets i Bild Förlag, 1954.

8508. "Bild and Bubbla." *Serieskaberen*. December 1989, p. 7.

8509. Hegerfors, Sture. "Seriemagasinet Karison." Exhibition Catalogue, Göteborg, December 11, 1965.

8510. Hegerfors, Sture. "Seriernas Kongress." *Kvällsposten* (Malmö). July 16, 1967.

8511. "Kalmar Seriefestival 90." *Seriejournalen*. September 1990, p. 23.

8512. "Pornoretssag Skraemmer Redaktører Bort fra Epix." *Seriejournalen*. September 1990, p. 11.

8513. "Swedish Museum of Comic Art." *Cartoonist PROfiles*. March 1977, pp. 18-23.

Animation

8514. "Birgitta i Vara Hjartan." *Story Board*. No. 6, pp. 2-6.

8515. "Disney Anlaegger Sag." *Seriejournalen*. March 1991, p. 7.

8516. Gordon, Mattias. "Gunnar Karlsson. Till Minnes." *Story Board*. No. 6, p. 18.

8517. Gordon, Mattias. "Sveriges Basta Animerade Film." *Story Board*. No. 7, 1988, p. 25.

8518. Hegerfors, Sture. "Jetson-Tecknarna Började Med Sadistika Kortfilmer." *Göteborgs-Posten*. July 17, 1964.

8519. Hegerfors, Sture. "TV Renässans för Tecknad Film, Raske Rudolf och Hacke Hackspett Ateruppstar." *Göteborgs-Tidningen*. October 21, 1964.

8520. Hegerfors, Sture. "Uppstanden Stalman Ater pa Filmdukarna." *Idom-Veckojournalen* (Stockholm). February 11, 1966.

8521. "Hemliga Gasten: Min Bild av Per Ahlin." *Story Board*. No. 2, 1988, pp. 18-19.

8522. Holmquist, Karl-Gunnar. "Debatt: Mojlighetodla Sararten." *Story Board*. 1, 1989, pp. 12-13.

8523. "I Sisyfos Fotspar." *Story Board*. No. 6, pp. 16-17.

8524. Jungstedt, Torsten. *Kapten Grogg Och Hans Vänner*. Stockholm: Sveriges Radios Forlag/Svenska Filminstitutet, 1973.

8525. Keller, J.R. Keith. "Scandis Work in the Shadow of Disney and U.S." *Variety*. November 5, 1990, p. 70.

8526. "Nancy Beiman Berattar om... Hur Det ar Att Vara Kvinnlig Animator Pa Cal Arts och Disney." *Story Board*. No. 6, pp. 9-10.

8527. O'Konor, Louise. *Viking Eggeling 1880-1925; Artist and Film-Maker; Life and Work*. Stockholm: Almqvist and Wiksell, 1971.

8528. "One Hundred Years." *Story Board*. No. 6, pp. 10-14.

8529. "Per Ahlin." *Story Board*. No. 2, pp. 3-17.

8530. Rehlin, Gunnar. "Swedes Try 'Turtles'—Again." *Variety*. May 20, 1991, p. 32.

8531. "Samtad Med Kjeld Simonsen." *Story Board*. No. 1, pp. 19-27.

8532. "Story Debatt: Per Ahlin om Dagslaget." *Story Board*. No. 6, p. 15.

8533. "Tecknarhander I Varlden." *Story Board*. No. 1, pp. 15-17.

8534. "The World of Animation." *Story Board*. No. 2, pp. 20-22.

Caricature

8535. Fogelström, Per Anders. *25 Svenska Skämttecknare*. Stockholm: Folket i Bild, 1954. Unpaginated.

8536. Gauguin, Pola, ed. *Världens Karikatyrer Fran Forntiden till Vara Dagar*. 2 Vols. Stockholm: Natur och Kultur, 1949.

8537. Laurin, Carl G. *Albert Engstrom (Caricaturiste Suédoïs)*. Paris: L'Art et les Artistes, No. 17, August 1906.

Blix (Hig-Hook)

8538. Blix (Hig-Hook). *Genom Gallerierna, Karikatyrer.* Stockholm: Artiebolaget Ljus Förlag, 1908.

8539. Hig-Hook (Blix). *Anno 1941* (efter Judas). Stockholm: Axel Holmströms Förlag, 1941.

8540. Hig-Hook (Blix). *1942-44.* Stockholm: Albert Bonniers Förlag, 1944.

8541. Lima, Herman. "A Caricatura e a Arte." (Paródias de Blix). *Rio Magazine* (Rio de Janeiro). May 1950.

Comics

8542. "The Aborted Foetus Strikes Back." *Nordic Comics Revue International.* Autumn 1992, p. 22.

8543. Allwood, Martin S. *Kalle Anka. Stålmannen och VI.* Stockholm: Institutet for Samhallsforskning, 1956. 77 pp.

8544. Andersson, Per A.J. "The Brat Pack Goes Splatter." *Nordic Comics Revue.* Winter 1992-1993, pp. 8-9.

8545. Andersson, Per A.J. "Talent Go West: Mikael Oskarsson Makes Comics for the US." *Nordic Comics Revue.* April 1992, pp. 8-9.

8546. Andersson, Per A.J. "Tegneserielandet Som Både er Storebror og Lillebror." *Serieskaberen.* September 1989, pp. 18-22.

8547. Andreasson, Lars and Per J. Andersson. "The Lundkvist Losers of Modern Society." *Nordic Comics Revue International.* Autumn 1992, pp. 20-21.

8548. Atterbom, Daniel. "Statsstøtte til Serier." *Seriejournalen.* September 1992, pp. 5-6.

8549. Becker, Hartmut and Andreas C. Knigge. "Interview mit Rolf Gohs." *Comixene. Das Comicfachmagazin.* 6:25 (1979), pp. 55-57.

8550. Bjurström, P. and Lena Johannesson. *Serier för Alla. Svenska Serier Och Serier Och Serietecknare.* Stockholm: Nationalmusei, 1979.

8551. Blomberg, Stig. "Fantomens Fantastika Come-Back." *Vecko Revya* (Stockholm). No. 22, 1967, pp. 15-42.

8552. "Book About Modern Comics To Be Written." *Nordic Comics Revue*. April 1992, p. 10.

8553. Bryman, Werner. "Seriemagasinen-ord Och Innehäll." *Folkskolan* (Stockholm). 1954, p. 123.

8554. Burgdorf, Paul. "Jan Lööf." *Comixene. Das Comicfachmagazin.* 6:23 (1979), pp. 47-48.

8555. "Den Svenske Tegneseriepris Urhunden 1989 Uddelt." *Serieskaberen*. December 1989, p. 7.

8556. Ehrling, Ragnar. "Vart Behov av Seriefigurer." *Studiekontakt* (Stockholm). 1965, p. 1.

8557. "80-Ernes Bedste Tegneserie." *Serieskaberen*. June 1990, p. 10.

8558. Elgström, Jörgen. "De Komiska Stryptagen." *Biblioteksbladet* (Stockholm). 1955, pp. 61-65.

8559. Fransson, Evald. "Serielitteraturen." *Folkskolan* (Stockholm). 1955, pp. 104-108.

8560. Fransson, Evald. "Serielitteraturen-Ett Uppfostringsproblem." *Folkskolan* (Stockholm). 9, 1953, pp. 198-208.

8561. Gustafson, Axel. "Seriemagasinen-en Samhällsfara." Stockholm: Förlaget Filadelfia, 1955.

8562. Hammarström, Nils. "Serier Och Politik." *Clarté* (Stockholm). 1964, p. 2.

8563. Haste, Hans. *Läsning för Barn?* Stockholm: Folket i Bilds Förlag, 1955.

8564. Hegerfors, Sture. "Apropo Kalle Anka!" *Göteborgs-Posten*. January 17, 1964.

8565. Hegerfors, Sture. "Ar den 'Sjuka' Humorn Rolig?" *Göteborgs-Posten*. October 1, 1961.

8566. Hegerfors, Sture. "Den Nya Serien i Frankrike." *Hufvudstadsbladet* (Helsingfors). September 12, 1967.

8567. Hegerfors, Sture. "Det Är Ganska-Människan Som Skaper Toppserier." *Ostersunds-Posten*. July 14, 1967.

8568. Hegerfors, Sture. "Eva Och Jag." *GT-Söndags Extra* (Göteborg). November 26, 1967.

8569. Hegerfors, Sture. "Flabba at Snobben Med Fitness!" *Göteborgs-Tidningen*. October 7, 1967.

8570. Hegerfors, Sture. "Fränna Franska Flickor." *Kvällsposten* (Malmö). August 30, 1967.

8571. Hegerfors, Sture. "Han Är den Mest Kände Dansken i Världen." *Kvällsposten* (Malmö). August 27, 1967.

8572. Hegerfors, Sture. "Handen Pa Hjartat: Visst Läser Ni Serier?" *Hund-Sport* (Stockholm). No. 8-9, 1967.

8573. Hegerfors, Sture. "Hohoho, en Polack." *Expressen* (Stockholm). April 24, 1966.

8574. Hegerfors, Sture. "Kalle Anka Egentligen Ett Plagiat." *GT Söndags Extra* (Göteborg). January 14, 1968.

8575. Hegerfors, Sture. "Krikelius, Fridolf och Bom." *Expressen* (Stockholm). December 10, 1966.

8576. Hegerfors, Sture. "Kronblan i Co., Hopsamlade." *Kvällsposten* (Malmö). January 7, 1968.

8577. Hegerfors, Sture. "Kronblom, 40... Och Slar Alla Tiders Svenska Serie-Record." *Expressen* (Stockholm). July 16, 1967.

8578. Hegerfors, Sture. "Läderlappen Och Robin." *Borlänge Tidning*. August 5, 1966.

8579. Hegerfors, Sture. "La Première Bande Dessinée Suédoise." *Phénix*. No. 7, 3. Trim. 1968, pp. 2-5.

8580. Hegerfors, Sture. "Ludde-Sonen Till Honan av Värld i Hannen av Folket." *Göteborgs-Tidningen*. December 10, 1967.

8581. Hegerfors, Sture. "Lulu From Modehuset." *Expressen* (Stockholm). March 23, 1967.

8582. Hegerfors, Sture. "Mannen Med Tio Tigrars Styska, Dragos." *Göteborgs-Tidningen*. October 2, 1967.

8583. Hegerfors, Sture. "Mannen Som Gjorde Vad Som Föll Honan in." *Kvällsposten* (Malmö). November 12, 1967.

8584. Hegerfors, Sture. "Mycket Väsen Om Knallhatten." *Göteborgs-Tidningen, Söndags-Extra*. August 20, 1967.

8585. Hegerfors, Sture. "När Kommer 91: An?" *Expressen*. March 28, 1966.

8586. Hegerfors, Sture. "När Serierna Drog i Krig." *Expressen*. November 6, 1966.

8587. Hegerfors, Sture. "Neger? Icke!" *Expressen*. January 28, 1967.

8588. Hegerfors, Sture. "Nenni i en Naken Kvinnas Armar." *Expressen.* August 2, 1967.

8589. Hegerfors, Sture. "Ni Kan Bli Miljonär Pa Serier!" *Kvällsposten* (Malmö). July 2, 1967.

8590. Hegerfors, Sture. "Nu Kommer Läderlappen i Co!" *Lektyr* (Stockholm). September 10, 1966.

8591. Hegerfors, Sture. *Pratbubblan!: en Bok om Serier.* Stockholm: Trevi, 1978.

8592. Hegerfors, Sture. "Satanik Och Pelle Svanslös." *Expressen.* November 6, 1966.

8593. Hegerfors, Sture. "Seriehäfte God Hjälp Att Na Pres-Identpost." *Göteborgs-Posten.* May 15, 1960.

8594. Hegerfors, Sture. "Serieläsning Berikar Vart Sprak." *Tidnings-Nylt* (Stockholm). No. 1, 1968.

8595. Hegerfors, Sture. "Seriemode Balsam för Var Själ?" *Idun-Veckojournalen* (Stockholm). No. 27, 1966.

8596. Hegerfors, Sture. "Serierna Var Tids Folk-Litteratur." *Göteborg-Tidningen.* April 11, 1966.

8597. Hegerfors, Sture. "Sex i Seriernas Värld." *GT Söndags-Extra.* July 12, 1967.

8598. Hegerfors, Sture. "Släng Inte Bort Gamla Allan Kämpe." *Expressen* (Stockholm). July 13, 1967.

8599. Hegerfors, Sture. "Som Nanna Näktergal Ställt Till Det!" *GT Söndags Extra* (Göteborg). August 20, 1967.

8600. Hegerfors, Sture. "Stalkvinnan?" *Expressen.* January 24, 1966.

8601. Hegerfors, Sture. "Storm-P Förfader Till Mumin?" *Expressen.* November 19, 1964.

8602. Hegerfors, Sture. "Suède." In *Histoire Mondiale de la Bande Dessinée*, edited by Pierre Horay, pp. 200-201. Paris: Pierre Horay Éditeur, 1989.

8603. Hegerfors, Sture. *Svish! Pow! Sock! Seriernas Fantastika Värld.* Lund: Verlag Corona, 1966. 122 pp.

8604. Hegerfors, Sture. "Tacksamma Spenatodlare i Texas Reste Staty över Karl-Alfred." *GT Söndags Extra* (Göteborg). November 12, 1967.

8605. Hegerfors, Sture. "Titta in i Pratbubblan!" *Expressen.* December 15, 1965.

8606. Hegerfors, Sture. "Tuffe Viktor Fyller Tio Ar." *GT-Söndags Extra*. 1967.

8607. Hegerfors, Sture. "Universitetet Och Lumpen Skapade den Trötte Wilmer." *GT Söndags-Extra* (Göteborg). January 21, 1968.

8608. Hegerfors, Sture. "Vara Serier Jubilerar." *Hemmets Vecko Tidning* (Hälsingborg). No. 52, 1967.

8609. Hegerfors, Sture. "Varför Läser Vi Tecknade Serier?" *Röster i Radio-TV* (Stockholm). No. 32, 1966.

8610. Hegerfors, Sture. "Var Man Flinta." *Expressen*. December 4, 1966.

8611. Hegerfors, Sture. "Var Tids Folkliteratur." *Borlänge Tidningen* (Göteborg). June 5, 1966.

8612. Hegerfors, Sture. "Varvär Gifte Sig Inte Fantomen?" *Idun-Veckojournalen* (Stockholm). No. 1, 1966.

8613. Hegerfors, Sture. "Visste Ni Att Dinnis Slass i Vietnam Nu?" *Göteborgs-Tidningen*. Söndags-Extra. December 17, 1967.

8614. Hegerfors, Sture. "Wham! Pow! Zowie!" *Expressen*. August 16, 1966.

8615. Hegerfors, Sture. "Woffa, Woffa, Rit-Ola." *Expressen*. December 3, 1966.

8616. Hegerfors, Sture and H. Sidén. *Sex + Serier*. Stockholm: 1970. 200 pp.

8617. "'Heroin 210g 65 Kronor.'" *Nordic Comics Revue*. Winter 1992-1993, p. 14.

8618. Hjertén, Henrik. "I Serielandet." *Samtid Och Framtid* (Stockholm). 1954, pp. 44-47.

8619. Johannesson, Lena. "Swedish Comics, Original Art and Handicraft in Mass Reproduction." *Nationalmuseum Bulletin* (Stockholm). 1:3 (1977), p. 121-134.

8620. Klingberg, Göte. "Undersökningar Rörande Seriemagasinens Sprak." *Folkskolan* (Stockholm). 1-2, 1954, pp. 15-21.

8621. Kochheim, Wilfried. "Adamson Oder die Sprachlosigkeit der Bildergeschichte: Mit Beiläufigen Erläuterungen zum Erzählenlernen im Deutschunterricht." *Diskussion Deutsch* (Frankfurt). 12:60 (1981), pp. 320-346.

8622. Köhlert, Adolf. "Bilderhefte in Schweden und Deutschland." *Jugendschriften-Warte* (Frankfurt). 1:6 (1955), p. 47.

8623. Köhlert, Adolf. "Bilderhefte in Schweden und Deutschland." *Verlags-Praxis* (Darmstadt). 2 (1955), pp. 241-242.

8624. "Kort Nyt." *Serieskaberen.* June 1990, p. 10.

8625. Larson, Lorentz. "Barn Matas Vald, Mord, Sadism." *Barn* (Stockholm). 1960, p. 7.

8626. Larson, Lorentz. *Barn Och Serier.* Stockholm: Almkvist och Wiksell, 1954.

8627. Larson, Lorentz. "Children and Comic Books." *Norsk Pedagogisk Tidsskrift.* 38, 1954, pp. 25-32.

8628. Larson, Lorentz. *Ungdom Läser.* Stockholm: 1947.

8629. Leijonhielm, Christer. "Har Inte Serierna Nagra Goda Sidor?" *Barn* (Stockholm). No. 6, 1954, p. 2.

8630. Leijonhielm, Christer. "Serietidningarnas Verkan." *Pedagogisk Tidskrift* (Stockholm). 1954, pp. 105-110.

8631. Leijonhielm, Christer. *Ungdomens Läsvanor.* Stockholm: 1955. 199 pp.

8632. Leistikow, Gunnar. "Kampen Mot Raketens Förhärligande." *Popular Tidskrift för Psykologi Och Sexualkonskap* (Stockholm). 1955, pp. 66-69.

8633. Lindberger, Örjan. *Bibeln i Bubblor.* Stockholm: 1955.

8634. Lundin, Bo. *Salongsbödlarna.* Lund: 1971.

8635. Madsen, Frank. "Det Stockholmske Blodbad." *Seriejournalen.* March 1992, pp. 20-21.

8636. Madsen, Frank. "Kraemmermarked." *Seriejournalen.* December 1991, p. 13.

8637. Mathiasen, Paw. "Gang i de Svenskealternativer." *Seriejournalen.* December 1991, p. 14.

8638. "1992 Adamsson Awards." *Nordic Comics Revue.* Winter 1992-1993, p. 14.

8639. Nirje, Bengt. "Valdets Pornografi." *Hörde Ni* (Stockholm). 1954, pp. 825-831.

8640. Runnquist, Ake. "Seriereaktioner." *Bonniers Litterära Magasin* (Stockholm). 1964. pp. 109-117.

8641. Runnquist, Ake. "Svish! Pow!" *Bockernas Värld* (Stockholm). 1967, p. 2.

8642. Runnquist, Ake. "Tankar Om Serier." *Bonniers Litterära Magasin* (Stockholm). 1948, pp. 430-437.

8643. Runnquist, Ake. "Till Stalmannens Miuve." *Bonniers Litterära Magasin* (Stockholm). 1967, pp. 222-225.

8644. "Schröder and His Mature Comics Find Difficult Times." *Nordic Comics Revue.* April 1992, p. 10.

8645. Skard, Granda Ase. "The Problem of the Comic Books." *Norsk Pedagogisk Tidsskrift.* 38, 1954, pp. 39-48.

8646. "Splasch Alive—After 10 Years of Silence." *Nordic Comics Revue.* April 1992, p. 10.

8647. Stenberg, Ingvar. "Att Läsa Serier." *Perspektiv* (Stockholm). 1952, pp. 256-267.

8648. "Svensk Semic Holder Seminar for Forfattere." *Serieskaberen.* March 1990, pp. 10-11.

8649. "Svenske Serier Genopstået." *Serieskaberen.* December 1989, p. 6.

8650. "Swedish Erotica Hits the US—Again!" *Nordic Comics Revue International.* Autumn 1992, p. 21.

8651. "Urhunden to Arne and Charlie—Second Time Around." *Nordic Comics Revue.* April 1992, p. 9.

8652. "U.S. Comics Strips in Sweden." *Cartoonist PROfiles.* No. 15, 1972, p. 2.

8653. Wahlöö, Per. "Visste Ni Detta om en Väldsfrälst Drömvärld?" *Barn.* 1957, p. 1.

8654. "A World Record That Guinness Isn't Sure of." *Nordic Comics Revue.* April 1992, p. 10.

Political Cartoons

8655. Griffer, Beng-Göran. *Fred & Miljo.* Sysslebäck, Sweden: Bokförlaget Sattern, 1986.

8656. Heimerson, Staffan. "Ewert Karlsson: Drawing the Line." *Scanorama.* September 1987, pp. 130-136.

8657. Karlsson, G.A.E. (EWK). *The International Pavilion of Humor of Montreal Presents "EWK," 1979 Cartoonist of the Year.* Montreal: 1979.

SWITZERLAND

General Studies

8658. Gaertner, Susanna. "Europe's Biggest and Best Cartoons Museum (The Collection of Caricatures and Cartoons, Basel)." *Connoisseur.* March 1988, pp. 162 +.

8659. Haëm, Hans. "A Cartoonist's Creative Apple." *WittyWorld.* Spring 1988, pp. 43-44.

8660. Lubbers, Frits. "Een Zwitsers Sprookje." *Sick.* 22/23 (1991), pp. 28-29.

8661. Nadkarni, Dev. "A Museum of Laughter." *Amusement Today and Tomorrow.* October/November 1990, pp. 16-17.

8662. Spahr, Jurg. "Where Laughter Reigns." *Indian Post.* January 21, 1990.

Cartoonists and Caricaturists

8663. Jacot, Pierre-A. *De Cas... en Ca... Ricatures!* Preface by Guy Fontanet. Geneva: Sociéte de Publications Nouvelles, 1985.

8664. *100 Dessins d'Urs. Frédéric Studer.* Lausanne: Éditions Rencontre, 1964.

Ceppi, Daniel

8665. "Le Guêpier, Daniel Ceppi." Lausanne: Les Éditions sans Frontières, 1977.

8666. Logoz, Dinu. "Comicographie." *Comic Forum. Das Magazin für Comicliteratur.* 8:33 (1986), p. 28.

8667. Logoz, Dinu. "Interview mit Paûle und Daniel Ceppi." *Comic Forum. Das Magazin für Comicliteratur.* 8:33 (1986), pp. 23-27.

8668. Logoz, Dinu. "Scene Schweiz. Teil 3: Daniel Ceppi." *Comic Forum. Das Magazin für Comicliteratur.* 8:33 (1986), pp. 17-22.

Cosey (Bernard Cosandey)

8669. Affolter, Cuno. "Interview Mit Cosey." *Comixene. Das Comicfachmagazin.* 8:40 (1981), pp. 7-9.

8670. Affolter, Cuno. "Und die Berge Singen für Dich. Ein Portrait des Schweizer Comic-Zeichners Cosey." *Comixene. Das Comicfachmagazin.* 8:40 (1981), pp. 4-7.

8671. Tschernegg, Markus. "Interview Mit Cosey." *Comic Forum. Das Österreichische Fachmagazin für Comicliteratur.* 4:15 (1982), pp. 47-49.

Derib (Claude de Ribaupierre)

8672. Affolter, Cuno. "Derib." *Comixene. Das Comicfachmagazin.* 8:42 (1981), pp. 4-7.

8673. Affolter, Cuno. "Interview Mit Derib." *Comixene. Das Comicfachmagazin.* 8:42 (1981), pp. 7-9.

8674. Delporte, Yvan. *Les Amis de Buddy Longway: Trente Clins d'Oeil à Buddy Longway: Interviews d'Yvan Delporte.* Brussels: Eds du Lombard, 1983.

8675. Ecken, Claude. "Entretien avec Derib." *Schtroumpf. Les Cahiers de la Bande Dessinée.* 50, 1981, pp. 5-22.

8676. Filippini, Henri. "Bibliographie de Derib." *Schtroumpf. Les Cahiers de la Bande Dessinée.* 50, 1981, pp. 47-49.

8677. Filippini, Henri. "La Vie Familiale Chez Derib." *Schtroumpf. Les Cahiers de la Bande Dessinée.* 50, 1981, pp. 38-39.

8678. Pernin, Georges. *Derib. Un Créateur et Son Univers.* Brussels: Eds. du Lombard, 1985.

8679. Roux, Antoine. "Derib ou: en Moins de Mots Qu'il ne Faut pour le Dire..." *Schtroumpf. Les Cahiers de la Bande Dessinée.* 50, 1981, pp. 40-46.

8680. Tschernegg, Markus. "Derib." *Comic Forum. Das Österreichische Fachmagazin für Comicliteratur.* 2:7/8 (1980), pp. 70-76.

Töpffer, Rodolphe

8681. Blondel, Auguste and Paul Mirabaud. *Rodolphe Töpffer: l'Écrivain, l'Artiste et l'Homme.* Paris: Hachette, 1886; Geneva: Slatkine, 1976.

8682. Chaponnière, Paul. *Notre Töpffer.* Lausanne: Libraire Pagot, 1930.

8683. Courthion, Pierre. *Genève, ou le Portrait des Töpffer.* Paris: Grasset, 1936.

8684. de Maistre, Xavier. *Lettres Inédites à Son Ami Töpffer. Recueillies et Accompagnées de Notes par Léon-A Matthey.* Geneva: Skira, 1945.

8685. Gallati, Ernst. *Rodolphe Töpffer und die Deutschsprachige Kultur.* Bonn: 1975.

8686. Gaullieur, Eusèbe. "Rodolphe Töpffer: Essai Biographique." In *Etrennes Helvétiennes, Album Suisse.* Bern and Geneva: 1856.

8687. Gautier, Léopold. *Un Bouquet de Lettres de Rodolphe Töpffer.* Lausanne: 1974.

8688. Gautier, Théophile. "Du Beau dans l'Art." *Revue des Deux Models.* 19 (1847), pp. 887-908.

8689. Horay, Pierre. *Rodolphe Töpffer: Histoires en Images.* Paris: Pierre Horay Éditeur, n.d. 288 pp.

8690. Joakimidis, Demetre. "Un Héritage de Töepffer." *Construire* (Geneva). October 2, 1968.

8691. Kunzle, David. "The Eyesight of Rodolphe Töpffer." *Historia Ophthalmologica Internationalis* (Bonn). 2 (1981), pp. 57-84.

8692. Kunzle, David. "Histoire de M. Cryptogame (1845): Une Bande Dessinée par Rodolphe Töpffer pour le Grand Public." *Genava.* 32 (1984), pp. 139-169.

8693. "Lexikalisches Über Rodolphe Töpffer." *Bulletin: Jugend + Literatur.* No. 2/71, 1971, pp. 41-42.

8694. Maschietto, Manuela. *Trois Histoires en Images: Les Amours de Monsieur Vieux Bois, Les Voyages et Aventures du Docteur Festus, Monsieur Cryptogame,* by Rodolph Töpffer. Paris: Club des Libraires de France, 1962.

8695. "Meldung Über R. Töpffer." *Süddeutsche Zeitung, Literaturbeilage* (Munich). December 7, 1967, p. 2.

8696. Metken, Günter. "Ahnherr der Comics: Rudolphe Töpffers Bildromane." *Stuttgarter Zeitung.* April 4, 1970, p. 52.

8697. Relave, Pierre Maxime, Abbé. *La Vie et les Oeuvres de Töpffer.* Paris: 1886.

8698. Sac, Claude. "Rodolphe Töpffer." *Pencil.* No. 1, 1968, pp. 3-11.

8699. Sainte-Beuve, C.-A. "M. Rodolph Töpffer." *Portraits Contemporains* (Paris). III (1870), p. 225.

8700. Schur, E. *Rudolph Töpffer.* Berlin: 1912.

8701. Töpffer, Rodolphe. *Der Kühle Bräutigam.* Hamburg: Rowohlt-Verlag, 1956.

8702. Töpffer, Adam. *Les Caricatures d'Adam Töpffer et la Restauration Genevoise.* Intro. by Eduard Chapuisat. Geneva: 1917.

8703. Töpffer, Rodolphe. *Enter: The Comics. Rodolphe Töepffer's Essay on Physiognomy and the True Story of Monsieur Crépin.* Trans. and ed. by E.Wiese. Lincoln: Nebraska: University of Nebraska Press, 1965. 80 pp.

8704. Töpffer, Rodolphe. *Essai de Physiognomonie*. Geneva: 1845.

8705. Töpffer, Rodolphe. *Notes. Paris 1820. Le Journal Intime de Rodolphe Töpffer.* Edited by Jacques Droin-Bridel and Monique Droin-Bridel. Offprint from *Geneva*. 1968.

8706. Töpffer, Rodolphe. *Oeuvres Complètes: Caricatures.* 11 Vols. (Edition du Centenaire). Geneva: 1943.

8707. Töpffer, Rodolphe. *Trois Histoires en Images.* Preface by Manuela Maschietto. Paris: 1962.

Wäscher, Hansrudi

8708. Dambacher, H.D. and Peter Orban, eds. *Hansrudi Wäscher: Die Geschichte Eines Comic-Künstlers; Eine Zusammenfassende Darstellung Seines Werdeganges und Seines Werkes, Erzählt von Ihm Selbst.* Frankfurt: Comic-Buch-Club, 1978.

8709. Hethke, Norbert, ed. *Bibliothek der Großen Comics. Sammlerausgabe: Hansrudi Wäscher.* Schönau: Norbert Hethke Verlag, 1980.

8710. Hethke, Norbert, ed. *Sigurd. Sammlerausgabe.* Schönau: Norbert Hethke Verlag, 1982.

8711. Hoffmann, Udo. "Deutsche Phantasie-Comics Oder: Nur im Abstand zur Realität Liegt das Glück." In *Fantasy. Studien zur Phantastik*, edited by Rolf Giesen, pp. 40-54. Schondorf: Roloff and Seeßleen, ed., 1982.

Animation

8712. Edera, Bruno. "Histoire du Cinéma Suisse d'Animation." *Travelling* (Lausanne). Spring 1978, pp. 51-52.

Caricature

8713. Barth, Wolf. *Karikaturen aus dem Nebelspalter.* Geneva: Nebelspalter-Verlag, 1970. 142 pp.

8714. Fosca, François. "La Caricature en Suisse." *Arts et Métiers Graphiques.* September 15, 1932, pp. 135-139.

8715. Rothe, Rolf. *Album Souvenir de la Société des Nations, à Genève, le 15-11-1920.* Genèva: Édition Atar, 1920. (115 drawings and caricatures of delegates).

8716. Steger, H.U. *Lasst Hupen aus Alterzeit*. Zurich: Diogenes Verlag, 1955.

Comics

8717. Affolter, Cuno, Urs Hangartner and Otto Janssen. "BD '85: Ein Internationales Festival im Aufwind." *Comic Forum. Das Magazin für Comicliteratur*. 7:29 (1985), pp. 24-29.

8718. Antonioli, J.A. "Les Bandes Dessinées: Littérature d'Expression Graphique ou Balbutiment d'Illettrés." *Tribune de Lausanne*. April 5, 1963, p. 3.

8719. Armand, Frédéric. "Comics als Spiegel und Mythos." *Weltwoche-Magazin* (Zurich). July 31, 1970, pp. 10-15.

8720. Brunner-Lienhart, Fritz. "Der Schlag ins Gesicht—Zu den Problemen um die Jugendgefährdenden Schriften." *Neue Zürcher Zeitung*. April 7, 1965.

8721. "Comic-Books." *Der Standpunkt* (Meran). June 4, 1954.

8722. "Comic-Phaenomen." *Sonntags-Journal* (Zurich). November 20, 1971.

8723. "'Comics' Oder die Züchtung des Unpolitischen Arbeitsmenschen." *Die Weltbühne* (Zurich). 10:32 (1955), pp. 1006-1009.

8724. Couperie, Pierre. "100,000,000 de Lieues en Ballon. La Science-Fiction dans la Bande Dessinée." Catalogue, Kunsthalle Bern, Bern, July 8-September 10, 1967, pp. 6-7.

8725. Couperie, Pierre. "Spiegelungen der Modernen Kunst im Comic Strip." *Graphis*. 28:159 (1972/1973), pp. 14-25; *Graphis-Sonderband*. 1972, p. 14-25.

8726. Couperie, Pierre. "Vorläufer und Definition des Comic-strip." *Graphis*. 28:159, 1972/1973, pp. 8-13; *Graphis-Sonderband* (Zurich). 1972.

8727. Crepax, Guido. *Valentina*. Bern: Lukianos-Verlag, 1971. 128 pp.

8728. Dahrendorf, Malte and Wolfgang Kempkes. "Comics Heute." *Schweizerische Lehrerzeitung* (Zurich). October 26, 1972, pp. 1665-1667.

8729. Daniels, Les. "Comic-Variationen." *Graphis*. 28:159 (1972/1973), pp. 62-75; *Graphis-Sonderband*. 1972, pp. 62-75.

8730. "Die Comics vor dem Strafrichter." *Schweizer Zeitschrift für Psychologie und Ihre Anwendungen* (Bern). 8:15 (1956), pp. 597-598.

8731. Eco, Umberto. "Nachwort-Comics." *Graphis*. Sonderband, 1972, pp. 118-119.

8732. "Editorial: Comics." *Pencil*. No. 1, G.E.L.D., 1968.

8733. Glaser, Milton. "Comics, Advertising and Illustration. Comics, Werbung und Illustration. Bande Dessinée, Publicité et Illustration." *Graphis* (Zürich). 28:160 (1972/1973), pp. 104-117.

8734. Görlich, Ernst J. "Die Comic-Books." *Civitas*. 10:11 (1955), pp. 567-568.

8735. "Heldin der Dritten Welt." *Die Weltwoche* (Zürich). December 16, 1966.

8736. Hensel, Georg. "Bilderbogen und Bilderdrogen. Zum Problem der Comic-Strips." *Schweizerisches Kaufmännisches Zentralblatt* (Basel). 51, 1955, p. 291.

8737. Herdeg, Walter and David Pascal. *The Art of the Comic Strip*. Zurich: Graphic Press, 1972.

8738. Hornung, Werner. "Optimistische Utopie." *Sonntags-Journal* (Zurich). No. 1, 1971, p. 27.

8739. "Ink!" *Comic Info*. May-June 1993, p. 45.

8740. Joakimidis, Demetre. "De la Nostalgie à la Renaissance." *Construire* (Geneva). September 25, 1968.

8741. Karrer-Kharberg, Rolf. *Wer Zeichner Wie?* Zurich: Diogenes-Verlag, 1963.

8742. "L'Art de la Bande Dessinée." *Graphis* (Zurich). Special Ed., Nos. 159/160, 1972.

8743. Lehner, René. "Scene Schweiz." *Comic Forum. Das Magazin für Comicliteratur.* 8:31 (1986), pp. 30-31.

8744. Lehner, René. "Scene Schweiz. Teil 2." *Comic Forum. Das Magazin für Comicliteratur.* 8:32 (1986), pp. 31-32.

8745. "Les Bandes Dessinées." *Tribune de Lausanne*. No. 21, 1965.

8746. *Les Bandes Dessinées Antichambre de la Culture*. Geneva: G.E.L.D., 1966. 45 pp.

8747. "Leserinnen und Leser Antworten zum Thema Comic-Strips." *Wir Eltern* (Zurich). March 1970, p. 5.

8748. Mauron, Sylvette. "Pleins Feux sur les Journaux pour Enfants et Adolescents." *Construire* (Geneva). February 21, 1968.

8749. "Mit Einem Kleinen Lächeln: 'Motus' von Jean-Pierre Gos." *Der Bund* (Bern). April 9, 1970.

8750. Moliterni, Claude. "Die Erzähltechnik der Comics." *Graphis*. 28:159 (1972/1973), pp. 26-43; *Graphis-Sonderband*. 1972, pp. 26-43.

8751. Morris, Marcus. "The Problem of the Comics." Manuscript. Internationaler Kongress für das Jugendbuch, Zürich, October 3, 1953.

8752. Netz, Robert. "Suisse." In *Histoire Mondiale de la Bande Dessinée*, edited by Pierre Horay, pp. 16-19. Paris: Pierre Horay Éditeur, 1989.

8753. Oberst, Helmut. "Plautus in Comics." Zurich: Artemis, 1971. 78 pp.

8754. Pascal, David. "Vorwort-Comics." *Graphis*. 28:159 (1972/1973), p. 7; *Graphis-Sonderband*. 1972, p. 7.

8755. Pasche, Daniel H. "Bandes Dessinées: Roman de Demain?" *La Tribune de Genève*. November 26/27, 1966, p. 11.

8756. Resnais, Alain. "Film und Comic-Strip." *Graphis-Sonderband*. 1972, pp. 96-103.

8757. "Resolution Über Comic-Strips." *Internationale Tagung für das Jugendbuch* (Aarau). 1953, p. 143.

8758. Sadoul, Jacques. "La Science-Fiction dans le Comic-Book." Catalog, Kunsthalle Bern, Bern, July 8-September 17, 1967, pp. 6-7.

8759. Schiele, J.K. "Was Sind Comics und Wie Stellen Wir uns Dazu?" Bericht der Internationalen Tagung für das Jugendbuch (Aarau). 1953, pp. 131-133.

8760. Schmidt, Heiner. *Bibliographie zur Literarischen Erziehung 1900-1965*. Zurich: 1967.

8761. "Schreckliche Kopfwäsche." *Sonntags-Journal*. November 20, 1971, pp. 52-53.

8762. Smith, Norman. "Was Macht die 'Comic-Strips' So Popular?" *Die Tat* (Zurich). April 20, 1964, p. 11.

8763. Versins, Pierre. "La Science-Fiction dans le Monde." Catalogue, Kunsthalle Bern, Bern, July 8-September 17, 1967, p. 3.

8764. Von Manteuffel, Claus Z. "Comic-Strips. Gedanken zu Einer Ausstellung." *Neue Zürcher Zeitung*. February 8, 1970.

8765. Weaver, Robert. "Experimente in Zeit-Kunst." *Graphis-Sonderband*. 1972, pp. 88-95.

8766. Werner, Harro. "Comics." *Helvetische Typographie* (Zurich). October 25, 1972.

8767. Wyss, Hedi. "Sind Comics Eine Gefahr für Unsere Kinder?" *Wir Eltern* (Zurich). March 1970, pp. 10-14.

8768. Zihler, Leo. "Die Herkunft der Bilderstreifen." *Neue Zürcher Zeitung*. May 6, 1961.

8769. Zulliger, H. "Sind die Comic-Strips Eine Gefahr?" *Pro Juventute*. 35, 1954, pp. 77-79; *Schweizerische Lehrerzeitung*. 26, 1962, pp. 803-805.

Political Cartoons

8770. Haëm, Hans. "Switzerland, Satire and Serious People." *WittyWorld*. Autumn, 1987, pp. 22-23.

TURKEY

General Studies

8771. Çakmak, Hüsseyin. "Magazine Editor Sentenced to 16 Months in Prison for Publishing a Cartoon About the President of His Country." *WittyWorld*. Summer 1993, p. 7.

8772. Cole, Marc, trans. "Cartoons Are Serious Stuff: Interview with Semih Balcioglu." *Apropos*. No. 3, 1986, pp. 134-135.

8773. *Çorum Haber. "Basin Özgürlüğü" ve "Kadin": Karikatür Albümü*. Corum: Corum Haber Basimevi, 1992.

8774. "Expressivité, Énergie de S. Undeger." *Limoges*. October 5, 1990, p. 5.

8775. Karabas, Seyfi. "Hairy Turkish Cartoons." *Humor: International Journal of Humor Research*. 3:2 (1990), pp. 193-216.

8776. "Karikatür Haberleri." *Akrep*. 1:1 (1988), p. 7.

8777. Kovachev, Roumen. "The Turkish Cartoon." *Apropos*. No. 3, 1986, pp. 129 +.

8778. "Ramiz Gökce." *Akrep*. 1:1 (1988), p. 10.

8779. Topuz, Hifzi. "Iletisim Olarak Karikatür." *Akrep*. 1:1 (1988), p. 5.

YUGOSLAVIA

General Studies

8780. Becker, Hartmut and Andreas C. Knigge. "Interview mit Walter Neugebauer." *Comixene. Das Comicfachmagazin*. 7:31 (1980), pp. 16-18.

8781. "Cartoons in Yugoslavia." *FECO News*. No. 4, 1987, p. 11.

8782. Dragič, Nedelko. *Lexikon für Analphabeten*. Berlin: Eulenspiegel, 1968.

8783. "From Animation to Thinking." *Kayhan Caricature*. October 1972.

8784. "The Golden Pen—Petričić." *FECO News*. No. 3, 1987, p. 13.

8785. Harrison, Hubert. "Mickey Mouse Is Banned by Censors in Yugoslavia." *New York Times*. December 1, 1937.

8786. "Hassan Talks of Himself." *Kayhan Caricature*. December 1992.

8787. "Jez—50 Years On." *Apropos*. No. 4, 1986, pp. 157-160.

8788. Lent, John A. "Yugoslav Cartooning Thrives Amidst Turmoil." *Comics Journal*. May 1992, pp. 37-39.

8789. "Srećko Puntarić Felix." *FECO News*. No. 4, 1987, pp. 8-9.

8790. Thurow, Roger. "Amid Their War, Serbs Bid Goodbye to Donald Duck—Disney Characters' Departure Spurs Some Soul-Searching Among Adults, Kids Alike." *Wall Street Journal*. January 27, 1993, p. A-1.

8791. "Who Killed Donald Duck?" *Comics Buyer's Guide*. March 5, 1993, p. 128. Reprinted from *Wall Street Journal*. January 27, 1993.

8792. "Yugoslavie." *FECO News*. No. 3, 1987, p. 11.

8793. "Yugoslavie Zdenko Puhin." *FECO News*. No. 4, 1987, p. 3.

Caricature

8794. Behrendt, Fritz. "Refined People—Drawn by Otto Reisinger." *Apropos*. No. 3, 1986, p. 101.

8795. "Borivoj Dovnikovic-Bordo: Caricaturist...." *Apropos*. No. 3, 1986, pp. 58 +.

8796. "Nikola Ugrin Angelkoski." *FECO News*. No. 12, 1991, pp. 2-4.

Comic Books

8797. "Captain America in Yugoslavia." *Comics Scene*. No. 9, 1989, pp. 69-70.

8798. Dutrey, Jacques. "Enki Bilal Wins Top Prize at Angoulême." *Comics Journal*. July 1987, p. 130.

8799. Furtinger, Zvonimir and Julio Radilovic. "Herlock Sholmes, Master of Disguise." *Cartoonist PROfiles*. No. 20, 1973, pp. 58-67.

8800. Millo, Stelio. "I Fumetti in Jugoslavia." *Comics World* (Genoa). No. 3, 1968, pp. 27-29.

8801. "Now Yugoslavs Will Be Reading Classic Comics." *International Herald Tribune*. August 18, 1967.

8802. Rustemagíc, Ervin. "La Bande Dessinée Yougoslave." *Phénix*. No. 38, June 1974.

8803. Rustemagíc, Ervin. "Yougoslavie." In *Histoire Mondiale de la Bande Dessinée*, edited by Pierre Horay; pp. 196-200. Paris: Pierre Horay Éditeur, 1989.

8804. Stanek, Heinz. "Comics in Jugoslawien." *Comixene. Das Comicfachmagazin*. 5:21 (1978), pp. 38-39.

8805. Urban, Peter. "Miki Mis&Co.—Groschenhefte in Jugoslawien." In "Titel, Thesen, Temperamente." 1. Deutsches Fernsehen, August 10, 1970, Frankfurt.

8806. Zograf, Aleksandar. "Hey, Kids! Comics." *Comics Journal*. March 1993, p. 117.

Comic Strips

8807. Ciment, Gilles. "YU Strip: Les Bandes Dessinées Yougoslaves." *Les Cahiers de la Bande Dessinée*. 70, 1986, pp. 52-53.

8808. Rovsek, Jernej. "Strip." *Cartoonist PROfiles*. September 1983, pp. 20-21.

8809. Stojak, Rudi. "Struktura Stripa (The Structure of Comics)." *Pregled*. 65:4 (1975), pp. 459-472.

Author Index

Abbà, A., 7063
à Beckett, Arthur W., 5997, 5998, 6585
Abraham, Abu, 6586
Abruzzese, Alberto, 7692
Acevedo, Juan, 5618, 8376
Adam, Marcele, 2620
Adhémar, Jean, 1339, 1528-1529, 1918-1923, 3231, 5850
Adler, Philippe, 3956
Adley, D.J., 5690
Aeschimann, Eric, 3228
Affolter, Cuno, 201, 299, 2741, 8669-8673, 8717
Agulhon, Maurice, 1530
Ajello, Nello, 6992, 7682
Akokalidi, George, 6929
Akoun, André, 2375
Alain, P., 3229
Alapetite, Bernard, 2845
Alber, Wolfgang, 340-342, 440, 2742, 4214, 5502, 5505, 7186, 7252
Alberelli, Christian, 1161, 2625, 3232
Albert, A., 5700
Albert, Claudia, 2857
Albertarelli, Rino, 7133, 7278-7279, 7337, 7424
Alberti, Walter, 7407

Aldebert, Bernard, 3168
Alderson, Connie, 6859
Alderson, Frederick, 5701
Aldridge, Alan, 5970, 6685
Alem, Conrado, 2175
Alemán Sainz, Francisco, 8138
Alessandrini, Ferruccio, 7346, 7425
Alessandrini, Marjorie, 44, 1162
Alessi-Conte, Andrea, 7134, 7572
Alexander, David, 5852
Alexandre, Arséne, 1340-1342, 1925, 1926, 2734
Alexandre, Pierre, 1809
Alhoy, Maurice M., 2307
Alix, Lefranc, 2547
Allard, John, 6537, 6538
Allaway, Jeremy, 6798
Allen, Ann Taylor, 4007
Allodoli, Ettore, 6661
Allwood, Martin S., 300, 8505, 8543
Altabella, José, 8172
Altarriba, Antonio, 740
Altick, Richard, 6587
Alvarez Villar, Alfonso, 8302, 8478-8480
Alvarus (Álvaro Cotrim), 1343, 1927, 1928, 2255, 2256, 2455, 2735,

6177, 6313, 6314
Amengual, Barthélemy, 3050, 3084
Ames, Winslow, 6892
Amiel, Vincent, 1302, 3491
Amutio, Robert, 3578
Anders, Günther, 4362
Andersch, Lothar, 5208
Andersen, Verner E., 6686
Anderson, J. Martin (Cynicus), 6087, 6088
Anderson, Paul, 6799
Andersson, Max, 6642
Andersson, Per A.J., 8506, 8544-8547
Andioc, René, 8265
André, Jean-Claude, 3492
Andreasen, Mogens Wenzel, 7877
Andreasson, Lars, 8547
Andres, Stefan, 5099
Andrevon, Jean-Pierre, 1766, 2286, 2287, 2779, 2780, 3860
Anglo, Michael, 6687
Ansa, Luis, 3136
Antal, Frederick, 6194
Antonioli, J.A., 8718
Antral, Louis, 6195
Apelt, Hans-Peter, 5209
Apfel, Alfred, 4363
Aping, Norbert, 4019, 4743
Apostolidi, Tasos, 6929
Apostolidés, Jean-Marie, 741-744, 742, 743
Appelbaum, Stanley, 1345, 4012
Appleby, Steven, 5999
Apunen, Matti, 1147
Arapu, Mircea, 8054
Arasse, Daniel, 1531
Arbesú, Faustino R., 6022, 7253, 8139-8143, 8205, 8206, 8222, 8223, 8252, 8298, 8301, 8303, 8334, 8340, 8377-8385, 8417
Arcos, René, 4364
Arfort-Cochey, Edith, 4834
Arias Terrón, Horacio, 3735
Armand, Frédéric, 8719
Armelhaut, J., 2308
Armengol, M.H., 5750
Armingeat, Jacqueline, 1929, 2086
Arnauldet, Thomas, 1532

Arndt, Walter, 4292
Arnold, Karl, 4820
Arrouye, Jean, 668, 1476, 1857, 3736, 3844, 3861, 7254, 7255
Asbury, Martin, 6534
Ashbee, C.R., 5854
Ashford, David, 6009
Ashford, Richard, 6689
Ashton, Dore, 4365
Ashton, J., 5855
Askew, Mary, 8266
Aspesi, Natalia, 7426, 7757
Assadolah Binakhahi, 943, 944
Assenin, Sergei, 1128
Atherton, Herbert M., 5856, 6196, 6909 6453-6454
Atterbom, Daniel, 7892, 8548
Atzert, Joachim, 4676
Auad, Manuel, 8224
Auclert, Jean-Pierre, 1572
Auffret, Hélène, 3703
Augusto, Sergio, 2859, 3235, 7187
Auquier, Jean, 137
Auriol, Jean-Georges, 3085, 3086
Austin, Alan, 5682
Auvray, Annie, 3579
Avello, Manuel F., 8246
Avelot, Henri, 1728-1729
Averanius, Ferdinand, 4061
Avermaete, Roger, 4366
Aymé, Marcel, 1581
Aziza, Claude, 1477

Babuchkina, A.P., 8059
Bac, Ferdinand, 1734-1748
Baccard, Erik, 2743, 2748
Bachand, Denis, 3834
Bachollet, Raymond, 1283, 1582
Backus, Dana, 5101
Bacon, Edward, 6849
Badert, A.G., 3172
Baer, Reto, 4677
Bailey, D.M., 6935
Bailey, Peter, 6491
Bairnsfather, Bruce, 6089-6093
Bajard, Annie, 1583
Baker, Rosemary, 5979

George, Hardy, 6027
George, M. Dorothy, 5684, 5880-5882, 5986
Georgel, Pierre, 1405
Gérard, Bertrand, 1230
Gerasimov, Bogomil, 891
Gerbault, Henri, 2362-2367
Gerin, Elisabeth, 1240
Gerlach, Peter, 3850
Gerosa, Ambrogio, 6976
Gerosa, Guido, 7370
Gerstenlauer, Wolfgang, 5253
Gessler, Alfred, 4074
Gettings, Frank, 4436
Ghébali, Catherine, 2590
Ghébali, Victor-Yves, 2590
Ghesquiere, Rita, 7871
Ghiringhelli, Zeno, 7698
Ghirotti, Gigi, 7015, 7488
Ghosh, Arup, 308
Giacardi, David, 6704
Giachi, Arianna, 4927
Giacobbi, Carole, 1776
Giammanco, Roberto, 7489, 7770
Gianeri, Enrico, 278, 6989, 7056, 7412
Giani, Renato, 7616
Giardino, Vittorio, 7212, 7213
Gib, 1629
Gibson, Ian, 6793, 6797
Gibson-Cowan, Ialeen, 5883
Giehrl, Hans E., 4147, 4148, 5410
Gielle, J., 587
Giese, Suzanne, 998
Giffhorn, Hans, 5130, 5131, 5254
Gifford, Denis, 154, 5685-5687, 5696, 5697, 5714-5720, 5822-5824, 5832, 5844, 5884-5886, 5941-5968, 5973-5977, 6028-6031, 6492, 6509, 6518, 6524, 6525, 6653, 6654, 6705-6722, 6885, 6895, 6896
Gil Roesset, C., 8181
Gila, Miguel, 8372
Giles, F.T., 6175
Gill, André, 2372
Gill, Andy, 3108
Gill, Ruben, 8011, 8012
Gillain, Joseph, 3327, 3641
Gillon, Paul, 2289

Gilloud, André, 8290
Gillray, James, 6180
Gilroy, Harry, 7839
Giménez, Carlos, 8217
Giménez, Juan, 8314
Gimferrer, Pedro, 8428
Giovannetti, Max, 7215
Giovannetti, Pericle Luigi, 7216-7219
Girard, Richard, 6212
Giraud, Jean (Moebius), 2388, 2389, 3019
Giraudoux, Jean, 3150
Girerd, J.P., 1631
Giromini, Ferruccio, 2747, 7413
Giroux, Renée-Héloïse, 480
Gisle, Jon, 1777
Giuffredi, E., 2957
Giuntoli, Ilio, 7771
Givens, Bill, 911, 5845
Glade, Dieter, 5132
Glaser, Milton, 8733
Glasser, Jean-Claude, 3559, 7380, 7855
Glaubitz, Joachim, 5255
Glénat, Jacques, 216, 309, 425, 445, 462, 471, 596-598, 603, 606, 607, 731, 1763, 1914, 2217, 2302, 2303, 2426, 2444, 2445, 2560, 2634, 2644, 2748, 2980, 2992, 3046, 3076, 3081, 3345, 3346
Glendenning, Nigel, 8272, 8273
Glietenberg, Ilse, 4929
Glodowski, Wlodzimierz, 7983
Gobin, Maurice, 2033
Godard, Christian, 2414, 2415
Goddin, Philippe, 481-483, 757, 1915, 1916
Godfrey, Richard T., 5852, 5887
Godin, Noel, 855, 856
Goergen, Helene, 708
Goergen, Jeanpaul, 4438
Goimard, Jacques, 1319, 3017, 7340
Gola, Guido, 3560
Goldkind, Igor, 6032
Goldstein, Ben, 2034
Goldstein, Robert J., 1406-1408
Goll, Ivan, 4439, 4440
Göllner, Lutz, 5480
Golowin, S., 5464

Meyer, Hans Georg, 4052
Meyer, R.-A., 4099
Meys, Lucien, 3622
Mézires, Jean-Claude, 1905, 2562-2565, 3077
Miani, Rozinaldo A., 2901
Micheli, S., 27
Michetz, Marc, 804
Mickethier, Knut, 4745
Middleton, L., 5990
Midgley, Carol, 6520
Midgley, Dominic, 6743
Mietzsch, Andreas, 735
Mige, Bernard, 3731
Mihr, Ulrich, 4326
Mikelbank, Peter, 2902
Milenkovitch, Michael M., 8130
Miller, Henry, 4511
Millet, Giles, 2641
Milligan, Pete, 6554
Millo, Stelio, 7677, 8800
Mills, Pat, 6555, 6786-6790
Mills, T.F., 221, 774
Milton, Freddy, 238, 1017, 1018, 1089, 7859, 7863
Milton, Ingo, 1012, 1090
Minte-König, Bianka, 5305
Minuzzo, Nerio, 7732, 8447
Miot, Bernard, 3797
Miotto, Antonio, 6999
Mira, J. Eduard, 8448
Mirabaud, Paul, 8681
Missfeldt, Wulf, 5306
Misyuchenko, Vladimir, 8105
Mitchell, Adrian, 6744
Mitchell, Hannah, 1553
Mitelberg, Louis, 3208, 3209
Mitry, Jean, 3120
Moeller, Michael Lukas, 4999, 5513, 5540
Moese, Willy, 4256
Mogensen, Jørgen, 1091
Mogensen, Kristoffer, 1062
Mohsen, Ibrahim, 2731
Moins, Philippe, 800
Moix, Ramón-Terenci, 8449, 8450, 8476
Moliterni, Claude, 46, 53, 222, 328,

736, 776, 864, 865, 1160, 1195, 1272-1274, 1487, 1516, 1517, 1682, 1893, 2198, 2304, 2369, 2398, 2448, 3051, 3431, 3432, 3499, 3525, 3661, 3798, 4933, 6192, 7011, 7020, 7266, 8750
Møller, Kurt, 1019, 1020
Mollica, Vincenzo, 7182, 7197, 7228, 7267, 7268, 7596
Mollino, Carlo, 4512
Monaco, Steve, 7499
Monet, Jack, 3732
Monfort Cañellas, Blas, 8259
Monnier, Albert, 2348
Monnier, Henry, 2569, 2570
Montañes, Luis, 8451
Monteiro, Mário, 2349
Moolenaar, Ab, 197
Moonie, George, 6510
Moorcock, Michael, 2965
Moore, Alan, 6791-6793
Moore, Linda, 8353
Moralejo Alvarez, María R., 8280
Morand, Claude, 2432
Moreau, René, 3052
Moreno Santabárbara, F., 8335
Moreno, Federico, 8452
Moreno, Pepe, 8319
Moretto, Mauro, 7166
Morgan, Vanessa, 5785
Morin, E., 777
Morin, Louis, 1196, 1554, 1555
Morin, Violette, 3154, 3799
Morris, 838
Morris, Frankie, 6444
Morris, Marcus, 5968, 6583, 6794, 8751
Morrison, Susan S., 4053
Morrissey, Ann, 2082
Mosca, Benedetto, 7103
Moscati, Massimo, 7597
Mose, 3213
Moser, G., 3870
Moser, Leopold, 356
Mosse, Hilde L., 5162-5164
Mouchel, Gérard-Guy, 1518
Mouerris, Alejandro G., 8482
Moulin, Patrick, 3641

Rehlin, Gunnar, 8530
Rehm, Dirk, 645, 667, 5480
Reichardt, Rolf, 1430
Reid, Arthur, 5735
Reid, G.W., 6153
Reimann, Hans, 4530
Reinecke, Lutz, 4177, 5383
Reinhardt, Helmut, 4755
Reinhardt, Manfred, 4261
Reinoss, Herbert, 4016
Reisner, M.E., 5925
Reitberger, Reinhold C., 15, 16, 3980, 5018, 5019
Relave, Pierre Maxime, 8697
Rémi, Georges (Hergé), 510-524
Remus, Heinz, 4972
Renard, Emmanuel, 2720
Renard, Jean-Bruno, 1522, 3446, 3711, 3858, 3894-3896
Renner, M., 4178
Rennie, Gordon, 6069, 6070
Renouvier, Jules, 1565
Rentmeister, Cäcilia, 2102
Reshef, Ouriel, 3161
Resnais, Alain, 3573, 7506, 8460, 8756
Ressano, Arnaldo, 7995
Rest, W., 5384
Restany, Pierre, 3528
Revel, Jean-François, 1453
Rey, Alain, 31, 3447
Rey, Robert, 2103-2106
Reyna Domenech, Consuelo, 8193
Ribaud-Moisan, André, 1692
Ribe, Göran, 7859
Ribeiro, Aquilino, 8001
Ribera, Julio, 2414, 2415
Ribeyre, Félix, 1284, 1886
Richard, Marius, 1566
Richard, Rob, 52
Richardot, J.C., 3625
Richardson, John, 5736
Richter, Dieter, 5167
Richter, Hans P., 5021
Richter, Peter, 3988
Richter, Wolfgang, 357
Rickwood, Edgell, 5994
Ridout, Cefn, 6754
Riegenring, Wilmar, 4262

Riely, John C., 6126
Riera, Marti, 8325
Ries, Gregor, 1693, 3991
Riesenberger, Dieter, 4179
Riewald, J.G., 6118
Rifas, Leonard, 8078, 8086, 8107, 8112
Rifkin, Adrian, 1577
Riha, Karl, 32, 920, 4180, 4181, 4474, 4532, 4790, 5022, 5514, 5583, 7105
Rim, Carlo, 2107, 2108
Rinaldi, Riccardo, 33
Ring, Max, 4011
Rio, Michel, 3806
Rioux, Lucien, 2915
Risley, John, 176
Riva, Javier, 8299
Riverain, Jean, 1455, 1456, 1457
Rivire, Franquin, 3712
Rivire, François, 425, 426, 454, 525-527, 568, 574, 610, 2400, 2635, 2826, 2840, 2841, 2967, 3448, 3656, 3712, 3807
Roberts-Jones, Philippe, 1458, 1567, 2109-2112
Robertson, Nan, 3947
Robida, Albert, 2649
Robida, Michel, 2650
Robin, Christian, 3626
Robinson, Dane, 6584
Robinson, David, 7416
Robinson, Heath, 6312
Robiquet, Jean, 2353
Roca, Javier, 8504
Rocha, Camile, 2281
Rodari, Gianni, 7721
Rodi, Rob, 6755, 6940
Rodier, Alain, 697
Roditi, Eduard, 4533
Rodrigo, Antonina, 8499
Rodríguez, Carlota, 6071
Rodríguez, Faustino, 6756, 8150, 8151
Rodríguez Diéguez, José Luis, 8461
Roe, F. Gordon, 6328
Roehricht, Karl-Hermann, 4263
Roge, Raymond, 1488
Roger, Milés L., 3218
Roger-Marx, Claude, 295, 296, 2113-2118, 2507, 3162, 8097

St.-James, Ashley, 1706
Saint-Michel, Serge, 1523, 3272, 3594, 7274
Saint-Ogan, Alain, 3082
Saint-Péron, Roland, 3616
Sainte-Beuve, C.-A., 2354, 2355, 8699
Sala, George A., 6230
Sala, Paolo, 7509, 7737
Saladrigas, Roberto, 8195
Salazar, Abel, 2132
Salmony, Alfred, 4537
Salmony, G., 4184
Salpeter, Harry, 4538
Salvucci, Giorgio, 7124, 7125, 7291
Sama, Dominic, 5663
Sambonet-Bernacchi, Luisa, 7510
Samson, Jacques, 1697, 3810, 3841
Samson, Mireille, 2133
Samu, Charles, 8091
Sanchez Abuli, Enrique, 8345
Sánchez Brito, Margarita, 8196
Sánchez Cantón, Francisco J., 8281
Sandberg, Herbert, 4054, 4651-4653
Sandberg, Tor, 7882
Sanders, Alain, 5, 1292, 1698, 2555-2557, 3461, 3657, 7275
Sanders, Andrew, 6622
Sanders, Jan, 178
Sanders, Rino, 5025
Sándor, Láncz, 4539
Sansoni, Gino, 7151
Santelli, Claude, 2978
Santucci, Luigi, 5026, 7667
Saouter Caya, Catherine, 1819, 2525, 3811, 7381
Sarcander, Alice, 5169
Sarjon, A., 3221
Sarrotte, Christophe, 3023
Sarto, Maria M., 8485
Sarzano, Frances, 6446
Sasturain, Juan, 8343
Saulnier, Adam, 1568
Saulnier, Claude, 3163
Saunier, Henri, 786, 2244
Sauret, André, 2134
Sautermeister, Gert, 5664
Sauvage, Léo, 4540
Saxer, Robert, 5318, 5319

Sayers, John, 534
Sayrem, Joel, 8326
Scarfe, Gerald, 6338
Schaaf, Ernst-Ludwig, 5027
Schaber, Will, 5680
Schad, Renate, 5419
Schaffer, Bernhard, 6074, 6165, 6546
Schaller, Horst, 5028
Schappacher, D., 5320
Schauer, Lucie, 5087
Scheckel, Rainer, 5321
Scheerer, Friedrich, 5030
Scheffler, Karl, 4541-4543
Scheibe, Wolfgang, 5170
Scheifley, W.H., 1569
Scheiwiller, Giovanni, 2135
Schelduk, Burkhardt, 5031
Scher, Hannelore, 3635
Scherf, Walter, 5171
Schiaffino, Gualtierno, 7795
Schiele, J.K., 8759
Schiff, Gert, 6330
Schifferstein, Mat, 7843, 7864
Schilling, Robert, 5172-5174, 5386, 5461
Schinkel, Erich, 3036
Schlichter, Rudolf, 4544
Schlirf, Yves, 2404
Schlocker, Georg, 5088
Schlüter, Paul, 980
Schmalenbach, Werner, 5089
Schmidmaier, Werner, 4185, 4798, 5032, 5033, 5090-5094, 5322, 5469, 5495, 5496
Schmidt, A.M.R., 4005
Schmidt, Heiner, 5175, 8760
Schmidt, Jürgen, 5095
Schmidt, Karl Eugen, 1460, 2623, 4330, 4331, 4733
Schmidt, Manfred, 4737, 4738
Schmidt, Paul F., 4545, 4546
Schmidt, W., 8067
Schmidt-Rogge, C.H., 5323, 5387
Schmitt, Erich, 4265
Schnackertz, Hermann J., 5584, 5665
Schnapper, Antoine, 2165
Schneede, Uwe M., 4547-4549
Schneider, Hagen, 1524

Subject Index

Fronval, Georges, 1698
Fuchs, Eduard, 4359, 4360
Furniss, Harry, 6024

Galindo, Federico, 8236
Galleppini, Aurelio, 7154
Gantriis, Henning, 996, 997
García López, José Luis, 8235
Garofalo, Romano, 7170
Gattia, 1620
Gaugun, Paul, 1691
Gavarni (Guillame Sulpice Chevallier),
   166, 1402, 1472, 1559, 1596, 1625,
   1628, 1646, 1663, 1686, 1938,
   2024, 2307-2361
Gawronkiewicz, Krzysztof, 7941
Genommen, Ernst, 4878
Georgiev, Chavdar, 899
Gerbault, Henri, 2362-2367, 3167
Ghezzi, Pier L., 7205-7210
Giacon, Massimo, 7172
Giardino, Vittorio, 7211-7214, 7381
Gibbons, Dave, 6015
Gibo, 1630
Giese, Suzanne, 998-1001
Gifford, Denis, 5686, 5692, 5821
Gigi, Robert, 1682, 2368, 2369
GIL, 973
Giles, Carl Ronald, 6172-6176
Gill, André (Louis Gosset de Guines),
   1699, 2370-2374
Gillain, 1708
Gillon, Paul, 1605, 2375-2381
Gillray, James, 6177-6190
Giménez, Carlos, 8257-8259
Gimmel, Paul, 4259
Giner, Eugenio, 8260-8264
Giovannetti, Pericle L., 7215-7219
Giraud, Jean (Gir, Moebius), 1682,
   2382-2408, 3020
Girerd, Jean Pierre, 1631
Gittins, 5767
Godard, Christian, 1696, 2409-2422,
   3047, 3540
Godfrey, Bob, 226
Goetzinger, Annie, 1614
Goffe, Toni, 6081

Gohs, Rolf, 8549
Gökce, Ramiz, 8778
Goll, Yvan, 4571
Gonzalez Casquel, Miguel, 8244
Goossens, Daniel, 2423-2425
Gos, Jean-Pierre, 8749
Goscinny, René, 688, 1627, 1696, 2426-
   2441
Gotlib, Marcel (Marcel Gotlieb), 1682,
   1714, 2442-2454
Gotta, Horst, 4230
Gould, Carruthers, 6007
Goupy, Joseph, 6084
Goya, Francisco, 333, 1691, 8265-8284
Graham, Alex, 6532
Grambert, 1672
Grandville (Jean Ignace Isidore Gérard),
   1364, 1663, 1938, 2455-2477
Grant, Alan, 6066
Grassier, 1598
Greaves, Andrew, 6027
Greg, Michel (Michel Régnier), 449,
   461-466
Grévin, A., 1402, 2478-2481
Griffin, 6010
Griset, Ernest, 6047
Grosz, Eva, 4378
Grosz, George (Georg Ehrenfried),
   4066, 4361-4580
Grun, 3167
Guérin, Raoul, 1639
Guillaume, Albert, 1598, 2482-2503,
   3167
Gulbransson, Jan, 4222
Gulbransson, Olaf, 7883-7890
Gus, 1641
Gutwirth, Marcel, 3437
Guys, Constantin, 2504-2507

Hahn, Albert, 7845
Halas, John, 6191-6193
Hassan, 8786
Heartfield, John, 4437, 4438, 4463,
   4465, 4501, 6075
Hebgen, Thomas, 5563
Hegenbarths, Josef, 4249
Hegerfors, Sture, 975

Xuasús, 8347, 8348

Zack, 3621, 4784-4787
Zig et Puce, 3081-3083
Zok Roarr Wumm, 32, 4788-4790
Zora, 8313
Zorry Kid, 7298

COMPANIES, FANZINES, and PERIODICALS

Almanach Vermot, 1335
Anuscha Mascha, 56
Apropos, 57
Association of Comics Enthusiasts Newsletter. Comic Cuts, 58
(A Suivre), 59, 1289, 1290, 1295

Bédésup, 60, 1261, 1290
Bild and Bubba, 62, 107
Black and White, 63
Bobbla, 107
Borsszem Jankó, 6956
Bulgaran, 888

Caricature et Caricaturistes, 64
Carlsen-Verlag, 5502-5504
The Cartoon Art Trust Newsletter, 65
The Cartoonist, 66
Charivari, 289, 1296-1298, 1874
Charlie Mensuel, 1289, 1290, 1294, 2991
Circus, 1289, 1290
Coccinelle, 837
Comic Art, 67
Comic Book Confidential, 1032
Comic Forum, 68
Comicgraph, 69
Comicguia, 70
Comic Media News, 71
Comic Reddition, 72
Comics Express, 73
Comics International, 74

Comics News Service from Poland, 75
Comic-Verlag Dupuis, 726, 860-862
Comikazin, 76
Comix, 77
Comixene, 78
Corto Maltese, 79
Crisis, 6872, 6873, 6875

Dargaud, 321, 3055, 3728, 3730
Dark Horse, 3482
Die Sprechblase, 80

EC, 6834
Éditions de Fleurus, 1287
Éditions Vaillant, 1286, 1501
Ehapa-Verlag, 5505, 5506
El·Wendigo, 81, 8136, 8137

Fan, 7927, 7972
Fantasy Advertiser (FA), 82
Fantazia. The Definitive Superhero Magazine, 83
Fat Comic, 84, 950, 1040, 1041, 1102, 1104
FECO News, 85
Fleetway, 6868, 6872, 6875
Fliegenden Blätter, 4003-4006
Fluide Glacial, 1289, 1290, 2984-2987
Fusion, 86
Futuropolis, 3729

Giff-Wiff, 87
Glénat, 1636, 3724, 6876
Graphixus, 88

Haga, 89
Hara-Kiri, 2305, 2990, 2991
Heavy Metal, 2394
Humo, 614

Icom Info, 90
Il Fumetto, 91

GENERAL SUBJECTS

Adamsson Awards, 8638
Adenauer, Konrad, 4809
adult comics, *see* alternative comics and
    eroticism
adventure comics, 163, 3649, 4675,
    4703, 5421-5429, 7682-7688, 8495,
    8498
advertising, 714, 858, 1548, 3721,
    3760, 7415, 7487, 8733; in
    Germany, 5511-5517, 5673; in Great
    Britain, 5723, 5781, 6314, 6658
Aesop, 8106
aesthetics, 3115, 6200, 6891, 7298,
    7700, 8298, 8324; in France, 1819,
    2079, 2081, 2716, 2720, 2780,
    3124, 3137, 3163, 3492, 3494,
    3508; in Germany, 5315, 5316,
    5591, 5671
Africa, 840, 1011, 3468, 7516
aggression, 5247, 5426, 5607, 5612
Akademie der Künste, 5083
Albania, 334, 335
Albert H. Wiggin Collection, 6322

allegory, 3883
alternative comics, 5430-5436, 6848,
    7955, 8441, 8637, 8644
American Revolution, 5896
Amos Anderson Museum, 1130
Amsterdam, 7828
Angoulême festival, 201, 1251-1260,
    1266, 1267, 1271, 1275, 1277,
    1278, 1282, 2383, 5798, 8798
animal comics, 709, 727, 3652-3658
animals, 2466, 2467, 2469, 2577, 2578,
    5853, 6231, 6662, 6681, 7681
animation, 252-272, 6361, 7805, 7985,
    8072, 8782; in Belgium, 403, 799,
    800; in Croatia, 911, 912; in
    Czechoslovakia, 942-946; in
    Denmark, 1023-1026; in Estonia,
    1128, 1129; in France, 1338, 2196,
    3084-3135; in Germany, 4058-4060,
    4791-4800; in Great Britain, 5840-
    5849, 6191-6193, 6642-6660; in
    Hungary, 6952, 6953; in Ireland,
    6961, 6962; in Italy, 7407-7418; in
    Netherlands, 7857-7859; in Norway,
    7891; in Poland, 7930-7932; in
    Russia, 8087-8092; in Scandinavia,
    226, 231-236, 239, 241-244, 247,
    248; in Spain, 8349-8356; in
    Sweden, 8514-8534; in Switzerland,
    8712
Annecy festival, 232-234, 268, 3089
anthologies, 3118, 3167-3227, 3480-
    3490, 3951-3955, 5750-5778, 6780-
    6797, 7570, 7571
anthropologist, 5901
anti-comics campaign, 6798-6830
anticonformism, 3897
antiquity, 1489, 1518
Arabic, 2885, 7485
archeology, 1475, 5177
architecture, 913, 5098; in France,
    2196, 3491, 3493, 3501, 3536, 3861
Aristophanes, 6929
art, 19, 23, 43, 143, 159, 257, 293,
    298, 1387, 2034, 2085, 3312, 3800,
    4109, 5099, 5772, 5914, 6194,
    6667, 7986, 7993, 8541, 8619,
    8688; in Belgium, 368, 372, 538,

About the Compiler

JOHN A. LENT began studying comics in 1963–1964 when he conducted a readership/causal relationship analysis of fourth graders in Syracuse, New York. Over the years, he has pursued cartooning, studying comic books as part of a larger mass communications project in the Philippines in 1964–1965, and presenting the featured address at the first comic art exhibition in Malaysia in 1973. In 1984, he founded the comic art working group within the International Association for Mass Communication Research, and in 1986, compiled the first international comic art bibliography published in the United States. He also founded the quarterly newsletter, *Berita*, of which he is editor, and the Malaysia/Singapore/Brunei Studies Group in the mid-1970s.

Dr. Lent has been managing editor of *WittyWorld International Cartoon Magazine* since its inauguration in 1987. The author or editor of 46 books and monographs and hundreds of articles, he also serves on the editorial boards of *Comics Journal*, *Big O Magazine*, *Studies of Latin American Popular Culture*, and other periodicals. Some of his works have concentrated on comic art, beginning with a 1966 monograph, *3 Research Studies*; followed by *Comic Art: An International Bibliography* (1986), a special issue of *Philippine Communication Journal* (1993); *Cartoonometer: Taking the Pulse of the World's Cartoonists*; *Asian Popular Culture*; and the four-volume bibliography of comic art worldwide (Greenwood, 1994). In preparation for a book on Asian comic and cartoons, Dr. Lent has interviewed about 190 cartoonists in 15 Asian countries; he has also interviewed cartoonists from Europe, North and South America, and the Caribbean.

A professor since 1960, Dr. Lent has taught at universities in the Philippines, where he was a Fulbright Scholar; in Malaysia, where he started the first mass communications program in that country; and has taught at universities and colleges in West Virginia, Wyoming, Wisconsin, and Pennsylvania.

ISBN 0-313-28212-9

90000>

EAN

9 780313 282126

HARDCOVER BAR CODE